THE COMPLETE BOOK OF
HOME
WORKSHOP
TOOLS

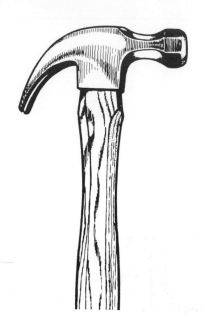

THE COMPLETE BOOK OF
HOME

McGRAW-HILL BOOK COMPANY

New York   St. Louis   San Francisco

Auckland	**New Delhi**
Bogotá	**Panama**
Düsseldorf	**Paris**
Johannesburg	**São Paulo**
London	**Singapore**
Madrid	**Sydney**
Mexico	**Tokyo**
Montreal	**Toronto**

WORKSHOP TOOLS

by Robert Scharff

A NORBACK BOOK

Library of Congress Cataloging in Publication Data

Scharff, Robert.
    The complete book of home workshop tools.

    Includes index.
    1. Woodworking tools.   2. Power tools.
I. Title
TT186.S3   684'.08   78-14822
ISBN 0-07-055042-5

The editors for this book were Robert A. Rosenbaum
and Carolyn Nagy, the designers were Robert Scharff
and Associates, and the production supervisor was
Thomas G. Kowalczyk.
It was set in Chelmsford by Robert Scharff and Associates.

It was printed and bound by Von Hoffmann Press, Inc.

CONTENTS

Dedicated to my wife Mary
for her untiring assistance and inspiration

PREFACE

This book was written for the homecraft person on the selection and use of the most important hand and power tools in the home workshop. It is a thorough, up-to-date reference book and guide which will prove invaluable to anyone who works with tools. In addition to a complete description of the various tools and how to use them correctly, there is information on how to employ them safely, how to care for them, and how to get the best use from them. However, it is not necessary to break down the subject matter any further in the Preface; the extent of the range of information, can be found in the Contents, Introduction, Index, and, of course, the text itself.

The compilation of this volume required the help of many people. For their technical help as well as for many of the illustrations, I wish to thank the following manufacturers: Goldblatt Tool Company; L. S. Starrett; Desa Industries, Ltd; Skokie Saw and Tool Company; Vermont American Corporation; Remington Arms Company, Inc.; Omark Industries, Inc.; Century Drill & Tool Company; Coastal Abrasive & Tool Company, Inc.; Howard Hardware Products, Inc.; Arco Products Corporation; Ridge Tool Company; James Neill, Inc.; X-Acto Company; Merit Abrasive Products, Inc.; Dresser Industries, Inc.; H. K. Porter Company, Inc.; William Dixon, Inc.; Daido Corporation; Homelite Division of Textron, Inc.; Channellock, Inc.; Adjustable Clamp Company; Dremel Manufacturing Company; Vaco Products Company; General Hardware Manufacturing Company; Wilde Tool Company, Inc.; Petersen Manufacturing Company; K-D Manufacturing Company; Frog Tool Company, Ltd.; Millers Falls Company; Brink & Cotton Manufacturing Company; Armstrong Brothers Tool Company; Baltimore Tool Works, Inc.; TRW, Inc.; Koehring Atomaster, Inc.; Grobet File Company; Utica Tool Company, Inc.; Warren Tool Corporation; Klein Tools, Inc.; Sanborn Manufacturing Company; Burgess Vibrocrafters, Inc.; Henry L. Hanson, Inc.; Bostitch, Inc.; Great Neck Saw Manufacturers, Inc.; Red Devil, Inc.; Skodco Inc.; Plumb Tools, Inc.; Oxwall Tool Company; True Temper Corporation; Greenlee Tool Company; American Gage & Manufacturing Company; Hoffco, Inc.; Roe International, Inc.; Diamond Tool and Horseshoe Company; Proto Tool Company; Skil Corporation; Magna Engineering Corporation; Duo-Fast Corporation; and Swingline Inc.

I would like to especially thank the following men and their companies for all the special help they gave us: John M. Sheehan of Rockwell International Corporation; Edward S. Benfield of Stanley Works; Robert L. Yale of Easco Tools, Inc.; Harold F. Hogrefe of The Cooper Group; Glenn Spoerl of Sears, Roebuck and Co.; Robert E. Davis of Turner Company; Carl Starner of Black & Decker Manufacturing Company; Dave Sauers of Bernz-O-Matic Corporation; Robert Sherwood of Vaughan & Bushnell

Manufacturing Company; and Morton Walters and Arnold B. Romney of *Family Handyman* magazine.

In addition, I would also like to give special thanks for their specific help and assistance in the following sections mentioned: Sears, Roebuck and Co. for permission to use data and illustrations from both of their two *Power Tool Know How* books published by Midwest Technical Publications that appear in Section 3; Rockwell International Corporation for certain information in Section 3 that originally appeared in their *Getting the Most From* series; the Hand Tool Institute for material that appeared in Section 1; Black & Decker Manufacturing Company for data from their *How To Choose and Use Power Tools* book that can be found in Section 2; the Stanley Works for information from their *How To Work With Tools and Woods* book that appeared in Sections 1 and 2; and the McGraw-Hill Book Company for permission to use illustrations from *Power Tool Woodworking for Everyone* by R. J. Cristoforo and *General Shop* by Chris H. Groneman and John L. Feirer that are found in Sections 1 and 3.

To the others who, inadvertently, may have been omitted from the above thank you's, please accept my deep apologies for such omissions.

ROBERT SCHARFF

INTRODUCTION

Tools are designed to make a job easier and enable you to work more efficiently. Tools can be your best friend when you undertake any home repair or improvement. But, if the tools are not used properly or cared for, their advantages will be lost.

Tools found in the home workshop can be either powered by hand or electricity. The latter type of tools are divided into two groups—portable and stationary. All three categories are thoroughly covered. Section 1 deals with hand tools, and the chapter headings describe the various tool functions: striking, woodcutting, metal-cutting, turning, holding, and measuring. There are also chapters on screwdrivers and miscellaneous hand tools.

Section 2 covers portable electric tools: drills, saws, routers, sanders, and miscellaneous other tools of this class. Section 3 details the stationary electric tools: table saw, radial arm saw, drill presses, lathes, jointers, shapers, sanders, grinders, and other stationary saws that are found in the home workshop. To clearly show the use and selection of tools, there are more than 1,200 illustrations.

It must be remembered that regardless of the type of work to be done, you must have, choose, and use the correct tools for doing your work quickly, accurately, and safely. Without the proper tools and the knowledge of how to use them, you waste time, reduce your efficiency, and may even injure yourself. This book explains the specific purposes, correct use, and proper care of the more common tools you may encounter in the home workshop.

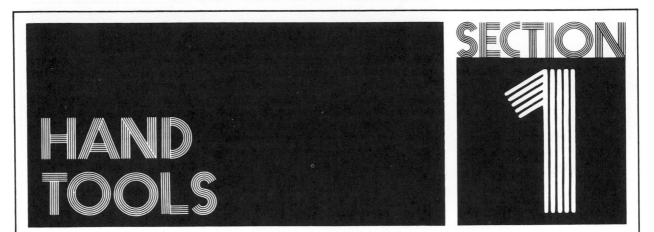

SECTION 1

HAND TOOLS

As stated in the introduction, this section is devoted to tools powered by your hands—striking tools, cutting tools, turning tools, holding tools, measuring tools, and so on. But it is very important to remember that your most important and most remarkable hand tool—one which is impossible to purchase—is your hands.

This fabulous tool is subject to injury by being caught in machines, crushed by objects, or cut by a variety of sharp-edged tools such as chisels, knives, and saws. Your hands can also be damaged by being burned, fractured, or sprained unless you are always alert.

Your hands are invaluable, but they cannot *think* for themselves; you must *protect them. Keep alert* while you work. *Think* as you work. Protect your hands from injury by following the applicable safety instructions whenever you use tools. You would be working under a severe handicap without the full use of both hands. Make it a habit to *follow all safety rules.*

When purchasing hand tools, remember that good ones are worth every penny of their cost, but they still cost money. Buying the wrong tool or the wrong size of tool is a waste. In order to select the right tool, you must first evaluate the job. When someone is to be hired for a job, the first thing the employer does is to set down the requirements of the job, or write up the job specifications for the personnel department. A person is then hired to fill those specifications. You have to do the same thing in buying tools. Once you have selected the right tool, a good general rule to follow is to buy the best tools you can afford.

Now let us take a look at the tools that are powered by your hands.

STRIKING TOOLS

Hammers and other striking tools are perhaps the most widely used, and probably the most often abused, of all hand tools. They are made in various types and sizes, with varying degrees of hardness and different configurations for specific purposes. A hammer should be selected for its intended use and used only for that purpose.

Hammers

A tool kit would not be complete without at least one hammer. In most cases, two or three are included, since they are designated according to weight (without the handle) and according to style or shape. The shape (Figure 1-1) varies according to the intended use. For instance, the nail or carpenter's hammer is designed for one purpose, while the ball peen hammer has other primary functions.

NAIL OR CARPENTER'S HAMMER

The primary use of the carpenter's hammer is to drive or draw (pull) nails. Note the names of the various parts of the typical carpenter's hammer shown in Figure 1-2. The "claw," which is at one end of the head, is a two-pronged arch used to pull nails out of wood. The carpenter's hammer has either a curved claw or a straight or "ripping" claw. The former is the most common and is best suited for general nail pulling. The ripping claw, which may be driven between pieces of wood, is used somewhat like a chisel to pry them apart. This type is often known as a "framing" hammer. Incidentally, all carpenter's hammers are frequently called "claw" hammers.

The face of a nail hammer may be flat (plain-faced), or it may be slightly rounded, or convex (bell-faced). The plain-faced hammer is easier for the beginner to learn to drive nails with. However, with this hammer, it is difficult to drive the head of the nail flush with the surface of the work without leaving hammer marks on the surface. The bell-faced hammer is generally used in rough work. When handled by an expert, it can drive the nailhead flush with the surface of the work without damaging the surface. Some heavy-duty nail hammers have checkered or milled faces designed to reduce the possibility of glancing blows and flying nails.

The head of a good nail hammer is forged of high-quality steel and is heat-treated to give the poll and face extra hardness. While the polls on most hammers are round, some carpenters prefer the more decorative octagon shape.

As mentioned earlier, the size of any hammer is determined by the weight of its head. The claw hammer is available in a range of from 7 to 28 ounces. Here are the recommended uses of the popular hammer weights.

7-ounce head. For light-duty driving; for brads, picture hanging; handy for women.
13-ounce head. For cabinetmaker's requirements; popular for households.
16-ounce head. For general use; most popular weight; standard for carpenters.
20-ounce head. For extra swing-weight requirement and bigger nails.
28-ounce head. For heavy duty; drives big nails fast; ideal for framing work.

Handles may be hickory, tubular or solid steel, or fiberglass. Tubular-steel, solid-steel, and fiberglass handles are generally furnished with perforated, neoprene-rubber type grips which are occasionally also used on hickory handles. These grips are more

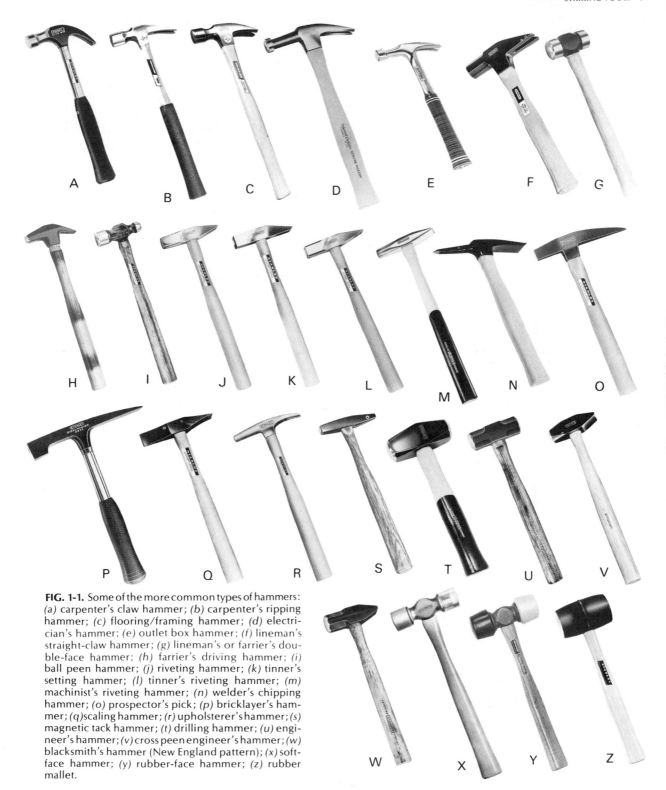

FIG. 1-1. Some of the more common types of hammers: (a) carpenter's claw hammer; (b) carpenter's ripping hammer; (c) flooring/framing hammer; (d) electrician's hammer; (e) outlet box hammer; (f) lineman's straight-claw hammer; (g) lineman's or farrier's double-face hammer; (h) farrier's driving hammer; (i) ball peen hammer; (j) riveting hammer; (k) tinner's setting hammer; (l) tinner's riveting hammer; (m) machinist's riveting hammer; (n) welder's chipping hammer; (o) prospector's pick; (p) bricklayer's hammer; (q) scaling hammer; (r) upholsterer's hammer; (s) magnetic tack hammer; (t) drilling hammer; (u) engineer's hammer; (v) cross peen engineer's hammer; (w) blacksmith's hammer (New England pattern); (x) soft-face hammer; (y) rubber-face hammer; (z) rubber mallet.

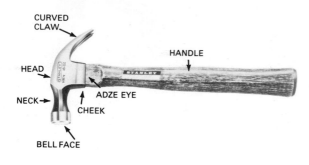

FIG. 1-2. Parts of a nail or carpenter's hammer.

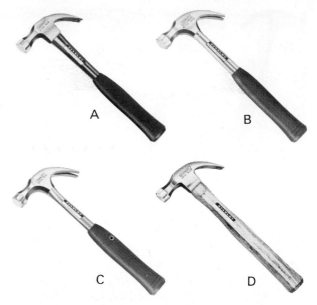

FIG. 1-4. The four major types of hammer handles: *(a)* fiberglass; *(b)* tubular steel; *(c)* solid steel; *(d)* hickory.

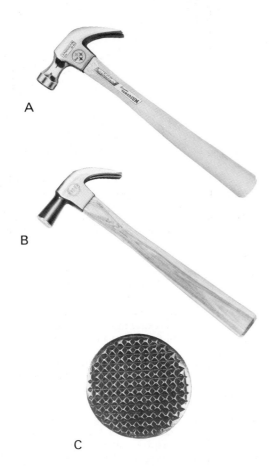

FIG. 1-3. Pattern faces of carpenter's hammers: *(a)* bell face; *(b)* plain face; *(c)* close-up of a milled face.

comfortable and seem to absorb the shock better than plain handles. Remember that the type of hammer handle affects the way it feels in your hand, as well as its balance. (The balance of a hammer depends on the weight of the head as compared with the weight of the handle.) When rested on a narrow board, a hammer with a wood handle will balance fairly close to the head. Those with tubular steel or fiberglass handles will balance somewhere in between the head and end of the handle.

Some special-duty claw hammers are available for use by various craftsmen. For example, the lineman's straight-claw hammer (Figure 1-1f) is heavy (it usually weighs between 32 and 36 ounces) and is used to drive lag bolts and to pull large nails. Another heavy hammer designed for line-pole work is the lineman's double-face type Figure 1-1g). Farriers often use this double-face hammer when shoeing horses.

USE OF NAIL HAMMERS To use a claw hammer, grasp the handle with the end flush with the lower edge of the palm (Figure 1-5a). Keep the wrist limber and relaxed. Grasp the nail with the thumb and forefinger of the other hand, and place the point at the exact spot where it is to be driven. Unless the nail is to be purposely driven at an angle, it should be held perpendicular to the surface of the work. Strike the nailhead squarely, keeping the hand level with the head of the nail. That is, to drive the nail, first rest the face of the hammer on the head of the nail; then raise the hammer slightly and give the nail a few light taps with a wrist movement, to start it. This helps give you proper aim and holds the nail in place during succeeding blows.

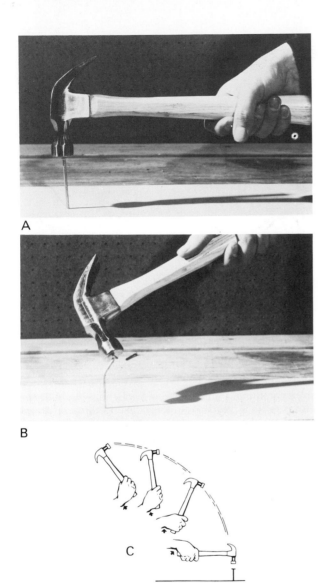

A

B

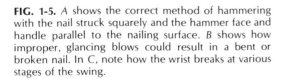

C

FIG. 1-5. *A* shows the correct method of hammering with the nail struck squarely and the hammer face and handle parallel to the nailing surface. *B* shows how improper, glancing blows could result in a bent or broken nail. In *C*, note how the wrist breaks at various stages of the swing.

Never use the cheek of the hammer for driving; the face has been specially processed for striking. Take the fingers away from the nail, and continue to drive the nail with firm blows with the center of the hammer face. The wrong way to drive a nail is shown in Figure 1-5*b*. Nails that do not drive straight or that bend should be pulled out and discarded. But, if after several attempts the nail still continues to bend or go in crooked, check to be sure

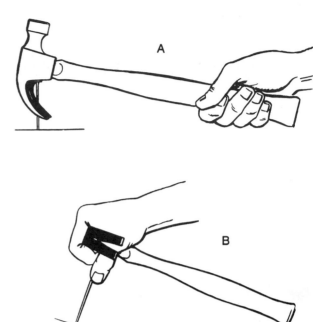

FIG. 1-6. Simple method of driving a nail with one hand.

that you are not trying to drive the nail into a knot or some other obstruction. If you are, drill a *small* hole through the obstruction and then drive the nail through.

There are times when it may be desirable to start a nail with one hand. This can be done in either of the following ways:

1. Insert the nail between the claws of the hammer, with the head of the nail resting against the head of the hammer (Figure 1-6*a*). Drive the nail slightly into the wood; then release it from the claw and finish driving in the usual manner.
2. Rest the head of the nail against the side of the hammer, and steady it in position with the fingers as shown in Figure 1-6*b*. Start the nail with a sharp tap of the hammer held in this manner; then finish driving in the usual manner.

A small nail can be held by piercing it through a piece of light cardboard that can be held comfortably. Another type of nail holder is made by attaching a pencil clip to a nail set. A small brad can be held between the clip and the base of the nail set, just as it might be held by a pair of pincers.

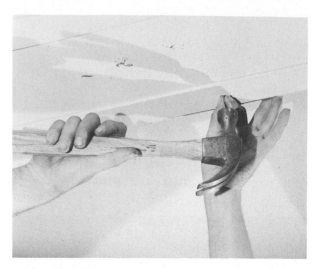

FIG. 1-7. (Left) The backhand grip is useful in tight corners. The grip is about halfway up the handle, and the stroke is as level as possible with the nail. (Right) When working on a ladder, a forehand stroke may throw you off balance. Use the backhand stroke with the hammer ahead of you.

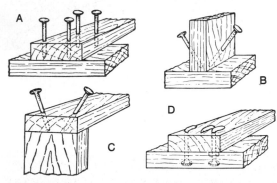

FIG. 1-8. Methods of nailing: (a) staggering; (b) toenailing; (c) skewing; (d) clinching.

If hardwood resists a brad, a hole can be drilled in the hardwood. Use, as a bit, a beheaded brad or a needle cut above the eye. Dipping a nail in paraffin will help it enter hardwood more easily. Some professional carpenters store paraffin in a hole drilled in the handle of a hammer. Hot paraffin is poured into the hole and allowed to cool.

Face nailing is used in accessible areas and is accomplished by driving the nail perpendicular to the surface. When driving several nails, it is best to stagger them (Figure 1-8a) to prevent the grain from splitting. In fact, a few staggered nails are stronger than a large number of nails.

Toenailing is the driving of nails obliquely (Figure 1-8b). It is used when it is impossible to face nail. The nail enters the wood at a slight angle. Keep in mind that the joint is

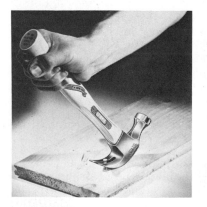

FIG. 1-9. While it is sometimes possible to pull nails directly (left), it is generally best to use a block of wood under the hammerhead for better leverage. This also keeps the hole from being enlarged. A nail puller is shown at the right.

stronger when two nails are driven in at opposite angles, so that they act as cleats. When nails are driven at an angle on a surface, the operation is called "skewing" (Figure 1-8c).

Clinched nails (Figure 1-8d) have more holding power than nails that are driven straight. Whenever possible, use a nail long enough to pierce the work and protrude about 1½ inches on the opposite side. Strike the protruding tip to bend it over; then finish the clinch with a sharp rap on the point, to sink it below the surface. Always clinch with the grain. When clinching nails, rest the work on a solid surface and be careful to prevent splitting of the wood.

To pull a nail, slide the claw of the hammer under the nailhead. Pull back on the handle until the handle is nearly vertical; then slip a block of wood under the head of the hammer, and pull the nail completely free (Figure 1-9). The claw hammer should not be used for pulling nails larger than 8d (8 penny). For larger nails, use a wrecking bar (see Chapter 8).

and forefinger, with the hand resting on the wood. Press the nail set onto the head of the nail and strike it, checking its position before each blow. This is particularly important when driving nails in moldings or corners, or when toenailing. The small surface hole created above the head of the nail can usually be plugged with putty if necessary.

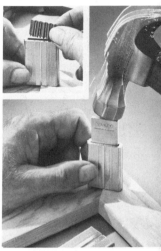

FIG. 1-11. When driving corrugated fasteners, use a medium-weight hammer and strike with evenly distributed light blows (left). It is important that the lumber being fastened together rest on a solid surface. To help drive corrugated nails quickly and accurately, a nail set such as the one shown at the right is very handy.

FIG. 1-10. A 20-ounce ripping hammer being used to rip apart forming lumber. The straight-claw or ripping hammer is specifically designed for this type of work. When ripping, insert the claw part of the hammer into a crack as near to a nail as possible. Use a quick, jolting movement to loosen each nail.

NAIL SET A nail set (Figure 1-12) is used to *set* (meaning to countersink slightly below the surface) the heads of nails in finish carpentry. The purpose of setting is to improve the appearance of the work by concealing the nailheads. A nail is set by placing the tip of the nail set on the head of the nail and striking the set a blow or two with the hammer. To keep from creating too big a hole when using a nail set, hold it firmly in the left hand, between thumb

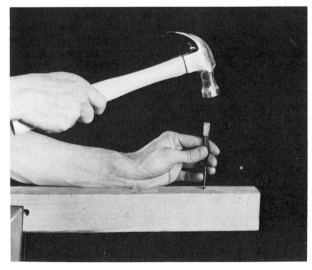

FIG. 1-12. Driving a nail all the way with the hammerhead will leave a dimple. Use a nail set or, in a pinch, a heavy spike.

The tips of nail sets are cupped, chamfered, and heat-treated for toughness. The heads are often untempered and soft, to prevent chipping when they are hit with a hammer. The bodies are either round along their entire length, with machine knurling for a good grip, or have square heads. The latter give a slightly larger striking surface and keep the tool from rolling when dropped.

The size of a nail set is determined by its tip diameter, which may be $\frac{1}{32}$, $\frac{1}{16}$, $\frac{3}{32}$, or $\frac{1}{8}$ inch. It is wise to use a nail set whose tip is slightly smaller than the nail that is being driven. If a larger nail set is used, you enlarge the nail hole unnecessarily. Incidentally, corrugated nail sets are available, for driving "wiggle" nails flush with the surface.

CABINETMAKER'S HAMMERS The claw hammer, which was designed basically for carpenters, is used for most woodworking jobs in the United States; however, there are several hammers designed especially for cabinet-makers (Figure 1-13). For instance, the Warrington joiner's hammer—a favorite with English cabinetmakers—is available in weights from 8 to 16 ounces; its small end, used to drive small brads, is more important than a claw. The cabinetmaker's hammer is used by cabinetmakers and joiners on the continent of Europe. The square head allows it to get into corners. The small end is used for driving small brads. These hammers range in weight from 140 to 520 *grams*. The veneer hammer (Figure 1-13c) is used to smooth down veneer when hot glue or contact glue is used; no press is needed. Another excellent small hammer is the long-handle pin hammer shown as *D* in Figure 1-13.

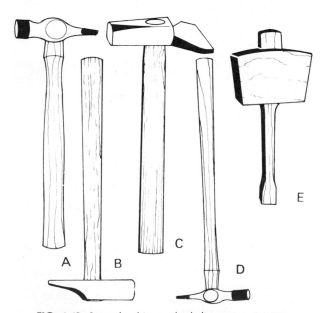

FIG. 1-13. Several cabinetmaker's hammers: *(a)* Warrington joiner's hammer; *(b)* cabinetmaker's hammer; *(c)* veneer hammer; *(d)* pin hammer; *(e)* square wooden mallet.

BALL-PEEN HAMMERS

The ball-peen hammer, as its name implies, has a ball which is smaller in diameter than the face. It is therefore useful for striking in areas that are too small for the face to enter.

Ball-peen hammers are made in different weights, usually 4, 6, 8, and 12 ounces and 1, 1½, 2, 2½, and 3 pounds. For most work, a 1½-pound and a 12-ounce hammer will suffice. However, a 4- or 6-ounce hammer is often used for light work. Handles may be hickory, tubular or solid steel, or fiberglass. The tubular-steel, solid-steel and fiberglass types are generally furnished with perforated, neoprene-rubber style grips which are occasionally also used on hickory handles.

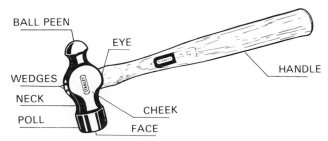

TO STRIKE HEAVY AND MEDIUM BLOWS, GRASP THE HAMMER FIRMLY NEAR THE END OF THE HANDLE AND SWING IT WITH A FREE GRACEFUL SWEEP, WELL OVER THE SHOULDER
TO STRIKE LIGHT BLOWS, AS IN DRIVING RIVETS, GRASP THE HANDLE NEARER THE HEAD AND SWING WITH A MOTION SLIGHTLY AT THE ELBOW BUT CHIEFLY AT THE WRIST.

FIG. 1-14. Parts of a standard ball peen hammer.

USING A BALL-PEEN HAMMER Ball-peen hammers (of the proper size) are designed for striking cold chisels and punches, and for riveting, shaping, and straightening metal. For striking another tool (cold chisel or punch), the face of the hammer should be proportionately larger than the head of the tool. For example, a ½-inch cold chisel requires at least a 1-inch hammer face. A hammer blow should always be struck squarely, with the hammer face parallel to the surface being struck. Always avoid glancing blows.

One of the most common faults in using a ball peen hammer is holding the handle too close to the head. This is known as "choking" the hammer, and it reduces the force of the blow. Choking also makes it harder to hold the head in an upright position. Except for light blows, hold the handle close to the end, to increase the lever arm and produce a more effective blow. Hold the handle with the fingers underneath and the thumb alongside or on top of the handle. The thumb should rest on the handle, and never overlap the fingers. Try to hit the object with the full force of the ball peen hammer. Hold the hammer at such an angle that the face of the hammer and the surface of the object being hit will be parallel. This distributes the force of the blow over the full face and prevents damage to both the surface being struck and the face of the hammer.

SOFT-FACE HAMMERS AND MALLETS

Soft-face hammers and mallets are made of various nonferrous materials (wood, rawhide, rubber, plastic, copper, brass, lead, etc.). Their heads are cylindrical with two flat striking faces. Their handles are usually hickory or fiberglass.

Soft-face hammers are intended for striking blows where steel hammers would mar or damage the surface of the work. Wooden mallets are properly used for striking wood- and plastic-handled chisels, gouges, wood pins, and small stakes, and to form or shape sheet metal. Rubber and plastic hammers are used for setting stone. Plastic hammers usually have replaceable tips, available in varying degrees of hardness. They are designed for use on metal and other hard materials where rebound and nonmarring properties are desired. Rawhide mallets are used for much the same tasks. Brass and copper mallets are excellent all-purpose nonmarring hammers. They are ideal for bushings, gears, transmissions, etc. Never use a soft-face hammer or mallet to drive nails, screws, or any object that may damage the face.

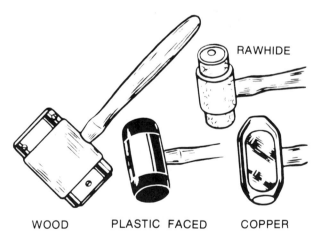

WOOD   PLASTIC FACED   COPPER

FIG. 1-15. Common soft-face and nonferrous hammers and mallets: *(a)* wood; *(b)* plastic-face; *(c)* rawhide; *(d)* copper.

SLEDGES

The sledge is a steel-head, heavy-duty striking tool that can be used for a number of purposes. There are several different types of sledges.

DOUBLE-FACE OR ENGINEER'S SLEDGE This is the most commonly used type of sledge hammer; it is made in slightly different head configurations by various manu-

facturers. All patterns have a crowned face with beveled edges and are forged from high-carbon or alloy steel and heat-treated. Head weights range from 2 to 20 pounds, with handle lengths from 15 to 36 inches.

Sledges are designed generally for striking wood and metal. Common uses are drifting heavy timbers and striking spikes, cold chisels, rock drills, hardened nails, etc. Never use this type of sledge to strike stone or concrete; instead, use a stone sledge or bush hammer.

STRAIGHT AND CROSS PEEN SLEDGES These heavy-duty hammers are designed primarily for use by blacksmiths in striking metal. Forged from high-carbon or alloy steel and heat-treated, their faces are crowned with beveled edges. Head weights range from 2 to 16 pounds, with handle lengths from 14 to 36 inches.

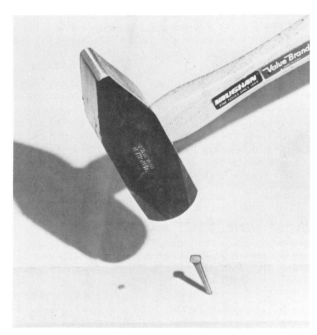

FIG. 1-16. Concrete or masonry nails should be driven with a blacksmith's hammer (shown) or a hand drilling hammer. The striking faces of these hammers are specially tempered to allow their use on hardened nails.

These peens are used for shaping (fullering) and bending metal. To strike a heavy or medium blow, grasp the hammer or sledge firmly near the end of the handle, and swing it with a free, graceful sweep, well over the shoulder. To strike a light blow, as in driving rivets, grasp the handle nearer the head; swing it with a slight motion at the elbow but with most of the motion at the wrist.

HAND-DRILLING OR MASH HAMMERS These heavy, short-handle hammers are made in slightly varying configurations by different manufacturers. The double-faced head has crowned and beveled striking faces, forged from high-carbon steel and heat-treated. Head weights range from 2 to 4 pounds, with hickory handles from 10 to 11 inches long.

Hand-drilling hammers are designed for use with cold chisels, brick chisels, star drills, hardened nails, etc. Their design permits heavy blows with limited swing—especially advantageous in restricted working areas.

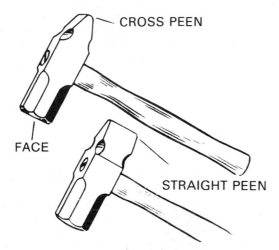

FIG. 1-17. The straight (a) and cross peen (b) hammers. When using either of these hammers to strike heavy or medium blows, grasp it firmly near the end of the handle, and swing it with a free, graceful sweep, well over the shoulder. To strike light blows, grasp the handle nearer the head and swing it with a slight motion at the elbow but chiefly at the wrist.

STONE SLEDGES AND SPALLING HAMMERS These stonemason's tools are made in slightly varying configurations by different manufacturers. The sledge usually has a crowned oval striking face with a napping face opposite. The lighter spalling hammer may be single- or double-faced. Stone sledges vary in head weight from 8 to 16 pounds, with hickory handles from 32 to 36 inches long. Spalling hammers weigh from 3 to 12 pounds, with handles from 16 to 36 inches long. The heads of both are forged from high-carbon steel and heat-treated.

Stone sledges are designed for breaking up stone and concrete. Spalling hammers are used for cutting and shaping concrete and stone. Never use these tools for striking metal.

BUSH HAMMERS Bush hammers are designed for a single purpose—roughing and chipping concrete. They are double-faced tools of compact, rectangular design having both faces milled with sharp, hardened teeth. They are forged from alloy steel and are heat-treated. The head weight is usually 4 pounds, with a 16-inch hickory handle.

OTHER HAMMERS

Hammers are made in a great variety of patterns intended for specific uses by specific tradesmen (floor layers, prospectors, linemen, upholsterers, bricklayers,

etc.). For example, body-and-fender hammers are highly specialized tools used almost exclusively by skilled automotive repairmen for bumping and dinging sheet metal on and off the dolly in the repair of car bodies and fenders. Prospecting picks are special-purpose tools generally used only by geologists, prospectors, and rock collectors. Some specialty hammers are very small—the watchmaker's hammer, for example—while others, such as some special blacksmith's types, are larger than the sledges already mentioned in this chapter. There is also a complete line of hammers—silversmith, embossing, planishing, chasing, and raising types—that are used by metal craftsmen and hobbyists. While most of these hammers are of little value in a so-called "general" craftsman's shop, some specific tradesman's hammers are quite useful.

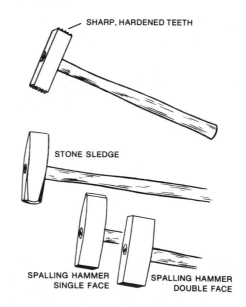

FIG. 1-18. (a) Typical toothed bush or concrete hammer; (b) stone sledge; (c) two types of spalling hammers.

BRICKLAYER'S HAMMERS The bricklayer's hammer is a special-purpose tool that is designed for setting and cutting (splitting) bricks, masonry tile, and concrete blocks, and for chipping mortar from bricks. The square face is flat with sharp corners. The blade has a sharp, hardened cutting edge. Head weights range from 10 to 24 ounces. Handles may be hickory, tubular or solid steel, or fiberglass and may be furnished with rubber-type grips. Never use these tools to strike metal or to drive struck or hammered tools (including brick sets and chisels). Use a ball peen hammer of the proper size or a hand-drilling or mash hammer.

When cutting a brick with a hammer, first cut a line all the way around the brick with light blows of the hammerhead (Figure 1-21a). When the line is complete, a sharp blow to one side of the cutting line will split the brick at the cutting line. Rough places are trimmed using the blade of the hammer, as shown in Figure 1-21b. The brick can be held in the hand while it is being cut.

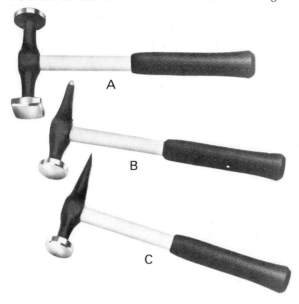

FIG. 1-19. Typical body-and-fender hammers: *(a)* bumping or dinging hammer, for fender and other panel dinging and bumping; *(b)* cross peen hammer, used on narrow-bend surfaces; *(c)* pecking or pointed pick hammer, with its pointed end, employed for pecking out small dents, and round, slightly crowned face for finishing.

FIG. 1-20. Bricklayer's hammer being used to chip mortar. This hammer is designed for use on brick or concrete blocks only. It should never be used to strike a brick chisel or other metal object because the corners of the striking face can be chipped by these hard objects.

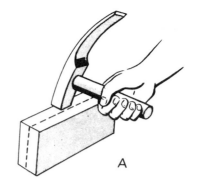

STRIKING BRICK TO ONE SIDE OF CUTTING LINE

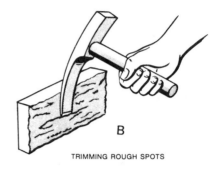

TRIMMING ROUGH SPOTS

FIG. 1-21. Cutting brick with a hammer.

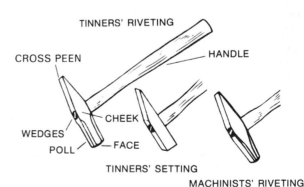

TINNERS' RIVETING

CROSS PEEN — HANDLE

CHEEK

WEDGES

POLL — FACE

TINNERS' SETTING

MACHINISTS' RIVETING

FIG. 1-22. Riveting and setting hammers.

If a brick is to be cut to an exact line, a brick chisel or set should be used, as described later in this chapter.

RIVETING AND SETTING HAMMERS These hammers are designed for machinist's and tinner's use. Their handles are usually made of hickory. The machinist's riveting hammer has a round poll with a slightly beveled, flat striking face and rounded cross peen. Head weights range from 4 to 12 ounces. The tinner's riveting hammer has an octagonal poll with a flat striking face and slightly beveled edges. The cross peen is slightly rounded. The face of the tinner's setting or paning hammer has sharp corners and no bevels. The cross peen has a sharp beveled edge. Head weights of 8 to 20 ounces are available.

The riveting hammer is designed for driving and spreading rivets in sheet-metal work (see Chapter 8). The setting hammer is designed for forming sharp corners, for closing and peening seams, lock edges, etc., and for use by glaziers in inserting glazier's points.

SCALING OR CHIPPING HAMMERS Scaling or chipping hammers are special-purpose tools designed for chipping welds, scale, rust, paint, etc. from metal. They are made in varying configurations by different manufacturers. The two patterns illustrated in Figure 1-23 are typical. Head weights usually range from 12 to 36 ounces, with hickory handles from 11¼ to 13 inches long.

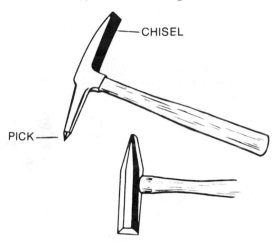

FIG. 1-23. Two patterns of scaling hammers.

MAGNETIC HAMMERS Magnetic hammers are usually made in the patterns illustrated in Figure 1-24. Their heads are forged from high-grade steel and weigh from 5 to 8 ounces. One end of the head is magnetized to hold tacks. Their handles are usually made of hickory.

The primary use of these light-duty hammers is holding and driving tacks. The tack hammer has a long, thin claw for pulling tacks in corners and along walls; it may also be used for removing light moldings. The heads of the other two patterns are designed for starting and driving tacks only. The magnetic end is used for starting the tack; the opposite end, for driving.

WOODCHOPPER'S MAUL This tool is designed for splitting wood. It is also used in conjunction with wood-splitting wedges (see page 19), first for making a notch with the splitting edge, and then to drive the wedge with the striking face opposite the splitting edge. Mauls are forged from high-carbon steel and heat-treated, and usually are made in 6- and 8-pound head weights with 32-inch hickory handles.

These and all specific-use hammers are very specialized tools. They should not be used for general-purpose work.

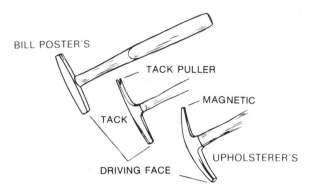

FIG. 1-24. Typical magnetic hammers.

FIG. 1-25. Striking a wood-splitting wedge with a woodchopper's maul.

AXES AND HATCHETS

Axes are made in various patterns and head configurations. The more widely used types are illustrated in Figure 1-26. Their heads are usually forged from carbon tool steel, and the blades or bits are heat-treated. Head weights vary from 1¼ to 5 pounds, with hickory handles from 14 to 36 inches long.

Hatchets are made in an even greater variety of patterns, since specific types are intended for use by various tradesmen (carpenters, roofers, dry-wall installers, rig builders, etc.). Their heads are usually forged from carbon tool steel and heat-treated. Their handles may be hickory, tubular or solid steel, or fiberglass. Tubular-steel, solid-steel, and fiberglass handles are generally furnished with rubber-type grips which are occasionally also used on hickory handles.

The double-bit axe is usually used to fell, trim, or prune

trees and to split and cut wood. It is also used for notching and shaping logs and timbers. The single-bit axe may be used for the same purposes; in addition, the poll is used to drive wood stakes. Hatchets are used for cutting, splitting, trimming, and hewing, and nails and stakes may be driven with the striking face.

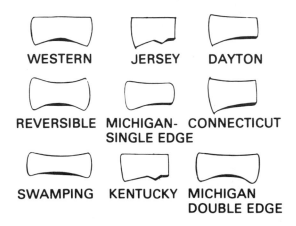

FIG. 1-26. Various axe-head configurations.

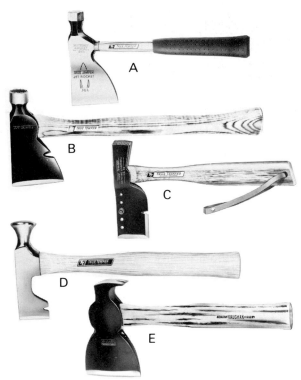

FIG. 1-27. Various types of hatchets: *(a)* half hatchet; *(b)* rig-builder's hatchet; *(c)* lathing-shingling hatchet; *(d)* wallboard hatchet; *(e)* claw hatchet.

Another hatchet-axe-like hand tool is the adz. It is used to smooth the surface of timber. Many interior exposed beams in houses, barns, and ships have received this treatment. The adz has a rather thin blade set at right angles to the handle and curved toward it. The gouge adz is used for forming gutters and removing large amounts of wood from timber, as in notching logs for log cabins.

The cutting edges of axes, hatchets, and adzes are designed to cut wood and equally soft materials. They should never be struck against metal, stone, or concrete. The striking faces of hatchets are properly hardened for driving common nails, but they should not be used to strike cold chisels, punches, rock drills, or other hardened metal tools, or for striking stone or concrete. Never use an axe as a wedge or a maul; do not strike with its sides.

SAFETY AND STRIKING TOOLS

The following safety precautions apply generally to all striking tools:

1. Check to see that the handle is tight before using any striking tool. Never use a striking or struck tool with a loose or damaged handle.
2. Always use a striking tool of suitable size and weight for the job. Do not use a tack hammer to drive a spike, nor a sledge to drive a tack.
3. Discard any striking or struck tool if the face shows excessive wear, dents, chips, mushrooming, or improper redressing. Directions for redressing hammers and other striking tools are given in Chapter 22.
4. Rest the face of the hammer on the work before striking, to get the *feel* or *aim*. Then grasp the handle firmly, with the hand near the extreme end of the handle.
5. Strike squarely, but lightly, until the nail or tool to be driven is set. Get the fingers of the other hand out of the way before striking with force.
6. A hammer blow should always be struck squarely, with the hammer face parallel to the surface being struck. Always avoid glancing blows and over-and-under strikes.
7. For striking another tool (cold chisel, punch, wedge, etc.) the face of the hammer should be proportionally larger than the head of the tool. For example, a ½-inch cold chisel requires at least a 1-inch hammer face.
8. Hardened steel-cut and masonry nails should never be driven with a nail hammer. These nails shatter under the force of an indirect or glancing blow. When such a nail is not to be driven through a piece of wood, a hole should be started with a small star drill or masonry bit. A heavy hammer with a large striking face is the proper tool to use.
9. Never use one hammer to strike another hammer.

10. Do not use the end of the handle of any striking tool for tamping or prying; it may split.

MAINTENANCE AND CARE OF STRIKING TOOLS

Broken hammer handles should be replaced, and loose handles tightened. If a handle is loose, set it by striking the end of the handle with a mallet, and then drive the wedges back into the handle. Wedges may be of either metal or straight-grained hardwood. Nails or screws should not be used. If a handle is broken, remove it, seat a new handle, and replace the wedges. If it is difficult to remove the old handle, saw it off close to the head and drive it through the larger end of the eye. The wedges should be saved and reused.

The hammer face should be kept clean and smooth. This usually can be done by rubbing it with emery cloth. If it becomes necessary to grind the face to restore it because it is in very bad condition, notice whether it is a bell or a plain face, and then grind it to the proper shape. Dip the head in water often to prevent burning and loss of temper while grinding. Do not grind the face more often than necessary or remove more material than necessary to restore the face. More on how to redress hammer heads can be found in Chapter 22.

Hammers, sledges, and mallets should be cleaned and repaired if necessary before they are stored. Before using the tool, ensure that its faces are free from oil or other material that would cause it to glance off nails, spikes, or stakes.

Never leave a wooden or rawhide mallet in the sun, as the head may dry out and crack. A light film of oil should be left on the mallet to keep the head moist.

FIG. 1-28. Shingling hatchet being used to establish the length of shingle "to the weather." A gauge pin in the hatchet is adjustable to the weather length desired. The striking face is beveled and tempered for nail driving.

Struck or Hammered Tools

Many tools are designed specifically to be struck or hammered. These include chisels, punches, drift pins, and wedges. It should be remembered that the striking or hammered surface of a tool is designed to direct the force of a blow toward the center or body of the tool. This is accomplished by (1) a crown radius on the striking or hammered surface, and (2) a generous bevel between this surface and the sides of the tool. Once the metal on the striking or hammered surface begins to move out of place, the crown radius begins to disappear, along with the bevel. In this condition, blows struck off center are no longer directed toward the body of the tool where they can be absorbed, but rather travel directly along the sides of the tool where there is insufficient backup material. The net effect is shearing, which is dangerous, rather than cushioning.

The angle and thickness of the cutting edges of tools are designed to give maximum cut and durability. When a cutting edge becomes dull, the cutting ability decreases and the durability is drastically reduced. Many failures are caused by dullness. Full details on how to sharpen various struck and hammered tools are given in Chapter 22.

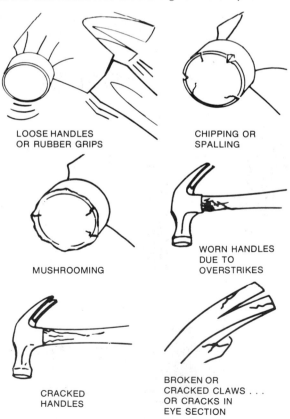

LOOSE HANDLES OR RUBBER GRIPS

CHIPPING OR SPALLING

MUSHROOMING

WORN HANDLES DUE TO OVERSTRIKES

CRACKED HANDLES

BROKEN OR CRACKED CLAWS . . . OR CRACKS IN EYE SECTION

FIG. 1-29. Never use a hammer with any of the faults illustrated.

CHISELS

There are well over 20 basic types of chisels with innumerable design variations, many with names that are the same or similar. Fortunately, however, the average craftsman need be concerned with only a few types.

A

B

FIG. 1-30. (a) All-steel wood chisel; (b) flooring electrician's chisel. The steel molding chisel looks like the electrician's chisel but is smaller.

WOODWORKING CHISELS A wood chisel is a steel tool fitted with a wooden or plastic handle. A hammer is never used with a woodworking chisel. Use either a soft-face mallet (the wood style is best) or your hand, depending upon the work to be done. Complete details on the selection and use of wood chisels with wooden or plastic handles are given in Chapter 2.

There are on the market all-steel wood chisels which are heavy-duty woodcutting tools designed for rougher work than the standard woodworking chisels. This type of wood chisel is forged from a single piece of tool steel. The blade, handle, and head comprise the forging. The usual blade widths range from $\frac{1}{2}$ to 4 inches. These chisels can be struck with a ball peen hammer or a small sledge.

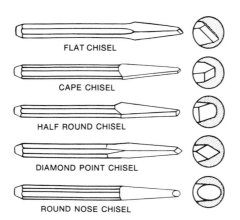

FLAT CHISEL

CAPE CHISEL

HALF ROUND CHISEL

DIAMOND POINT CHISEL

ROUND NOSE CHISEL

FIG. 1-31. Various metal-cutting chisels.

The two most popular all-steel wood chisels are the so-called "flooring" and "electrician's" chisels. These chisels have broad blades and tapered or V-shaped edges. Flooring chisels are about $2\frac{1}{2}$ inches wide and are used to remove rotted or damaged pieces of hardwood flooring. The hardened steel can easily cut through floor nails. This type of chisel is also used to trim or cut through wood shingles and clapboard siding.

The electrician's chisel is a larger version of the flooring type and has a 4-inch blade. It is not actually used only by electricians; its name stems from the fact that it is often used when a beam or joist has to be trimmed or cut to provide a channel for Romex or armored electric cable. It is one of the widest chisels made and is the best hand tool to use where a lot of wood has to be removed rapidly. For removing trim, use an all-steel molding chisel. Its offset blade is 2 inches wide and has a beveled nail slot.

Another popular chisel is the wide but thin glazier's chisel, which is used primarily for removing window trim and molding. Its thin blade allows trim or molding to be removed without any appreciable damage to painted surfaces.

METAL-CUTTING CHISELS Cold metal-cutting chisels are designed for cutting and chipping cold metal (steel, cast and wrought iron, aluminum, brass, copper, etc.). They will cut any metal that is softer than the material of which they are made. These chisels are made from a good grade of tool steel and have hardened cutting edges and beveled heads. Cold chisels, as these tools are frequently called, are classified according to the shapes of their points; the width of the cutting edge denotes their size. The most common shapes of chisels are flat, cape, half-round, diamond-point, and round-nose. Cold chisels may have a cut width of from $\frac{1}{4}$ to $1\frac{1}{2}$ inches.

The type of chisel most commonly used is the flat cold chisel, which serves to cut rivets, split nuts, chip castings, and cut thin metal sheets. The cape chisel is used for special jobs such as cutting keyways, narrow grooves, and square corners. Round-nose and half-round chisels make circular grooves and chip inside corners with a fillet. Finally, the diamond-point chisel is used for cutting V grooves and sharp corners.

As with other tools, there is a correct technique for using a chisel. Select a chisel that is large enough for the job. Be sure to use a hammer that matches the chisel; that is, the larger the chisel, the heavier the hammer. A heavy chisel will absorb the blows of a light hammer and will do virtually no cutting.

As a general rule, hold the chisel in the left hand with the thumb and first finger about 1 inch from the top. The chisel should be held steadily but not tightly. The finger muscles should be relaxed, so that if the hammer strikes the hand, the hand will slide down the tool and lessen the effect of the blow. Keep your eyes on the cutting edge of the chisel, not on the head, and swing the hammer in the same plane as the body of the chisel. If you have a lot of chiseling to do, slide a piece of rubber hose over the

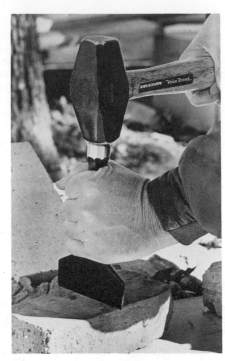

FIG. 1-32. Hand drilling or "mash" hammer being used with a cold chisel to shear rivet heads (left); with a star drill to make a hole in cement block (center); and with a brick chisel or set to cut brick (right).

chisel. This will lessen the shock to your hand.

When using a chisel for chipping, always wear goggles to protect your eyes. If other people are close by, protect them from flying chips by erecting a screen or shield to contain the chips. Remember that the time to take these precautions is before you start the job.

The blacksmith's cold chisel looks like a hammer (see Figure 1-17) but it cuts the metal directly. It is forged from a solid piece of alloy steel, weighs from 2 to 5 pounds, and is usually fitted with a hickory handle from 16 to 32 inches long.

HAND PUNCHES

A hand punch is a tool that is held in the hand and struck on one end with a hammer. There are many kinds of punches, designed to do a variety of jobs; Figure 1-33 shows several types. Most punches are made of tool steel. The part held in the hand is usually octagonal in shape, or it may be knurled. This prevents the tool from slipping around in the hand. The other end is shaped to do a particular job. The lengths of hand punches vary from 4½ to 20 inches.

There are two things to remember when you use a punch:

1. When you hit the punch, you do not want it to slip sideways over your work.

2. You do not want the hammer to slip off the punch and strike your fingers.

You can prevent both these troubles by holding the punch at right angles to the work and striking the punch squarely with your hammer.

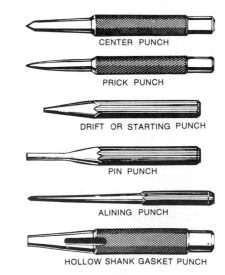

FIG. 1-33. Various types of punches.

The center punch, as the name implies, is used for marking the center of a hole to be drilled. If you try to drill a hole without first punching the center, the drill will "wander" or "walk away" from the desired center.

Another use of the center punch is to make corresponding marks on two pieces of an assembly to permit reassembling in the original positions. Before taking a mechanism apart, make a pair of center-punch marks in one or more places to help in reassembly. To do this, select places where matching pieces are joined. First clean the places selected. Then scribe a line across the joint at each place. Center punch the line on both sides of the joint with single and double marks as shown in Figure 1-34, to eliminate possible errors. In reassembling the pieces, first refer to the sets of punch marks to determine the approximate positions of the parts. Then line up the scribed lines to determine the exact positions.

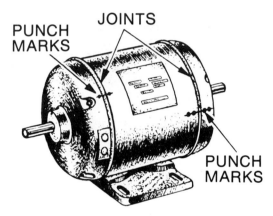

FIG. 1-34. Punching mating parts of a mechanism.

Automatic center punches are useful for layout work. They are operated by pressing down on the shank by hand. An inside spring is compressed and released automatically, striking a blow on the end of the punch. The impression is light but adequate for marking, and it serves to locate the point of a standard punch when a deeper impression is required.

The point of a center punch is accurately ground to be concentric with the shank, usually at a 60 to 90° angle, and is difficult to regrind by hand with any degree of accuracy. It is, therefore, advisable to take good care of center punches, and not to use them on extremely hard materials. When extreme accuracy is required, a prick punch is used. Compare the point angle of the center and prick punches.

To mark the intersection of two layout lines, bring the point of the prick punch to the exact point of intersection, and tap the punch lightly with a hammer. If inspection shows that the exact intersection and the punch mark do not coincide, as at *A* in Figure 1-35, slant the punch as shown at *B* and again strike with the hammer, thus

enlarging the punchmark and centering it exactly. When the intersection has been correctly punched, finish the mark with a light blow on the punch while holding it in an upright position (*C* shows the corrected punch mark).

Drift punches, sometimes called "starting punches," have a long taper from the tip to the body. They are made that way to withstand the shock of heavy blows. They may be used for knocking out rivets after the rivet heads have been chiseled off, or for freeing pins which are "frozen" in their holes.

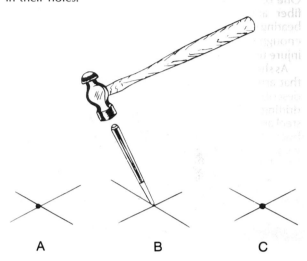

FIG. 1-35. Marking the intersection of lines with a prick punch.

After a pin has been loosened or partially driven out, the drift punch may be too large to finish the job. The follow-up tool to use is a pin punch. It is designed to follow through the hole without jamming. Always use the largest drift or pin punch that will fit the hole. These punches usually come in sets of three to five assorted sizes. Both punches have flat points, never edged or rounded.

To remove a bolt or pin that is extremely tight, start with a drift punch that has a point diameter that is slightly smaller than the diameter of the object you are removing. As soon as it loosens, finish driving it out with a pin punch. Never use a pin punch to start a pin, because the punch has a slim shank, and a hard blow may cause it to bend or break. Rivet punches are similar to pin punches in both design and use.

For assembling units of a machine, an alignment (aligning) punch or long taper punch is invaluable. It is usually about 1 foot long and has a long, gradual taper. Its purpose is to line up holes in mating parts.

Hollow-shank metal-cutting punches are made from hardened tool steel. They are made in various sizes and are used to cut holes in light-gauge sheet metal. Others are available for cutting gasket holes in rubber, cork, leather, and composition metal. Such gasket punches usually come in sets of various sizes to accommodate standard bolts and studs. The cutting end is tapered to a sharp edge to produce a clean, uniform hole. To use the gasket punch, place the gasket material to be cut on a piece of hardwood or lead, so that the cutting edge of the punch will not be damaged. Then strike the punch with a hammer, driving it through the gasket where a hole is required.

Other punches have been designed for special uses. One of these is the soft-face drift. It is made of brass or fiber and is used for such jobs as removing shafts, bearings, and wrist pins from engines. It is generally heavy enough to resist damage to itself, but soft enough not to injure the finished surface on the part that is being driven.

As shown in Figure 1-36, there are blacksmith's punches that are completely different from the punches already described. The blacksmith's round punch is designed for drifting and aligning. It is forged from a solid piece of alloy steel and heat-treated. The punch is tapered from point to body. Punch diameters range from $\frac{1}{4}$ to 1 inch; head weights range from $1\frac{1}{2}$ to $3\frac{1}{4}$ pounds. The hickory handles are usually 16 inches long.

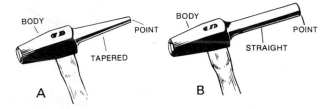

FIG. 1-36. *(a)* Blacksmith's round punch; *(b)* backing-out punch.

The blacksmith's backing-out punch is designed for backing out bolts, rivets, and pins. It is forged from a solid piece of alloy steel and heat-treated. The punch is the same diameter from point to body. Diameters range from $\frac{3}{8}$ to 1 inch; head weights range from 1 to $3\frac{1}{2}$ pounds. The hickory handles are usually 16 inches long.

DRIFT PINS

Drift pins are designed for aligning holes in metal. They are made from round steel stock in diameters of $\frac{9}{16}$ to $1\frac{1}{16}$ inches, for holes $\frac{1}{2}$ to 1 inch in diameter. The plug or

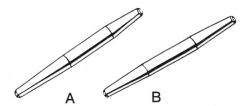

FIG. 1-37. The two types of drift pins: *(a)* standard; *(b)* barrel.

standard type has an abrupt taper at one end and a longer taper at the other end. The barrel type has equal tapers at both ends.

STAR DRILLS

Star drills are designed for drilling holes in masonry (stone, concrete, brick, etc.). They are usually hand-forged from high-carbon steel and hardened and tempered. The cutting end resembles four chisels joined at their edges to form a cross (star). Popular sizes range from $\frac{1}{4}$ to $1\frac{3}{4}$ inches in diameter by 12 to 48 inches in length.

A star drill should be struck squarely with a heavy hand-drilling hammer or sledge, and it should be rotated after each blow as it goes through the masonry. Special rubber head cushions are available; they slip over the handle to protect your hand while you are hitting the end of the drill with a hammer or sledge.

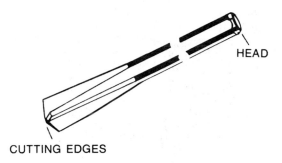

FIG. 1-38. Typical star drill.

BRICK CHISELS OR SETS

The brick chisel or set (also called a "brick bolster") is designed for scoring and cutting bricks and concrete or cinder blocks. The set is used for adjusting and trimming bricks to size without shattering them. These tools are forged from tool steel, heat-treated, and tempered. Their heads are crowned and beveled to reduce mushrooming. Blade widths are usually 3 to 4 inches. The chisel has a double bevel; the set, a single bevel.

As mentioned earlier, if a brick is to be cut to an exact line, the brick chisel or set should be used. When a single-bevel chisel—the most popular type—is used, the straight side of the cutting edge should face the part of the brick to be saved and face the user. One blow of the hammer on the brick chisel should be enough to break the brick. Extremely hard brick will have to be cut roughly with the head of a bricklayer's hammer (described earlier in this chapter) in such a way that there is enough brick left to be cut accurately with a brick set.

There are several other brick-cutting chisels, but the two most used are the dooking chisel and the plugging chisel. The latter is used for cutting slots in brickwork for wall fixtures, etc. The dooking chisel is employed for cutting holes in brick and stone; its relieved shank allows free movement of the chisel within the recess. A concrete point chisel is another important tool for masons and is used for breaking up concrete.

Brick chisels and sets should be struck with a hand-drilling or mash hammer—not a bricklayer's hammer. Never use these tools on metal; they, like the star drill, are strictly masonry tools.

WEDGES

The wedge is forged from a solid piece of high-carbon steel and may be heat-treated. Wedges are made in various patterns, the ones illustrated being the most commonly used. Weights range from 3 to 8 pounds.

Square-head, Oregon splitting, and stove wedges are designed for splitting logs, firewood, staves, and other wood products. Always use a woodchopper's maul or an axe to make a starting notch. A wedge should be struck with a sledge or woodchopper's maul having a striking face that is larger than the head of the wedge.

Discard any wedge, chisel, star drill, punch, or pin with a chipped, battered, or mushroomed head. The cutting edges on these tools may be resharpened by filing or grinding; their original bevel or shape must be maintained. Instructions for grinding these tools can be found in Chapter 22.

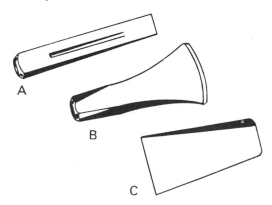

FIG. 1-39. Three major types of wedges: (a) square head; (b) Oregon: (c) stave.

STUD DRIVERS

The stud driver, or drive tool as it is sometimes called, will set tempered-steel studs in concrete, blocks, bricks, and even soft metal, thus eliminating the need to drill a hole when using fasteners such as expansion shields, plugs, or toggle bolts in such materials. The driver tool is designed to give the control and support needed to hammer threaded studs or pins into these materials.

Stud fasteners from $\frac{3}{4}$ to $3\frac{1}{2}$ inches are usually available. When selecting the proper size, remember that the fastener should be long enough to penetrate at least $\frac{3}{4}$ inch into hard concrete and 1 inch into mortar or

masonry. When fastening 2 x 4's to any of these surfaces, allow for at least $1\frac{1}{4}$ inches of stud penetration. While the studs can be driven with a carpenter's hammer, it is best to use a 2- or 3-pound double-faced sledge, especially if you have many studs to drive. Of course, if you are driving a great many studs, it may pay to purchase or rent a power-actuated stud driver. This tool uses .22 cartridge loads to literally "fire" the stud fasteners into the concrete or masonry. Operational instructions for the so-called "velocity" stud driver are in the applications manual which comes with the tool. Be sure to follow these instructions closely at all times.

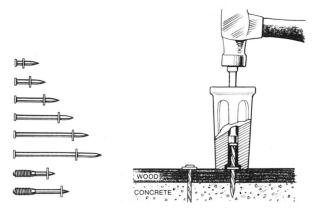

FIG. 1-40. Typical stud driver in use.

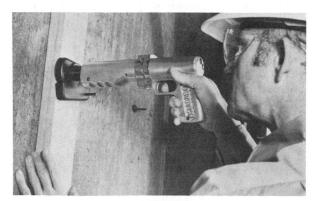

FIG. 1-41. Two types of powered stud drivers.

WOODCUTTING TOOLS

Many different tools are used to cut wood. They include handsaws, chisels, planes, spokeshaves, drawknives, scrapers, wood files, rasps, abrasive papers, bits, drills, and knives. Let us see how they perform their jobs.

Handsaws

The handsaw is one of man's oldest tools, dating back to prehistoric times. Because they have been around so long, the various handsaws in use today have evolved to a state of near perfection. All the common types of woodcutting handsaws consist of a steel blade with a handle at one end. In the two most used types—crosscut saw and ripsaw—the blade is narrower at the end opposite the handle. This end of the blade is called the "point" or "toe." The end of the blade nearest the handle is called the "butt" or "heel." One edge of the blade has teeth which act as two rows of cutters. When the saw is used, these teeth cut two parallel grooves close together. The chips (called "sawdust") are pushed out from between the grooves (the "kerf") by the beveled part of the teeth.

The teeth are bent alternately to one side or the other, to make the kerf wider than the thickness of the blade. This bending is called the "set" of the teeth. The number of teeth per inch, the size and shape of the teeth, and the amount of set depend on the use to be made of the saw and the material to be cut. Woodcutting handsaws are described by the number of tooth points per inch. There is always one more point than there are teeth per inch. A number, usually stamped on the blade under the manufacturer's trademark, gives the number of points of the saw.

While most saw blades are still silvery in color, the black Finish Teflon blades are increasing in popularity. Teflon-coated steel blades offer rust resistance and self-lubricating, nonstick qualities that allow cutting with minimum effort. And, on the subject of extra qualities, manufacturers claim that stainless-steel blades stay sharp five to ten times longer than the conventional steel-bladed saws. Incidentally, the back edge of the blade of a ripsaw or crosscut saw may be either skew or straight. (The edge opposite the teeth of a skewback saw is curved in order to lighten its weight without reducing the stiffness.) While both have their advocates, the straight or ribboned back is the most popular in the United States.

In addition to crosscut saws and ripsaws, the other common woodcutting saws include the compass saw, the coping saw, the backsaw, and the dovetail saw. When selecting a saw, purchase one of good quality—not necessarily the most expensive, but not the cheapest you can find either—and get a saw that is designed for the job you have in mind. The so-called "multipurpose" tools do not really do any one job successfully. Saws are no exception to the basic axiom of tool buying: Get a good one to begin with, and it will give better performance and last longer.

CROSSCUT SAWS AND RIPSAWS

Ripsaws are used for cutting with the grain, and crosscut saws are for cutting across the grain. The major difference between a ripsaw and a crosscut saw is the shape of the teeth. A tooth with a square-faced chisel-type cutting edge, like the ripsaw tooth shown in Figure 2-2, does a good job of cutting with the grain (called "ripping"), but a poor job of cutting across the grain (called "crosscutting"). A tooth with a beveled, knifelike cutting edge, like the crosscut saw tooth shown in Figure 2-3, does a good job of cutting across the grain, but a poor job of cutting with the grain. The set of the teeth lets the two parallel rows make cuts on each side of the kerf so that the wood in between is crumbled out as the teeth move back and forth. The crosscut saw actually cuts slightly on the back stroke, as well as on the forward stroke, but most of the work is done on the forward stroke.

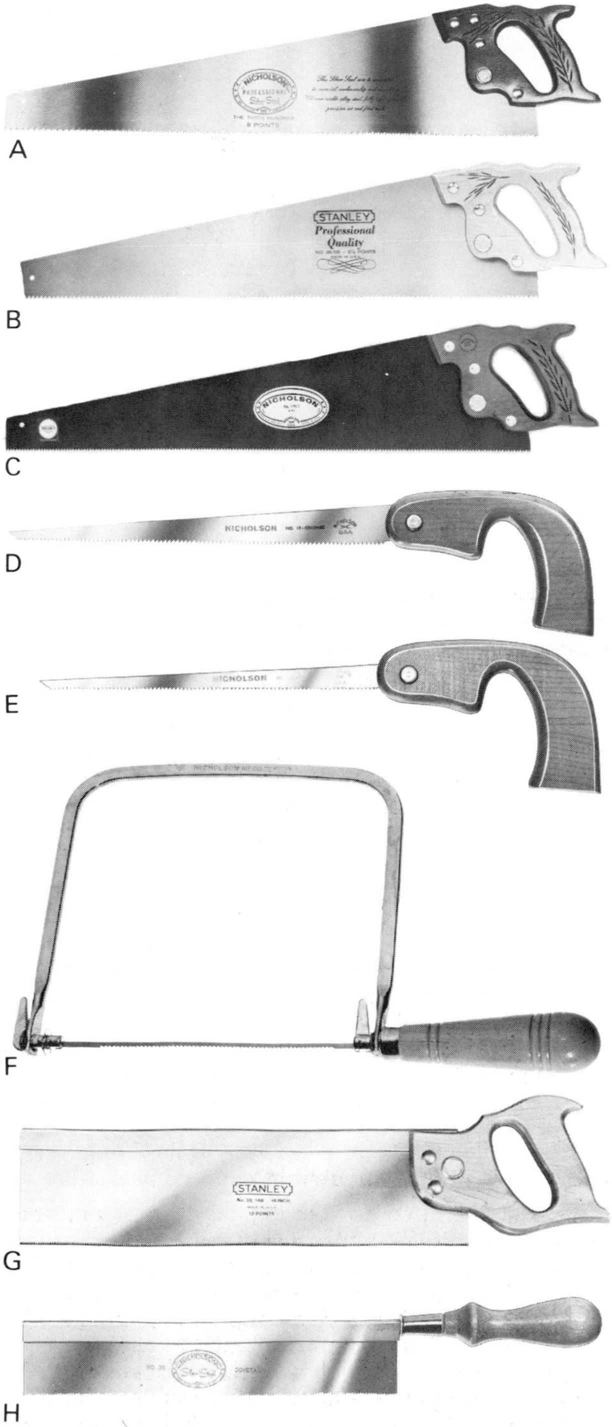

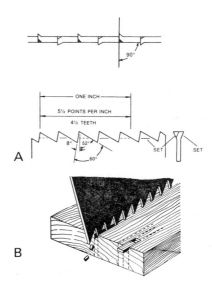

FIG. 2-2. Ripsaw teeth. *(a)* The teeth are usually set alternately to the right and left for a "set" of one-third of their thickness. The 90° angle is often increased slightly to give the tooth a negative rake. *(b)* Ripsaw teeth, like chisels, cut chips on the forward stroke.

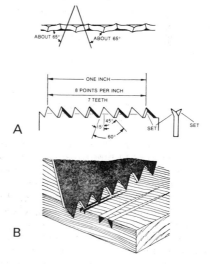

FIG. 2-3. *(a)* The proper set for crosscut teeth; *(b)* crosscut saw teeth, like knives, cut two parallel grooves on the forward and backward strokes. The edges of the teeth pare the groove and clear away sawdust.

FIG. 2-1. Common handsaws: *(a)* ribbon-back crosscut; *(b)* straight-back rip; *(c)* Teflon crosscut; *(d)* compass; *(e)* keyhole; *(f)* coping; *(g)* backsaw; *(h)* dovetail.

A

B

C

D

E

F

G

H

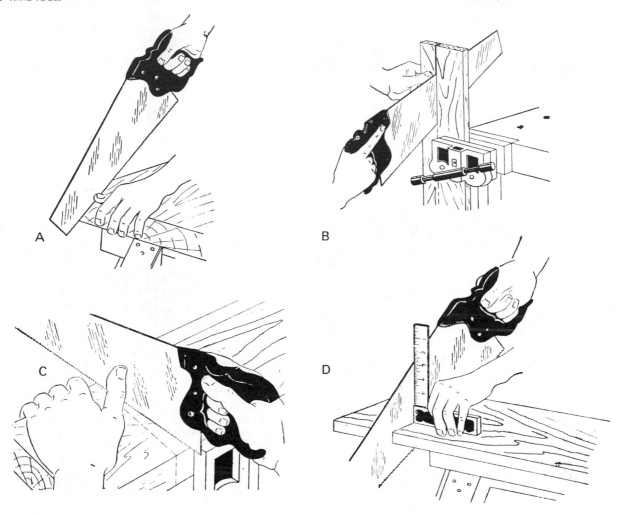

FIG. 2-4. Hints regarding the use of handsaws: (a) starting to rip a board on a sawhorse; (b) wood held in a vise while ripping; (c) board held in a vise for crosscutting; (d) testing a saw cut with a try square.

The teeth on a ripsaw are filed straight across at the front, with this front cutting edge almost perpendicular (about 8°) to the length of the blade (unlike the crosscut saw, where the front edge slants back at about a 15° angle from the blade). As a result, its teeth act like a gang of tiny sharp chisels arranged in an almost straight line. Thus, instead of slicing the wood out the way a crosscut saw does, a ripsaw chips out small pieces from alternate sides, and then pushes them out through the kerf.

The amount of set given a saw is highly important because it determines the ease with which the saw runs; it ensures cutting accuracy; and it helps keep the saw sharp for a longer time. The nature and character of the wood to be cut also must be considered. Green or wet wood requires a saw with coarse teeth and a wide set, with 7 or 8 points to the inch, while a 10-, 11-, or 12-point saw with light set will work better on dry, well-seasoned lumber.

For ordinary crosscutting, the 8- or 10-point saw is most in demand. Ripsaws are coarser and generally have either 5½ or 6 points to the inch. This helps give them the faster cutting action that most people want, since ripping cuts are generally longer than crosscuts. While flat-ground blades are available, the better-quality saws generally have their blades ground to a taper so that they are slightly thinner along the back edge than they are along the toothed or cutting edge. The blade is also thinner at the tip than at the butt or handle end. This taper provides added clearance for the blade to prevent binding in long cuts, and it minimizes the amount of set required on the teeth. In addition, it makes sawing a great deal easier when you work with gummy or green wood.

The length of either a ripsaw or a crosscut handsaw is measured from point to butt on the cutting edge. Crosscut saws are made in different lengths. Some patterns of crosscut saws are made with blades 20, 22, 24, and 26 inches long; and ripsaws, with blades 26 inches long. Saws 24 inches and shorter are also known as "panel saws." The 20-inch, 10-point crosscut saw is most popular among the shorter panel saws.

USING CROSSCUT SAWS AND RIPSAWS To saw across the grain of the stock, use a crosscut saw; to saw with the grain, use a ripsaw. Study the teeth in both kinds of saws so you can readily identify the saw that you need.

Place the board on a sawhorse or some other suitable object, or in a vise. Hold the saw in the right hand, and extend the first finger along the handle as shown in Figure 2-4a and b. When crosscutting, grasp the board as shown in Figure 2-4c, and take a position so that an imaginary line passing lengthwise along the right forearm will be at an angle of approximately 45° with the face of the board (Figure 2-5a). Be sure the side of the saw is plumb, or at right angles, with the face of the board. Place the heel of the saw on the mark. Keep the saw in line with the forearm, and pull it toward you to start the cut. When ripping, the best saw angle is about 60° (Figure 2-5b).

Well-made saws are designed to make starting cuts easily. Ripsaws are usually one point finer at the tip than at the butt, so start the cut with the tip end of the blade. In crosscutting, start with a draw stroke at the butt end of the blade. Repeat once or twice until a groove is started; then use full strokes. That is, to begin with, take short, light strokes, gradually increasing the strokes to the full length of the saw. Do not force or jerk the saw; such a procedure will only make sawing more difficult. The arm that does the sawing should swing clear of your body so that the handle of the saw operates at your side rather than in front of you.

Use one hand to operate the saw. You may be tempted to use both hands at times, but if your saw is sharp one hand will serve you better. The weight of the saw is sufficient to make it cut. If the saw sticks or binds, it may be because the saw is dull and is poorly "set." The wood may have too much moisture in it, or you may have forced the saw and thus caused it to leave the straight line.

Keep your eye on the line, rather than on the saw, while sawing. Watching the marked line enables you to see instantly any tendency to leave the line. If the saw veers away from the marked line, a slight twist or flex of the handle, and taking a few short strokes while sawing, will bring the saw back. But do not flex it much or it may "oversteer" and veer across to the other side. (Also, too much flex could cause the saw to jam or buckle, causing permanent damage.) Blow away the sawdust frequently, so you can see the marked layout line. The final strokes of the cut should be taken slowly. Hold the waste piece in your other hand so the stock will not split when you take the last stroke.

When it is important that your cut be perfectly square, use a small try square as a guide (Figure 2-4d). Another way to keep the cut true and square is to clamp a piece of scrap stock to your work and use it as a guide. For accurate

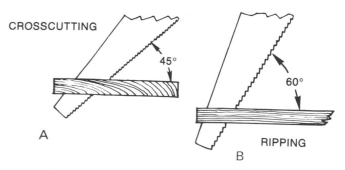

FIG. 2-5. Proper sawing angles. When ripping—that is, cutting with the grain—keep the saw at a 60° angle. The proper sawing angle for crosscutting is about 45°.

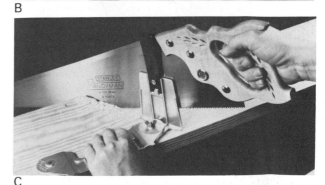

FIG. 2-6. When cutting angles, miters, and square cuts, it is wise to use a (a) wood or (b) plastic miter box or (c) an angle guide. All are relatively inexpensive.

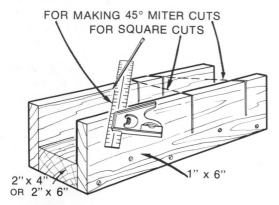

FOR MAKING 45° MITER CUTS
FOR SQUARE CUTS

2" x 4"
OR 2" x 6"

1" x 6"

FIG. 2-7. It is an easy job to build your own miter box, but remember, its accuracy depends on accurate workmanship. Be sure the base is square and straight, and the sides parallel, straight, and flush. With a combination square, mark off both the 45° miter cuts and 90° square cuts. Cut the slots from top to base.

bevel cuts, clamp a length of 2 X 4 stock parallel to the cut line—far enough to one side so that, with the block in place, you control the angle. By the way, like a miter saw or backsaw, the crosscut saw can be used for miter cutting (Figure 2-6). Take slow strokes to avoid saw-tip whip.

When cutting plywood or wallboard panels, place the material on edge with guide boards securely clamped at top and bottom as shown in Figure 2-8b. Clamp these guides to the board that is to be cut, making the distance betwen the guides equal to the width of the sawteeth. Then saw with the blade between the clamped boards, and your cut will be straight and true.

Short boards may be placed on one sawhorse for sawing. Place long boards on two sawhorses, but do not saw so that your weight falls between them or your saw will bind. Place long boards so that your weight is directly on one end of the board, over one sawhorse, while the other end of the board rests on the other sawhorse.

Short pieces of stock are more easily cut when they are held in a vise. When ripping short stock, it is important that you keep the saw from sticking, so it may be necessary to take a squatting position. The saw can then cut in the upward direction and thus work easily. At times, when ripping long lengths, you may encounter trouble with the kerf closing and binding the blade. To prevent this, simply insert a wedge or a large nail or the blade of a screwdriver in the kerf, keeping it just behind the action of the blade. End whipping (of the work), another annoyance on long cuts, is eliminated by clamping the ends of the work together.

When sawing across the grain, if the nature of the work permits, place the board as shown in Figure 2-10b. This avoids splintering at the last resin ring, as sometimes happens when the board is placed as shown in Figure 2-10a.

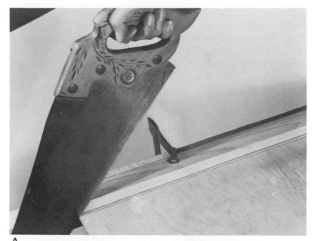

A

B

FIG. 2-8. (a) Using a guide to keep the work square. (b) Method of clamping guides when cutting plywood or wallboard panels.

When ripping or crosscutting, keep the saw on the waste side of the marked line—do not try to saw on the line, or "saw out the line." This ensures that the board will be of the right width or length after it is cut (see Figure 2-10c). When cutting on the line, you cut into the board as well as the waste, as shown in Figure 2-10d. The same principle applies when cutting a mortise. Remember that accuracy is essential in good carpentry. Measure carefully, saw straight, keep within the waste material, and your pieces will fit together smoothly.

KEYHOLE, COMPASS, AND PLUMBER'S SAWS

The "nested saws" shown in Figure 2-11 consist of a handle and three blades which are a compass saw, a keyhole saw, and a plumber's saw. The handle is of wood and is shaped somewhat like a pistol grip. Each of the

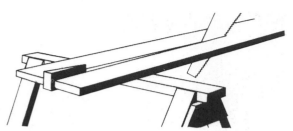

FIG. 2-9. In ripsawing a long board, the kerf may close sufficiently to cause the saw to bind. To avoid this, insert a small wedge at the start of the cut.

blades has a slot in the heel, by which it can be fastened to the handle. The handle has a thumb nut which is tightened to hold the blade securely in place.

The *compass-saw* blade is designed for sawing curves. It is also used for starting cuts to be completed by larger saws, particularly interior cuts. The blade is tapered, usually from less than 1 inch wide at the butt to a point at the tip, and is from 12 to 14 inches long. The teeth—usually 8 or 10 points per inch—are filed in such a manner that the saw may be used either for crosscutting or for ripping. The kerf left by this saw is wider than that of either the crosscut saw or the ripsaw, in order to provide freedom so the blade can turn when it is cutting curves.

The *keyhole-saw* blade is much narrower than the compass-saw blade and is usually 10 to 12 inches in length. The point is narrow enough to enter a $\frac{1}{4}$-inch hole. Generally having 10 points per inch, it is commonly used for cutting keyholes for fitting locks in doors, and for small cuts. Like the compass saw, it cuts a wider kerf than either the crosscut saw or the ripsaw, so that the blade may turn in making curved cuts.

The *plumber's-saw* blade is a heavy blade with fine teeth (usually 15 points per inch), designed for cutting nails or soft metal. The blade, which is usually 16 to 18 inches long, is thick enough to permit a woodcutting saw to pass freely through the cut it makes in a nail. Some nests of saws include a general utility or nail-cutting blade in place of the plumber's-saw blade. This blade is of the same length and design as the compass saw, but it has fine teeth (usually 13 to 15 points per inch). Of course, these

saws are not only sold in nested-saw sets; compass saws, keyhole saws, and plumber's saws are sold as individual saws with their handles permanently fastened to the blade.

To use a compass saw or a keyhole saw, first bore a hole with an auger bit. Insert the compass or keyhole saw into the hole and start to cut, working slowly and carefully with a minimum of pressure. Keep your eye on the saw to avoid flexing; these narrow-bladed saws bend easily. When the cut is long enough to permit it, remove the compass saw or keyhole saw and finish the cut with a standard crosscut saw or ripsaw.

The plumber's saw is used to cut through any nail encountered while sawing. The cut is then continued with a standard woodcutting saw.

There are several other saws that perform duties similar to those of the compass and plumber's saws. Among the more popular of these are the floor saw, electrician/plumber's saw, wallboard saw, and dry-wall saw. The latter has specially designed rounded teeth and gullets to prevent clogging when cutting dry-wall products. The wallboard saw is designed especially for plasterboard—making cutouts for electric outlets—and is self-starting (the point is sharpened for plunge cuts). The flooring type is a short (the blade is about 12 inches long), strong saw with fine teeth (about 15 points per inch) that continue around the nose and up onto the back of the saw. The electrician/plumber's saw is about 12 inches long; it has 12-point teeth on one edge, with no set, for cutting light metal, conduit, BX cable, etc. The opposite blade edge is toothed at 8 points per inch for fast woodcutting.

A variation of the compass and keyhole saws is the spiral-blade "stickle-back" saw. It is a combination hand drill and saw which requires no predrilling of lumber to make an interior cutout. It is particularly useful for cutting holes in wall panels for switch or outlet boxes.

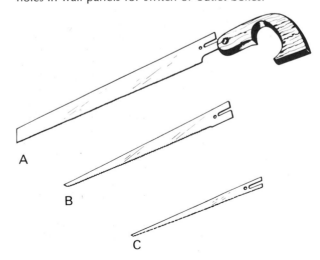

FIG. 2-11. Nested saws: *(a)* plumber's saw; *(b)* compass saw; *(c)* keyhole saw.

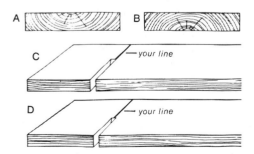

FIG. 2-10. More hints regarding the use of handsaws.

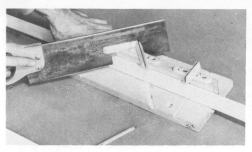  

FIG. 2-12. The backsaw is frequently used in conjunction with a miter gauge (left) or a miter box (center). With the miter machine (right) any miter joint can be cut, glued, and nailed for tight, close-fitting corners. It is used with a miter saw.

BACKSAWS

The backsaw is a crosscut saw designed for sawing a perfectly straight line across the face of a piece of stock. That is, the blade is not tipped downward in cutting, like the crosscut or rip types, but is kept parallel to the surface throughout the cut. A heavy steel backing along the top of the rectangular blade keeps the blade perfectly straight. These saws have fine teeth—11 to 16 points per inch—so they cut cleanly without splintering. The backsaw is generally used with either a miter gauge or miter box (Figure 2-12).

Backsaws vary from 10 to 30 inches in length, although the most widely used model, and the one you will most likely want for use with a simple miter box, is the one that measures about 12 inches in length. (Some factory-made, adjustable miter boxes such as the one shown in Figure 2-15a require a miter-box saw, which is just a backsaw in the 24- to 30-inch length range.) The handle on the backsaw is set at an angle for comfort while working with a miter box, but you will find many other jobs for which the backsaw is handy—for instance, to trim off molding that is nailed flush against a surface.

To start a backsaw cut, make a slight groove along the cut on the waste side; then make a kerf on the waste side of the mark. Be sure to check the accuracy of the angle of the line; then hold the backsaw against the whole length of the cutting line. It is best to support the board being cut from below with a piece of scrap wood. The saw must be kept level at all times. Some factory-made miter boxes, like the type shown in Figure 2-15a, keep the saw level automatically.

If a miter gauge or miter box is not used, it is advisable to support the workpiece with a bench hook (Figure 2-13). For long material, two bench hooks are necessary.

DOVETAIL SAWS

The dovetail saw is a special type of backsaw with a thin, narrow blade (usually only about 6 to 10 inches long and approximately $1\frac{1}{2}$ inches wide) and a file- or chisel-type handle. As its name implies, it was principally designed for cutting dovetails (and tenon joints), but it is used for exceedingly fine cutting (it has about 15 points per inch)

such as is needed for small moldings and veneer work, as well as for trimming woodwork in tight corners where most other saws would not fit. The razor saw, which looks exactly like a dovetail saw, has a smaller blade (4 to 6 inches long and about 1 inch wide) and has up to 70 teeth per inch. It is used to make hairline cuts in metal, wood, and plastic without chipping, splitting, or leaving burred surfaces.

To get the utmost cutting precision from a dovetail saw, score the line to be cut three or four times with a sharp-pointed knife. Use the knife to peel away a portion of the wood on the waste side of the line, and then place the saw flush against the remaining straight side of the knife cut. This procedure ensures an accurate cut.

COPING SAWS

The coping saw (often incorrectly called a jigsaw) is a close relative of the compass saw, for it too is used to cut curves, circles, and interior cutouts. However, this saw is used mainly with thin lumber, preferably $\frac{1}{2}$ inch or thinner. It can also be used to shape the ends of moldings and to cut exact patterns of ornamental scroll designs. Replaceable blades, in widths of $\frac{1}{8}$ inch and less, are available for cutting wood, metal, and plastic.

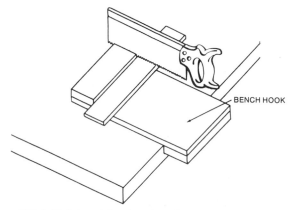

FIG. 2-13. A bench hook such as the one shown is ideal for holding work for backsawing.

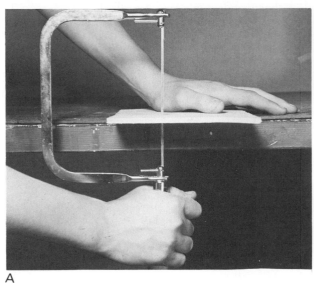

A   B

FIG. 2-14. Two methods of holding the coping-saw work. (*a*) For cutting at a table with the work held flat, the teeth should point downward so that the cut is made on the downstroke. (*b*) For working with thicker stock held vertically in a vise, the teeth should point away from you so that the cut is made on the push stroke.

The coping saw's light bow- or U-shaped frame holds the blade taut between its ends. Most coping saws are designed so that the blade can be turned at any angle—up, down, or sideways—to permit cutting in tight corners where the frame might get in the way. In fact, the blade may be revolved in the frame by turning the end fittings, so the cutting edge may be set at the desired angle. This allows the frame to be swung over the nearest wood edge without changing the cutting direction. Although used primarily on thin and narrow material, it can be used on thicker stock; actually the coping saw is limited by the depth of the throat, which is usually between 4¾ and 6¾ inches. To reach into the centers of larger workpieces, special deep-throated models of 10 inches or more (often called "scroll" or "fret" saws) are also available. A smaller version of the coping saw—called the "piercing" or "jeweler's" saw—is frequently used to cut small metal jewelry designs. The throat depth of these saws is from 2 to 3½ inches.

For most coping-saw work, the blade should be mounted so that the teeth point toward the handle rather than away from it as on most saws. In other words, you do your maximum cutting on the "pull" stroke (Figure 2-14*a*) rather than on the "push" stroke. The exception to this basic rule is shown in Figure 2-14*b*.

One of the major uses of the coping saw is to make coped joints. There are two ways to make these joints. The first method is to make a miter cut on the molding, and then cut away the excess wood using the edge of the miter cut as a guide (Figure 2-15*a*). A coping saw is used for this operation, which is why it is called a coped joint. However, instead of cutting at an exact angle to the face of

the molding, ease the saw slightly backwards so that the back of the molding is somewhat shorter than the front (see Figure 2-15*b*). This is done for clearance. This type of coped joint is always used when the back of the molding does not have a plain, flat surface—which is always the case with the crown molding used for ceiling work.

The second method of making a coped joint is somewhat easier than the first. It can only be used with molding that has a flat surface on the back. Cut a short piece of molding, about two or three inches long, and trace its outline on the back of the molding you want to cope. Hold it true and perpendicular, and use a sharp pencil to make the outline, Next, tape the front to avoid splintering, as you will be cutting from the back. Place the molding in a vise. Use the coping saw to cut through the molding, following the pencil line on the back (Figure 2-15*c*). Again cut at a slight backward angle for clearance. By either method, the coped molding will perfectly fit the molding to which it has been coped. Figure 2-15*d* is a view from "behind" the wall showing the fit between the two pieces.

For a ceiling job, you will have to cope the other end of the molding as well. Carefully measure the length of molding required, making allowance for waste and the thickness of the saw cut. Cope this end the way you did the opposite end. Finish by nailing the joint together.

A coped joint or a mitered joint can be used in an interior corner (Figure 2-15*e*). However, only a mitered joint can be used for exterior corners. Regardless of which type of molding joint is being made, a good miter box and sharp backsaw are a must to get the square ends necessary to start any joint (Figure 2-15*f*).

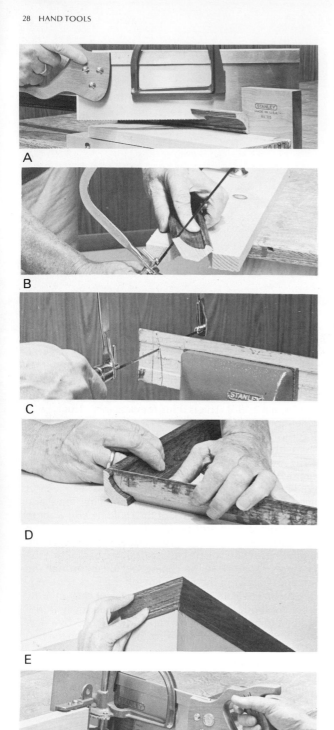

A

B

C

D

E

F

FIG. 2-15. Steps in coping a molding.

Other woodcutting saws frequently seen in wood-working shops are the pad saw, bow saw, and veneer saw. The versatile *pad saw* is handy for difficult cuts and cuts in awkward places; it works much like a conventional keyhole saw but is easier to use. It is used with short strokes. The *bow-saw* handles swivel so the saw can cut at any angle to the frame. The blade, which is usually about 10 inches long, can curve patterns 5½ inches deep in the

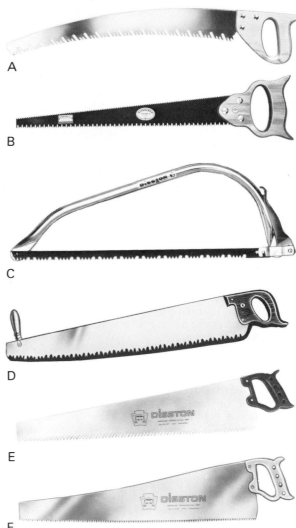

A

B

C

D

E

F

FIG. 2-16. Pruning saws such as the curved pruner *(a),* double-edge pruner *(b),* bow saw *(c),* and one-person crosscut saw *(d)* are good additions to a home workshop, especially if you have any number of trees on your grounds. All these saws are designed for fast cutting of small limbs and logs. Other heavy-duty saws are the skew-backed docking saw *(e),* and the mine and utility saw *(f).*

same way as a bandsaw (see Chapter 16). With fine teeth (about 13 points per inch), it is a useful hand tool for anyone who has ever needed a power band saw but did not have one. The craftsman's bow saw should not be confused with a pruning bow saw (Figure 2-16c).

The *veneer saw* is primarily designed for trimming thin sheets of wood veneer. It has fine teeth on both sides of the blade (on one side they are tapered, and on the other they are straight) and a projecting handle attached to the flat of the blade. Thus, a veneer saw can be used to cut off veneer flush with a surface or for any other delicate work requiring a saw that can cut in a corner.

SAW PRECAUTIONS

A good saw deserves care. After using it, wipe the blade with a rag saturated with light oil to prevent rust, and hang the saw up or stow it in a toolbox to protect the teeth from accidental damage. A toolbox designed to store saws has notches that hold them on edge, teeth up. When saws are stowed loose in a toolbox, the sawteeth may become dulled or bent through contact with other tools. Protection against moisture is an absolute must, to preserve the specially tempered steel blade. Rust causes rapid pitting of the blade, which in turn makes the roughened blade surface drag when cutting. After each use, rub your saw lightly with linseed oil or fine machine oil. Keep an oilcan and a linen cloth in the saw cabinet as a constant reminder. After a time, proper treatment will become automatic. If your saw is already pitted, treat it at once. Rub the spots thoroughly with a cloth dampened with oil. Repeat this after a few days; then give it a rubbing with lump pumice and water. If some rust still remains, remove it with fine emery cloth, and apply oil again. Then keep it oiled and carefully stored.

Care must be taken that the saw is not kinked. If the saw binds in the cut, and pressure is then applied to force it through the wood, a kink is almost certain to result. A kinked saw is useless. Make certain that nails, spikes, and other foreign objects are removed from wood before it is sawed. When sawing out a strip of waste, do not break out the strip by twisting the saw blade. This dulls the saw and may spring or break the blade.

When sawing, be sure that the saw will go through the full stroke without striking the floor or some other object. If the work cannot be raised high enough to obtain full clearance for the saw, you must carefully limit the length of each stroke. Always support the waste side of the work to prevent splitting off.

Make sure that, if the saw slips from the work, it will not cut your hands or other portions of your body. Lay the saw down carefully when it is not in use, in a position such that no one can brush against the teeth and be cut.

Proper use will keep your saw sharp longer, but any saw will dull eventually. While a few craftspeople sharpen their own saws, it is better to have this job done professionally (your hardware store or home center operator can usually have it done for you).

Woodworking Chisels

As was stated in Chapter 1, a woodworking chisel is a steel tool fitted with a wooden or plastic handle. It has a single beveled cutting edge at the end of the steel part, the blade. According to their construction, chisels are divided into two general classes: *tang* chisels, in which part of the chisel enters the handle, and *socket* chisels, in which the handle enters into a part of the chisel. A socket chisel is designed for striking with a wooden mallet (never a steel hammer), whereas a tang chisel is designed for hand manipulation only.

Wood chisels are also divided into types depending upon their weights and thicknesses, the shape or design of their blades, and the work they are intended to do. The shapes of the more common types of wood chisels are shown in Figure 2-17. The *firmer* chisel has a strong, rectangular-cross-section blade, designed for both heavy and light work. The blade of the *tang paring* chisel is relatively thin and is beveled along the sides for fine paring work. The *butt* chisel has a short blade, designed for work in hard-to-get-at places. The butt chisel is commonly used for chiseling the gains (rectangular depressions) for butt hinges on doors; hence its name. The *mortising* chisel is similar to the socket firmer but has a narrow blade designed for chiseling out the deep, narrow mortises for mortise-and-tenon joints. This work requires a good deal of levering out of chips; consequently, the mortising chisel is made extra thick in the shaft to prevent breaking. A *framing* chisel is shaped like a firmer chisel, but has a very heavy, strong blade designed for work in rough carpentry. The sizes of all woodworking chisels are designated by the width of the cutting edge.

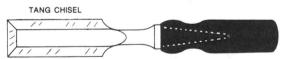

TANG CHISEL

THE SHANK OF THE CHISEL HAS A POINT THAT IS STUCK INTO THE HANDLE. THE POINT IS CALLED A TANG AND THE CHISEL IS CALLED A TANG CHISEL

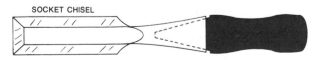

SOCKET CHISEL

IF THE SHANK OF THE CHISEL IS MADE LIKE A CUP, THE HANDLE WILL FIT INTO IT. THIS IS CALLED A SOCKET CHISEL

FIG. 2-17. Tang and socket wood chisels.

SAFETY AND WOODWORKING CHISELS

These are a few basic precautions that you should observe at all times when using a chisel.

1. Secure the work so that it cannot move.
2. Keep both hands back of the cutting edge at all times.
3. Do not start a cut on a guideline. Start slightly away from it, so that there is a small amount of material to be removed by the finishing cuts.
4. When starting a cut, always chisel away from the guideline toward the waste wood, so that no splitting will occur at the edge.
5. Never cut toward yourself with a chisel.
6. Make the shavings thin, especially when finishing.
7. Examine the grain of the wood to see which way it runs. Cut with the grain. This severs the fibers and leaves the wood smooth. Cutting against the grain splits the wood and leaves it rough. This type of cut cannot be controlled.

USING WOOD CHISELS

For light cuts in softwood, the chisel can usually be operated with hand pressure only. For most hardwood, however, a soft-face hammer or mallet is employed to force the chisel into the wood. The chisel is held in one hand, beveled edge down against the wood, and the end of the handle is struck lightly with the mallet, which is held in the other hand. For finish work, the chisel is used with the beveled edge of the blade turned away from the finished surface. Whether striking or hand pressure is employed, be sure to secure the work.

When using hand pressure, the chisel should be held and guided by the left hand and powered with the right. Do not start to cut directly on the marked line, but a little away from it, so that any accidental splitting will occur in the waste portion rather than in the finished work. Cut with the grain as much as possible, since then the chisel's cutting edge tends to sever the wood fibers cleanly, leaving the wood fairly smooth. Cutting against the grain splits the fibers of the wood, leaving it rough. That is, the chisel acts as a wedge, forcing the fibers apart in advance of the cutting edge. The cut thus cannot easily be controlled.

In cutting with a chisel, be very careful (especially when finishing) to make the shavings thin and to cut with the grain of the wood so the surface will be left smooth and bright. Hold the chisel, when possible, at a slight angle to the cut, instead of square across the direction of motion. This gives a paring or sliding cut that is easier to make, and one that leaves the work smoother both on the end grain and with the grain.

The two principal chisel cuts are horizontal and vertical paring. To chisel horizontally with the grain, always hold the tool turned toward one side, and push it with your

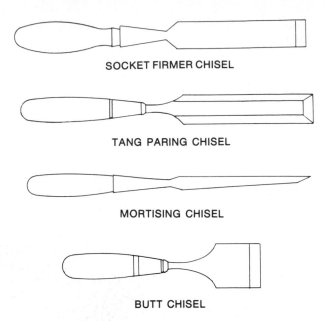

FIG. 2-18. Shapes of common types of wood chisels.

SOCKET FIRMER CHISEL

TANG PARING CHISEL

MORTISING CHISEL

BUTT CHISEL

A

B

FIG. 2-19. (a) To cut horizontally with the grain, hold the chisel slightly turned to one side, and then push it away from yourself. Hold it with the bevel down for a roughing cut, and with the bevel up for a paring cut. (b) To cut horizontally across the grain with the workpiece held in the vise, press your forefinger and thumb together on the chisel to act as a brake. To avoid splintering the corners, cut halfway from each edge toward the center.

hand (Figure 2-19*a*), removing moderate or small portions of the wood. To chisel horizontally against the grain, press your forefinger and thumb together on the chisel to act as a brake while you push the chisel with your other hand (Figure 2-19*b*). To avoid splintering the corners, cut halfway from each edge toward the center, and remove the center stock last. While a chisel is frequently used for roughing, it is usually better to remove as much waste as possible with a saw.

To cut vertically against the grain, the chisel can either be tilted to one side, or held straight and moved to a side as the chisel cuts down into the wood. If the surface to be cut is wider than the chisel, part of the chisel should be pressed against the portion just cut out. This helps to guide and keep in line the part of the chisel cutting out a new portion of the work.

To chisel vertically with the grain, keep the chisel slanted as you would when cutting across the grain. If you are working along an edge of a board, work from the guideline toward the end so that the wood will split away from the line. If you work from the end toward the guideline, you could ruin your work if the wood splits too far.

To cut curves on corners or edges, first remove as much waste as possible with a saw. A coping saw may be used for curves in thin wood, a compass saw or a keyhole saw for curves in thick wood, and a backsaw or crosscut saw for straight, oblique cuts. A chisel should then be used to finish the work. For example, to cut a concave curve, hold the chisel with the bevel on the work, and make the cut by pushing down and then pulling back on the handle. For a convex cut, hold the chisel with the flat side of the tool on the work and the beveled side up; hold the tool and applying the necessary pressure with the left hand, while the right hand guides it and acts as a brake at the same time. To secure a clean shearing cut, hold the chisel tangent to the curve and move from side to side.

When paring on corners and ends, observe the direction of the grain, and work *with* the grain from the edge toward the thicker end; otherwise the board may split along the grain. Round corners are pared in the same manner. When making a shearing cut, bring the chisel from a straight to a slanting position, sliding it from side to side as you press it down on the work. To clean a corner in a notch, tilt the handle away from you, and move the chisel toward you, using the chisel as a knife while holding the wood with the left hand.

A chisel can be used to cut a chamfer, a stopped chamfer, or a rabbet, but a spokeshave or bullnose rabbet plane will do the work better and more easily. Only the ends need be cut with a chisel. For straight and convex cuts, the chisel must be held with the flat side on the work and the bevel up. The left hand holds the chisel; the right hand guides it, applies the power, and acts as a brake. On occasion, an exception may be made to this method. When a long groove or a dado is being cut in wide wood, the chisel may cut in too deeply. It should then be turned

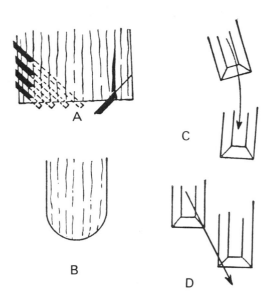

FIG. 2-20. Vertical paring on corners and ends: *(a)* Observe the grain, and start cutting at the edge to avoid splitting the wood. *(b)* A round corner or end can be pared in the same manner. *(c)* A shearing cut can be made by bringing the chisel from a slanting to a vertical position. *(d)* The chisel can also be slid to one side as it is pressed down.

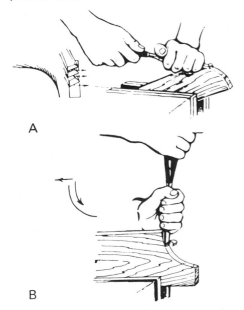

FIG. 2-21. *(a)* To cut a round corner, move the chisel sideways across the work, making a series of cuts close together, each one tangent to the curve. *(b)* A concave curve may be cut by pressing down on the chisel and at the same time drawing back on the handle. Observe the grain.

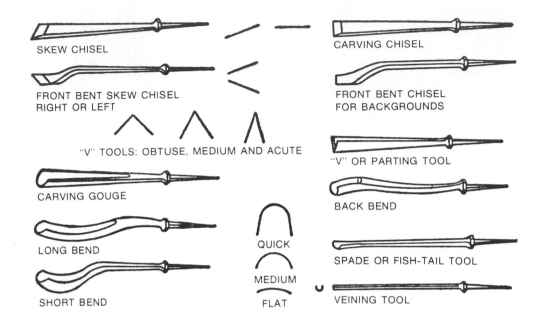

FIG. 2-22. Various woodcarving chisels.

so the bevel is down; this will allow clearance for the handle.

In cutting into plywood, cut only the depth of one ply with vertical cuts; remove that layer, and cut the following layers one at a time.

A chisel should not be used to cut metal, and care must be taken that no foreign substance such as a nail damages the blade. The chisel should be oiled to prevent rust. Always make sure that your chisel is sharp before you begin to work. A dull chisel is difficult to guide and dangerous to use. The method of sharpening a woodcutting chisel is given in Chapter 22.

WOODCUTTING GOUGES

Gouges are, of course, also chisels, the most important difference being that they are rounded, with curved cutting edges. They are classified as firmer and paring gouges and furnished with either a flat, medium, or regular sweep from $\frac{1}{8}$ to 2 inches wide.

Firmer gouges are made with the bevel ground either on the inside or on the outside, and with tang or socket handles. They are used for cutting hollows and grooves. *Paring* gouges are inside ground (that is, the bevel is on the inside), and they have tang handles. They may have offset handles. Paring gouges are used to cut surfaces or ends needed to match irregular forms, as, for instance, moldings. Patternmakers use these gouges to finish shaping core boxes and for similar work.

The woodcarver's tools and gouges differ from the ordinary tools in that the sides, instead of being parallel, taper toward the shoulder and are beveled on both sides. In ordinary practice, gouges come with 11 different sweeps or curves, ranging from those that are almost flat to those with a deep U shape.

The small, deep, U-shaped gouges are called "veiners." The larger ones with quick turns are called "fluters." Those with slight curves are called "flats." There are three V-shaped tools—acute, medium, and obtuse—called "V" or "paring" tools. The chisels are square or oblique on the ends and are known as "firmers" and "skew firmers." Skew firmers with bent shanks are available for either the right or left hand.

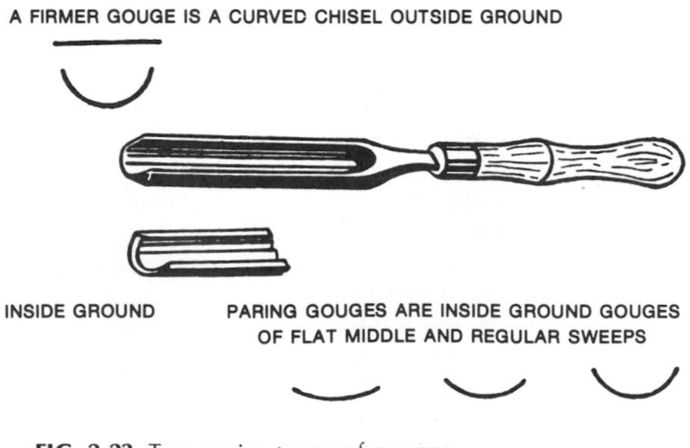

A FIRMER GOUGE IS A CURVED CHISEL OUTSIDE GROUND

INSIDE GROUND   PARING GOUGES ARE INSIDE GROUND GOUGES OF FLAT MIDDLE AND REGULAR SWEEPS

FIG. 2-23. Two major types of gouges.

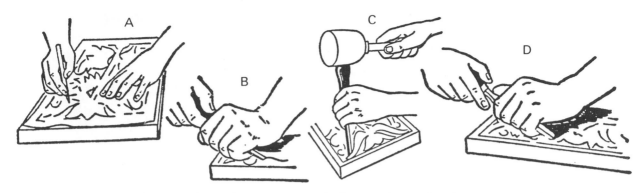

FIG. 2-24. Steps in making a simple wood carving: (a) Trace the design on the wood, or draw it geometrically if its character permits. (b) Outline the design with a gouge or veiner. Be sure to cut the outline on the background side of the line. (c) Set down the outline with a mallet and gouges of suitable sweeps, to fit the curves of the design. (d) Cut out the background with a flat gouge. Model the surface, add detail, and clean up corners to complete the carving.

There is no machine that will do carving for you. There is no substitute for steadiness of hand and eye and long practice. Probably more tools have been designed for wood carving than for any other mechanical operation. Each of the tools is, of course, a kind of chisel, and the fundamental requirement of wood carving is to be able to use a chisel skillfully and successfully.

The various chisels are made in 18 sizes ranging from $\frac{1}{32}$ to 1 inch, with straight, long-bend, or short-bend shanks. Veiners are made as small as $\frac{1}{64}$ inch. The other tools are made in six sizes between 1 and 2 inches. Most of the small sizes are either spade- or fishtail-shaped, and that enhances their usefulness in modeling. Greater clearance is built in just behind the cutting edge.

Wood carving is the kind of thing that people spend a lifetime doing and is, of course, one of the great arts. A great deal has been written on the subject, and anyone who wishes to go into it in depth should by all means use the public library to find whatever books are available.

Planes

It was probably some medieval craftsman who first came up with the idea of mounting a sharp chisel in a block of wood so that it would be held firmly at a constant angle while the blade was used to trim lumber to a specific size or shape (and who thus invented the first wood plane). Since then, professional and amateur carpenters alike have found that no other woodworking tool can match the accuracy and the smoothness of finish that can be achieved with a correctly sharpened and properly adjusted plane. Of course, modern precision-built planes have steel rather than wood blocks. And instead of blade adjustment by hammer and wedge, thumbscrews and levers control the blade. With such workmanship devoted to tool construction, precision work is within the scope of the most amateur carpenter. A few easily mastered rules are all that is required.

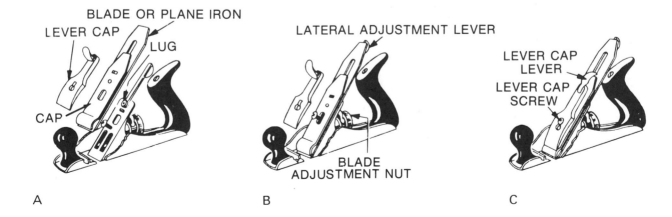

FIG. 2-25. Parts of a bench plane.

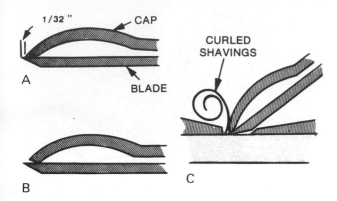

FIG. 2-26. Plane iron and plane-iron cap.

TYPES OF PLANES

More than a score of different planes are made, each designed to do a special kind of work. For example, there are three types of bench planes: the smooth plane, the jack plane, and the jointer plane (sometimes called the "foreplane" or the "gauge plane"). But before going into their various uses, let us look at the principal parts of a typical bench plane (Figure 2-25). The part at the rear that you grasp to push the plane ahead is called the "handle"; the part at the front that you grasp to guide the plane along its course is called the "knob." The main body of the plane, consisting of the bottom, the sides, and the sloping part which carries the plane iron, is called the "frame." The bottom of the frame is called the "sole," and the opening in the sole, through which the blade emerges, is called the "mouth." The front end of the sole is called the "toe"; the rear end, the "heel."

A plane-iron cap, which is screwed to the upper face of the plane iron, deflects the shavings upward through the mouth, as indicated in Figure 2-26, and thus prevents the mouth from becoming choked with shavings. The edge of the cap should fit the back of the iron as shown in Figure 2-26a, not as shown in Figure 2-26b. The lower end of the plane-iron cap should be set back $\frac{1}{32}$ inch from the edge of the blade top, as shown in Figure 2-26a. The iron in a bench plane goes in bevel down.

The edge of the plane iron is brought into correct cutting position by manipulating first the adjusting nut and then the lateral-adjustment lever, as shown in Figure 2-27. The adjustment nut moves the edge of the iron up or down; the lateral-adjustment lever cants it to the right or left. To adjust the plane, hold it upside down, sight along the sole from the toe, and work the adjusting nut until the edge of the blade appears. Then work the lateral-adjustment lever until the edge of the blade is in perfect alignment with the sole, as shown in Figure 2-27b and e. Finally, use the adjusting nut to give the blade the amount of protrusion you want. This amount will depend, of course, upon the depth of the cut you intend to make.

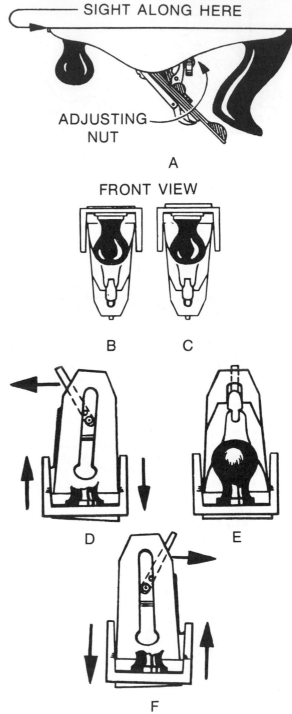

FIG. 2-27. (a, b, and c) Manipulation of the adjustment nut moves the plane iron up or down. (d, e, and f) The effect of manipulation of the lateral adjustment lever.

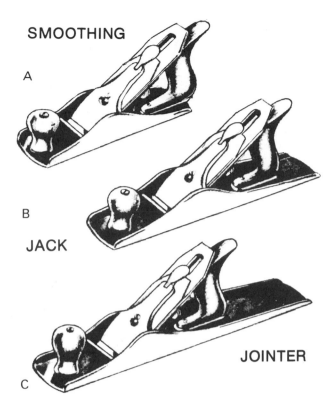

SMOOTHING

A

B

JACK

JOINTER

C

FIG. 2-28. Types of bench planes.

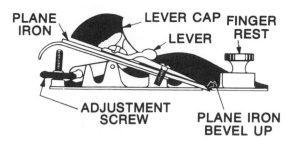

PLANE IRON   LEVER CAP FINGER REST
LEVER
ADJUSTMENT SCREW   PLANE IRON BEVEL UP

FIG. 2-29. Block-plane nomenclature.

All bench planes are used primarily for shaving and smoothing with the grain; the chief difference among them is the length of the sole. The sole of the smooth plane is about 7 to 10 inches long, the sole of the jack plane about 12 to 15 inches long, and the sole of the jointer plane from 18 to 24 inches long. The longer the sole of the plane, the more uniformly flat and true the planed surface will be. Consequently, which bench plane you should use depends upon the requirements with regard to surface trueness. The smooth plane is, in general, a smoother only; it will plane a smooth, but not especially true surface in a short time. It is also used for cross grain smoothing and the squaring of end stock.

The jack plane is the general "jack of all work" of the bench-plane group. It can take a deeper cut and plane a truer surface than the smooth plane. The jointer plane is used when the planed surface must meet the highest requirements with regard to trueness.

Another type of plane that you will find useful is different from the others. The *block* plane is used to smooth end grain, especially for beveling and chamfering. The blade is set at a lower angle (12° from the horizontal) because end grain is much more difficult to cut. The block plane is small (generally about 6 inches in length) and light enough to be held in one hand. Because it is usually held at an angle to the work, the block plane is used chiefly for cross grain squaring of end stock. It is also useful, however, for smoothing all planed surfaces on small work. For very small pieces, the trimmer or modelmaker's plane is ideal. Looking like a miniature block plane (only about 3½ inches long), it comes in several designs, but one of the most popular types has a slightly convex bottom, curved both lengthwise and sidewise. The curvature enables the cutting edge to reach into hollows of the work.

FIG. 2-30. The rabbet plane is designed to cut a rectangular recess along the edge of a piece of wood. This one is a duplex rabbet with two seats for the cutter blade. One is used for regular work, the other for close quarters which could not otherwise be reached. An adjustable fence, which can be used on either side of the plane, controls the width of the rabbet. The fence is also removable.

FIG. 2-31. The combination or plow plane has a variety of interchangeable cutter blades that enable you to form practically any shape along edges and surfaces in a single operation. It can be used for producing fancy decorative effects on wood or for shaping a variety of moldings.

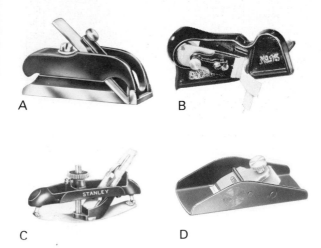

A   B

C   D

FIG. 2-32. Other useful planes: (a) bullnose or cabinetmaker's rabbet plane; (b) edge-trimming block plane; (c) circular plane; (d) trimmer or model-maker's plane.

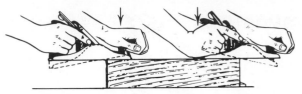

FIG. 2-33. To cut a smooth, straight edge, push the plane with the grain; that is, in the uphill direction of the fibers. To keep the plane straight, press down on the knob at the beginning of the stroke, and on the handle at the end of the stroke. Avoid dropping the plane as shown by the broken lines. It rounds the corner.

Another particularly useful small plane is the edge-trimming block type that makes the job of squaring up a board easy. The plane is machined to a perfect 90° angle, and the cutter blade is set at an angle to make cutting easier. Wood blocks with various bevels may be attached to allow cutting at angles other than 90°.

On the other side of the work, the scrub plane with its rounded cutting edge is ideal for taking heavy cuts to reduce the width of a board quickly when the material to be removed is not quite enough to be ripsawed off, but too much for ordinary planing in a reasonable amount of time. In other words, the scrub plane, which looks like a jack plane but is only 8 to 10 inches long, is good for rough planing and is frequently used to create a hand-hewn appearance on exposed beams.

The rabbet plane is a special plane designed to cut a rectangular recess or groove on the edge or end of a board. This type of plane is fitted with an adjustable guide bar to permit cutting a "step" or rabbet along the edge of a piece of lumber. The guide bar can be adjusted for cutting either right or left. This plane greatly simplifies cabinetwork, panel joining, and such jobs as cutting rabbets in doors for weatherstripping. The standard rabbet plane can be equipped with a "spur" which permits it to cut across the grain—a handy feature for rabbeting frames or joints. Of course, several variations of this plane are available, including duplex, cabinetmaker's, and bench rabbet planes, each of which cuts a special kind of groove. The duplex rabbet plane has unique flexibility. It has two seats for the plane iron—one seat for the ordinary cutting of a rabbet, and the other for close corners or perpendicular cutting. Special adjustable guides make it easy to cut the right width. A spur on the rear seat (which can be raised when not required) is used to score the fibers for cutting across the grain.

FIG. 2-34. It is easier to plane a long edge straight with a long plane than with a short plane. A long plane bridges the low parts and does not cut them until the high spots are removed.

FIG. 2-35. To obtain a smooth surface, plane with the grain. If the grain is torn or rough after the first stroke, reverse the work. If the grain is cross or curly, sharpen the plane iron carefully (see Chapter 22), set the plane-iron cap as near the cutting edge as possible, and adjust the plane iron to take a very thin, even shaving.

A cabinetmaker's rabbet plane has a bullnose that permits it to be used close to an obstruction for a stopped rabbet (one that does not extend to the end of the board). It is especially useful for fine work in which extreme accuracy is essential. An adjustable throat opening is set narrow for fine work and opened for coarse work.

The side rabbet plane is used for smoothing the sides of a groove or for trimming dadoes or moldings. This device contains two small adjustable knives on the sides, facing in opposite directions so that cutting takes place on both the forward and backward strokes. Reversing the plane allows the left and right sides to be trimmed. Some side rabbet planes have a bullnose which allows the plane to cut very close to an obstruction (usually both blades are then set in the same direction).

The router plane is used when a dado or groove has been sawed or cut out. Giving the groove a smooth finish presents some problems for the ordinary plane, and a router plane is used for this purpose. This tool has L-shaped cutters that, in appearance, resemble an offset screwdriver. These cutters are attached to a cutting post and extend below the surface of the board on which the plane rests. The cutters may face front for ordinary planing, or back for bullnose work. Like other planes, the router plane has adjustments to control the size of the shaving, the side of the cut, and the depth of the cut. A small rectangular version of the router plane is also made for inlay work, lock plates, small dadoes, and various model-making tasks.

If you ever have to plane a curve, you will appreciate the value of circular planes that will smooth a circular edge, either concave or convex. Built with flexible bottoms, they can be adjusted to form a curve to fit the work (20 inches minimum radius). That is, an adjusting screw varies the curvature as required and holds it as set. Once adjusted to the surface, the plane is used in the normal manner. Separate planes are used for convex and concave work.

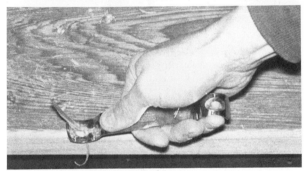

FIG. 2-36. Edges can be chamfered with a plane as shown in the top illustration. Or, as shown in the lower one, a chamfered cutter or cornering tool can be used.

FIG. 2-37. The block plane is used with one hand. It is the handiest tool for planing corners and chamfers on small pieces of wood.

A very specialized plane is the dado plane, which can be used only to cut grooves or dadoes. The width of the blade determines the size of the groove. There is one handle on either side of the blade to guide the plane when it is cutting.

A combination or "universal" plane (also called a "plow plane") will "plow," rabbet, and cut dadoes as well as virtually every type of molding profile and shape. Its more than 50 interchangeable, adjustable cutter blades or

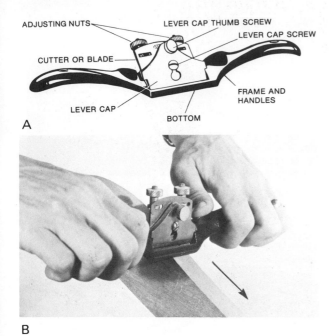

FIG. 2-38. (a) Parts of a spokeshave. (b) The spokeshave is usually pushed. Care must be exercised to cut with the grain of the wood.

guides make possible a wide variety of edge trims for decorating cabinetwork. Cutters are held by special clamps and turned down gradually by a thumbscrew as work progresses. The so-called "molding plane" is a deluxe version of the universal type. It can cut on panel edges as well as on wood strips to be used for molding.

We have not mentioned all the planes available to the home carpenter. Other planes are used for special types of work, but usually only by the professional or the advanced hobbyist. For example, woodworkers claim that steel-body planes are no substitute for the wood-body type. There is little question that the wood sole will not mar the work surface, and the wood-to-wood contact between the sole and the stock lets the plane slide easier than a steel-body plane. Also, because a wooden plane is lighter than a comparable steel plane (superior planing is accomplished by pushing a sharp blade *through* the wood, not into it), it is less fatiguing to use. Wood-body planes are available in the types already described, plus some 30 to 40 other styles.

USING THE PLANE

A plane is simply a chisel held in a metal base so that you can use both hands and work much more rapidly, taking off a very thin shaving with each stroke. Using a plane, you begin to feel the real joy of carpentry; the smell of the wood rises in your nostrils; beautiful curling shavings rise from the blade; the surface behind the plane (provided you are planing with the grain, as you should be) is smooth and slick.

Before adjusting the plane, it may be best to inspect the blade. Remove the lever cap, and you will notice that the blade can be readily removed from the plane. The blade has a cap iron screwed to it which should rest slightly back from the cutting edge on the unbeveled side. The cap iron acts as a shaving deflector. The sharp edge of the cap iron and the small flat surface that bears next to the cutter should lie tightly along the entire width of the blade when they are screwed together. This prevents shavings from working between them.

Before replacing the blade in the plane, be sure the cap iron is on the unbeveled side of the blade and the cap iron is uppermost in the plane. Replace the lever cap, locking it with the small cam at the top.

You will now want to adjust your plane for planing a working face (if you do not have a good milled surface) or for planing an edge square to the working face. Hold the plane by the knob at the front end, bottom side up, with the left hand, so that the bottom or sole is level with the eye. With the right hand, move the adjusting lever to the right or left until the corners of the blade are parallel with the sides of the throat. Then turn the adjusting nut until the blade projects *slightly* through the throat, above the bottom of the plane. This position may be determined by touching the sole across the throat lightly with the fingers. A common mistake is to set the blade too far out. Take off

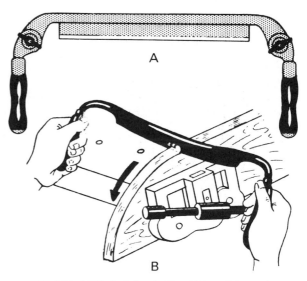

FIG. 2-39. (a) Typical drawknife; (b) how it is used.

really thin shavings that are not thicker on one edge than on the other, and you will obtain good results without gouging the work or clogging the throat of the plane with thick shavings.

Another adjustment that should be made on most planes is the throat opening. The throat opening is the distance between the blade and the front edge of the opening; this determines how long a shaving will run without being broken and, thus, how smooth the cut will be. The finer the planing, the narrower the throat should be. The adjustment is made by moving (forward or backward) the frog supporting the blade. The more nearly horizontal a blade is, the less the resistance of the wood to it. Thus, end-grain planes are set at a low angle. Larger planes usually have blades set at a fixed angle.

When beginning to plane, take a firm position in front of the bench or table, with one foot forward. Make certain that the work to be smoothed is held securely—either clamped in a vise with the board butting against a stop of wood tacked onto the bench, or with the board clamped to a sawhorse. Position the board so that it can be planed with the grain. Hold the plane with both hands—the left hand on the knob for controlling direction, and the right hand on the handle for powering the plane. Press on the knob when you begin the stroke; then exert equal pressures on both knob and handle. As you finish the stroke, lighten the pressure. That is, at the beginning of each stroke, the pressure and driving force are exerted by the left hand. As the stroke progresses, the pressure of the left hand is gradually lessened, and that of the right correspondingly increased, until the pressures of both hands are approximately equal. As you continue the stroke, continue increasing the pressure of the right hand. At the end of the cut, the right hand will be exerting the

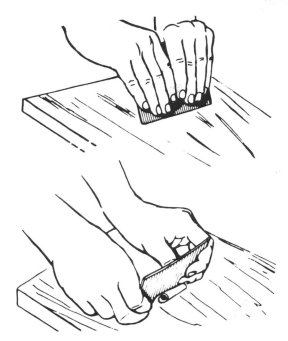

FIG. 2-41. The hand scraper can be either pushed or pulled, as the grain of the wood demands or whichever is more convenient.

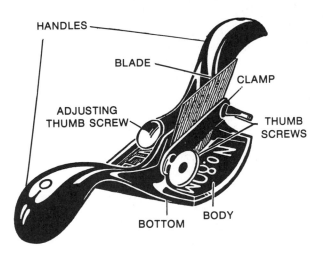

FIG. 2-40. Typical cabinet scraper.

HANDLES

BLADE

CLAMP

ADJUSTING THUMB SCREW

THUMB SCREWS

No. 80 M

BOTTOM

BODY

power and driving the plane, while the left hand will be guiding the tool (Figure 2-33). A common fault is dubbing, or rounding, the ends of the work by forgetting to lessen the pressure. Stay above the work as you plane.

To make planing easier when you are taking a rough cut, slant the plane across the stock diagonally from corner to corner as you push it forward. This method allows the cutting edges of the plane to slice off the shavings. For large surfaces use the largest plane available to ensure a flat surface and speedier work (Figure 2-34). At various stages, test the flatness of the surface in various positions with a try square or a steel square. The edge should lie flat at all points. High spots should be marked with chalk or pencil and planed away.

For finishing, plane lightly with the grain, using a very thin chip adjustment of the blade. Proceed carefully to get a smooth, square edge, testing frequently for straightness by sighting its length, and for squareness with the try square.

Planing a working face smooth and flat is easy, and making the edge square is no more difficult. It requires nothing more than a little practice. If your hands are skillful enough to hold the plane square to the working face, you will go through the operation rapidly. Besides having your cutter sharp and set to take a fairly fine shaving, and holding the tool as square as you can while you work, there is really little to think about when planing a larger surface—except that, again, at the beginning of each stroke, you put a little more downward pressure on the knob of the plane than on the handle. In the middle of the stroke, the pressures are equal. At the end of the stroke, you apply pressure with your right hand on the handle and practically no pressure on the knob. (These directions are for a right-handed user.) In this way you make a cut of approximately the same thickness from

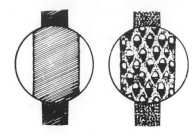

FIG. 2-42. Comparison of a single-cut metal-cutting file (left) and a woodcutting rasp.

beginning to end and ensure the straightness of the edge.

Planing an end is more difficult. While a jack plane or smooth plane can be used, a block plane is better because it is especially designed for cutting end grain. Its plane iron, or blade, is set at a very small angle with the bottom of the bed to aid it in cutting across the grain. The block plane is designed to be held in one hand; grasp the sides of the tool between the thumb and the second and third fingers, with the forefinger resting in the hollow of the finger rest at the front of the plane, and with the lever cap under the palm of the hand. When planing an end, begin at the outside of the board and plane toward the center; then reverse the board and work from the opposite side. If the plane is pushed all the way across an end grain, the corners and the edge of the work are apt to split off. Press down and forward at the start of each stroke, and maintain an even pressure throughout the forward motion. Since this procedure takes time, you should always saw as close as you dare to your guide mark, leaving only minimum finishing to be done at the end with the block plane.

Planing a narrow edge presents the problem of an irregular cut caused by tilting of the plane. To overcome this, clamp a strip of scrap wood in the vise alongside the work, to provide a base sufficiently wide to keep the plane in position.

If the wood has an irregular grain, it may be necessary to plane one end of the board in one direction, and the other end in the opposite direction. On a fairly rough job like a workbench, this will not bother you. The first cutting on a long surface really requires a jack plane. Its long bottom surface, or sole, rides over the low places and enables you to take off the high places, preserving the general plane of the surface. The cutter on the jack plane (Figure 2-28b) is ground in a slightly convex shape which facilitates the removal of thick shavings and, at the same time, avoids a rectangular shaving that would tend to choke up the throat of the plane. Thus, all parts of the blade coming in contact with the work cut smoothly, even shavings. This is also true for the cutter of a jointer plane, except it is slightly less convex (Figure 2-28c). The convex cutters of both planes will leave a series of slight grooves, but these are easily removed with a smoothing plane. That is, finishing is usually done with a smoothing plane.

CARE OF PLANES

Planes will do their job only when their edges are sharp. Unfortunately, it does not take much to dull or nick the tempered steel enough to require that the blade be reground. But taking reasonable care and following a few rules will keep a blade sharp for long periods of use and require only a few minutes of occasional whetting on an oilstone to bring it back to razor keenness for smooth, effort-free woodworking. Of course, the edges should never be allowed to bump other metal objects. Do not toss planes onto a workbench where they can be chipped by nails or by other tools. Have a specific place to keep your planes when they are not in use. A good practice with planes is to retract the blade edge into the mouth when not in use. Also, when assembling a plane, do not drag the plane iron across the cutting edge.

The greatest damage to plane blades comes from nails or other metal objects embedded in the wood, which nick the bevel. Such nicks must be completely removed by grinding; otherwise the plane will leave ridges in all your work. Complete information on how to sharpen plane blades is given in Chapter 22.

Spokeshaves, Drawknives, and Scrapers

The spokeshave is a sort of two-handled plane with a short bottom and a wide throat particularly suited for regular or curved surfaces. The handles permit the tool to be guided more accurately than the ordinary plane for cutting curved surfaces. Many variations of the spokeshave are convenient for special types of work. Models come with a curved or straight bottom. The latter is used on convex or concave edges where the curves have a long sweep.

Most spokeshaves have adjusting nuts that set the depth of the blade, but some have thumbscrews or ordinary screws that loosen the blade to permit manual adjustment. A slight tap on the blade will help adjust it. When using a spokeshave, hold it at a slight angle and make the cut in the "uphill" direction of the grain. When the grain changes direction, the direction of the stroke should be changed. Deep cuts may be made for quick material removal, but for smooth, finished contours the final cuts should be light ones. While the tool can be pulled or pushed, the latter is usually preferred because it permits better control (Figure 2-38b).

The drawknife is a two-handled cutter like the spokeshave, but it is pulled toward your body for cutting (Figure 2-39). The blade has a single-bevel edge, like that of a plane iron, chisel, or spokeshave. The drawknife is used principally for rough-shaping cylindrical timbers, but it is also useful for removing a heavy edge cut prior to finish planing.

Another wood cutter that looks like a spokeshave is the cabinet scraper, used to prepare surfaces for sanding. The beveled blade, which is set in a two-handled metal frame, can be removed by loosening the adjusting screw and the clamp thumbscrew. Once the blade is adjusted properly, hold the cabinet scraper in both hands and either push or pull it over the surface of the work.

A hand scraper produces finer shavings than a cabinet scraper. These are made in two styles, rectangular and curved. (The latter are used on moldings.) They are made of highly tempered steel in various sizes and are available with both square and beveled edges. The square-edge type produces a flatter and smoother surface, is not as fast as the bevel-edge type, and becomes dull sooner. Square-edge scrapers are used for furniture, moldings, and cabinetwork. Bevel-edge scrapers are used for scraping floors and other large areas.

When using a hand scraper, hold it with both hands at a 75° angle and apply pressure according to the thickness of shaving required. It may be either pushed or pulled.

Other wood scrapers are described in Chapter 8.

Wood Files and Rasps

There is frequently confusion between a rasp and a file, and the use of one where the other is called for can only lead to trouble. For smoothing edges and small shaping problems, for instance, the wood file is an essential tool. Files come in lengths from 4 to 14 inches. The cut of a file—that is, the angle and spacing of its teeth—determines its best use. Single-cut files have teeth running diagonally in parallel lines; double-cut files have two sets of crossing parallel lines, making a grid. Files are classified as coarse, bastard, second, and smooth, each (in order) representing a smaller distance between the lines and therefore creating a smoother finish on the work. The distance between the lines of teeth is also proportional to the size of the file, so that smaller files have closer lines that permit smoother finishes. The shape of the file is designed to fit the space in which it must work. The blade may be flat, half-round, round, triangular, or square. The shape may vary: it may be blunt or it may taper. (The taper permits the cutting area to increase gradually and permits working in smaller grooves.) More information on files can be found in Chapter 3.

Rasps, which have deeper, coarser cuts than files, have triangular teeth rather than parallel lines of teeth like files. The rasp cut also differs from both the single and double cuts of files in that the teeth are individually formed and disconnected from each other. A rasp takes away wood particles at a rapid rate. Yet its shape—a square edge, a flat back, and a curved face—makes it useful on almost any surface.

Half-round wood rasps have one flat side and one round side; the flat side is used for flat cuts, and the round side for making curved and irregular cuts. It also comes in various lengths and in smooth and bastard cuts. The round wood rasp is for enlarging holes. It is especially useful on very small holes, where a half-round rasp will not fit. It is available in various lengths, but only with bastard-cut teeth. The shoe rasp, also known as the "four-in-hand," is another type worth considering. It is really

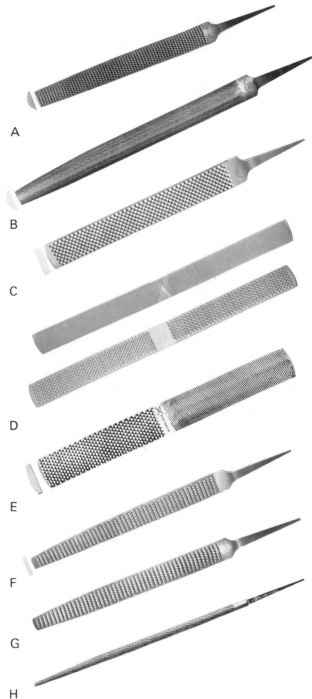

A

B

C

D

E

F

G

H

FIG. 2-43. Various woodcutting files: (a) Half-round cabinet rasp; (b) coarse wood file, half-round; (c) tanged horse rasp; (d) double-ended horse rasp; (e) shoe rasp; (f) wood rasp, flat bastard; (g) wood rasp, half-round bastard; (h) wood rasp, round bastard.

half rasp and half file, with one side half round, and the other flat. It is available with bastard, smooth, or second-cut teeth (between bastard and smooth in coarseness). While it is convenient to have a two-in-one tool, the shoe rasp also has disadvantages. It does not have a tang for a handle, which some craftsmen say reduces control, and it is slower than other rasps because you cannot take long strokes with its shorter working surfaces. The shoe rasp is available in 8-, 9-, and 10-inch lengths, while the others can be found in 8-, 10-, 12-, and 14-inch lengths. As with any rasp, the length to select is the one you find most comfortable.

Many shaping and smoothing operations are performed with a new tool manufactured in a variety of shapes. Known as "Surform tools," they are used for shaping, trimming, and forming wood, plastics, and soft metals. With a surface that looks a little like a roughened colander and a little like a file, Surform tools have many tiny cutting teeth which work like individual planes. One Surform tool is in the shape of a file, with a flat-blade surface. The front of the tool has a ribbed section that permits use of the tool with both hands. It is used in place of a rasp. A similar instrument, cylindrical in shape, is used for enlarging holes. For shaping large surfaces, a Surform tool comes in the shape and style of a plane. A pocket Surform plane, 5½ inches long, is useful for trimming rough edges on the job. All Surform tools have replaceable blades, both flat and curved. Special blades are made for cutting metals in the same fashion. An appropriate Surform tool can be used for almost any shaping problem; they are especially valuable for

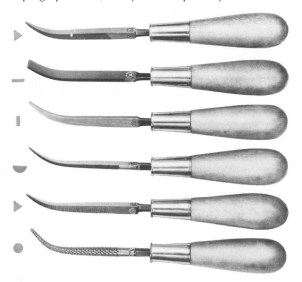

FIG. 2-44. Bent riffler files are used principally by wood carvers and metal and stone workers for shaping and finishing in and about the many irregular parts of patterns. While made many different shapes, the ones shown here are the most commonly used.

patternmaking, shaping a chair or table leg, or finishing any intricate shape, from a gunstock to a mirror frame.

The shaper tool, similar to a Surform tool, is used for final speed shaping. It forms, trims, and smooths wood and plastic, and works particularly well on metal. Straight or half-round replaceable blades are used.

USING SURFORM TOOLS, FILES, AND RASPS

Craftsmen use a Surform file or woodworker's file on wood, and a regular file for work on their tools. But it is usually not considered good practice to file wood. The Surform tool or file is used to enlarge round holes and to finish curved work that has been sawed nearly to the final size. To the craftsman this is permissible only when the work is exceedingly difficult to reach with a chisel or a spokeshave.

A

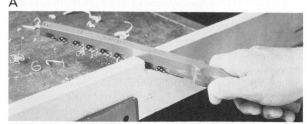

B

C

D

FIG. 2-45. The four major types of hand Surform tools: (a) plane type; (b) file type; (c) shaver type; (d) round type.

When working with a Surform tool or a file, hold it at the level of your elbow. The handle should be grasped in the right hand, against the fleshy part of the palm, with the thumb extending on top of the tool. The front end of the tool should be held with the thumb and first two fingers of the left hand, with the thumb on top. These tools are made to cut in only one direction, so that pressure should be applied only on the forward stroke. The amount of stock removed can be controlled by varying the angle of the stroke. To make finishing cuts on long, narrow work, hold the tool at a right angle and move it back and forth. In filing a curve, use a sweeping motion diagonally across the grain to avoid making grooves and hollows in the work. This also tends to prevent chipping of the edges. Many of the filing techniques given in the next chapter for metal hold for cutting wood with a file.

It is a good idea to equip all files (both wood and metal types) with handles. Many accidents occur when a file without a handle meets resistance and the tang pierces the user's skin. Metal and wooden handles are available; they are usually removed when the file is not in use. Of course, some files may be purchased with a handle already attached. But, to attach a small handle, insert the file with the handle on the bench, striking the point of the file until the fit is firm. Be careful not to strike too hard, or the handle will split. To remove the handle, place the ferrule at the edge of the bench so that the handle is above the bench and the file is free; then tap the file against the bench.

The teeth of a Surform tool are delicate and easily broken. Careless handling of files will dull them. The oil on a new file can be removed by covering it with chalk or charcoal before using it. All files will last much longer if they are cleaned with a file card or brush every time they are used (see Chapter 3). This does not sharpen the file but will restore its usefulness.

Abrasive Papers

Abrasive papers (sandpaper) can cut wood. The various types of abrasive papers are fully described in Chapter 12. But, for hand sanding, keep the following points in mind. The general rule in all sanding operations is to work from a coarser grit through progressively finer grits until you get the degree of smoothness you require. To avoid doing any more work than is absolutely necessary, never start with a grade that is coarser than it has to be. In other words, if the surface is not in too bad a condition, start with medium or possibly fine grit; then finish with very fine grit. There is no sense in starting out with a coarse paper that leaves deep scratches which you will only have to smooth out later.

Always sand parallel to the grain; sanding across the grain tears and roughens the fibers and leaves scratches that will ruin the final finish—especially if the wood is to be stained. Wherever possible, use a sanding block or holder of some kind, instead of holding the sandpaper in your hand. When you sand with your fingers you are

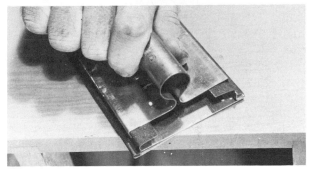

FIG. 2-46. Three types of sanding blocks.

bound to apply more pressure with your fingertips than with the rest of your hand, so you may wind up with gouges or wavy marks in the finish if you are not careful. You can use a scrap piece of wood for a block, and (1) simply wrap the sandpaper around it to hold it in place, or (2) fasten the sandpaper to the sides or top of the block with tacks or staples. However, for best results, face the block with a small piece of carpet or felt to give it some resiliency. Then, if any grit breaks loose or if there are any high spots on either the block or the surface being sanded, you will not wind up with glazed marks and scratches when the loose grit gets caught between the two hard surfaces. The resilient backing absorbs the loose pieces and does a better job of rubbing down high spots without skipping. Even better than a homemade wood block are several different types of commercially available sandpaper holders. They may be made of metal, wood, plastic, or hard rubber, but they all provide a means for gripping a sheet of sandpaper securely while providing a comfortable grip for your hand.

When you get down to the final rubbing, judge the smoothness of the surface by feeling lightly with your fingertips, rather than by merely looking. Examining the surface with light aimed at a low angle across the surface also helps. To keep edges square, use a small block, and keep it flat against the edge by letting your fingertips ride against one side of the piece so that you can tell whether or not the block is being rocked to either side as you rub.

Boring Holes in Wood

When working with wood, you will frequently be required to bore holes. It is important, therefore, that you know the proper procedures and tools to use for this job. Auger bits and a variety of braces and drills are used extensively for boring purposes.

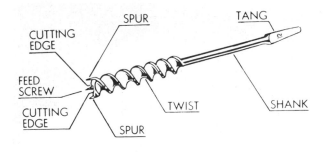

FIG. 2-47. Nomenclature of auger bits.

THE BRACE AND AUGER BITS

Bits are used for boring holes for screws, dowels, and hardware, as an aid in mortising (cutting a cavity in wood for joining members), in shaping curves, and for many other purposes. As with saws and planes, bits of various shapes and structure are used for different types of jobs. Some of the most common bits are described in this section.

Auger bits are screw-shaped tools consisting of six parts: cutter, screw, spur, twist, shank, and tang (Figure 2-47). The twist ends with two sharp points called the spurs, which score the circle, and two cutting edges which cut shavings within the scored circle. The screw centers the bit and draws it into the wood. The threads of the screw are made in three different pitches: steep, medium, and fine (Figure 2-48). The steep- (or fast-) pitch screw makes for quick boring and thick chips, and the fine- or slight-pitch screw makes for slow boring and fine chips. For end-wood boring, a steep- or medium-pitch screw bit should be used, because end wood is likely to be forced in between the fine screw threads, and that will prevent the

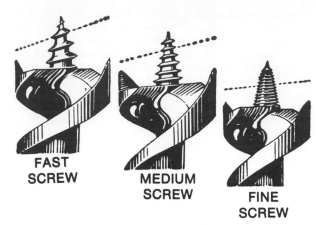

FIG. 2-48. The three bit pitches.

screw from taking hold. The twist carries the cuttings away from the cutters and deposits them in a mound around the hole. For fast cutting in green or gummy work, the single-thread form (threads farther apart) is best. The standard double-thread feed screw (threads close together) is preferred for general work with seasoned wood and for most cabinetmaking work. The diamond point (no screw thread) is used for machine boring with power feed.

Auger bits are made in either single or double twist. The most commonly used is the single-twist bit, which is best for fast, easy boring. It has a single spur and a single cutting lip. The single twist clears itself of chips more readily and quickly than the double-twist type. The double-twist type is, however, better for smooth, accurate boring, but it works slower than the single-twist type. It has two spurs and two cutting lips. The single-twist type is used for hard and gummy woods, while the double-twist type is employed with softwoods. Other differences in standard auger-bit features are not of critical importance.

The sizes of auger bits are indicated in sixteenths of an inch and are stamped on the tang. The number 10 means $\frac{10}{16}$ or $\frac{5}{8}$ inch; number 5 means $\frac{5}{16}$ inch; and so on. The most common woodworker's auger-bit set ranges in size from $\frac{1}{4}$ to 1 inch. Standard auger bits up to 1 inch in diameter are from 6 to 9 inches long. Short auger bits that are about $3\frac{1}{2}$ inches long are called "dowel bits." Long bits are made up to 18 inches in length.

Expansive auger bits have adjustable cutters, for boring holes of different diameters (Figure 2-50). Expansive bits are generally made in two different sizes: one for boring holes from $\frac{1}{2}$ to $1\frac{1}{2}$ inches in diameter, and the other for boring holes from $\frac{7}{8}$ to 4 inches in diameter. They have adjustable cutting blades which can be set to bore holes of any diameter within their range. A scale on the cutter blade indicates the diameter of the hole to be bored. However, it is always wise to check the accuracy of the adjustment by making a test bore through a piece of scrap wood.

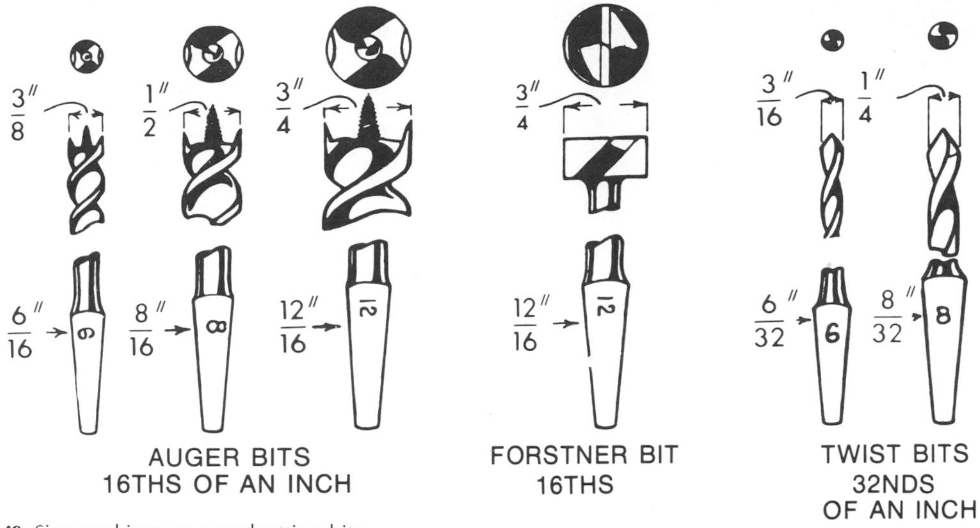

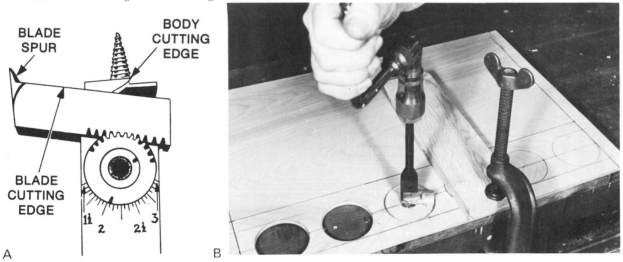

3″/8
1″/2
3″/4
6″/16
8″/16
12″/16
AUGER BITS
16THS OF AN INCH
3″/4
12″/16
FORSTNER BIT
16THS
3″/16
1″/4
6″/32
8″/32
TWIST BITS
32NDS
OF AN INCH

FIG. 2-49. Size markings on woodcutting bits.

BLADE
SPUR
BODY
CUTTING
EDGE
BLADE
CUTTING
EDGE
1½
2
2½
3
A
B

FIG. 2-50. *(a)* Parts of an expansive bit; *(b)* how it is used.

A
B
C
D

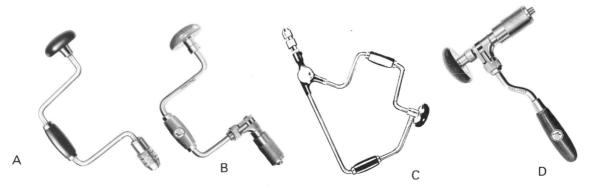

FIG. 2-51. Four types of carpenter's braces: (a) common or plain; *(b)* ratchet; *(c)* corner ratchet; *(d)* right angle or short.

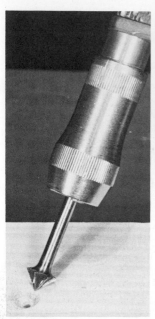
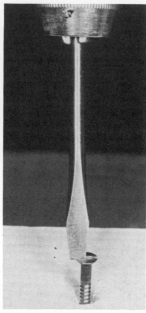

FIG. 2-52. The countersink bit (left) and screw bit (right) are good additions to your boring equipment.

Another wood-boring bit is the Forstner type. This bit does not have a feed screw but must be fed by pushing while turning. The rim projects slightly and prevents the bit from creeping when in use. There is no tendency to split the wood as is often the case with screw-feed bits. Forstner bits, because of the absence of a feed screw, will bore holes almost through a board without defacing the opposite side of the board. A Forstner bit can also be used to bore a larger hole where a smaller hole has previously been bored. (This cannot be done with an ordinary auger bit without first plugging up the smaller hole.) These bits are made in sizes up to 2 inches in diameter, with the size indicated in sixteenths of an inch on the tang in the same manner as for auger bits. To center or start a Forstner bit, scribe a circle the size of the hole with dividers, and press the rim of the Forstner bit into it.

Another bit that is sometimes used is the "gimlet" bit. Being 18 to 24 inches in length, the gimlet bit is used to bore holes through very thick timbers and planks in heavy construction work. Some gimlet bits have neither spur or screw. (A gimlet itself is a small wood-boring tool that has a wooden handle attached at right angles to a small gimlet bit.) Wood-boring drills which are similar to twist drills are also available.

The auger bit is the tool that actually does the cutting in the wood; however, it is necessary that another tool be used to hold the auger bit and give you enough leverage to turn the bit. The tool most frequently used is the carpenter's brace. Figure 2-51 shows several of the most common types of carpenter's braces: the plain, the ratchet, the corner, and the short brace. All braces have an adjustable chuck which receives bits from $\frac{1}{4}$ up to $1\frac{1}{8}$ inches in diameter and will also receive most special bits, such as the expansive auger bit, Forstner bit, wood drill, and gimlet bit. For most general uses a brace with a well-balanced, heavy-duty ratchet is recommended. The ratchet feature, of course, makes it possible to work in close quarters, where half turns and quarter turns are all that the clearance allows. With a reverse ratchet, you can take out tightly set screws easily. A ball-bearing head for easy turning and long wear, a self-opening chuck with automatic centering, and a deep-sweep frame for maximum leverage are features of the better makes of braces.

On both plain and ratchet braces, the head is centered above the bit chuck. The whimble brace is similar to the standard ratchet brace except that the head is located off center on the opposite side of the sweep from the crank handle. In this position, it serves as a second crank handle rather than a center grip. This allows you to apply turning force with both hands for the power needed on difficult boring jobs. In corners and other inaccessible places, the corner brace is used. The centerline of its sweep is at about a 45° angle to the centerline of the chuck. Another brace ideal for cramped quarters is the short type. The bit is turned with a back-and-forth movement of the handle.

In addition to the bits already mentioned, there are two others that help to make the brace even more versatile. They are the countersink bit and the screwdriver bit. The latter will prove immensely helpful in driving screws—particularly when a large number must be driven, or when the wood is hard. Also, in withdrawing screws that are tightly set, the screwdriver bit is of great aid.

A depth-gauge bit can be set to drill holes to an exact depth; this is essential in dowel work, setting adjustable shelf pegs, and many other forms of cabinetwork. While ready-made gauges (Figure 2-53a) are available, one can be made from a small block of wood. Bore a hole in the block, slightly larger in diameter than the auger bit. Cut the block to the proper height, which will vary inversely with the depth of the hole that is to be bored (Figure 2-53b). Slip depth gauge over the bit before boring the hole.

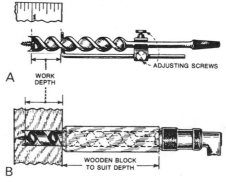

FIG. 2-53. (a) Ready-made or commercial depth gauge; (b) improvised depth gauge.

FIG. 2-54. Another valuable gauge or jig is this one, which is used in doweling work. Graduations permit direct reading and accurate setting of the jig to the centerline of the work.

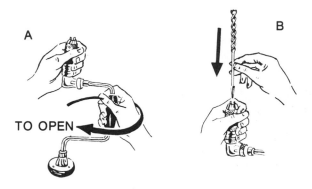

A

TO OPEN

B

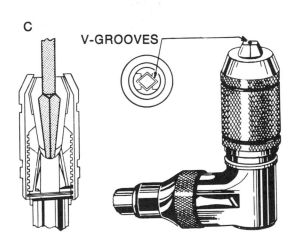

C

V-GROOVES

FIG. 2-55. Placing an auger bit in a chuck.

BORING HOLES THROUGH WOOD

To bore a hole in wood with an auger bit, first select the proper bit, as indicated on or near the square tang. Then insert the auger bit into the chuck.

To chuck the bit, hold the shell of the chuck (Figure 2-55a) as you turn the handle to open the jaws. When the jaws are apart far enough to take the square tang of the bit, insert it (Figure 2-55b) until the end seats in the square driving socket at the bottom of the chuck. Then tighten the chuck by turning the handle to close the jaws while holding the bit in place.

With a chuck having no driving socket (a square hole which is visible if you look directly into the chuck), additional care must be taken to seat and center the corners of the tapered shank in the V grooves of the chuck jaws. (See Figure 2-55c.) In this type of chuck, the jaws serve to hold the bit in the center and to prevent it from coming out of the chuck.

After placing the point of the feed screw at the location of the center of the hole you will bore, steady the brace against your body, if possible, with the auger bit square with the surface of the work. Generally, it is a good idea to first make an impression in the wood with an awl or a center punch (Figure 2-56a).

To bore a horizontal hole in stock held in a bench vise, hold the head of the brace with one hand, steadying it against your body, while turning the handle clockwise with the other hand. Scrap stock placed behind the job will prevent splintering (Figure 2-56b).

When it is not possible to make a full turn with the handle of the brace, turn the cam ring clockwise until it stops. This will raise one of the two ratchet pawls, allowing clockwise ratchet action for rotating the bit. For counterclockwise ratchet action, turn the cam ring counterclockwise as far as it will go.

A   B

FIG. 2-56. (a) Always center the screw tip accurately on the point where the center of the hole should be. For accuracy, make a pilot hole with an awl or a center punch. (b) In boring a hole, back up the workpiece with a scrap board, and bore through into it to avoid tearing the back of the stock with the emerging tip.

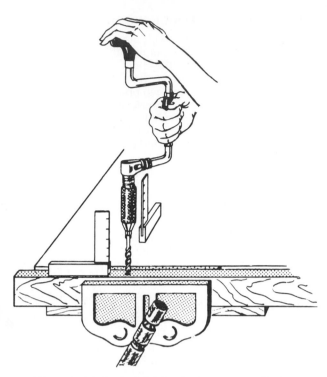

FIG. 2-57. Method of sighting in for a perpendicular hole.

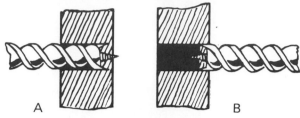

FIG. 2-58. Boring a through hole by reversing direction.

To bore a vertical hole in stock in a bench vise, hold the brace and bit perpendicular to the surface of the work. Placing a try square near the bit, alternately in the two positions shown in Figure 2-57, will help you sight it in.

Another way to bore a through hole without splitting out on the opposite face is to reverse the bit one or two turns when the feed screw just becomes visible through this opposite face (Figure 2-58a). This will release the bit. Remove the bit while pulling it up and turning it clockwise. This will remove the loose chips from the hole. Finish the hole by boring from the opposite face. This will remove the remaining material, which is usually in the form of a wooden disk held fast to the feed screw (Figure 2-58b).

The feel of the brace and the effort required to turn it will indicate whether the parts of a bit are working together. If the chips are uniform in thickness, the two cutting lips are in the right relation to each other. If both thick and thin chips come from the hole, the cutters are not sharing the work equally. Also, if the edges of the chips are rough, the spurs are not doing their part. If the screw fills with fiber and releases, the threads are not smooth and are not properly joined with the cutting lips. The proper method of resharpening the spur and cutters is given in Chapter 22. Remember that the spurs on bits are brittle so that they will keep a sharp cutting edge. They can be damaged by banging against other spurs if tossed

FIG. 2-59. Drilling a hole with a hand drill.

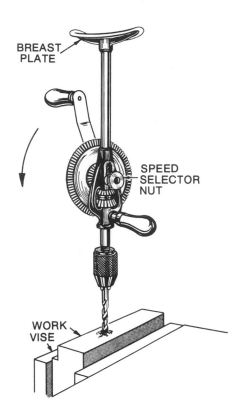

FIG. 2-60. Drilling a hole with a breast drill.

BREAST PLATE

SPEED SELECTOR NUT

WORK VISE

loosely in a drawer. It is better to get into the habit of racking them, in order of size.

To keep braces in good working order, oil them periodically. Bits should also be oiled before storing, since rust quickly blunts their sharp edges and damages the screw tips.

DRILLING HOLES WITH A TWIST DRILL

An ordinary twist drill may be used to drill holes in wood. Select a twist drill of the size required, and secure it in the chuck of a drill. (Complete information on the various sizes and types of twist drills can be found in Chapter 3.) Twist drills may be driven with either a hand drill or a breast drill and may be used to drill plastic and metal as well as wood.

In Figure 2-59, the twist drill has been chucked. Notice that the work (a piece of plastic) is secured to the table with a clamp. Beneath the workpiece is a block of wood. In drilling through the workpiece, the backup block is used to ensure a clean hole at the bottom of the job.

Figure 2-60 shows a hole being drilled with a breast drill. Turn the crank handle with one hand as you hold the side handle with the other hand. This will steady the breast drill while you apply feed pressure by resting your chest on the breast plate (Figure 2-60). Notice, too, that the breast drill can be set for high or low speed with the speed-selector nut.

In drilling a horizontal hole with the hand drill shown in Figure 2-61, operate the crank with the right hand. With the left hand, guide the drill by holding the handle which is opposite the chuck end of the drill.

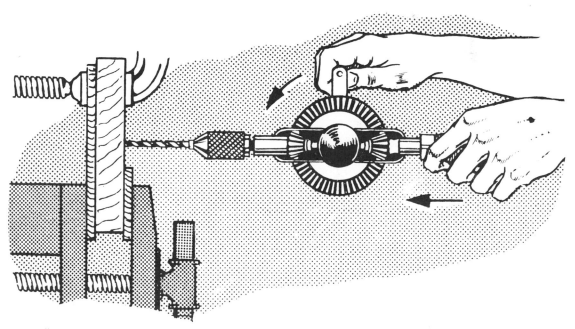

FIG. 2-61. Drilling a horizontal hole with a hand drill.

DRILLING HOLES WITH A PUSH DRILL

The push or automatic drill can be used to drill either horizontal or vertical holes when the accuracy of the right angle with the work is not critical. The bit point used in push drills is a straight flute drill. Sharpen its point on the grinder, and provide only slight clearance behind the cutting edge. It will drill holes in wood and other soft materials.

To select a drill for use in a push drill, hold the handle of the drill in one hand and release the magazine by turning the knurled screw as shown in Figure 2-63a. This will permit you to drop the magazine. Figure 2-63b shows the drill magazine lowered to expose the drills, from which the proper size can be selected. To chuck the drill, loosen the chuck several turns and insert the drill as far as it will go. Turn the drill until it seats in the driving socket in the bottom of the chuck. Then tighten the chuck to hold the drill in place (Figure 2-63c).

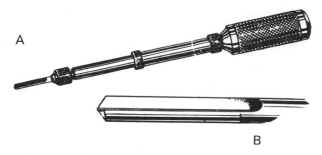

FIG. 2-62. *(a)* Push drill; *(b)* drill point.

To drill a vertical hole with this drill (Figure 2-64a), place the job on a flat surface and operate the push drill with alternating up and down strokes. If it is necessary to hold the work in place while it is being drilled, use some mechanical means, if possible. If you must hold the job with your hand, grasp the material as far as possible from where the drill is drilling.

In drilling horizontal holes with the push drill, as in Figure 2-64b, secure the job in a vise. The back-and-forth strokes rotate the drill, advancing it into the work on the forward stroke as the drilling proceeds. The index finger, extended along the body of the tool, will help guide the drilling at a right angle to the work.

For faster, more accurate boring, keep bits and drills sharp by honing their cutting edges as described in Chapter 22. Keep the moving parts of a brace or drill well oiled.

Knives

Most knives are used to cut, pare, and trim wood, leather, rubber, and similar materials. The types you will probably encounter most frequently are the shop or utility knife, pocketknife, and various hand knives. Other knives that may be found in a workshop are described in Chapter 8.

The utility knife finds a hundred uses in a home workshop—cutting shingles, scoring asphalt tile, cutting dry wall, trimming, and so on. The knife is especially important for marking a thin line on wood more exactly than with a pencil, and for cleaning areas where a chisel cannot be used. The knife blade should be of good steel

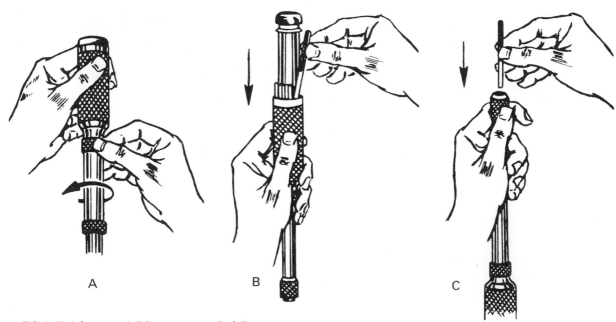

FIG. 2-63. Selecting a drill for use in a push drill.

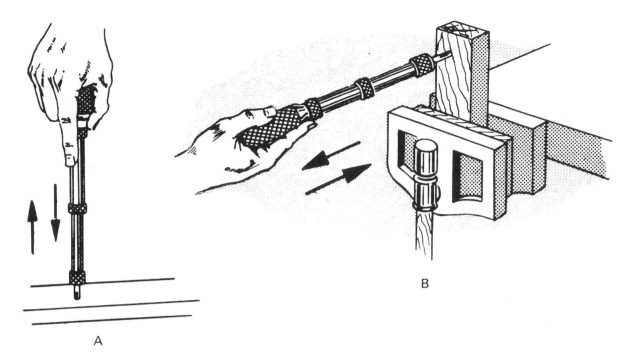

A

B

FIG. 2-64. Drilling horizontal and vertical holes with a push drill.

and always kept sharp. The most satisfactory utility or shop knife is one with a retractable blade and a button that prevents unintended sliding. The blade should be adjustable at two or more cutting positions so that a small cut or groove can be made without using the entire blade. Some knives have a hole in the handle for convenient hanging. Other models can be converted into scrapers for removing paint or stickers, and some others have substitute saw blades.

Pocketknives are used for light cutting, sharpening pencils, cutting strings, etc. They are unsuited for heavy work. Multipurpose knives have an assortment of blades, designed for forcing holes, driving screws, and opening cans, as well as cutting. The blades are hinged and should be contained within the case when not in use. They are spring loaded to keep them firmly in place when open or closed.

Linoleum, vinyl, carpet, tar-paper, and roofing knives are all similar in design, but their blades vary slightly in shape, depending on the material to be cut. The hawkbill blade usually varies from $2\frac{1}{2}$ to $3\frac{1}{2}$ inches in length.

Safety with knives is essential. Do not use knives larger than can safely be handled. Use knives only for the purpose for which they were designed. Always cut away from your body. Do not carry open knives in your pocket or leave them where they may come into contact with, or cause injury to, others. Put knives away carefully after use to keep their sharp cutting edges from contacting other hard objects.

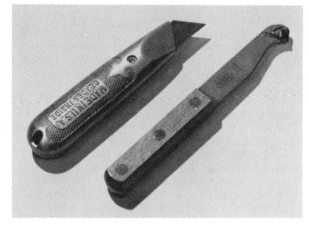

FIG. 2-65. Two styles of utility knives.

METAL-CUTTING TOOLS

Many hand tools have been designed for the specific purpose of cutting metals quickly and accurately. This chapter describes some metal-cutting operations that can be performed with snips and shears, hacksaws, chisels, files, drills, taps and dies, reamers, and pipe and tubing cutters.

Snips and Shears

Snips and shears are used for cutting sheet metal and steel of various thicknesses and shapes. Normally, the heavier or thicker materials are cut with shears.

One of the handiest tools for cutting light (up to $\frac{1}{16}$ inch thick) sheet metal is the hand snips (tin snips). The straight hand snips shown in Figure 3-1a has blades that are straight and cutting edges that are sharpened to an 85° angle. Such snips can be obtained in different sizes, ranging from the small 6-inch to the large 14-inch snip. Straight tin snips will also work on slightly heavier gauges of soft metals such as aluminum alloys.

In addition to the straight snips, there are duckbill-pattern snips (good for cutting moderately tight curves to the left or right in light stock as well as cutting straight), scroll-pivoter snips (used to cut out small arcs and circles or sharp irregular curves), curved-blade or circular snips (good for any curves except really small ones), hawkbill snips (useful for making curved cuts in large sheets), combination snips (provide greater ability to cut wide curves), trojan snips (make most cuts well, but are best for curved cuts in heavier material), and bulldog snips (have greatest cutting power for notching, nibbling, or trimming heavy stock). While most snips, like the straight type, are designed for cutting softer metals, some will do a good job on stainless steel and Monel metal. These special cutting snips have inlaid alloy cutting edges, and their handles are usually stamped "for stainless-steel use only."

Of course, the most popular of all metal-cutting snips is the aviation or compound leverage-action type shown in Figure 3-1e, f, and g. There are also light snips (Figure 3-1h) that are compact, handy snips popular in the electronics and appliance industries.

Snips will not remove any metal when a cut is made. There is danger, though, of causing minute metal fractures along the edges of the metal during the shearing process. For this reason, it is better to cut just outside the layout line. This procedure will allow you to dress the cutting edge while keeping the material within the required dimensions.

Cutting extremely heavy-gauge metal always presents the possibility of springing the blades. Once their blades are sprung, hand snips are useless. When cutting heavy material, use the rear portion of the blades. This procedure not only avoids the possibility of springing the blades but also gives you greater cutting leverage.

Many snips have small serrations (notches) on the cutting edges of the blades. These serrations tend to prevent the snips from slipping backward when a cut is being made. Although this feature does make the actual cutting easier, it mars the edges of the metal slightly. You can remove these small cutting marks if you allow proper clearance for dressing the metal to size. There are many other types of hand snips, for special jobs, but the snips discussed here can be used for almost any common type of work.

SAFETY AND SNIPS

While snips are very safe tools, you should keep the following tips in mind:

1. Learn to use snips properly. They should always be oiled and adjusted to permit ease of

cutting and to produce a surface that is free from burrs. If the blades bind, or if they are too far apart, the snips should be adjusted.

2. Never use snips as screwdrivers, hammers, or pry bars. They break easily.
3. Do not attempt to cut heavier materials than those that the snips are designed for. Never use tin snips to cut hardened steel wire or similar objects. Such use will dent or nick the cutting edges of the blades.
4. Never toss snips in a toolbox where the cutting edges can come into contact with other tools. This dulls the cutting edges and may even break the blades.
5. When snips are not in use, hang them on hooks or lay them on an uncrowded shelf or bench.

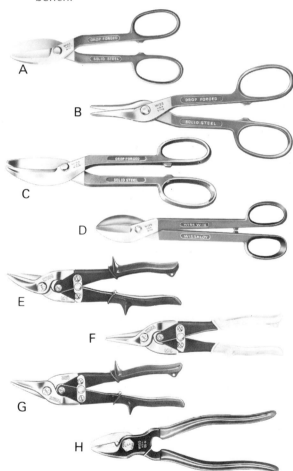

FIG. 3-1. Various snips: *(a)* tinner's straight pattern snips; *(b)* circular cutting or duckbill snips; *(c)* combination bulldog pattern; *(d)* curved blade pattern; *(e)* aviation snips, left cut; *(f)* aviation snips, right cut; *(g)* aviation snips, straight cut; *(h)* snips.

CUTTING SHEET METAL WITH SNIPS

It is hard to cut circles or small arcs with straight snips. Some snips are especially designed for circular cutting. They are called circle snips, hawkbill snips, trojan snips, duckbill snips, and aviation snips. To cut a large hole in a light gauge of sheet metal, start the cut by punching or otherwise making a hole in the center of the area to be cut out. With an aviation snips, as shown in Figure 3-2a, or some other narrow-bladed snips, make a spiral cut from the starting hole out toward the scribed circle, and continue cutting until the scrap falls away. Right-handed snips have the right shear blade on the top and cut counterclockwise. Left-handed snips are the reverse. Combination aviation snips can cut either way.

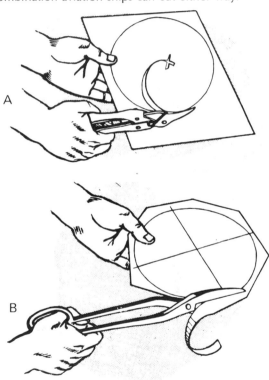

FIG. 3-2. *(a)* Cutting an inside hole with snips; *(b)* cutting a disk out of sheet metal.

Bolt Cutters

Bolt cutters are made in lengths of 18 to 36 inches. The larger ones (Fig. 3-3) will cut mild-steel bolts and rods up to $\frac{1}{2}$ inch in diameter. The material to be cut should be kept as far back in the jaws as possible. Never attempt to cut spring wire or other tempered metal with bolt cutters. This will cause the jaws to be sprung or nicked. Adjusting screws near the middle hinges provide a means for ensuring that both jaws move the same amount when the handles are pressed together. Keep the adjusting screws just tight enough to ensure that the cutting edges meet along their entire length when the jaws are closed. The hinges should be kept well oiled at all times.

When using bolt cutters, make sure your fingers are clear of the jaws and hinges. Take care that the bolt head or piece of rod that is cut off does not fly and injure you or someone else. If the cutters are brought together rapidly, sometimes the bolt head or piece of rod being cut off will fly some distance.

Bolt cutters are fairly heavy, so make sure that they are stored in a safe place where they will not fall and injure someone.

FIG. 3-3. Typical bolt cutter.

Hacksaws

Hacksaws are used to cut metal that is too heavy for snips or bolt cutters. Metal bar stock can be cut readily with hacksaws.

There are two parts to a hacksaw, the frame and the blade. Common hacksaws have either adjustable or solid frames; the former are by far the most popular. For the "home mechanic," the market offers various acceptable models and qualities of hacksaw frames, with "pistol" and "handsaw" grips and with conventional notched-extension and wing-nut adjustments for blade length and tension. But for skilled-trades or shop mechanics, ruggedness, rigidity, and good alignment are of prime importance. The round-solid or tubular frame back and the slip-slide grip heighten those qualities and are very popular. Adjustable frames can be made to hold blades from 8 to 16 inches long, while those with solid frames take only the length blade for which they are made. This length is the distance between the two pins that hold the blade in place.

HACKSAW BLADES

Good work with a hacksaw depends not only upon proper use of the saw, but also upon proper selection of the blades for the work to be done. Sawtooth correctness embraces design (shape), coarseness (number per inch), degree of toughness and hardness, and the way the teeth are "set." The three major types of set used with hacksaw blades are:

1. *Alternate*, in which one tooth is bent to the right, the next to the left, and so on. This set is found principally in wood-saw blades.
2. *Raker*, which is characterized by a straight (unbent) chip-clearing tooth between alternate right- and left-bent cutting teeth. This set is used

principally in the coarser-tooth metal-cutting blades.

3. *Wavy*, which is formed by alternately bending two or more teeth to the right and to the left in graduated degrees. This set is most commonly found in the finer-tooth saw blades used in cutting thin-metal and hard-steel stocks.

It is important that the right- and left-bent teeth be balanced; otherwise the blade will not cut straight. Raker and wavy sets are most commonly found in coarse- and fine-tooth metal-cutting blades.

Hand hacksaw blades generally come in 10- and 12-inch (hole-to-hole) lengths, with 14, 18, 24, and 32 teeth to the inch. Coarse teeth are required on thick cross sections to facilitate chip clearance (teeth that are too fine will clog), and fine-tooth blades are to be preferred for thin sections (excessive coarseness may "shell" the teeth). Here are some general recommendations on tooth selection.

14-tooth. For cutting stock 1 inch or over in cross section; for soft materials where maximum chip clearance is needed

18-tooth. For general shop use, when the same blade is used on several jobs

24-tooth. For $\frac{1}{16}$- to $\frac{1}{4}$-inch cross sections, such as pipe, angles, and small drill rod

32-tooth. For cutting stock up to $\frac{1}{16}$ inch, such as sheet metal, light tubing, and BX cable

For more detailed specifications, use Table 3-1.

Table 3-1 Hacksaw Blade Specifications

Material	Teeth per inch	Strokes per minute
Ferrous metals		
BX*	32	60
Conduit, rigid*	24	60
Drill rod	18–24	40
Cast iron	14	60
Pipe*	18–24	60
Rails	14	40
Sheet metal*	24–32	60
Steel, machinery	14–18	60
Steel, tool	18–24	50
Structural shapes, heavy	14–18	60
Structural shapes, light	18–24	60
Tubing, light*	24, 32	60
Non-ferrous metals		
Aluminum	14	60
Brass and bronze	14–24	60
Brass tubing*	24	60
Copper	14	60
Structural shapes	14–24	60
Non-metal		
Asbestos	14	60
Fibre	14	60
Slate	14	60

*Special shatterproof blades of coarser teeth than specified may be used with excellent results on thin sections.

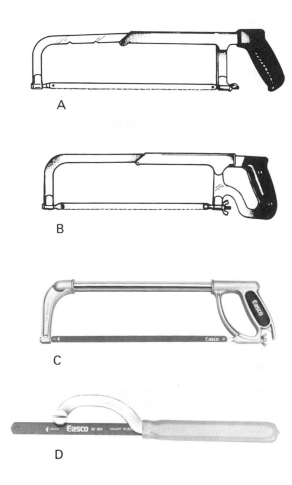

FIG. 3-4. Various types of hacksaw frames: *(a)* pistol-grip adjustables; *(b)* D-type grip; *(c)* tubular adjustable; *(d)* minihacksaw.

Most manufacturers produce five blade types:

1. *Flexible standard.* This is a low cost all-around steel blade for all-purpose cutting, especially on nonferrous metals and low-carbon steels. Because the teeth are hardened and the gradually softened back remains flexible, breakage is reduced to a minimum, even when the work is done in cramped or awkward positions.
2. *Special shatterproof.* Specially hardened to include toughness, this steel blade is virtually indestructible when properly used. Recommended for cutting thin sections. Its extreme toughness permits the 18- and 24-tooth blades to withstand the cutting of thin materials.

3. *Flexible molybdenum.* Its combination of toughness and flexibility is further endowed with high resistance to the heat generated in sawing hard alloys. It is a shatterproof blade.
4. *Hard molybdenum.* When the workpiece can be firmly positioned and the operator needs the best blade for straight cuts and long life, this blade is the logical choice. It gives excellent results on abrasive or tough materials in the tool-steel categories.
5. *Hard tungsten.* This premium-price blade is specifically for cutting the toughest materials with the utmost efficiency. While relatively few cutting jobs demand the exceptional qualities built into this blade, they nevertheless make its selection advantageous. It is extremely effective on stainless and high-manganese steels and on certain bronzes.

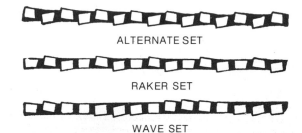

FIG. 3-5. Set of hacksaw blade teeth.

All blades have a hole at each end which hooks onto a pin in the frame. All hacksaw frames which hold the blade either parallel to or at right angles to the frame are provided with a wing nut or screw to permit tightening and removing the blade. The hacksaw blade should always be taut but not overstrained. A properly strained blade, when "thumbed," gives a clear humming note which, once heard, is readily remembered. After a few cuts with a new blade, the tension should be checked and increased slightly. Remember that a loose blade is likely to "slip" and therefore will not cut straight. All-hard blades should generally be kept at full tension and should never be put under a twisting strain. Otherwise, even a moment's carelessness creates the hazard of breakage.

The hacksaw frame should be inspected from time to time to see that it is giving adequate support to the blade. Adjustable frames have a tendency to twist when the blade is tightened. The frame should be rigid enough to allow proper tensioning of the blade and to hold it straight. The pins on the frame can also become badly worn, putting a severe strain on the pin holes of the blade, which also could lead to breakage. If the pins are worn, they should be replaced or a new frame should be used.

Mount the blade in the frame as shown in Figure 3-6. Hand hacksaws are designed to cut on the forward or "push" stroke (away from the handle). Only rarely do conditions necessitate a "pull" cutting stroke. But in either case, make certain that the blade is inserted with the teeth pointing in the direction of the cutting stroke (the teeth point away from the handle of the hacksaw in Figure 3-6b). The one possible exception, for which the blade can be dragged on the backward stroke, is when nonferrous metals of the softer varieties are being cut. A light backward drag, with no more pressure applied than the weight of the tool itself, is extremely helpful in alleviating clogging.

Keep your reserve supply of blades dry, preferably in their original carton or wrapping. Moisture attacks their delicate tooth points.

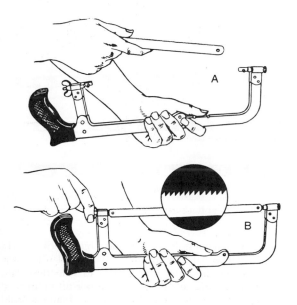

FIG. 3-6. Installing a hacksaw blade.

USING HACKSAWS

In cutting with a hacksaw, the rigidity of the work is as important as that of the blade. If possible, the work should be locked securely in a vise and positioned to engage the maximum number of sawteeth during the cut. Also keep in mind that a minimum of overhang will reduce vibration, give a better cut, and lengthen the life of the blade. Have the layout line outside the vise jaw, so that the line is visible while you work. In general, the vise should be at about elbow height. If the work is of a fine or delicate nature, it should be raised near eye level.

The proper method of holding the hacksaw is depicted in Figure 3-7. Note how the index finger of the right hand, pointed forward, aids in guiding the frame. When cutting, let your body sway ahead and back with each stroke. Apply pressure on the forward stroke, which is the cutting stroke, but not on the return stroke. From 40 to 60 strokes

per minute is the usual speed. Higher speeds, particularly on hard, tough metals, "heat up" the teeth, dulling them rapidly. Long, slow, steady strokes are better.

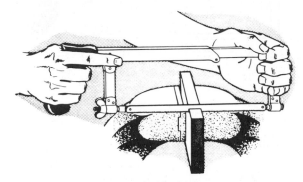

FIG. 3-7. Proper way to hold a hacksaw.

A cut should be started off the edge (Figure 3-8a), never against it (Figure 3-8b). That is, never start your cut on a sharp corner. Use a blade with a tooth spacing that allows at least two teeth in the work on the initial cut. For sawing narrow cross sections and sharp corners, a fine-toothed blade with 24 or 32 teeth per inch should be selected. It is important to remember that the initial strokes of a blade greatly affect the cutting life of its teeth. If the blade does not begin cutting immediately, the teeth will be dulled by the resulting rubbing action. Begin with light pressure and a steady forward stroke. After the first few strokes, the down feed on the forward stroke can be increased. Feed hard enough so that you can feel the teeth cutting; if they slide over the work and do not cut, they will wear out rapidly. Usually the weight of the hacksaw frame itself is enough to begin the proper cutting action of the blade. However, where extreme accuracy is required, on harder materials, it is sometimes desirable to begin the cut with a triangular file having toothed edges as well as sides. Always relieve all feeding pressure on the return stroke. Hacksaw blades, as mentioned earlier, are made to cut only on the forward stroke; they will dull rapidly if allowed to drag on the back stroke.

For long cuts, rotate the blade in the frame so that the length of the cut is not limited by the depth of the frame. Hold the work with the layout line close to the vise jaws, raising the work in the vise as the sawing proceeds. On larger cross sections, the pressure may be increased after the blade has engaged a wider cutting area. Apply sufficient pressure to keep the teeth cutting throughout the stroke, which, whenever possible, should carry the whole length of the blade. Relaxing the pressure on the cutting stroke causes the teeth to become prematurely dull. On the other hand, excessive pressure can also hasten dullness—and damage teeth as well. At the end of the cutting stroke, relieve the pressure completely to avoid dragging the teeth over the material on the reverse stroke.

A

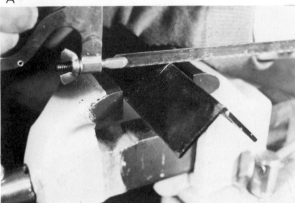

B

FIG. 3-8. Avoid starting a cut on a sharp corner if possible. If it is unavoidable, begin with light pressure. Use a steady, forward stroke.

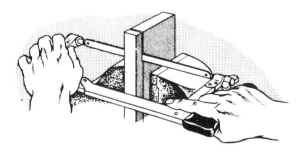

FIG. 3-9. Making a long cut near the edge of the stock.

Saw thin metal as shown in Figure 3-10a. Notice the long angle at which the blade enters the saw groove (kerf). This permits several teeth to cut at the same time.

Metal which is too thin to be held can be placed between blocks of wood (Figure 3-10b). The wood provides support for several teeth as they are cutting. Without the wood, as shown at C in Figure 3-10, teeth will be broken owing to excessive vibration of the stock and

because individual teeth have to absorb the full power of the stroke.

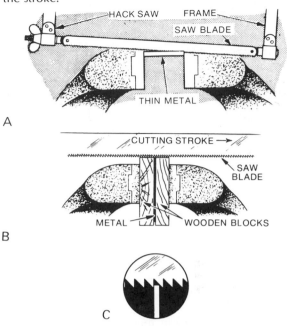

FIG. 3-10. (a) Cutting thin metal with a hacksaw; (b) cutting thin metal between two wooden blocks; (c) without the wood, individual teeth must absorb excessive strain.

Cut thin metal with layout lines on its face by placing a piece of wood behind it (Figure 3-11). Hold the wood and the metal in the jaws of the vise, using a C clamp when necessary. The wood block helps support the blade and produces a smoother cut. Using wood only in back of the metal allows the layout lines to be seen.

If the saw starts to make a crooked cut, do not attempt to straighten the cut by twisting the saw frame. Instead, turn the piece over and start cutting from the other side. Also, remember that a new blade should not be used in an old cut. Again, turn the stock over and cut from the other side.

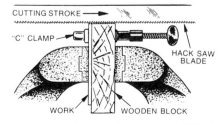

FIG. 3-11. Cutting thin metal using a wood block with layout lines.

To remove a frozen nut with a hacksaw, saw into the nut as shown in Figure 3-12. Start the blade close to the threads on the bolt or stud and parallel to one face of the nut, as shown in Figure 3-12a. Saw parallel to the bolt until the teeth of the blade almost reach the lock washer. Lock washers are hard and will ruin hacksaw blades, so do not try to saw them. Figure 3-12b shows when to stop sawing. Then, with a cold chisel and hammer, remove this one side of the nut completely by opening the saw kerf. Put an adjustable wrench across this new flat and the one opposite, and again try to remove the frozen nut. Since very little original metal remains on this one side of the nut, the nut will either give or break away entirely and permit its removal.

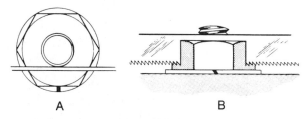

FIG. 3-12. Removing a frozen nut with a hacksaw.

To saw a wide kerf in the head of a cap screw or machine bolt, fit the hacksaw frame with two blades side by side, with their teeth lined up in the same direction. With slow, steady strokes, saw a slot approximately one-third the thickness of the head of the cap screw, as shown in Figure 3-13. Such a slot will permit subsequent holding or turning with a screwdriver when it is impossible, owing to close quarters, to use a wrench.

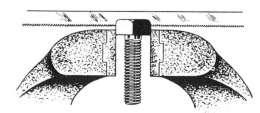

FIG. 3-13. Cutting a wide kerf in the head of a cap screw or bolt.

If the blade sticks in the cut, remove the saw and examine the teeth. If chips are sticking in the gullets, you are using too fine a tooth spacing on soft material. If the blade jams and cuts noisily, it is quite possible you are using too coarse a tooth spacing. Other hacksaw problems that you may encounter and their solutions are as follows:

BLADE BREAKAGE

1. Lack of tension: Tighten until taut.

2. Too much tension: Loosen slightly.
3. Cutting in awkward position: Use flexible-type blades.
4. Jamming in cut: Hold the work securely; the stock should fall free after a cut. In soft material the teeth may be binding because they are too fine.

PINHOLE BREAKAGE

1. Too much tension: Loosen slightly.
2. Worn pins causing pressure on eyeholes: Replace the pins.

ROUNDED TEETH (PREMATURE WEAR)

1. Blade not cutting: Use a slower stroke and apply heavier feed.
2. Dragging on return stroke: Lift the saw.
3. Material too hard: Select the proper blade.

CROOKED CUTTING

1. Too much pressure: Reduce the feed.
2. Blade out of alignment: Check the frame and blade tension.
3. Blade worn out: Replace.

TOOTH BREAKAGE

1. Teeth too coarse: Keep at least two teeth in the work.
2. Too much feed, teeth loading: Ease the feed pressure.
3. Teeth too fine, clogging: Change to a coarser tooth.
4. Starting cut on sharp corner: Reposition the work.

Worn hacksaw blades cannot be resharpened, at least not in a practical manner. Their teeth, being infinitely harder than those of non-metal-cutting saws, would ruin the conventional saw file in short order. Any resharpening at all would require "dehardening" (annealing) the blade so it could be filed. Then it would require rehardening, which, especially in the case of the soft-back–hard-teeth type blade, is a process that only expert technical experience and special equipment can accomplish adequately. Buying new blades costs much less than "reconditioning" old ones.

HACKSAW SAFETY

The main danger in using hacksaws is injury to your hand if the blade breaks. The blade will break if too much pressure is applied, when the saw is twisted, when the cutting speed is too fast, or when the blade becomes loose in the frame. Additionally, if the work is not tight in the vise, it will sometimes slip, twisting the blade enough to break it.

ROD SAWS

An improvement in industrial technology provides us with a tool that can cut material an ordinary hacksaw cannot even scratch. The rod saw, like a diamond, can cut hard materials such as stainless steel, inconel, titanium, carbon phenolics, ceramic tile, slate, glass, asbestos-cement, and various masonry items.

The rod saw cuts through material with hundreds of tungsten-carbide particles that are permanently bonded to the rod (see the magnified portion of Figure 3-14). The rod saw cuts through stainless steel and files with ease. A unique feature of this saw is its capability of cutting on the forward and reverse strokes. Available in 10- and 12-inch lengths, rod-saw blades fit a standard hacksaw frame.

There are also *tungsten-carbide* hacksaw blades (Figure 3-15a), which will cut the same materials as a rod saw. These blades, like those of the rod saw, cut on both forward and back strokes.

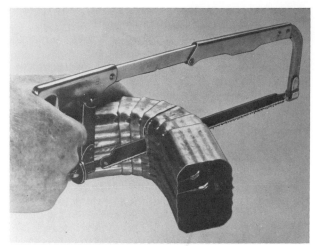

A

B

FIG. 3-15. *(a)* Tungsten hacksaw blades are available to make cutting easier. *(b)* The metal-cutting handsaw is specially constructed for cutting nonferrous metals.

OTHER SAWS

Cross-cut saws are available that are specially constructed for cutting nonferrous metals. The blades of such metal-cutting handsaws (Figure 3-15b) usually have fine teeth with about 15 points per inch and are approximately 20 inches long. There are also sheet-metal saws on the market which are designed to cut metal sheets, both plain and corrugated, of steel, brass, copper, aluminum, etc. They will also cut thinner sheets of asbestos, plastic, slate, and similar materials. Sheet-metal saws come with 12 and 15 points per inch.

Chisels

As stated in Chapter 1, cold chisels are tools that can be used for chipping or cutting metal. Also illustrated in that chapter are the common shapes of cold metal-cutting chisels: flat, cape, half-round nose, and diamond point. As was mentioned, the type most commonly used is the flat cold chisel, which serves to cut rivets, split nuts, chip castings, and cut thin metal sheets. The cape chisel is used for special jobs such as cutting keyways, narrow grooves, and square corners. Round-nose chisels make circular grooves and chip inside corners with a fillet. Finally, the diamond-point chisel is used for cutting V grooves and sharp corners.

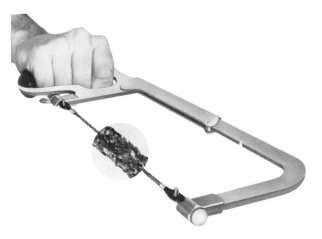

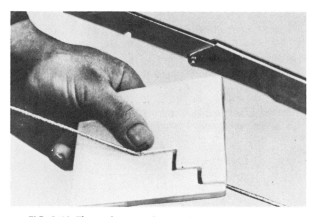

FIG. 3-14. The rod saw and operations.

USING METAL-CUTTING CHISELS

The general use of the cold chisel is described in Chapter 1. However, there are some special techniques that can be handy at times. For example, when cutting wire or round stock with a cold chisel, mark off a guideline on the stock and place the work on the top face of an anvil or other suitable working surface. Place the cutting edge of the chisel on the mark, in a vertical position, and lightly strike the chisel with a hammer. Check the chisel mark for accuracy. Continue to strike the chisel until the cut is made. The last few blows of the hammer should be made lightly to avoid damage to the anvil, supporting surface, or chisel.

Heavy stock is cut in the same manner, except that the cut is made halfway through the stock; the work is then turned over and the cut is finished from the opposite side. To cut rod or small bar stock to rough size, nick it on opposite sides and bend it back and forth until it breaks.

To chip a broad surface, that is, to remove surplus material preparatory to smoothing with a file, both a cape chisel and a flat chisel are used. First, chip grooves across the surface of the work with the cape chisel. The grooves should be slightly closer together than the width of the flat chisel. Chip the stock from both sides toward the center to avoid fracturing the metal at the edges. Hold the cape chisel at an angle that will bring the lower bevel parallel to the surface of the work. Grasp the chisel firmly enough to guide it, but loosely enough to ease the shock of the hammer blows imparted to the hand through the chisel.

Once the grooves have been cut, chip away the material between the grooves with a flat chisel. Hold the chisel at an angle that will bring the lower bevel parallel to the surface of the work. It is not necessary to lubricate the chisel when chipping cast iron. When chipping wrought iron or steel, lubricate the chisel every few blows by touching the edge to a piece of oil-soaked waste.

To cut out a hole in metal, use a narrow chisel so the shape of the cut will conform closely to the guideline, reducing the amount of filing necessary for finishing.

To cut off a rivet or bolt head with a chisel, hold the work in a heavy vise or secure it some other way so that the work will not move. Place the cold chisel with one face of the bevel flat on the surface of the job. Strike the head of the chisel with the hammer as you loosely hold and guide the chisel (Figure 3-16).

To cut off a rivet head with a cape chisel, use a chisel of about the same size as the diameter of the rivet. Cut through the center of the rivet head, holding one face of the bevel flat on the surface of the job. Then sever the center of the head from the shank or body, as shown in Figure 3-17.

To cut off a rivet head with a side-cutting chisel, place the chisel nearly flat on the surface of the work, with its single bevel upward. Drive the cutting edge under the edge of the rivet head, just as you would if you were using a cold chisel. (See Figure 3-18a.) Notice in Figure 3-18b

that the cutting edge of the chisel has a slight radius which will tend to prevent the corners from cutting undesirable grooves in the surface of the work.

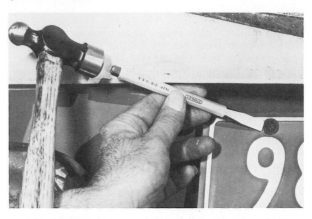

FIG. 3-16. Removing a machine screw with a flat chisel. The bonded vinyl covering effectively cushions the impact of hammer on chisel, short-circuiting the numbing vibrations through fingers and forearm that cause fatigue and inaccuracy. And, on cold days, the grip insulates the hand from the metal tool.

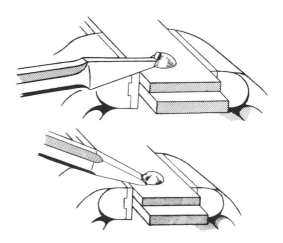

FIG. 3-17. Cutting off a rivet head with a chisel.

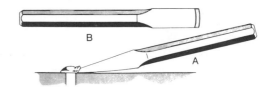

FIG. 3-18. Cutting off a rivet head with a side-cutting chisel.

To remove a rivet head (Figure 3-19) when there is not room enough to swing a hammer with sufficient force to cut the rivet, first drill a hole about the size of the body of the rivet in and almost to the bottom of the rivet head. Then cut off the head with a cold chisel.

When using a cold chisel, keep the head of the chisel and the face of the hammer clean and free of oil. Make sure to let the grip of the thumb and forefinger be loose enough to give if the hammer should slip and hit them. If the head of the chisel should become turned over or burred in use, grind the burr away to prevent injury to the hands and to prevent particles of the burr from flying off into your eyes. Of course, use goggles to protect your eyes.

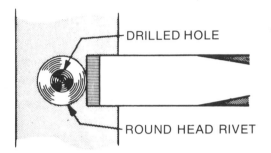

FIG. 3-19. Removing a rivet head in a hard-to-reach position.

Files

The file is one of the oldest known tools. It was probably developed when prehistoric man wanted a better cutting edge for crude stone axes. The first file was probably a rough stone used as an abrasive to make the edge of an axe thinner and sharper. With the advent of the metal age centuries later, files were made from bronze or iron. These were a great step forward, and they form the basis for today's highly efficient file and its use as a cutting tool. The first files made from metal were forged completely by hand, with only the crudest type of heat treating. They were made in this manner for centuries.

Improvements occurred only as iron was refined into what we now know as steel. The teeth were cut into files with a hammer and chisel. Each tooth was made by striking a chisel at the proper angle and spacing. Making an entire file, which might have hundreds of teeth, was a long and tiresome job. Near the end of the fifteenth century, a file-cutting machine was designed. However, the first successful machine was not put into use until the middle of the eighteenth century. The power source for these early machines was water. This was later changed to steam, and finally to today's electric power. Modern file manufacturing represents a unique blend of the craftsman's skill and current technology to produce a consistently superior precision instrument.

CUTS AND SHAPES OF FILES

There are four standard American-pattern file cuts: single cut, double cut, curved cut, and rasp cut. The latter was fully discussed along with wood-cutting files in Chapter 2. The other three are primarily used in metal cutting.

A single-cut file has a single set of diagonal rows of file teeth. These rows are parallel to each other and extend across the working face of the file. The teeth themselves are set at an angle of about 65° with the centerline. Single-cut files are used for sharpening tools, finish filing, and drawfiling. They are also the best tools for smoothing the edges of sheet metal.

A double-cut file has two sets of diagonal rows. The first set of teeth is called the "overcut." On top of these rows of teeth, a second set of teeth is cut, at a different angle with the file axis. This is known as the "upcut;" it is finer than the overcut. The two cuts form teeth that are diamond-shaped and fast cutting. Double-cut files are used for quick removal of metal and for rough work.

A curved cut is an arrangement of file teeth in curved contours across the working face of the file. The teeth are milled with a decided undercut (or positive rake).

American-pattern files are graded according to the spacing of the file teeth, or the number of teeth per inch. Tooth spacing varies with the shape and length of the file. The spacing of the teeth increases as the length of the file is increased. A coarse-cut file has the fewest number of teeth per inch. The bastard cut has more teeth per inch, and the second cut has still more teeth per inch. The smooth-cut file has the greatest number of teeth per inch. Note that, in defining the degree of coarseness, the terms coarse, bastard, second, and smooth are comparable only when files of the same length and shape are being considered.

The length of the file exclusive of the tang (the narrow pointed portion of the file which fits into the file handle) is generally from 4 to 16 inches, depending upon the file type. Sizes in general move up in 2-inch steps, with a few exceptions. Many files are tapered; that is, there is a reduction in the dimensions of the file from the heel (the part of the file where the tang begins) to the point (the front end of the file). A file may taper in width, in thickness, or in both. On some files, one edge has no teeth and is known as a "safe" edge. The safe edge is handy to file in corners.

There are three basic classifications of files: mill, machinist's and Swiss pattern. Mill files are so named because they are widely used for sharpening mill or circular saws. These files are also useful for sharpening large crosscut saws and mowing-machine knives, for lathe work and drawfiling, for working on compositions of brass and bronze, and for smooth-finish filing in general. Mill files are single cut and are tapered slightly in width for about a third of their length; the 12-, 14-, and 16-inch mill files are also tapered in thickness.

Machinist's files, as the name indicates, are widely used

Table 3-2

	ILLUSTRATED FILE FINDER FOR SPECIAL-PURPOSE FILES				
Cross-Section	Name	Shape	Character Of Teeth	Taper	General Uses
	Brass	Flat Rectangular	Made in one cut only. Sharp teeth, with open cut.	Tapered.	Filing brass, bronze, copper, aluminum.
	Brass	Half-Round	Made in one cut only. Sharp teeth, with open cut.	Slightly tapered.	Filing brass, bronze, copper, aluminum.
	Aluminum	Flat Rectangular	Made in one cut only. Fast-cutting teeth.	Tapered.	Filing aluminum alloys and other soft metals.
	Aluminum	Half-Round	Made in one cut only. Fast-cutting teeth.	Slightly tapered.	Filing aluminum alloys and other soft metals.
	Lead Float	Flat Rectangular	Single-cut; coarse teeth.	Almost blunt.	Filing lead, aluminum, brass and other soft metals.
	Lead Float	Half-round	Single-cut; coarse teeth.	Slightly tapered.	Filing lead, aluminum, brass and other soft metals.
	Foundry	Flat Rectangular	Short, stubby, sturdy teeth.	Tapered.	Rough filing, castings, harder metals generally.
	Foundry	Half-Round	Short, stubby, sturdy teeth.	Slightly tapered.	Rough filing, castings, harder metals generally.
	Long Angle Lathe	Flat Rectangular	Made in one cut only. Both edges safe.	Slightly tapered.	Lathe work where smooth finish is desired. Also soft metals.
	Plastic File	Flat Rectangular	Teeth leave no serrations on plastic surface.	Slightly tapered.	Plastics.
	Stainless Steel File	Flat Rectangular	Exceptionally sharp.	Slightly tapered.	Stainless steels and high-chrome tool steels.

by machinists and repair shops; by automobile, truck, tractor, and other machinery manufacturers; and by ship, aircraft, engine, and ordnance builders—in short, throughout industry, wherever metal must be removed rapidly and finish is of secondary importance. Table 3-2 gives the shape, character of teeth, and general uses of the more common special-purpose files.

The so-called Swiss-pattern files constitute a vast group of files. They are used by tool- and diemakers, jewelers, model makers, delicate-instrument-parts finishers, and home craftsmen. In short, everyone who does superfine precision filing will have many uses for Swiss-pattern files. They are primarily finishing tools—used for removing burrs left over from previous finishing operations; for truing up narrow grooves, notches, and keyways; for rounding out slots and cleaning out corners; for smoothing small parts; and for the final finishing on all sorts of delicate and intricate pieces. While American-pattern files are available in three cuts, Swiss precision files are made in much finer cuts, ranging from No. 00 (the coarsest) to No. 8 (the finest). Here is a comparison of Swiss cuts with American-pattern cuts:

Swiss Pattern	No. 00	No. 0	No. 2
American Pattern	Bastard	Second cut	Smooth cut

There are no American-pattern files equivalent to the Swiss-pattern cuts numbered from No. 4 to No. 8.

Today, Swiss precision files and rifflers are made in over 700 shapes. Most of them are available in a considerable range of sizes. Swiss precision rifflers alone are available in over 600 variations. Table 3-3 gives the shape, character of teeth, and general uses of the more common Swiss-pattern files.

Swiss precision rifflers may be shaped like buttonhooks or trowels and may have gentle or sharp curves with needle or bayonet points. Many of them are extremely narrow and delicate, while others are reasonably heavy. Each has a different profile and contour. They range in lengths from 6 to 12 inches and in cuts from No. 0 to No. 6. There are diesinker's, diemaker's, silversmith's, and toolmaker's rifflers, so called because they were originally hand forged by these craftsmen. Others are designed for patternmaking and cabinetwork. Now, though the traditional names persist, rifflers are selected by contour, size, and cut for the particular job to be accomplished.

There are also special-purpose files for use on special materials such as brass, aluminum, lead, stainless steel, and plastic. These files usually carry the name of the material they cut: i.e., brass files, aluminum files, etc.

Table 3-3

Cross-Section	Name	Shape	Character Of Teeth	Taper	General Uses
			ILLUSTRATED FILE FINDER FOR SWISS PATTERN FILES		
	Hand	Rectangular	Double-cut on two flat faces and one edge. Other edge safe or uncut.	Uniform in width.	Flat surfaces.
	Pillar	Width narrower than Hand File	Double-cut on two flat faces. Both edges safe.	Uniform in width.	Flat surfaces, slots.
	Warding	Thin Rectangular	Double-cut on two flat faces. Single-cut on two edges.	Tapered in width uniform in thickness.	Slots, locks and keys.
	Square	Square	Double-cut.	Tapered.	Corners, holes.
	Three-Square	Triangular (Equilateral)	Double-cut on three faces. Single-cut on edges.	Tapered.	Corners, holes.
	Round	Circular	Double-cut.	Either tapered or uniform (straight).	Corners, holes.
	Half-Round	Third-Circular	Double-cut.	Tapered.	Corners, holes.
	Knife	Knife-Shaped	Double-cut on flat faces. Single-cut on edges.	Tapered.	Slots.
	Crossing	Oval, with unequal radii	Double-cut.	Tapered.	Corners, holes.
	Equalling	Rectangular	Double-cut on flat faces. Single-cut on edges.	Uniform through-out length.	Slots, corners.
	Barrelle	Trapezoidal	Cut only on wide flat face. Other faces safe.	Tapered.	Corners, flat surfaces, burring gear teeth.
	Crochet	Flat, with round edges	Double-cut.	Tapered.	Slots, flat surfaces, rounded corners.
	Cant	Triangular, (Isosceles)	Double-cut on three faces. Single-cut on two sharp edges.	Tapered.	Corners.
	Slitting	Flat Diamond	Double-cut on four faces. Single-cut on two sharp edges.	Blunt.	Slots, corners.
	Pippin	Apple Seed	Double-cut.	Tapered.	Rounded corners, holes.

FILING OPERATIONS

Filing is an operation that is nearly indispensable in working with metal. You may be cross-filing, drawfiling, using a file card, or even polishing metal. Let us examine these operations.

After you have used a file, it may be necessary to use an abrasive cloth or paper to finish the job. Whether this is necessary depends on how fine a finish you want on the work. Most work that is filed is held in a vise. Unless it is held firmly, chattering and vibration will result. This causes the file teeth momentarily to lose contact with the surface, and the depth of cut to vary; the results will be unsatisfactory, and the file will probably be damaged. The top of the vise should be on the same level as the elbow when the arm is bent. However, the work should be lowered if heavy filing is to be done. In die- and toolmaking, much of the work is small and delicate. As this requires simply a movement of the arms or of one hand and arm alone, the vise and work should be higher—not only so that the work can be more closely scrutinized and the file more accurately guided, but also so the filer can stand erect.

The high finish obtained after much time-consuming effort may easily be marred if the work is held in the vise carelessly. Polished work and soft metal can be protected with pieces of copper, brass, zinc, tin, or other soft metals placed between the jaws of the vise and the work. Pieces of wood are best for aluminum or lead workpieces. For highly polished work on mild steel or for screw threads, pieces of leather are recommended.

For best results when filing, keep your feet spread well apart, with the left foot about 24 inches in front of the right foot. You should have the full free swing of your arms from the shoulder. Any separate movement of the wrist and elbow should be avoided if possible. The handle of the file should be held in the right hand, and the tip held with the left hand. Although the position of the left hand varies with the type of work to be done, the right-hand position remains the same. (For a left-handed person, the hand positions should be reversed.) The file handle should rest in the palm of the right hand; the thumb should lie along the top of the handle, with the fingers curling around the handle and pointing upward, and all the fingers falling into a natural grip. When the tip of the file is gripped in the left hand, with the ball of the thumb pressing upon the top of the file and lying in line with the file axis, and with the fingers winding around the file, a powerful grip is secured that enables the maximum pressure to be applied and a large quantity of material to be removed.

The grip described above is generally used with a medium or long file. When a lighter stroke is wanted and less pressure is to be applied, the direction of the left thumb is changed more and more until it lies at right angles, or nearly so, with the length of the file. The tip of the file is then held between the thumb and only the first two fingers of the left hand.

CROSS-FILING For flat or straight cross-filing, the thumb and fingers of the left hand are stretched as far apart as possible and pressed evenly against the file. This assures a uniform distribution of pressure over the whole file length. As a result, the file tends to remain horizontal, and any unevenness in the surface can be readily detected. This position also permits the use of the file's full length, since the left hand is not in the way of the work.

For very accurate work, or when curved surfaces are to be filed, the tip of the file should be held by just the thumb and index finger of the left hand. This grip allows for maximum guidance and control. When the file can be held with one hand, the index finger of the right hand is generally placed on top of the handle so it lies as nearly as possible in the direction of the file. The thumb and other fingers fall into a natural grip.

When filing a narrow piece, it is often easier to obtain and hold a flat surface if the file is held diagonally to the work. As the file is pushed forward, it is moved to the right from one end of the piece to the other. After a few such strokes, the process is repeated, but to the left, so that an absolutely level, smooth finish is obtained.

The teeth of the file should cut only on the forward stroke. Accordingly, the file should be carried forward on an almost straight line, with the pressure first applied by the left hand at the beginning of the stroke, then later with both hands equally in the middle of the stroke, and finally with the right hand alone at the end of the stroke. If pressure is applied on the return stroke, the teeth are dulled and the file is quickly ruined. Except in working on soft metals, the return stroke should be made with the file lifted clear of the work.

If too much pressure is employed on the forward stroke, the teeth are liable to clog or even to shell off. Just enough pressure should be applied to keep the file cutting efficiently. It is well to remember that, at the beginning of the stroke, the leverage favors the right hand and the file tends to round off the near side of the work. As the stroke is completed, the leverage favors the left hand and so the file is brought down harder on the far side of the work. The tendency, then, is for the file to develop a curved surface instead of a flat one. This may be minimized by carefully following the directions given above. With practice, patience, and perseverance, it is possible to file a surface that is absolutely true and square.

The reason for most defective filing is that the beginner allows the file to rock or seesaw, thereby producing a convex surface instead of the level surface desired. To avoid this, the body should be kept still and the arms made to pivot about the shoulders. Also, the filer should not try to remove too much metal in one stroke. In other words, take it easy.

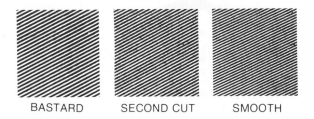

BASTARD SECOND CUT SMOOTH

FIG. 3-21. Comparative coarseness of 10-inch mill files.

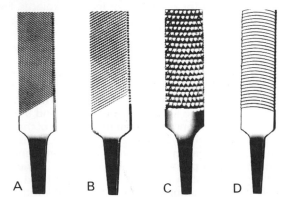

FIG. 3-20. Kinds of teeth: *(a)* single cut; *(b)* double cut; *(c)* rasp cut; *(d)* curved cut.

FIG. 3-22. How the length of a file is measured.

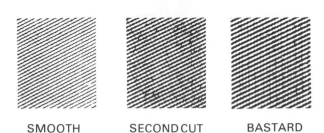

SMOOTH SECOND CUT BASTARD

FIG. 3-23. The actual coarseness of No. 12 mill files.

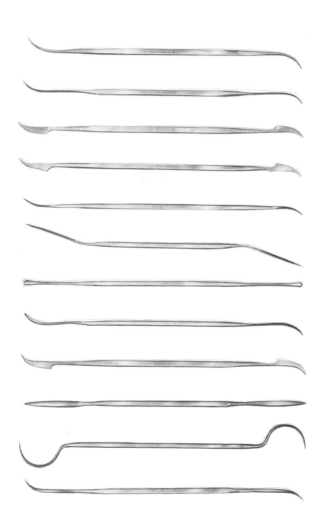

FIG. 3-24. Typical metal-cutting precision rifflers.

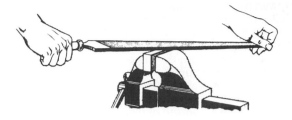

A. CROSSFILING A PIECE OF MILD STEEL

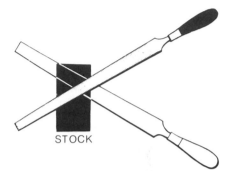

STOCK

B. ALTERNATING POSITIONS WHEN FILING

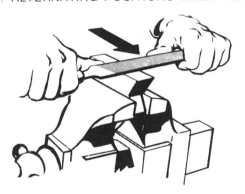

C. DRAWFILING A SMALL PART

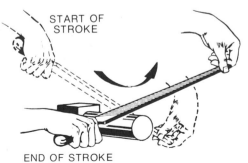

START OF STROKE

END OF STROKE

D. FILING ROUND METAL STOCK

FIG. 3-25. Various filing operations.

DRAWFILING Drawfiling is defined as operating a file in such a way that its length is transverse to the direction of motion. It is employed where a smooth, level surface is desired on planes or edges of the work. The file is held with both hands, with the fingers on the edge away from the body and the thumbs on the edge toward the body of the filer. The file is alternately pulled toward the body and then pushed away, across the work, with an even pressure. One advantage of drawfiling is that the file can be held steady. As a result, a fine surface finish is obtained without scoring or scratching.

Ordinarily, a single-cut mill bastard file or a long-angle lathe file should be used, so the metal is cut with a true shearing or shaving action and scoring is avoided. If metal is to be removed rapidly or in comparatively large amounts, as, for example, on the end of a metal plate or sheet, a flat or hand bastard file may be employed. This roughing down may then be followed by finishing with a mill file.

In drawfiling, the beginner has a tendency to apply the most effort when the file is in the middle of its stroke. In consequence, the surface is likely to develop a hollow spot. This must be guarded against by careful testing after filing. Such a hollow area may be removed by applying a few more strokes at the ends of the work.

To remove the sharp wire edge that drawfiling frequently produces on the work, hold the file at an angle and run it lightly down each edge.

USE OF FILE CARD As you file, the teeth of the file may "clog up" with some of the metal filings and scratch your work. This condition is known as "pinning." You can prevent pinning by keeping the file teeth clean. Rubbing soft chalk between the teeth will help prevent pinning too, but the best method is to clean the file frequently with a file card or brush. A file card (Figure 3-26) has fine wire bristles. Brush with a pulling motion, holding the card parallel to the rows of teeth.

Always keep the file clean, whether you are filing mild steel or other metals. Use chalk liberally when filing nonferrous metals. Chalking is also advantageous during the finishing of any metal, as otherwise the pins are likely to scratch the work.

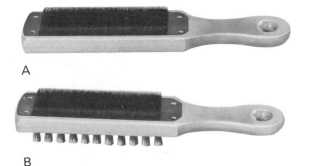

A

B

FIG. 3-26. Typical file brush and card.

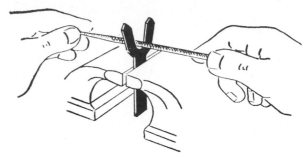

FIG. 3-27. Using a jeweler's file for small work.

FILING ROUND METAL STOCK Figure 3-25d shows that, as a file is passed over the surface of round work, its angle with the work is changed. This results in a rocking motion of the file as it moves over the work. This rocking motion permits all the teeth on the file to make contact and cut as they pass over the surface; it tends to keep the file much cleaner and does better work.

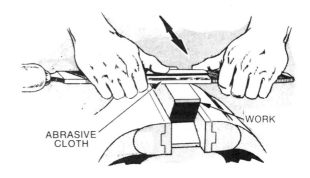

ABRASIVE CLOTH

WORK

FIG. 3-28. Polishing metal with the abrasive cloth wrapped around a file.

PRECISION FILING The finishing and smoothing of metal in the various narrow grooves and depressions of tools, dies, molds, jigs, and fixtures calls for precision filing at its best. The small rifflers used for this purpose are held in much the same manner as a pen or pencil. Larger rifflers are held in the hand with the index finger on the safe side to exert the proper cutting pressure. When necessary, on very fine and delicate work, the left hand is used to control the direction and, in some cases, the stroke of the riffler. With the large range of shapes, sizes, and cuts now available in precision files and rifflers, logic and experience will suggest the contour and profile most suited for the job.

POLISHING A FLAT METAL SURFACE When polishing a flat metal surface, first drawfile the surface as shown in Figure 3-28. Then, when the best possible drawfiled surface has been obtained, proceed with abrasive cloth, often called "emery cloth." Select a grade of cloth suited to the drawfiling. For example, if the drawfiling was well done, only a fine cloth will be needed to do the polishing.

If your cloth is in a roll, and the job you are polishing is of a size that should be held in a vise, tear off a 6- or 8-inch length of cloth, 1 or 2 inches width. If you are using sheets of abrasive cloth, tear off a strip from the long edge of the 8 X 11 inch sheet.

Apply a thin film of lubricating oil to the surface being polished. Wrap the cloth around the file (Figure 3-28) and hold the file as you would for drawfiling. Hold the end of the cloth in place with your thumb. To polish, apply pressure on both the forward and backward strokes. (Note that this is different from the drawfiling stroke in which you cut with the file in only one direction.) When further polishing does not appear to improve the surface, you are ready to use the next finer grade of cloth. Before changing to the finer grade, however, reverse the cloth so that its back is toward the surface being polished. Work the reversed cloth back and forth in the abrasive-laden oil as an intermediate step between grades of abrasive cloth. Then, with the solvent available in your shop, clean the workpiece thoroughly before proceeding with the next finer grade of cloth. Carefully cleaning between grades helps to ensure freedom from scratches. For the final polish, use a strip of crocus cloth—first the face and then the back—with plenty of oil. When the polishing is completed, again carefully clean the work with a solvent and protect it, with oil or other means, from rusting.

Figure 3-29a shows another way to polish in which the abrasive cloth is wrapped around a block of wood. In Figure 3-29b, the cloth has simply been folded to form a pad from which a worn, dull surface can be removed by simply tearing it off to expose a new surface.

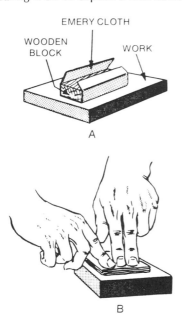

FIG. 3-29. Alternative methods for polishing a metal surface.

POLISHING ROUND METAL STOCK In Figure 3-30, a piece of round stock is being polished with a strip of abrasive cloth which is seesawed back and forth as it is guided over the surface. Remember that the selection of grades of abrasive cloth, the application of oil, and the cleaning between grades apply regardless of how the cloth is held or used.

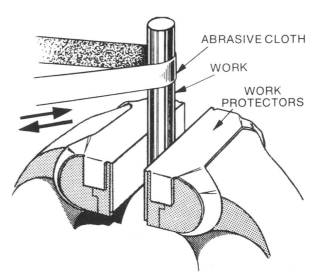

FIG. 3-30. Polishing round metal stock.

CARE OF FILES

A new file should be broken in carefully. To do this, use it first on brass, bronze, or smooth cast iron. Just a few of the teeth will cut first, so use a light pressure to prevent tooth breakage. Do not break in a new file by using it first on a narrow surface.

Protect file teeth by hanging your files in a rack when they are not in use, or by placing them in drawers with wooden partitions. Your files should not be allowed to rust; keep them away from water and moisture. Avoid getting the files oily. Oil causes a file to slide across the work and prevents fast, clean cutting. Files that you keep in your toolbox should be wrapped in paper or cloth to protect their teeth and prevent damage to other tools.

Never use a file for prying or pounding. The tang is soft and bends easily. The body is hard and extremely brittle. Even a slight bend or a fall to the floor may cause a file to snap in two. Do not strike a file against a bench or vise to clean it—use a file card.

SAFETY AND FILING

Never use a file unless it is equipped with a tight-fitting handle. If you use a file without the handle and it bumps something or jams to a sudden stop, the tang may be driven into your hand. To put a handle on a file tang, drill a hole in the handle, slightly smaller than the tang. Insert the tang end, and then tap the end of the handle to seat it firmly. Make sure you get the handle on straight.

Metal Cutting with Drills

Making a hole in a piece of metal is generally a simple operation, but in most cases is an important and precise job. A large number of tools and machines have been designed to make holes speedily, economically, and accurately in all kinds of material; of the hand tools, the hand drill and the breast drill (see Chapter 2) do the best job.

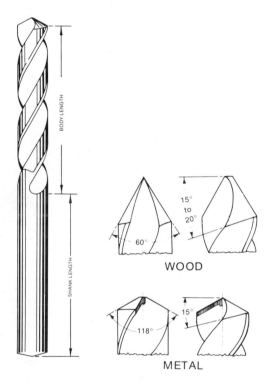

WOOD

METAL

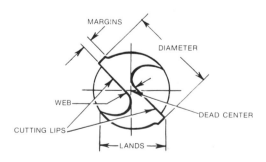

FIG. 3-31. Drill-bit nomenclature for a standard twist drill, and point shapes. Note particularly the great variation in drill-tip angles for metal and wood.

To be able to use these tools efficiently, it is a good idea to become acquainted with them. The most common tool for making holes in metal is the twist drill. It consists of a cylindrical piece of steel with spiral grooves. One end of the cylinder is pointed, while the other end is shaped so that it may be attached to a drilling machine. The grooves, usually called "flutes," may be cut into the steel cylinder, or the flutes may be formed by twisting a flat piece of steel into a cylindrical shape.

The principal parts of a twist drill are the body, the shank, and the point. The dead center of a drill is the sharp edge at the extreme tip end of the drill. It is formed by the intersection of the cone-shaped surfaces of the point and should always be in the exact center of the axis of the drill. The point of the drill should not be confused with the dead center. The point is the entire cone-shaped surface at the end of the drill.

The lip or cutting edge of a drill is that part of the point that actually cuts away the metal when a hole is drilled. It is ordinarily as sharp as the edge of a knife. There is a cutting edge for each flute of the drill. The lip clearance of a drill is the surface of the point that is ground away or relieved just back of the cutting edge of the drill. The strip along the inner edge of the body is called the "margin." It is the greatest diameter of the drill and extends the entire length of the flute. The diameter of the margin at the shank end of the drill is smaller than the diameter at the point. This allows the drill to revolve without binding when deep holes are drilled.

The shank is the part of the drill which fits into the socket, spindle, or chuck of the driving tool. Several types exist (Figure 3-32).

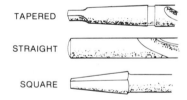

TAPERED

STRAIGHT

SQUARE

FIG. 3-32. Representative shanks.

A tang is found only on tapered-shank drills. It is designed to fit into a slot in the socket or spindle of a machine. It may bear a portion of the driving torque, but its principal use is to make it easy to remove the drill from the socket of the driving machine.

Twist drills are provided in various sizes. They are sized by letters, numerals, and fractions. Table 3-4 illustrates the relationship, by decimal equivalents, of all drill sizes (letter, number, and fractional) from No. 80 to ½ inch. Note how the decimal size increases as the number of the drill decreases. Drills are available in sets, usually according to the way in which the sizes are stated, that is as sets of "letter drills" or sets of "number drills." However, twist drills of any size (letter, number, or fraction) are available individually if desired.

Table 3-4 Decimal Equivalents of Drill Sizes

Drill	Diameter, inches	Drill	Diameter, inches
80	0.0135	20	0.161
79	0.0145	19	0.166
1/64	0.0156	18	0.1695
78	0.016	11/64	0.171875
77	0.018	17	0.173
76	0.02	16	0.177
75	0.021	15	0.18
74	0.0225	14	0.182
73	0.024	13	0.185
72	0.025	3/16	0.1875
71	0.026	12	0.189
70	0.028	11	0.191
69	0.0292	10	0.1935
68	0.031	9	0.196
1/32	0.03125	8	0.199
67	0.032	7	0.201
66	0.033	13/64	0.203125
65	0.035	6	0.204
64	0.036	5	0.2055
63	0.037	4	0.209
62	0.038	3	0.213
61	0.039	7/32	0.21875
60	0.04	2	0.221
59	0.041	1	0.228
58	0.042	A	0.234
57	0.043	15/64	0.234375
56	0.0465	B	0.238
3/64	0.046875	C	0.242
55	0.052	D	0.246
54	0.055	E	0.25
53	0.0595	1/4	0.25
1/16	0.0625	F	0.257
52	0.0635	G	0.261
51	0.067	17/64	0.265625
50	0.07	H	0.266
49	0.073	I	0.272
48	0.076	J	0.277
5/64	0.078125	K	0.281
47	0.0785	9/32	0.281125
46	0.081	L	0.29
45	0.082	M	0.295
44	0.086	19/64	0.296875
43	0.089	N	0.302
42	0.0935	5/16	0.3125
3/32	0.09375	O	0.316
41	0.096	P	0.323
40	0.098	21/64	0.328125
39	0.0995	Q	0.332
38	0.1015	R	0.339
37	0.104	11/32	0.34375
36	0.1055	S	0.348
7/64	0.109375	T	0.358
35	0.11	23/64	0.359375
34	0.111	U	0.368
33	0.113	3/8	0.375
32	0.116	V	0.377
31	0.12	W	0.386
1/8	0.125	25/64	0.390625
30	0.1285	X	0.397
29	0.136	Y	0.404
28	0.1405	13/32	0.40625
9/64	0.140625	Z	0.413
27	0.144	27/64	0.421875
26	0.147	7/16	0.4375
25	0.1495	29/64	0.453125
24	0.152	15/32	0.46875
23	0.154	31/64	0.484375
5/32	0.15625	1/2	0.5
22	0.157		
21	0.159		

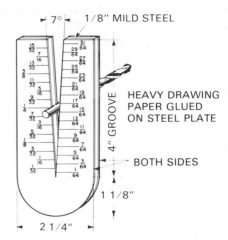

FIG. 3-33. While commercial drill-bit gauges are available, this simple gauge can be made.

METAL-CUTTING PROCEDURE WITH DRILLS

In drilling any metal, several general steps should be followed, after you have selected the correct drill size. First, mark the exact location of the hole. Second, secure the work properly. Then use the correct cutting speed and appropriate cutting oil or other coolant, where applicable. Finally, apply pressure on the drill properly.

The exact location of the hole must be marked with a center punch. The punch mark forms a seat for the drill point, thus ensuring accuracy. Without the punch mark, the drill may have a tendency to "walk off" before it begins to cut into the metal. As shown in Figure 3-34a, if, in starting, a drill has run off the center of the layout, the error can be corrected if the spot is not too deep. Chip the heavy side of the spot with a round-nose or diamond-point chisel, as shown in Figure 3-34b. The drill will bite

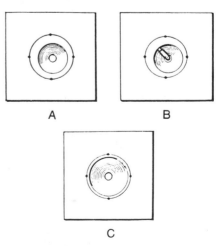

FIG. 3-34. Method of drawing a drill or hole.

deeper on this side, thus drawing the spot to the center, as shown in Figure 3-34c. This process is termed "drawing the drill." It can only be accomplished before the full diameter of the cut is reached.

Most work is held for drilling by some mechanical means, such as a vise or clamps. It is mandatory that the work be well secured. If not, the work or stock may rotate at high speed or fly loose, becoming a high-speed projectile endangering all personnel within its range. Various securing procedures are discussed in Chapters 11 and 17 for power drills; many of them can be used with hand drills.

If you are required to hold thin metal, place it on a block of wood to provide support directly beneath the place where the hole is to be drilled. This support will also help minimize drill breakage when the feed pressure is applied. Secure in a vise as shown in Figure 3-35, and drill through the metal and into the wood. Stop drilling when wood chips appear.

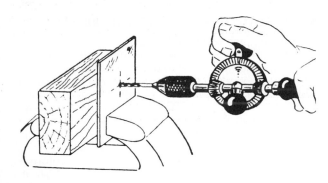

FIG. 3-35. Proper technique for metal drilling.

It is necessary to use a cutting oil to cool the drill when drilling steel and wrought iron. Cast iron, aluminum, brass, and other metals may be hand-drilled dry. For complete information on coolants, see Chapter 9.

Always apply pressure on a line which goes straight through the axis of the drill. (Side pressure will enlarge the hole and can break the drill.) Keep the drill steady, and apply enough pressure to keep it cutting.

When drilling large holes, do so in stages. A pilot hole is a good idea, since it serves as a guide for the larger drill and helps to increase accuracy. More on metal cutting with drills can be found in Chapters 11 and 17.

COUNTERSINKS

Countersinking, as already mentioned, is the operation of beveling the mouth of a hole with a rotary tool called a "countersink." The construction of the typical countersink is similar to that of the twist drill. There are four cutting edges, which are taper ground to the angle marked on the body.

A countersink is used primarily to set the head of a screw or rivet flush with the material in which it is being placed. Countersinks are made in a number of sizes. One size usually take care of holes of several different diameters. For example, the same countersink can be used for holes from $\frac{1}{4}$ to $\frac{1}{2}$ inch in diameter.

Select the countersink with the lip angle that corresponds to the screw or rivet head being used. Countersinks can be turned by any machine that will turn a twist drill. Remove only enough metal to set the screw or rivet head flush with the material. If you remove too much material, the hole will enlarge and weaken the work.

REAMERS

Reamers are used to enlarge and true a hole. The reamer consists of three parts: the body, the shank, and the blades. The shank has a square tang, to allow the reamer to be held with a tap wrench (Figure 3-37a) or a T-handle pipe reamer for turning. The main purpose of the body is to support the blades.

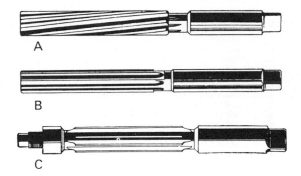

FIG. 3-36. Common types of straight reamers: (a) solid spiral flute; (b) solid straight flute; (c) expansion.

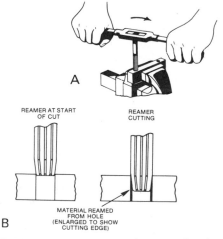

FIG. 3-37. (a) Using a tap wrench to turn a hand reamer. (b) Reaming a hole with a straight hole reamer.

Reamers of the types shown in Figure 3-36 are available in any standard size. They are also available in size variations of 0.001 inch for special work. The solid straight-flute reamer lasts longer and is less expensive than the expansion reamer. However, the solid spiral-flute reamer is preferred by craftsmen because it is less likely to chatter.

For general purposes, an expansion reamer is the most practical. This reamer can usually be obtained in standard sizes from $\frac{1}{4}$ to 1 inch, by thirty-seconds of an inch. It is designed to allow the blades to expand $\frac{1}{32}$ inch. For example, the $\frac{1}{4}$-inch expansion reamer will ream a $\frac{1}{4}$ to a $\frac{9}{32}$-inch hole. A $\frac{9}{32}$-inch reamer will enlarge the hole from $\frac{9}{32}$ to $\frac{5}{16}$ inch. This range of adjustment allows a few reamers to cover sizes up to 1 inch.

To operate the reamer, secure the work in a vise so that the hole to be reamed is perpendicular to the top of the vise jaws. Position the reamer at the top of the hole (Figure 3-37b). Straight-hole reamers have a slight taper at the end so they will fit into the hole easily. Turn the wrench clockwise very slowly, until the reamer is centered in the hole.

After the reamer is centered in the hole, turn the wrench clockwise with a steady, firm pressure until the reamer has been turned all the way through the hole. When reaming steel, use cutting oil or machine oil to lubricate the tool. When reaming soft iron, do not lubricate the tool. When you are reaming a hole, turn the reamer in the cutting direction only. This will prevent chipping or dulling of the blades. Great care should be used to ensure even, steady turning. Otherwise, the reamer will "chatter," causing the hole to become marked or scored. To remove the reamer from the hole, turn the wrench clockwise and raise the reamer simultaneously.

Reamers are made of carbon steel and high-speed steel. In general, the cutting blades of a high-speed reamer lose their keenness more quickly than those of a carbon-steel reamer. However, after that keenness is gone, it will last longer than the carbon-steel reamer. The blades of a reamer are made of steel and hardened to such an extent that they are brittle. For this reason you must be careful, when using and storing the reamer, to protect the blades from chipping. To prevent damage to the reamer while it is not in use, wrap it in an oily cloth and keep it in a box.

Taps and Dies

Taps and dies are used to cut threads in metal, plastics, or hard rubber. Taps are used for cutting internal threads, and dies to cut external threads. There are many different types of taps; the most common are the taper, plug, bottoming, and pipe taps (Figure 3-38).

The taper (starting) hand tap has a chamfer length of 8 to 10 threads. These taps are used when starting a tapping operation and when tapping through holes. Plug hand taps have a chamfer length of 3 to 5 threads and are designed for use after the taper tap. Bottoming hand taps

are used for threading the bottom of a blind hole. They have a very short chamfer length of only 1 to $1\frac{1}{2}$ threads, for this purpose. This tap is always used after the plug tap has already been used. Thus, both the taper and plug taps should be used before the bottoming hand tap.

Pipe taps are used for pipe fittings and other places where extremely tight fits are necessary. The tap diameter, from end to end of threaded portion, increases at the rate of $\frac{3}{4}$ inch per foot. All the threads on this tap do the cutting, as compared to the straight taps where only the nonchamfered portion does the cutting.

Dies are made in several different shapes and are of the solid or adjustable type. The square pipe die will cut American Standard Pipe Thread only. It comes in a variety of sizes for cutting threads on pipes with diameters of $\frac{1}{8}$ to 2 inches.

The rethreading die is used principally for dressing over bruised or rusty threads on screws or bolts. It is available in a variety of sizes for rethreading American Standard Coarse and Fine threads. These dies are usually hexagonal in shape and can be turned with a socket, box, or open-end wrench, or any wrench that will fit. Rethreading dies are available in sets of 6, 10, 14, and 28 assorted sizes in a case.

TAPER PIPE

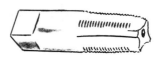

TAPER HAND   CHAMFER
                               LENGTH

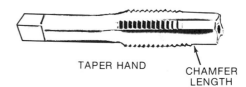

PLUG HAND-NATIONAL
COARSE

BOTTOMING HAND

FIG. 3-38. Types of common taps.

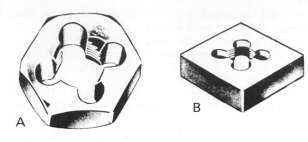

FIG. 3-39. Types of solid dies: *(a)* rethreading; *(b)* square pipe.

Round split adjustable dies (Figure 3-40) are called "button" dies and can be used in either hand diestocks or machine holders. The adjustment in the screw-adjusting type is made by a fine-pitch screw which forces the sides of the die apart or allows them to spring together. The adjustment in the open adjusting types is made by means of three screws in the holder, one for expanding and two for compressing the dies. Round split adjustable dies are available in a variety of sizes to cut American Standard Coarse and Fine threads, special-form threads, and the standard sizes of threads that are used in Britain and other European countries. For hand threading, these dies are held in diestocks. One type of diestock has three pointed screws that will hold round dies of any construction, although it is made specifically for open adjusting type dies.

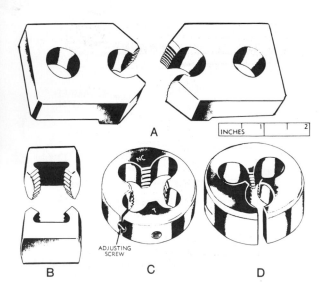

FIG. 3-40. Types of adjustable dies: *(a)* two-piece rectangular pipe die; *(b)* two-piece collet die; *(c)* screw adjusting type; *(d)* open adjusting type.

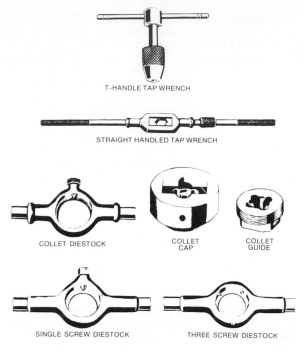

FIG. 3-41. Diestock, die collet, and tap wrenches.

Two-piece collet dies are used with a collet cap and collet guide. The die halves are placed in the cap slot and are held in place by the guide which screws into the underside of the cap. The die is adjusted by means of setscrews at both ends of the internal slot. This type of adjustable die is available in various sizes to cover the cutting range of American Standard Coarse and Fine and special-form threads. Diestocks to hold the dies come in three different sizes.

Two-piece rectangular pipe dies are available to cut American Standard Pipe Threads. They are held in ordinary or ratchet-type diestocks. The jaws of the dies are adjusted by means of setscrews. An adjustable guide serves to keep the pipe on alignment with respect to the dies. The smooth jaws of the guide are adjusted by means of a cam plate; a thumbscrew locks the jaws firmly in the desired position.

Threading sets are available in many different combinations of taps and dies, together with diestocks, tap wrenches, guides, and the screwdrivers and wrenches needed to loosen and tighten adjusting screws and bolts. Figure 3-42 shows a typical threading set for pipe, bolts, and screws.

Never attempt to sharpen taps or dies. The sharpening of taps and dies involves several highly precise cutting processes which affect the thread characteristics and chamfer. These sharpening procedures must be performed by experienced personnel, to maintain the accuracy and cutting effectiveness of the taps and dies.

Keep taps and dies clean and well oiled when not in use. Store them so that they do not contact each other or other tools. For long periods of storage, coat taps and dies with a rust-preventive compound, place them in individual boxes or standard threading-set boxes, and store them in a dry place.

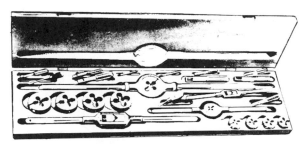

PIPE THREADING SET WITH RECTANGULAR ADJUSTABLE DIES, DIESTOCK, WRENCH, GUIDES AND TAPS

BOLT AND SCREW THREADING SET WITH ROUND ADJUSTABLE SPLIT DIES, DIESTOCKS, TAPS, TAP WRENCHES, AND SCREWDRIVERS

FIG. 3-42. Typical threading sets.

CUTTING MACHINE THREADS WITH A TAP

A 50-50 mixture of white lead and lard oil, applied with a small brush, is highly recommended as a lubricant when tapping in steel. When using this lubricant, tighten the tap in the tap wrench and apply the lubricant to the tap. Start the tap carefully, with its axis on the center line of the hole. The tap must be square with the surface of the work, as shown in Figure 3-43a.

To continue tapping, turn the tap forward two quarter turns, back it up a quarter turn to break the chips, and then turn forward again to take up the slack. Continue this sequence until the threads are cut. After you have cut for the first two or three full turns, you no longer have to exert downward pressure on the wrench. You can tell by the feel that the tap is cutting as you turn it. Do not permit chips to clog the flutes or they will prevent the tap from turning. When the tap will not turn and you notice a springy feeling, stop trying immediately. Back up the tap a quarter turn to break the chips, clean them out of the flutes with a wire are shown in Figure 3-43b, add some more lubricant, and continue tapping. When the tap has cut threads through the hole, the tap will turn with no resistance.

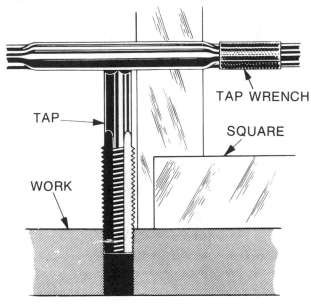

FIG. 3-43. (a) Using a square to ascertain that a tap is square with the work. (b) Using a wire to clear chips from the flute of a tap.

To tap a blind hole, start with the taper tap. For a blind hole you will need all three types—the taper, plug, and bottoming taps. (Be sure they are of the size and thread series you need, and that the tap hole is the size called for by Table 3-5.) Begin with the taper tap. Handle it as described and shown above. Figure 3-44a shows the taper tap just starting to cut. In Figure 3-44b it has cut a little farther. In Figure 3-44c it has bottomed in the hole after having cut several full threads near the top of the hole. This completes the work to be done with the taper tap.

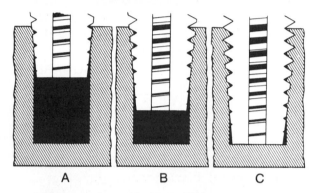

FIG. 3-44. Tapping a blind hole with a taper tap.

TABLE 3-5 Tap Drill Sizes: National Fine (NF) and National Coarse (NC).

| NO. OR FRAC-TION | TAP | | TAP DRILL | | DRILL FOR CLEARANCE |
	NC	NF	NC	NF	
0		80		$3/64$	51
1	64	72	53	53	47
2	56	64	50	50	42
3	48	56	47	45	37
4	40	48	43	42	31
5	40	44	38	37	29
6	32	40	36	33	26
8	32	36	29	29	17
10	24	32	25	21	8
12	24	28	16	14	1
$1/4$	20	28	7	3	Same as tap
$5/16$	18	24	F	I	Same as tap
$3/8$	16	24	$5/16$	Q	Same as tap
$7/16$	14	20	U	$25/64$	Same as tap
$1/2$	13	20	$27/64$	$29/64$	Same as tap
$9/16$	12	18	$31/64$	$33/64$	Same as tap
$5/8$	11	18	$17/32$	$37/64$	Same as tap
$3/4$	10	16	$21/32$	$11/16$	Same as tap
$7/8$	9	14	$49/64$	$13/16$	Same as tap
1"	8	14	$7/8$	$15/16$	Same as tap

In Figure 3-45a the plug tap has entered the few full threads cut by the taper tap. In Figure 3-45b it has continued these threads a little farther down into the hole. In Figure 3-45c it has bottomed in the hole. This is all the work that you can do with the plug tap. It has cut full threads about halfway down the tap hole before bottoming.

In Figure 3-46 the bottoming tap has been substituted for the plug tap. In Figure 3-46a it has been run down the full threads cut by the plug tap and is ready to cut more full threads. In Figure 3-46b it has cut a few more threads, and in Figure 3-46c it has bottomed in the hole. The blind hole has now been completely tapped.

Because these threads are being tapped in a blind hole, the chips must be removed differently. To remove the chips, back the tap completely out of the hole very frequently, invert the stock, if possible, and jar out the chips or work them out of the hole with a wire while the stock is in the inverted position. Until these chips are removed, none of the three taps can complete its work. In tapping blind holes, alternate tapping and chip removal until each of the three taps bottoms in the blind hole.

When you have finished using the three taps, brush the chips out of their teeth, oil them well with lubricating oil, wipe off the surplus oil, and replace them in the threading set.

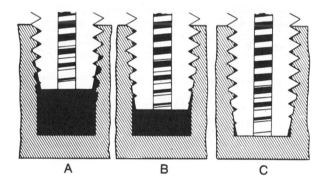

FIG. 3-45. Tapping a blind hole with a plug tap.

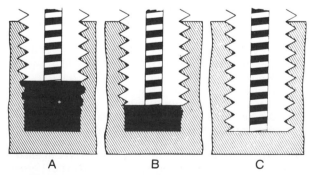

FIG. 3-46. Finish tapping a blind hole with a bottoming tap.

CUTTING MACHINE THREADS WITH DIES

To cut threads on a piece of round stock, first grind a chamfer on the end of the rod. Then hold the rod vertically in a vise to cut the threads. The adjustable round split die shown in Figure 3-47 has an adjusting screw at A. Tightening this screw spreads the die slightly so it will cut less deeply into the rod, and the fit in the tapped hole will be tighter. The shallow hole at B is placed in the diestock opposite the adjustable handle E and serves as a drive hole. Also, when the adjustable handle is tightened, it holds the split die together and against the adjusting screw to maintain the setting while the die is cutting. The threads or cutting teeth of the die are chamfered or relieved at C to help start the die squarely on the round stock. The die is put into the diestock so that the face with the unchamfered teeth is against the shoulder D.

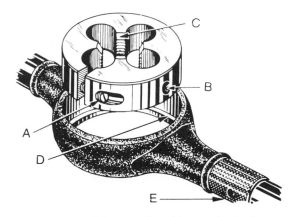

FIG. 3-47. Assembling an adjustable round split die to the diestock.

Figure 3-48 is a plain round split die and diestock. At A, where the die is split, there is no adjusting screw. There are shallow holes at B and C, on both sides of the split, opposite which there are setscrews in the diestock at D and E. F is the adjusting screw, which is pointed, and which enters the split A in the die. D and E are the holding setscrews. They have flat points and are tightened after the setting is made with F. D and E hold the adjustment and furnish the drive as they enter the shallow holes B and C shown in Figure 3-48.

Figure 3-49 shows a section of the die in the diestock and its relation to the chamfer on the end of the work. The taper on the face of the die will accept the chamfer on the end of the work to start the threads square with the common centerline.

To thread the work, brush some 50-50 white lead and lard oil on the rod. Start the die square with the work. Hold one handle with each hand, apply downward pressure, and turn clockwise until you feel that the thread has been started. When the die has started to cut, rotate the diestock two quarter turns, back it off one quarter turn to break the chips, and repeat the cutting (Figure 3-

50). When you have cut enough threads so that the rod comes through the back of the die, remove the die and try the rod in the tapered hole.

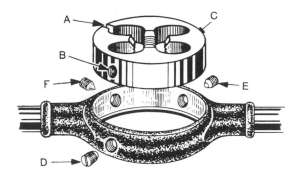

FIG. 3-48. Assembling a plain round split die to the diestock.

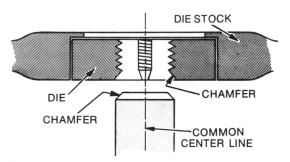

FIG. 3-49. Position of a diestock in relation to the chamfer on the end of the work.

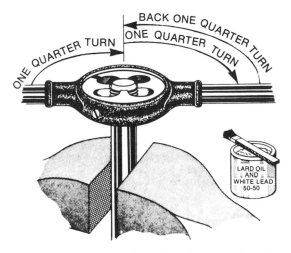

FIG. 3-50. Cutting outside the threads on round stock.

Adjusting a threading die to produce a thread of the proper fit is a trial-and-error procedure. This was a trial run. If the fit is too loose, cut off and discard the portion of the rod that you threaded. Then expand the die by tightening the pointed setscrews (or the adjusting screw) so the die will cut shallower threads on the rod and produce a tighter fit.

If the fit is too tight, it will not be necessary to discard the threaded portion of the rod. Contract the die by backing off (loosening) the pointed setscrew (or the adjusting screw) to decrease the size of the split in the die. This will cause the die to remove more metal when cutting, and produce a looser fit. Then run the die down the cut threads that were too tight. Now test the fit again by turning the threaded end into the tapped hole.

When you have finished the threading job, remove the die from the diestock, carefully clean out all the loose chips, and apply plenty of oil. Wipe off the surplus oil and put the die and diestock away in the threading set, where it will be protected and ready for the next job.

THREAD CHASERS AND RESTORERS

Thread chasers are threading tools that have several teeth and are used to rethread (chase) damaged external or internal threads. These tools are available to chase all standard threads. The internal thread chaser has its cutting teeth located on a side face. The external thread chaser has its cutting teeth on the end of the shaft. The handle end of the tool shaft tapers to a point.

To recondition machine threads when the damage is not serious, you may use the proper *threading die*. Start the die with the chamfered face of the die the position shown in Figure 3-49. Put it in a diestock, and run over the threads that are damaged. For steel, lubricate with a 50-50 mixture of white lead and lard oil, lard oil alone, or lubricating oil if the others are not available. Use no lubricant for brass and copper.

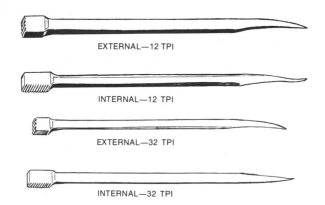

EXTERNAL—12 TPI

INTERNAL—12 TPI

EXTERNAL—32 TPI

INTERNAL—32 TPI

FIG. 3-51. Thread chasers. Size is marked in threads per inch.

The thread restorer resembles a square file. Each face is designed to match a cerain pitch of screw thread. This tool is available in two sizes, each covering eight different machine-thread pitches. Together they cover a range of from 9 threads per inch through 32 threads per inch. Use this thread restorer as you would a file, maintaining the proper angle (that of the threads) as you go over the damaged threads.

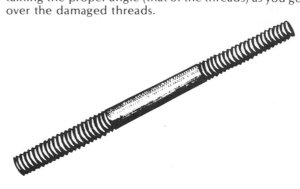

FIG. 3-52. Thread restorer.

Tools of this type are available for external pipe threads as well as for machine threads. The thread restorer (Figure 3-52) for internal pipe threads is similar to a tap. This type of thread restorer, whether internal or external, removes metal. Therefore, the thread that remains as a restored thread will not be a perfect or full thread. Where the crest of the original thread was battered over, the crest of the restored thread will be noticeably flat. Threads restored in this manner are, for practical purposes, as strong as new threads and will again enter a nut or tapped hole.

SCREW AND TAP EXTRACTORS

Screw extractors are used to remove broken screws without damaging the surrounding material or the threaded hole. Tap extractors are used to remove broken taps.

Some screw extractors are straight (Figure 3-53a), having flutes from end to end. These extractors are available in sizes for removing broken screws with $\frac{1}{4}$- to $\frac{1}{2}$-inch outside diameters. Spiral tapered extractors are sized to remove screws and bolts with $\frac{3}{16}$- to $2\frac{1}{8}$-inch outside diameters. Most sets of extractors include twist drills and a drill guide. Tap extractors are similar to screw extractors and are sized to remove taps ranging from $\frac{3}{16}$ to $2\frac{1}{8}$ inches outside diameter.

To remove a broken screw or tap with a spiral extractor, first drill a hole of the proper size in the screw or tap. (The size of hole required for each screw extractor is stamped on it.) Then insert the extractor in the hole, and turn it counterclockwise to remove the defective component. If the tap has broken off at the surface of the work, or slightly below the surface of the work, the straight tap extractor shown in Figure 3-53 may remove it. Apply a liberal amount of penetrating oil to the broken tap. Place the tap extractor over the broken tap, and lower the upper collar to insert the four sliding prongs down into the four flutes of the tap. Then slide the bottom collar down to the surface of the work so that it will hold the prongs tightly against the body of the extractor. Tighten the tap wrench on the square shank of the extractor, and carefully work the extractor back and forth to loosen the tap. It may be necessary to remove the extractor and strike a few sharp blows with a small hammer and pin punch to jar the tap loose. Then reinsert the tap remover and carefully try to back the tap out of the hole.

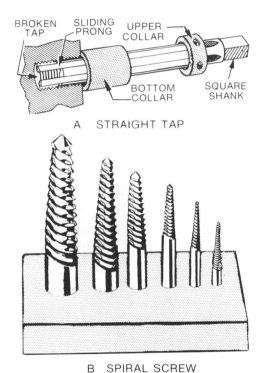

FIG. 3-53. Screw and tap extractors: *(a)* straight tap; *(b)* spiral screw.

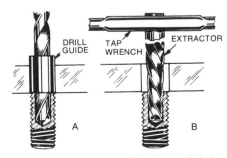

FIG. 3-54. Removing a stud broken off below the surface.

Pipe and Tubing Cutters and Flaring Tools

Pipe cutters are used to cut pipe made of steel, brass, copper, wrought iron, and lead. Tube cutters are used to cut tubing made of iron, steel, brass, copper, and aluminum. The essential difference between pipe and tubing is that tubing has much thinner walls. Flaring tools are used to make single or double flares in the ends of tubing.

PIPE CUTTING

Two sizes of hand pipe cutters are generally used. The No. 1 pipe cutter has a cutting capacity of $\frac{1}{8}$ to 2 inches, and the No. 2 pipe cutter has a cutting capacity of 2 to 4 inches. The pipe cutter has a special alloy-steel cutting wheel and two pressure rollers which are adjusted and tightened by turning the handle.

Figure 3-55 shows three methods of measuring threaded pipe to determine desired lengths. In the end-to-end method, the threaded portions of the pipe are included, and the pipe is measured from end to end. The end-to-center method is used on a section of pipe that has a fitting screwed on one end only; measure from the free end of the pipe to the center of the fitting at the other end of the pipe. The center-to-center method is used when both ends of the pipe have fittings; measure from the center of one fitting to the center of the other fitting at the opposite end of the pipe. The approximate length of thread on $\frac{1}{2}$- and $\frac{3}{4}$-inch wrought-iron or steel pipe is $\frac{3}{4}$ inch. On 1-, $1\frac{1}{4}$-, and $1\frac{1}{2}$-inch pipe, the threaded portion is approximately 1 inch long. On 2- and $2\frac{1}{2}$-inch pipe, the threaded length is $1\frac{1}{8}$ and $1\frac{1}{2}$ inches, respectively.

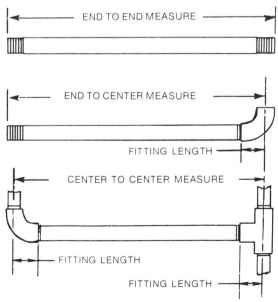

FIG. 3-55. Proper method for measuring pipe to desired lengths.

To determine the length of pipe required, take the measurement of the installation by one of the three methods—for example, center to center if the pipe requires two fittings. Measure the size of the fittings as shown in Figure 3-55. Subtract the total size of the two fittings from the installation measurement. Multiply the approximate thread length by 2, and add the result to the length obtained. This will give you the length of pipe required.

After the length of the pipe has been determined, measure the pipe and mark the spot where the cut is to be made with a scriber or crayon. Lock the pipe securely in a pipe vise. Inspect the cutter to make sure that there are no nicks or burrs in the cutting wheel. Open the jaws of the cutter by turning the handle counterclockwise. Position the cutter around the pipe at the marked point. Make sure the cutting wheel is exactly on the mark, and close the jaws of the cutter lightly against the pipe by turning the cutter handle clockwise. After the jaws make contact, turn the cutter handle clockwise one quarter turn more. This will put a bite on the pipe.

Grasp the cutter handle and rotate the cutter as a whole, one complete revolution, swinging it around the pipe in the direction indicated in Figure 3-56. Turn the cutter handle clockwise one quarter turn more to take another bite on the pipe, and rotate the cutter another complete revolution. Keep the cutter perpendicular to the pipe at all times, or the wheel will not track properly. Repeat this operation until the pipe is cut. Remove the small shoulder on the outside of the pipe with a file, and remove the burr on the inside with a reamer (Figure 3-57).

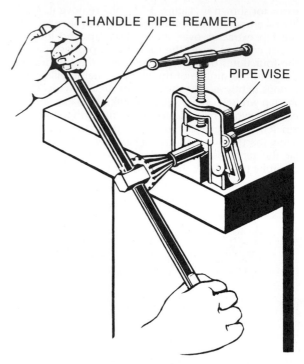

FIG. 3-57. Using a pipe reamer to remove burrs from a pipe.

To begin thread cutting, put the diestock on the pipe so that the pipe passes through the guide and enters the tapered face of the pipe die. Turn the diestock clockwise for right-hand threads, applying pressure only when starting. (After the die has taken hold, it will feed itself.) It

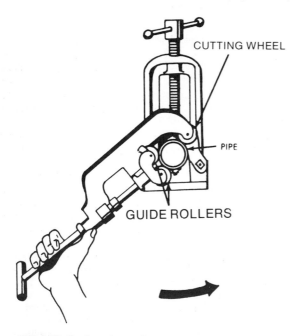

FIG. 3-56. Cutting pipe with a pipe cutter.

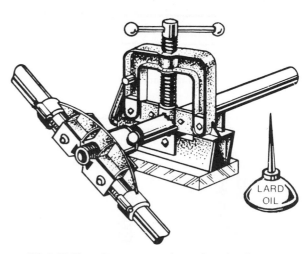

FIG. 3-58. Threading an external pipe thread with a pipe die.

is not necessary to back up the die, as you do when cutting machine threads. Pipe-threading dies can cut continuously because they cut only as many threads on the pipe as there are on the die itself and because there is plenty of room in a pipe die for the chips to escape. When cutting threads on steel pipe, apply lard oil to the pipe and die where the cutting is actually taking place. Continue turning until the end of the pipe has gone through the die and is flush with the near face (Figure 3-58).

TUBE CUTTING

Most tube cutters closely resemble pipe cutters, except that they are of lighter construction. A hand-screw-feed tubing cutter of ⅛- to 1¼-inch capacity (Figure 3-59) has two rollers with cutouts located off center so that cracked flares may be held in them and cut off without waste of tubing. It also has a retractable cutter blade that is adjusted by turning a knob. The other tube cutter shown (Figure 3-60) is designed to cut tubing up to and including ¾ and 1 inch outside diameter. Copper tubing is one kind of metallic tubing that you can cut readily with a tube cutter.

To cut tubing, place the tube cutter with the cutting wheel on the mark where the cut is to be made. Move the cutting wheel into light contact with the tubing. (See Figure 3-59a.) Then swing the handle around the tubing as you feed the cutting wheel a little for each revolution by turning the screw adjustment. Different wall thicknesses, kinds, and diameters of metallic tubing require different feeds. Figure 3-59b indicates the direction of rotation. The feed pressure is correct when it keeps the wheel cutting but does not flatten the tubing.

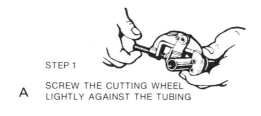

A STEP 1
SCREW THE CUTTING WHEEL LIGHTLY AGAINST THE TUBING

B STEP 2
ROTATE THE CUTTER KEEPING A SLIGHT PRESSURE AGAINST THE CUTTING WHEEL WITH THE SCREW ADJUSTMENT

FIG. 3-59. Steps in cutting tubing with a tube cutter.

The design of some tubing cutters will permit cutting off a flared end close to the base of the flare. In Figure 3-60a, notice the groove in the backup roller. Place the flare in this groove so that the cutting wheel rides at the base of the flare. Then cut off the flare as you would cut tubing. Burrs may form, similar to those formed in pipe cutting. Remove the inside burr with the reamer attached to the tubing cutter, opposite the handle (Figure 3-60b). In some cases a three-cornered scraper, pocketknife blade, or round file may work better than the reamer. After reaming, clean out the chips. Then remove any outside burr with a file.

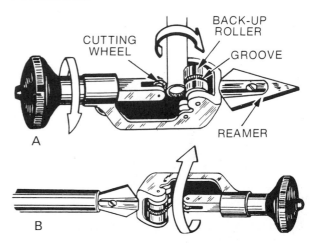

FIG. 3-60. (a) Cutting a tube close to the base of a flare. (b) Reaming the burrs from a piece of tubing.

FLARING METAL TUBING

Flaring tools are used to flare soft copper, brass, or aluminum. The single flaring tool consists of a split die block that has holes for ³⁄₁₆-, ¼-, ⁵⁄₁₆-, ⅜-, and ½-inch tubing, a yoke with a screw and a flaring cone, plus five adapters for the different sizes of tubing, all in a metal case.

To flare the end of a piece of tubing, first check to see that it has been cut off squarely and that the burrs have been removed from both inside and outside. Remember to slip the flare nut on the tube before you make the flare. Then, as shown in Figure 3-62a, open the flaring tool at the die which corresponds to the size of the tubing being flared. Insert the end of the tubing so it protrudes slightly above the top face of the die blocks. The amount by which the tubing extends above the block determines the finished diameter of the flare. The flare must be large enough so that it will seat properly against the fitting, but small enough so that the threads of the flare nut will slide over it. You determine the correct size by trial and error. Then as shown in Figure 3-62b, close the die block and secure the tool with the wing nut. Use the handle of the yoke to tighten the wing nut. Then place the yoke over the end of the tubing (Figure 3-62c), and tighten the handle to force the cone into the end of the tubing. The completed flare should be slightly visible above the face of the die block.

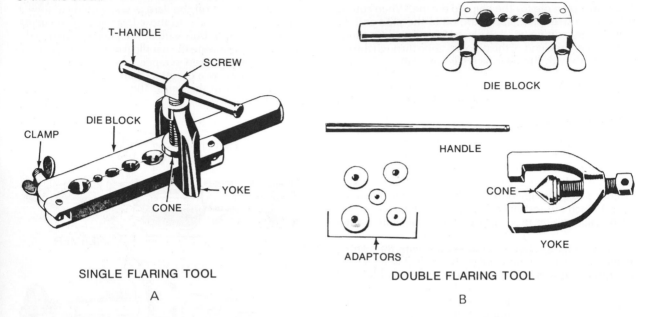

FIG. 3-61. (a) Single and (b) double flaring tools.

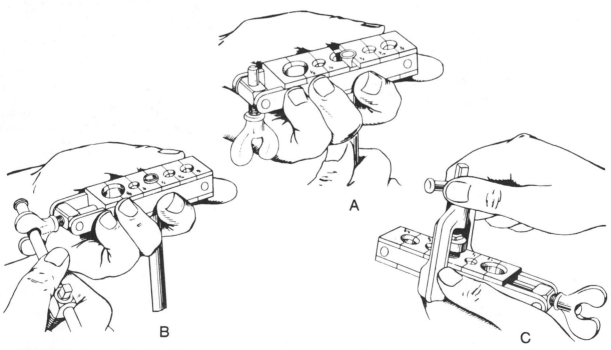

FIG. 3-62. Flaring metallic tubing.

BENDING METAL TUBING

The objective in tube bending is to obtain a smooth bend without flattening the tube. Tube bending is usually accomplished with one of the tube benders discussed below. In an emergency, however, aluminum tubing under ¼ inch in diameter may be bent by hand.

SPRING BENDERS External spring-type benders, shown in Figure 3-63a, come in sizes to bend ¼-, ⁵⁄₁₆-, ³⁄₈-, ⁷⁄₁₆-, ½-, and ⅝-inch outside-diameter soft copper, aluminum, and other soft metallic tubing. To bend tubing with this type of bender, first select the size that will just slip over the size of tubing you want to bend. Then slip it over the tubing so that it centers at the middle of the proposed bend. Grasp the bender with both hands, and make the bend. (See Figure 3-63b.) The restraining action of the bender will prevent the tubing from collapsing at the bend and will produce a smooth curve. To remove the bender, grasp the belled end and pull it off the tubing.

Internal spring-type benders, shown in Figure 3-63c, come in sizes to bend ³⁄₈-, ½-, and ⅝-inch outside-diameter tubing. This type can be used when both ends of a length of tubing are flared and the external type cannot be applied. To bend tubing with an internal spring-type bender, select the proper size bender and slip it inside the tubing. Insert it so that the center of its length is at the center of the proposed bend. Grasp the tubing with both hands, and make the bend. If the bender sticks out of the end of the tubing, remove it by pulling it out. If not, remove it with a fish wire or other simple means.

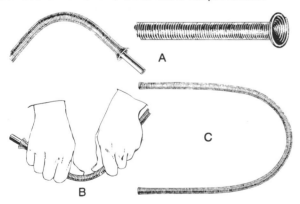

FIG. 3-63. Bending tubing with spring-type tube benders.

HAND TUBE BENDER The hand tube bender shown in Figure 3-64 consists of four parts: the handle, radius block (mandrel), clip, and slide bar. The radius block is marked in degrees of bend, ranging from 0 to 180°. The slide bar has a mark which is lined up with the zero mark on the radius block. The tube is inserted in the tool and, after the marks are lined up, the slide bar is moved around until the mark on the slide bar reaches the number indicating the desired bend (in degrees) as marked on the radius block. Follow the procedure indicated in Figure 3-64.

This type of bender is furnished in ³⁄₁₆-, ¼-, ⁵⁄₁₆-, ³⁄₈-, and ½-inch sizes. For larger sizes of tubing, similar mandrel-type benders are used. The only difference is that these larger benders are geared for greater mechanical advantage.

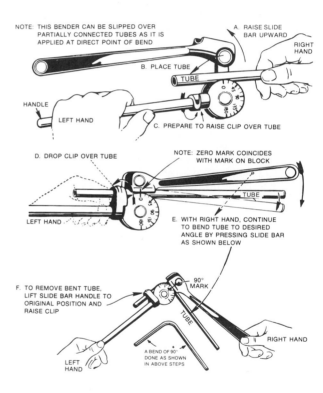

FIG. 3-64. Typical hand tube bender.

SCREWDRIVERS

The screwdriver is one of the most basic and essential of all hand tools. It is also the most frequently misused and abused of all hand tools. It is designed for one function—to drive and remove screws. But all too often it is used as a pry bar to pry nails and tacks from boards, lids from paint cans, etc. Using a screwdriver as a pry bar tends to round the corners of the tip, put nicks into it, and distort its shape so that it will no longer fit well in a screw slot; it then becomes almost useless for turning screws. Admittedly, a screwdriver does make a very handy little pry bar, but the best way to meet this need is to keep an old one around that you no longer use for screws.

Screws come in a variety of sizes, each of which has a slot of specific width and depth. To work well, the tip of the screwdriver should fit the slot as closely as possible. Since the slots vary in size, so must the screwdriver tips, if you are to get a close fit. There are two basic types of screwdrivers: the standard or slotted-head screwdriver and the recessed-head screwdriver.

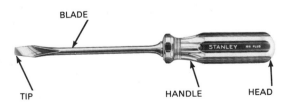

FIG. 4-1. Screwdriver nomenclature.

STANDARD SCREWDRIVERS

There are three main parts to a standard or "common" screwdriver. The portion you grip is called the handle, the steel portion extending from the handle is the shank, and the end which fits into the screw is called the blade (Figure 4-2a). The steel shank is designed to withstand considerable twisting force in proportion to its size, and the tip of the blade is hardened to keep it from wearing. The blade of the standard screwdriver fans out just back of the tip. While this offers the convenience of a better grip on the screwhead when extra leverage is needed, it also prevents the tip from following a screw into its hole. When you wish to recess screws in deep holes, use a "cabinet" blade (Figure 4-2b) instead of the standard or keystone blade. The cabinet blade (also known as the "gunsmith's" blade) does not fan out; its tip is no wider than its shank.

Standard screwdrivers are classified according to the combined length of the shank and blade and by blade size. The most common sizes range in length from $2\frac{1}{2}$ to 12 inches. The blade size varies from $\frac{3}{32}$ to $\frac{1}{2}$ inch. However, the following sizes will be good match for average slotted-head screw sizes: $\frac{3}{32}$-inch tip with 3-inch shaft; $\frac{1}{4}$-inch tip with 4-inch shaft; $\frac{5}{16}$-inch tip with 6-inch shaft; and $\frac{3}{8}$-inch tip with 10-inch shaft. You also should have a stubby $1\frac{1}{2}$-inch screwdriver with a $\frac{1}{4}$-inch tip for working in very tight places. There are, of course, many smaller and some larger screwdrivers, for special purposes. The diameter of the shank and the width and thickness of the blade are generally proportional to the length, but again there are special screwdrivers with long thin shanks, short thick shanks, and extra-wide or extra-narrow blades. As a rule, however, blades and handles are proportioned in size to withstand any torque to which they are subjected in normal use.

Table 4-1 Slotted-Screw Tool Selector

Screw Size	Blade Size, Inches	Screw Size	Blade Size, Inches
0	$3/32$	9	$5/16$
1	$3/32$	10	$5/16$
2	$1/8$	12	$3/8$
3	$5/32$	14	$3/8$
4	$3/16$	16	$7/16$
5	$3/16$	18	$7/16$
6	$1/4$	20	$1/2$
7	$1/4$	24	$1/2$
8	$5/16$		

While handles are made of transparent plastic these days, some are still made of wood or metal. When metal handles are used, there is usually a wooden hand grip placed on each side of the handle. In some types of wood- or plastic-handled screwdrivers the shank extends through the handle; in others, the shank enters the handle only a short way and is pinned to the handle. Most handles have flat-topped ridges that give you a better grip. Some manufacturers make their plastic handles thicker to give you more leverage, and others add a black rubber sleeve for the same purpose and for better gripping. In some small screwdriver kits, there is an extra handle that slips over the top of the midget screwdriver to provide a larger gripping surface, extend the reach, and increase the driving power. One company makes oversized plastic handles with a triangular shape and rounded ridges for these purposes.

For heavy work, special types of standard screwdrivers are made with a square shank which can withstand greater turning torque than round ones. Another advantage of a square shank is that you can put a wrench on it and supply some added torque when you have a rusted or frozen screw that is hard to turn. Some screwdrivers with round shafts have two flats on the shaft close to the handle for this purpose.

When using a standard, or slotted, screwdriver, it is very important to select a screwdriver of the proper length whose tip is fitted properly to the screw. This proper fit is important because the tip tends to slip out of the slot if it is too thin, and it sometimes mars the work surface. More important, when the slot is too wide for the tip, the blade has room to twist in the slot and shave away fine slivers of steel from its edges. Since screws are made of relatively soft steel, the slot edges can be worn down in no time at all; then the screwdriver becomes useless because its blade has nothing to press against.

The width of the tip is as important as its thickness. If the tip is wide enough to protrude beyond the edges of the head of the screw, it will cut into the work surface as the screw is driven home. This is especially true when flat-head screws are driven flush.

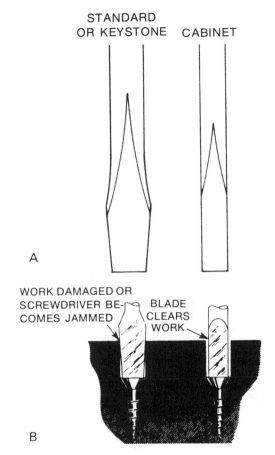

FIG. 4-2. Standard or keystone blade and cabinet-tip blade.

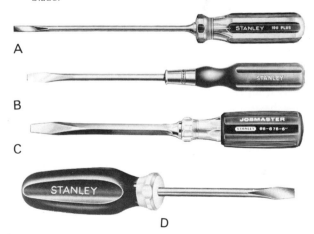

FIG. 4-3. Types of handles: *(a)* plastic with a cabinet-tip blade; *(b)* wood with a standard tip; *(c)* rubber sleeve grip with a mechanic's square shank; *(d)* triangular grip with a round shank.

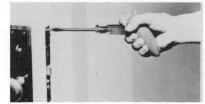

FIG. 4-4. Other types of handle devices to provide increased leverage.

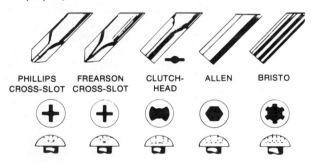

TOO NARROW   TOO THIN   TOO WIDE   CORRECT

FIG. 4-5. Make sure the screwdriver bit fits the screw slot properly.

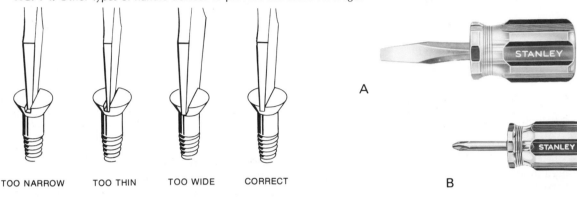

A

B

FIG. 4-7. *(a)* Stubby standard tip; *(b)* stubby Phillips-head-screw tip.

PHILLIPS   FREARSON   CLUTCH-   ALLEN   BRISTO
CROSS-SLOT   CROSS-SLOT   HEAD

FIG. 4-6. Several of the more common recessed-head type screws.

RECESSED-HEAD SCREWDRIVERS

Recessed screws are now available in various shapes. They have a cavity formed in the head and require a specially shaped screwdriver. These screwhead types include the familiar Phillips and the Pozidriv, Frearson (Reed and Prince), clutch, Robertson, Allen, Bristol, spline, hex, Scrulox, and Torq-set screws. Of them all, the most common is the Phillips-head screw which, of course, requires a Phillips-type screwdriver.

The head of a Phillips-head screw has a four-way slot into which the screwdriver fits. This prevents the screwdriver from slipping. Five standard-size Phillips screwdrivers handle a wide range of screw sizes. Their ability to hold helps to prevent damaging the slots or the work surrounding the screw. It is poor practice to try to use a standard screwdriver on a Phillips screw, because both the tool and screw slot will be damaged. But when using a Phillips screwdriver, you must exert somewhat more downward pressure to keep the screwdriver in the slots. A worn Phillips screwdriver will tend to slip out of the slots and should be discarded, for it cannot be sharpened easily. As with the flat-bladed screwdriver, always use the correct size.

Phillips-head screwdrivers are sized by number from No. 0 (smallest) to No. 4. Generally, the sizes that the average craftsman is most likely to need are Nos. 2 and 3, with 4- and 6-inch shafts, respectively. A stubby 1½-inch Phillips screwdriver with a medium point (No. 2) is also useful for screws of this type in a tight place.

While the Phillips-head screw looks similar to the Frearson (also called the Reed-and-Prince screwhead), the two screwdrivers are *not* interchangeable. Therefore, you should always use a Frearson screwdriver with Frearson screws and a Phillips screwdriver with Phillips screws, or a ruined tool or ruined screwhead will result. Also Torq-Set machine screws are similar in appearance to the more familiar Phillips machine screws. But a Phillips driver could easily damage a Torq-Set screwhead, making it difficult if not impossible to remove the screw even if the proper tool were used later.

The other types of recessed-head screws must have their own special screwdrivers if the screwhead is to remain undamaged. The exception is Allen and hex-recess screws, for which both Allen and hex wrenches and Allen-bladed and hex-bladed screwdrivers may be used.

Table 4-2 Phillips Screwdrivers

Point size	Blade diameter inches	Wood Screw		Machine screw		Sheet metal	
		Flat, oval	Round	Flat, oval, binding	Round, fillister	Truss, brazier, button	Flat, round, oval, stove, binding
0	⅛	0, 1	0, 1	0, 1	0, 1		
1	³⁄₁₆	2, 3, 4	2, 3, 4	2, 3, 4	2, 3, 4	2, 3, 4, 5	2, 3, 4
2	¼	5, 6, 7, 8, 9	5, 6, 7 8, 9, 10	5, 6, 8 10	5, 6, 8 10	6, 8, 10	5, 6, 7 8, 10
3	⁵⁄₁₆	10, 12 14, 16	12, 14 16	12, ¼″	12, ¼″ ⁵⁄₁₆	12, ¼″	12, 14
4	⅜	18, 20 24	18, 20 24	⁵⁄₁₆″, ⅜″, ⁷⁄₁₆″, ½″	⅜″, ⁷⁄₁₆″, ½″	⁵⁄₁₆″, ⅜″, ⁷⁄₁₆″, ½″	

Incidentally, screwdrivers having clutch-head tips lock tightly in the screwheads when turned clockwise. The screwdriver is unlocked simply by turning it in the opposite direction.

Recessed-head screwdrivers are available with metal, wood, and plastic handles. The latter are the most popular, and they have the same features as standard screwdrivers. While the shanks of most recessed-head screwdrivers are round, the larger sizes are available with heavy-duty square shanks.

Combination screwdrivers are available that consist of a single handle with detachable blades. Some of these multibit screwdrivers come as sets with an assortment of standard (slotted), recessed-head, hex-nut head, and other blades. Usually, they all provide two sizes of Phillips and standard (slotted) screwdriver blades in one tool. One kind has four screwdriver bits which fit into a hexagonal recess and are held in place by a magnet. The spare bits are stored inside the handle or in a kit box. With other models the blade is held in perfect alignment by spring locks. Other kinds have double-ended shafts which can be snapped into the handle and reversed when a different size is wanted, or a different shank can be inserted in the handle when a Phillips type is wanted instead of the standard type. The main advantage of the combination reversible screwdriver is that you do not have to hunt up another tool if you find that you have the wrong size or type.

SCREWDRIVER FEATURES

The two types of screwdrivers just discussed are so important that they should be considered absolute musts in any shop or toolbox. But there are a number of others that make tempting additions.

RATCHET SCREWDRIVERS For fast easy work the ratchet screwdriver (Figure 4-9) is extremely convenient, as it can be used one-handed and does not require the bit to be lifted out of the slot after each turn. There are several different styles of ratchet screwdrivers, but they are all of two basic types, standard or simple ratchet and spiral ratchet. The handle of the standard-ratchet screwdriver turns back and forth in the direction set, to drive or extract screws. A slide button adjusts the handle to turn in either direction or locks it to perform as an ordinary screwdriver. Because it permits a steady grip, it is easy on the hands and is especially good in cramped quarters where normal hand movement is difficult. Blades of various sizes and types can be obtained.

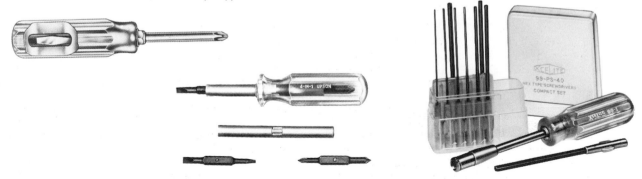

FIG. 4-8. (Left) Combination reversible screwdriver. (Center) The handle cutaway shows the standard tip up in the handle while the Phillips side of the reversible blade is ready for use. Typical four-in-one screwdriver set. (Right) Allen hex-type multiblade screwdriver kit; all the blades fit into the same handle.

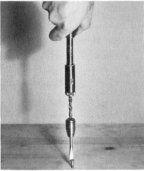

FIG. 4-9. (Left) Standard (or simple) ratchet screwdriver; (right) spiral ratchet screwdriver.

The most popular of the ratchet screwdrivers is the spiral type. Operating like a push drill, it may be fitted with either a standard-type bit or a special bit for recessed heads of various size. In addition, drill bits, countersinks, and socket bits for nuts are available. These bits snap into a holder at the end of the shaft. All you have to do is push the handle down several times (a spring returns the handle to its top position), and with each push the bit turns. In a couple of seconds the screw is driven home. The ratchet can be reversed so that you can back screws out, or it can be fixed so that the bit turns either way like an ordinary screwdriver. In addition, there are drill bits which can be used for pilot holes (which will be discussed later). There are a large and a small size of spiral-ratchet screwdriver, the smaller one having the advantage of storing its bits in a cavity in the handle.

As mentioned in Chapter 2, there is also a type of screwdriver which fits into a brace. Actually, no other screwdriver combination has as much leverage as this one. It is ideal for driving long, large slotted screws. Another advantage is that the ratchet in the bit brace permits its use in tight quarters, since the handle can be swung in short arcs (Figure 4-10). The ratchet can also be reversed to back screws out.

FIG. 4-10. Carpenter's bit brace can be fitted with a bit good for driving big screws.

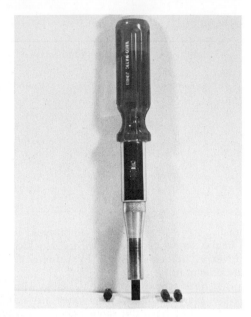

FIG. 4-11. The magnet built into the shank of this ratchet screwdriver holds the interchangeable bits and holds the screw. The extra bits are stored inside the handle.

OFFSET SCREWDRIVERS An offset screwdriver may be used where there is not sufficient vertical space for a standard or recessed screwdriver. Offset screwdrivers are constructed with one blade forged in line with, and another blade forged at right angles to, the handle. Both blades are bent at 90° to the handle. By alternating ends, one can seat or loosen most screws even when the swinging space is very restricted. Offset screwdrivers are made for either standard or recessed-head screws, or both. Some even have small 4-inch ratchet handles with reversible bits at right angles to the handle.

WEDGE-TYPE SCREWDRIVERS These screwdrivers have a split shaft and tip. A metal sleeve on the shaft, when pushed forward, forces one part of the split tip slightly behind the other. This wedges both parts tightly in the screw slot, which is very handy if you do not happen to have a standard screwdriver that fits the screw slot closely. It will hold the screw tightly enough for one-hand use where you cannot hold the screw with your other hand.

TORQUE SCREWDRIVERS Torque-limiting screwdrivers offer the most reliable means of tightening small threaded fasteners. When the set torque is reached, the screwdriver goes into a freewheeling condition that prevents further torquing of the screw. The control mechanism engages and disengages four or eight times (depending on the particular model) during each revolution of the handle, in either the right- or left-hand direction. Adjustable models usually have a calibrated micrometer scale. Preset models must be set on a suitable torque tester. For more on torque-set tools, see Chapter 5.

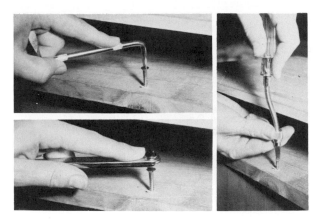

FIG. 4-14. The wedge-type screwdriver has a split tip which will expand in the screw slot and hold it tightly. This is very handy when you must work with one hand in a tight place.

FIG. 4-12. Offset screwdrivers come in handy when you have to work in cramped spaces and where limited room above the screw prevents the use of an ordinary screwdriver. The offset screwdriver at the top left is the simplest type, having a blade at each end at right angles to the shank. The one at the bottom left combines the offset feature with a ratchet handle which makes it a more versatile tool. When all else fails, the screwdriver shown at the right can be used to reach the most inaccessible screws. The shank is flexible and can be bent in any direction.

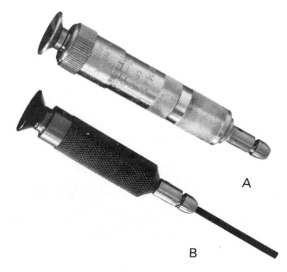

A

B

FIG. 4-15. (a) Adjustable and (b) preset torque chuck-type screwdrivers.

SPRING-JAW HOLDERS An attachment to a standard, or slotted-head, screwdriver consists of a pair of curved steel arms with V-shaped notches that grip the screw shank just under the head and hold it on the screwdriver tip. A coil spring above the arms holds them tightly together. The attachment is mounted at the factory and is part of the screwdriver. The purpose of this gadget is to allow one-hand use in an awkward or tight place.

There are several screw starters for both slotted and Phillips-head screws on the market. They hold the screw so that it can be started into a threaded hole to the point where a standard screwdriver can take over final tightening. The same holding capability of the tool can be used to lift out a loosened screw, to ensure that it is not dropped and lost. And, for screws that are dropped, most screw starters have a magnet mounted on the back end for easy retrieval. The screw starter shown in Figure 4-17 does its work with a unique three-section tip. The two outer sections are stationary. A spring-loaded center section can rotate. When the tip is cocked for use, the three sections are aligned to slip into the screw slot. When

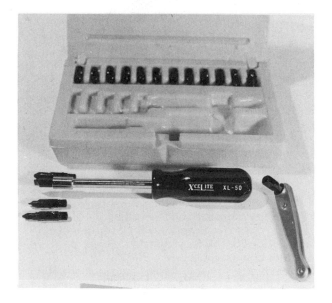

FIG. 4-13. A 19-piece midget reversible ratchet offset screwdriver set, an all-purpose set that is simple and easy to use in all kinds of assembly, disassembly, adjustment, and repair work involving Allen, hex, Phillips, and slotted screws. The offset ratchet fits a square socket in the end of the handle.

the screw is pressed against the tip, the spring-loaded mechanism uncocks, turning the center section of the tip against the sides of the screw slot. As the screw is turned into a threaded hole, increasing pressure on the tip again cocks the tool and lets it disengage from the screwhead, ready for the next screw. Screw starters are usually available with both slotted- and Phillips-screw tips.

FIG. 4-16. Standard and Phillips screwdrivers can be obtained with spring-jaw holders that hold the screw on the tip of the screwdriver.

SPECIAL SCREWDRIVERS There are a great many special-purpose screwdrivers on the market. For instance, there are so-called "insulated" electrician's screwdrivers, on which the handle and/or blade is coated with plastic to protect the user against accidental shorts. A good insulated electrician's screwdriver will withstand up to 5000 volts. Some screwdrivers of this type feature a handle that lights up to indicate a hot wire or side. You should never use an ordinary screwdriver to check an electric circuit.

There is also a special-purpose screwdriver that will test whether or not a spark plug is receiving power. Just touch the terminal with the blade tip; if it is working, a light will flash in the clear plastic handle. And, there are types that look like screwdrivers but whose tips are actually small sockets in various sizes, for turning hex nuts, hex screws, or Allen heads. They are much faster than wrenches.

For electronic work, there are screwdrivers that are made of nonmetallic material so that they can be used to tune sensitive gear that might be affected by the metal type. There are magnetized screwdrivers which will pick up and hold screws. Then, there are beryllium-copper screwdrivers which are nonmagnetic, nonsparking, and rust and corrosion resistant. These special screwdrivers are excellent safety tools for electrical and electronic assembly and servicing, as well as for work where they may be exposed to moisture, salt air, weather, chemicals, or chemical fumes, or wherever volatile or explosive materials are present. Beryllium-copper screwdrivers are available in slotted and Phillips types as well as with interchangeable blade sets.

While not a member of the screwdriver family, a ratchet-drive socket wrench (see Chapter 5) is needed for driving lag screws. And, at the other extreme of size, you can get a set of jeweler's screwdrivers, usually a single handle with four or five snap-in blades, the smallest of which has a tip so tiny you can hardly see it with the naked eye. In fact, there are so many special types of

screwdrivers that it is impossible to name them all in this book.

FIG. 4-17. Typical screw starter at work.

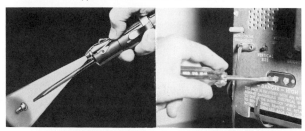

FIG. 4-18. The flashlight screwdriver shown at the left is perfect for emergencies, when the light on the work is bad. It operates on ordinary flashlight batteries and directs a strong beam of light around the tip of the screwdriver. The screwdriver at the right has a tube filled with neon gas encased in its handle. The neon gas glows when the tip comes in contact with any voltage.

SCREWDRIVER SAFETY

The screwdriver is a very safe tool; it only presents a hazard when misused or when the user lacks the knowledge or skill to use it. Keep the following safety tips in mind:

1. Do not hold your work in your hand while using a screwdriver; if the point slips, it can cause a bad cut. Hold the work in a vise, with a clamp, or on a solid surface. If that is impossible, you will always be safe if you follow this rule: *Never get any part of your body in front of the screwdriver blade tip.* That is a good safety rule for any sharp or pointed tool.
2. All screwdrivers should have smooth, firm handles, and the blades should be kept in good condition; the screwdriver becomes useless and dangerous if the blade is broken.
3. Do not use screwdrivers as chisels, hammers, can openers, crowbars, or for any purpose other than to turn screws.
4. Never try to turn a screwdriver with a pair of pliers.

5. Employ the right screwdriver for the job. That is, always use a screwdriver with a blade that fits the screw to be turned. The blade of the screwdriver should be seated squarely against the bottom of the screw slot.
6. Screwdrivers with insulated handles and/or blades should be used for electrical repairs or installations. Be sure the current is off before attempting such work.

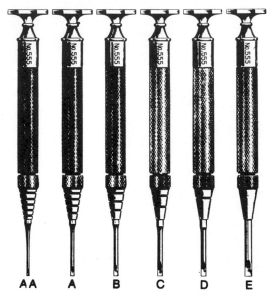

FIG. 4-19. Set of five jeweler's screwdrivers made with slender shanks and blades for delicate watch and camera repair work. Their overall lengths are from 3 to $3\frac{5}{8}$ inches, and blade sizes range from (a) 0.025 to (e) 0.100 inch.

PROPER USE OF SCREWDRIVERS

The most common error in driving a wood screw is applying too much pressure on the screwdriver when starting the screw. Without a starting hole, ordinary screws tend to follow the grain of the wood and are difficult to drive straight. But providing a pilot hole eliminates this problem and prevents the wood from splitting, especially near the edges and ends of the stock. If the screw is a small one, use a brad awl or screw-hole starter tool. Larger screws require pilot holes made with bits or twist drills.

1. For softwoods (pine, spruce, etc.), drill a hole only half as deep as the threaded part of the screw, or use the size hole recommended in Table 4-3.
2. For hardwoods (oak, maple, birch, etc.), drill the hole as deep as the screw, following the recommendations given in Table 4-3.

3. For large screws being driven into hardwoods, follow this procedure: First drill a pilot hole which is slightly smaller than the threaded part of the screw. Use a second drill to enlarge the hole at the top; this drill should be the same diameter as the upper (unthreaded) portion of the screw.

Table 4-3 Table of Screw Sizes and the Drill Gauge Numbers to Be Used for Maximum Holding Power

Screw No.	Pilot Holes		Shank Clearance Holes
	Hardwoods	Softwoods	
0	66	75	52
1	57	71	47
2	54	65	42
3	53	58	37
4	51	55	32
5	47	53	30
6	44	52	27
7	39	51	22
8	35	48	18
9	33	45	14
10	31	43	10
11	29	40	4
12	25	38	2
14	14	32	D
16	10	29	I
18	6	26	N
20	33	19	P
24	D	15	V

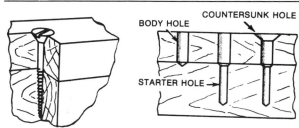

FIG. 4-20. Pilot holes for screws.

For flat-head screws, the shank hole should be countersunk so that the screwhead will seat flush with the surface. When a screw is used to attach metal to wood, the upper part of the pilot hole is often enlarged to accommodate the screw shank, especially in hardwood or when using large screws.

DRIVING SCREWS When driving any screw, remember these important points:

1. Use the blade which fits the screw slot exactly. Never use a round-tipped blade; it slips easily and may cause injury. Also, if the tip is rounded or beveled, it will rise out of the slot, spoiling the screwhead.

2. Use the longest screwdriver convenient for the job. More power can be applied to a long screwdriver than a short one, with less danger of its slipping out of the slot.

3. When starting a screw, place it on the screwdriver tip and hold screw and tip together with the fingers of one hand, while grasping the handle with the other hand so it rests comfortably in the palm. Then put the screw point in the starting hole, retaining the same grip but permitting the hand holding the screw to rest on the work. The handle of a good screwdriver, as mentioned previously, is rounded and smooth at the end (dome) to provide a comfortable palm rest, and the stopped flutes have rounded edges to minimize irritation and skin abrasion. A rubber crutch tip fitted over the handle of screwdriver will make driving large screws easier and prevent palms from blistering.

4. To drive the screw *in*, turn the handle *clockwise*. To *remove* a screw, turn it in the opposite direction, *counterclockwise*. The screw should be at right angles to the surface unless the work requires that it be driven at an angle. Apply very little pressure on the driver at first, while turning it in a clockwise direction until the screw point engages the wood. As soon as the screw holds firmly, transfer your fingers to the screwdriver blade, letting it slip between them to keep the tip centrally on the screw shank. Apply just enough pressure on the driver to keep it in the slot, and hold the driver blade directly in line with the screw. Tilting the driver when starting a screw causes it to go in at an angle, while tilting it after the screw is fully engaged may cause the driver to slip out of the slot. When cross-slot drivers are tilted, one of the wings is likely to break off because of the unequal pressures.

5. If no hole is bored for the threaded part of the screw, the wood is often split or the screwhead is twisted off. If a screw is difficult to turn, back it out and enlarge the hole. Wax or paraffin rubbed on the screw will take most of the effort out of screwdriving. A candle is perfect for this purpose. Never use soap, because the moisture in the soap will rust the screw, weaken the joint, and cause discoloration of paint or varnish finishes. Do not use oil either; it will penetrate and stain the wood grain for some distance around the screwhead.

6. To ease the driving of a machine screw in metal, use a little graphite or a bit of oil. In fact, it is a good idea always to use graphite or oil when driving a machine screw, as insurance against the screw rusting in place and preventing its removal.

7. You can set a screw into concrete so that it can

FIG. 4-21. The proper technique for driving a screw.

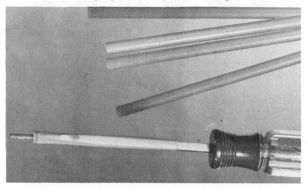

FIG. 4-22. Plastic soft-drink straws come in handy when you need a screwdriver with a screw-holding device. Cut a length of straw about an inch shorter than the driver shank. Slip it over the shank, and slide the straw over the head of the bolt or screw. When the straw end becomes tattered, snip it off to expose a new end.

be driven or removed by first dipping it into melted paraffin, and then setting it in position in the fresh concrete. The paraffin coating prevents the concrete from adhering to the screw. It can be backed out after the concrete has hardened, leaving a permanent thread in the hole.

8. To speed up the driving of screws, there is sometimes a temptation to start them with a hammer. *Do not* do so. This pushes the wood fibers ahead of the screw and prevents it from taking a firm grip. It will not support its intended load.

9. Since a screw is often used with the idea that it may later be removed and replaced, it is well to bear in mind that, when withdrawn, it will leave a much larger hole than a nail will. Before the screw can be replaced, the hole must be filled to provide a firm gripping area. You can fill it with wood putty and reset the screw in this new

material, or use plastic plugs driven into the old screw holes. Both provide an excellent base. Also, you can use a longer screw as the replacement.

10. To prevent flathead screws from working loose after they have been seated, try striking the head near the rim with a punch or a nail. The displaced metal serves as an anchoring wedge.

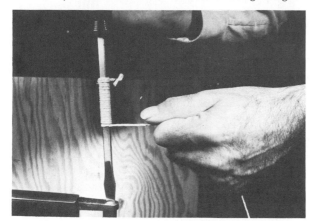

FIG. 4-23. Sometimes, when it is necessary to run in a screw which is located in a corner, the need for making hundreds of partial turns can be eliminated by wrapping a piece of stout cord around the shank of the screwdriver, and pulling on the string to turn the screw in or out. Care must be used to keep the screw from slipping out of the slot.

CONCEALING SCREWS On occasion, you will wish to conceal a screw with a wooden dowel plug, to match or contrast with the surrounding wood. Follow these steps:

1. Bore a hole at least $\frac{3}{8}$ inch deep for the plug.
2. Bore a pilot hole for the screw, and then a clearance hole.
3. Drive the screw in place, as far as it will go.
4. Select the proper size of dowel plug, apply glue to its sides, and insert it so that the grain on the end of the plug runs in the same direction as the grain on the surface of the surrounding wood.
5. Drive the plug in as far as it will go.

REMOVING A TIGHT SCREW There is an accepted procedure for removing tight screws, and this must be rigidly adhered to.

1. Select a blade with perfectly parallel sides, one which fits the slot exactly.
2. Turn the blade counterclockwise. If this does not work, turn the screw slightly in the direction which drives it in further.
3. Then, back the screw out. Follow this by turning it to drive it in. An application of penetrating oil will often help to free a machine screw.

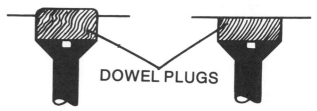

FIG. 4-24. Concealing screwheads with dowel plugs.

If you work the screw both ways, you will often find that the screw will back up a bit more each time, until it is entirely out. Use pliers to remove a screw that is partly out if its slot has been "chewed up."

In extreme cases, you may have to tap on the screwdriver handle. Do not use the common type of screwdriver for this job. Use the type favored by mechanics and machine repairmen. The shank of this type goes all the way through the handle, so that there is no danger of splitting the handle when you tap on it. Sometimes a screw is rusty, and the tip of the blade can be seated in the slot only by hitting the handle with a hammer. Use this special type of screwdriver in such emergencies. There are also:

1. Heavy-duty machinist's screwdrivers equipped with a handle on which you can get a double grip.
2. Heavy-duty types with a square shank; you can use a wrench on this shank and apply enough force to turn and loosen large, rusted screws.

FIG. 4-25. A small wrench may be used to apply force to a square-shank screwdriver to loosen a stubborn screw.

If the slot is worn or torn open, back out the screw one turn, and cut a new slot across the old one with a few strokes of a hacksaw. Incidentally, wood screws frozen in place can often be freed by applying the heat of a soldering iron to their heads.

CARE OF SCREWDRIVERS

A screwdriver does not have to be sharpened, but it does have to be dressed and kept in perfect condition. Occasionally, it must be ground on an emery wheel, or the sides must be filed with a flat file. Details on how to dress a screwdriver properly are given in Chapter 22.

TURNING TOOLS (WRENCHES)

Wrenches are among the most widely used hand tools. Their main function is to hold and turn nuts, bolts, cap screws, plugs, and various threaded parts. Since a screw (thread) in use acts as a remorseless wedge, it is possible to strip threads or damage parts by applying excessive torque. Quality wrenches, regardless of their type, are therefore designed to keep leverage and intended load in safe balance.

Standard wrench types are available for almost every conceivable operation and service, with both American Standard and metric openings. Special wrenches are also available for servicing and overhauling certain widely used equipment. Today's mechanic need not improvise to find the proper tool for a particular job. Although the variety of types of wrenches manufactured is practically infinite, two rather broad categories can be established: general-use wrenches and special-use or single-purpose wrenches. The latter, if ever needed by the do-it-yourselfer, should probably be begged, borrowed, or rented rather than purchased, because they may never be used again.

Which particular ones belong in your workshop depends, of course, on you and the types of jobs you enjoy or anticipate doing. For example, if you service your own car engine as well as the lawnmower, outboard, minibike, bicycle, and anything else mechanical, by all means include a good and complete set of socket wrenches. In addition, if you do such work, you may find S-shaped car wrenches, half-moon manifold box wrenches, and open-end ignition wrenches most valuable. If you prefer to do your own plumbing, you will need a couple of pipe wrenches as well as some special wrenches such as basin wrenches. But, whatever your specific needs, you should know a little bit about all types of wrenches, so that you can fit the right one to whatever

job you may have at hand.

The best wrenches are made of chrome vanadium steel. Wrenches made of this material are light in weight and almost unbreakable. This is an expensive material, however, so the common wrenches found in most shops are made of forged carbon steel or molybdenum steel. These latter materials make good wrenches, but they are generally built a little heavier and bulkier in order to achieve the same degree of strength as chrome vanadium steel. The best grades of wrenches are usually marked "drop forged." This process, when applied to the right kinds of steel alloys, ensures toughness and durability.

The sizes of wrenches used on bolt heads or nuts are given by the size of the opening between the jaws of the wrench. The opening of a wrench is manufactured slightly larger than the bolt head or nut that it is designed to fit. Hex nuts (six-sided) and other types of nut or bolt heads are measured across opposite flats (Figure 5-1). A wrench that is designed to fit a $\frac{3}{8}$-inch nut or bolt usually has a clearance of from 5 to 8 thousandths of an inch (0.005 to 0.008 inch). This clearance allows the wrench to slide on and off the nut or bolt with a minimum of "play." If the wrench is too large, the points of the nut or bolt head will be rounded and destroyed.

As already mentioned, there are many types of wrenches. Each type is designed for a specific use. Let us discuss some of the more used "general-use" wrenches.

OPEN-END WRENCHES

The most common wrench is the open-end wrench. This is a one-piece tool with nonadjustable, elongated C- or half-moon openings at both ends. Usually they come in sets of from 6 to 10 wrenches, with sizes ranging from $\frac{5}{16}$ to 1 inch. Wrenches with small openings are usually shorter than wrenches with large openings. This

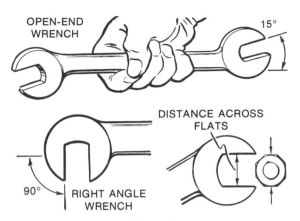

FIG. 5-1. Basic open-end wrenches.

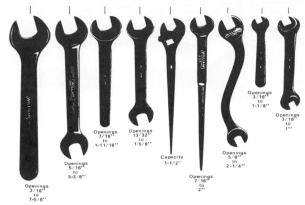

FIG. 5-3. Special-pattern open-end wrenches and their general size range.

proportions the lever advantage of the wrench to the bolt or stud and helps prevent wrench breakage or damage to the bolt or stud.

The heads of most open-end wrenches are placed at an angle to the shank. This angle is usually 15°, but it may be as much as 22½°. This variation in the angle permits selection of a wrench suited for places where there is room to make only a part of a complete turn of a hex nut or bolt. If the wrench is turned over after the first swing, it will fit on the same flats and turn the nut farther. That is, it allows you to "flop" the wrench, gaining a "swing" or turn twice as great as would be possible if the head were not angled.

Open-end wrenches are available in both single and double head patterns; double head patterns have different openings in the two heads. For instance, a double head type may be described as a 5/16 X 3/8 inch open-end wrench. This means that the wrench has a 5/16-inch opening in one end and a 3/8-inch opening in the other.

The handles of most open-end wrenches are usually straight, but some may be curved. Those with curved handles are called S or car wrenches. The square nuts used in many autos normally require a 90° swing for

complete rotation with most open-end wrenches. The S design permits flopping the wrench to reduce the swing to 45°. Other open-end wrenches may have offset handles. This allows the head to reach nut or bolt heads that are sunk below the surface.

While the standard open-end wrenches just described are designed for a wide variety of work, open-end wrenches are also made for special types of service (Figure 5-3). Electronics wrenches are thinner and have openings set at 15 and 60° (or 75°) to the centerline of the handle. Ignition wrenches which are very similar in design to electronics wrenches, are small, thin wrenches having openings at 15 and 60°. Tappet wrenches, both single and double head, have openings at 15° angles and are longer and thinner. Construction wrenches have a single 15° opening and a drift handle for aligning bolt holes. Structural wrenches are similar to construction wrenches except they have straight openings and an offset handle. Check-nut wrenches are thinner. Setscrew and heavy S wrenches have openings at a 22½° angles, rather than 15°.

These special-pattern wrenches are intended for the type of service which their name implies. For instance, both construction and structural wrenches have long handles for extra leverage and are tapered for easy

FIG. 5-2. The strong, slim, narrow jaws at a 15° angle to the handle permit the open-end wrench complete rotation of hex nuts in a 30° swing by flopping the head.

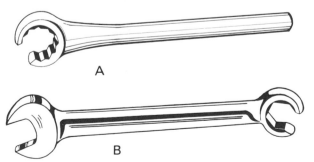

FIG. 5-4. Flare-nut wrenches are available as *(a)* a single-head wrench or *(b)* a combination with an open end. In the latter design, both openings are the same size; the nominal openings usually range from 3/8 to 1⅛ inches.

FIG. 5-5. Typical bulldog-type wrenches.

insertion in bolt holes to bring them in line. The structural pattern has the additional advantage of an offset handle for clearing obstructions. Steel construction and flange work are among their popular uses. On the other hand, extremely thin lock or adjustment nuts are often best serviced with tappet wrenches. Their thin heads and extra long handles are a decided convenience when servicing industrial engines, both gasoline and diesel types, such as are found on construction equipment.

For assembly, adjustment, and repair of electrical components and instruments, midget 15° and 15-75° wrenches offer a choice of opening angle to meet the many peculiarities of this type of equipment. Check-nut or thin wrenches are designed for the thin adjusting nuts and locknuts found on industrial machinery. Single and double head styles allow you to choose the type most convenient or economical for a particular application. Still another light-duty wrench is the setscrew type. The head heights of setscrews are greater than those of ordinary bolt heads and, therefore, require wrenches of more than average head thickness. Jigs, fixtures, and machine tools involving frequent adjustment most often use hardened setscrews. Setscrew wrenches wear longer by providing three points of contact, rather than the two offered by most open-end wrenches.

Some wrenches are designed for special nuts. For example, flare-nut wrenches are designed especially for use on nonferrous flare nuts and fittings on hydraulic and pneumatic tubing and on air-conditioning equipment. The open end slips over the tubing and has a thick head face to prevent marred fittings in final tightening.

Another differently designed open wrench is the bulldog or alligator type. These wrenches will grip pipe, and square, hexagonal, and round shapes, and any other shapes that will fit between their strong, tough jaws. They are often used for holding while nuts, sleeves, collars, and connectors of various types are being turned.

BOX WRENCHES

Box wrenches (Figure 5-6) are safer than open-end wrenches since there is less likelihood they will slip off the work. They completely surround, or box, a nut or bolt head.

One advantage of the fixed box wrench is its thin-wall construction. It is more suitable for turning nuts that are hard to get at with an open-end wrench. Another

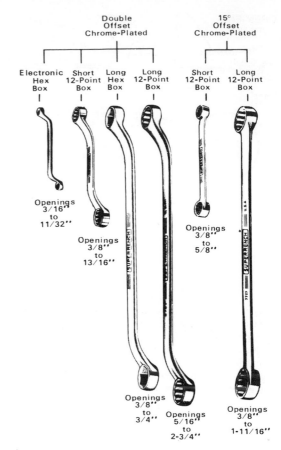

FIG. 5-6. Common patterns and sizes of fixed box wrenches.

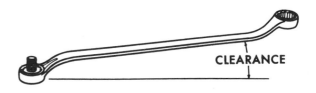

FIG. 5-7. Typical 15° offset box wrench (top) and double-offset box wrench (bottom).

advantage is that the wrench will operate between obstructions, where the space for handle swing is limited. A very short swing of the handle will turn the nut far enough to allow the wrench to be lifted and the next set of points fitted to the corners of the nut. Still another is that box wrenches are frequently offset so they can reach recessed bolt heads that are otherwise inaccessible; this often saves wear and tear on the hands. They usually give longer and better service than open-end wrenches because the points that grip the nuts on the box wrench do not wear and enlarge the way the jaws on an open-end wrench do. The one disadvantage of fixed box wrenches (and the open-end type) is that they must be completely lifted off the work and replaced after each swing.

The most frequently used fixed box wrench has 12 points or notches arranged in a circle in the head; it can be used with a minimum swing angle of 30°. Six- and 8-point wrenches are used for heavy work; 12-point wrenches for medium; and 16-point for light duty only. Box wrenches are also available with hex and square openings, in both regular- and heavy-duty patterns.

Box-wrench sizes are similar to those of open-end wrenches. The double types have different openings in each head. Generally, one end of the wrench differs from the other by $\frac{1}{16}$ inch, although some sets come in graduations of $\frac{1}{32}$ inch or $\frac{1}{8}$ inch. Box wrenches are, of course, made in long, short, and electronics patterns with double offset and 15° offsets. In the case of the latter wrenches, the 15° offset offers obstruction clearance with ample space for the mechanic's hand. But this box wrench will continuously rotate nuts in only a 30° swing of the wrench. On the other hand, the double-offset type—often referred to as the 45° wrench—offers better obstruction clearance, as well as all the other features of the 15°-offset type. This, the most popular of the box wrench styles, is made in short, long, and heavy-service models, with openings usually ranging from about $\frac{5}{16}$ to $2\frac{3}{4}$ inches.

While the ratcheting box wrench does not offer the clearance advantages of the fixed-box type, its ratcheting feature is a decided convenience. The smaller sizes require only 18° of swing to completely rotate hex nuts; the larger sizes require only 15° of swing. With most designs, the low back-drag torque causes the ratcheting action to start early. With the fully reversible style ratchet box wrench, there is no need to remove the wrench from the nut or bolt to reverse direction. A push knob near each end of the wrench normally controls the direction. Ratcheting box wrenches should not be used in heavy-duty applications. By the way, an occasional lubrication with light oil should keep the ratcheting mechanism in satisfactory working order.

Box wrenches in the regular pattern are designed for general service. The heavy-duty and striking-face patterns are designed for the services indicated by their names. Incidentally, the latter, which is made in both straight and offset patterns with 12-point openings, is the only wrench

that should be struck with a hammer. Striking-face wrenches are designed for heavy work where large nuts must be set up tight, or frozen nuts loosened. Use a ball peen or sledge type hammer when hitting a striking-face wrench. The heavy-duty-style box wrenches, which are completely safe under extreme torquing, provide extra strength in limited areas through their higher head walls, which also give full contact with large hex nuts. Another heavy-duty box wrench is the structural pattern, which is very similar to the open-end pattern except that it has a 12-point box opening.

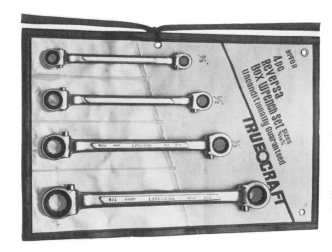

FIG. 5-8. A typical set of fully reversible ratcheting wrenches.

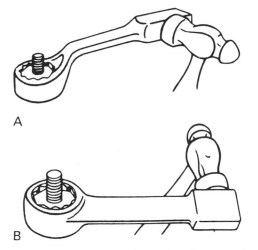

FIG. 5-9. Hitting (a) an offset-striking-face wrench and (b) a straight-striking-face wrench with a ball peen hammer. Unless obstructions require the use of the offset style, it is better and safer to use the straight pattern.

The midget electronic hex box patterns are designed for the lighter service encountered in electronic, carburetor, and ignition work. Obstruction clearance and extra strength are among the advantages of midget box wrenches over midget open-end styles. This style provides the additional strength and firm grip required to loosen corroded or frozen nuts as sometimes encountered in the range of service provided by these wrenches. Another handy light-duty wrench is the split-box style.

OPEN-END-BOX COMBINATION WRENCHES

The combination wrench has one open end and one box, both the same size, so that it is possible to break a tight nut with the box and then use the open end to loosen it. In tightening the nut, you can go most of the way with the open end and then secure it tightly with the box end. The box end of the wrench is sometimes designed with an offset in the handle.

The open-end–box combination may be the ultimate in wrench convenience, but you need twice as many of them, because each one represents only a single size, rather than the two sizes of the other basic wrenches. The purchase expense is therefore twice as great. Whether or not they are worth the extra cost depends on the type of work you do most frequently.

The most widely used patterns are made in long and short types having a 15°-angle open end and a 12-point box opening of the same size. The box opening is offset at a 15° angle to the handle for clearance. Special-service types include the following tools. The split-box or flare-nut pattern is for use on tube fittings and should not be used for high-torque applications. This type has a 6- or 12-point opening offset 15° from the plane of the handle, with a tube-opening slot at 22½° to the axis of the handle. This pattern is also available with openings of different sizes at the ends. The electronics pattern is thinner and slimmer, with a 15° hex box opening.

There are several special combination wrenches. One of these—the tool-post wrench—is preferred by many craftsmen over the straight style because of the clearance provided. The open end is generally used for making lathe tailstock adjustments, thus eliminating the necessity of using two wrenches when you do lathe work. Another special combination wrench is the lineman's style. Each end has two different sizes of openings; the hole provided at the larger end is for turning in standard pole steps. These wrenches are particularly suited for use on heavier three-bolt guy clamps on which clearance is

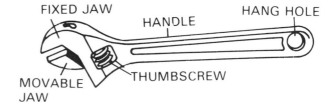

FIG. 5-11. Old-style monkey wrench in use.

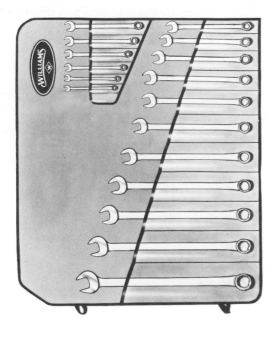

FIG. 5-10. Typical set of 18 open-end–box combination wrenches.

FIXED JAW   HANDLE   HANG HOLE
MOVABLE JAW   THUMBSCREW

FIG. 5-12. Parts of an adjustable wrench.

limited. Possibly one of the most useful combination wrenches, at least for the average craftsman, is the flex combination, which features an open end and a 12-point flexible socket wrench.

The correct use of open-end and box-end wrenches can be summed up in a few simple rules, the most important of which is to be sure that the wrench properly fits the nut or bolt head. When you have to pull hard on the wrench, as in loosening a tight nut, make sure the wrench is seated squarely on the flats of the nut. Pull on the wrench; *do not push*. Pushing a wrench is a good way to skin your knuckles if the wrench slips or the nut breaks loose unexpectedly. If it is impossible to pull the wrench, and you must push, do it with the palm of your hand, and hold your palm open.

Only actual practice will tell you if you are using the right amount of force on the wrench. The best way to tighten a nut is to turn it until the wrench has a firm, solid "feel." This will turn the nut to the proper tightness without stripping the threads or twisting off the bolt. This "feel" is developed by experience alone; practice until you have mastered it.

Attempts to repair box or open-end wrenches are not recommended. Discard any wrench with spread, worn, or mutilated jaws on the open end or rounded or damaged points on the box end. Also discard wrenches with bent handles.

ADJUSTABLE WRENCHES

There are two types of adjustable wrenches: the monkey wrench and the crescent-type wrench. The latter, named after the original manufactured by the Crescent Tool Company, is by far the most popular. As a matter of fact, if you are lucky enough to have one of the old-style monkey wrenches, keep it because they have practically disappeared from tool supply stores. These adjustable F-shaped wrenches have flat, smooth jaws that open much wider in proportion to the length of the handle than any adjustable wrenches available today. This makes them ideal for chrome-plated or polished plumbing fixtures of fairly large size, since the smooth jaws will not damage a polished finish, and they open wide enough to fit on large hex caps and threaded

coupling rings like those that hold U traps in place under sink basins. The jaws, which make an angle of 90° with the handle, should always point in the direction of the pull.

The crescent-type wrench, which is now manufactured by many companies, is a handy all-around wrench. But this open-end wrench is not intended to take the place of the regular solid open-end wrench. Additionally, it is not built for use on extremely hard-to-turn items. The usefulness comes from its capability of fitting odd-sized nuts. One jaw of the adjustable open-end wrench is fixed, and the other jaw is moved along a slide by a thumbscrew adjustment (Figure 5-12). By turning the thumbscrew, the jaw opening may be adjusted to fit various sizes of nuts.

Adjustable wrenches are available in varying sizes, ranging from 4 to 24 inches in length. The size of the wrench selected for a particular job is dependent upon the size of nut or bolt head to which the wrench is to be applied. As the jaw opening increases, the length of the wrench increases. The angle between the opening and the handle on most adjustable wrenches is $22\frac{1}{2}°$. High-dielectric-insulation handle types are widely used by linemen and other electrical workers. But ordinary plastic dipped handles are for comfort only, and are not electrically insulated.

There are several special types of adjustable wrenches. One of the more novel is the caliper wrench, which features an unusual locking mechanism: the lower jaw is adjusted by pressing up on the bottom of the tooth wedge; when it has been moved against a nut or bolt head, it is tightened and cam-locked by pressing in the wedge from the opposite sides. The stationary jaw has a scale reading from zero to $1\frac{1}{2}$ inches, in graduations of $\frac{1}{32}$ inch, which permits the wrench to double as an outside caliper.

Adjustable wrenches are often called "knuckle busters," because mechanics frequently suffer these consequences as a result of improper use of these tools. To avoid accidents, follow four simple steps. First, choose a wrench of the correct size; that is, do not pick a large 12-inch wrench and adjust the jaw for use on a $\frac{3}{8}$-inch nut. This could result in a broken bolt and a sore hand. Second, be sure the jaws of the correct size wrench are adjusted to fit snugly on the nut. Third, position the wrench around the nut until the nut is all the way into the throat of the jaw. Otherwise, the result is apt to be painful. Fourth, pull the handle toward the side having the adjustable jaw (Figure 5-13). This will prevent the adjustable jaw from springing open and slipping off the nut. If the location of the work will not allow all four steps to be followed with an adjustable wrench, then select another type of wrench for the job.

Practically all manufacturers supply parts assortments, repair kits, and instructions for their adjustable wrenches. Periodic inspections should be made to detect damaged jaws, knurls, pins, and springs. Damaged parts should be replaced. Discard any wrench with a spread or damaged fixed jaw or bent handle.

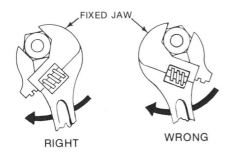

FIXED JAW

RIGHT   WRONG

FIG. 5-13. Proper procedure for pulling adjustable wrenches.

PIPE WRENCHES

There are four basic types of pipe wrenches: the Stillson or pipe wrench, chain wrench, strap wrench, and internal wrench.

STILLSON ADJUSTABLE PIPE WRENCH When rotating or holding round work, an adjustable Stillson pipe or jaw-type wrench may be employed. The movable jaws on a pipe wrench are pivoted to permit a gripping action on the work. But a Stillson pipe wrench is made for pipes alone—it has sharp teeth that grip pipes firmly. It should never be used on nuts, bolts, chrome-plated fixtures, etc. There is usually some deliberate slippage on such a wrench, since the jaws are tapered inward. Thus, the jaws should be adjusted so the bite on the work will be taken at about the centers of the jaws.

The Stillson offset-handle pattern (Figure 5-14b) is ideal for close quarters, where the normal swing of a straight handle is limited. If possible, always pull rather than push on the wrench handle.

CHAIN PIPE WRENCH A different type of pipe wrench is the chain pipe wrench (Figure 5-15). This tool works in one direction only but can be backed partly around the work, and a fresh hold taken, without freeing the chain. To reverse the operation, the grip is taken on the opposite side of the head. The chain wrench is designed for the same service as the jaw type.

The chain pipe wrench is particularly useful in unusually close quarters. Certain types of oil filters are also best serviced with this style of wrench. The teeth must be kept sharp. The head is usually double-ended and can be reversed when the teeth on one end are worn. When worn, they can be easily resharpened with a medium-toothed file.

STRAP WRENCH The strap wrench is similar to the chain pipe wrench, but it uses a heavy webbed strap in place of the chain. This wrench is used for turning pipe or cylinders when you do not want to mar the surface of the work. In use, the webbed strap is placed around the cylinder and passed through the slot in the metal body of the wrench. The strap is then pulled up tight. As the mechanic turns the wrench in the desired direction, the webbed strap tightens further around the cylinder. This gripping action causes the cylinder to turn.

INTERNAL PIPE WRENCH These are used inside, rather than outside, the pipe. They are especially convenient for use on chrome pipe and fittings where an ordinary pipe wrench may leave toothmarks. The internal pipe wrench is also invaluable when removing broken pipe, closed nipples, or other fittings when it is impossible to get an external grip. With this wrench, turning the mandrel forces the gripping dogs against the inside of the fitting or pipe; then it is turned with a wrench or, in some models such as the one shown in Figure 5-14f, with a handle that is integral with the tool.

Another valuable plumber's tool is the basin wrench illustrated in Figure 5-16. This tool is designed to get at out-of-the-way nuts and bolts such as those that hold sink

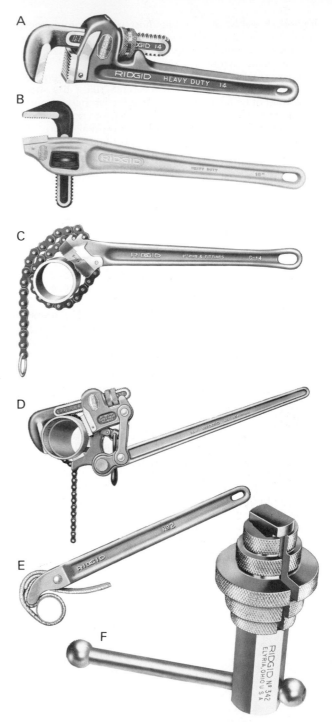

FIG. 5-14. Typical pipe wrenches: *(a)* straight pipe wrench; *(b)* offset pipe wrench; *(c)* heavy-duty chain wrench; *(d)* compound-leverage wrench; *(e)* strap wrench; *(f)* internal wrench.

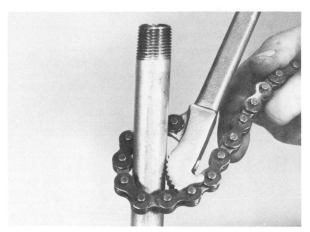

FIG. 5-15. Light-duty chain wrench in use.

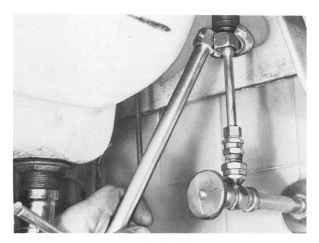

FIG. 5-16. Basin wrench in use.

basins to the wall or hold the front legs of the basin. Some have telescoping handles for greater versatility.

Practically all manufacturers supply repair parts and instructions for their pipe wrenches. Periodic cleaning is important, and inspections should be made to detect worn or unsafe parts; damaged parts should be replaced. Replacement pins and chains for chain wrenches and replacement straps for strap wrenches are available. Discard any wrench with a bent handle or broken housing.

SPANNER WRENCHES

The British call almost every wrench a "spanner." However, spanner wrenches, as they are known in the United States, are special wrenches used mainly in machine shops. They are used on machine tools for adjusting collars, locknuts, rings, spindle bearings, face-plate draw nuts, etc.

Many nuts are made with external splines or notches cut into their outer edges. For these nuts a "hook spanner" is required. This wrench has a curved arm with a lug or hook on the end. This lug fits into one of the notches of the nut, and the handle is turned to loosen or tighten the nut. This type of spanner may be made for just one particular size of notched nut, or it may have a hinged arm to adjust to a range of sizes.

Another type of spanner is the "pin spanner." Pin spanners have a pin in place of a hook. On either the regular or adjustable pin spanner, this pin fits into a hole in the outer part of the nut or adjusting collar.

Face pin spanners are designed so that the pins fit into holes in the face of the nut or collar.

When you use a spanner wrench, you must ensure that the pins, lugs, or hooks make firm contact with the nut while the turning force is transferred from the wrench to the nut. If this is not done, damage will result to either personnel, tools, or equipment.

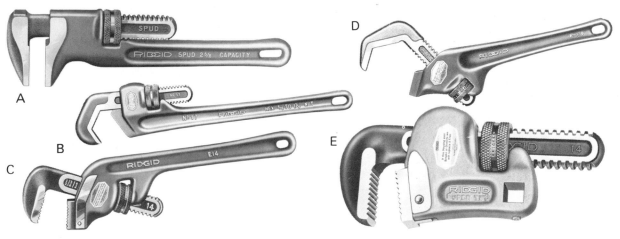

FIG. 5-17. Other wrenches for plumbing use: (a) speed wrench; (b) straight hex wrench; (c) end hex wrench; (d) offset hex wrench; (e) vertical pipe wrench.

TORQUE WRENCHES

Torque wrenches are designed to permit an operator to determine the torque being applied to bolts, nuts, and other fasteners. There are times when, for engineering reasons, a definite force must be applied to a nut or bolt head. In such cases a torque wrench must be used. For example, equal force must be applied to all the head bolts of an engine. Otherwise, one bolt may bear the brunt of the force of the internal combustion and ultimately cause engine failure.

Torque wrenches measure torque in ounce inches, pound inches and pound feet, as well as in metric measures. However, many manufacturers express torque in foot pounds (rather than pound feet) since this nomenclature is more familiar to the average tool user. Metric-measure torque wrenches register in meter kilograms or centimeter kilograms.

The three most commonly used adjustable torque wrenches are the *deflecting-beam, dial-indicating,* and *micrometer-setting* types (Figure 5-19). On the deflecting-beam and dial-indicating torque wrenches, the torque is read visually on a dial or scale mounted on the handle of the wrench.

To use the micrometer-setting type, unlock the grip and adjust the handle to the desired setting on the micrometer-type scale; then relock the grip. Install the required socket or adapter on the square drive of the handle. Place the wrench assembly on the nut or bolt, and pull in a clockwise direction with a smooth, steady motion. (A fast or jerky motion will result in an improperly torqued unit.) When the torque applied reaches the torque value, which is indicated on the handle setting, a signal mechanism will automatically issue an audible click, and the handle will release or "break" and move freely for a short distance. The release and free travel is easily felt, so there is no doubt about when the torquing process is complete. Torque screwdrivers, mentioned in Chapter 4, operate on this same basic principle, except that they release when the set torque is reached. Figure 5-23 illustrates some other adjustable and preset wrenches.

Manufacturers' and technical manuals generally specify the amount of torque to be applied. To ensure the

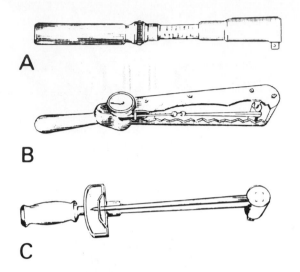

FIG. 5-19. The three major types of torque wrenches: *(a)* deflecting beam; *(b)* dial indicating; *(c)* micrometer setting.

SCALES PROPERLY POSITIONED. NO UPSIDE-DOWN READING FOR EITHER RIGHT OR LEFT HAND PULL.

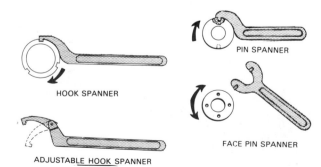

FIG. 5-18. Popular types of spanner wrenches.

HOOK SPANNER

PIN SPANNER

ADJUSTABLE HOOK SPANNER

FACE PIN SPANNER

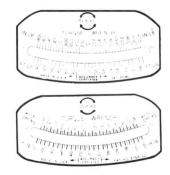

FIG. 5-20. Beam torque wrench in use, and typical scale.

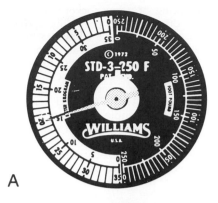

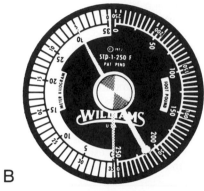

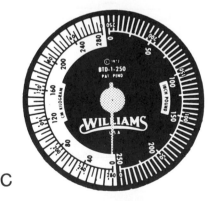

correct amount of torque on the fasteners, it is important that the wrench be used properly, in accordance with the manufacturers' instructions. Generally, however, use that torque wrench which will read about midrange for the amount of torque to be applied. Be sure that the torque wrench has been calibrated before you use it. Remember, too, that the accuracy of torque measurements depends a lot on how the threads are cut and on the cleanliness of the threads. Make sure you inspect and clean the threads. If the manufacturer specifies a thread lubricant, it must be used to obtain the most accurate torque reading. When using a deflecting-beam or dial-indicating wrench, hold the torque at the desired value until the reading is steady.

Torque wrenches are delicate and expensive tools. The following precautions should be observed when using them:

1. When using the micrometer-setting type, do not move the setting handle below the lowest torque setting. However, the tool should be placed at its lowest setting before it is returned to storage.
2. Do not use a torque wrench to apply a torque greater than its rated capacity. That is, avoid overtorquing. A torque wrench will permit tightening to the exact torque required for best performance, economy, and safety.
3. Do not use a torque wrench to break loose bolts which have previously been tightened. If you wish to set a previously tightened nut to a given torque, back off the nut a turn or two with a nontorque wrench, and then retighten it to the correct torque with an indicating torque wrench.
4. Do not drop the wrench. If it is dropped, its accuracy will be affected; it should be checked on a torque tester before use. Torque wrenches should be periodically checked for calibration accuracy when they are used frequently or continuously. Most manufacturers provide repair and calibration service. The manufacturer will advise whether the tool can be repaired or should be replaced.

FIG. 5-21. Three styles of dial torque-wrench scales: (a) single-pointer combination dial set for U.S.C.S. readings; (b) single-pointer combination dial set for metric readings; (c) follower-needle combination dial set for U.S.C.S. readings. Most dial faces permit measurement of torque in either U.S.C.S. or metric values, in either the left- or right-hand direction. The single-pointer style indicates the torque value directly. The follower-needle style has an additional "memory" needle which remains at the highest torque value attained, for positive verification. When its reading is no longer needed, the follower needle is reset to zero.

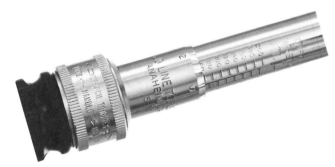

FIG. 5-22. Closeup of a microadjustable wrench scale.

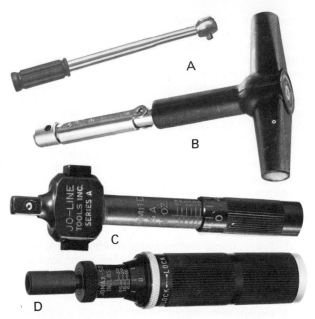

FIG. 5-23. Other torque-type tools: *(a)* preset limiting wrench; *(b)* preset no-hub soil-pipe wrench; *(c)* adjustable minitorque wrench; and *(d)* microadjustable screwdriver.

SOCKET WRENCHES

The socket wrench got its start as the wrench that is still used to remove the lugs from an automobile wheel in the event of a flat tire. The socket in this case was forged as part of the handle, which was shaped like a T, L, or X, depending on how it was to be used. While nondetachable socket wrenches are still being manufactured for specific applications, with both hex and square openings, detachable socket wrenches have replaced them in general use. Actually, today there are three basic types of detachable sockets—hand, power, and impact—all different in design and hardness. This chapter is concerned only with hand sockets, which should never be used on power-drive or impact wrenches (see Chapter 13).

A complete modern socket-wrench set consists of several types of handles along with bar extensions, adapters, and a variety of sockets (Figure 5-26).

A socket has a square opening cut in one end to fit a square drive lug on a detachable handle. In the other end of the socket is a 4-point (square opening), 6-point (hex opening), 8-point, or 12-point opening, very much like the opening in the box-end wrench. Regular 4- and 8-point sockets are designed expressly for square nuts and bolt heads, such as are found on set, machine, and lag screws and stove bolts and nuts. Single-hex sockets are better than 12-point sockets for servicing undersized or badly worn nuts. They also wear longer. Rapid seating on nuts is a feature of the 12-point socket, which requires

only half the swing of a hex socket when used with a nonratcheting driver. Extra-heavy-duty sockets have a cross hole for a sliding bar and safety attachment device for positive locking with various types of drivers. Incidentally, the 12-point socket needs to be swung only half as far as the 6-point socket before it has to be lifted and fitted on the nut for a new grip. It can therefore be used in closer quarters, where there is less room to move the handle. (A ratchet handle eliminates the necessity of lifting the socket and refitting it on the nut again and again.)

Sockets are classified by size, according to two factors. One is the size of the square opening, which fits on the square drive lug of the handle. This size is known as the "drive size." The other is the size of the opening in the opposite end, which fits the nut or bolt. The standard toolbox can be outfitted with sockets having $\frac{1}{4}$-, $\frac{3}{8}$-, and $\frac{1}{2}$-inch-square drive lugs. Larger sets—up to 1 inch—are available. The openings that fit onto the bolt or nut are graduated by sixteenths of an inch and are also available in metric sizes.

In addition to the standard sockets, there are extra-deep sockets for such uses as getting at nuts set well down on protruding bolts. Extra-deep 8-point sockets are particularly useful in running down and taking off locknuts. Under certain conditions, it is possible to avoid the use of an extension by using an extra-deep socket. Extra-deep 6- and 12-point sockets have all the advantages

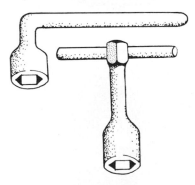

FIG. 5-24. Typical nondetachable socket wrenches.

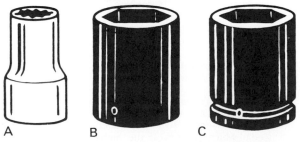

FIG. 5-25. Three types of sockets: *(a)* hand; *(b)* power; and *(c)* impact.

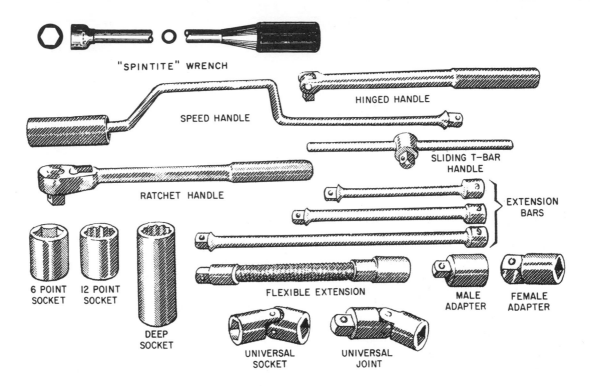

"SPINTITE" WRENCH

HINGED HANDLE

SPEED HANDLE

SLIDING T-BAR HANDLE

RATCHET HANDLE

EXTENSION BARS

6 POINT SOCKET

12 POINT SOCKET

DEEP SOCKET

FLEXIBLE EXTENSION

MALE ADAPTER

FEMALE ADAPTER

UNIVERSAL SOCKET

UNIVERSAL JOINT

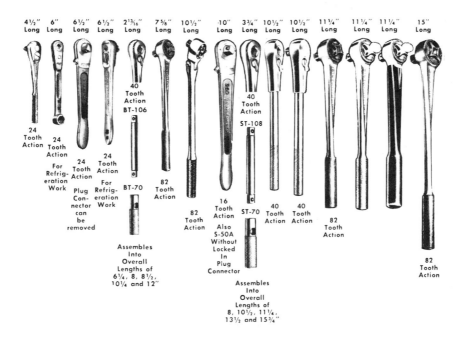

4½" Long — 24 Tooth Action

6" Long — 24 Tooth Action — For Refrigeration Work

6½" Long — 24 Tooth Action — Plug Connector can be removed

6½" Long — 24 Tooth Action — For Refrigeration Work

2¹³⁄₁₆" Long — 40 Tooth Action — BT-106 — BT-70 — Assembles Into Overall Lengths of 6¼, 8, 8½, 10¼ and 12"

7⅝" Long — 82 Tooth Action

10½" Long — 82 Tooth Action

10" Long — 16 Tooth Action — Also S-50A Without Locked In Plug Connector

3¾" Long — 40 Tooth Action — ST-108 — ST-70 — Assembles Into Overall Lengths of 8, 10½, 11¼, 13½ and 15¾"

10½" Long — 40 Tooth Action

10½" Long — 40 Tooth Action

11¼" Long — 82 Tooth Action

11¼" Long

11¼" Long

15" Long — 82 Tooth Action

FIG. 5-26. Socket set components (top) and types of ratchet handles (bottom).

noted above under regular sockets. In addition, they can be used on spark plugs and nuts, where the bolt or stud extends considerably beyond the surface of the nut face. Cross holes are provided, for use with a bar.

Many socket sets contain a special socket for spark plugs. It is often impossible to remove a spark plug without this type of socket because the plug is usually in a recess. Spark-plug sockets also have a rubber insert inside them, which grips the ceramic upper part of the plug so that the plug can be withdrawn after being loosened.

Another very useful socket is the universal or flex type. Nuts in very restricted areas can sometimes be reached only with a universal socket (Figure 5-29a). The operating range is approximately 130°. Spring tension maintains the working angle.

SOCKET HANDLES Four basic types of handles are used with these sockets. Each type has its advantages, and the experienced worker chooses the one best suited for the job at hand. The square driving lug on the socket-wrench handle has a spring-loaded ball that fits into a recess in the socket receptacle. This mated ball-recess feature keeps the socket engaged with the drive lug during normal usage. A slight pull on the socket, however, disassembles the connection.

Ratchet The ratchet handle has a reversing lever which operates a pawl (or dog) inside the head of the tool. Pulling the handle in one direction causes the pawl to engage in the ratchet teeth and turn the socket. Moving the handle in the opposite direction causes the pawl to slide over the teeth, permitting the handle to back up without moving the socket. This allows rapid turning of the nut or bolt after each partial turn of the handle. With the reversing lever in one position, the handle can be used for tightening. With the lever in the other position, it can be used for loosening.

Ratchets with dielectric insulation handles are available for linemen's use. Also, extra-heavy-duty ratchet wrenches are made in 24-, 36-, and 48-inch lengths. Both hex and square sockets are available with openings from 1 to $3\frac{1}{8}$ inches. As with other precision tools, reversible ratchets should receive care for best service and longest tool life. It is recommended that ratchets be regularly immersed in light machine oil overnight. Rotate or spin the ratchet to flush out dirt and hardened lubricant and to remove excess oil. By following this procedure, it is possible to avoid complete dismantling of the ratchet for extensive cleaning.

Flex Handle The flex or hinged handle is also very convenient. To loosen tight nuts, swing the handle at right angles to the socket. This gives the greatest possible leverage. After loosening the nut to the point where it turns easily, move the handle into the vertical position and then turn the handle with the fingers. Maximum leverage in relation to drive size is generally "built in" on most flex handles. Any additional leverage gained by extending the handle is sure to cause damage. Occasional lubrication of the flex joint and retaining ball and spring

FIG. 5-27. Single- and double-end jeweler's socket wrenches. These miniature wrenches are most useful in the average shop.

will ensure smooth action and reduce wear.

Sliding T-Bar Handle When using the sliding-bar or T handle, the head can be positioned anywhere along the sliding bar. Select the best position for the job at hand. Actually, the nature of the work itself generally indicates the best use of the sliding T handle, whether it be as an offset tool, a spinner, or for two-hand use. This type of driver combines readily with sockets, extensions, universal joints, and adapters to make a wide variety of highly useful tool combinations in all drive sizes.

Speed Handle The speed or speeder handle is worked like the woodworker's brace. After the nuts are first loosened with the sliding-bar handle or the ratchet handle, the speed handle can be used to remove the nuts more quickly. In many instances the speed handle is not strong enough to be used for breaking loose or tightening the nut. Speeders combine readily with the various extensions and universal joints to reach many otherwise inaccessible places. An unusually useful tool can be made in the $\frac{1}{2}$-inch drive by combining the ratchet adapter with a speeder. The speed socket wrench should be used carefully to avoid damaging the nut threads. Frequent lubrication of the revolving grips will flush out dirt particles and ensure free action.

FIG. 5-28. Typical wrench sockets. The top two are considered regular, while those on the bottom are extra long (deep).

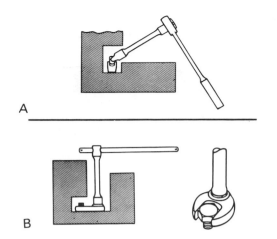

FIG. 5-29. Two useful socket items at work: (a) universal socket; (b) crowfoot attachment.

Table 5-1 Drive-Size Adapters

DOWN* (can be adapted to drive sockets in this drive size)	Originating drive size	UP (can be adapted to drive sockets in this drive size)
—	1/4	3/8
1/4	3/8	1/2
3/8	1/2	3/4
1/2	3/4	1
3/4	1	—

*Caution must be exercised not to use the full leverage of drivers when adapting sockets of a smaller drive size.

ACCESSORIES To complete the socket-wrench set, there are several accessory items, including extension bars, adapters, flexible joints, and various bits such as hex, slotted, and Phillips. Extension bars of different lengths are made to extend the distance from the socket to the handle. Extensions will engage with sockets and drivers more readily if the ball and spring on the male end are occasionally oiled and the female end is cleaned. Use the shortest extension possible on any job to ensure the most rigid tool possible.

The flex or universal joint allows the nut to be turned with the wrench handle held at an angle. While universal joints may be used up to angles of 65°, smaller angles give more efficient operation. Universal joints should never be used as right-angle drivers. This type of work should be done with flex or sliding T handles. Occasional lubrication will retard wear.

Some nuts are only accessible with crowfoot attachments (Figure 5-29b). These are usually made in 3/8-inch drive only, with openings from 3/8 to 11/16 inch. By coupling them with extensions and drivers, such as offset and flex handles, you can work them into some extremely tight spots.

Another valuable accessory is the regular or Phillips screwdriver attachment, which is ideal where leverage is required beyond that provided by the average screwdriver. The offset combinations possible with various drivers, and the convenience of ratcheting action, make these attachments highly useful in a number of automotive and industrial applications.

Still another accessory item is an adapter which allows you to use a handle having one drive size with a socket having a different drive size. These adapters allow the matching of drive sizes as indicated in Table 5-1.

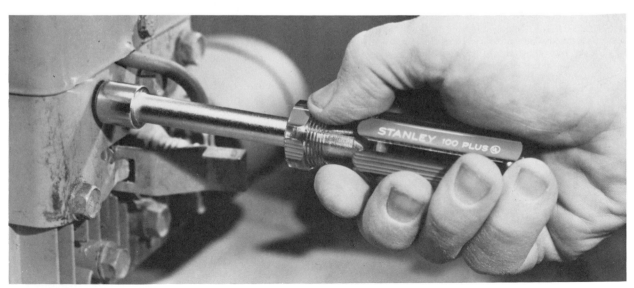

FIG. 5-30. Typical nut driver in use.

In any assembly using the ratchet adapter, it is preferable to place the adapter as close to the operator as possible for convenient access to the shift lever. The care and lubrication instructions given above for regular ratchets apply also to the ratchet adapter.

The use of universal joints, bar extensions, ratchet adapters, and universal sockets in combination with appropriate handles makes it possible to form a variety of tools that will reach otherwise inaccessible nuts and bolts.

NUT DRIVERS

Nut drivers are screwdriver-type tools which, in their simplest form, have a one-piece shank and socket secured in a fixed handle. The socket heads have openings for hex nuts, bolts, and screws up to ¾ inch nut size. The shafts may be solid, drilled partway, or full hollow, and plain or magnetic (for holding small fasteners). So-called "automatic" nut drivers such as the one shown in Figure 5-31 are also available.

Handles, both regular and reversible ratcheting, are available to accommodate interchangeable shanks for recessed-head screws such as Phillips, Pozidriv, Robertson, clutch, Frearson, hex, spline, and Scrulox and for slotted screws as well as for standard ¼-inch drive sockets. These tools either fit or they do not; there is no sharpening or adjustment.

FIG. 5-31. The locking mechanism allows a nut to be turned with slight pressure. To operate it, position the chuck over the nut. Push toward the nut; the collet fingers automatically engage the flats. Turn to tighten or loosen a nut. The revolving knurled chuck sleeve may be held to steady the driver.

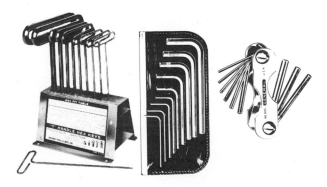

FIG. 5-32. Three styles of setscrew wrench.

SETSCREW WRENCHES

While most wrenches grip the fastener by fitting over it, there are types that must be inserted into a recess in the head of the fastener. The most used wrenches of this type are the Allen (hex) wrenches and the Bristol wrench.

Recessed-head screws usually have a hex-shaped (six-sided) recess. To remove or tighten this type of screw requires a special wrench that will fit in the recess. This wrench is called an Allen-type wrench. Allen-type wrenches are made from hexagonal L-shaped bars of tool steel. They range in size up to ¾ inch. When using an Allen-type wrench, make sure you use the correct size, to prevent rounding or spreading of the head of the screw. A snug fit within the recessed head of the screw is an indication that you have the correct size.

The Bristol wrench is made from round stock. It is also L-shaped, but one end is fluted to fit flutes or little splines in the Bristol setscrew.

These, then, are the wrenches used by the average craftsman. There are a multitude of other wrenches, most of which we shall never need to use; nor is there room in this book to catalog all the special-use and single-purpose wrenches available.

SAFETY RULES FOR WRENCHES

Here are a few basic rules that you should keep in mind when using wrenches:

1. Keep wrenches clean and free of oil. Dirt and grit will prevent them from seating firmly around a nut. Oil and grease will make them slippery.
2. Do not use a wrench to do the job of another tool. You will not do the job as well, and you might damage or even break the wrench. Using a wrench as a hammer or a pry bar or as anything but a wrench can be dangerous. Take the time to get the right tool.
3. Never use a wrench opening that is too large for the fastener. This can spread the jaws of an open-end wrench and batter the points of a box or socket wrench. A too-large wrench opening can also spoil the points of the nut or bolt head. And, when selecting a wrench for proper fit, take special care to use inch wrenches on inch fasteners, and metric wrenches on metric fasteners.
4. Match the wrench to the job, using box or socket wrenches for heavier jobs, open-end wrenches for medium-duty work, and adjustable wrenches for light-duty jobs and odd-sized nuts. A pipe wrench should only be used on pipes, never on a nut, for its teeth will damage the nut. Always use a straight, rather than offset, handle if conditions permit.

5. Never push a wrench beyond its capacity. Quality wrenches are designed and sized to keep the leverage and intended load (torque) in safe balance. The use of an artificial extension (such as a pipe "cheater") on the handle of a wrench can break the wrench, spoil the work, and hurt the user. Instead, get a larger wrench or a different kind of wrench to do the job. The safest wrench is a box or socket type. (To free a "frozen" nut or bolt, use a striking-face box wrench or a heavy-duty box or socket wrench. Never use an open-end wrench. And apply penetrating oil beforehand.)

6. Determine which way a nut should be turned before trying to loosen it. Most nuts are turned counterclockwise for removal. This may seem obvious, but even experienced people have been observed straining at the wrench in the tightening direction when they wanted to loosen it.

7. If possible, always *pull* on a wrench handle, and adjust your stance to prevent a fall if something lets go. That is, assume a natural stance that will allow correct motion of the tool without endangering you if something should slip. There may be situations, of course, in which you can only push a wrench handle to loosen or tighten a nut or bolt. But you should always pull on a wrench to exert even pressure and avoid injury if the wrench slips or the nut breaks loose unexpectedly. (If you must push the wrench, do it with the palm of your hand, and hold your palm open.)

8. Never expose a wrench to excessive heat. Direct flame can draw the temper from the metal, weakening and possibly warping it, and making it unsafe to use.

9. Place the tool in its correct position. For instance, never cock or tilt an open-end wrench. Always be sure the nut or bolt head is fully seated in the jaw opening, for both safety and efficiency. A box or socket wrench should be used on hard-to-reach fasteners. Adjustable wrenches should be tightly adjusted to the work and pulled so that the force is applied to the fixed jaw.

10. Do not depend on plastic-dipped handles to insulate you from electricity. Ordinary plastic-dipped handles are for comfort and a firmer grip. They are not intended for protection against electric shock. (Special high-dielectric-strength handle insulation is available, but it should only be used as a secondary precaution.)

HOLDING TOOLS

Holding tools can be placed in either of two basic categories: hand-held holding tools (pliers), and vises or clamps. Let us first look at pliers.

Pliers

Pliers of various types are used by practically every mechanic, both amateur and professional. They are made in many styles and sizes and are used to perform many different operations. Pliers are used for cutting purposes as well as for holding and gripping small articles in situations where it may be inconvenient or impossible to use hands.

While most plier types are versatile, there is no such thing as a single pair of pliers that performs all the tasks of its cousins. To help prove the point, about 125 standard types and sizes of pliers are made by one manufacturer alone. There are pliers designed especially for textile weavers and knitters, telephone technicians, aircraft assemblers, and radio and electronics workers, among many others. Fortunately, however, for the average craftsman the pliers mentioned in this chapter will offer a tremendous variety of services.

SLIP-JOINT PLIERS

Slip-joint pliers (Figure 6-1a) are pliers with straight, serrated (grooved) jaws; the screw or pivot with which the jaws are fastened together may be moved to either of two positions, to better grasp small or large objects.

To spread the jaws of slip-joint pliers, first spread the ends of the handles apart as far as possible. The slip joint, or pivot, will now move to the open position. To close, again spread the handles as far as possible; then push the joint back into the closed postion.

Slip-joint combination pliers (Figure 6-1b) are similar to the slip-joint pliers just described, but with the additional feature of a wire cutter at the junction of the jaws. This cutter consists of a pair of square-cut notches, one on each jaw, which act as a pair of shears when an object is placed between them and the jaws are closed.

The cutter is designed to cut material such as soft wire and nails. To use the cutter, open the jaws until the notches on the jaws are lined up. Place the material to be cut as far back as possible into the opening formed by the cutter, and squeeze the handles of the pliers together. Do not attempt to cut hard material such as spring wire or hard rivets with the combination pliers. This will spring the jaws; and, if the jaws are sprung, it will be difficult thereafter to cut small wires with the cutters.

Slip-joint pliers are available with or without wire cutters in sizes from 5 to 10 inches in length and with jaw capacities from $\frac{3}{4}$ to $1\frac{1}{2}$ inches. They are available in

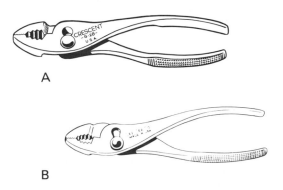

A

B

FIG. 6-1. *(a)* Slip-joint pliers; *(b)* slip-joint combination pliers.

several patterns: standard, heavy-duty, thin-nose, and bent-nose. In the latter, the jaws are offset 30°; they can grasp flush objects, yet the angle puts the handles far enough from the flush surface to provide plenty of clearance for turning.

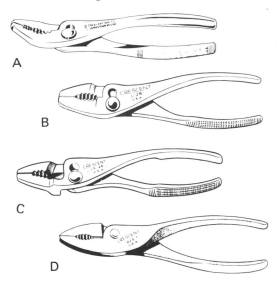

FIG. 6-2. Other types of slip-joint pliers: *(a)* thin bent-nose combination; *(b)* thin straight-nose combination; *(c)* slip-joint side cutting; *(d)* slip-joint heavy-duty side cutter.

UTILITY PLIERS

A first cousin to slip-joint pliers are utility pliers. These wide-capacity pliers, which are sometimes called "engineer's pliers," are made with both the tongue-and-groove adjustment design and a multiposition slip-joint adjustment. (The latter type were at one time called "water-pump pliers" because they were originally designed for tightening or removing water-pump packing nuts.)

Self-locking, the jaws of both designs of utility pliers can be set at a series of openings, in parallel, making them ideal grippers for things like bonnets on sink faucets. Owing to this jaw design and the necessarily long handles, you can exert considerable leverage and holding power. These are the pliers to use for tightening garden-hose couplings, removing an outside faucet, adjusting bicycle handlebars, or for removing the spark plug from some lawnmowers. For light use on plumbing projects, utility pliers will do a handy job as a pipe wrench, providing the pipes are neither too large nor require too much leverage. Actually, the smallest of the so-called utility pliers is the ignition style. That is, the jaw capacities of utility pliers range from about ¾ to 4½ inches, while lengths range from 9½ to 16 inches. Jaws may be smooth,

straight, or curved-toothed. As a rule, utility pliers have the same size of teeth running the lengths of both jaws, for a firm, evenly distributed grip.

FIG. 6-3. Typical utility pliers.

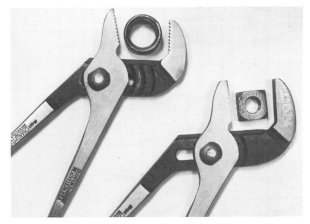

FIG. 6-4. The jaws of utility pliers are available toothed (left) or smooth (right).

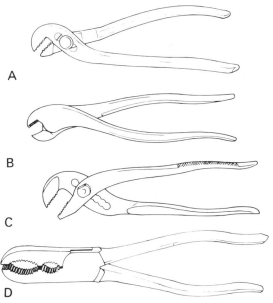

Fig. 6-5. Variations of special utility pliers: *(a)* ignition pliers; *(b)* battery pliers; *(c)* water-pump and electrician's lock-nut pliers; *(d)* gas and burner pliers.

SIDE-CUTTING PLIERS

Side-cutting pliers (side cutters) are principally used for holding, bending, and cutting thin materials or small-gauge wire. Side cutters vary in size from 5 to 9½ inches in length and are designated by their overall length. The jaws are hollowed out on one side, just forward of the pivot point of the pliers. Opposite the hollowed-out portion of the jaws are the cutting edges.

Square-nosed and with serrated tips, side-cutting pliers are available in two head patterns: standard and New

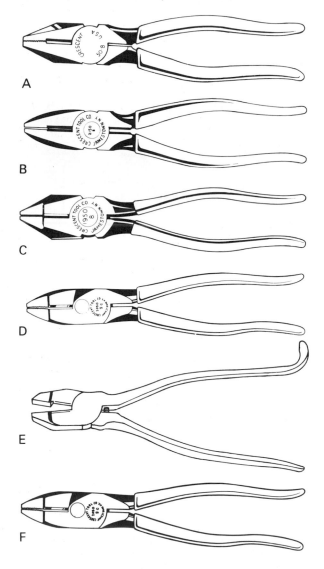

FIG. 6-6. Side-cutting pliers: *(a)* standard; *(b)* New England or round nose; *(c)* heavy-duty side cutting; *(d)* heavy-leverage pliers; *(e)* ironworker's *(f)* Button lineman's pliers.

England, or round nose, which is more streamlined. Handles may be plain, slip-on molded plastic, plastic-dipped, or high-dielectric insulated. High-leverage patterns are also available, as are pliers incorporating sleeve twisters and threaded bolt-holding openings. Another design—called the "parallel-jaw" pliers—has a special joint which permits the jaws of the pliers to remain parallel regardless of the extent of the opening. These pliers are particularly effective in holding square stock or holding the parallel sides of a nut.

For holding or bending light metal surfaces, the jaw tips are used to grasp the object. When holding wire, grasp it as near one end as possible because the jaws will mar the wire. To cut small-diameter wire, use the side cutting edge of the jaws, near the pivot. Never use side cutters to grasp large objects, tighten nuts, or bend heavy-gauge metal, since such operations will spring the jaws.

Sidecutters are often called electrician's or lineman's pliers. They are used extensively for stripping insulation from wire and for twisting wire when making a splice. Incidentally, ironworker's pliers are very similar to lineman's pliers, except that they have a hook bend on one handle and have a coil spring to hold the jaws open. Sizes range from 7 to 9 inches in length, and they are available in standard and high-leverage patterns.

Another style of pliers similar to the lineman's type is the Button pliers. These electrical pliers have a curved gripping portion in their jaws. The cutting action, which is accomplished on the outside of the jaws, is a shearing action similar to that in slip-joint pliers. But these fixed-pivot pliers do a much better job.

The electrician's wiring pliers are specially designed to speed the installation of electrical outlets. Their wire-stripping notches for 12- and 14-gauge wire will strip insulation quickly and cleanly without nicking the wire.

When stripping the insulation from wire with side-cutting pliers, nick the insulation all around, being careful not to break through to the wire itself. The index finger should be kept between the handles of the pliers, close to the joint. This affords better control over the cutting edges so that there is less chance that the insulation will be broken completely through. When the nick has been made all around the wire, press your thumb against the side of the pliers to break the insulation at the nick. Without changing your grip on the pliers, strip the short length of insulation off the end of the wire. Care must be exercised to avoid cutting too far through the insulation and nicking the wire.

DIAGONAL CUTTING PLIERS

Diagonal cutting pliers (often called "dikes") are used for cutting light material, such as wire and cotter pins, in areas which are inaccessible to larger cutting tools. Since they are designed for cutting only, they can cut larger objects than slip-joint pliers.

As the cutting edges are diagonally offset approximate-

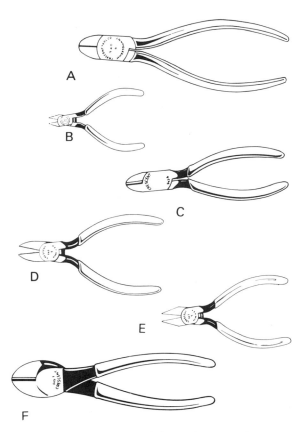

FIG. 6-7. Various types of diagonal-cutting pliers: *(a)* short-nose diagonal; *(b)* midget semiflush diagonal; *(c)* standard diagonal; *(d)* taper-nose diagonal; *(e)* full-flush-cutting diagonal; *(f)* heavy-duty diagonal cutting.

ly 15°, diagonal pliers are adapted to cutting small objects flush with a surface. The inner jaw surface is a diagonal, straight-cutting edge. Diagonal pliers should never be used to hold objects, because they exert a greater shearing force than other types of pliers of a similar size. The sizes of diagonal cutting pliers are designated by the overall length of the pliers, which ranges from 4 to 8 inches.

Diagonal cutters are made in several patterns ranging from the high-leverage, heavy-duty pattern down to the midget pattern for electronic work. They are available with and without a top bevel on the knives for flush cutting. Some have wire-skinning holes; some have coil springs to open the jaws. Handles may be plastic-dipped, slip-on molded plastic, or plain. Some diagonal cutters have a plastic insert between the jaws that holds the cut-off end of a wire until the jaws are opened up. This is an important aid for working on electronic assemblies, since the clipped ends could fall into the chassis and cause short circuits.

END-CUTTING PLIERS

End-cutting pliers or nippers range in size from heavy-duty, high-leverage patterns down to the traverse end cutter. The long jaws of the latter can reach into confined areas and cut wires at their tips. The cutting edges on these pliers are on the front of the jaws, rather than at the side. This permits cutting behind other wires and around small electronic components.

The regular end-cutting pliers have wide blades and powerful mechanical leverage which make them more useful than diagonal cutters for heavy-duty work. They snip wire of all kinds, and even cut nails. Nipper sizes range from 4½ to 8 inches in length.

The wire-cutting type of end cutters will cut baling wire, wire box strapping, concrete reinforcing wires, aerial and ground wires, etc. The jaws are tapered so the wire is drawn toward their base and not pushed out. Their short jaws will cut close to surfaces.

A special type of end-cutting nippers is employed for cutting ceramic tile and similar materials. When these nippers are completely closed, the jaws are still approximately ⅛ inch apart and, unlike those of ordinary end-cutting pliers, are off center.

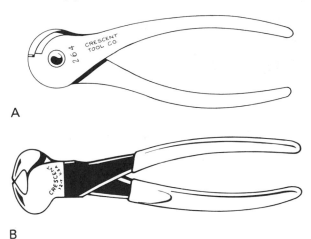

FIG. 6-8. End-cutting pliers: *(a)* wire cutting; *(b)* end-cutting nippers.

FLAT-NOSE PLIERS

Often referred to as "duckbills," these pliers have flat noses in various widths. They are available with plain or plastic-dipped handles in sizes from 4½ to 8 inches in length. Duckbills are used in confined areas where the fingers cannot be used. The jaw faces of the pliers are scored to aid in holding an item securely. Duckbills have diverse uses in the electrical, telephone, and electronic fields, among others. They are extensively used in typewriter repair and assembly work and in textile weaving and knitting operations.

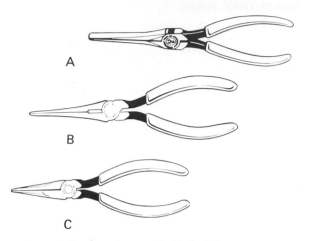

FIG. 6-9. Flat-nose pliers: *(a)* duckbill; *(b)* long flat nose; *(c)* long chain nose with side cutter.

LONG-NOSE PLIERS

This type of pliers embraces three nose configurations: needle, round, and chain. Needle-nose pliers are used in the same manner as duckbill pliers. However, there is a difference in the design of the jaws. Needle-nose jaws are tapered to a point, which makes them adapted to installing and removing small cotter pins. They have serrations at the nose end and a side cutter near the throat. Needle-nose pliers may be used to hold small items steady, or to do numerous other jobs which are too intricate or too difficult to be done by hand alone. Curved needle-nose pliers, which have their long thin noses bent at an angle, are handy for working in out-of-the-way corners.

Round-nose pliers are designed for bending and holding curved wires and strips. They can easily form loops and eyes in wire, because both jaws are round and tapered toward the end. Curves of small radius are bent at the tips of the jaws, while curves of larger radius are bent at the base of the jaws. Chain-nose pliers are similar in design to round-nose pliers and are used in much the same manner.

Long-nose pliers are available with and without side cutters and with tip cutters notched for stripping insulated wire. Needle-nose pliers with side-cutting edges at the tip, for example, can cut wires that are normally inaccessible to other types of cutter, and are most useful in electronic assembly work. The cutting edges are flush with the side of the jaws and leave no wire stub.

The handles of long-nose pliers may be plain, slip-on plastic, or dipped. Sizes range from 4 to 8 inches in length. Duckbill and long-nose pliers are especially delicate. Care should be exercised when using these pliers to prevent springing, breaking, or chipping of the jaws. Once these pliers are damaged, they are practically useless.

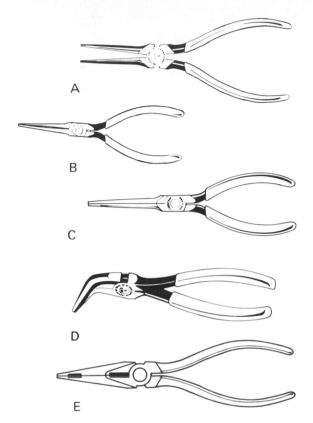

FIG. 6-10. Typical needle-nose pliers: *(a)* long needle nose; *(b)* very fine needle nose; *(c)* extra-thin long needle nose; *(d)* curved needle nose; *(e)* needle nose with side cutter near the end.

LOCKING WRENCH PLIERS

Locking wrench pliers, also known as clamps and by two popular trade names—vise grip and grip-lock—can be used for holding objects of odd shape. A screw adjustment in one of the handles makes them suitable for several different sizes. The jaws of wrench pliers may have standard serrations as in the pliers just described, or they may have clamp-type jaws. The clamp-type jaws are generally wide and smooth and are used primarily when working with sheet metal.

Wrench pliers have an advantage over other types of pliers in that you can clamp them on an object and they will stay. This leaves your hands free for other work.

A craftsman uses this tool a number of ways. It may be used as a clamp, speed wrench, portable vise, or wherever locking, plier-type jaws are needed. For best results with any locking wrench pliers, it is important that you learn to adjust them as directed by their manufacturer. To use pliers such as those shown in Figure 6-13, proceed as follows:

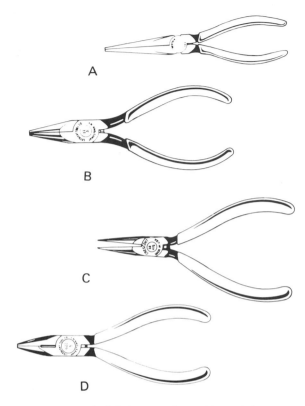

FIG. 6-11. Typical chain-nose pliers: *(a)* Long chain nose; *(b)* short chain nose; *(c)* midget chain nose; *(d)* short chain-nose side cutting.

1. When the jaws are locked, place one hand around the pliers, as shown in Figure 6-14a. Then, hook the fingers of the other hand around the screw end of the pliers, and push the release with the thumb.
2. To lock the jaws onto the work, grasp the tool as shown in Figure 6-14b, with the lever slightly open. Then, with the other hand, adjust the end screw until the jaws just slip over the work. Tighten your grip on the lever. The jaws will then snap closed, and the pliers are locked on the work.
3. To grip tightly without locking, adjust the end screw so the jaws will not quite snap shut. Simply use the tool as pliers (Figure 6-14c) or with a ratchet action. The tool will open automatically when the grasp is released.
4. The jaws of pliers equipped with wire cutters can easily cut ordinary wire (Figure 6-14d). For heavy wire or small bolts, adjust the end screw so the cutter jaws cut only partly through; make the cut, and then adjust the end screw for a deeper bite. Repeat until the cut is complete.

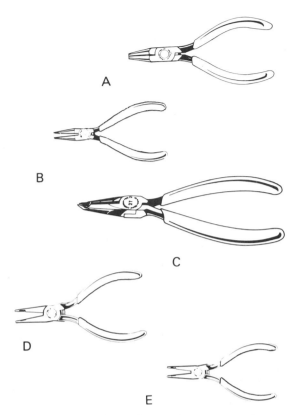

FIG. 6-12. Typical round-nose pliers: *(a)* round-nose wire loop; *(b)* short flat nose; *(c)* short-nose tip cutters; *(d)* tip cutter; *(e)* cutting and looping.

In addition to being available in several sizes, with straight and curved jaws as well as with or without wire cutters, locking wrench pliers are also made for various other holding tasks. As shown in Figure 6-15, the vise-grip principle is used in locking C clamps, sheet-metal clamps, pinch-off tools, welding clamps, and locking chain clamps. The latter hold and lock around items of any size and any shape that their chain can be wrapped around.

Locking wrench pliers should be used with care, since the teeth in the jaws tend to damage the object on which they are clamped. They should not be used on nuts, bolts, tube fittings, or other objects which must be reused. Do not expose wrench pliers to the direct heat of welding torches or allow them to contact welding electrodes. When subjected to severe vibration, such as is encountered during riveting, locking wrenches or clamps holding the workpieces should be wired or taped closed, to prevent accidental opening. Do not use pipe, other extensions, or hammering to increase the torque applied to these tools. An occasional drop of oil on all points of wear will ensure better operation and prolong the life of the tool.

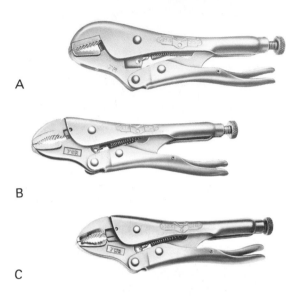

A

B

C

FIG. 6-13. Locking wrench pliers with *(a)* straight jaws; *(b)* curved jaws; *(c)* curved jaws with wire cutters.

OTHER PLIERS

There are literally hundreds of other kinds of pliers, many so specialized that they perform only one task. These, of course, would have value in specialty crafts shops, but there are a few others that are handy to have around.

For electrical work, *wire-stripper* pliers are available to cut the insulation but not the wire. An adjustable stop allows them to handle various wire sizes, usually from 12 to 26 gauge. There are also combination *wire-stripping, crimping,* and *cutting* pliers available that do a neat, quick job of preparing a wire and attaching a lug to it. The lug is then slipped under a screw terminal to make a perfect, tight connection. Its jaws also have cutting edges.

Burner pliers, also called "gas pliers," have a series of oval openings in the jaws that grip the small brass and copper fittings found on furnaces and similar equipment. *Battery* pliers are fixed-joint self-gripping pliers with long handles. Three sets of teeth engage the work, giving additional holding power on round rods or badly corroded battery bolts. *Spark-plug-terminal* pliers, with their insulated jaws and handles, are used for removing plug wires with the engine running. The angled jaws of these pliers cover a wide range of wire and terminal sizes and permit access to hard-to-reach spark plugs. *Hose-clamp* pliers are designed especially for applying and removing spring hose clamps. The recesses in the jaws grip the ends of the spring so it cannot slip or twist. The pliers grip with either the end or side of the jaw, for reaching easily into tight places. The slip ring on the handle allows the mechanic to remove a hand from the

pliers to adjust a hose.

If you do any motor work on your car or garden equipment, *retaining-ring* pliers are handy for installing or removing internal and external retaining or snap rings. Both straight and angle tips are available. The straight-type pliers simplify the horizontal installation or removal of the ring; the angle-type pliers are designed for maximum efficiency for vertical installation or removal of the ring.

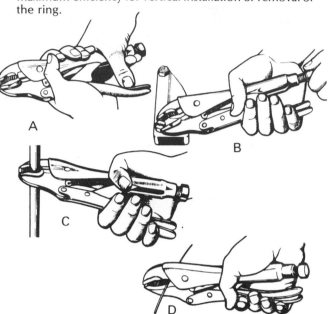

A

B

C

D

FIG. 6-14. How to use locking wrench pliers.

Snap-ring pliers and *lock-ring* pliers are also useful to the mechanic. The latter (also called "horseshoe pliers") spread the snap lock rings used on brakes, transmissions, pedal shafts, clutch shafts, and machine tools. They can also be used to spread piston rings. Of course, one of the most valuable tools is the *brake-spring* pliers. This combination tool can be used for the removal and replacement of Bendix, Lockheed, and other hydraulic and mechanical brake springs. On some pliers of this type, one handle has a socket end for removing a spring set over a post, and the other has a guide for replacing springs.

If you expect to put up any wire fencing, there are special pliers—*fence* pliers—that are designed to make fence building and repairing an easier job. They can be used to pull out stubborn staples and to stretch wire taut before fastening. The broad face is used as a hammer to drive staples. The cutting jaws on the neck of the tool cut through fence wire easily. One of the more interesting types of pliers is the *wire twisters*. These pliers are extremely useful in the safety wiring of such items as jet engines, aircraft communications gear, racing-car engine components, private, commercial and military aircraft components, and the like. The tool is also finding growing usage in the farming market (for tying fencing), the boating market (tying mesh for concrete boats) and in automobile and motorcycle racing (tying crankcase drain plugs).

Both jaws of the *glass-cutting* pliers are smooth and accurately finished. The flat upper jaw supports the top surface of the glass, while the humped lower jaw, developing powerful leverage under the slightest pressure from the handles, cleanly severs the glass at a scored line.

Jeweler's pliers are so called because they are miniature in size and therefore suitable for precision work. Each of these types of pliers is similar to a type that was described earlier, but much smaller. They are used for electronic wiring and assembly work, as well as hobby and craft work. *Optician's* pliers are also small pliers, in conventional shapes, that have value in such work.

Locking needle-nose pliers are really a medical "forceps" adapted to electronic assembly work. The long, narrow jaws are particularly suited for holding electrical components and wires together while they are being soldered. The scissor-shaped handles are held in the locked position by wedge-type serrations. The tool is very

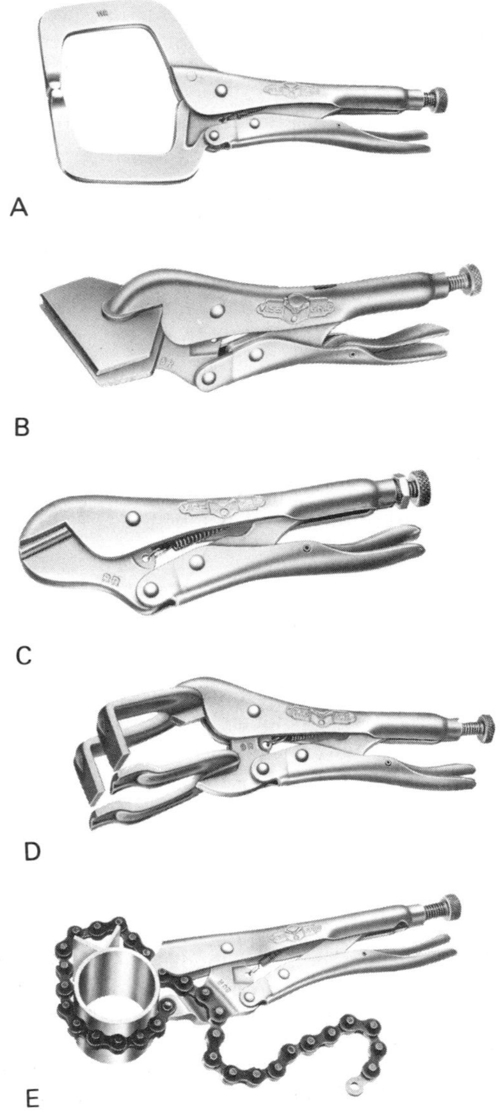

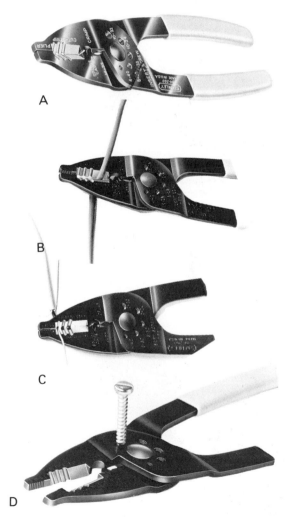

FIG. 6-15. Various special locking wrench pliers: *(a)* C clamp; *(b)* sheet-metal clamp; *(c)* pinch-off tool; *(d)* welding clamp; *(e)* chain clamp.

FIG. 6-16. Cutter-stripper-crimper pliers *(a)* serve many purposes. They cut electrical wire *(b)*; strip insulation *(c)*; and cut bolts and screws *(d)*.

useful for soldering components onto printed-circuit boards, since it acts as a "heat sink," drawing away excess heat which might damage the circuit board.

When purchasing any pliers, make sure that the jaws meet flush. The pivots (except in the case of slip-joint types) should allow the handles to open and close smoothly, with little effort, yet not be so loose that they wobble. Cutting edges should be smoothly honed and meet along their entire length. Hold the pliers up to the light, and you will immediately see if there are gaps in the cutters. Smooth jaws should be just that—smooth. Engraved, or milled, jaws should be evenly milled. The finish of the tool is another way to judge quality. A well-made tool looks and feels good; a cheap one often has rough surfaces and, generally, a crude finish.

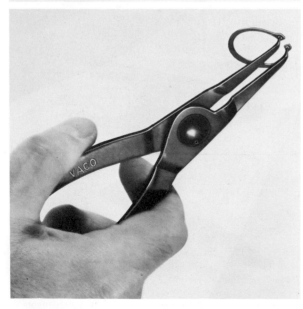

FIG. 6-17. (Top) The range of sizes of retaining-ring pliers. (Bottom) How retaining-ring pliers hold.

SAFETY RULES FOR PLIERS

The following basic safety rules should be applied to the use of pliers:

1. Pliers should not be used for cutting hardened wire unless specifically manufactured for this purpose.
2. Never expose pliers to excessive heat. This may draw the temper and ruin the tool.
3. Always cut at right angles. Never rock the tool from side to side or bend the wire back and forth against the cutting blades.
4. Do not bend stiff wire with light pliers. Needle-nose pliers can be damaged if the tips are used to bend too large a wire. Use a sturdier tool.
5. Never use pliers as a hammer, or use a hammer on the handles. They may crack or break, or the blades may be nicked by such abuse.
6. Ordinary plastic-dipped handles are designed for comfort, not electrical insulation. Tools having high-dielectric insulation are available and are so identified. Do not confuse the two.
7. Never extend the length of the handles to secure greater leverage. Use a larger pair of pliers or a bolt cutter.
8. Pliers should not be used on nuts or bolts. A wrench will do a better job with less risk of damage to the fastener.
9. Safety glasses should be worn when cutting wire, etc., to protect the eyes from being struck by the end of the object being cut.

CARE OF PLIERS

Nearly all side-cutting pliers and diagonals are designed so that the cutting edges can be reground. Some older models of pliers will not close if material is ground from the cutting edges. When grinding the cutting edges, never take any more material from the jaws than is necessary to remove the nicks. Grind the same amount of stock from both jaws. (*Note:* When jaws on pliers do not open enough to permit grinding, remove the pin that attaches the two halves of the pliers so that the jaws can be separated.)

The serrations on the jaws of pliers must be sharp. When they become dull, the pliers should be held in a vise and the serrations recut with a small three-corner file.

Pliers should be coated with light oil when they are not in use. They should be stored in a toolbox in such a manner that the jaws cannot be injured by striking hard objects. Keep the pin or bolt at the hinge just tight enough to hold the two parts of the pliers in contact, and always keep the pivot pin lubricated with a few drops of light oil.

Vises and Clamps

Vises are used for holding work that is being planed, sawed, drilled, shaped, sharpened, or riveted, or wood that is being glued. Clamps are used for holding work which cannot be satisfactorily held in a vise because of its shape and size, or when a vise is not available. Actually, the major difference between the two is that clamps are portable and move about on the job while the vise is stationary. Both, however, employ the same basic idea of applying pressure equally from opposite ends toward the center. Both employ the screw as a means of applying controlled pressure in measurable amounts.

TYPES OF VISES

There are several types of vises suitable for use by the craftsman, but the one selected will generally depend on the work done in the shop. Here are some of the more popular vises.

WOODWORKING BENCH VISE Probably the vise most commonly used by the handyman and craftsman is the woodworking bench vise. It is designed to hold work for planing, sawing, or chiseling at the bench (Figure 6-18). Turning the screw (by means of the handle) causes the movable jaw on the vise to move in or out on the slide bars (sometimes called the guide bars). On a vise with a continuous screw, the movable jaw must be turned all the way. On a vise with an interrupted screw (which is called a "quick-acting" vise), the movable jaw can be moved rapidly in or out when the screw is in a certain position. When the jaw is in the desired position against the work, the quick-acting vise can be tightened by a partial turn of the handle.

Most woodworking vises are equipped with a dog as shown in the illustration. The dog, which can be raised as shown or lowered flush with the top of the vise, is used in conjunction with a bench stop to hold work which is too wide for the maximum span of the vise.

MACHINIST'S BENCH VISE Often simply called a "bench" vise, this is a steel vise with scored jaws that prevent the work from slipping. Most of these vises have a swivel base with jaws that can be rotated, while others cannot be rotated. A similar light-duty model is equipped with a cutoff. These vises are usually bolt-mounted onto a bench.

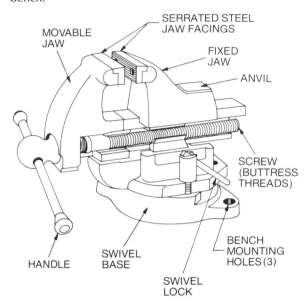

FIG. 6-19. Parts of a typical machinist's vise.

BENCH AND PIPE VISE This vise, sometimes called a "utility" bench vise, has integral pipe jaws for holding pipe from ¾ to 3 inches in diameter. The maximum working main-jaw opening is usually 5 inches, with a jaw width of 4 to 5 inches. The base can be swiveled to any position and locked. These vises are equipped with an anvil and are also bolted onto a workbench.

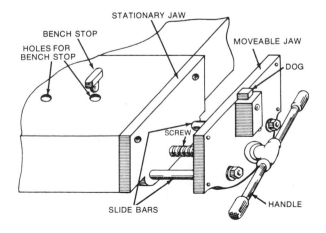

FIG. 6-18. Woodworking bench vise with a typical dog–bench-stop arrangement.

CLAMP-BASE VISE The clamp-base vise usually has a smaller holding capacity than either the standard machinist's or utility vise and is usually clamped to the edge of the bench with a thumbscrew. These vises have a maximum holding capacity varying between 1½ and 3 inches. They normally do not have pipe-holding jaws.

The so-called "carpenter's" vise is a small clamp-on version of the woodworker's vise. This portable vise has 5½-inch-long L-shaped jaws which open to 2¾ inches. It can hold work either horizontally across the bench or vertically at its end.

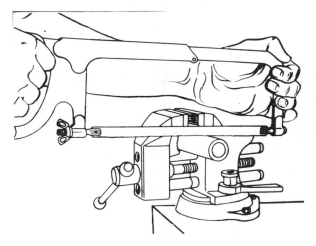

Fig. 6-20. Bench-and-pipe type vise in use.

There are, of course, many specialized vises, designed to do certain jobs better than any other vise. For example, there is the *drill-press* vise, made to hold small items (particulary metal) at any angle and in any position so that work can be drilled in the press. For small, delicate work, there is the *jeweler's* vise. The *miter* vise will hold two pieces perfectly at a right angle for nailing, gluing, or other fastening operations. This type of vise is ideal for making picture frames. For plumbing work, the *pipe* vise is a must, since it is designed to hold standard pipe for cutting and threading. There are also small *hand-held* vises as well as such holding devices as the *third hand*.

USE OF VISES

The correct way to use a vise is also the safest way. A little care and know-how is all it takes to avoid a damaged job. For safety's sake, keep in mind the fact that even the smallest vise is capable of developing hundreds of pounds of pressure between its jaws—so be sure to keep your fingers out of harm's way when closing the jaws.

Do not open the jaws of a vise beyond their capacity, as the movable jaw will drop off, possibly causing personal injury or damage to the jaw. Also, regardless of the material in the vise, never extend the vise handle with a length of pipe to increase leverage. Most vises are

designed to withstand only the maximum pressure that can be applied directly on the handle. To prevent vibration and movement, work as close to the vise jaws as possible. Vibration can cause a hammer or chisel to slip or glance off the workpiece and ruin hours of labor. Odd-shaped work should always be clamped in a jig, to keep it steady.

When holding heavy work in a vise, place a block of wood under the work as a prop to prevent it from sliding down and falling on your foot.

Before placing a piece of work in a vise, it is generally necessary to protect it from crushing or marring. This holds true for both woodworking and metalworking vises. Softwoods and soft metals damage easily under

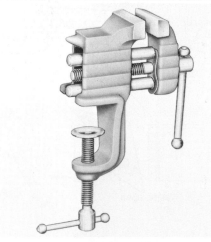

FIG. 6-21. Two styles of clamp-base vises.

pressure. It is worth the effort to make removable jaw facings that will protect delicate work. Sandwiching the work between large blocks of wood or sheets of plywood will serve to distribute the vise pressure over a greater area and prevent crushing of the work. A piece of aluminum or other soft material can also be employed to provide a smooth surface when needed. Always try to hold the part in the center of the vise jaws so as not to put too much strain on the movable jaw and its sliding guide. Do not overtighten the jaws. Doing so could damage the work or the vise screw.

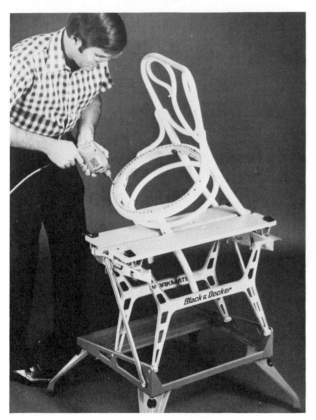

FIG. 6-22. All-purpose portable work bench with vise arrangement.

CARE OF VISES

Keep vises clean at all times. They should be cleaned and wiped with light oil after using. Never strike a vise with a heavy object, and never hold large work in a small vise, since these practices will cause the jaws to become sprung or otherwise damage the vise. Keep the jaws in good condition, and oil the screws and the slide frequently. Never oil the swivel base of a swivel jaw joint; its holding power will be impaired. When the vise is not in use, bring the jaws lightly together or leave a very small

gap. (The movable jaw of a tightly closed vise may break if the metal is expanded by heat.) Leave the handle in a vertical position.

TYPES OF CLAMPS

There are many different types of clamps, but virtually all are used for the same purpose—to hold two pieces of work together for convenience or during the drying of an adhesive. Among the clamps which the craftsman might use in the shop are the following.

C CLAMPS Most commonly used in the workshop is the C clamp. It is shaped like the letter C. It consists of a steel frame threaded to receive an operating screw with a swivel head. C clamps are made for light, medium, and heavy service with a variety of openings from $\frac{5}{8}$ to 12 inches.

FIG. 6-23. C clamps are perhaps the most widely used of all clamps. This is because they are inexpensive, long lasting, quick acting, and easy to use. They come in a wide range of sizes and shapes, differing in the depth of throat and the width of the jaws. They are adaptable to many uses, some of which include holding edging on veneer strips, clamping work on a drill press, and holding rabbeted glued corners. A C clamp can also be used as an auxiliary vise.

HAND-SCREW CLAMPS These clamps consist of two hard maple jaws connected with two operating screws. They are a generally preferred holding device for nearly all types of shop projects and repair work. They grip and hold odd shapes securely, and will not mar highly finished surfaces.

To use hand-screw clamps correctly, learn the habit of grasping the "end" spindle (Figure 6-24a and b) with the right hand; then the direction for "swinging" or rotating the handscrew to open the jaws will always be the same.

Rapid adjustment of the handscrew is obtained by proper swinging. Hold the handles firmly, arms extended, and, with a motion of the wrists only, make the jaws revolve around the spindles. When the jaw opening is approximately correct, place the hand screw on the work with the "end" spindle either to your right or in the upper position, and with the "middle" spindle as close to the work as possible. Adjust either or both handles so that the jaws grip the work easily and are slightly more open at the end. Turn the end spindle clockwise to close the jaws onto the work. Final pressure is applied only by means of the end spindle. The middle spindle acts as a fulcrum. Make certain that pressure is applied all along the entire length of the jaws, not just at the end or at the edge of the work.

A   B

FIG. 6-24. Proper use of spindle hand-screw clamps.

BAR CLAMPS Bar clamps are long (the standard maximum opening ranges from 2 to 8 feet) precision clamps normally used for making fine furniture. They adjust by means of a movable jaw at one end of a metal or wood bar and a crank that turns a screw at the other end. Scrap wood pads must be employed under their jaws to prevent marring.

PIPE CLAMPS Pipe clamps operate in the same manner as bar clamps except that they slide on pipe. These clamps are available to fit either ½- or ¾-inch-diameter iron pipe. Only one end of the pipe need be threaded. The craftsman should have several different lengths of pipe to use with the clamps. While you can use a long pipe for all jobs, the excess pipe might get in your way. The pipe, of course, must be straight and smooth.

SPRING CLAMPS Resembling large clothespins, these handy clamps are available in sizes that open from 1 to 4 inches. They are the extra hands around the shop that hold your work in position while you are busy with another part of the job. They can be used where light pressure is adequate. Some spring clamps have plastic-

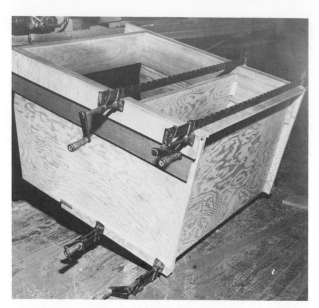

FIG. 6-25. Metal bar clamps in use.

FIG. 6-26. Wood bar clamps are favorites of many woodworkers.

covered tips to minimize marring of the work.

BAND CLAMPS These clamps solve the knotty problem of clamping round or irregular shapes where uniform pressure is required simultaneously at several joints. They are especially efficient for clamping furniture, as shown in Figure 6-29 (left). The canvas or steel band encircles the work and is pulled tight from either end through a screw-clamp device. The self-lock cams of the clamp hold the band securely without slippage while final screw pressure is applied. Slight pressure on the cam extensions releases the band instantly. The canvas band, which is usually

FIG. 6-27. Typical pipe clamp.

about 2 inches wide, is recommended for most applications.

Web clamps are lightweight, low-priced band clamps with innumerable uses. The 1-inch-wide nylon band (which is usually 12 to 15 feet long) can be placed around any regular or irregular shape to apply clamping pressure all around the work—drum tables, chair frames (Figure 6-29, right), picture frames, etc. With the band so located, it is drawn snug by hand, and final pressure is applied by means of a wrench or screwdriver applied to the hex-head slotted tightening bolt.

THREE-WAY EDGING CLAMPS Three-way edging clamps provide a convenient, practical method for applying "right-angle" pressure to the edge, or side, of the work. A unique three-screw design permits the right-angle screw to be centered or positioned above or below center, on varying thicknesses of work.

MITER CLAMPS There are several types of miter clamps. They are used in picture-frame making. The miter clamps shown in Figure 6-31 (top) are designed for mitering flat casing where a $\frac{5}{8}$-inch-diameter blind hole can be bored in the back of each piece. It forces the two ends being mitered directly against each other, no matter what the angle, with no tendency for the ends to creep along or away from each other.

The corner clamp is a flat triangular device used to clamp the corners of furniture frames, picture frames, and the like. The frame is set into the clamp, and a diagonal bolt then pushes it against the corner. In a variation of this device, pressure is exerted by two bolts which tighten against the outside corners of the frame (Figure 6-31, bottom).

The miter clamp shown in Figure 6-32 is an interesting "one-evening" project that will provide you with an uncomplicated clamping jig with many advantages for mitering picture frames and similar objects. It is adjustable to any size of frame; it applies uniform pressure to all four joints simultaneously; it leaves joints visible so you can be sure they are straight and tight; it is light and easy to handle, minimizing the danger of damage to new frames or those precious old ones in need of restoration; and it eliminates the necessity of buying a separate clamp for each joint. This practical jig overcomes the disadvantages of most other miter clamps which hold work of a limited size range and apply little, if any, pressure to the joint itself.

BENCH HOLD-DOWN CLAMPS These hold-down clamps can be installed in wood or metal surfaces. This is a distinct advantage over conventional clamps and vises, which function only near the edge of a workbench or table. Without the use of tools of any kind, the clamp slides onto a prespotted holding bolt, ready to go to work instantly. That is, as shown in Figure 6-34, it will hold work in the middle or near the edge of metal or wood benches, T slot or machine tables. Pressure is applied to the work by a screw adjustment. The clamp slides off the bolt head to be stored when not in use. When the hole is countersunk, the bolt head drops below the surface, leaving the work

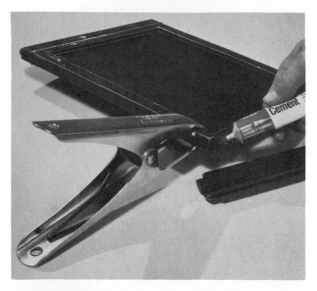

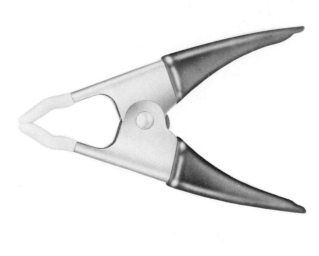

FIG. 6-28. Standard spring clamp (left) and plastic-tipped type (right).

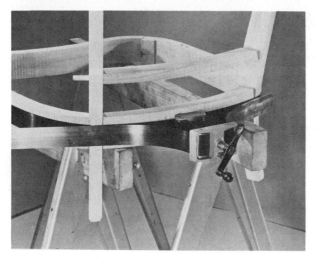

FIG. 6-29. Band clamp (left) and web clamp (right) in use.

area clear and uncluttered. The clamp swivels 360° around the holding bolt to secure the work in position at just the right spot or angle. One clamp, with several bolts installed at strategic locations, will perform work-holding service in many places throughout the shop. When the device is installed along the side of a bench for use as a vise, a cotter pin (furnished) run through holes in the clamp base holds the clamp on the bolt head to keep it in place when the screw pressure is released. Press screws are similar and are used frequently in the making of a veneer press.

Two different style veneer presses are shown in Fig. 6-35. Two or more frames are required to make up a press; there is no limit to the length of the work that may be handled. For average work, frames should be set about 9 inches apart; allow one screw for each 80 square inches. Thus, the top frame illustrated in Fig. 6-35, having four screws bearing on the work, will produce very satisfactory results over an area of 320 square inches.

EDGE CLAMPS. These handy attachments (Fig. 6-36) provide pressure at right angles to the axis of the bar of the clamp used. They are used to apply moldings to

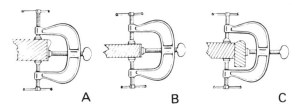

FIG. 6-30. Three-way edging clamp and how it may be applied with the right-angle screw off center (a) or centered (b), or to clamp around returns (c).

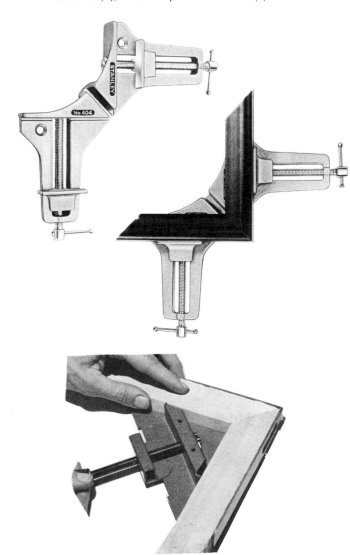

FIG. 6-31. (Top) Typical miter clamp; (center) typical miter overall clamp; (bottom) typical corner clamp and how it holds.

FIG. 6-32. A mitering jig that uses hand screws to apply equal pressure simultaneously at all four corners of the frame. On very large frames, the swivel bars may be a considerable distance apart, in which case a bar clamp can be used.

edges, drawing joints together, or for applying pressure to the middle of board areas.

USE AND CARE OF CLAMPS

When using clamps, first consider your clamping requirements, and then select the clamp best suited to your needs by ascertaining (1) the opening required; (2) the depth required; (3) the strength and weight required; (4) whether or not a full-length screw is essential (if not, the constant hindrance of the screw extending beyond the frame can be eliminated by selecting a clamp with a screw length proportionate to your needs; (5) the type of handle best suited to your needs; and (6) the balance of clamp operating time versus clamping needs, i.e., do you require a spring clamp, C clamp, bar clamp, or some other type. This appraisal of your clamping needs will assure you of getting the most from your clamps by saving time and money and enhancing the life of the clamps.

With all clamps (except possibly the hand-screw type), it is well to remember that heavy pressures crush

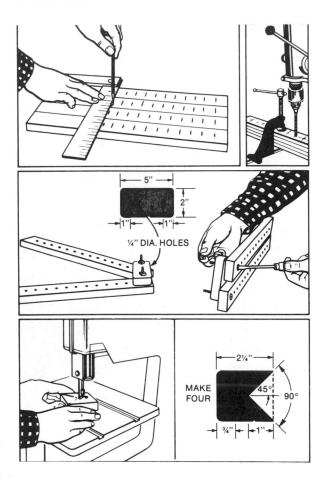

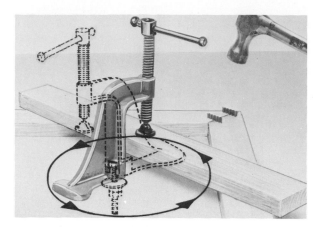

FIG. 6-34. Bench hold-down clamps in use.

FIG. 6-33. Steps in making a mitering jig: (a) Use straight, clear hardwood strips 1 X 2 X 18 inches (or as much longer as desired). Locate the centers accurately at 1-inch intervals, and drill ¼-inch-diameter holes. (b) If you prefer, the four legs can be "stacked," clamped, and drilled simultaneously. Corners should be rounded, and all holes counterbored, to accommodate flathead machine screws. (c) Swivel blocks (two required) are made from 1 X 2 inch stock, cut 5 inches long. Drill and assemble as shown. (d) Corner blocks (four required) are made from 1 X 2 inch stock, cut 2¼ inches long. Drill, cut, and assemble the entire jig as shown in Figure 6-32.

softwoods. To keep from ruining the workpiece, large blocks are used to distribute the pressure over a wider surface. Provide yourself with a stock of blocks of assorted sizes, thicknesses, and lengths, preferably of hardwood such as maple or birch.

Use clamps in pairs on both ends of the work. This will prevent one end from separating while the other is being joined. For large surfaces, additional clamps are needed.

Apply even pressure on all clamps. Tighten as far as possible with the handle. After a few minutes, take a few extra turns on the clamp handle, if possible. However,

FIG. 6-35. Typical veneer press frames.

avoid pressing in the sides of the workpiece. When closing the jaws of a clamp, avoid getting any portion of your hands or body between the jaws or between one jaw and the work.

Occasionally lightly lubricate all moving parts for longer service and smoother operation. Make sure there is no oil on any part(s) that will come in contact with the workpiece. The threads of C clamps must be clean and free from rust. The swivel head must also be clean, smooth, and grit-free. If the swivel head becomes damaged, replace it as follows: Pry open the crimped portion of the head, and remove the head from the ball end of the screw. Replace it with a new head, and recrimp.

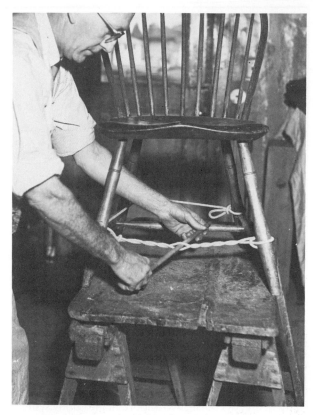

FIG. 6-37. Rope and sticks can be used as clamps under certain conditions.

FIG. 6-36. Edge-clamp fixtures in use.

MEASURING TOOLS

Before any sort of project begins, materials must be measured. In other words, the craftsman who wants a project to turn out well must first learn to measure materials accurately and mark lines where cuts must be made on that material. Shoddy measuring means inaccurate cuts. And the result can be a lopsided affair instead of an item to be proud of.

There are, of course, two important measuring systems in the world today—the U.S. Customary System (U.S.C.S.), which is most commonly used in the United States, and the International System of Units (SI), which is used in most other countries of the world. The United States, too, is now under the process of converting to the metric system.) The two systems are interconvertible. One meter equals 39.37 inches, and 1 inch equals 25.4 millimeters. (Full details on conversion between the two systems are given on the end papers of this book.) The length standards of both systems are today based on the distance between waves of light.

There are many different types of measuring tools. After reading this chapter, you should be able to select the appropriate measuring tool to use in doing a job and be able to operate a variety of measuring instruments properly.

Rules and Tapes

Figure 7-1 shows some of the more popular rules and tapes used by craftsmen. Of all measuring tools, the simplest and most common is the steel (or fiberglass) rule. This rule is usually 6 or 12 inches in length, although other lengths are available. Steel or bench rules, as they are sometimes called, may be flexible; but the thinner the rule, the easier it is to measure accurately, because the division marks are closer to the work. Yardsticks are sometimes used as bench rules.

Generally, a rule has four sets of graduations, one on each edge of each side. The longest lines are the "inch marks," representing inches. On one edge of one side, each inch is divided into 8 equal spaces, so each space represents ⅛ inch. The other edge of this side is divided into sixteenths. The ¼- and ½-inch marks are commonly made longer than the smaller division marks to facilitate counting, but the graduations are not, as a rule, numbered individually; they are sufficiently far apart to be counted without difficulty. The opposite side is similarly divided into 32 and 64 spaces per inch, and it is common practice to number every fourth division for easier reading.

There are many variations of the common rule. Sometimes the graduations are on one side only; sometimes a set of graduations is added across one end for measuring in narrow spaces, and sometimes only the first inch is divided into sixty-fourths, with the remaining inches divided into thirty-seconds and sixteenths. Steel machinist's rules, which are popular variations of the common rule, are thin blades of steel of varying lengths, widths, and thicknesses, usually graduated in inches and various subdivisions of the inch on each edge of both sides (and often at the ends). The makers term the various subdivisions of the inch with graduation numbers; for example, the No. 4 graduation has sixty-fourths on the first edge, thirty-seconds on the second edge, sixteenths on the third edge, and eighths on the fourth edge. By means of sliding or fixed attachments, a great variety of length measurements may be made with the ordinary steel rule. U.S.C.S. rules offer a great variety of both fractional and decimal increments as fine as one one-hundredth of an inch (0.010 inch), which is about the limit of the resolving power of the eye. Metric scales are normally graduated by millimeters (0.039 inch) and half millimeters (approximately 0.020 inch). Most manufacturers now make many of their linear measuring devices with both metric and U.S.C.S. graduations. This will be of help in the transition to the metric system occurring in the United States.

A metal or wood folding rule may be used for measuring purposes. The simple folding rule is usually 2

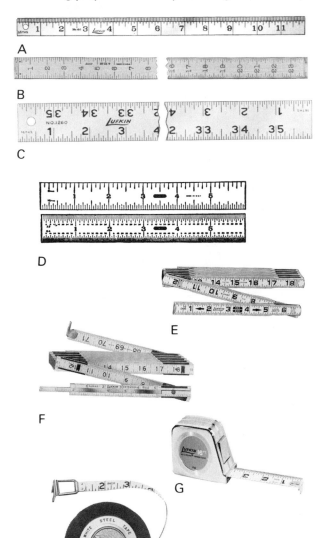

FIG. 7-1. Some common types of rules and tapes: *(a)* steel rule; *(b)* bench rule; *(c)* yardstick; *(d)* steel machinist's rule; *(e)* zigzag folding rule; *(f)* zigzag folding rule with extension; *(g)* power tape rule; *(h)* tape.

feet long, while the multiple-folding or "zigzag" wood rule is 6 feet long. The sections are so hinged that it is 6 inches from the center of one hinge joint to the center of the next, which makes the sections roughly 8 inches in length. It is graduated in sixteenths of an inch. Some zigzag rules have a thin metal extension rule built into one of the end sections; it is particularly useful for inside measurements. The reading on the extension is simply added to the length of the opened rule.

Several special folding rules are used by the various trades. For instance, there are brickmason's rules, used by bricklayers for spacing brick courses; modular-spacing rules designed for masonry work such as laying concrete and glass blocks, facing tile, and special brick; and plumber's rules. As shown in Figure 7-3, with the plumber's rule turned to the 10-inch graduation on the standard inch side, the graduation directly opposite indicates the center-to-center distance of the fittings to be $14\frac{1}{8}$ inches. Actually the length of the pipe will vary, as allowances must be made for the type of pipe and fitting used. All other size offsets are calculated in the same manner. Where the offset is longer than the length of the rule, you add the 45° scale measurement of the extra distance to the last scale reading on the rule ($101\frac{13}{16}$ inches). Incidentally, folding rules cannot be relied on for *extremely* accurate measurements because a certain amount of play develops at the joints after they have been used for a while.

Fiberglass or steel tapes are made from 6 to 100 feet in length. The shorter lengths are frequently made with a curved cross section so that they are flexible enough to roll up, but remain rigid when extended. Long, flat tapes require support over their full length during measuring, or the natural sag will cause an error in the reading.

The flexible/rigid tapes are usually contained in metal cases into which they wind themselves when a button is pressed, or into which they can easily be pushed. A hook provided at one end can be hooked over the object being measured, so one person can handle the rule without assistance. On some models, the outside of the case can be used as one end of the tape for measuring inside dimensions. "Pull-push tapes," as this type is commonly called, usually come in lengths of 6 to 16 feet, graduated in feet, inches, and fractions of an inch down to $\frac{1}{16}$ inch.

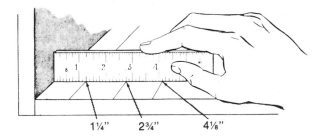

FIG. 7-2. Measuring with and reading a common rule.

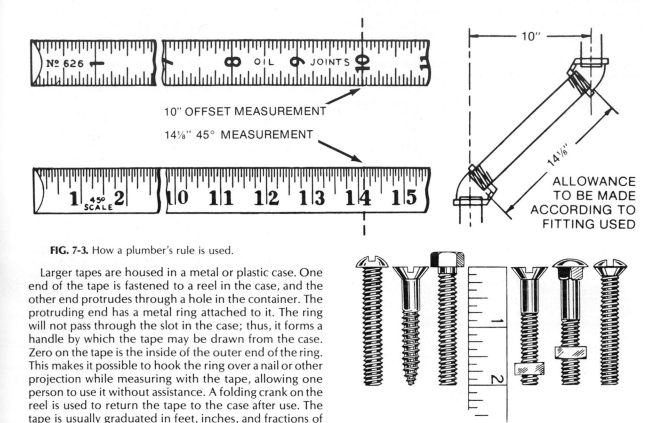

FIG. 7-3. How a plumber's rule is used.

Larger tapes are housed in a metal or plastic case. One end of the tape is fastened to a reel in the case, and the other end protrudes through a hole in the container. The protruding end has a metal ring attached to it. The ring will not pass through the slot in the case; thus, it forms a handle by which the tape may be drawn from the case. Zero on the tape is the inside of the outer end of the ring. This makes it possible to hook the ring over a nail or other projection while measuring with the tape, allowing one person to use it without assistance. A folding crank on the reel is used to return the tape to the case after use. The tape is usually graduated in feet, inches, and fractions of an inch down to $\frac{1}{8}$.

MEASURING PROCEDURES

To take a measurement with a common bench rule, hold the rule with its edge on the surface of the object being measured. This will eliminate parallax and other errors which might result due to the thickness of the rule. Read the measurement at the graduation which coincides with the distance to be measured, and state it as being so many inches and fractions of an inch. Always reduce fractions to their lowest terms; for example, $\frac{6}{8}$ inch would be called $\frac{3}{4}$ inch. A hook or eye at the end or a tape or rule is normally part of the first measured inch.

The lengths of bolts or screws are best measured by holding them against a rigid rule or tape. Hold both the bolt or screw to be measured and the rule up to your eye level, so that your line of sight will not affect the measurement. As shown in Figure 7-4, bolts or screws with countersink-type heads are measured from the top of the head.

To measure the outside diameter of a pipe, it is best to use some kind of rigid rule. A folding wooden rule or a steel rule is satisfactory for this purpose. As shown in Figure 7-5a, align the end of the rule with one side of the

FIG. 7-4. Measuring the length of a bolt or screw.

pipe, using your thumb as a stop. Then, with one end held in place with your thumb, swing the rule through an arc and take the maximum reading at the other side of the pipe. For most practical purposes, the measurement obtained using this method is satisfactory. It is necessary that you know how to take this measurement, as the outside diameter of pipe is sometimes the only dimension given on pipe specifications.

To measure the inside diameter of a pipe with a rule, hold the rule so that one corner of the rule just rests on the inside of one side of the pipe (Figure 7-5b). Then, with one end thus held in place, swing the rule through an arc and read the diameter across the maximum inside distance. This method is satisfactory for an approximate inside measurement.

To measure the circumference of a pipe, a flexible rule that will conform to the cylindrical shape of the pipe must be used. A tape rule or a steel tape is adaptable for this job. When measuring pipe, make sure the tape has been wrapped squarely around the axis of the pipe (i.e., the measurement should be taken in a plane perpendicular

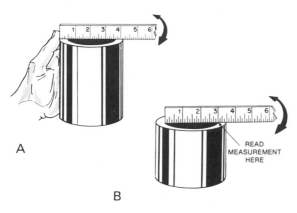

FIG. 7-5. *(a)* Measuring the outside diameter of a pipe. *(b)* Measuring the inside diameter of a pipe.

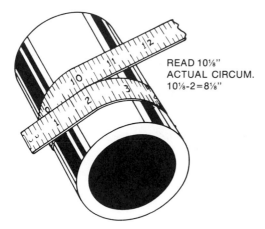

FIG. 7-6. Measuring the circumference of a pipe with a tape.

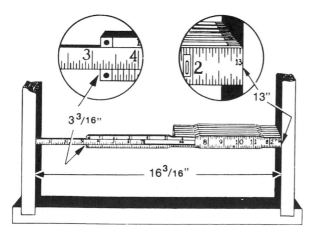

FIG. 7-7. Using a folding rule to measure an inside dimension.

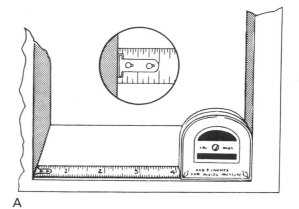

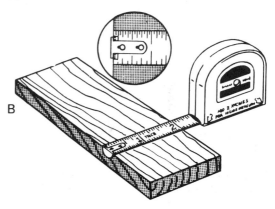

FIG. 7-8. *(a)* Measuring an inside dimension with a tape rule. *(b)* Measuring an outside dimension using a tape rule.

to the axis) to ensure that the reading will not be more than the actual circumference of the pipe. This is extremely important when measuring large-diameter pipe.

Hold the rule or tape as shown in Figure 7-6. Take a reading using the 2-inch graduation, for example, as the reference point. In this case the correct reading is found by subtracting 2 inches from the actual reading. The first 2 inches of the tape, serving as a handle, enable you to hold the tape securely.

A folding rule that has a 6- or 7-inch sliding extension is one of the best measuring tools for taking an inside measurement, such as the inside of a box. To take the measurement, first unfold the rule to the approximate dimension. Then extend the end of the rule, and read the length by which it is extended, adding that to the length on the main body of the rule (Figure 7-7). In this illustration the length of the main body of the rule is 13 inches, and the extension is pulled out $3\frac{3}{16}$ inches. The total inside dimension being measured is thus $16\frac{3}{16}$ inches.

In Figure 7-8a, notice in the circled insert that the hook at the end of the particular rule shown is attached to the rule so that it is free to move slightly. When an outside dimension is measured by hooking the end of the rule over an edge, the hook locates the end of the rule even with the surface from which the measurement is being taken. Being free to move, the hook will retract away from the end of the rule when an inside dimension is taken. To measure an inside dimension using a tape rule, extend the rule between the surfaces as shown, take a reading at the point on the scale where the rule enters the case, and add 2 inches. The 2 inches is the width of the case. The total is the inside dimension being measured. To measure the thickness of stock through a hole with a hook rule, insert the rule through the hole, hold the hook against one face of the stock, and read the thickness at the other face (Figure 7-9).

To measure an outside dimension using a tape rule, hook the rule over the edge of the stock. Pull the tape out until it projects far enough from the case to permit measuring the required distance. The hook at the end of the rule is designed so that it will locate the end of the rule at the surface from which the measurement is being taken (Figure 7-8b). For a measurement of length, the tape is held parallel to the lengthwise edge. For measuring widths, the tape should be at a right angle to the lengthwise edge. Read the dimension on the rule exactly at the edge of the piece being measured.

It may not always be possible to hook the end of the tape over the edge of the stock being measured. In this case it may be necessary to butt the end of the tape against another surface or to hold the rule at the starting point from which the measurement is to be taken.

Steel or fiberglass reel tapes are generally used for making long measurements. Secure the ring or hook end at the starting point, either by slipping it over a nail or by other means. Walk in the direction to be measured, letting the tape be pulled from the case as you walk. Stretch the slack out of the tape, making sure it is parallel to the surface or edge to be measured. Read the graduation which falls at the end of the distance to be measured.

There are valuable *tricks* that can be performed with measuring devices. For example, suppose you wish to make a 45° angle and have nothing but a folding rule. Bend the rule down at the 6- and 12-inch joints, until the metal end tip touches 16$\frac{3}{8}$ inches. The small angle at the 6-inch end will be exactly 45° (Figure 7-11a). Obviously, any measurable angle can be arrived at by moving that first 6-inch length up or down. The angles you might want, and the placements of the rule tip to get them, are:

At 14$\frac{13}{16}$ inches, for 30°
At 16$\frac{3}{8}$ inches, for 45°
At 17$\frac{3}{4}$ inches, for 60°
At 18$\frac{9}{16}$ inches, for 70°
At 20$\frac{1}{4}$ inches, for 90°

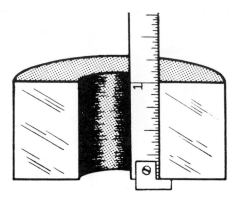

FIG. 7-9. Measuring the thickness of stock through a hole.

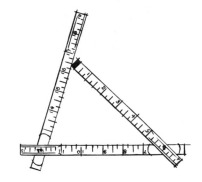

FIG. 7-10. Measuring and marking with a folding rule.

A

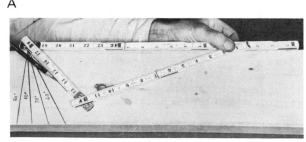

B

FIG. 7-11. Using a folding rule to find various angles.

This idea has been developed into a specially marked rule that points out the right spots for you. It does most of the arithmetic on a lot of other calculations that take time and brainwork. As the photo shows, it is useful in marking rafters and other intricate angled cuts.

Another useful trick with a folding rule consists first of boring a $\frac{1}{16}$-inch hole exactly centered on the 1-, 2-, 3-, and 4-inch lines. Then, if you butt the folded portion against a board edge and insert a sharp pencil in one of the holes, the rule becomes a scribing tool. Or, elaborating on this process, a hole at a more distant section, through which a pin can be anchored to a tabletop, converts the rule into a circle scriber. Exact radii can be arrived at in this fashion, and any circle or arc easily drawn.

CARE

Rules and tapes should be handled carefully and kept lightly oiled to prevent rust. Never strike the edges of measuring devices with hard objects, as they will be nicked. They should preferably be kept in a wooden box when not in use.

To avoid kinking tapes, pull them straight out from their cases; do not bend them backward. With the windup type, always turn the crank clockwise; turning it backward will kink or break the tape. With the spring-wind type, guide the tape by hand. If it is allowed to snap back, it may become kinked, twisted, or otherwise damaged. Do not use the hook as a stop. Slow down as you reach the end.

Calipers

Calipers are important shop measuring tools. They range from the simple spring calipers to more complicated vernier calipers and micrometers.

SPRING CALIPERS

Simple spring calipers are used in conjunction with a rule to measure diameters. The spring calipers most commonly used in the crafts shop are shown in Figure 7-12.

Outside calipers for measuring outside diameters are "bowlegged"; those used for inside diameters have straight legs with the feet turned outward. Calipers are adjusted by pulling or pushing the legs to open or close them. Fine adjustments are made by tapping one leg lightly on a hard surface to close them, or by turning them upside down and tapping on the joint end to open them.

Spring-joint calipers have the legs joined by a strong spring hinge and linked together by a screw and adjusting nut. For measuring chamfered cavities (grooves), or for use over flanges, transfer calipers are available. They are equipped with a small auxiliary leaf attached to one of the legs by a screw. The measurement is made as with ordinary calipers; then the leaf is locked to the leg. The legs may then be opened or closed as needed to clear the obstruction, then brought back and locked to the leaf again, to restore them to the original setting.

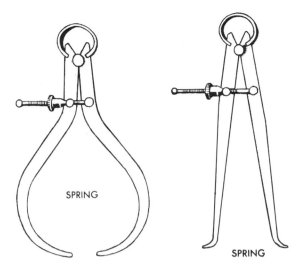

FIG. 7-12. Simple caliper, noncalibrated.

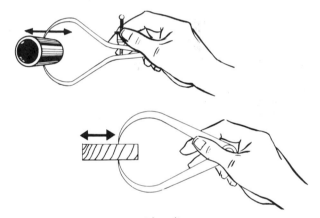

FIG. 7-13. Using an outside caliper.

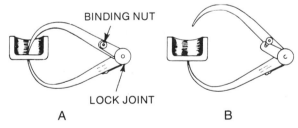

FIG. 7-14. Measuring the thickness of the bottom of a cup.

A different type of caliper is the hermaphrodite, sometimes called the "odd-leg" caliper. This caliper has one straight leg ending in a sharp point, sometimes removable, and one bow leg. The hermaphrodite caliper is used chiefly for locating the center of a shaft, or for locating a shoulder.

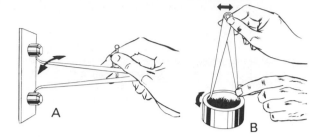

FIG. 7-15. Measuring the distance between two surfaces with an inside caliper.

A caliper is usually used in one of two ways. Either the caliper is set to the dimension of the work, and the dimension is transferred to a scale; or the caliper is set on a scale, and the work is machined until it checks with the dimension set up on the caliper. To adjust a caliper to a scale dimension, one leg of the caliper should be held firmly against one end of the scale; the other leg is adjusted to the desired dimension. To adjust a caliper to the work, open the legs wider than the work and then bring them down to the work.

To measure the diameter of round stock, or the thickness of flat stock, adjust the outside caliper so that you feel a slight drag as you pass it over the stock (Figure 7-13). After the proper "feel" has been obtained, measure the setting of the caliper with a rule. In reading the measurement, sight over the leg of the caliper after making sure the caliper is set squarely with the face of the rule.

To measure an almost inaccessible outside dimension, such as the thickness of the bottom of a cup, use an outside transfer firm-joint caliper as shown in Figure 7-14. When the proper "feel" is obtained, tighten the lock joint. Then loosen the binding nut, and open the caliper enough to remove it from the cup. Close the caliper again, and tighten the binding nut to seat in the slot at the end of the auxiliary arm. The caliper is now at the original setting, representing the thickness of the bottom of the cup. The caliper setting can now be measured with a rule.

To measure the distance between two surfaces with an inside caliper, first set the caliper to the approximate distance being measured. Hold the caliper with one leg in contact with one of the surfaces being measured (Figure 7-15a). Then, as you increase the setting of the caliper, move the other leg from left to right. Feel for the slight drag indicating the proper setting of the caliper. Then remove the caliper and measure the setting with a rule.

To measure the diameter of a hole with an inside caliper, hold the caliper with one leg in contact with one side of the hole (Figure 7-15b) and, as you increase the setting, move the other leg from left to right, and in and out of the hole. When you have found the point of largest diameter, remove the caliper and measure the caliper setting with a rule.

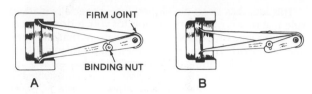

FIG. 7-16. Measuring a hard-to-reach inside dimension with an inside caliper.

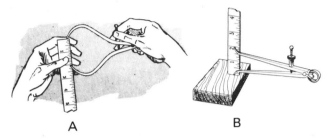

FIG. 7-17. (a) Setting an outside spring caliper. (b) Setting an inside spring caliper.

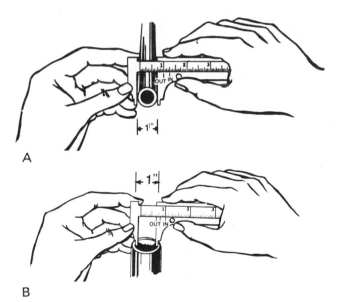

FIG. 7-18. (a) Measuring an outside dimension with a pocket slide caliper. (b) Measuring an inside dimension with a slide caliper.

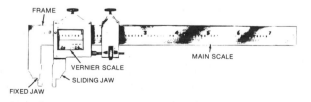

FIG. 7-19. Typical vernier caliper.

To measure a hard-to-reach inside dimension, such as the internal groove shown in Figure 7-16, a lock-joint inside caliper should be used. The procedure for measuring a hard-to-reach outside dimension is used.

To set a particular reading on an outside spring caliper, first open the caliper to the approximate setting. Then, as shown in Figure 7-17a, place one leg over the end of the rule, steadying it with index finger. Make the final setting by sighting over the other leg of the caliper, squarely with the face of the rule at the reading, and turning the knurled adjusting nut until the desired setting is obtained.

To set an inside spring caliper to a particular reading, place both caliper and rule on a flat surface, as shown in Figure 7-17b. The rule must be held squarely, or normal (90° in both directions) to the surface, to ensure accuracy. Adjust the knurled adjusting nut, reading the setting on the rule with line of sight normal to the face of the rule at the reading.

CARE OF CALIPERS

Keep calipers clean and lightly oiled; do not overoil the joint of firm-joint calipers, or you may have difficulty in keeping them tight. Do not throw them around or use them for screwdrivers or pry bars. Even a slight force may spring the legs of a caliper so that other measurements made with it are never accurate. Remember, they are measuring instruments and must be used only for the purpose for which they are intended.

SLIDE CALIPERS

The main disadvantage of ordinary calipers is that they do not give direct readings. As explained earlier, you must measure a caliper setting with a rule. To overcome this disadvantage, use a slide caliper. This instrument is occasionally called a "caliper rule."

Slide calipers can be used for measuring outside, inside, and other dimensions. One side of the caliper is used as a measuring rule, while the scale on the opposite side is used in measuring outside and inside dimensions. Graduations on both scales are in inches and fractions thereof. A locking screw is used to hold the slide-caliper jaws in position during use. Stamped on the frame are two words, "in" and "out." These are used in reading the scale while making inside and outside measurements, respectively.

To measure the outside diameter of round stock, or the thickness of flat stock, move the jaws of the caliper into firm contact with the surface of the stock. Read the measurement at the reference line stamped "out" (see Figure 7-18a).

To measure the inside diameter of a hole, or the distance between two surfaces, insert only the rounded tips of the caliper jaws into the hole or between the two surfaces (Figure 7-18b). Read the measurement on the reference line stamped "in." Note that two reference lines are needed if the caliper is to measure both outside and inside dimensions, and that they are separated by an

amount equal to the outside dimension of the rounded tips when the caliper is closed.

Pocket models of slide calipers are commonly made in 3- and 5-inch sizes and are graduated to read in thirty-seconds and sixty-fourths. Pocket slide calipers are valuable for checking squares and rounds, bits with markings that have become obscured, and stock thicknesses, and for confirming dado measurements.

VERNIER CALIPERS

The vernier, named after Pierre Vernier, its inventor in 1631, is in effect a combination of steel rules which permits exceedingly accurate readings. In the vernier caliper, one of the contact points is a fixed part of a graduated steel bar, while the other is a part of a graduated movable jaw mounted upon the blade of the first. Perhaps the most distinct advantage of the vernier caliper over other types of caliper is its ability to provide very accurate measurements over a large range. It can be used for both internal and external surfaces. Pocket models usually measure from zero to 3 inches, but sizes are available all the way to 4 feet. In using the vernier caliper, you must be able to measure with a slide caliper and be able to read a vernier scale. Full instructions are usually included with the tool and should be followed.

CARE OF THE VERNIER CALIPER

The inside faces of the jaws and the outside of the tips must be treated with great care. If they become worn, or the jaws bent, the tool will no longer give accurate readings. The accuracy of vernier calipers should be checked periodically by measuring an object of known dimension. Vernier calipers can be adjusted when they are not accurate, but the manufacturer's recommendations for this adjustment must be followed. Keep vernier calipers lightly oiled to prevent rust, and keep them stored away from heavy tools.

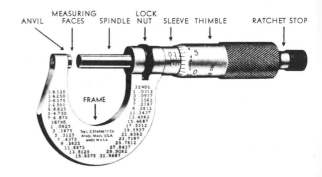

FIG. 7-20. Nomenclature for outside micrometer caliper.

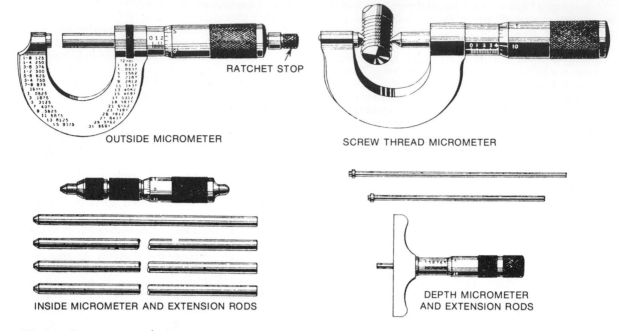

FIG. 7-21. Common types of micrometers.

MICROMETER CALIPERS

In much wider use than the vernier caliper is the micrometer, commonly called the "mike." It is important that a person who is working with machinery, or in a machine or metal shop, thoroughly understand the mechanical principles, construction, use, and care of the micrometer. Figure 7-20 shows an outside micrometer caliper with the various parts clearly indicated. Micrometers are used to measure distances to the nearest one-thousandth of an inch. The measurement is usually expressed or written as a decimal, so you must know the method of writing and reading decimals.

There are three types of micrometers that are most commonly used: the outside micrometer caliper (including the screw-thread micrometer), the inside micrometer, and the depth micrometer (Figure 7-21). The outside micrometer is used for measuring outside dimensions, such as the diameter of a piece of round stock. The screw-thread micrometer is used to determine the pitch diameters of screws. The inside micrometer is used for measuring inside dimensions, as, for example, the inside diameter of a tube or hole, the bore of a cylinder, or the width of a recess. The depth micrometer is used for measuring the depths of holes or recesses.

The types of micrometers commonly used are made so that the longest movement possible between the spindle and the anvil is 1 inch. This movement is called the "range." The frames of micrometers are, however, available in a wide variety of sizes, from 1 inch up to as large as 24 inches. The range of a 1-inch micrometer is

from 0 to 1 inch; in other words, it can be used on work where the part to be measured is 1 inch or less. A 2-inch micrometer has a range from 1 inch to 2 inches, and will measure only work between 1 and 2 inches thick; a 6-inch micrometer has a range from 5 to 6 inches and will measure only work between 5 and 6 inches thick. It is necessary, therefore, that the mechanic first find the approximate size of the work to the nearest inch, and then select a micrometer that will fit it. For example, to find the exact diameter of a piece of round stock, first use a rule to find the approximate diameter of the stock. If it is found to be approximately $3\frac{1}{4}$ inches, a micrometer with a 3- to 4-inch range would be required to measure the exact diameter. Similarly, with inside and depth micrometers, rods of suitable lengths must be fitted into the tool to get the approximate dimension within an inch, after which the exact measurement is read by turning the thimble. The size of a micrometer indicates the size of the largest work it will measure.

The sleeve and thimble scales of the micrometer caliper have been enlarged in Figure 7-22. To understand these scales, you need to know that the threaded section on the spindle, which revolves, has 40 threads per inch. Therefore, every time the thimble completes a revolution, the spindle advances or recedes $\frac{1}{40}$ inch (0.025 inch). Notice that the horizontal line on the sleeve is divided into 40 equal parts per inch. Every fourth graduation is numbered 1, 2, 3, 4, etc., representing 0.100 inch, 0.200 inch, etc. When you turn the thimble so that its edge is over the first sleeve line past the zero on the

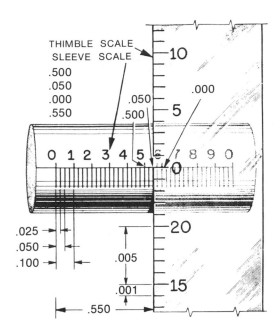

FIG. 7-22. Sleeve and thimble scales of a micrometer (enlarged).

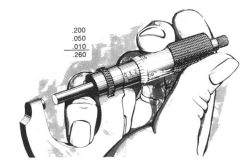

FIG. 7-23. How to read a micrometer caliper.

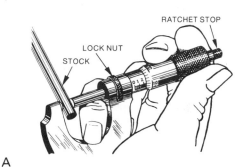

A

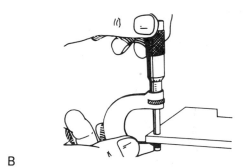

B

FIG. 7-24. (a) Measuring round stock with a micrometer caliper. (b) Measuring flat stock with a micrometer caliper.

thimble scale, the spindle has opened 0.025 inch. If you turn the spindle to the second mark, it has moved 0.025 inch plus 0.025 inch or 0.050 inch. You use the scale on the thimble to complete your reading when the edge of the thimble stops between graduated lines. This scale is divided into 25 equal parts, each part representing $\frac{1}{25}$ of a turn. And $\frac{1}{25}$ of 0.025 inch is 0.001 inch. As you can see, every fifth line on the thimble scale is marked 5, 10, 15, etc. The thimble scale therefore permits you to take very accurate readings to thousandths of an inch; and, since you can estimate between the divisions on the thimble scale, fairly accurate readings to the ten-thousandths of an inch are possible.

The closeup in Figure 7-23 will help you understand how to take a complete micrometer reading. Count the units on the thimble scale, and add them to the reading on the sleeve scale. The figure shows a sleeve reading of 0.250 inch (the thimble having stopped slightly more than halfway between 2 and 3 on the sleeve), with the tenth line on the thimble scale coinciding with the horizontal sleeve line. Number 10 on this scale means that the spindle has moved away from the anvil an additional 10 X 0.001 or 0.010 inch. Add this amount to the 0.250-inch sleeve reading, and the total distance is 0.260 inch.

CARE OF MICROMETERS

Keep micrometers clean and lightly oiled. Make sure they are placed in a case or box when they are not in use. Anvil faces must be protected from damage and must not be cleaned with emery cloth or other abrasive.

Squares

Squares are used primarily for testing and checking the trueness of an angle or for laying out lines on materials. Most squares have a rule marked on their edge. As a result, they may also be used for measuring. There are several types of squares commonly used in any workshop.

FRAMING OR CARPENTER'S STEEL SQUARE

The framing or carpenter's steel square (sometimes called a "rafter" square) consists of a wide, long member called the "blade" and a shorter member, called the "tongue," which forms a right angle with the blade. The outer corner, where the blade and tongue meet, is called

A

B

FIG. 7-25. (a) Carpenter's framing steel square in use. (b) Part of the square's blade.

the "heel." The "face" of the square is the side one sees when the square is held with the blade in the left hand and the tongue in the right hand, with the heel pointed away from the body. The manufacturer's name is usually stamped on the face. The blade is usually 24 inches long and 2 inches wide, and the tongue varies from 14 to 18 inches long and is 1½ inches wide, as measured from the heel.

The outer and inner edges of the tongue and the blade, on both face and back, are graduated in inches. The first thing you must do is memorize the manner in which the inch is subdivided in the scales on the back of the square. In the scales on the face, the inch is subdivided into the usual fractions (eighths or sixteenths of an inch). On the back of the square, however, the outer edge of the blade and outer edge of the tongue are graduated in inches and twelfths of inches; the inner edge of the tongue is graduated in inches and tenths of inches; and the inner edge of the blade is graduated in inches and thirty-seconds of inches on most squares.

The framing square is used most frequently to find the length of the hypotenuse (longest side) of a right triangle when the lengths of the other two sides are known. This is the basic problem involved in, for example, determining the length of a roof rafter, a brace, or any other member which forms the hypotenuse of an actual or imaginary right triangle.

Figure 7-26 shows you how the framing square is used to determine the length of the hypotenuse of a right triangle when the other sides are each 12 inches long. Plane a true, straight edge on a board, and set the square on the board so as to bring the 12-inch mark on the tongue and the 12-inch mark on the blade even with the edge of the board. Draw the pencil marks shown in the second view. The distance between these marks, as measured along the edge of the board, is the length of the hypotenuse of a right triangle with other sides each 12 inches long. You will find that the distance, which is called the "bridge measure," is just a shade under 17 inches. To

be exact, it is 16.97 inches, as shown in the figure, but for most practical purposes 16.97 inches may be rounded off to 17 inches.

Actually, the problems that can be solved with this steel square are so varied that books have been written on the square alone. Thus, the craftsman who desires to take full advantage of the square's capacities for solving a whole host of construction problems should obtain and study one of the books on the square. Figure 7-27, however, illustrates one of the most common uses of the framing square—laying out risers and stringers.

TRY SQUARES

The try square (Figure 7-28) consists of two parts at right angles to each other: a thick wood or metal handle and a thin steel blade. Most try squares are made with the blades graduated in inches and fractions of an inch. The blade length varies from 3 to 12 inches. This square is used

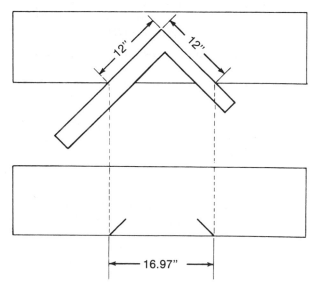

FIG. 7-26. A basic problem solved with a framing square.

for testing the squareness of ends and edges of stock; held upside down on a flat surface, it may be used to check for warp; held against the inside corner of a workpiece, it may be used to check a right angle. It can also be used to measure sections (not exceeding the length of the blade) and to scribe across the face of the work.

A try-miter square is similar to the conventional try square except that it has a cross beam that permits its use as a quick mitering guide, in either the right- or left-hand position, in addition to its squaring function.

COMBINATION SQUARES

There are two basic types of combination squares: the carpenter's combination square and the engineer's or machinist's combination square.

CARPENTER'S COMBINATION SQUARE The carpenter's combination square (Figure 7-29) looks a lot like a try square, but it can perform more tasks. The square head may be adjusted to any position along the 12-inch blade and clamped securely in place. Since the blade is graduated in inches and fractions of inches, the combination square can thus serve as a depth gauge, height gauge, or marking gauge. Two of the faces of the head are ground at right angles to each other, and a third face at 45°. This means that the combination square can be used as an inside and outside try square, as well as a miter square. A small spirit level is built into the head for checking whether surfaces are plumb, and a small scriber is housed in a hole in the end of the head for marking layout lines. Of course, without the square head, the square can be used as a straightedge.

Some carpenter's combination squares have a center head that can be slid onto the blade in place of the square head. This is a V-shaped member so designed that the center of the 90° V lies exactly along one edge of the blade. This attachment is useful when locating the exact center of round stock.

ENGINEER'S COMBINATION SQUARE An engineer's combination square (Figure 7-31) is equipped with movable heads called the square head, protractor head, and center head. These combine the functions of several

tools and serve a variety of purposes. Normally, only one head is used at a time.

The square head may be adjusted to any position along the scale and clamped securely in place. The combination square can thus serve as a depth gauge, height gauge, or scribing gauge. Two of the faces of the head are ground at right angles to each other, and the third face at 45°. A small spirit level is built into the head for checking

FIG. 7-28. Try square in use.

FIG. 7-29. The carpenter's combination square has a so-called "square head" with 90 and 45° angles, which slides along the blade. This square head contains a bubble level and a metal scriber.

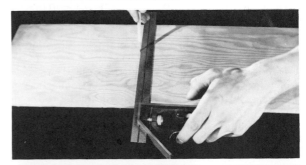

FIG. 7-30. Two of the main functions of a carpenter's combination square: (top) squaring a line on stock; (bottom) laying out a 45° angle.

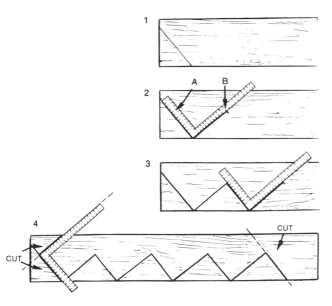

FIG. 7-27. Steps in laying out risers and stringers: (1) Mark the tread size on the width of the board, the riser on one side. Connect the points to form a triangle. (2) Lay the framing square on the line; mark the riser height at *A*, the tread width at *B*. (3) Place the square with the point at the edge of the stringer, and the riser width meeting *B*. Draw the lines, and repeat to the end of the board. (4) The dotted lines indicate the cutoff points for the top and bottom of the stringer.

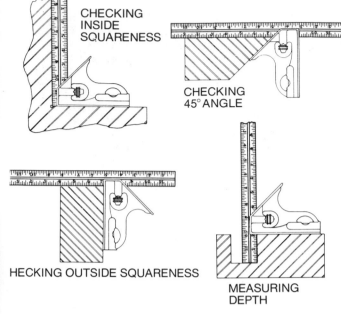

FIG. 7-31. Some of the many uses of an engineer's combination square.

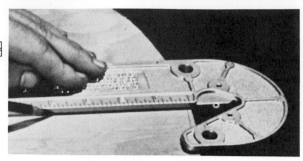

FIG. 7-32. Typical center square in use.

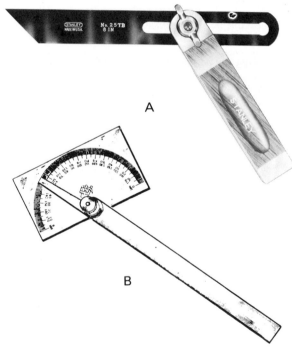

FIG. 7-33. (a) Sliding T bevel; (b) shop protractor.

whether surfaces are plumb, and a small scriber is housed in a hole in the end of the head for marking layout lines.

The center head can be slid onto the blade in place of the square head. This is a V-shaped member so designed that the center of the 90° V lies exactly along one edge of the blade. This attachment is useful when locating the exact center of round stock.

The protractor head, commonly called a "bevel protractor," can be attached to the scale, adjusted to any position on it, and turned and locked at any desired angle. Angular graduations usually read from 0 to 180° both ways, permitting the supplement of the angle to be read. A spirit level may be included on some models, forming, in effect, an adjustable level that works at any required angle.

CENTER SQUARE

The center square (Figure 7-32) can be used to locate the center of a circular workpiece as large as a patio tabletop or as small as a chair leg or dowel. It can be used as a square to draw an exactly straight guideline for a saw. Or it can be used as a protractor to mark off any desired angle at any point on a workpiece.

There are other types of squares available to the craftsman. For instance, the T square is excellent for drafting, layout work, and general-purpose use. They range in size from 12 to 48 inches in length. The large size is generally used for dry-wall material marking and cutting.

CARE OF SQUARES

Make certain the blades, heads, dials, and all accessories are clean. Apply a light coat of oil to all metal surfaces to prevent rusting when not in use. Do not use squares for purposes other than those intended. When storing a square or bevel for a long period of time, apply a liberal amount of oil or rust-preventive compound to all its surfaces, wrap it in oiled paper or cloth, and place it in a container or on a rack, away from other tools.

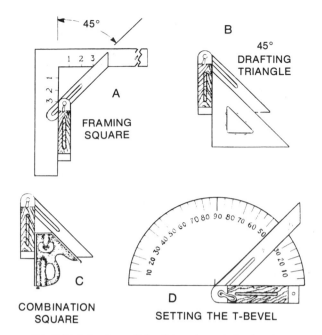

FIG. 7-34. Adjusting a sliding T bevel to a desired setting.

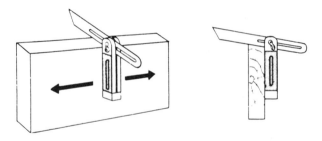

FIG. 7-35. Testing the trueness of a bevel.

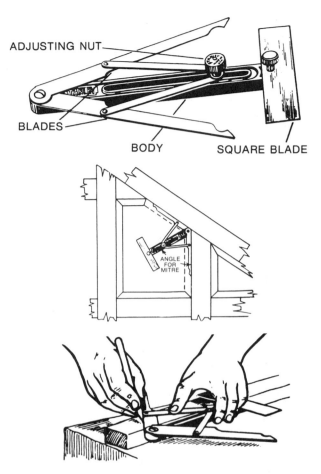

FIG. 7-36. A typical angle divider and how to measure a miter with it.

SLIDING T BEVEL

The sliding T bevel (Figure 7-33) is an adjustable try square with a slotted, beveled blade. The blade is normally 6 or 8 inches long. The sliding T bevel is used for laying out angles other than right angles, and for testing constructed angles such as bevels. It is made with either a wood or metal handle.

To adjust a sliding T bevel to a desired setting, loosen the blade screw, at the round end of the handle, just enough to permit the blade to slide along its slot and to rotate with little friction.

To set the blade at a 45° angle, hold the handle against a framing square, as shown in Figure 7-34a, with the blade intersecting equal graduations on the tongue and blade of the square. Or, hold the bevel against the edges of a 45° drafting triangle, as shown in Figure 7-34b. When using a drafting triangle for setting a sliding T bevel, a different size of triangle must be used for each different setting. A 45° angle can also be set by using the squaring head of a

combination set, as shown in Figure 7-34c.

A sliding T bevel can be set to any desired angle with a protractor. Loosen the blade screw as before. Hold the bevel with its blade passing through the graduation selected, and the center of the protractor as shown at D in Figure 7-34.

To test a chamfer or bevel for trueness, set the T bevel to the required angle, and hold the handle to the working face of the stock being tested. Face a source of light, and with the blade brought into contact with the surface to be tested, pass the blade along the length of the surface. The appearance of light between the blade and the surface of the stock indicates where the angle is not correct. Figure 7-35 indicates the checking of a bevel; the trueness of a chamfer is tested in the same manner. A bevel or shop protractor (Figure 7-33b) will perform many of the same tasks as the sliding T bevel and is very handy for marking angles accurately.

The angle divider shown in Figure 7-36 is a double-bevel tool that functions in somewhat the same manner as a T bevel in marking off identical angles on several pieces of work. It is also used to take off and divide angles for the miter cut in one operation, or to find the center of two pieces of wood joined at an angle. The handle is graduated on the back for laying off 4-, 5-, 6-, 8-, and 10-sided work. Incidentally, the square blade may be used as a try square.

Gauges and Indicators

Gauges are measuring devices. They are special tools used because they are more convenient to handle or easier to read than the conventional rules or micrometers. Of course, there are many types of gauges. Some are standard and are used frequently in machine-shop or woodworking-shop projects. Others are special and are used only by the advanced craftsman and the professional. Let us take a look at some of the more common gauges and indicators.

MARKING GAUGES

Marking gauges are used to mark off guidelines parallel to an edge, end, or surface of a piece of wood or metal. They are made of metal or wood (Figure 7-37) and consist of a graduated beam about 8 inches long on which a head slides. The head can be fastened at any point on the beam by means of a thumbscrew. The thumbscrew presses a brass shoe tightly against the beam and locks it firmly in position. The steel pin or spur that does the marking projects from the beam about $1/16$ inch.

To draw a line parallel to an edge with a marking gauge, first determine the required distance of the line from the edge of the stock. Adjust the marking gauge by setting the head the desired distance from the spur. Although the bar of a marking gauge is graduated in inches, the spur may work loose or bend. If this occurs, accurate measurements should be made with a rule between the head and spur (Figure 7-38a). To draw a line after setting the gauge, grasp the head of the gauge with the palm and fingers as shown in Figure 7-38b; extend the thumb along the beam toward the spur. Press the head firmly against the edge of the work to be marked, and, with a wrist motion, tip the gauge forward until the spur touches the work. Push the gauge along the edge to mark the work, keeping the head firmly against the edge of the work.

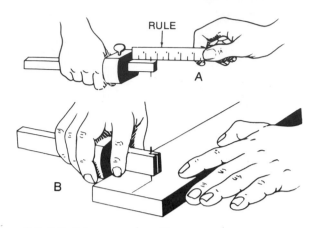

FIG. 7-38. Using a wood marking gauge.

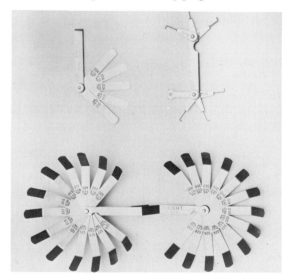

FIG. 7-39. Various types of thickness or feeler gauges.

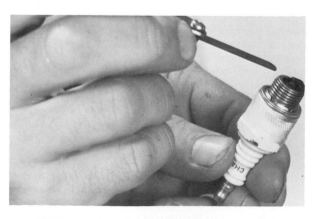

FIG. 7-40. Feeler gauge in use.

FIG. 7-37. Marking gauges: *(a)* steel; *(b)* wood.

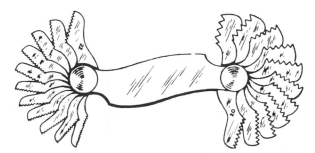

FIG. 7-41. Typical screw-pitch gauge.

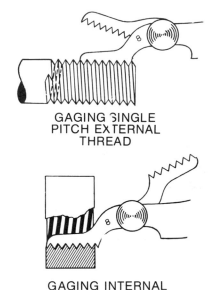

GAGING SINGLE
PITCH EXTERNAL
THREAD

GAGING INTERNAL
THREAD

FIG. 7-42. Using a screw-pitch gauge.

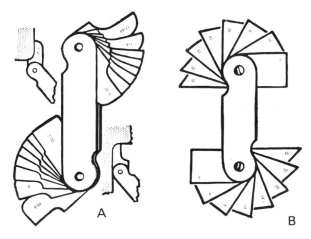

FIG. 7-43. (a) Radius gauge; (b) angle gauge.

THICKNESS (FEELER) GAUGES

Thickness (feeler) gauges are used for checking and measuring small openings such as contact-point clearances and narrow slots between spark plugs. These gauges are made in many shapes and sizes; as shown in Figure 7-39, thickness gauges can be made with multiple blades (usually 2 to 26). The thickness of each blade is a specific number of thousandths of an inch. This allows one tool to be used to measure a variety of thicknesses. Some thickness-gauge blades are straight, while others are bent at 45 and 90° angles at the ends. Thickness gauges can also be grouped so that there are several short and several long blades together. Before using a feeler gauge, remove any foreign matter from the blades. You cannot get a correct measurement unless the blades are clean.

When using a feeler gauge consisting of a number of blades, insert various blades or combinations of blades between the two surfaces until a snug fit is obtained. The thickness of the individual blade or the total thickness of *all the blades used* is the measurement between the surfaces. The secret of checking "gaps" and clearances accurately with a feeler gauge is your ability to "feel" the tension on the blade when you move it back and forth in the space that is being measured. The best way to develop this feel is to practice measuring clearances of known dimensions.

CARE OF THICKNESS GAUGES Handle the blades with care at all times. Keep from forcing the blades into openings that are too small for them. Some blades are very thin and can be bent or kinked easily. Blade edges and polished surfaces are also easy to damage. When a thickness gauge is not in use, keep it closed.

THREAD GAUGES

Thread gauges (screw-pitch gauges) are used to determine the pitch and number of threads per inch of threaded fasteners (Figure 7-41). They consist of thin leaves whose edges are toothed to correspond to standard thread sections.

To measure the unknown pitch of a thread, compare it with the standards of the screw-pitch gauge. Hold a gauge leaf to the thread being measured (Figure 7-42), substituting various sizes until you find an exact fit. Look at the fit toward a source of light for best results.

The number of threads per inch is indicated by the numerical value on the blade which fits the unknown threads. Using this value as a basis, you can select the correct sizes of nuts, bolts, taps, and dies, for use.

ANGLE AND RADIUS GAUGES

Angle gauges and radius gauges also have blades, but here it is the blade outline that is important. Angle-gauge blades all have the same thickness, but each blade has a different end angle. They are substitutes for the bevel protractor and are indispensable for measuring angles in restricted areas where you could not possibly use the protractor.

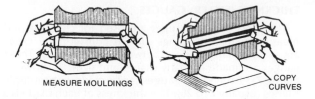

FIG. 7-44. A contour pattern gauge permits the lifting of complicated shapes so that they may be copied. The adjustable wires of the gauge conform to any shape they are pressed against.

A radius gauge (or "fillet gauge," as it is sometimes called) has two sets of blades. The rounded corner of each blade is the arc of a circle. The radius of that arc is stamped on the blade. As shown in Figure 7-43a, the blades can be used to check outside radii as well as inside radii.

CONTOUR PATTERN GAUGES

The contour pattern gauge (Figure 7-44) is used for measuring and marking off irregular and unusual shapes. Its thin adjustable wires can be fit to any such surface to pick up its exact conformation. Then, after the gauge has been set to match the irregular surface, it is laid on the new work, and the pattern is traced with a pencil.

DEPTH GAUGES

A depth gauge is an instrument for measuring the depths of holes, slots, counterbores, and recesses, and the distance from a surface to some recessed part. The rule depth gauge, the micrometer depth gauge and vernier depth gauge are the most commonly used. Details on their operation are usually found in the instruction booklet that comes with these tools.

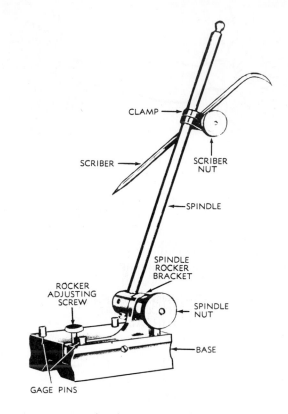

FIG. 7-46. Typical surface gauge.

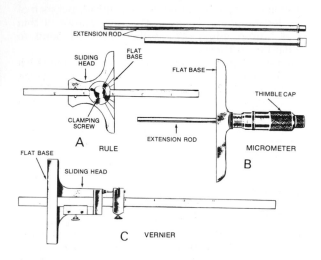

FIG. 7-45. Types of depth gauges: *(a)* rule; *(b)* micrometer; *(c)* vernier.

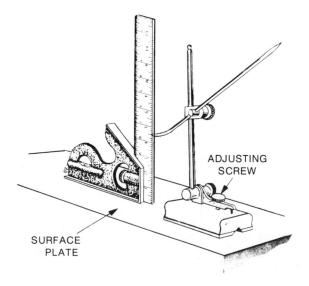

FIG. 7-47. Setting a surface gauge.

SURFACE GAUGES

A surface gauge is a measuring tool generally used to transfer measurements to work by scribing a line, and to indicate the accuracy or parallelism of surfaces. It consists of a base with an adjustable spindle to which may be clamped a scriber or an indicator. Surface gauges are made in several sizes and are classified by the length of the spindle, the smallest spindle being 4 inches long, the average 9 or 12 inches long, and the largest 18 inches long. The scriber is fastened to the spindle with a clamp. The bottom and the front end of the base of the surface gauge have deep V grooves cut in them to allow the gauge to be seated on a cylindrical surface.

The spindle of a surface gauge may be adjusted to any position with respect to the base and tightened in place with the spindle nut. The rocker adjusting screw provides for finer adjustment of the spindle by pivoting the spindle rocker bracket. The scriber can be positioned at any height and in any desired direction on the spindle by tightening the scriber nut. The scriber may also be mounted directly in the spindle and nut mounting, in place of the spindle, and used where the working space is limited and the height of the work is within range of the scriber.

To set a surface gauge for height, first wipe off the top of a layout table or surface plate and the bottom of the surface gauge. Use either a combination square or a rule with rule holder to get the measurement. A rule alone cannot be held securely without wobbling, and consequently an error in setting generally results. Because a combination square is generally available, its use for setting a surface gauge is explained in this section.

Place the squaring head of a combination square on a flat surface, as shown in Figure 7-47, and secure the scale so that the end is in contact with the surface. Move the surface gauge into position, and set the scriber to the approximate height required, using the adjusting clamp that holds the scriber onto the spindle. Make the final adjustment for the exact height required (4½ inches in this case) with the adjusting screw on the base of the gauge.

SURFACE PLATE

A surface plate provides a true, smooth, plane surface. It is a flat-topped steel or cast-iron plate that is heavily ribbed and reinforced on the underside. It is often used in conjunction with a surface gauge, as a level base on which the gauge and work are placed to obtain accurate measurements. The surface plate can also be used for testing parts that must have flat surfaces.

To test a surface for flatness, carefully clean it and remove all burrs. Then place the surface on a flat area such as the surface plate in Figure 7-48. Any rocking motion indicates a variance from flatness.

For very fine work, lightly coat the surface plate with Prussian blue (bearing blue), and move the piece being tested across the blue surface (Figure 7-49). The low spots

FIG. 7-48. Testing a surface for flatness.

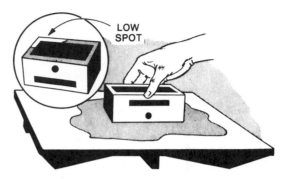

FIG. 7-49. Using Prussian blue to aid in testing a flat surface.

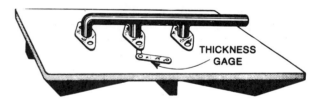

FIG. 7-50. Checking the conformity of a flat surface.

on the surface being tested will not take the blue; the high spots will. See the insert in Figure 7-49.

To determine how much variation there is from flatness—and where it is—you can insert leaves of a thickness gauge to determine the amount of variation of flatness. Remember to add the thicknesses of all leaves together to get the total variation (Figure 7-50).

A surface also may be tested for flatness with a straightedge. To do this, clean the surface thoroughly, and hold the straightedge on the surface in several places as you look toward a source of light. Light showing between the surface and the straightedge indicates variance from flatness.

WIRE AND SHEET GAUGES

The wire gauge shown in Figure 7-51 is used for measuring the diameters of wires or thicknesses of sheet metal. This gauge is circular in shape, with cutouts in the outer perimeter. Each cutout gauges a different size, from No. 0 to No. 36. Examination of the gauge will show that the larger the gauge number, the smaller the diameter or thickness.

Gauges similar to the one shown in Figure 7-51 are available for measuring a variety of wire and sheet-metal thicknesses. There are several standards for wire gauges, such as the United States Standard, American (Brown & Sharpe), Washburn & Moen, and Birmingham. Before using any of these gauges, be sure to remove the burrs from the wire or sheet metal that you are measuring.

To measure wire size, apply the gauge to the wire as shown in Figure 7-51. Do not force the wire into the slot. Find a slot that refuses to pass the wire without forcing. Then, try the next larger slot, until one is found that passes the wire. This is the correct size. (Remember, your measurements are taken at the slot portion of the cutout rather than the inner portion of the gauge.) Now that you have the gauge number, turn your gauge over and read the decimal equivalent of that number.

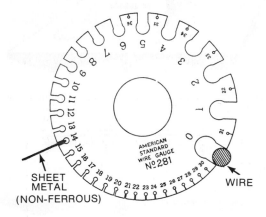

FIG. 7-51. Using a wire gauge to measure wire and sheet metal.

To measure the gauge of a piece of metal, first remove any burrs from the place where you intend to apply the gauge. Then select the appropriate gauge for the metal to be measured. After the gauge has been selected, apply the gauge to the edge of the sheet, as shown in Figure 7-51. The number opposite the slot that fits the wire or sheet is its gauge number. The decimal equivalent is stamped on the opposite face of the gauge.

The drill and wire gauge (see Chapter 4) is used to verify the exact size of a drill bit. This is handy when the marked size of the bit has been worn away or the drill bit is unmarked. Another similar gauge, mentioned in Chapter 4, is the screw gauge, which is used to check the thickness or gauge of a screw.

DIVIDERS

Dividers have many uses. They are absolutely necessary for scribing a line when matching a workpiece (perhaps a wall panel) to an irregular edge such as brick or stone

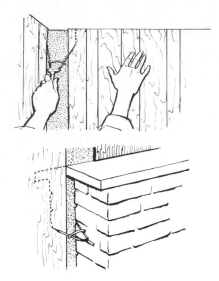

FIG. 7-52. Dividers may be used to scribe a line to match an irregular surface, masonry, or woodwork.

masonry. Dividers can also be used to step off a measurement several times accurately, as well as for scribing circles and arcs.

To lay out a circle with dividers, set the dividers at the desired radius, using a rule as shown in Figure 7-53a. Note that the 3-inch radius being set here is being taken at a central portion of the rule, rather than at the end. This reduces the chance of error, as each point of the dividers can be set on a graduation. Place one leg of the dividers at the center of the proposed circle, lean the tool in the direction it will be rotated, and rotate it by rolling the knurled handle between your thumb and index finger (Figure 7-53b).

Trammel points (Figure 7-55) are used to lay out the distance between two points and to scribe circles beyond the capacity of dividers. Some trammel points are made to slide over a metal or wooden beam, while others are in the form of C clamps and fasten to one side of a straight board. Some trammel points are even designed with a special socket for a carpenter's pencil, for marking.

PLUMB BOB

A plumb bob is a pointed, tapered brass or bronze weight which is suspended from a cord for determining the vertical or plumb line to or from a point on the ground. Common weights for plumb bobs are 6, 8, 10, 12, 14, 16, 18, and 24 ounces.

A plumb bob is a precision instrument and must be cared for as such. If the tip becomes bent, the cord from which the bob is suspended will not show the true plumb line over the point indicated by the tip. Many plumb bobs have a detachable tip, so that if the tip should become damaged it can be renewed without replacing the entire instrument.

The plumb bob is used in carpentry to determine true verticality for erecting the vertical uprights and corner posts of framework. Surveyors use it for transferring and lining up points. To locate a point which is exactly below a particular point in space, secure the plumb-bob string to the upper point, such as A in Figure 7-57. When the bob stops swinging, the point indicated at B in the illustration will be exactly below A.

To plumb a structural member or an electrical conduit, as shown in Figure 7-58, secure the plumb line A so that you can look at both the line and the piece behind the line. Then, by sighting, line up the member or conduit with the plumb line. If this cannot be done, it may be necessary to secure the plumb line at some point such as B, and then measure the offset from the line to the piece at two places so that, for example, C and D in Figure 7-58 are equal. If the distances between C and D are not equal, adjust the structural member or conduit until they are.

CHALK LINE

Long straight lines between distant points are marked by snapping a chalk line as shown in Figure 7-59a. The line is first chalked by holding the chalk in the hand and

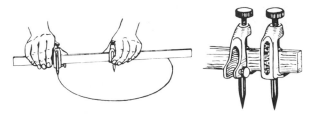

FIG. 7-55. Typical set of trammel points.

FIG. 7-56. Popular weights and sizes of plumb bobs: (left to right) 12, 8, 5 ounces.

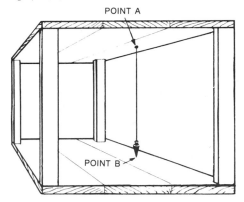

FIG. 7-57. Locating a point with a plumb bob.

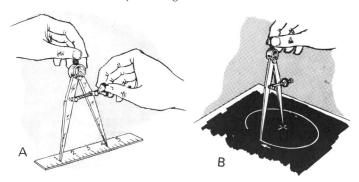

FIG. 7-53. (a) Setting dividers to a desired radius; (b) scribing a circle with dividers.

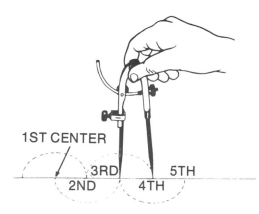

FIG. 7-54. Dividers are used to step off a measurement accurately several times.

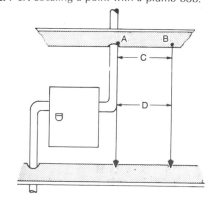

FIG. 7-58. Plumbing a structural member with a plumb bob.

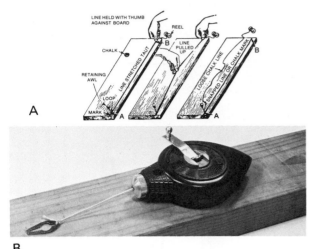

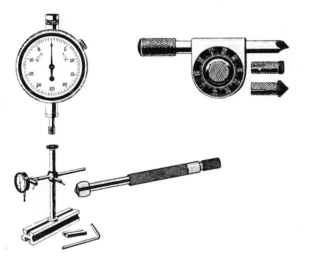

FIG. 7-59. (a) How to snap a simple chalk line; (b) chalk line tool.

FIG. 7-60. Typical speed indicators.

drawing the line across it several times. The line is then stretched between the points and snapped as shown. For an accurate line, never snap the chalk line for a distance greater than 20 feet.

SPEED INDICATOR

When you need to know the number of revolutions per minute (rpm) of an electric motor, a line shaft, or other revolving part, you can easily secure the information with a speed indicator. It is also known as a "revolution counter." This tool has a set of interchangeable rubber tips that fit on the spindle. Cone-shaped, flat-end, and vacuum tips are usually supplied with the indicator. The cuplike vacuum tip works best on the flat end of a shaft; the cone tip is best if the shaft has a countersunk end.

When you use one of these indicators, the time element must be considered. You can use a wristwatch that has a second hand for timing, but you will get better results with a stopwatch. A "tachometer" is a type of revolution counter that constantly indicates the revolutions per minute of an engine or motor. It resembles an automobile speedometer. Some tachometers record the engine speed on a time chart.

There are other gauges that some craftsmen find especially valuable. For instance, if you plan to hang several doors, a butt gauge would be very helpful. This gauge assists in laying out all the necessary dimensions for hanging a door with butt hinges.

GENERAL CARE OF GAUGES AND INDICATORS

All precision tools and instruments must be handled with the greatest care, and should be cased in their own boxes or containers when they are not in use. Precision tools will not retain their accuracy if allowed to become rusty, bent, or dented. That is why you must keep precision equipment coated with a thin film of clean oil to prevent rust, and adequately cased to prevent damage. Never use emery cloth, sandpaper, steel wool, or any other abrasive to clean the moving parts of a precision tool or instrument. Those moving parts are machined and ground to exceptionally close tolerances. If you wear away some of the metal, you ruin the fit of the parts and impair the accuracy.

Levels

Levels are tools designed to determine whether a plane or surface is truly horizontal or vertical. Some precision spirit levels are calibrated so that they will indicate, in degrees, minutes, and seconds, the angle of inclination of a surface in relation to the horizontal or vertical. They are made in a variety of materials—aluminum, steel, plastic, hardwood, and softwood. Aluminum levels are lightweight, rustproof, and warpproof; they are preferred for general construction use. Wood levels, carefully used, will not scratch fine woodwork.

There are four basic types of levels of interest to the average craftsman: line level, carpenter's level, torpedo level, and pocket level.

LINE LEVEL

The line level (Figure 7-61a) consists of a bubble tube set into a metal case with a hook at each end, to permit it to be hung on a line or cord. The line level is used to test whether or not a line or cord is level. It is particularly useful when the distance between two points to be checked for level is too long to permit the use of a mason's or carpenter's level. However, the line level has a disadvantage in that at long distances the line has a tendency to sag. To use the level, stretch a cord between the two points which are to be checked for level. Hang the line level on the cord, and see whether the bubble is in the middle of the tube. If it is not, raise the end of the

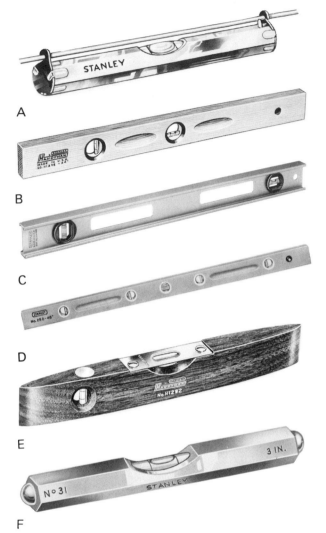

A

B

C

D

E

F

FIG. 7-61. Various types of levels: (a) line level; (b) carpenter's level (wood); (c) carpenter's level (metal); (d) mason's level; (e) torpedo level; (f) pocket level.

cord which is toward the lower end of the bubble, until the bubble rests in the middle of the tube. Unhook the level, turn it end for end, hang it on the cord, and retest. Continue testing until the bubble rests in the same relative position in its tube when the level is turned end for end. Remember, to make the bubble rise in the tube, lift that end of the cord which is toward the lower end of the bubble.

The line level is a delicate instrument; therefore, it must be kept in a box when not in use, to protect the bubble tube from being broken and the hooks from being bent. Never clean the level with water or any liquid, because condensation will appear.

CARPENTER'S LEVEL

The carpenter's level is usually either a 24-inch wood block (Figure 7-61b) or of metal I-beam construction (Figure 7-61c) with true surface edges. While this type of level may have two or more vials, there are two important bubble tubes in it. One is in the middle of one of the long edges. The other is at right angles to this, and parallel to the end of the level. The bubble tubes are glass vials nearly filled with alcohol. They are slightly curved. As a bubble of air in such a tube will rise to the highest point, the bubble will be in the middle of the tube only when the tube is in a horizontal position. Scratch marks at equal distances from the middle of the tube mark the proper position of the bubble when the surface on which the tube rests is level. Incidentally, some I-beam levels feature a magnetic strip that holds the level fast to metal surfaces, leaving the user's hands free for work.

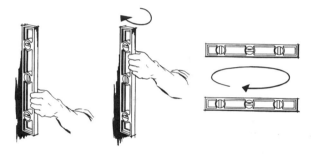

FIG. 7-62. You can check a level by placing it firmly against a surface and carefully noting the location of the bubble. Then turn the level (end for end when checking the horizontal indicator; edge for edge keeping the same vial upright when checking the vertical), and place it in exactly the same position. Any discrepancy between the two readings indicates a misalignment of the vial, nicks on the straightedge surface of the level, warpage, or some other problem that may be corrected or taken into consideration when using the level.

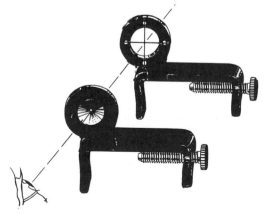

FIG. 7-63. Level sights fit on a carpenter's level and are used in conjunction with it for sighting and aligning grades, walls, fences, and the like.

The carpenter's level is used to determine whether a surface is level. "Level" usually describes a horizontal surface which, throughout its extent, lies on a line corresponding to that of the horizon. "Plumb" means vertical, or at right angles to "level."

To test for the levelness of a surface, lay the carpenter's level on the surface and see where the bubble comes to rest. If the surfaces are level and the level is in adjustment, the bubble will come to rest exactly between the two scratch marks mentioned above. Turn the level end for end, and recheck. The bubble should come to rest in the same place. If it does not, raise the end of the surface being tested which is toward the low end of the bubble, until it checks level.

To check for plumb, set the long side of the carpenter's level against the upright to be tested, and use the bubble which is set in the end in the same way as described above. Turn the level end for end to ensure accuracy, as mentioned above.

Mason's levels are very similar in design to carpenter's levels, except that they are longer—usually 48 to 80 inches long—and usually have more bubble vials. Mason's levels are available in either wood or metal I-beam construction. The better I-beam levels are made of magnesium.

TORPEDO LEVEL

Smaller than the carpenter's level, the torpedo level (Figure 7-61e) is nevertheless a useful addition to a tool chest. It has two advantages over the larger models: first, a bevel bubble for checking 45° angles, and second, a grooved base for unassisted positioning on shafts, pipes, and similar rounds. The hole at one end is simply for hanging the tool for storage.

POCKET LEVEL

For small spaces as well as handy pocket carrying, this level (Figure 7-61f) is of enormous value. It is limited to horizontal use only but is very convenient in tight spots.

Another handy pocket device is the magnetic three-way plumb and level shown in Figure 7-67a. It attaches to straightedge or straight board of any length and is designed for use as a temporary or extra long level. It is especially desirable for use by masons and cement workers. Still another handy pocket tool is shown in Figure 7-67b. This device combines features of such tools as a level, a square, a protractor, a rise-and-fall gauge, and a handy rule. It has two magnetic plumbs and one magnetic edge for reading at various angles. The reverse side has a pitch gauge showing rise and fall in inches per foot, such as is sometimes required for steam and radiator pipes, drainpipes, etc.

Levels must be checked for accuracy. This is readily accomplished by placing the level on a true horizontal surface and noting the vial indication. Reverse the level end for end. If the bubble appears on one side of the graduations on the first reading and on the other side for the second reading, the level is out of true and must be

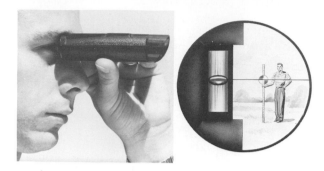

FIG. 7-64. The sighting level works on the same principle as precise surveying instruments. It enables the user to establish a true level line of sight in relation to a definite object. From this line of level sight, measurements may be obtained to determine proper levels, grades, or slopes.

FIG. 7-65. Over considerable distances (as when laying out foundations, grading, excavating, landscaping, laying out walks and drives, or determining level points on opposite walls), a liquid-filled hose with glass or plastic tube inserts becomes a long-distance level. The level of water at each end indicates the true horizontal plane.

FIG. 7-66. A position level attached to either a hand or power tool allows the user to guide the tool in a determined direction without using a jig. The level is a small plastic liquid-filled partial sphere, with a flange at 45° that clips to the tool; it is etched with circles spaced at 22½°, permitting accurate work at almost any angle.

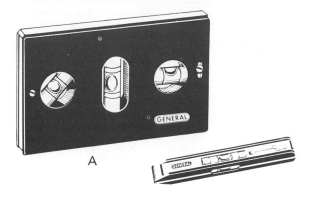

FIG. 7-67. Two handy leveling devices.

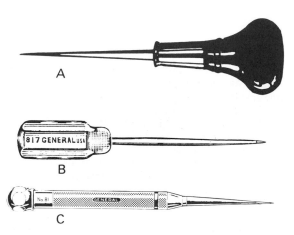

FIG. 7-68. (a) Typical awl; (b) scratch awl; (c) scriber.

adjusted.

Do not drop a level or handle it roughly. To prevent damage, store it in a rack or other suitable place when it is not in use.

Marking Devices

There are many shop tools that can be used for marking work. While pencil, pen, crayon, and chalk are the most common "tools" for such purposes, there are also specialized marking tools. The marking gauge, chalk line, contour pattern gauge, and dividers were described earlier in this chapter. Also, the punches detailed in Chapter 1 could be considered marking tools. The most popular marking tools in most shops, however, are the awl, and scriber.

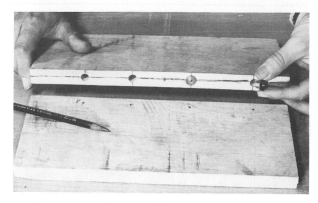

FIG. 7-69. Typical dowel centering points in use.

The awl, or scratch awl as it is often called, is a sharp-pointed piece of steel, like an ice pick, which is used to score metal or wood. It is true that lines for cuts may be drawn on stock with a sharp pencil, tilted to bring the point close to the straightedge. However, the line will be more accurately located if you scribe the stock with a scratch awl like the one shown in Figure 7-68a and b. A utility knife or trimming knife (Chapter 2) is also often used to mark the surfaces of wood and similar materials.

The awl is also used for making pilot holes for screws and nails. It is particularly useful in making pilot holes for brads, or small nails, when an exact position is required. In many ways, the awl serves the same function as a small drill bit, but the hole it makes becomes larger in diameter as the point is forced further into the wood.

The scriber (Figure 7-68c) is used for marking lines on metal, especially when you are measuring with a rule. Centers can be located by using it to draw two intersecting lines and then using a prick punch (see Chapter 1). A bent end is convenient for marking the insides of cylindrical objects or partially closed recesses. Keep the scriber sharp, and use it like a pencil, with only enough pressure to make a clear mark.

There are some special marking devices, too. Among the more commonly used are dowel centers, which are employed to locate the centers of holes to be drilled for blind dowel joints. After drilling the holes for the dowels in one piece of wood, you insert dowel centers in these holes. Then you align the two pieces of wood as they will be joined. When you press them together, the points on the dowel centers mark the second piece of wood. Now it is possible to drill holes at these center marks; when the pieces are connected with dowels, the blind dowel joint is perfectly aligned. Dowel centers come in assorted sizes to fit holes from $\frac{1}{8}$ to 1 inch in diameter.

MISCELLANEOUS HAND TOOLS

There is a whole group of hand tools which are rather difficult to place in specific categories. They are valuable tools nevertheless and are described in this chapter.

Staplers, Tackers, and Nailers

Today, mechanical staplers and nailers perform a variety of operations formerly done by hand. They provide an efficient method of attaching insulation, roof material, building paper, screening, underlayment, weatherstripping, upholstery material, ceiling tile, and many other products.

Staplers are two-pointed fasteners made of wire. While staples over 1 inch in length are available, most manufacturers produce them for average use in five standard leg lengths of from ¼ to ⁹⁄₁₆ inch. Table 8-1 gives general recomendations for the use of standard staples. But your own judgment must dictate the proper choice in some instances. Which length you use depends principally on the thickness of the materials being stapled, and the number of staples used depends upon the weight of the material and the stress placed upon the tacking in use. Keep in mind, however, that most staplers will take staples produced only by the manufacturer of the tool. Staples made by other manufacturers will not fit. Thus it is important not only to select a good stapler, but also one that will take all the sizes and kinds of staples you wish to use.

Three of the basic types of stapling tools or tackers have applications in the average shop or around the home. They are: (1) the staple gun, (2) the hammer tacker, and (3) the plier stapler. The latter is used primarily for fastening thin sheets of material together. Both sides of the material must be accessible, since the tool bends the staple legs closed on the reverse side.

Of the two stapling tools that are exclusively used for nailing, the staple gun is the most commonly used. While specific light-, medium-, and heavy-duty staple guns are available, many of the newer ones have variable power drives. That is, by turning a knob or moving a lever, you can change the stapler from light duty for soft surfaces to heavy drive for hard ones, or vice versa. This makes the tool more versatile by permitting a wider range of materials to be fastened. In recent years, the electric staple gun has entered the picture. This push-button-operated tool makes it very easy to drive the longest of staples into a hard surface.

| 1/4" | 5/16" | 3/8" | 1/2" | 9/16" |

Table 8-1A. Actual Staple Sizes

Table 8-1 Staple Uses by Leg Length

¼-inch leg	⁵⁄₁₆-inch leg	⅜-inch leg	½-inch leg	⁹⁄₁₆-inch leg
Light upholstering, shelf trimming, screens, window shades, decorations, valances, etc.	Thin insulation, storm windows, draperies, upholstery, heavy fabrics	Weatherstripping, roofing papers, light insulation, electrical wires, wire mesh	Canvas, felt stripping, underlayments carpets, fiberglass	Ceiling tile,* fencing, insulation board, metal lathing, roofing

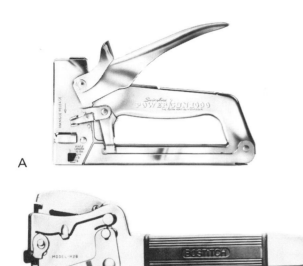

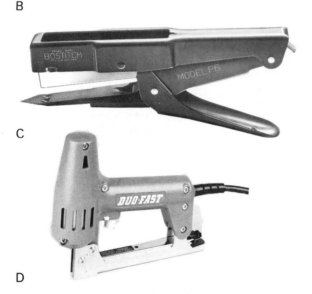

FIG. 8-1. The basic stapling tools: *(a)* staple gun; *(b)* hammer tacker; *(c)* plier stapler; *(d)* electric staple gun.

There are specialty staple guns that are used to fasten electric wires, cables, and copper tubing up to ½ inch in diameter. Still another staple gun shoots a flared staple which enters soft material and locks inside without penetrating through the material. Some staple-gun kits feature attachments to make them more versatile. For instance, there may be a window-shade attachment to fit round shapes, another to keep screening taut while stapling, and a centering device for making small-wire fastening easy. Most kits also contain a staple lifter for removing staples; in some guns this is a built-in-feature.

To load a typical staple gun, proceed as follows:

1. With the operating lever or handle locked, hold the gun in the normal firing position. Push the loading latches forward on both sides simultaneously, and pull out on the staple channel with the other hand.
2. Holding the staple gun upside down, pull back on the staple channel until the spring pulls the feeding bar completely back. Then put the staples in the staple pocket with the legs pointing up.
3. Lower the staple channel, pull back on the loading latches, push the channel securely into place, and release the latches, making sure the channel is secure.
4. When you are ready to use the gun, release the handle lock and allow the handle to open. Your staple gun is now ready to fire when you depress the handle. This procedure may vary slightly with different makes of guns.

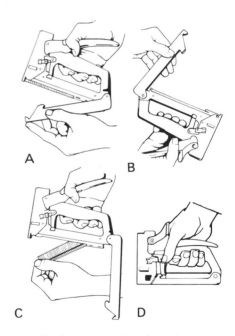

FIG. 8-2. The four steps of staple-tool operation: *(a)* open; *(b)* load; *(c)* close; and *(d)* fire.

To use the hammer tacker, swing it like a hammer; when it hits the surface, it automatically drives a staple. While you do not have accurate aim with a hammer tacker as you do with a staple gun, the jobs it is used for— tacking up building paper, vapor barriers, and insulation and attaching shingles, underlayment, etc.—do not require it. The hammer tacker is generally loaded in the same manner as the staple gun.

FIG. 8-3. Hammer tacker in use.

Nailers or nail guns look and basically operate in the same manner as staple guns, except that instead of staples they drive small brad-type nails, usually about $1\frac{1}{32}$ inches long (18 gauge). The nail gun operates on the lever principle, lifting an internal ram that is driven forward with great force by a ram spring. (The safety guard locks the ram.) The nail driver is only slightly larger than the nailhead, making countersinking nearly invisible. Each nail is placed precisely and accurately with a single blow of the hardened steel driver. This means you can nail at much faster speeds with no surface damage, no mars, and no hammer dents. These devices are especially useful for paneling, fine finishing, curved molding, and hard-to-get-at places in corners or near floors and ceilings. The nails are available in wood-tone colors and in off white.

Riveters

Riveting is used extensively for joining and fastening metal sheets when brazing, welding, or locking techniques will not provide a satisfactory joint. Rivets are also used for many household repairs.

The major types of extensively used rivets include the standard type and pop rivets. Standard rivets must be driven using a bucking bar, whereas pop rivets have a self-heading capability and may be installed where it is impossible to use a bucking bar.

STANDARD RIVETS Wherever possible, rivets should be made of the same material as the material they join. They are classified by lengths, diameters, and their head shape and size. Some of the standard head shapes are shown in Figure 8-4.

Selection of the proper length of rivet is important. If too long a rivet is used, the formed head will be too large, or the rivet may bend or be forced between the sheets being riveted. If too short a rivet is used, the formed head will be too small or the riveted material will be damaged. The length of the rivet should equal the sum of the thicknesses of the metal plus $1\frac{1}{2}$ times the diameter of the rivet, as shown in Figure 8-5.

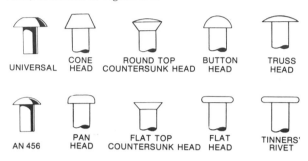

FIG. 8-4. Some common types of rivets.

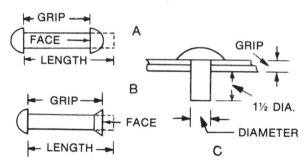

FIG. 8-5. What is meant by the "grip" of a rivet.

When using tinner's rivets, refer to Table 8-2 as a guide in selecting rivets of the proper size for the different gauges of sheet metal.

Table 8-2 Guide for Selecting Rivet Sizes for Sheet-Metal Work

Gauge of sheet metal	Rivet size (weight in pounds per 1000 rivets)
26	1
24	2
22	$2\frac{1}{2}$
20	3
18	$3\frac{1}{2}$
16	4

The riveting procedure for the standard type of rivet involves three operations; drawing, upsetting, and heading, as shown in Figure 8-6. The sheets are drawn together by placing the deep hole of the rivet set over the

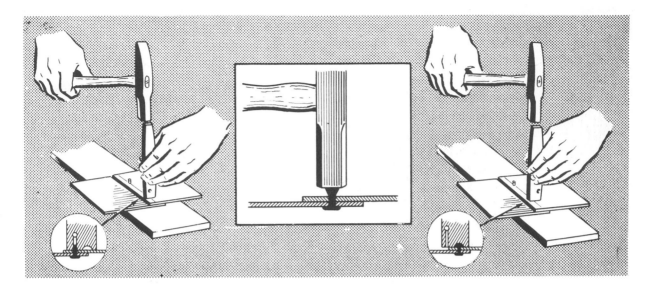

FIG. 8-6. Drawing, upsetting, and heading a rivet.

rivet and striking the head of the set with a rivet hammer (see Chapter 1). Upon removal of the set, the end of the rivet is struck lightly to upset the end of the rivet. Finally, the heading die (dished part) of the rivet set forms the head of the rivet when the hammer again strikes the head of the rivet set. The results of correct and incorrect riveting are shown in Figure 8-7.

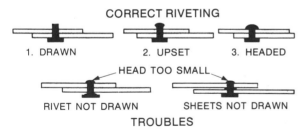

FIG. 8-7. Correct and incorrect riveting.

POP RIVETS Pop or squeeze-type rivets have two advantages over standard rivets: they can be set by one person, and they can be used for blind fastening. This means that they can be used where there is limited access or no access to the reverse side of the work.

To determine the proper size of pop rivet, first determine the size of the predrilled hole. Use the rivet that matches the size of the hole; for example, a ⅛-inch rivet for a ⅛-inch hole. On jobs requiring the drilling of new holes, the rivet diameter is best determined by the strength requirement. Pop rivets are usually available in steel and aluminum, and in a variety of diameters (usually from ⅛ to ¼ inch) and lengths that can be used for work up to ½ inch thick. Steel rivets are much stronger than

aluminum ones. Use steel rivets for very-heavy-duty jobs and when riveting steel to steel. Employ aluminum rivets for lighter-weight jobs such as aluminum to aluminum, fabrics, plastics, etc. A few companies make copper rivets which should be used for repairing and fastening copper items. Neither copper nor aluminum rivets will rust.

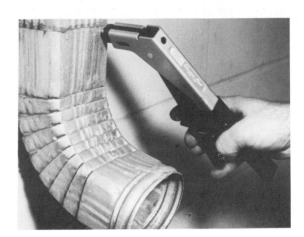

FIG. 8-8. Pop-rivet tool in use.

There are two basic designs of pop rivets, closed end and open end (Figure 8-9). The closed-end rivet fills the need for blind rivets which seal as they are set. They are gastight and liquidtight when used properly, since a high degree of radial expansion provides excellent hole-filling characteristics, and the mandrel head is within the core of the rivet body.

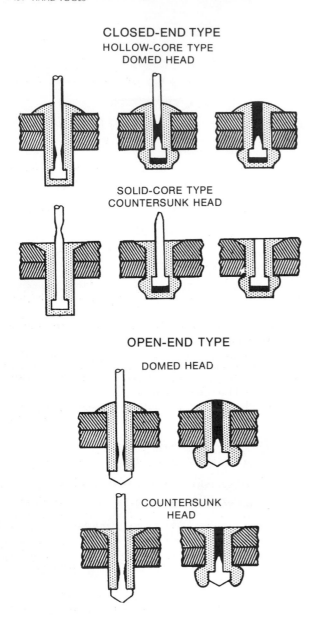

CLOSED-END TYPE
HOLLOW-CORE TYPE
DOMED HEAD

SOLID-CORE TYPE
COUNTERSUNK HEAD

OPEN-END TYPE

DOMED HEAD

COUNTERSUNK
HEAD

FIG. 8-9. Pop rivets.

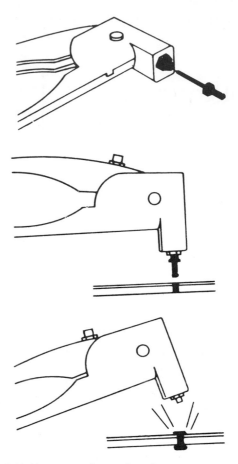

FIG. 8-10. How a pop-rivet tool works.

The open-end type is not liquidtight because the mandrel head which remains in the rivet body is not enclosed within that body as in the closed-end type. This obviously leaves room for possible seepage of liquid or gas.

There are special rivets with extra–large flanges for large holes in soft materials, countersunk rivets for flush surfaces, threaded rivets for setting threaded holes in various materials, and white rivets for repairing white-colored objects.

The operation of the riveter (often called a "riveting plier") is simple. After the holes have been drilled in the parts to be riveted, the rivet is inserted into the riveter by opening the handles of the plier completely and setting the pointed end of the rivet into the hole of the nose piece as far as it will go. (Most pop riveters have interchangeable nose pieces to accept rivets of different diameters.) The bulbous head portion of the rivet is inserted through the holes in the material being fastened. Then the handles of the tool are squeezed firmly until the rivet stem is broken off. This action is repeated if the stem does not separate on the first squeeze. The squeezing action helps to flare out the rivet on the other end.

To remove the separated stem from the tool, open the handles completely and turn the tool over. The separated stem will fall out of the riveting pliers. (*Caution*: Be sure to remove the separated stem so the riveter will accept the next rivet, and to prevent the separated stem from being expelled into the air.)

When rivet holes become enlarged, deformed, or otherwise damaged, use the next larger size rivet as a

Table 8-3 General Sizes of Bars Used in Construction Work

Tool name	Length, inches	Uses
Crowbar	36–60	For heavy-duty prying, lifting, and concrete breaking. When lifting, you must provide your own fulcrum. Being straight, it offers better control than an angled bar.
Digging bar	60–72	Similar to a crowbar in shape, it is used mainly in post-hole digging operations. Frequently has a mushroom top that can be struck with a sledge.
Straight ripping bar	24–36	For rough work involving wrecking, prying, and nail pulling. The flat claw lets you get in and pull nails a hammer could not reach.
Offset ripping bar	16–24	To drive under nailheads or pry and pull nails. You can pound with a hammer on the end of its shaft if you have to. It is made in $\frac{3}{4}$-inch hex shaft and flat bar models.
Gooseneck ripping bar	12–36	Same as for straight ripping bar. It has tremendous leverage but requires a long swing.
Stripping bar	24–36	To strip concrete forms, disassemble scaffolding, and other rough work involving prying, wrecking, nail pulling, and lifting. It is especially good for the latter. Because it has a shallower hook than a gooseneck, it can get up close to vertical surfaces.
Jimmy bar (also called a lining-up bar)	15–20	For prying and aligning jobs—especially in metal work. The end with the long slim taper is used to line up rivet and bolt holes.
Wrecking bar	12–36	Because of its offset chisel end, it is fine for prying. The gooseneck end is designed for pulling up tough nails and spikes.
Pry bar	5–18	Available in several shapes, it is used to pry loose molding and loose boards, pull out nails, and scrape paint. In some designs both ends of the tool have scraping edges, with one end curved and the other end a flat, sharp blade. The small-size pry bar is often called a "barracuda" bar.
Nail puller or nail claw bar	8–14	To drive under nailheads and to pull nails. Available hexagonal or round, the claw ends of these tools have varying degrees of curvature or offset. The curve or offset serves as a fulcrum.
Tack puller	5–8	Used primarily to pull tacks.

replacement or use a backing plate for added holding power. Metal backup plates or washers are also recommended for use in soft materials such as canvas, fabric, plastic, and leather. Incidentally, to remove a pop rivet, just drill out the head. There is little danger of damaging the work, as in removing most standard rivets.

Several attachments for standard vise pliers (see Chapter 6) can be used to clinch standard rivets, snaps, and grommets in metal, plastic, canvas, and leather. As shown in Figure 8-11, the various anvils for rivet, snap, and grommet fasteners are attached to the jaws of the vise pliers. For snaps and grommets, the tool punches the material and clinches the fastener all in one operation. For riveting, the holes must first be drilled, and then the rivet is clinched by the tool.

MAINTENANCE OF RIVETING PLIERS

Occasionally a drop of oil on the moving parts is desirable. Also, it is advisable to clean the jaws. The jaws are generally easily removed by unscrewing a retainer screw. Remove the spring, jaw pusher, and jaws. Wipe the jaws clean. (This simple procedure will prolong the life of the riveter.) Be sure to put the unit together properly.

Ripping Bars, Pry Bars and Nail Bars

In Chapter 1, we mentioned flooring and electrician's chisels and stated that they were used for removing wood rapidly. Actually, these two tools could be classified in a group of tools known as ripping bars, pry bars and nail bars. Figure 8-12 illustrates the various bars employed in construction work, while Table 8-3 lists their general sizes and possible uses.

In using any bar, the principal hazard is encountered when the tool slips, causing the user to fall or the bar to fall on the foot. This is generally due to improper placing of the bar under the object to be moved, or the bar not readily gripping the object.

Paintbrushes and Rollers

Paintbrushes and rollers are very important hand tools in any shop or home. Both are used to apply finishes of various kinds.

PAINTBRUSHES

The proper use of a brush ensures good contact between the paint or other finish and pores, cracks, and crevices. Brushing is particularly recommended for applying primer coats and exterior paints. It is also the most effective way of painting windows, doors, and intricate trim work.

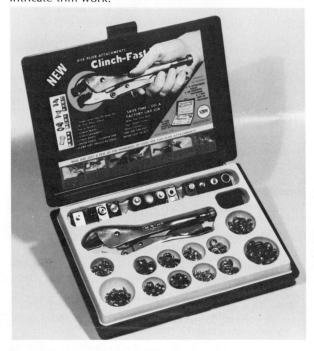

FIG. 8-11. Typical kit, available for standard vise pliers, that will allow the clinching of standard rivets, snaps, and grommets.

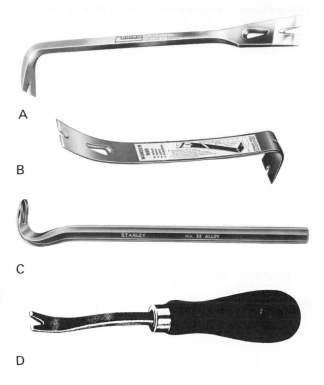

A

B

C

D

FIG. 8-13. Other popular bars: *(a)* wrecking bar; *(b)* pry bar; *(c)* nail puller; *(d)* tack puller.

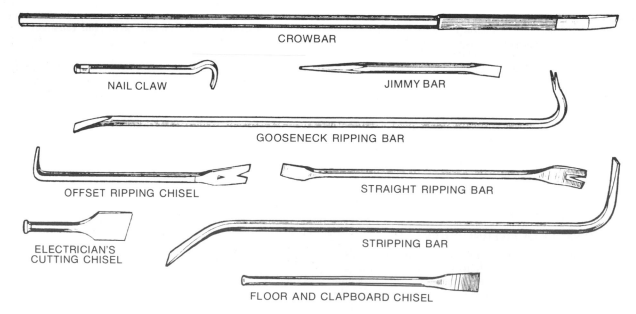

CROWBAR

NAIL CLAW

JIMMY BAR

GOOSENECK RIPPING BAR

OFFSET RIPPING CHISEL

STRAIGHT RIPPING BAR

ELECTRICIAN'S CUTTING CHISEL

STRIPPING BAR

FLOOR AND CLAPBOARD CHISEL

FIG. 8-12. Various ripping and wrecking bars employed in construction work.

There are three categories of brushes: (1) wall size; (2) medium-size sash and trim; and (3) small-size sash and trim. Of the three, the medium and small sizes are available in either flat or oval shapes. Wall brushes are used primarily for painting large areas indoors and outdoors, including walls, siding, ceilings, foundations, decks, floors, and roofs. These brushes are known as either flat wall brushes or as calcimine brushes. Flat wall brushes come in 3- to 6-inch widths; all are suitable for painting exterior surfaces. Comfort in handling should be the deciding factor here. For painting interior surfaces, however, a flat wall brush 3 to 4 inches wide is recommended because paint spattering is kept to a minimum—the wider the brush, the more mess. Calcimine brushes, used primarily for the application of calcimine and masonry paint, are available in 6-, 7-, and 8-inch widths. But if you think this is too much brush to handle, get a good-quality flat wall brush of a smaller size.

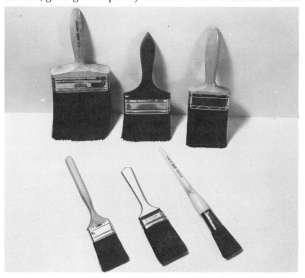

FIG. 8-14. Six brushes that will fulfill most shop jobs.

Medium-size sash-and-trim brushes of the flat type are manufactured in 2-, 2½-, and 3-inch widths, and your selection depends on what is to be painted. For example, you would not use a 3-inch sash-and-trim brush to paint a 2-inch baseboard. They are used for painting baseboards (as noted), cabinets, cupboards, doors, eaves, gutters, wide-sash windows, moldings, picket fences, and shutters. As shown in Figure 8-15, the oval shape produces a thicker accumulation of bristles, making this design ideal for irregular surfaces. By comparison, the traditional flat brush is ineffective on an irregular surface, the thinner distribution of bristles parting at the first contact. Therefore, use the oval-shaped brush on things like trellises, pipe, inside corners, and decorative iron grillework. Medium-size oval sash-and-trim brushes are referred to as No. 8, No. 10, and No. 12 brushes; the smaller the number, the smaller the brush.

Small-size sash-and-trim brushes of the flat type are available in 1- and 1½-inch widths, for use in narrow inside corners and for painting narrow window sash, small-size moldings, and similar delicate work. Small-size oval designs, No. 2, No. 4, or No. 6, are your best bet for painting narrow, rounded surfaces.

Brush prices vary considerably; the greatest difference between brushes lies in the bristle stock, which can be made from either natural or synthetic materials. Natural-bristle brushes are made with hog hair. This type of brush was originally recommended for applying oil-base paints, varnishes, lacquers, and other finishes, because natural fibers resist strong solvents.

Synthetic-bristle brushes are made from a synthetic fiber, usually nylon. Today's nylon brushes are recommended for both latex (water-soluble) and oil-base paints, because this tough synthetic fiber absorbs less water than natural bristles do, while resisting most strong paint and lacquer solvents. In addition, nylon bristles are easier to clean than natural bristles.

Brush quality determines painting ease, and the quality of the finished job. A good brush holds more paint, controls dripping and spattering, and applies paint more

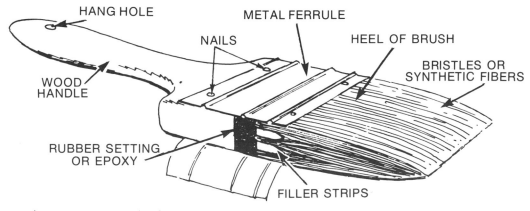

HANG HOLE

METAL FERRULE

NAILS

HEEL OF BRUSH

BRISTLES OR SYNTHETIC FIBERS

WOOD HANDLE

RUBBER SETTING OR EPOXY

FILLER STRIPS

FIG. 8-15. The anatomy of a paintbrush.

smoothly to minimize brush marks. To ensure that you are buying a quality brush, check the following factors:

1. Flagged bristles (Figure 8-16a) have split ends that help load the brush with more paint, while permitting the paint to flow on more smoothly. Cheaper brushes have less flagging, or none at all.
2. Tapered bristles (Figure 8-16b) also help paint flow and provide smooth paint release. That is, tapered bristles give the brush flexibility. Check to see that the base of each bristle is thicker than the tip. This helps give the brush tip a fine painting edge for more even and accurate work.
3. The fullness of a brush is important too (Figure 8-16c). As you press the bristles against your hand, they should feel full and springy. If the divider in the brush setting is too large, the bristles will feel skimpy, and there will be a large hollow space in the center of the brush.
4. Bristle length should vary (Figure 8-16d). As you run your hand over the bristles, some shorter ones should pop up first, indicating a variety of bristle lengths for better paint loading and smoother release.
5. A strong setting is important for bristle retention and maximum brush life. Bristles should be firmly bonded into the setting with epoxy glue, and nails should be used only to hold the ferrule to the handle.

BRUSHING TECHNIQUE

Hold the brush by gripping the wide part of the handle between your fingertips near the metal ferrule. The rest of the handle should be held between your thumb and forefinger, as you would grip a pencil. This is the best way to hold the brush, except when working overhead. In that case, wrap your hand around the handle, with the thumb resting against the handle's inside curve. Use long, steady strokes and moderate, even pressure; excessive pressure or "stuffing" the brush into corners and cracks may damage the bristles.

Always work toward the "wet edge," the previously painted area, making sure not to try to cover too large a surface with each brush load. When loading the brush with paint, do not dip more than half the bristle length into the paint. Tap the bristle tips lightly against the inside rim of the can to remove the excess. Never wipe the brush edgewise across the rim. This removes more paint than necessary, causes the brush to separate or finger, and causes tiny bubbles that make it hard to get a smooth job.

BRUSH CARE

A good brush is a relatively expensive tool, and it pays to invest the time and effort necessary to take care of it properly. Clean brushes immediately after use, with a thinner or special brush cleaner recommended by your paint or hardware store. Use turpentine or mineral spirits to remove oil-base paints, enamels, and varnish; alcohol to remove shellac; and special solvents to remove

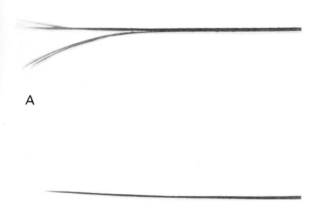

A

B

C

D

Fig. 8-16. Quality factors in the make-up of paint brush.

lacquer. Remove latex paints promptly from brushes with soap and water. If any type of paint is allowed to dry on a brush, a paint remover or brush-cleaning solvent will be needed. Use the following procedure to clean paint brushes:

1. After removing the excess paint with a scraper, soak the brush in the proper thinner, working it against the bottom of the container.
2. To loosen paint in the center of the brush, squeeze the bristles between thumb and forefinger; then rinse the brush again in thinner. If necessary, work the brush in mild soap suds, and rinse in clear water.
3. Press out the water with a stick.
4. Twirl the brush in a container so you will not get splashed.
5. Comb the bristles carefully, including those below the surface. Allow the brush to dry by suspending it from the handle or by laying it flat on a clean surface. Then wrap the dry brush in the original wrapper or in heavy paper to keep the bristles straight. Store the brush either suspended by its handle or lying flat.

PAINT ROLLERS

Paint rollers are faster than brushes for working on large, flat surfaces. It has been estimated that this comparatively new painting tool is today being used to apply over 75 percent of all interior wall and ceiling paint, and it is being used in an impressive share of outdoor painting tasks as well.

As with paint brushes, it is important to choose the proper type of roller for the particular job to be done. Modern paint rollers are available in various sizes and with handles of different lengths. Many are built so that extensions can be screwed into their handles. This makes it possible to paint ceilings or stairwells as high as 12 feet while standing on the floor, or to paint the floor without stooping. You can enamel a baseboard much faster with a roller than a brush, and thus will have to spend less time in an uncomfortable position. Be sure to protect the wall and floor when you paint the baseboard.

Roller covers are available in a variety of widths suitable for use on different areas (Figure 8-17). For walls and ceilings, the best size roller for the amateur is the 7- or 9-inch model. For finished woodwork, doors, and trim, the best choice is the 3-inch model. There are smaller sizes available to cut in corners and for use on window frames and moldings. There are even doughnut-shaped rollers that will coat both sides of a corner at the same time. To help you paint a wall without getting paint on the ceiling, there are special edging rollers, too. Flat painting "pads" (some with guide wheels) are available for use on fencing, siding, shakes, and other hard-to-get-at surfaces.

Most paint trays are designed for use with a roller up to 9 inches wide. Roller frames can have a compression-type

cage, or the roller cover can be held on with an end cap held by a wing nut. Compression frames permit easier and faster roller-cover mounting or removal. If you apply floor or ceiling paint with your roller, be sure the frame handle has a threaded end that will permit an extension pole to be added.

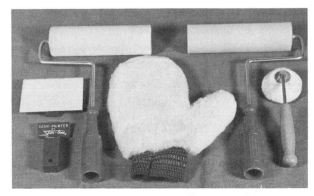

FIG. 8-17. The two 7-inch rollers (from left to right) are made of mohair and polyurethane, respectively. The other tools shown are also used to apply paint.

The fabric on the roller cover should conform to the type of paint to be applied. Lamb's-wool rollers are excellent for oil-base paints, but they should not be used with water-thinned latex paints. Water softens and swells rayon and lamb's wool. These roller fabrics lose their resilience, and the fibers mat together, when they are used for latex paints. Oil or alkyd paints and varnishes are usually thinned with mineral spirits or turpentine. Roller fabrics of all types remain unaffected by these thinners. Toluol and xylol are sometimes used as thinners, however, and these may swell polyurethane foam covers. Lacquers and two-component epoxy enamels are generally thinned with solvent mixtures that contain ketones. Ketone solvents will degrade dynel, acetate, and polyurethane foam roller covers. Mohair rollers can be used with any type of interior flat paint, but are recommended especially for applying enamel and wherever a smooth finish is desired. Rollers made from synthetic fibers can be used with all types of flat paint, inside and out.

In buying a roller, be sure the roll can easily be removed and changed. If both oil and water paints are to be applied, get a roll for each. Make sure that neither water nor oil will soften the tube (frequently treated cardboard) that supports the fabric. It may be better to get a roll with the material stretched over a plastic tube.

Walls can be made unique and attractive by using a special roller to stipple a contrasting color over another one. Stippling rollers come in a wide assortment of design-producing sleeves. With these rollers, however, a different rolling technique must be used. The roll should be started at the left-hand side of the wall at the ceiling line, and the roller drawn evenly in a straight line to the floor. The second stroke should not overlap, but simply fit against, the edge of the first.

Another factor to consider when choosing a roller is the length of the nap or pile. This can range from $\frac{1}{16}$ to $1\frac{1}{2}$ inches. A handy rule to remember is the following: The smoother the surface, the shorter the nap; the rougher the surface, the longer the nap. Use short-napped rollers for most walls, ceilings, and woodwork and smooth concrete. The longer naps are for rough masonry, brick, stucco, wire fences, and other irregular surfaces. Your paint dealer can help you with this choice or you can use the following chart:

Pile	Application
Standard: $\frac{1}{4}$ or $\frac{3}{8}$ inch	Most ceiling, wall, or floor work
High: $\frac{3}{4}$ or $1\frac{1}{2}$ inch	Exceptionally rough surfaces, such as stucco, masonry, brick, and wire fences
Stipple (carpet weave)	For a stipple-textured finish or rolling on mastic materials

ROLLER TECHNIQUE

Before applying the paint with a roller, first cut in the edges of the wall and hard-to-reach areas with a brush or with an edging roller, taking care not to get paint on the ceiling or the adjacent wall.

Some roller models have a roll that may be filled with paint, which then soaks through a perforated backing into the pile cover. However, most rollers used by amateurs are manually loaded from a tilted tray, which usually has a corrugated bottom. Before paint is poured into the roller tray, it should be thoroughly mixed in the can to ensure even pigment distribution. The tray should be propped so that about two-thirds of the bottom is covered with paint.

Next, dip the roller into the tray. Dip it into the edge of the paint, rolling the tool back and forth over the slanting corrugated section of the tray to distribute the paint evenly over the entire surface of the roller and to remove excess paint. If the roller drips when lifted from the tray, it is overloaded. The excess should be wiped off on the dry side of the tilted tray before you begin your stroke.

Apply even pressure when rolling paint on a surface. Even if the general direction of the painting is downward, make your first stroke upward to avoid dripping. Work up and down first, doing about three strips; then work the roller horizontally to ensure even coverage. As you progress, always start in a dry area and roll toward one just painted, blending in the laps.

ROLLER CARE

Rollers should be thoroughly cleaned after each use. You should use the cleaning liquids recommended for brushes with the various types of bristles. Pour the liquid into a shallow pan, and roll the tool back and forth in it.

Then roll out the paint and thinner on newspaper. The roller cover can also be cleaned by putting it into a large-mouth jar filled with thinner (or water, if you are using a water-thinned paint) and then shaking the jar.

The paint tray should also be cleaned after each use. If, before use, you line it with newspaper held in place with masking tape, then your cleaning job will be much easier. (Tin or aluminum foil serves better with water-base paints, since newspapers may disintegrate when wet with water.) After the roller has been washed, wipe it with a clean, dry cloth, and wrap it in aluminum foil. This will keep it soft until the next time it is used.

OTHER PAINT AND FINISHING APPLICATORS

There are some other paint and finishing applicators which ought to come in handy—for example, a triangular-shaped edger fitted with three small wheels and a handle for getting into corners with a neatly painted line. There is a variation of this device (actually, an earlier development) which is rectangular and two-wheeled and performs the same function. Still another variation is a small, flat pad (no wheels) for painting narrow sash, called the "sash painter." And then there is the painter's mitt, which is a lamb's-wool glove that is slipped onto your hand and dipped into paint, making it an easy chore to coat just about any irregular or partly inaccessible surface.

OTHER PAINT-RELATED TOOLS

There are several paint-related tools that would make good additions to your shop. These include putty knives, wire brushes, scrapers, caulking guns, and ladders. A putty knife is used, of course, for applying putty to window sashes when the panes of glass are set in. The blade has a wide, square point available in different lengths and widths; the $1\frac{1}{4}$-and 3-inch blade widths are the most popular. Paint scrapers, which look like putty knives, are available in several sizes, but the 3- or 4-inch scraper is handiest for most work. Both putty knives and scrapers come with flexible and stiff blades. The latter type is usually considered best for such things as pressing wood filler into holes, while the flexible is best for applying putty. Also, the more flexible the blade, the better the tool is for scraping. When it comes to scraping paint from glass, however, nothing beats the handy metal razor-blade scraper. A push button locks the blade into the scraping position and retracts the blade back into the handle.

Woods scrapers are available in blade sizes ranging from 1 to 6 inches and are very handy for removing paint from wood surfaces. The 5- or 6-inch size is used for large areas such as floors and boat decks and hulls whereas the 1-inch size is best for removing paint from narrow surfaces in the home, including sash, window frames, and flat trim. Paint may be scraped from moldings with curved and deep-cut grooves with a molding scraper. This scraper, with a $9\frac{3}{4}$-inch-long handle, has a triangular blade with three scraping edges and a teardrop blade. Of course, one of the quickest ways to remove paint from large areas is with an electric paint remover. This remover is pulled across the surface slowly until the paint is softened; a scraper then is employed to remove the softened paint. Another electric device that is very handy is a putty softener, which makes the removal of rock-hard putty an easy task.

When using a wood scraper, remember that it is pulled at an angle into the paint. Never push a scraper into the paint, as this quickly dulls the blade. A shaving motion is preferred for best results and to keep blades sharper longer. Putty knives and paint- and wood-scraper blades must be kept sharp if they are to be effective. Most wood scrapers have replaceable blades.

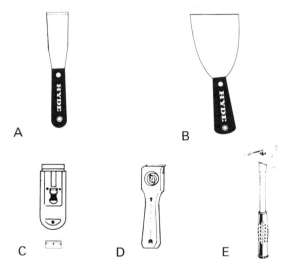

FIG. 8-18. Various paint-related tools: *(a)* putty knife; *(b)* paint scraper; *(c)* razor-blade scraper; *(d)* wood scraper; *(e)* molding scraper.

Joint knives look like putty knives. The blades of these knives range from 3 to 10 inches in width, and they are used to apply spackling compound for finishing wallboard joints. The smaller 4- and 5-inch sizes are used to start the job, and the 10-inch-wide knife is employed to finish the work. To finish inside corners, a corner knife is employed for tape application as well as to apply the final coat of joint compound. This tool has a 4-inch-wide flexible steel blade with a 103° angle to fit tightly in corners.

A caulking gun is used to apply caulking compound to waterproof the areas around windows, doors, and gutters. While there are several different types on the market, the most popular for the average user are the ones with replaceable cartridges.

Other tools that are handy when painting are paint shields for keeping paint off glass, paint-can hooks, and even a window-opener tool for opening paint-stuck

windows and paint-bound sliding doors. This triangular steel tool with small, sharp sawtooth edges is pushed between the sash and the frame to cut the paint seal.

Ladders are important tools, and they should be treated like any others in the shop. A good aluminum or wood stepladder and a 12- to 28-foot extension ladder are needed around almost any house. They must be used safely like any other tool, and must be maintained so that they do not become defective.

If you hang any amount of wall covering, you want to have available a paste brush, a smoothing brush, a seam roller, shears, a wallpaper table with straightedge, and a razor knife or trimmer. The measuring tools mentioned in Chapter 7 (plumb bob, chalk line, ruler, level, and square) also are handy for hanging wall coverings.

Glass Cutters

In glass cutting, the importance of a perfect tool cannot be overemphasized. Use caution in purchasing a glass cutter. Buy only those that are individually packaged. Tools stocked loosely in bins are likely to have nicks in the cutting wheel, or be corroded by atmospheric changes. Test the cutter on a piece of glass before purchase. If the scored line shows a series of dots and dashes or skips, discard the cutter as worthless. Find one that emits a continuous sound as you score a line on glass with it. Once you have found a perfect cutter, keep it in good condition by storing it in a glass jar with a pad of cloth or felt in the bottom, and about 1 inch of kerosene over this pad. The pad protects the wheel from nicks, and the kerosene prevents oxidation.

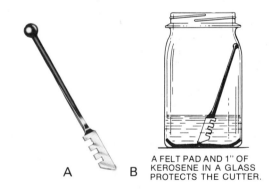

A FELT PAD AND 1" OF KEROSENE IN A GLASS PROTECTS THE CUTTER.

FIG. 8-19. *(a)* Typical glass cutter; *(b)* method of storage.

Glass, for cutting, should be clean. Dust and grime interfere with the cutting wheel. Your working table should be covered with a single layer of a not-too-thick blanket or similar base. This keeps the table level, evens up any irregularities on the top, and prevents scratches which might be caused by the glass slipping on the hard tabletop. A china-marking crayon, or a piece of sharpened soapstone, is ideal for marking the line on the reverse side of the glass where the cut is to be made.

A good method to use to anchor your straight-edged cutting guide is to drive two brads into the table and set the guide against them (Figure 8-20). Metal makes the best guide.

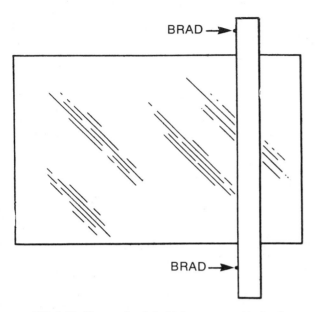

FIG. 8-20. The two brads hold the cutter guide firmly.

Hold the glass cutter firmly, though in a more perpendicular position than you would hold a pencil. Keep the cutting wheel away from your body. The cutting line starts just inside the farther edge of the glass. Use an even pressure to draw the cutter toward your body and past the nearer edge.

Only experience and practice will tell you how much pressure is necessary. The slow, deliberate speed of the cutter will make an even sound which indicates the quality and depth of the cut. You will gradually learn to cut by "ear" as well as by hand.

After the line is scored, gently tap the underside of the cut near the edge of the window glass with the reverse end of the cutter. This will start the cleavage, or split. The split will continue through the entire length of the glass if the break is forced by pressure.

Another way to complete the break is to place a pencil or guide on the table under the scored line on the window glass, and press down on each side of the scored line. Cut only one line at a time. That is, do not score two lines crossing each other without breaking.

The cutting procedure for heavier glass is the same as that for window glass—with one additional step: Apply a thin film of lubricating oil on the line to be cut. But do not apply oil to the backing side of a mirror, as it may damage the mirror.

The notched edge of the glass cutter is used only for chipping off narrow strips of glass. It is used after the line has been scored and the reverse side tapped. Then fit the glass edge into the appropriate notch and snap downward.

Sharpening Stones

Sharpening stones are either natural or artificial. Some natural stones are oil-treated during and after the manufacturing processes. The stones that are oil-treated are sometimes called "oilstones." Artificial stones are normally made of silicon carbide or aluminum oxide. Natural stones have very fine grains and are excellent for putting razorlike edges on fine cutting tools. Most sharpening stones have one coarse and one fine face. Some of these stones are mounted; and the working faces of some sharpening stones are a combination of coarse and fine grains. Stones are available in a variety of shapes, as shown in Figure 8-21

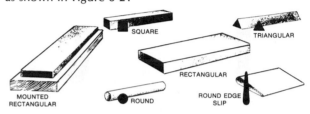

FIG. 8-21. Shapes of sharpening stones and oilstones.

A fine cutting oil is generally used with most artificial sharpening stones; however, other lubricants such as kerosene may be used. When a tool has been sharpened on a grinder or grindstone, a wire edge or a feather edge is usually left by the coarse wheel. A sharpening stone is used to hone this wire or feather edge off the cutting edge of the tool. Do not attempt to do a honing job with the wrong stone. Use a coarse stone to sharpen large and very dull or nicked tools. Use a medium-grain stone to sharpen tools that do not require a finished edge, such as tools for working soft wood, cloth, leather, and rubber. Use a fine stone and an oilstone to sharpen and hone tools requiring a razorlike edge.

Prevent glazing of sharpening stones by applying light oil while using the stone. Wipe the stone clean with a wiping cloth or cotton waste after each use. If the stone becomes glazed or gummed up, clean it with aqueous ammonia or dry-cleaning solvent. If necessary, scour the stone with aluminum-oxide abrasive cloth or flint paper attached to a flat block.

At times, stones will become uneven from improper use. True the uneven surfaces on an old grinding wheel or on a grindstone. Another method of truing the surface is to lap it with a block of cast iron or other hard material covered with a waterproof abrasive paper, dipping the stone in water at regular intervals and continuing the lapping until the stone is true.

Stones must be carefully stored in boxes or on special

racks when not in use. Never lay them down on uneven surfaces or place them where they may be knocked off a table or bench, or where heavy objects can fall on them. Do not store them in a hot place.

Complete instructions for the use of sharpening stones are given in Chapter 22.

Trowels

There are many different trowels that can be used around the shop and home. Figure 8-22 illustrates some of the more common trowels, while Table 8-4 lists their sizes and possible uses.

In addition to the hand tools already mentioned as being used for concrete and brickwork (bricklayer's hammer, drilling hammer, mason's rule, chalk line, trowels, cold chisels, levels, etc.), there are a number of other tools that come in handy for this type of work. For instance, in brickwork there are the tuck-pointer's rake for digging mortar out of brick joints; an 8 X 8 inch hawk for holding and feeding new mortar into a joint; jointers (V-shaped raker or convex) for compacting the mortar in the joints; and line twigs and pins to hold a line securely during this work. For concrete work, a groover is used for creating patterns or joints on a plain slab of concrete; an edger for finishing the concrete edges; step tools which are matched for inside and outside corners of steps; a radius edger to edge curved slabs; and a wood float for rough finishing. A mortar box or cement boat plus a mortar hoe, or a small electric- or gasoline-powered cement mixer, are needed for the mixing of cement, unless you plan to buy ready-mixed concrete. A contractor's wheelbarrow that holds $4\frac{1}{2}$ to $5\frac{1}{2}$ cubic feet, shovels, and rakes are needed to transport and spread the concrete at the work site. Frequently, cement mixers are available for rent. A stiff-fiber brush, wire brush, and whisk broom are useful in masonry work, as well as for many other tasks around the shop.

Table 8-4 Types, Sizes, and Uses of Trowels

Trowel type	Approximate size, inches	Uses
Angle	6X2½X2½, 6X4X4	Clean, fast and easy inside corner forming
Brick	Blades 8, 9, 10, 10½, and 11 long	Scoop and spread mortar over wide area when laying brick
Bucket	Blades 6 long	Scoop and hold mortar, cement, or plaster while doing small patching jobs; the diagonally cut blade makes it easy to get into the bucket or mortar box
Cement finishing	Blades 10½, 11, 11½, 12, 13, 14, and 16 long	Shape and smooth cement after it has been laid
Caulking	6X¼; 6X½; 6X¾; 6X1	Fill flat and flush brick joints
Dry-wall joint	8X4½; 10X4½; 12X4½; 14X4½	Similar in design to plastering trowel, but with a concave bow in the blade that allows excellent regathering of "mud" used for plastering dry-wall joints
Floor	Classified by tooth size; check mastic container for tooth size called for by the particular mastic	Apply floor and wall mastics
Fresno	24X5; 30X5; 36X5	Very large blade, usually with a long handle, to smooth large cemented areas.
Margin	5X1½; 5X2; 8X2	Finishing plastered and cemented corners
Midget	7½X3	Plastering in small areas such as around window sills and inside closets
Pipe	3X10½	Plastering in hard-to-get-at places, such as around pipes
Plastering	Blades 10½, 11, 11½, and 12 long	Similar in design to cement finishing trowel, but with a larger support bar to hold, spread, and smooth plaster on vertical areas
Pointing	Blades 3, 3½, 4, 4½, 5, 5½, and 6 long	Similar in design to brick trowel, but smaller; used for painting masonry joints
Pool	10X3; 12X3½; 14X4; 16X4	Mortaring pool walls; easily bent to the configuration of the walls; the silo trowel is very similar but is smaller
Roofing	Classified by tooth size; check mastic container for tooth size called for by the particular mastic	Applying roofing mastic; same design as floor trowel, except pointed teeth make the size grooves required

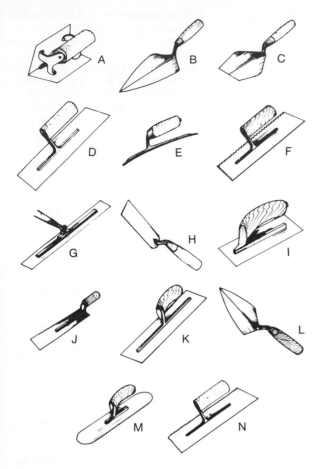

FIG. 8-22. Some of the more common trowels: *(a)* angle; *(b)* brick; *(c)* bucket; *(d)* cement finishing; *(e)* dry-wall joint; *(f)* floor; *(g)* fresno; *(h)* margin; *(i)* midget; *(j)* pipe; *(k)* plastering; *(l)* painting; *(m)* pool; *(n)* roofing.

Plumbing Hand Tools

In addition to the various wrenches, tubing cutters and pipe benders, flaring tools, reamers, etc., already mentioned, there are a few other plumbing specialty tools that are good to have around any home shop. For example, no home can be without a force cup (also known as a plunger or "plumber's friend"). It is used to force a clogging substance free so that it can be washed down the drain. In addition to the standard force cup, there are now power drain cleaners that shoot a blast of air to clear out blockages. The discharged air comes from a carbon-dioxide bulb which is loaded into the cleaner. It will work on drain openings of up to 6 inches.

An auger, better known as a "snake," is another important tool used to open clogged drains. The closet auger, which is 5 to 6 feet long and has a protective rubber guard, is primarily used to free clogged toilets. For

cleaning other drains and traps, there are hook-end or corkscrew-tipped augers ranging from 15 to 50 feet in length. Some feature a crank feed-rewind arrangement and self storage in a rust-resistant canister, which helps to make the auger easier to use and prolongs its life. Sewer rods, which come in lengths up to 150 feet with blades $\frac{3}{4}$ inch wide are used to clear blockages in sewers. Some augers are made of thin clock-spring steel, while others are of coiled spring steel. The latter are flexible in every direction. There are also power augers which work in conjunction with $\frac{1}{4}$-, $\frac{3}{8}$- and $\frac{1}{2}$-inch electric drills. These electric snakes, 6, 15, and 25 feet in length, work best with drills that have variable speed and a forward-reverse switch. For most home use, an auger 15 to 25 feet long is best.

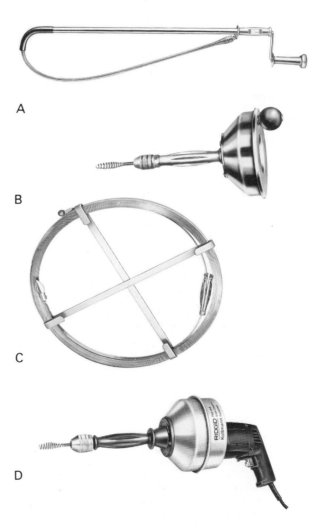

FIG. 8-23. Pipe and drain cleaning tools: *(a)* closet auger; *(b)* hand spinner auger; *(c)* flat steel sewer tape; *(d)* portable electric drain cleaner.

Frequently, replacing a worn faucet washer is only half the job, if the seat onto which it fits is rough or pitted. In such cases, the only way to smooth the unevenness and seat the washer properly is to use a tool known as a "faucet-seat dresser" (Figure 8-24).

The plumber's toolbox also contains a group of tools that look like cold chisels but are called "calkers" and "yarning irons." These are used to pack and calk cast-iron pipe fittings to prevent leakage. There are also other plumber's hand tools on the market, but they are very specialized.

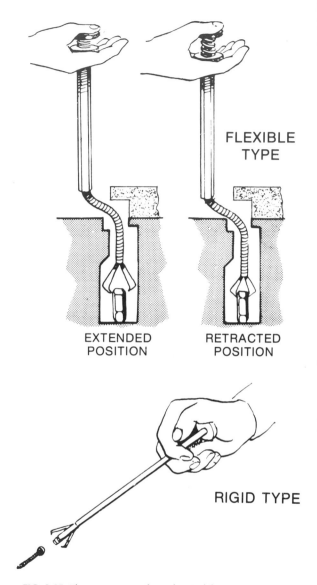

FLEXIBLE TYPE

EXTENDED POSITION   RETRACTED POSITION

FIG. 8-25. The two types of mechanical fingers.

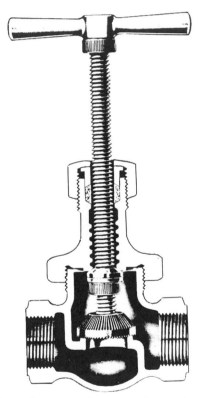

FIG. 8-24. A faucet-seat dresser can frequently restore seats so they work properly.

RIGID TYPE

Other Tools

Many other items will come in handy in any shop. Small articles which have fallen into places where they cannot be reached by hand may be retrieved with the "mechanical fingers" or "pickup tongs." This tool is also used to start nuts or bolts in difficult areas. The mechanical fingers, shown in Figure 8-25, have a tube containing flat springs which extend from the end of the tube to form clawlike fingers, much like a screw holder. The springs are attached to a rod that extends from the outer end of the tube. A plate is attached to the end of the tube, and a similar plate, to be pressed by the thumb, is attached to the end of the rod. A coil spring placed around the rod between the two plates holds them apart and retracts the fingers into the tube. When the bottom plate is grasped between the user's fingers and enough thumb pressure is applied to the top plate to compress the spring, the tool fingers extend from the tube in a grasping position. When the thumb pressure is released, the tool fingers retract into the tube as far as the object they hold will allow. Thus, enough pressure is applied on the object to hold it securely. Some mechanical fingers have a flexible end on the tube to permit their use in close quarters or around obstructions. *Note*: Mechanical fingers should not be used as a substitute for wrenches or pliers. The fingers are made of thin sheet metal or spring wire and can easily be damaged by overloading.

In addition, a good flashlight is always useful; an adjustable inspection mirror aids greatly in making detailed checks where the human eye cannot directly see the inspection area; a magnifying glass or an eye loupe is useful for reading or working under certain conditions; tweezers are handy for servicing and repairing electronic and other subminiature assemblies; scissors are used for cutting paper and cloth; and oil cans and oilers of various sizes are needed for easy dispensing of lubricants. Another valuable tool, especially for metalwork, is magnets. They can perform holding, attracting, and lifting duties. Magnets for shopwork fall mainly into the following two categories (but there is no sharp dividing line between the two):

1. *Gripping* magnets, that exert maximum grip on workpieces placed on them but do not attract objects from a distance. Pot magnets are best for such duty.
2. *Tractive* magnets, that attract ferrous matter from a distance (depth of field) but do not need maximum grip. In general, the greater the depth of field required, the greater should be the gap between the poles. Thus, large horseshoe magnets have greater depths of field than small ones, but all the horseshoe types are basically tractive magnets.

Gripping or holding magnets are used to keep metal objects in place for welding. Pot magnets usually have some type of nonmagnetic straps to complete the holding jig.

Handy in any shop are the machinist's jack, jackscrew, and jack lift. The machinist's jack and jackscrew look alike, but the latter is larger and is used for heavier-duty work. The machinist's jack, which usually has a lifting capacity of approximately 1000 pounds, is used on drill presses, shapers, milling machines, planers, and any place where leveling is necessary. It can also be used for leveling radiators, electrical appliances, etc.

The jackscrew, because of its greater capacity, can be used to support a house sill when a pier supporting the house has to be replaced. It also is used to support the ceiling joints when a picture window is being installed in an outside wall, or a bearing wall is being removed and added support is being set in its place. In the workshop, a jackscrew (or even a machinist's jack) can be used for clamping; the jackscrew is set up so that it exerts pressure on the surface of a board pressed against the surface that is being glued. Two or four jackscrews or machinist jacks can be used as a substitute for a press screw when gluing a veneer surface in place.

With capacities of 1 ton and up, jack lifts are great time and strength savers. The one shown in Figure 8-26

weighs only about 6½ pounds, but it can lift, slip, slide, or pull up to 2000 pounds.

FIG. 8-26. A typical jack lift.

It is, of course, impossible to list all the hand tools that could be used in a shop. As has been stated several times, many specialized shops have special tools. For example, a shop where upholstering is done would have such items as an upholsterer's tack hammer (see Chapter 1), webbing stretchers, webbing pliers, skewers, spring clippers, regulators (heavy needles), and shears or scissors. In shops specializing in leather work, there would be tooling instruments, tracer-molders, leather trimming tools and cutting knives, various leather designing punches, revolving punch pliers, eyelet setters, and various types of needles. On the other hand, an electronics or electrical shop would have specialized test equipment, including various meters. Speaking of the latter, every shop should have some type of troubleshooting checker for testing simple electric circuits. It might be a simple continuity checker, a neon current tester, a volt-ohmmeter (VOM), or a clamp-on amp-voltmeter. The continuity checker and ohmmeter are always used on disconnected equipment, never on live circuits; the other testers are used on live circuits. At least one of these testers should be in every shop.

FIG. 8-27. Sawhorses are very valuable tools that can perform several tasks. These have metal legs which can be folded when the tool is not in use, for storage on a wall.

In metal shops, in addition to the hand tools already mentioned in Chapters 1 and 3, various sheet-metal stakes (Figure 8-28) would be needed for bending and forming. Of course, a great deal of sheet-metal bending can be done over pieces of pipe or between wooden or angle-iron jaws. Always use a rawhide or wooden mallet to do the bending and shaping on sheet metal. The bar folder (Figure 8-29a) is also used to bend metal, to make a hem to stiffen an edge, to make an open fold for a folded or grooved seam, and to make a rounded fold in preparation for wiring an edge.

The slip-roll forming machine (Figure 8-29b) presents the quickest way to form cylindrical parts. Also available are groovers for making seams, modeling tools for tooling foil, various punches and forming tools for shaping operations, and chasing tools for creating a diversity of patterns and designs. If a great deal of metal cutting must be done, a metal shear and rod cutter or a squaring shear is a shop must. The latter has a guillotine-like blade that cuts metal when the foot pedal is pressed down. One item—an anvil—is a must item in any metal shop or, as a matter of fact, in any shop.

FIG. 8-28. Common sheet-metal stakes: *(a)* square; *(b)* double seaming; *(c)* hatchet (for sharp right-angle bends); *(d)* conductor; *(e)* creasing; *(f)* blowhorn (for funnels and other conical shapes); *(g)* breakhorn; *(h)* candle-mold; *(i)* hollow mandrel.

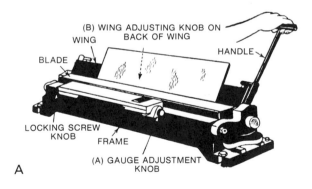

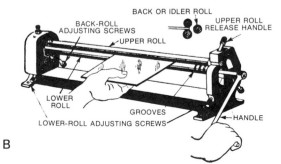

FIG. 8-29. Using *(a)* a bar folder and *(b)* a slip-roll forming machine.

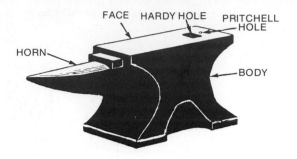

FACE HARDY HOLE PRITCHELL
HOLE

HORN

BODY

FIG. 8-30. Typical anvil and its parts.

For a shop geared to automotive or engine activities, hand tools that could be considered specialized items would include gear pullers, various valve tools, hydraulic valve-lifter pullers, piston-ring compressors, gasket and carbon scrapers, spark-plug and battery cleaners, oil-filter removal tools, ignition-point files, distributor wrenches, etc. As you can see, there are specialized hand tools for every trade or craft.

PORTABLE POWER TOOLS

The introduction of portable power tools to the manual trades brought a great many changes and a number of problems. For instance, the portable power saw changed the direction in which a saw cut is made. The handsaw is used to cut from the far side of the wood toward the worker. The table saw also cuts in this direction, and from the top of the board down. But the portable power saw cuts from the bottom of the board up and from the worker side to the far side. This and other differences in the operation of these new tools demand a different approach in laying out work, in marking, clamping, and setting up for working, and in the actual operations.

Safety, both for the worker and for the material being worked on, is another important factor that has changed materially with the advent of portable power tools. In the design of the tools, manufacturers have, in every case, included safety guards over blades, ground wires to reduce electric-shock hazards, automatic slip clutches to prevent kickback, fingertip controls, and other devices that reduce the hazards of using electric power.

The one outstanding feature of portable tools that makes them so valuable in use also makes them more dangerous to use. The power saw cuts many times faster than the handsaw. The electric drill turns up to 2000 times per minute, as compared with the hand-drill speed of around 120 turns per minute. Router bits run at a speed of up to 28,000 revolutions per minute. *Speed* is the one big feature that makes these tools so valuable. Not only do they cut faster at high speed, but they make a smoother and more accurate cut. But, because of this speed factor, both the tools and the materials on which they are used must be handled more carefully than was necessary with hand tools. Mistakes can be made just as rapidly as an accurate cut.

Electric power tools are precision built and manufactured, as a rule, to satisfy the highest standards. For maximum performance, long tool life, and your safety, follow these instructions carefully:

VOLTAGE WARNING

Before connecting a tool to a power source (receptacle, outlet, etc.), be sure the voltage supplied is the same as that specified on the nameplate of the tool. A power source with a voltage greater than that specified for the tool can lead to serious injury to the user, as well as damage to the tool. If in doubt, do not plug in the tool. Using a power source with a voltage lower than the nameplate rating is harmful to the motor.

Tool nameplates also bear a figure with the abbreviation "amps" (for *amperes*, a measure of electric current). This refers to the input of electrical energy. On the surface, it would seem that the higher the input current, the more powerful the motor should be. But since this figure increases with the load (and is greatest on stall, when the motor is so burdened it cannot turn), the ampere rating on a nameplate is not of itself a true indication of a tool's capacity.

Look for the Underwriter's Laboratories (UL) label on any hand power tool you buy. It tells you, first, that an original sample was examined by UL and found to meet all established electrical codes. Second, it is your guarantee that UL is checking this tool periodically, to see whether the manufacturer is maintaining the standard set by the original sample. As a part of such inspections, UL measures the input current with the tool loaded to approximate the severest normal use for which it is meant. In the case of an electric drill, for example, UL standards call for measuring the input current with the largest drill that will fit the chuck while making holes in mild steel as thick as the drill diameter. A buyer can also be sure that the rated input current is a safe one—that under the severest use mentioned, the tool will not heat up beyond stringent limits set by Underwriter's Laboratories. The temperature is checked not only on the housing, but also at strategic points inside the tool where maximum heat is developed.

GROUNDED OUTLETS

Three-pronged plugs will be found on all UL-listed tools unless they have a nonconducting housing or a self-contained power source (cordless types). The latter two types of tools are covered fully in the next chapter. Power tools with three-pronged plugs will not fit the familiar household outlet with two holes. They do fit modern grounding-type receptacles. When inserted in such receptacles, these plugs "ground" the tool housing.

If the only outlet available is of the old two-hole type, you should do two things to use power tools safely: (1) find out whether your wiring is the kind that grounds the outlet boxes in the walls (ask your electrician if you are not sure); (2) buy a special grounding adaptor. This has two prongs on one end (to fit the two-hole outlet) and three holes at the other end (for the three-pronged tool plug.) The adaptor also has a very important little pigtail of wire that is connected to the grounding socket inside it. If you leave this pigtail hanging in the air, the tool is not grounded.

The pigtail must be grounded; with BX armored cable and conduit wiring, this is simple: Loosen the screw holding the outlet cover plate, and hook the pigtail lug under the screwhead. Tighten it well, and see that it stays tight to maintain the grounding protection.

If your outlet boxes are not grounded (as may be the case in some rural areas with knob-and-tube wiring or nonmetallic cable) the pigtail must be connected to a water pipe, steam pipe, faucet, or other valid ground. It is probably too short to reach such a connection, but you can attach it, with a small bolt and nut, to a piece of sturdy single-conductor wire (or even standard two-wire cord with the wires twisted together at both ends). A ground strap can be used to connect the other end of the wire to a pipe or faucet body.

Grounding adaptors are illegal in Canada, being forbidden by the Canadian Electrical Code. The Canadian tool buyer should install one or more grounding outlets, if they are not already installed, to use for electric tools.

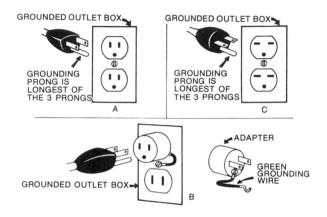

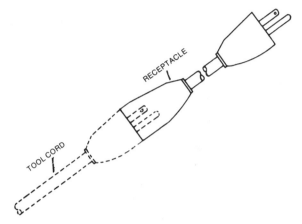

FIG. II-1. If your power tool requires less than 150 volts it has a plug that looks like *A*, it will fit directly into the proper type of three-wire grounding receptacle. The unit is then grounded automatically each time it is plugged in. Shown in *B* is a special grounding adapter (not allowed in Canada by the Canadian Electrical Code) which is available from your dealer and will permit using a two-wire receptacle. The green grounding wire extending from the side of the adapter must be connected to a permanent ground. If a tool requires from 150 to 250 volts, it has a plug like *C*. No adapter is available, and the plug must be used in the proper three-wire grounding receptacle.

FIG. II-2. Extension cords should be of the three-wire type with approved connector caps to ensure continuity of the tool ground wire. Also, the wire should be of the correct gauge to maintain adequate voltage at the tool.

EXTENSION CORDS

When using an extension cord, be sure it is heavy enough to carry the current your tool will draw. An undersized cord will cause a drop in line voltage, resulting in loss of power or overheating. Table II-1 shows the correct size to use, based on cord length and nameplate amperage rating. If in doubt, use the next heavier size. (*Note:* The smaller the gauge number, the heavier the cord.) Repair or replace damaged cords.

Extension cords must be of the three-wire type, with grounding plugs and sockets, and connected to a grounding outlet or a properly grounded adaptor, to keep unbroken the chain that protects you against shock. This is especially important because extensions are most often needed for outdoor work, where the possibility of shock is greatly increased because the user stands on more or less damp ground. Do not risk using an ungrounded tool under such conditions.

Table II-1 Recommended Minimum Gauge for Extension Cords for Portable Electric Tools

Amperes	Volts			Length of cord, feet						
rating	120 →	25	50	100	150	200	250	300	400	500
range	240 →	50	100	200	300	400	500	600	800	1000
0–2		18	18	18	16	16	14	14	12	12
2–3		18	18	16	14	14	12	12	10	10
3–4		18	18	16	14	12	12	10	10	8
4–5		18	18	14	12	12	10	10	8	8
5–6		18	16	14	12	10	10	8	8	6
6–8		18	16	12	10	10	8	6	6	6
8–10		18	14	12	10	8	8	6	6	4
10–12		16	14	10	8	8	6	6	4	4
12–14		16	12	10	8	6	6	6	4	2
14–16		16	12	10	8	6	6	4	4	2
16–18		14	12	8	8	6	4	4	2	2
18–20		14	12	8	6	6	4	4	2	2

GENERAL SAFETY RULES

While we are on the subject of safety, you should read the instructions below, as well as those given in the chapters concerning specific types of tools. These general safety rules apply to both portable and stationary power tools.

1. *Keep the work area clean.* Cluttered areas and benches invite accidents.
2. *Avoid dangerous environments.* Do not expose power tools to rain. Do not use power tools in damp or wet locations. Keep the work area well lit.
3. *Keep children away.* All visitors should be kept at a safe distance from the work area.
4. *Store idle tools.* When not in use, tools should be stored in a dry, high or locked area—out of the reach of children.
5. *Do not force any tool.* It will do the job better and safer at the rate for which it was designed.
6. *Use the right tool.* Do not force a small tool or attachment to do the job of a heavy-duty tool.
7. *Wear the proper apparel.* Do not wear loose clothing or jewelry that can get caught in moving parts. Rubber gloves and footwear are recommended when working outdoors.
8. *Use safety glasses.* Wear safety glasses when you work with most tools. Also wear a face or dust mask if a cutting operation is dusty.

9. *Do not abuse power cords.* Never carry a tool by its cord, or yank a cord to disconnect it from a receptacle. Keep cords away from heat, oil, and sharp edges.
10. *Secure the work.* Use clamps or a vise to hold the work. It is safer than using your hand, and it frees both hands to operate the tool.
11. *Do not overreach.* Keep the proper footing and balance at all times.
12. *Maintain tools with care.* Keep your tools sharp and clean, for best and safest performance. Follow the instructions for lubricating and changing accessories.
13. *Disconnect tools.* Tools should be unplugged when not in use, before servicing, and when you change blades, bits, cutters, etc.
14. *Remove adjusting keys and wrenches.* Form the habit of checking to see that keys and adjusting wrenches are removed from tools before turning them on.
15. *Avoid accidental starting.* Do not carry a plugged-in tool with your finger on the switch. Be sure the switch is *off* before you plug in any tool.

PURCHASING POWER TOOLS

Unfortunately, price is a poor indication of value, as you will find out when you shop for power tools. This is a serious matter to all craftsmen, because it is necessary to have good tools in order to turn out good work. Generally, portable power tools cost more than hand tools, and a mistake in their purchase is more to be regretted than a simple error in buying the wrong chisel or screwdriver. The durability and reliability of the tool are of utmost importance. The design and construction of the tool are important in relation to the type of use for which it is intended. Light shopwork demands a tool that is light and easy to handle, well balanced, and accurate for working on small stock. Farm work, building, and the heavier trades require a stronger tool that is not tiring to use. It must be accurate, with control settings that are easy to use yet stay in place. The frame must be such that it is not easily damaged around busy work areas.

When inspecting a tool before you buy, look at the adjusting devices to see if they are well marked and do actually measure the degree of the setting. Inspect the threads of bolts and setscrews to determine whether they can be easily damaged. Soft materials in such places can easily be stripped of threads, bent, or otherwise rendered useless by even a slight accident. Is the metal of the base substantial, or can it easily be bent out of shape or alignment? Do the clamping or holding devices on the tool fasten securely, or will they be easily pulled out of position? This is especially important for sanders.

Further inspection should concern the matter of personal safety. On saws, do the guards close completely around the blade and work freely? Is the switch located so that it can be used easily but not accidentally turned on or off? Balance the tool in your hand; run the motor, and check for vibration (if any), noise, and how it starts and stops. Finally, there is that all-important factor called the "feel" of the tool. This cannot be defined. You have to use the tool and like it. Its companion is the thing called "pride of ownership." The sales clerk knows what it is but cannot explain it to you. You just have to feel good about using and owning the tool to be really satisfied.

All the tools discussed and illustrated in this book were selected because they come nearest to satisfying all the requirements of good portable power tools. Furthermore, all the directions apply to all good tools. Whatever make of tool you happen to own or buy, if it is made to meet the standards of precision and quality that are demanded by all trades, you will find that the comments and suggestions in this book apply to your tools as well as the ones actually shown. As you look at the pictures and diagrams, you will learn to recognize the necessary and desirable qualities of really good tools, so that, whatever you buy, you will have a standard of value by which to judge.

As is true for hand tools, you should use power tools that meet your specifications. What type of work are you going to do? How often will you be running the machine? How frequently will you be using it? Will you be cutting light or heavy materials? Will the motor be running steadily or intermittently? Is wood the only material involved, or will you be working on metals, stone, plastic, or composition materials? Is the work simple, or will you need a variety of accessories and adapters for special tasks? These questions must all be answered; and, as you go through this section, many others will come to mind as you consider the tools you need.

There is one aspect of buying tools, and particularly portable power tools, that cannot be overstressed. It is the reliability of the manufacturers of the tools and their service arrangements with local dealers. As for the makers of the tools and their reputations, you can easily check a few stores that sell to professional workers. Ask around in the trade, to find out what the everyday worker thinks of different brands of tools. Then check with your dealers and learn whether they carry good stocks of accessories, extra blades, spare parts, and other tools made by the same manufacturers. Nothing is more disconcerting than to find out that you have to ship a tool 800 to 1000 miles to have it repaired. Good distribution today demands authorized service centers in every large city. Good dealerships also demand a good supply of tools, parts, and accessories.

Make sure that you can get good service before spending your money for a particular tool. The best way to do this is to look at and read the manufacturer's literature which comes with the tool. Make sure that it includes a repair sheet and spare-parts list for that particular model. Also make sure that it includes a list of the authorized repair stations, with complete addresses. Buy as good a tool as you can afford, but be sure that it will meet your requirements. It need not be more tool than you require, but more mistakes are made in buying insufficient power and quality than otherwise. Remember that a small or poorly powered tool cannot do a heavy-duty job. The better tool can always do the lighter job with no trouble.

TOOL RENTAL

Today there is no need to put off a project because you do not have the proper portable power equipment. The entire line of portable power tools is now available on a rental basis.

Power tools may be rented from most retail tool stores and from many hardware stores. In addition, certain types of equipment can be leased from lumber yards. The advantages of portable tool rentals are:

1. The best portable power tools are placed at your disposal.
2. New tools, with improvements over older models, are always being added to the line.
3. You have at your disposal equipment you might otherwise never be able to acquire.
4. If you are planning to purchase, you can first try out the tool for the relatively small rental fee, and then decide whether it fits your needs.

Rental costs are low for most portable power tools. Thus, as you read this section, remember that you can rent as well as buy tools that you do not own.

PORTABLE POWER DRILLS

One of the earliest power tools invented, and a most popular tool today, is the electric portable drill. Although it is designed for drilling holes, various attachments and accessories allow you to adapt it for many different jobs. Sawing, sanding, polishing, buffing, screwdriving, wire brushing, grinding, and paint mixing are examples of possible uses. As a matter of fact, there are so many attachments available, you can literally have a small but complete light-duty home power workshop driven by this one tool, the portable electric drill.

Drills come in more varieties and are made by more manufacturers than any other power tool. Essentially, a drill consists of a motor, a trigger switch to control the motor, and a chuck into which you insert the shafts of twist drills, bits, and your choice of attachments. But each of a drill's ingredients is subject to countless variations, and that makes all the difference. For instance, home-use sizes of drills are $\frac{1}{4}$, $\frac{3}{8}$, and $\frac{1}{2}$ inch. A drill may weigh a little more than 2 pounds or almost 10 pounds. Its top speed may be 600 or 2500 rpm. Its case may be plastic or metal, and its appearance may vary to some degree.

SIZES AND SPEEDS The size of a portable electric drill is determined by the maximum size of straight-shank drill the chuck will hold. That is, a $\frac{1}{4}$-inch drill will hold straight-shank drills up to and including a $\frac{1}{4}$-inch drill. The $\frac{3}{8}$-inch drill will hold all the small drills and others up to $\frac{3}{8}$ inch in diameter, while the $\frac{1}{2}$-inch drill will take straight-shank drills up to and including $\frac{1}{2}$ inch.

The free-running speed of a typical $\frac{1}{4}$-inch drill is about 2000 rpm; the $\frac{3}{8}$-inch size has a top speed of 1000 rpm; and $\frac{1}{2}$-inch tool is limited to a maximum of 700 rpm.

The rpm rating is an indication of the number of gear sets in the tool and the type of work for which it is best suited. For example, a $\frac{1}{4}$-inch drill rated about 2000 rpm usually has one gear set and is appropriate for rapid drilling in wood and for use with sanding and polishing accessories. A drill with more gears would have a lower rpm rating and work more slowly, but it could make bigger holes in hard metals or masonry without stalling or overloading. Under load, all electric drills lose speed; thus, a drill can be overloaded to such an extent as to reduce its operating speed to the danger point. If not immediately corrected by the operator, this will eventually result in a burned-out motor. Any craftsman, after using a hand drill for only a short time, can tell from the sound of the motor whether or not it is being overloaded. Another indication of overload is excessive heating of the drill while it is being used.

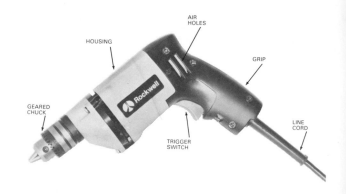

FIG. 9-1. Major parts of a typical portable drill.

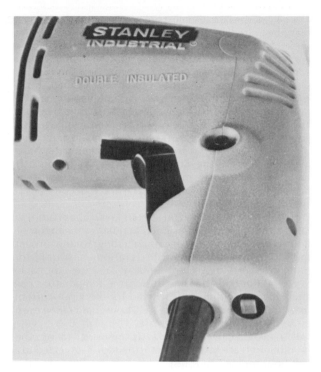

FIG. 9-2. Industrial-rated drills are usually so marked on the drill, while household drills carry no label. The drill shown above is also double insulated and has a circuit breaker built in at the base of the handle.

The causes of overloading are trying to do a job too fast (that is, applying too great a pressure on the hand drill to force the operation) and using bits, drills, or other attachments that were designed for heavier equipment. The remedy in each case is quite obvious: Take the time to let the machine do its own work, or provide yourself with a heavier hand drill if heavy work is to be done. You cannot expect one horse to do the work of two in the same length of time, nor can you expect one horse to pull a load that should be handled by two.

Some modern drills have speed controls; the speed remains constant no matter how hard you push your tool. Few people realize that, as a motor turns, it generates its own electric current, completely apart from the current that is feeding into it. In a constant-speed drill, this generated current goes to a "solid-state" control. The nature of the control is that the more generated current coming to it, the less current it will feed the drill motor. When a drill starts running more slowly and generates less current, the control supplies more current to the motor.

Many portable drills are available with a variable-speed feature. The speed at which such drills run usually depends upon how far you pull the trigger switch. For a ¼-inch drill, for instance, this can be any speed from 0 to about 2000 rpm. The slow speed is used to drive screws without any special attachments. It also lets you tighten bolts and nuts. And, you probably know how a drill can jump around when you start to drill into a hard material. The slow speed lets you start drilling hard materials, such as tile or steel, without first scratching or punching a starting point.

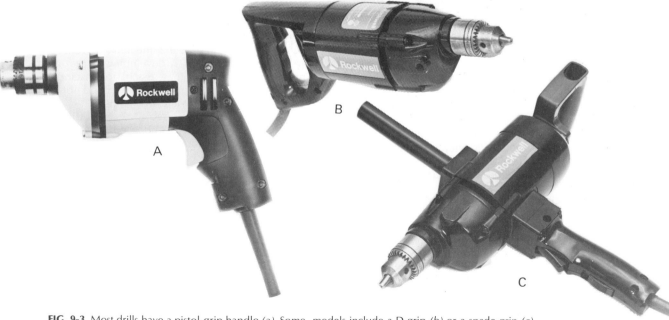

FIG. 9-3. Most drills have a pistol-grip handle (a). Some models include a D grip (b) or a spade grip (c).

Some variable-speed drills have an arrangement with which you can set the maximum speed. A full pull on the trigger then gives you this speed. It eliminates guesswork and the possibility of damaging work by accidental overspeeding. In addition to *infinitely* variable-speed drills, you can get two- to six-speed drills. Typical multispeed ³/₈-inch models have ranges from 0 to 1000 rpm. At least one offers dial-controlled speeds from 1000 to 2500 rpm. Other two-speed varieties may give you a choice of 800 or 1750 rpm. Still another, a six-speed drill, lets you dial or preset speeds of 450, 750, 900, 1050, 1200, and 1350 rpm.

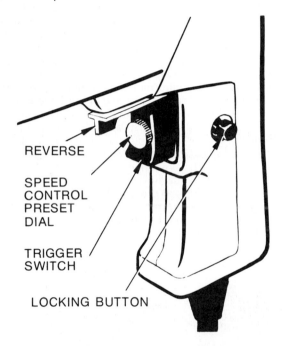

REVERSE

SPEED
CONTROL
PRESET
DIAL

TRIGGER
SWITCH

LOCKING BUTTON

FIG. 9-4. Control and switches on a typical variable-speed drill.

Another feature that should be considered is *reversing*. A drill that has this feature lets you extract screws or loosen nuts with the same efficiency as driving them, because the reversing speed is completely controlled too. The reversing feature is a good one if you do a lot of work involving screws or thread-cutting.

A drill motor's power rating is indicated by its ampere rating or (less frequently) by its horsepower. Actually, both are confusing, because different manufacturers have different methods of arriving at these ratings; as a rule, they are only useful in comparing tools of the same brand. For example, a manufacturer may offer four different ¼-inch drills. The cheapest will be rated ¹/₇ horsepower and 1.9 amperes. Next up the line is one rated at ¹/₅ horsepower and 2.5 amperes. A still higher-quality ¼-inch drill will be rated at ¼ horsepower and 2.8 amperes.

The best of the line, usually tagged as "commercial duty," may be rated ¼ horsepower at 3.2 amperes. But remember that a motor's ampere rating indicates only the amount of current it will draw under "normal" load conditions. A drill will run under such conditions without overheating. Under a greater-than-normal load, however, the current draw in amperes will be greater than the rating, and the drill will deliver up to its maximum power. This maximum power will, however, overheat the tool. If you operate the drill beyond this limit, it will draw even more amperage, but its power will decline until the point is reached where the drill stalls. When this occurs, the motor still draws the maximum current; but since the current cannot be converted into work, it becomes heat and the motor burns out.

Here is another thing you should know about ampere ratings: A tool may be designed to qualify for either a UL household rating or a UL industrial rating. For the former, the UL temperature test calls for running a drill, for example, with no load until it reaches a stable temperature, and then measuring the temperature rise after drilling six holes as specified for the input-current measurement. Any tool with a UL household rating must be so marked on the nameplate.

If a manufacturer wants a UL industrial rating, the requirements are tougher. Here, the tool is subjected to a half-hour temperature test at a steady load equal to the rated amperage. To keep the tool from overheating under this strenuous condition, the input current must generally be less for an industrial tool than for one of the same size with a household rating. Thus, the stronger tool with an industrial rating, capable of doing hard work over longer periods, will actually show a lower current draw. Obviously, this figure alone does not tell the complete story. A high input rating can be misleading, especially if the tool is not labeled by UL standards.

It is also interesting to note that the initial current surge when the motor starts and is developing its maximum turning power or torque may reach, for instance, ¼ horsepower. But, under normal operating conditions, it is usually far below the ¼-horsepower rating.

Most manufacturers of portable electric drills offer tools in the "good," "better," and "best" categories in each size. The soundest advice is to get the best drill your budget allows for the kind of work you do. Generally, the higher-priced drills have more power, more durability, and added versatility. Most companies today classify all their portable power tools as consumer (household standard or utility) duty or industrial (professional or commercial) duty. Unless you have special needs, you will be concerned only with the standard variety.

SHOCKPROOF DRILLS Some portable drills (and a few other portable power tools) are "double-insulated" and "shockproof." That is, no matter what goes wrong inside the drill, you cannot get an electric jolt. This safety feature also has several extra advantages, particularly for the person working in damp areas or where the necessity of properly grounding the tool presents a problem. Double-insulated tools do not require grounding and thus have a standard two-prong plug. Drills that are not double insulated have a three-prong plug.

All or most of the case of a shockproof tool is made of plastic. Besides being a nonconductor of electricity, plastic has three other advantages. It makes drills more colorful and appealing to the eye. The color makes them easy to locate. Further, the plastic safeguards the drill against damage if it is dropped. Finally, it is more pleasant to the touch. But remember that, to preserve the finish of the tool housing, certain cleaning agents must be avoided. These agents include chlorinated cleaning solvent and gasoline. Kerosene and ethyl alcohol are recommended for cleaning the housing of grease and oil. Household detergents that do *not* contain ammonia can also be used.

HANDLES Most drills have pistol-grip handles. The handle should be comfortable and well balanced and have fingerholds in front for nonslip gripping. Some models include spade grips or side handles. These may be attached so that the drill can be grasped with both hands for heavy work or while it is held in an unusual position. A rear handle on the case is especially convenient for many types of drilling jobs; it should be adjustable to vertical or horizontal positions and removable for close work in crowded places.

The connecting cord, which is usually about 8 feet long, should enter the machine case through the extreme end of the pistol-grip handle. This helps to keep the cord clear of the working end of the tool and out of the way of the operator.

SWITCHES AND CONTROLS The trigger switch, which starts the drill, is usually on the pistol-grip handle. Many models include a switch lock for continuous operation. You activate the lock by pressing a button; the lock instantly releases if you tighten your squeeze on the trigger switch. Incidentally, be sure to release the switch locking button before disconnecting the plug from the power supply. Failure to do so will cause the tool to start immediately the next time it is plugged in. Damage or injury could occur.

Variable-speed drills, as mentioned previously, usually have trigger switches that allow you to vary the bit speed from zero to the maximum speed with trigger-finger pressure. Some drills have controls that allow you to preset the maximum speed.

Drills with a reversing feature have separate reverse controls, located in different positions on different brands. In most cases, the reverse control is a slide switch. If the slide switch is set between the forward and reverse positions, the unit will not operate. Simply push the slide switch fully to either the forward position or the reverse position, and the unit will operate when the trigger is depressed.

To protect the motor on any drill, allow the drill to come to a full stop before reversing it. Do not run the drill continuously in reverse; the cooling fan functions most efficiently in the forward position.

CHUCKS All portable drills are equipped with some form of chuck to hold the tools that are to be driven by the machine. There are three types of chucks, as shown in Figure 9-5. These are the *hand-tightened* chuck, which, as its name implies, is tightened onto the tool simply by turning the sleeve by hand; the *hex-key* chuck, which is tightened with the aid of an Allen key; and the *three-jaw geared* chuck. The latter, also known as the "Jacobs chuck," is the most popular and is considered best. In use, its collar is first hand closed onto the shank of a bit. Then the geared key is inserted into the chuck body and turned in the clockwise direction to tighten the three jaws simultaneously. To release the bit, turn the chuck key counterclockwise. On some three-hole geared chucks, it is necessary to tighten the bit by turning the key in all three holes; to release the bit, it is only necessary to turn the key in one hole. A key is supplied with the geared or keyed chuck when the portable drill is purchased.

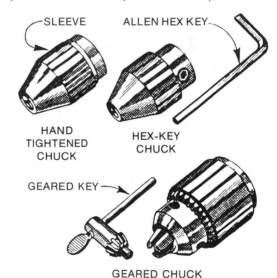

FIG. 9-5. Types of chucks.

Always remove the key *immediately* after you use it. Otherwise the key will fly loose and perhaps cause serious injury when the drill motor is started. Some models have a holder for the key, or it can be taped to the line cord; if it is not, make sure you put it in a safe place where it will not get lost.

To remove a geared chuck from most drills (to use a threaded shank accessory or to replace the chuck), first unplug the tool. Open the chuck, and remove the screw in the bottom of the chuck (it has a left-hand thread). Insert the key in the chuck, and tap it sharply in the direction in which the tool normally rotates (see Figure 9-6). This will loosen the chuck shank threads, and the chuck may then be unscrewed by hand.

FIG. 9-6. Method of removing a geared chuck.

CORDLESS ELECTRIC DRILLS Most drill manufacturers now produce cordless portable drills. If your work takes you onto a roof, into trees, out in the woods, or to other places where electricity is not readily available, a battery-operated drill is for you. The power supply is usually a nickel-cadmium battery pack, located in the handle or in a separate case which you can slip on your belt. An important advantage of the battery-operated drill is that it can be used with absolutely no danger of shock in the rain, on soaked ground, in damp cellars, or on a wet boat dock.

The number of holes that can be drilled with one battery charge varies with bit sharpness, the material being drilled, and the way you handle the tool. Typically, a charge will drill 100 half-inch or 250 quarter-inch holes in ¾-inch fir plywood. It will drill 75 eighth-inch holes in ¼-inch cast iron. For keeping the drill's power up, there is a compact charger to which the drill can safely be left connected when not in use. It keeps the drill ready to go, but will not overcharge or damage it. A typical ¼-inch cordless drill runs at 800 rpm and recharges in 10 hours.

Several manufacturers are producing power packs which are interchangeable among several power tools. That is, a single rechargeable power pack can be used to drive several cordless power tools, such as drills, screwdrivers, solder guns, grass shears, shrub trimmers, and garden sprayers. Most power packs have a greater reserve power than the conventional cordless tools. To recharge the power pack, follow the maker's directions to the letter.

DRILLS AND BITS

Today, you can purchase a drill bit to make a hole in almost any material—wood, metal, plastic, glass, ceramic, stone, and masonry. However, the bits most often used in electric portable drills are called "twist drills."

Twist drills are made of either carbon or high-speed steel. High-speed steel drills—made of an alloy containing tungsten, chromium, and vanadium—are designed expressly for work on metal and can take considerable heat without weakening or becoming dull.

Usually, high-speed drills can do their work without the use of a coolant. The carbon-steel drills are softer and are used solely on wood and soft metals or plastics. They cost much less than the harder steel drills but will wear quickly and become distorted if overworked. On soft metals, they require a flow of water, oil, or other cooling liquid on the tip, to prevent burning. Never put water or other liquids on the electric drill itself. When it is necessary to work without a flow of coolant into the hole, the drill bit must be withdrawn frequently and dipped into a bath of cold water. Do not cool a high-speed drill bit in this manner or it is likely to crack.

FIG. 9-7. (Top) Conventional battery-operated cordless drill; (bottom) power-pack-operated cordless drill.

Here is a general guide giving the drill speed and coolant to use for various materials encountered in the shop (¼- to ½-inch drills):

Cast iron. Dry, at a speed of about 500 rpm
Wrought iron. Lard oil* at about 1500 rpm
Hard steel. Turpentine* at a speed of 450 rpm
Machine steel. Soluble sulphurized oil* at 450 to 800 rpm
Aluminum. Kerosene at a speed of up to 2000 rpm
Brass. Paraffin* or dry at 1500 rpm
Plastic. Dry at speeds over 1000 rpm
Hardwood and softwood. Dry at any speed

*If not available, kerosene or light machine oil may be used.

As described in Chapter 3, the twist drill has no spur or screw at its end to pull it into the work. It cuts away the material at the bottom of the hole as the drill is pushed into the work while it turns very rapidly. Naturally, the most attention must be given to the condition of the tip of the drill. Dull and broken tips heat very rapidly and will not cut straight, clean holes.

As also noted in Chapter 3, twist-drill sizes are denoted by three different systems. Table 3-4 shows that the smallest drills are numbered by wire-gauge sizes from 1 to 80, the largest being number 1, which is 0.228 inch in diameter. Number 80 measures 0.0135 inch in diameter. Letter-size twist drills are commonly known as "jobber's drills" and range from size A, which is 0.234 inch, to Z, which is 0.413 inch in diameter. The third series of twist drills overlaps the other two, but without duplication. These are denoted in fractional sizes, increasing by sixty-fourths of an inch from 1/16 to 1/2 inch. Straight-shank and straight fluted drills for wood and soft metal are made in sets of 16 sizes from 1/32 to 1/2 inch. It is usually necessary to

have a complete set of twist drills on the workbench. For the average home craftsman, the set of fractional-size drills does very well. They should be kept in a drill stand, however, so that the correct size can readily be selected. Inexpensive drill stands are available with the size marked alongside each hole.

Small holes in wood (hard or soft), from 1/16 inch to about 1/2 inch, can be drilled with an electric drill and ordinary twist drills. Drilling in softwood or boards up to 1 inch thick poses no problems. Drilling in hardwood or drilling deep holes can cause the bit to bind if the drill bit is thin, and the chance of the bit breaking is great. To prevent this from happening, all you have to do is relieve (remove) the accumulated chips. This is done by drilling a short distance into the wood and, with the drill still running, drawing the bit out. This will relieve the chips. Then drill a little further, repeat, and continue until the hole is completely bored through.

To drill larger holes in wood, the *spade* or *speed-type* bit is generally recommended. Bits of this style range from about 3/8 inch to as large as 1½ inches. They relieve the chips easily, and binding is not much of a problem. Spade or speed bits have a tendency to split not only the front surface of the wood, but the back surface as well. The front surface can be drilled clean by starting the hole slowly. (That is, do not press too hard.) Also be sure the bit goes in square to the wood.) The back surface can be drilled clean (with no splintering) by either of two methods. First, as soon as the pilot of the bit comes through the back, stop drilling. Complete the hole by drilling from the back. Or, second, clamp a piece of scrap to the back, and drill through both pieces.

Holes larger than 1½ inches can be cut with a hole saw. This is literally a saw bent into a circle. It will make clean, prefectly round holes in anything a hacksaw will cut, including metal, plastic, composition board, and asbestos. Its pilot bit can be centered on a punch mark to locate the

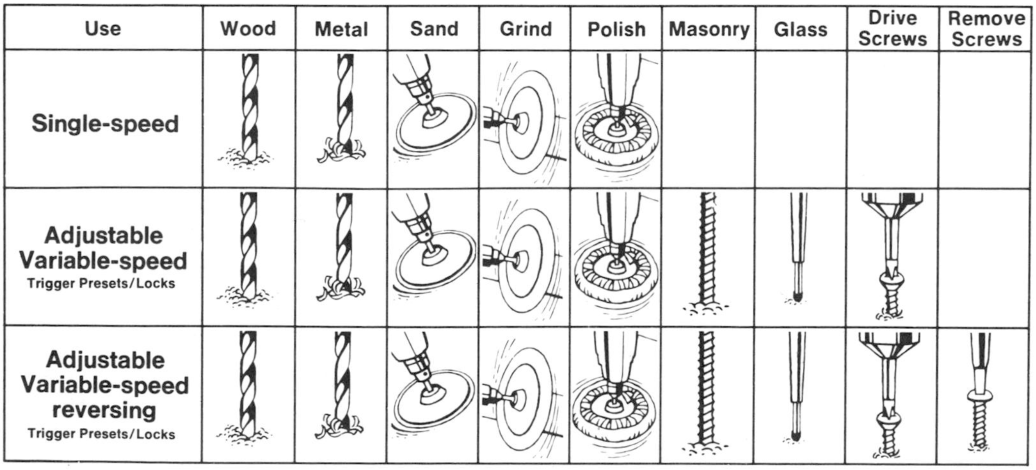

Use	Wood	Metal	Sand	Grind	Polish	Masonry	Glass	Drive Screws	Remove Screws
Single-speed									
Adjustable Variable-speed Trigger Presets/Locks									
Adjustable Variable-speed reversing Trigger Presets/Locks									

FIG. 9-8. With the proper drill or bit, it is possible to drill almost any material, including (left to right) wood, metal, masonry, and glass.

large hole with great accuracy. Although hole saws are available in a size range from about ½ to 6 inches in diameter, most ¼- and ⅜-inch drills are not strong enough to cut large holes with hole saws. The approximate drill-size ranges for hole saws are as follows:

¼-inch drills. Hole saws up to 1½ inches
⅜-inch drills. Hole saws up to 2½ inches
½-inch drills. Hole saws up to 4 inches
Heavy-duty industrial ¼-inch drills. Hole saws up
　　to 6 inches

One-size hole saws are rather costly. More economical is the type with a shaft or mandrel on which saws of various sizes can be mounted. The cuplike saw shells range from ¾ to 2½ inches in diameter and are deep enough to cut through ¾-inch-thick material. (A few are designed to cut up to 2 inches.) Mandrels that fit ¼-inch chucks take saws up to 1⅛ inches in diameter; those for larger saws fit ⅜-inch drill chucks. Be sure to tighten the chuck key in all three holes for maximum grip when using a hole saw, since its large diameter puts great stress on the shank. At any angle other than 90°, the saw will start cutting at one point instead of all around, so take pains to start the pilot drill straight. Use a cutting oil on metal, as you would for twist drills. In thick or hard wood, withdraw the saw occasionally to clear the chips and help cool the saw and the drill motor.

Fly-cutter type circle makers are also available, for cutting holes from ½ to 8 inches in diameter. Actually, the size of the hole is controlled by loosening a setscrew and then sliding the cutter blade in or out. For best results when cutting circles in wood, cut halfway through each side of the wood, or back up the wood, so that the cutting blade does not tear and splinter the wood as it comes through. The cutter blade should be set back behind the center drill bit approximately ½ inch (where the flutes end on the drill bit), so that the blade will be held firmly in place when it begins to bite into the wood. Since the circle cutter has an off-center load, it works more smoothly and with less vibration at slower speeds. When using a fly cutter, be sure that the workpiece is securely clamped to a solid surface.

With either the hole saw or fly cutter, splintering of the far side of the work will be prevented if you bore the hole about halfway through and then finish cutting it from the other face of the work. The pilot hole, having passed through the work, centers the tool for its second cut.

There are other types of bits for drilling holes in wood, such as the spur, auger, self-feed, and Forstner bits. The spur machine bit has a brad and lip point and is one of the cleanest, fastest-cutting bits for dowel holes. These bits come in standard sizes from ¼ to 1 inch and are generally marked thirty-seconds of an inch. The multispur bits give best results for larger holes, from ½ to 1½ inches.

Power auger bits for portable drills have a straight shank and a brad point; they never have a tang. They come in sizes as small as ¼ inch and as large as 2 inches. (Those larger than 1 inch are primarily for industrial use.) Common power auger bits are made either with a solid center or double-spur tips. Because of their efficient chip ejection, auger bits are best for drilling deep holes. That is, the lips on the auger score the circumference of the hole and then cut out the shavings as they revolve. These bits bite deeply into the wood, and the work should be held securely with clamps or a vise to prevent mistakes. Boring the hole from both sides or clamping a block of wood to the back of the work will prevent the bit from splitting the wood as it breaks through. Never use an ordinary screw-point auger in an electric drill; the point will screw itself into the wood and jam there, stalling the motor or wrenching the tool out of your grasp. Such screw-point augers are meant for turning by hand, with the screw helping to feed the bit into the work.

Self-feed bits are used for drilling very-large-diameter holes in wood. They have a threaded point that draws the bit into the wood. For this reason they should only be used in drills with slow speeds. The Forstner bit is similar to the self-feed bit except that it has a brad point. (A brad point is a short projection that does not draw itself into the

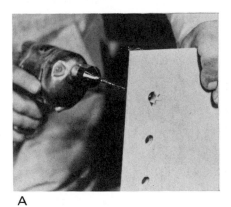

A　　　　　　　　　　B　　　　　　　　　　C

FIG. 9-9. To make large holes in wood, use a: *(a)* power- spade-type bit; *(b)* hole saw; or *(c)* fly or circle cutter.

work.) Forstner bits are used for drilling blind holes—holes that do not go all the way through the work. They leave the bottom of the hole flat. They can, of course, be used to drill completely through. For electric-drill use, they come in all sizes, up to as large as 4 inches in diameter.

Another bit that is good for enlarging holes and making circles and scrolls is the *router* type. Its ¼-inch shaft contains sharp milled flutes that are designed for cutting any shape in plywood, lumber, laminated plastic, wallboard, and nonferrous metals. Used like a round file or rasp, the router drill cuts its own starting hole and will cut any shape in any direction in which the tool is moved.

As mentioned in Chapter 4, it is a good idea, before driving screws in wood, to drill a pilot hole. Not only is it much easier to drive a screw with a pilot hole (especially with a hand screwdriver), but the pilot hole also prevents splitting of the wood. There is a correct size (diameter) of pilot hole for every size of screw. For hardwoods, pilot holes are slightly larger and a little deeper than for softwoods. This is because hardwoods tend to split more easily. If you use twist bits to drill pilot holes, consult the chart in Chapter 4 for the number of the bit to be used to drill the correct size of hole for each size of screw. There are also special profile bits, made for drilling pilot holes.

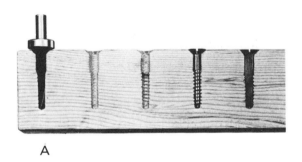

A

B

FIG. 9-10. Two special wood bits for setting screws.

Each is stamped with the number or size of the screw for which they are intended. Most will also bevel the hole for the flush fit of flathead screws (Figure 9-10a). There are also a few which will drill countersink holes for wood plugs to conceal the screwheads (Figure 9-10b). By the way, plug cutters are available as attachments for electric drills (Figure 9-11).

FIG. 9-11. Plug cutter at work.

Bit extensions are available for power drills; they range in length from 12 to 24 inches. Most of these extensions will hold only twist drills, but they permit easy reach into out-of-the-way places.

For drilling masonry, carbide-tipped bits are available in sizes ranging from ⅛ inch to over 1 inch. The larger sizes can only be used with ½-inch drills. Never try to drill masonry with an ordinary drill; even the high-speed variety will quickly succumb to such use. Masonry bits are of ordinary steel except for the cutting lips or edges, which are made of super-hard carbide. The shank may have flutes or a spiral of wire to carry chips out of the hole. It is usually shouldered down to fit a small chuck.

SAFETY TIPS FOR USING PORTABLE DRILLS

In addition to the safety tips already given for the use of portable electric drills, keep the following points in mind:

1. Select the correct drill or bit for the job to be done. For *wood*, use twist drill bits, spade bits, power auger bits, self-feed bits, Forstner bits, spur bits, and hole saws. For *metal*, use high-speed twist drill bits, machine spur bits, or hole saws. For *masonry*, such as brick, cement, and cinder block, use carbide-tipped bits. Use sharp drill bits only.

2. Be sure the material to be drilled is anchored or clamped firmly. When drilling thin material, use a wood backup block to prevent damage to the material.

3. Mount the bit securely in the chuck, and connect the drill to a properly grounded outlet (this is not a concern with the double-insulated type) with the switch in the OFF position. Incidentally, always unplug the drill when attaching or changing bits or accessories.

4. Turn on the switch for a moment, to check whether the bit is properly centered in the chuck and is running true.

5. With the switch in the OFF position, place the point of the bit in the punched layout hole. With variable-speed drills there is no need to center-punch the point to be drilled. Use a slow speed to start the hole, and accelerate by squeezing the trigger harder when the hole is deep enough to drill without the bit skipping out.

6. Hold the drill firmly in one or both hands and at the correct drilling angle. Then turn on the switch and feed the bit into the work. Always apply pressure in a straight line, along the shank of the bit. Use enough pressure to keep the drill biting, but do not push hard enough to stall the motor or deflect the bit. Be sure to brace yourself against the twisting action of the drill.

7. If the drill stalls, it is usually because it is being overloaded or improperly used. Release the trigger immediately to stop the drill, remove the drill bit from the work, and determine the cause of the stalling. Do not click the trigger off and on in an attempt to start a stalled drill: this can damage the drill.

8. When drilling deep holes, especially with a twist drill, withdraw the drill several times to clear the cuttings. Keep the motor running when you pull the bit back out of a drilled hole. This will help prevent jamming.

9. To minimize stalling and breaking through the material, reduce the pressure on the drill, and ease the bit through the last part of the hole.

10. Always remove the bit from the drill as soon as you have completed the work.

DRILLING METAL

The portable electric drill was originally designed for drilling holes in metal—in workpieces that could not be moved to a drill press. Today, this is still an important function of these machines, as almost any home craftsman can testify. Any twist drill having a shank small enough to fit the chuck of a hand drill can be used in the machine. Since all hand-drill chucks are equipped with three jaws, only those drills having a round shank can be used successfully. But, when using twist drills, keep in mind that they are brittle and will break if enough bending stress is applied. To avoid stressing the drill bit, try extending your index finger along the side of the drill housing, with your middle finger on the trigger. Guide the tool—do not force it. Should the tool become overheated, run it unloaded at maximum speed. The drill will cool faster when it is run without a load.

For drilling holes in metal with a hand drill, the same procedure should be followed as when drilling holes in this material with any other equipment (see Chapters 3 and 17). After the hole has been located, a center-punch mark should be placed at the point at which the hole is to be made. Before the power is turned on, the point of the drill should be placed on the center-punch mark. Apply a slight pressure to keep the point of the drill in contact with the metal; then throw the switch to operate the drill. With a variable-speed drill, start the hole at slow speed and increase it to the proper speed as soon as the bit grabs hold. Use the proper lubricant or coolant (as recommended earlier in this chapter) when drilling metals.

Because of its spiral flutes, a twist drill often "grabs" as it breaks through thin material. The lip edges bite into the paper-thin edge formed when the drill has penetrated partway, and the piece tries to ride up the flutes like a nut on a screw. If caught this way, a piece of sheet metal that is not securely held will rotate with the drill and become as dangerous as a whirling knife. Sheet metal should always be clamped down tightly on a workbench, chair, or other firm support. A piece of wood can be placed under the work if you want to avoid drilling into the supporting surface. Never drill sheet metal while holding it with your fingers. The larger drills readily go through sheet stock, but they are even more likely to grab than small drills. When a clean hole is wanted, clamp the sheet metal to the working surface with a piece of wood on top of it. Boring a hole in this way will enable you to spot the drill precisely on the punch mark made in the metal (Figure 9-12).

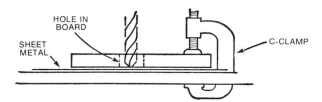

FIG. 9-12. Method of holding a piece of sheet metal.

When drilling any hole, the angle at which the hand drill is held will determine the direction of the hole. If the hole is to be at a right angle to the surface, it is necessary to hold the hand drill in this position. Keep a steady and even pressure on the bit, but only enough to keep the tip cutting. If too much pressure is applied, the tip will dull quickly, and the smaller sizes of twist drills are quite likely to bend or even break. In either case, the hole will be imperfect and you may spoil the work. If the bit bends, the sides of the drill will enlarge the diameter of the hole. When the hole is to go all the way through the material, ease up on the pressure as you approach the other side. Let the bit cut its way through, instead of breaking out of the other side. Do not allow the drill to go any farther than necessary in finishing the hole. Keep it turning as it is withdrawn. It is at this breakthrough stage that the bit is most likely to jam and break. The drill should rotate as long as it is in contact with the metal; keep the power on until the drill is completely free of the hole.

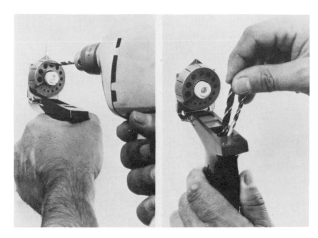

FIG. 9-13. An aid to drilling straight. The dial rotates to sizes of drills up to ¼ inch in diameter. You hold the guide on the work with one hand, and operate the drill with the other. A nonslip rubber base on the guide keeps the drill from walking or scratching while you drill horizontally or vertically on any flat surface. Drills are stored in the handle.

Never hold the work in your lap or hands, or against your chest while using any kind of drill. Remember that the electric drill works many times faster than the ordinary hand drill. Fasten the work securely in a vise, or clamp it to the work table or a sawhorse before starting to drill. When the work is well clamped, grabbing can be controlled to some extent by holding back on the feed pressure as the drill begins to break through; but shut off the power immediately if it seizes. Always have a good hold on the drill so it will not twist out of your grasp. You can sometimes clear out the jagged hooks remaining in the hole by feeding the drill in very lightly, for an instant at a time; however, it is likely to snag again. A better and safer way is to turn a T-handled taper reamer in the hole by hand. This will both clean out the ragged edges and bring the hole to final size.

To convert a portable hand drill to a lightweight drill press, all that is required is a bench stand similar to the one shown in Figure 9-14. The manufacturers of various hand drills have designed stands to take their particular machines. In most cases, a stand designed to take one manufacturer's hand drill will not hold the hand drill of some other maker.

FIG. 9-14. Drill-press stand for a portable drill.

In operation, all bench stands are alike; to use them, all that is required is to place the chuck end of the drill in the yoke at the bottom of the drill bracket and secure it in place by whatever means has been provided. The base of the stand should be fastened to the bench with screws. The bracket can be adjusted to any height from the base and swung around to any desired position. The feed-handle leverage is advantageous for tough drilling and for smoother feeding for delicate work.

DRILLING WOOD

Holes in wood can be made with the same twist drills used for metal. In thick stock there is considerable friction, and the wood waste does not pass up the flutes easily. Carbon drills may overheat unless pulled out frequently to clear the chips from the flutes. For larger holes, use the woodcutting bits and tools mentioned earlier in the chapter.

To start the hole accurately, make an indentation with a center punch, the blunt-pointed punch called a "nail set," or even an ordinary nail. However, even with an indentation, the drill may drift from a hard section to a softer section or run along a grain line in the wood. Where hole location is critical, it is a good idea to lay it out with cross lines, punch-mark the intersection, and inspect the depression made by the drill before it has fully entered. The cross marks will show up any shift, even though the drill has obliterated the original punch mark.

When thin material or material that is apt to splinter is to be drilled, the workpiece should be backed up with a block of scrap wood so that the bit will have a good bed to bite into. Let up on the pressure just before the tip cuts through; this will give a good clean hole. When drilling deep holes in wood, lift the bit partly out of the hole several times. This will clear the chips from the flutes of the drill bit and greatly speed up the work. It will also aid in making the hole more exactly to size.

There are several methods for gauging the depth of a hole that is not to go all the way through the material. A short piece of copper tubing or a piece of scrap wood can be slipped over the drill bit to expose only enough of the bit to make the correct depth of hole. Or, a short rubber band or piece of string can be fastened around the drill to mark the proper depth.

SPECIAL DRILLING JOBS

As mentioned earlier in the chapter, carbide-tipped masonry drill bits should be used when making holes in soft stone, cement, brick, cinder block, stucco, and similar materials. When you use these hard-tipped bits, however, take care not to break or dull the tip. Carbide tips are brittle and breakable. Do not ram the drill hard against the work. Maintain a steadily increasing pressure as the bit enters the work. Do not let the drill ease up or run idly in the hole. Once the hole is started, increase the pressure as the bit cuts away at the material. If you should get tired (or to free the bit of debris), pull it out of the hole for a minute, but do not let up on the pressure while the drill is working. Actually, for all practical purposes, how much pressure should be used depends directly upon the hardness of the material being drilled. Coolants are not necessary, as a general rule. It may be desirable, however, when hard material such as tile or porcelain is being drilled, to use water or turpentine as a coolant. When a coolant is used, the entire drill point should be kept wet.

Keeping the hole free of dust is important when using a masonry drill. A drill having a flute or twist along the body will, itself, remove the cutting dust; however, when excessive moisture is encountered, particularly in horizontal or downward drilling, it may be necessary to lift the drill slightly from time to time to clean the hole. If the hole is deep, blow it out from time to time (a syringe or pump is best, to avoid getting dust in the eyes), or flush it out with water from a small syringe.

The drilling of small holes is never a problem, whether the material is hard or soft. Large-diameter holes, however, should first be drilled to a small diameter and then either to a larger or to the desired diameter, depending upon the hardness of the material and the diameter of the hole. When drilling holes in reinforced concrete, examine the hole occasionally to avoid drilling through large pebbles. If a pebble is encountered, it is best to break it with a center punch and hammer to protect the drill point.

FIG. 9-15. Drill bits used for drilling in brick, stone, concrete block, and concrete should have carbide tips. Heavy pressure should be applied when drilling these hard materials. A drill revolving with too little pressure will soon have a dull or glazed cutting point, which makes drilling difficult thereafter. Once a certain amount of pressure has been applied, it should be maintained or increased, but never reduced. If you get tired, remove the drill from the work and rest, rather than let up on the pressure.

When you have the problem of drilling a series of holes in wood or metal at the same angle, make a jig from a piece of 2 X 4 by drilling one hole through it at the correct angle. This block can then be clamped into position over the mark to start each hole; after the hole is started, the block can be removed for drilling to depth. Each hole will be at the same angle. When starting any hole at an angle to the surface, make a deep mark with the punch, and start the drill into the material *vertically*. When the tip has entered, change the angle of the machine to the desired angle for the hole.

Wooden alignment jigs can be useful, but only in proportion to the care with which they are made. In a square-cut wood block about 2 inches thick, bore true holes with the bits you most commonly use. This should be done on a drill bench stand or drill press if possible. With a square, carry (mark) the centerlines of the holes down all four edges so that they can be aligned with cross lines on the work surface to spot the holes where you want them (Figure 9-16a). A similar block with the guide hole at an angle is useful for boring holes to fit furniture legs. Draw the centerline down two edges for alignment with guidelines on the workpiece. If these are laid out parallel to the work edges, the legs will be angled the same way. If they are drawn diagonally, the legs will spread out cornerwise as shown in Figure 9-16b.

When any quantity of work is to be done—a number of holes in either one piece or several similar pieces—arrange the work so that all the holes of one size can be drilled at one time. This will speed up the work and make for greater accuracy. If called for, perhaps a drill jig can be devised which will make all the holes uniform and precise. A piece of soft steel or hardwood with holes drilled at the desired intervals will be of help in spacing and locating accurately. Any piece which serves as a pattern in making duplicate holes will serve as a drill jig. Heavy cardboard or thin plywood will do very well for large areas.

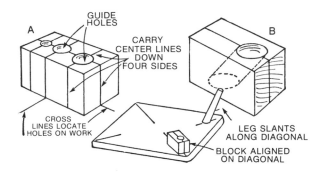

FIG. 9-16. Simple wooden alignment jig.

DRILL ACCESSORIES

With a variety of accessories, a portable electric drill can also turn wood, grind, sand, pump water, drive or remove screws, chisel wood, mix paint, saw, trim hedges, and perform many other tasks. Although the function of the drill is simply to provide power for these accessories, not all drills can do all jobs. There are two limiting factors: speed and power.

Speed is far less a problem these days than it was a few years ago. Variable-speed drills are common today, at reasonable prices. Power, however, is something else. It is the real limitation on a drill's ability to do all the other jobs. For example, a given drill may easily drive a hedge trimmer but may not be powerful enough for a chain saw that is supposed to cut down a tree. Nor would you think of hitching up a drill to a cement mixer, with its heavy load of gravel, sand, water, and cement. Fortunately for us, however, most accessory manufacturers are well aware of these limitations and do not make accessories which are beyond a drill's capability. But even within this area, you cannot leave it to the manufacturer to decide for you. You must match the accessory to your drill or perhaps burn it out.

Two accessories that illustrate this point are the hole saw and the sanding disk. Any ¼-inch, 2000-rpm drill will handle a 1-inch hole saw without undue strain. Some of the better ones can even go beyond this. With the same drill, you can use sanding disks up to about 5 inches in diameter. If you need larger disks and hole saws, you will have to use a ⅜-inch drill, which operates with more power and less speed. For very large hole saws and bigger sanding disks you must go to ½-inch drills. As drills get bigger, their speed is generally reduced, and their power increased. The reduction in speed and the increase in power are accomplished by gear reduction and not by reducing the speed of the drill motor itself. The speeds of the motors of most ¼-, ⅜-, and ½-inch drills are almost the same (10,000 to 15,000 rpm). It is the gear reduction that changes the speed and at the same time increases the power (torque). So keep in mind that a variable-speed drill that is run at one-half its top speed does not have twice the torque (power). It will have the same torque as it would have at top speed. How do you know, then, whether an accessory is safe to use on your drill? Here are a few simple rules:

Small-diameter accessories require less power than large ones. For example, a ¼- or ⅜-inch drill is usually powerful enough to run any of the following accessories:

> Screwdrivers for up to No. 8 screws
> Nut runners and sockets
> Flexible-shaft drivers
> Contour sanders
> Grinding and honing stones up to 3 inches
>   in diameter
> Lawn-mower sharpeners
> Wire wheels up to 4 inches
> Cutting wheels for metal, masonry, and ceramic
>   tile
> Sanding disks
> Orbital-sander attachments
> Bevel and bead molding cutters
> Earth augers
> Saber-saw attachments, up to 4-inch blades
>   (softwood only)
> Small circular-saw attachments
> Buffing pads up to 5 inches
> Polishing pads up to 5 inches
> Rotary power files
> Right-angle drives
> Router attachments
> Router-type cutters
> Chisel-type cutters
> Small lathe units
> Small plug cutters
> Compass hole cutters (can cut holes up to 12
>   inches in diameter)
> Paint mixers
> Small sanding drums and rasps
> Hedge trimmers no more than 12 to 13 inches
>   long
> Grass shears
> Water pumps for intermittent use

A

B

C

D

E

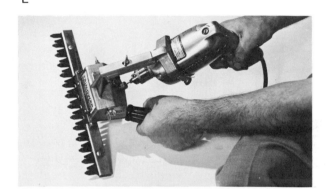

F

G

H

FIG. 9-17. Popular drill accessories: *(a)* wire wheel for rust-removal jobs; *(b)* paint mixer; *(c)* right-angle drive for hard-to-reach locations; *(d)* buffing pad being used in a horizontal stand; *(e)* woodcutting drum rasp; *(f)* hedge trimmer; *(g)* water pump; *(h)* disk sander; *(i)* pad sander; *(j)* earth auger; *(k)* polisher; *(l)* contour sander.

K

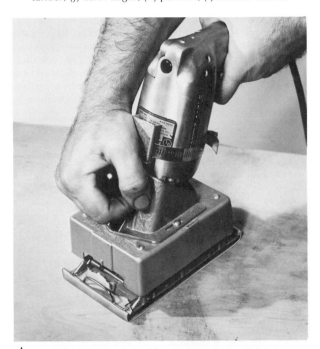

I

L

J

Although the accessories listed above are fine to use with most ¼- or ⅜-inch drills, they can harm the drill if they are misused; to prevent this, follow the maker's instructions. For example, if you have a 4-inch circular-saw attachment and you try to cut ¾-inch pine with a dull blade, you will burn out your drill. This also applies to hole saws in hardwood or metal and hedge trimmers being used to cut heavy bushes.

There are three ways to know if you are overburdening your drill. Any one or more of these signals means *stop;* something is wrong, and any further work will destroy the drill.

1. The job is just not getting done.
2. The drill is straining too hard; it is groaning and/or turning too slowly, it is twisting and jerking in your hand, and it just does not sound right.
3. The drill is getting hot in your hand. The best way to make drill manufacturers rich is to overcome the hot-drill problem by wrapping the drill in rags or by wearing a pair of gloves so as not to burn yourself. When any portable tool gets that hot, it is telling you to stop work instantly.

If you burn out a small ¼-inch drill, it will cost you more to replace the burned-out motor than to purchase a new drill. This is reason enough to take note of the three warnings mentioned above. Here is how to overcome these three problems:

1. If the accessory being used has a cutting edge, check to be sure that the edge is sharp and free of chips, gums, and resins. Also check to be sure the accessory is in good order. See that it is well oiled and that its bearings are in good condition.
2. Take it easy; reduce the feed or pressure you are applying. Also remember that a light-duty ¼-inch drill is for light work only. A heavy-duty ¼-inch drill can take more punishment.
3. If the drill gets hot, you may have already damaged it, probably because it is underpowered for the job at hand. To overcome this problem, you must invest in a larger tool, such as a ⅜-inch drill. Some accessories for which larger drills should be used are sanding disks (up to 6 inches), wire wheels (up to 6 inches), grinding wheels (up to 5 inches), screwdriver bits to drive No. 10 screws, nut runners up to ⅜ inch, small lathe attachments, pumps, and hacksaw attachments.

Naturally, any accessories that are compatible with a ¼-inch drill will do no harm to a ⅜-inch drill. Not many accessories are designed for the ½-inch drill. It is too slow for good grinding and sanding, but it works well in driving wire plumber's snakes for pipe cleaning and very large hole saws. See the manufacturer's catalog for information on the accessories available for particular drill brands and models.

DRILL MAINTENANCE

No more important message could be given regarding the use of any tool than this simple advice: *Read the instructions carefully.* Your portable electric drill is simple to operate and is built for many years of trouble-free performance. Satisfactory results, personal safety, and good performance depend on your knowledge of your work and the tools you use. A few minutes spent in reading the manufacturer's instructions will save many headaches later on. If trouble should develop, by all means contact your nearest authorized dealer and have repairs made promptly. Your dealer is the only one who can make adequate and guaranteed repairs to your portable electric drills. It is up to you to keep your tools clean and free of dust and dirt.

LUBRICATION Most electric drills today have self-lubricating bearings, which means that periodic relubrication is not required. But if a tool is not of this type, two or three drops of a high-grade lubricating oil should be added to the commutator end bearing once a month through the oil hole in the top of the motor housing.

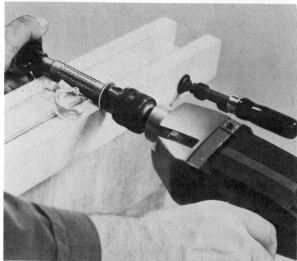

FIG. 9-18. Two router-type cutters in use.

DRILL CHUCK Always bottom the drill bit in the chuck. The chuck jaws must grip the shank fully and firmly so that the bit will be centered exactly. Use all three holes in the chuck body to tighten the jaws. Insert the chuck key in each hole in turn, and tighten as much as possible. Use only the chuck key to tighten or loosen the chuck jaws.

DRILL CARE Make it standard practice to inspect new bits or drills before you buy them, and periodically check your old ones. Keep all drill bits in a drill rack or box holder, and keep them in proper order. Pick each one up by the shank end, and examine the condition of the cutting edge. Look directly at the point to determine whether the center is correct. Look at the lip of the drill and at the radial clearance. Inspect the shank to see whether it is dented or chewed to such an extent that it will not center properly in the chuck. Finally, roll the drill bit across a smooth surface to determine whether it is bent. If repairs are required, make them at once so the drills will be in good shape when needed. In Chapter 22 of this book, we explain how to sharpen and care for your twist drills and bits.

FIG. 9-19. An electric chisel attachment cuts a mortise (top) in a furniture leg to fit a tenon cut in a side rail (bottom). An adjustable ring on the tool seats on the guide strip when the desired depth of cut is reached.

A   B   C

FIG. 9-20. Power screwdriver and accessories: (a) variable-speed 3/8-inch drill with screwdriver bit; (b) bit with finder sleeve that snaps into clutch, which engages when the drill is pushed down; (c) speed reducer that adds torque for driving screws (for drills without enough power.)

PORTABLE POWER SAWS

There is no doubt about handsaws being basic to any workshop; they are convenient to use and certainly less expensive than power saws. But sooner or later, if you do any quantity of work at all, you are certain to want one or more of the four portable power saws—circular, saber, reciprocating, and chain saws—that are now available. You will save hours of time and arm-tiring effort. For instance, with 132 strokes of a handsaw, sharpened and properly set, you can cut diagonally across a 2 X 10 to form a roof rafter. With a portable circular saw you can make this same cut in 16 seconds. You have saved 116 seconds plus the effort involved. True, if you are a home handyman, you may not value your time or effort in dollars and cents, but you can pause between strokes of the handsaw to think about it. Of course, for the professional, the time spent in prolonged cutting operations can now be cut to one-tenth or even less. In the cutting of joists, studs, and rafters for a house, one carpenter can easily do the work of 10 with an efficient portable circular saw.

In most operations where wood is involved, the accuracy of the sawing is of utmost importance. If a piece is cut unevenly or cut too short, it cannot be used without considerable alteration of the structure or the creation of an unsightly or weak member. The electric portable saw makes straight, accurate cuts in almost any type of material. With a little practice, the average person can cut with a portable saw with far greater accuracy and precision than a skilled worker with a handsaw.

Circular Saws

The workhorse of all power saws is the portable circular saw. In general, it saves 50 to 90 percent (in time) for most operations and, proportionate amount of energy. But most important, by taking some of the drudgery out of the work, it makes most carpentry more interesting and satisfying. Your own effort is limited to lifting the saw and guiding it along the markings.

FIG. 10-1. Major parts of a typical portable circular saw.

GENERAL FEATURES OF CIRCULAR SAWS

The sizes and prices of portable electric circular saws vary a great deal, and there is probably no one size and type that will be fully satisfactory for all workers. The saw is sized according to the diameter of the circular blade that it uses. Since there are quickly interchangeable blades for cutting all kinds of materials and for all kinds of cuts, the saws themselves are not designated by cut as are ordinary handsaws.

Electric saws range in size from small 4-inch-blade types up to heavy-duty 10- and 12-inch-blade types for construction work. The 6½- to 7½-inch sizes are probably the most popular and most generally useful saws for home shop and general cutting operations. In practice, there is not as much difference between the cutting capacities of a 6½- and a 7½-inch saw as one might think. As a rule, you gain only about ⅛ inch of cutting depth with each ½-inch increase in blade diameter. Therefore, it is important to check not only on the blade diameter, but on the actual thickness of stock a saw can handle. Remember, too, that you will be making many 45° angle cuts, which call for greater capacity than straight-through sawing. In general, a 6½-inch saw, tilted to 45°, can penetrate a stock thickness of 1$\frac{13}{16}$ to 1⅞ inches, and bevel-cut 2 X 4s with ease. A 7¼-inch saw will angle-cut to a depth of about 2 inches, and an 8-inch saw to 2$\frac{3}{16}$ inches. These three sizes are capable of 90° cuts of 2$\frac{3}{32}$ inches, 2$\frac{7}{16}$ inches, and 2$\frac{23}{32}$ inches, with some slight variation among models.

The motor used in most saws is a universal 120-volt, motor that has a free-running no-load speed of anywhere from 4400 to 7000 rpm. Theoretically, the faster a blade turns, the smoother will be its cut. The question is, how well does a blade maintain its speed under load? The only way to find out is to try the saw yourself. What you will probably discover is that the higher the horsepower, the more drive and the less stalling there is. The big danger in using portable saws used to be stalling and kickback. When a saw struck tough going and could not go forward, it usually jumped back. This hazard has largely been eliminated by the use of a slip clutch. Typically, this is a

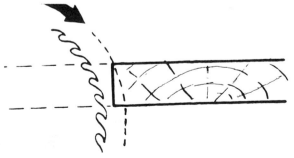

FIG. 10-2. The cutting action of a portable circular saw is exactly opposite that of a stationary table circular saw. The portable saw cuts from the bottom up.

spring washer under the blade nut. If the blade binds in the cut, the washer allows the blade to slip while the motor continues to turn. There is no kickback. It is safer for you and easier on the motor windings. For the record, the normal slowdown from a free-running speed of 5500 rpm is to about 3200 rpm under full load.

Generally, the more power a saw has, the smoother and faster it is likely to cut and the easier and safer it is to handle. You will find 7¼-inch saws with 1, 1¼, 1½, 2, and 2½ horsepower (hp). Does that mean a saw with 1½ hp is automatically more powerful than one with 1 hp? Not necessarily. For one thing, horsepower is not an absolute standard. Different manufacturers have different ways of evaluating it. A motor's ampere rating is, in some cases, a more accurate indication of its power. (Most 6½- to 7½-inch consumer type saws draw from 9 to 10 amperes.) For another, the kind and number of bearings, plus the saw's construction and design are extremely important factors in power. Horsepower rating is, however, a fairly reliable way of ranking the saws of one manufacturer with each other.

When selecting a portable circular saw, study it carefully. For instance, with the saw in cutting position, check how well you can see where the blade is. Can you see it from either side? Usually, you follow a line by watching where the blade is cutting. Check the blade guard. Generally, the upper blade guard is an integral part of the saw housing. The lower blade guard is made to cover the lower part of the blade when the saw is not cutting; it retracts into the upper blade guard as the saw enters the work. Thus, as much as possible of the blade is guarded. When the blade is cutting, however, the portion of it below the work is exposed. Some more expensive portable saws have a ball-bearing guard in their telescopic action. This device allows the blade to enter a cut smoothly at angles as small as 5° right or left, at very slight pressure.

Almost all standard-make portable saws have a housing that serves as a guard against the blade below. Base or shoe plates on which the saws ride are pivoted so that square and angular cuts can be made easily. This base or shoe may be wraparound, or on one side of the blade only. The design of the base plate determines how closely you can saw to vertical surfaces. For extra-close cutting, one saw permits detaching of the wraparound base and makes use of a special built-in, flush-cut base. Most good saws have some type of rip guide. In most cases, this rip guide is a side extension to the shoe that guides the saw blade parallel to the edge of the work. Some saw models include a rip guide; for others, it is an accessory.

Portable circular power saws have switches that will only operate when they are squeezed. That is, the saw is turned on and off by a trigger-type switch located in the pistol-grip handle. This arrangement provides an efficient way to grip the saw, work with it, and control it with minimum fatigue.

The depth of cut on some saws is controlled by sliding the motor and blade up and down. On others, the power unit is pivoted at the front of the shoe. Either method is sound, provided it includes a scale for quick depth setting and allows the blade to be pulled almost all the way up to make very shallow dado cuts. If the blade cannot be retracted this far, the shallowest groove, rabbet, or dado you can make is the saw's minimum projection below the shoe. The other adjustment to consider is that for tilting the blade to make angle cuts.

Some saws have housings that are all or part plastic. This usually indicates the saw is double-insulated and "shockproof." Its plug will have two prongs instead of three. Saws with three-prong plugs usually come with an adapter so they can be plugged into ungrounded outlets. Few people ever bother to connect the adapter properly, so the grounding feature is worthless. With a double-insulated tool this is never a problem, and you are always protected. A plastic housing is as tough or tougher than metal. A plastic handle also has a thermal advantage. It is not quite so icy cold to the touch in freezing weather, or blistering in hot weather.

Other factors that should guide you in choosing a saw are its weight and duty cycle. Is its weight such that you will be able to use it as long at a time as is necessary? Makers have worked miracles in lightening these tools, and a competent one need not be overly heavy. Good 6½- and 7½-inch saws weigh only 10 to 11 pounds. An 8-inch heavy-duty machine usually weighs under 14 pounds.

Most consumer type circular saws have bronze sleeve bearings, which require periodic lubrication and cleaning. Ball bearings are lubricated for their expected life and equipped with seals. However, as the gearbox does require cleaning and greasing, the saw has to be opened up periodically, regardless of the type of bearings. Therefore, for occasional home use a consumer or utility type saw is more than adequate. If you plan major construction work that will keep a saw humming for hours at a time, consider an industrial or professional heavy-duty type with ball bearings and an industrial Underwriters' Laboratories listing.

BLADE TYPES

The portable electric circular saw is designed primarily for the rough work of construction and home alterations and improvements. It is not meant for fine finish work. However, it can be very useful to the home craftsman because of its versatility. What makes it so versatile is the great variety of blades and cutting wheels that can be used with it.

With the proper saw blade, you can cut almost any material—wood, metals (iron, steel, aluminum, brass, bronze), plastics, fiberglass, ceramics (tile), brick, cement block, and slate. Naturally, in order to cut such a large variety of materials, you need a selection of blades.

The three basic blade types are crosscut, rip, and combination.

1. Crosscut blades have teeth that angle alternately to the left and right. The inside of each tooth is filed like a knife-edge, so it slices wood fibers. There is no better blade for crosscutting operations.
2. Rip blades have teeth that are individual chisels. They chip away the wood. There is no better blade for ripping.
3. Combination blades both slice and chip, so they can be used either for ripping or crosscutting. They do not crosscut as well as crosscut blades or rip as well as rip blades, but they do both well enough to make them the most popular blades around. When you purchase a new saw, a combination blade generally comes with it.

FIG. 10-3. The four commonly used blades: (top) flooring blade; (left) crosscut blade; (right) plywood blade; (bottom) combination blade. Profiles of the other blades mentioned in this chapter can be found in chapter 14.

In addition to these three basic blades, there are the following specialized types.

Miter or *planer* blades are combination blades that have been hollow-ground or flat-ground to produce especially smooth cuts. They are for cabinet and trim work. They make almost invisible joints and leave no tooth marks.

Plywood blades have very fine teeth—typically 150, in contrast to 20 to 24 in a combination blade. They produce smooth, splinter-free cuts. Plywood blades have no set, and their rims are typically taper-ground (to make them thinner than the rest of the blade) or flat-ground. The extra-fine teeth mean a smooth cutoff. A plywood blade, in addition to doing a clean job on plywood, also works well with flakeboard or chipboard, hardboard, and fiberboard, as well as copper, brass, bronze, and lead. When cutting any of these soft metals, lubricate the blade with tallow.

Flooring blades have teeth that are larger than those of the plywood blade and are designed to cut best across the grain. The teeth are quite hard and will stand up quite well if the blade cuts through an occasional nail or two. These blades are good for cutting up old or used lumber, ripping up old floors, or cutting through plaster walls. (Incidentally, when cutting through a wall, keep the protrusion of the blade at just the thickness of the plaster or wallboard you are cutting. It can be disastrous if you cut through a hidden electric cable or water pipe.)

Nonferrous blades usually have even finer teeth than plywood blades—typically 168. Use them for aluminum, bronze, copper, lead, other soft nonferrous metals, and tough materials.

Sheet-metal blades will cut metal roofing and iron. It is essential to wear goggles when using them.

Cutoff wheels are used for cutting metals, either nonferrous or ferrous (iron, steel, stainless steel). They are disks made of small grains of abrasive embedded in reinforced plastic. When purchasing one of these wheels, be sure it is marked "reinforced," "shatterproof," or "flexible." Also be sure it is marked with a speed rating of over 4000 rpm (the speed of the average portable saw). Metal cutoff wheels will also cut any ceramic, brick, slate, stone, cement, etc. If, however, the bulk of your cutting is in these materials, get a cutoff wheel especially designed for masonry. It will be basically the same as the metal-cutting wheel, with a different grit and binder. Needless to say, if you have a masonry wheel and you must cut an occasional piece of metal, you can do so with the masonry wheel.

Friction wheels are used only to cut iron and steel. They are hard-steel blades that have no teeth; they cut by friction and burn their way through the material.

Some circular-saw blades are made of special metal or have a special finish. For example, Teflon-coated blades are perhaps the newest development. They are available in crosscut, rip, combination, plywood, planer, and other styles. Coated with self-lubricating, self-healing Teflon S, these saw blades cut faster and smoother, and require less motor power. Teflon blades resist rust and stay sharp longer. They can be resharpened and reset.

A black-oxide finish identifies a hard-tooth "disposable" blade. Each tooth edge is induction-hardened and holds an edge even when encountering an occasional nail. These blades are so cheap you can afford to discard them when they dull. You cannot sharpen them with a file; it has to be done by grinding. The teeth cannot be reset. These blades are good for framing cuts, but not for fine work or finish cabinetry.

Tungsten carbide is one of the hardest cutting materials known. Tungsten-carbide-tipped blades cost nearly three times as much as standard blades but may last up to 20 times longer. You can get one with 8 or 12 silver-brazed

FIG. 10-4. Cutoff wheel (left) and friction blade (right) in use.

carbide teeth for rough cutting, or with 24 to 60 teeth for smoother cutting. Despite their hardness, they are not for masonry, ferrous metals, or where nails may be encountered; any of these will damage the teeth.

Circular-saw blades, like those on any saw, get dull and must be resharpened. The first sign of dullness is the blade's inability to cut easily. Hitting a nail, even a small one, will diminish the blade's ability to cut properly. (A blade that creeps to the right or left while cutting has been improperly sharpened.) Good-quality blades are cheaper to own than cheap blades in the long run. Blades with chromium plating on the teeth are harder and last longer than blades without the chrome finish. However, when they are sharpened the first time, the chrome finish is removed by the file; since the rest of the blade is comparatively soft, it will not hold an edge any more.

The time it takes to change to the proper blade is well worth the resulting better performance. Here are two tricks to keep in mind when changing the blade of a circular saw:

1. Use a box wrench to turn the arbor nut counterclockwise, holding the blade stationary by means of a small block of wood wedged between the teeth and the shoe. When the nut is off, you can remove the blade. Or, if the blade teeth are too small to get a bite on the wedge block, you will find that the blade has a small hole into which you can insert a nail or rod; rotate the blade until this metal wedge "locks" the blade against the shoe. Then turn the nut.

2. As mentioned earlier, most good saws have a slip clutch: you can turn the nut, but you will only succeed in rotating it without loosening it. For this type, place the box wrench on the nut; then sharply rap its opposite end with a hammer. One or two blows should free it for further loosening by turning. If the nut is extremely tight (it gets tighter as you saw), do not give up. Keep rapping; it will come off. When mounting a blade, make sure the saw teeth face in the proper direction.

SAFETY FIRST WITH A POWER CIRCULAR SAW

The following safety rules must be observed when you use a portable circular saw:

1. Wear goggles or a face shield while using the saw and while cleaning up debris afterward.
2. Hold the saw firmly with one hand. Care should be taken that the saw does not break away, thereby causing injury. If you are guiding the saw with two hands, keep the second hand on the motor housing, not near the blade.
3. Inspect the blade at frequent intervals, and always after it has locked, pinched, or burned. The electrical connection should be broken before this examination. Remember, never use a dull saw blade. Pinching or binding indicates a dull blade. Details on sharpening saw blades can be found in Chapter 22.
4. Do not overload the saw motor by pushing too hard or cutting stock that is too heavy.
5. Before using the saw, carefully examine the material to be cut, and free it of nails and other metal substances. Avoid cutting into or through knots as far as possible.
6. All portable power-driven saws should be equipped with guards which will automatically adjust themselves to the work when in use, so that none of the teeth protrude above the work. The guard over the blade should be adjusted so that it slides out of its recess and covers the blade to the depth of the teeth when the saw is lifted off the work. All guards have some form of rubber bumper to absorb the shock when the guard jumps back into place. If this bumper is lost or worn out, metal will bang against metal, and sooner or later something will crack. When you put the saw down after a cut, the blade is still spinning. If the guard does not cover the bottom of the blade quickly, the spinning blade will touch the floor or workbench, and the saw will kick back at you. When you put the saw down, it should rest on the lower guard and one edge of the shoe. The shoe is quite sturdy, but the lower guard is not, so be sure not to drop the saw down on it. A broken lower guard can be dangerous and is fairly expensive to repair. If the saw is accidently dropped, check the lower guard by lifting it to make sure it moves freely and does not touch the saw blade. Incidentally, never clamp or tie the lower guard into the open position.
7. Check the shoe and bevel-angle adjustments to be certain that they are tight. Plug the cord into a grounded outlet (unless the saw is double insulated), and be sure that the cord will not become tangled in the work.

8. The electric plug should be pulled before any adjustments or repairs are made to the saw. This includes changing the blade. Also make certain that the switch snaps off immediately once it is released. Never tape the switch so it will stay on. If you find that the switch sticks, even a little, change it.

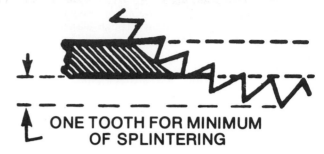

ONE TOOTH FOR MINIMUM OF SPLINTERING

FIG. 10-5. Not more than one tooth of the blade should extend below the material to be cut for minimum splintering. Depths beyond one tooth should be used only when splintering is no problem.

USING THE PORTABLE CIRCULAR SAW

The portable electric circular saw is a right-handed tool and is used very much like the handsaw. The difference is that the cut is made in the opposite direction: the blade cuts from the bottom to the top of the work, and the speed of the machine does the cutting. Hold the saw with the right hand, and the work with the left. Make sure that the work is safely supported and in a position that allows comfortable sawing. The ideal height for sawing is about midway between the knees and the hips, or just below the hips. This height allows the body to lean forward and slightly over the work so that the guideline of the cut can be clearly seen. The height of the work should also be such that you can move the saw all the way across the width of the board without an extended reach. Never stand directly behind the saw when operating it. Stand off to one side, and keep your other (left) hand well out of the line of cut. Never hold the work with a finger underneath the work, and do not become careless when you reach the end of the cut. Remember that the lower blade guard will not return until the blade is clear of the material.

Supporting the work properly is of considerable importance in any kind of sawing, but with the portable circular saw it is especially so. Sawhorses make good supports and are about the right height for most ordinary sawing. Place them far enough apart so that the material has a solid support, and place one of them close to the left side of the line of the cut so the saw will not bind. The only thing to be careful of here is leaving enough clearance so that the saw blade can complete the cut without sawing the support. When plywood or other light material is to be sawed, it will help considerably to place the stock on the worktable, with scrap 1 X 2 material used to space it up from the table surface. If you allow the blade less than 1 inch of clearance below the material, the saw will easily clear the top of the table and will have a solid support to ride on. Never support the saw on the work that is to be cut off. If you do, the saw will not be supported at the end of the cut. Position the work, the saw, and yourself so that the saw is supported by the work during and after the cut. If you cannot hold any work firmly with one hand, use clamps or a vise to do so. Do not try to hold short pieces by hand. Never run the saw while carrying it at your side.

Place the work with its "good" side—the one on which appearance is more important—down. The portable circular saw cuts upward, so any splintering that occurs will be on the face that is up when you saw it. Set the depth of cut $\frac{1}{4}$ to $\frac{1}{2}$ inch greater than the thickness of the stock to be cut. A good rule of thumb is that the blade should protrude through the work by one tooth depth. More protrusion will only increase the cutting friction and, in some cases, make for a rougher surface. The exception is carbide-tipped blades, for which only half a tooth tip should project below the material. Be sure to tighten the wing nut well, after making the depth adjustment.

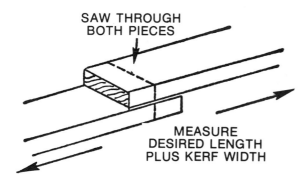

FIG. 10-6. Cutting parallel edges.

Always maintain a firm grip on the handle, and operate the switch with a decisive action. Place the saw base on the stock, with the blade clear, before turning on the switch. That is, the saw should be running at full speed before the blade contacts the work. Advance the saw into the wood. The telescoping lower guard will swing back by itself. Feed the tool at the speed at which the blade cuts willingly. Never force the saw. Always use a light and continuous pressure. Remember that hardness and roughness can vary even in the same piece. A knotty or damp section can put a heavy load on the saw; when this happens, feed more slowly. Your ear and your muscles will tell you when the saw is overloaded; feed hard enough to keep it working without much decrease in speed. Forcing it beyond this makes for rough cuts, inaccuracy, and overheating of the motor.

Should your cut begin to go off the line, do not try to force it back on. It is best, of course, to make errors on the waste side of the line. Then you can withdraw the saw, sight anew, and start a new cut a trifle inside the wrong one. In any event, withdraw the saw if you must shift the cut. Forcing a correction inside the cut can stall the saw, cause kickbacks, and perhaps spoil the work. Also, never attempt to remove a portable circular saw from the work while the blade is in motion, or kickback may occur. When making an incomplete cut or when the cut is interrupted, release the switch and hold the saw motionless in the material until the blade comes to a complete stop.

For a straight or right-angle cut, use the right side of the alignment slot that appears on the base or foot of most saws. For bevel cuts, use the left side. The alignment slot will give an *approximate* line of cut. A sample cut should be made in scrap lumber to verify the actual line of cut. This is needed because of the number of different blade types and thicknesses available.

CROSSCUTTING OPERATIONS Crosscutting may be done with a combination blade for ordinary work, with a crosscut blade for a finer cut, or with a planer or plywood blade if a really smooth edge is desired. In any case, be sure the blade is sharp, and adjust the depth so that the blade just cuts through the work. On very thin or very thick materials, the depth adjustment is important in order to (1) prevent any tendency to kick and (2) obtain a smoother cut.

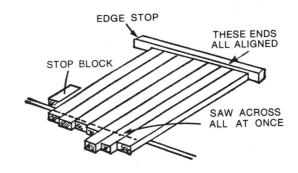

FIG. 10-7. Crosscutting to the same length.

Whenever possible, place the board to be cut so that the mark is at the right of the support. You should always cut on the right side of the line and lay out the work so that the saw base plate will be on the supported side of the material. Rest the front of the saw base on the work so that the guide mark lines up with the saw blade. Keep the blade well back of the work and start the motor, letting the blade come up to full speed. Advance the saw steadily through the work, following the cutting mark with the guide at the bevel edge of the front plate. When you reach the end of the cut, release the trigger switch and allow the blade to follow through as the machine is lifted out and away from the work. Do not allow the blade to keep running, and do not twist the machine at the end of the cut, or the work can be badly scored. To prevent any sudden jamming or binding of the blade as you reach the center of the cut in a wide board, insert the tip of a screwdriver or any small wedge in the kerf at the near end. This will keep the cut open as the saw moves across.

Several types of crosscut gauges and guides can be used for sawing, and these will be discussed later in the chapter. As you acquire some experience with your portable power saw, you will find that freehand cutting across the board is quite easy and can be very accurate. One of the most important factors in obtaining this accuracy is the manner in which the saw is held. Let the saw balance itself in the hand. Get to know the feel of the movement required to keep the blade cutting. Never push or force the blade into the work. Let it cut easily and at good speed. Hold the machine firmly in your grasp, but let your grip be relaxed. Let the saw do the cutting, with your arm merely guiding and feeding the material as the saw moves across the work.

A good way to cut two pieces that are to be butted endwise is to lay one on top of the other with their edges parallel, as in Figure 10-6. The blade, set to cut through both at once, can be guided freehand, for the cut edges will match up whether they are at exactly 90° or not. But remember that the kerf has width; add this to any measured length where fits are critical.

Construction workers cut 2 X 4s and the like to length by nailing a stop to the supporting surface, aligning all the pieces at one end, and sawing across the whole lot of them toward the stop, as in Figure 10-7. You can trim fence pickets or pieces of odd length to uniform size in the same way.

RIPSAWING Ripping can be done with the combination blade or the ripping blade. The latter gives a much smoother edge. Adjust the blade depth to slightly more than is normally used in crosscutting. Attach the rip gauge, set the knurled thumbscrew so that the gauge will give the proper distance to the blade, and start the motor as in the crosscutting operation.

Generally, a slightly different type of work-holding arrangement will be needed in ripping. One must be careful not to cut toward the sawhorse or other support without making sure of the clearance underneath. Ripping a wide board presents few difficulties, because there is room to allow good support for the saw and a good holddown with the left hand. Place the board so that the cut can be run out to the limit of a reasonable reach. Release the trigger, but be careful not to move the saw. Now slide the board toward you so that the cut can be extended further, and insert a small wedge in the cut to hold it open. When you reach a point somewhere beyond the middle, it may be necessary to move the board along to complete the cut and allow good support for the work. When cutting narrow pieces, it is usually necessary to use

FIG. 10-8. An edge guide (often called a rip guide) enables the operator to cut off (top) or rip (bottom) pieces to the same size without following a line.

a straightedge and some kind of clamping device to make a secure base for the saw. Some of these devices will be described later in the book.

Of particular importance in ripsawing is the matter of the kerf, or the width of the cut made by the blade. The teeth of the saw blade are set at opposing angles to each other; they remove material to a width about twice the thickness of the blade. This loss of material can be very important if the cut is made on the inside of the line, that is, on the "good" side of the mark. The resulting piece of lumber could be short by $3/16$ inch. In all types of sawing, this loss must be remembered, although it is not quite so critical in framing and heavy work. When ripping a piece of wood, be sure that you have figured out which piece you want to use; then set the gauge or straightedge so that the cut will be on the "right" side of the mark. The best method of making the rip cut accurately is to make the settings and place the saw against the guideline so that the blade touches the wood. Without starting the motor, lean over and look at it carefully from the front, so you can see where the blade will enter the wood. When you are pretty sure that the cut will be exactly alongside the mark, turn on the motor and cut about ¼ inch into the wood. Pull the saw back and make a final check before going ahead.

FIG. 10-9. Board is used as a guide for ripping.

BEVEL SAWING Making a bevel cut with the portable circular saw requires a somewhat different approach. First of all, remember that the depth of cut possible with the saw set at a bevel angle is not as great as that with the saw set for a straight cut. When you are working near the capacity of the saw, check the thickness first to make sure that the cut can be made in one pass. If it cannot, it may be best to decrease the depth so that about half the necessary depth is cut on the first pass. Then you can turn the piece over and complete the cut with a second pass. You must remember, however, to keep the same angle of blade on the opposite side, and to guide the bed of the saw along on the other side of the mark, so that the two kerfs will be lined up. When you make bevel cuts, the saw must always be guided to the *outside* of the mark, or the *long* side of the bevel. Remember that the saw blade tilts under the base plate of the saw, and the short side will be at the bottom of the cut.

Bevel cutting is sometimes confused with the mitering cut, which is actually an ordinary, straight-blade cut made at a 45° angle across the board. More care must be taken in starting the blade into this type of cut, and the work must be held securely in place. A bevel cut that is made at an angle to the edge of the board is called a "compound angular" or "compound miter" cut and always should begin with a good mental picture of the finished result. Set the saw blade at the necessary angle, and mark the long side of the bevel across the surface of the wood. It is a good plan, especially in the beginning, to make a trial cut with a piece of scrap and try the fit first. Once the angle and bevel are correct, the finish cut can be made accurately the first time.

DADO AND GROOVE CUTS To make a dado or a groove, merely set the blade to the required depth and make two parallel cuts. The groove can then be cleared either with a chisel or by making additional cuts between the two edges. If the groove to be cut is too shallow for the depth gauge, clamp a piece of hardwood over the face and saw through it. As in all cuts, a guide fence clamped to one side of the saw makes for more accurate cutting. The same fence can be used for the second side of the dado if a strip that is the width of the dado is added to it (but allow for the width of the kerf). Some model saws have grooving cutters.

Adjust the shoe for the depth of cut you want; mark the two sides of the dado with pencil, and make the two outlining cuts with the blade just inside the line on either side. For greater accuracy, clamp a guide strip on the work for one cut, and then reclamp it for the other cut. Any stock remaining between the outlining cuts can be removed by making careful freehand cuts, as many as necessary, or by reclamping the guide strip for each pass with your saw.

FIG. 10-10. Dado grooves can be cut by adjusting the depth of the blade and then cutting a series of cuts for the desired width.

For rabbet cuts, which are L-shaped cuts, use the same procedure as for dado cuts. This is easier than trying to cut in from the edge of the piece. If, however, you have a large rabbet to cut and it is easier to cut in from the edge, then use guide blocks clamped to the edge of the piece to help support the saw.

Rabbet cuts can best be made by cutting first from the edge of the stock, and then from the face of the stock. This provides maximum support for the saw. Stock that is 1 inch thick will not support the saw at the beginning and end of the cut, so an additional waste piece must be attached either to the stock or to the edge of the workbench. If the strip is added to the bench, room for a guide strip can also be provided.

To cut notches, make two parallel cuts to the desired length and knock away the material between them. If the notch is wide, make a number of cuts. If the bottom of the notch has to be square, hold the board on its side in a vise, and make the cuts by passing the saw over it, holding the saw level by hand. Many boards can be notched in this way at the same time. Where appearance is not important, intersecting cuts are made by overcutting slightly with the saw. When no overcutting is permitted, cut up to the intersection but not beyond; then complete the cut with a handsaw. Notching cuts take special planning because the saw must be supported for both cuts. The cuts should be made with the largest possible blade so that the cleaning cut is kept shallow. Where you cannot overcut, the sawing must be finished by hand.

PLUNGE OR POCKET CUTS The portable saw is ideally suited to making the plunge, pocket, or interior cut. In fact, no other tool or method can make this type of cut as easily and neatly as the portable saw. These cuts are made in the middle area of a board, floor, or wall, rather than at the end or edge. The area to be cut out should be marked exactly to its corners, with good, clear lines on all sides. Start near the corner of one of the sides, and set the saw down so that the front of the base is resting solidly on the work and the blade rests on the waste side of the mark. Adjust the blade depth so that the teeth will just cut through the other side. If there happens to be sufficient clearance at the opposite face, greater depth will give a closer corner cut, but this is not often possible. The blade guard will have to be held back at the start of this cut, but once the blade is down on the material, the guard will stay out of the way.

Start the blade a short distance out from the near corner; with the front of the base steadying the machine on the work, and the blade lifted about $\frac{1}{2}$ inch away from

FIG. 10-11. How a plunge or pocket cut is made.

the board, start the motor. After the saw has reached full speed, lower the rear end to let the blade enter the work. The front end of the foot resting on the work acts as a hinge point. When the foot rests flat on the work surface, proceed forward to the end of your cut. Release the switch, letting the saw come to a complete stop; then remove the saw from the work and start another cut. Never, under any circumstances, pull the saw backward; the saw should be turned around and the cut finished in the normal manner. Do the other three sides, and the pocket cut is complete. You may have to use a keyhole saw or handsaw to clean out the corners, because the blade of the saw is round; if two cuts meet exactly at their tops, they will not meet at the bottom of the cut.

SAW GUIDES While the circular saw is generally employed freehand, there are times when accuracy demands a guide of some sort. The problem is mostly one of starting the saw cut straight; once the cut is started, it is difficult (if not impossible) to change the direction without binding the blade. The simplest guide is a scrap of wood clamped to the work for the base plate to ride against.

There are several cutting guides on the market, but one of the most useful is the protractor or miter style. As shown in Figure 10-12, there are two basic designs. In one (Figure 10-12a), the tool can be locked at any angle between 0 and 90°, and thus can be used to make miter and compound angular cuts as well as for crosscutting. In use, the leg underneath is held firmly against the edge of the work farthest from you (with the left hand), and the saw is guided along the long leg. If you hold the protractor against the nearer work edge, you will have to handle the saw with your left hand, which is less convenient for most right-handed persons. Whichever you do, try to hold the guide against the part of the stock that remains supported, not against the cutoff.

The other design (Figure 10-12b) works in much the same manner. It makes crosscutting and angular and compound angular cuts easy and accurate.

Another popular cutting guide that can be purchased is the try-square arrangement. It is made of an aluminum alloy; the arm that places the square exactly perpendicular to the edge of the board extends far enough to locate the exact position of the cut. You will find this type of square an excellent guide for all ordinary cutting where a truly square and straight edge is wanted. You can make one for yourself if you need a longer guiding edge or one that will guide a straight cut at angles other than 90° to the edge of the board.

A cutoff square such as the one shown in Figure 10-13 can easily be made. Properly assembled, it will give you accurate 45 and 90° cuts (the two angles most commonly used). A large carpenter's square is helpful in making the guide accurately. Corrugated or miter-joint fasteners may be used to join the parts at the apex. Common nails will do for fastening on the crossbars. If a guide lock screw or any other part protrudes above the saw base on either side,

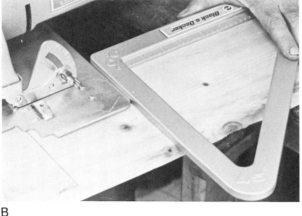

FIG. 10-12. Two styles of a protractor or miter type cutting guide.

the crossbars may be inset from the edge of the long guide leg a trifle to clear it, as shown. Both crossbars must, of course, be fastened at exactly 90° to the long leg and at 45° to the other. The advantage of having two crossbars is that you can flip the guide over for making a 45° cut that slants the other way, or cut at 90° with the guiding edge at the right or left of the saw as you please. For greater durability, you may want to glue all the joints, fasten them with wood screws instead of nails, and give the finished guide several coats of shellac.

Another type of crosscut guide can be made with the perpendicular aligning edge at the top (Figure 10-14). The part that lies on top of the workpiece must be thin enough for all parts of the saw to clear it. Use glue and wood screws to attach the T head, with one piece extending from the crossbar a greater distance than the width of the wide part of the saw base. In use, hold the T head firmly against the far edge of the work with your left hand, and guide the left-hand edge of the saw base against the right-hand edge of the crossbar. Make a first cut with the saw through the T head, thus cutting it somewhat shorter. The cut end of this piece is now an accurate alignment guide; set it on the cutting line, and the saw will trim exactly right.

A longer and more elaborate square will be needed for making accurate cuts on large sheets of plywood,

hardboard, etc. This frame can be made of straight-grained hardwood, but redwood is lighter, is straight grained, and is not likely to warp or twist out of shape. Pick out a 6-foot piece that has a perfectly straight and smooth edge. Use 1 X 3 inch stock which you can rip accurately with the ripping gauge, and plane the edges smooth. The squaring piece that forms the base of the triangle should be no more than ¾ inch thick and at least 30 inches long. A large carpenter's square will help in locating the two principal pieces at a 90° angle. You might want to check further by using the right-triangle formula:

$$A^2 + B^2 = C^2$$

Measure a distance of 9 inches along the foot from the point of joining, and a distance of 12 inches along the vertical side of the triangle. Make a distinct mark at the two points. If the angle is truly 90°, the distance between the measured points will be exactly 15 inches. Leave the end of the footing piece just a bit longer, say 2 inches, than the width of the base of the saw. Nail the pieces together, and brace them by joining the ends with a light strip on the side of the triangle away from the guide edge. Be sure that the pieces do not overlap at the top end to make a total thickness which will not go under the motor of the saw.

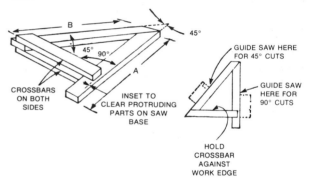

FIG. 10-13. Simple cutting guide. Dimensions A and B may vary from 15 to 48 inches, but both must be the same.

Sometimes it is necessary to use a longer straightedge than that afforded by the guides you have bought or made. When you rip a wide board, the crosscut guides will not serve very well. In such cases, any straight piece that is thin enough to lie under the motor housing of the saw will serve very well. It can be clamped to the work or, if large enough, can be held in place by hand while the saw is guided along its edge. A handy guide can be made from a piece of hardboard and a strip of wood nailed to it along the top of the left edge. This serves very well for ripping to a line, because the saw rests on the base of the guide and holds it in place at the same time. Any convenient width of hardboard can be used because the saw will cut off the excess, and the edge will thereafter

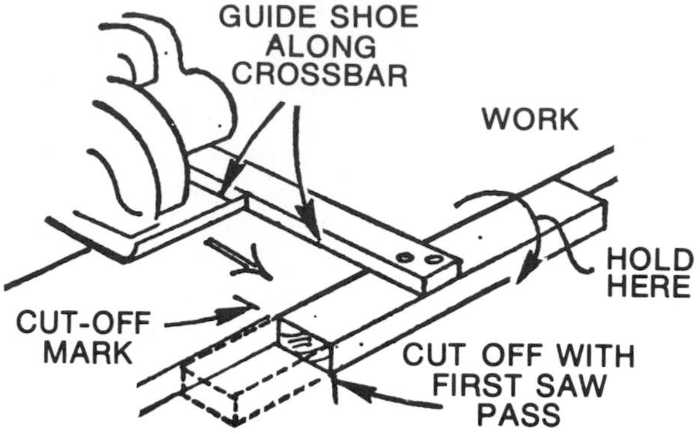

FIG. 10-14. Simple T cutting guide.

mark the line of the cut. The width of the base, from the guide strip out to the cutting line, will be exactly right for the saw for which it was made.

The several saw tables and attachment arrangements on the market make circular saws even more useful in the shop and for light work such as furniture making and cabinetmaking. While they operate in slightly different ways, the principal advantage of these accessories is their ability to handle small pieces which cannot be accurately located or handled while the saw is held in the hand.

FIG. 10-15. Commercial cutting guide that comes in a standard 5-foot length but will adjust to widths from 6 to 48 inches. The built-in locks and blade-guide blocks make this a handy tool.

CARE AND MAINTENANCE

As do other power tools, circular saws require some routine maintenance. After each use, blow the sawdust from the air vents. The motors of these saws need all the cooling they can get. Sawdust can also pile up inside the blade guard, where it can interfere with the action of the telescoping lower guard, so check there too. Whenever you have a blade out, check the guard return spring and clear out any sawdust and debris.

The motor brushes should be inspected after 50 hours of operation or 1 year, whichever comes first. If you remove the brushes for inspection or cleaning, pull them out one at a time, and be sure you do not turn them around when you put them back—they fit only one way.

FIG. 10-16. There are special accessories that help decrease the work involved in patching splintered or feathered edges of plywood, veneer plywood, or panel doors. The one shown above can be adapted to any portable circular saw.

FIG. 10-17. Typical panel-saw arrangement employing a circular saw. All you have to do is guide the tool up and down the tracks.

If the brushes are less than $\frac{1}{4}$ inch long, they should be replaced. It is normal for the motor brushes to spark, but any time you see a ring of fire around the commutator, there is trouble. It could be nothing more than a dirty commutator or brushes sticking in their spring-loaded holders, but it could be something more serious: an open, shorted, or grounded winding, a rough commutator, or brushes worn beyond their useful life. Do not operate the saw with this kind of arcing. Find out what is wrong.

Clean off the saw housing occasionally, but chlorinated cleaning solvents, gasoline, or household detergents containing ammonia should not be used on plastic. Use kerosene, ethyl alcohol, or a little soap and water.

Lubrication is important. Follow the manufacturer's directions. Usually, unless the saw has ball bearings, the motor end bearing will require a few drops of SAE 20 or 30 oil periodically. Do not overoil or the oil will leak onto the commutator and brushes. Of course, many of the saws produced today have sealed bearings and cannot be lubricated by the owner. However, the reduction gear drive from motor to blade is usually packed with grease which can and should be replenished or replaced every 75 to 100 hours of use. Liquid graphite is used to lubricate the spring guard (oil is bad here because sawdust can cling to it). Periodically tighten all screws and nuts on the saw, as cutting vibration tends to loosen them. But the most important maintenance is to keep a sharp blade—it is safer, it cuts faster, and it causes less wear on the motor.

Do not attempt any repairs not recommended by the manufacturer in the service manual. This may void your warranty.

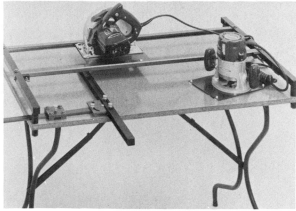

FIG. 10-18. Two of the many table or guide setups that do a great many special cutting operations. The lower one can also be used with a router.

Saber Saws

What it lacks in outright cutting speed as compared to a circular saw, the saber saw (also called the "portable jigsaw" or "bayonet saw") more than makes up with its ability to do so many jobs well. It can handle almost any operation of which the circular saw is capable, except dadoing and rabbeting. Riping, crosscutting, mitering, and beveling are its meat—to say nothing of the tool's ability to make plunge cuts, large or small arcs and circles, scrolls, and other cuts. In fact, if you were limited to only two power tools, the drill and the saber saw would be excellent choices.

SABER-SAW FEATURES

In principle, all saber saws are the same. Differences are due to their refinements. For instance, less expensive models may have either vibratory or rotary motors and reciprocating, or up-and-down, blade motion. On some of the more expensive heavier-duty models with rotary motors, the blade swings out from the work on the downstroke and into the work for cutting on the upstroke. This orbital motion provides faster cutting, easy feeding, and longer blade life.

If you intend to cut only simple shapes, a one-speed saber saw will be satisfactory. Its high speed is best suited for softer materials like softwood, plastics, composition board and light, soft metals. Where a low speed is needed for cutting hard, dense materials (laminates, brittle plastics, and relatively light metals) the two-speed models are better. Of course, the variable-speed saber saw is best suited to the complete range of work, from softwood to harder, thicker metals. Its infinite control of speed allows it to be matched to the material for maximum control. It is best for intricate scrollwork.

Actually, the simplest measure of a saber saw's work capacity is its maximum depths of cut in different materials. Some manufacturers list these for each model in their sales literature. Many manufacturers also list maximum blade strokes per minute (spm) and the lengths of blade strokes in inches. Both differ according to saw design and are hard for the layman to relate to work capacity. But, as a general rule, the maximum depths of cut of an inexpensive, light-duty saber saw are about $1\frac{1}{2}$ inches in softwood, 1 inch in hardwood, and $\frac{1}{8}$ inch in soft metal. Such a saw has approximately a $\frac{1}{6}$-hp motor (2.1 to 2.5 amperes rating) with a $\frac{1}{2}$-inch stroke and one speed of about 3200 spm. The middle-price, medium-duty saw has about a $\frac{1}{4}$-hp motor (2.5 to 3 amperes rating) with a $\frac{3}{4}$-inch stoke and a special switch that lets you select either of two speeds, for example, 3400 and 2700 spm. Heavy-duty models can cut up to 2 inches of softwood, $1\frac{1}{2}$ inches of hardwood, $\frac{1}{4}$ inch of soft metal, and $\frac{1}{8}$ inch of hard metal. Such saws usually have a full 1-inch stroke and a hearty $\frac{1}{2}$-hp motor (3 to 5 amperes rating) with a selection of speeds that run from about 1300 to 3400 spm.

Most models have a D-shaped handle on top and may or may not have auxiliary bars or knobs for steadying the

HANDLE

SWITCH

HOUSING

AIR HOLE

Rockwell

DOUBLE INSULATED

BLADE CHUCK

SHOE (BASE)

BLADE GUIDE

FIG. 10-19. Parts of a typical saber saw.

saw or guiding the blade. Other models simply have a palm grip on the housing. Slide, toggle, or trigger switches turn saber saws on and off. The first two are self locking for continuous operation and have no "instant off." In contrast, the trigger switch must be locked on by pressing a button, and it releases instantly when you squeeze the trigger. In variable-speed models, a trigger switch that changes the blade speed in response to trigger-finger pressure is convenient. On models with slide or toggle switches, a separate speed control is provided.

The base or shoe of the saber saw consists of skids, a cutting-angle adjustment in all but the least expensive models, and a place to attach rip or circle guide accessories. The skids should provide stable support and extend at least $\frac{1}{4}$ inch in front of the blade to prevent the saw from tipping forward as you guide it through the work. The blade slot should be small or provided with inserts so that the skids can help hold wood fibers in place (prevent splintering) around the sawing blade. A few skids can be reversed for making cuts flush up to a perpendicular surface. While a few saber saws are still made with fixed base, the vast majority are adjustable to cut miters and bevels. The cutting-angle adjustment is, as a rule, a large scaled hinge, between the skids and the housing, that allows precision angle cuts up to 45°. The hinge is loosened by means of a lever, a wing nut, screws, or a small hex key. Then the skids are tilted to the desired angle, and the hinge is retightened. A few models have a quick-acting cam lock which is easy to use and positive in

its action. The scale should be accurate and easy to read. If you have any question about accuracy, check the angle between the blade and the tilted skids by means of a protractor.

FIG. 10-20. There are three basic types of construction for portable tools. The two on the right are called "clamshells." (The one at the far right is opened up to show the two halves of the case.) The one on the left is a machined casting. The double-insulated type is illustrated in Figure 10-19.

A rip fence for guiding the saw blade parallel to the edge of the work can be quickly attached, adjusted, or removed by turning screws. Some designs can also be used as circle guides. A rip fence is included with some models and available as an accessory for most others.

A saber saw may have a metal or plastic housing, or a combination of both. Some operators prefer the solid weight of metal. Others like the feel of plastics, their color, and their lightness. The plastics used for housings are guaranteed breakproof. Saber saws with plastic housings may also be double insulated and shockproof. They have two-pronged plugs; these fit any outlet without the need for a special grounding-plug adaptor. Saws that have plugs with three prongs need grounding for safety. Most saber saws are for ac operation only. A few models are available which operate on either ac or dc.

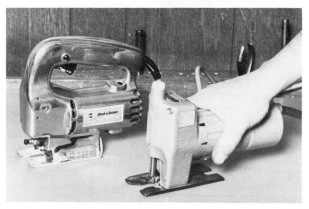

FIG. 10-21. Two basic grips are used on saber saws: (left) top or D handle; (right) motor or palm grip.

A feature of every saw is a blower that keeps the path of the blade clear, and the cutting line visible. The blower force depends on the motor speed; slow a multi-speed tool and you also slow the speed of the airstream. A few models even have a built-in light to eliminate shadows and permit accurate guideline cutting. Some have deflectors to keep chips from flying upwards. These are all points to consider.

FIG. 10-22. The saber saw at the left does not tilt. The shoe tilts on the saw in the middle. Only the head tilts on the saw at the right.

SABER-SAW BLADES

Blades for saber saws are of four general types: woodcutting blades, metal-cutting blades, toothless tungsten-carbide blades, and knife blades. The latter slice through a variety of soft materials, such as rubber, leather, cork, and insulation board. Woodcutting blades may have from 6 to 10 teeth per inch. Six-tooth blades are for rough cutting. Seven-tooth blades are for softwoods, 1 X 4s, 2 X 4s, plasterboard, and ripping. Ten-tooth blades are for hardwoods, wallboard, and general crosscutting. There is also a special 10-tooth blade with a tapered back edge for finish cuts in plywood and veneer. Another special blade has only 5 teeth per inch. It is called a "skip-tooth" blade and is for very fast, rough cuts in wood. The finer the blade (the more teeth), the smoother the cut; but finer blades work best in stock no more than $^{13}/_{16}$ inch thick (or what is called 1-inch lumber).

Blades for cutting metal have 14 to 24 teeth per inch. Use blades with more teeth per inch for cutting harder, thinner metals; blades with *fewer* teeth for thicker, softer metals. A coarse metal-cutting blade is good for cutting wood when there is danger of running into nails. There is also an all-purpose blade for both wood and metal which has 14 teeth per inch.

Some blades have teeth that are set—meaning that they splay out slightly from the otherwise flat blade. Some teeth are set so that the edge is a wavy line. Blades that have no set may be hollow-ground or taper-ground. Both kinds of grinding produce a thinner edge, and such blades are usually for very smooth cuts. Blade lengths may vary from 2½ to 6 inches. The extra-length blades are for tree branches, wall partitions, etc., and fit only certain saw models.

Good blades come sharpened and ready to use. Unless you know exactly how to resharpen saw teeth, worn or dull blades are best discarded. Using a poor blade puts you and the tool under a severe handicap and is a poor way to save money.

Tungsten-carbide saber-saw blades, although more costly, will outlast standard toothed blades by as much as 10 to 1. In additon to both hardwood and softwood, toothless blades will cut asbestos cement, brick, slate, ceramic tile, stainless steel, counter-top material, and many other problem materials. As noted in Table 10-1, there are three types of tungsten-carbide blades: fine grit, medium grit, and coarse grit. Use fine-grit blades when a smooth cut is desired in thin, hard materials and where precision is important, particularly where chipping, splitting, or delamination could be a problem. Employ medium-grit blades where faster cutting is needed or when fine-grit blades become loaded. Use coarse-grit blades to cut thick or softer materials faster and where a rougher finish is acceptable. Coarse-grit blades will permit up to a 30 percent smaller radius cut.

Table 10-1 Types of Tungsten-Carbide Blades and Their Uses

Material to be cut	Fine grit	Medium grit	Coarse grit
Plywood, hardwood-veneer plywood	X*	XX†	
Asbestos cement, nail-embedded wood, plaster and nails			XX‡
Ceramic tile, slate, cast stone	XX	X	
Fiberglass (silicones, epoxies, polyesters, malamines)	X	X	XX
Chalkboard, clay pipe, brick	X	XX	
Stainless-steel trim, Sheet metal to 18 gauge, ducting, counter-top materials, tempered hardboard.	X		

*X denotes a use of the grit size.
†XX denotes the most popular grit size for each material.
‡Use the slower speeds of variable-speed saber saws for these materials.

As mentioned earlier, the screws that hold a saw blade are loosened or tightened with a screwdriver, a small hex key, or a special clamp. In any case, loosen the chuck screws. Insert the proper blade for the material to be cut, pushing it as far as it will go into the chuck. Follow the manufacturer's directions for tightening the setscrews with the wrench furnished. In two good saws, for example, the front screw is tightened only until it is firm, to line up the blade with the chuck shaft. The side screw is then tightened to grip it. Tightening the wrong screw first, undertightening, or overtightening may result in blade breakage.

BLADE APPEARANCE	RECOMMENDED USES	WIDTH	LENGTH	TEETH PER INCH
	Cutting non-ferrous metals (aluminum, copper, etc.)—1/8" to 1/4" thick.	1/4"-1/2"	3"-4"	14
	Cutting ferrous (iron) metals—1/64" to 3/16" thick.	1/4"	3"	24
	Cutting ferrous (iron) metals—1/64" to 3/16" thick.	1/4"	3"	32
	Cutting non-ferrous metals (aluminum, copper, etc.)—1/16" to 1/8" thick.	3/16"	3 1/4"	14
	Cutting soft woods. For fine finish applications. Not for scroll work.	1/4"	2 1/4"-3"	7-8
	Cutting hard or thinner woods less than 3/4" thick.	1/4"	3"	10
	Cutting green or wet woods—3/16" to 1-5/16" thick. Blade thickness tapers front (tooth edge) to back for cut relief; easier cutting.	1/4"	3"	10
	Intricate cutting (circles and other scroll work). For use on wood, plastic, plywood 1/4" to 1" thick.	1/4"	2"-2 1/2"	14
	Fast cutting of soft woods—3/4" or thicker.	1/4"-1/2"	3"-3 1/4"	5-6
	Fast, smooth finish cutting of hard woods less than 3/4" thick.	1/2"	3"-3 1/4"	10
	Remington toothless tungsten carbide blades. Fiberglass, ceramic tile, hidden nails, plastic laminates, steel trim.	3/8"	3"	None
	Fast, coarse cutting of soft woods.	1/2"	6"	3
	Medium to fast cutting of soft woods, medium finish.	1/2"-3/4"	6"-6 1/2"	3-7
	Knife blade, cutting paper, cardboard, rubber, leather, linoleum, styrofoam, other materials cut with knife.	1/4"-3/8"	2"-3 1/2"	None
	Offset or flush cutting blades for cutting to perpendicular surface or obstruction.	1/4"-1/2"	2"-3"	7-10

Always use the shortest blade practical for piercing to start internal cuts.

FIG. 10-23. How to pick the right blade.

With any blade, surface splintering can be minimized by feeding slowly. Usually, too, one face of the work is the "good side," whose appearance is more important than that of the other. In such a case, it pays to lay out the cutting lines on the back face and saw with the good side down. Any splintering will occur on the back (the up side), leaving the critical face much smoother than if it were up during sawing.

SAFETY AND THE SABER SAW

While the saber saw is considered a rather safe tool, there are some precautions that should be taken.

1. Make certain the saber saw is properly grounded through the electric cord, unless it is of the double-insulated type. The switch must be in the off position before the tool is connected to the power source.

2. Select the correct blade for your work, and be sure it is properly mounted.

3. Disconnect the saber saw from the power source before changing blades or making adjustments.

4. Place the base of the saw firmly on the stock before starting a cut. Make sure the work is well supported, and do not cut into sawhorses or other supports. Turn on the motor before the blade contacts the work.

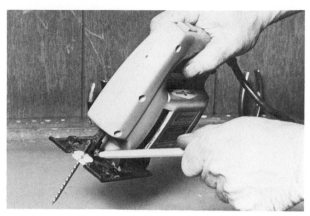

FIG. 10-24. Some saber saws have an insert straddle plate (shown). This insert keeps splintering down, particularly when cutting plywood panels. A hollow-ground blade should be used with a straddle plate.

USING THE SABER SAW

The workpiece or stock should be firmly clamped, held securely in a vise, or supported on sawhorses, chairs, or some other solid base. If you are using a saber saw for the first time, by all means clamp the piece so that you are free to concentrate on using the tool. Make sure that *all* parts of the line you plan to cut along are clear of the supporting surface and clamps. *Never* try to hold small workpieces by hand; anything shorter than 18 inches should either be clamped or laid across blocks that leave ample blade clearance below.

Before cutting long pieces or large panels, give thought to the shifting of weight when an unsupported segment is partly cut off. The end of a board, for example, will begin to sag and may break off before the saw can cut it free; this will ruin the edge. You can prevent this by holding up the cut-off part with your free hand until the blade cuts through.

FIG. 10-25. Cutting ceramic tile (left) or wood filled with nails (right) is easy with tungsten-carbide saber-saw blades.

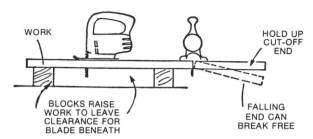

FIG. 10-26. Method of supporting small work when sawing.

A plywood panel bridging two supports will sag more and more in the middle as the cut proceeds (Figure 10-27). Eventually it will pinch the blade in the kerf, making it very difficult to feed. It helps to support the work close to the cutting line; but to prevent the difficulty already mentioned—an outboard section breaking free of its own weight—you may need extra supports under a big panel. A simple means of keeping the kerf open behind the blade is to drive in a wedge. Some control of sagging between the parts of a large panel is gained by clamping a block across the start of the cut, as shown in Figure 10-28.

Pick up the saber saw with the thumb and three fingers, keeping your forefinger straight and off the switch until the tool is fully in your grip. Making this a habit can spare you the jolting surprise of having the tool start before you are ready to control it, or having the blade jab into things on the workbench. Swing the electric cord well behind the saw, out of line with the projected cut, underneath as well as on top of the work.

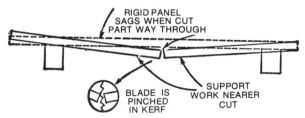

FIG. 10-27. To prevent the work from sagging, the work must be supported.

Holding the tool handle firmly, set the front of the saw base on the work edge, with the blade not quite touching the cutting line. Switch on the motor, and move the blade into the work edge. Take care to keep the base, or shoe, parallel to the work surface at this time. Once it is on the work, correct any tendency to tilt the base up at either end. Keep it firmly down, flat on the work. For the most efficient cutting with cycloidal action, put downward pressure on the saw. With a good blade, only light forward pressure should be needed to make the saw cut steadily. Do not force it; let the blade cut at its own speed. Pushing harder will not increase the cutting speed much, but it will make a rougher cut and may overload the blade and motor.

FIG. 10-28. Method of supporting larger work when sawing.

The cutting speed will vary, of course, with the material and its thickness. Experience will soon show you how fast you can feed in different kinds of stock. A slower rate is to be expected in cutting thick wood, hardwood, and metal. The cutting speed often varies within the same piece of wood, as the blade passes from soft areas to cross-grained or knotty ones. Maintain just enough feed pressure on the saw to keep it cutting at its own speed as the material permits. Sudden hard going is sometimes due to the cord snagging somewhere while you are intent on the job, or to having run the blade into a hidden edge or corner of the workbench or other supporting surface.

If the workpiece starts to vibrate or flutter, stop cutting long enough to secure it properly. Whenever possible, clamp or support the work close to the line of cut. When the cut is completed, shut off the power and lay the saw aside before loosening the work.

CROSSCUTTING WITH A SABER SAW Crosscuts are simply a matter of guiding the saber saw on a line at an angle of 90° to the work edge. You can mark the cut with a try square and carefully follow it by eye, but it is easier and more accurate to use a guide such as the simple crosscut type shown in Figure 10-13, or a smaller version of the protractor style illustrated in Figure 10-12. Be sure to hold either of these guides against the part of the stock that remains supported, not against the cut-off part.

RIPSAWING WITH A SABER SAW A coarse-toothed blade can be used for ripping if smoothness of cut is not essential; otherwise a slower-cutting 10-tooth blade is best. The saber saw is ideal for cutting one edge of an apron, or a soffit or fill piece that must fit closely against a ceiling, a wall, or any similar not-quite-straight line. Hold the piece to be so fitted firmly alongside the surface it is to match. With a pair of dividers set firmly at any convenient spacing, and the legs held at right angles to the work surface, scribe the cutting line as shown in Figure 7-52. The pencil line will follow both large and small irregularities. Guide the jigsaw along it by eye.

If the board to be ripped has a true straight edge, you can use the rip guide. This may be inserted from either side of the saw base to put the guiding head on the right or left side, whichever best suits the job at hand. With the power cord disconnected, measure from the side of the blade nearest the fence head to the head to set the desired cutoff width. (It is always best, on critical work, to make a trial cut in a bit of scrap wood and check this measurement.)

Starting the rip cut requires special care, as only the end of the guide is in contact with the work edge at first. Once the guide head is touching along its full length, you can use one hand to hold it in contact. Keep your eyes on the guide rather than on the blade, which will obediently follow where the guide head leads it. Since there is no marked guideline, watching the blade will not immediately show you that it is off line.

FIG. 10-29. Two methods of ripping a long piece of material: ripping fence (left) and straightedge (right).

If the board to be ripped is rough or irregular, or has a splintered edge, you can cut that part off along a straight line. If the piece is not too wide, set the rip guide to follow along the other (presumably) straight edge. If the stock is wide or has no straight edge at all, the job is still easy. Tack a straight-edged piece of wood to the upper surface, its edge one-half the saw-base width inside the intended cutting line, as in Figure 10-30. (Use enough nails to hold this strip firmly all along its length, but sink them only partway in, leaving enough protruding to make them easy to pull out.) Remove the rip fence if it is in the saw base. Then guide the jigsaw directly against the wood strip. It is an advantage to have the guide strip longer than the work so that it projects at both ends. This guides the saw fully, both before it starts the cut and through the end of the cut (Figure 10-30).

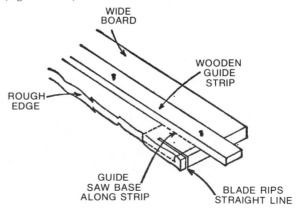

FIG. 10-30. Method of ripping irregular stock.

The saber saw can make an easy job of some of the more difficult joints, including mortise and tenon, dovetail, and miter. To make a mortise-and-tenon joint with a saber saw, proceed as follows:

1. To cut the tenon on a narrow strip, clamp it between scrap pieces to give the shoe riding space. Cut the tenon on the narrow edges of the strip first (Figure 10-31a).
2. Next turn the strip with the wide side up, and make the cuts to the correct depth (Figure 10-31b). Then complete the tenon by cutting out the scrap from the sides.
3. Make the mortise by boring a hole at one end and running the saw from the hole to either end (Figure 10-31c). A series of parallel saw cuts will remove the scrap.
4. A firm joint requires a snug fit. Cut the tenon slightly oversize, and test it on the mortise (Figure 10-31d); then "shave" the tenon with the saw blade to make it fit.

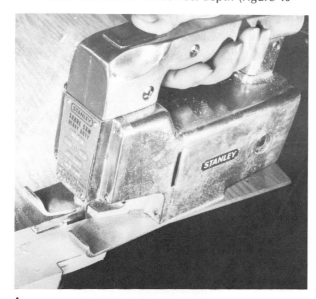

A

C

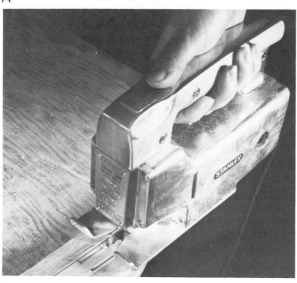

B

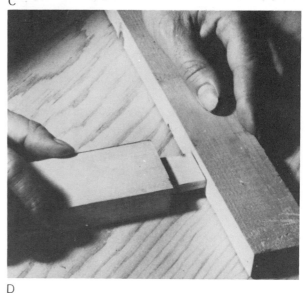

D

FIG. 10-31. Steps in making a mortise-and-tenon joint.

A dovetail joint can be made with a saber saw as follows:

1. Draw the dovetail outlines, and mark the cutouts to avoid error. Cut as shown in Figure 10-32a to remove the scrap. Set the blade to full depth for this.
2. The guidelines are easy to follow, but hold the saw firmly against the stock at all times (Figure 10-32b).
3. Hold the cutout on the edge of the piece that it is to mesh with, and mark the outlines (Figure 10-32c). Even if the first cuts were poor, this

method will match them.

4. Clamp the stock, and set the saw blade to the exact depth of the cut. Then follow the marked lines exactly, removing the lines with the saw cuts (Figure 10-32d).
5. Remove the center stock as before. Then hold the saw nose at an angle to cut out the corner stock (Figure 10-32e), setting the saw blade at the full depth for the job.
6. The assembled joint is firm and interlocking. The joint shown in Figure 10-32f has been sanded to illustrate how a joint made with a saber saw looks when finished.

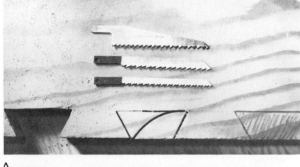

A

B

C

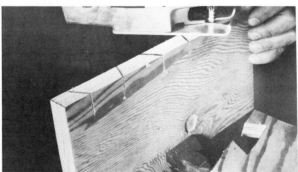

D

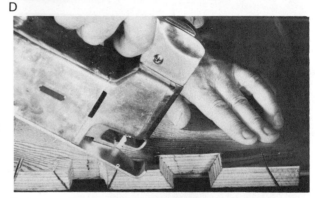

E

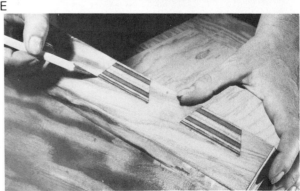

F

FIG. 10-32. Steps in making a dovetail joint.

The simplest and easiest way to make a miter joint is to overlap the two pieces at right angles, hold them with a brad, and run the saw down the miter as shown in Figure 10-33a. This gives a perfect square and fit, even if the saw cut is crooked. With a saber saw, it is possible to make curved miter joints such as that shown in Figure 10-33b. Such joints are made in the same way; the saw follows the wavy line (Figure 10-33c).

A

B

C

FIG. 10-33. Steps in making a miter joint.

BEVEL SAWING The cuts already discussed have all been made with the blade straight down, at a 90° angle to the work surface. Bevel cuts are those made at some smaller angle to the face of the work, which means the blade has to saw through a greater thickness than at 90°. The saw will therefore cut more slowly; and, because the blade thrust is partly toward the horizontal, it has more of a tendency to wander sideways than in straight-through cuts, especially at the start.

Some saws have a separate tilt base that must be mounted in place of the standard one. Others have the tilt feature built right in. In either case, use two hands for bevel sawing along a guideline or with a rip guide. For safety, keep the thumb of the left hand behind the guide lock screw or some other base projection, well back of the blade. For bevel sawing across a board (to make a box with mitered joints, for example), it is not a bad idea to tack a guide block fast to the work. Use a try square to set it accurately, and drive the nails in far enough to hold well. Another method, with hand-held guides, is to drive a stout nail into the work for the side of the guide to butt against. This prevents the tool from slipping sideways, as it otherwise tends to do no matter how firmly it is held. You can also, of course, clamp the guide to the workpiece.

Bevel cuts must be made slowly; forcing will only aggravate the tendency to wander off the cut. Take pains to keep the saw base absolutely flat on the work surface throughout; if it lifts, the cut will not be true. The work itself should always be clamped tightly to some supporting surface, the cut overhanging the edge. However, angle cuts are very deceptive because it is hard to tell where the bottom of the blade will be traveling. Therefore take pains to check that it will not run into the edge of the support, or against any of the clamps.

POCKET OR PLUNGE CUTS A pocket cut is an easy method of making an inside cut. The saw can be inserted directly into a panel or board; there is no need to drill a lead or pilot hole. Measure the cut, and mark it clearly with a pencil. Next tip the saw forward until the front end of the shoe sits firmly on the work surface. Switch the tool on, and allow it to attain maximum speed. Grip the handle firmly, and lower the back edge of tool until the blade cuts smoothly into material. Always be sure the blade reaches its complete depth, with the shoe flat against the work, before starting a forward cut. If the cutout is circular, then you just proceed in one direction to complete the cut. When square corners are desired, slant toward a line and then to a corner. Back out, and then slant to an adjacent line so you can make a second cut at right angles to the first one. This operation will have to be repeated at each corner. If the corners are rounded, then, of course, you can just make a turn. In such cases, it frequently is a good idea to drill holes at the corners. This will give the corners the desired shape and eliminate the need for plunging.

CUTTING CIRCLES True rounds, such as wooden wheels and table tops, can be sawed to almost any size with a circle-cutting attachment. The one provided with the saw

FIG. 10-34. Making a pocket or plunge cut. This technique can also be used for scrollwork.

is a bar that slides into a socket on the saber-saw base and can be locked at the desired radius. The head of this bar has a hole in which a nail can be inserted as a pivot. With this nail driven in at the center of the desired circle cut, the saw will track around back to its starting point.

To saw a round opening wholly inside a piece of stock such as a plywood panel, first drill a $\frac{5}{16}$-inch starting hole, or make a plunge cut, well inside the cutting circle. Run the saw carefully out to the cutting line, stopping with the blade aligned with it (that is, at right angles to a radius). Attach the circle-cutting guide, and lock it at the proper radius. If this is done with a rule, measure from the blade to the pivot hole in the guide, and be sure to take the width of the kerf into account.

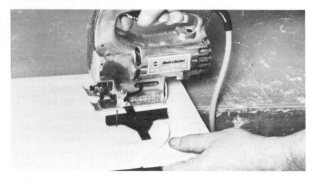

FIG. 10-35. Cutting a circle on an auxiliary table. This table can be used for many other tasks.

While the rip fence may be inserted from either side of the saw, the circle-cutting attachment must be put in from the right of the saw as shown, with the ripping-guide head *up* instead of down. This allows the saw to be set flat on the work, and brings the pivot hole at one end of the head straight across from the blade teeth, a critical point for smooth circle cutting. With the blade in the starting hole or kerf, drive as heavy a nail as will fit the pivot hole into the center of the cutting circle. Then start the saw and feed it clockwise until the cut is completed.

To make a wheel, you would, of course, drill the starting hole outside the circle. Sometimes you may want both a

round hole and a clean, unmarred disk; in other words, neither piece is to be wasted. With a carefully made plunge cut, which puts a kerf no bigger than the saw blade through the stock, you can do this.

You may sometimes want to saw big disks for such things as coffee-table or garden-furniture tops. The standard circle-cutting guide is limited in radius, but you can improvise a longer one in several ways. If you can get a strip of metal that closely fits the guide slots in the saw base, make one like that in Figure 10-36 . The short leg at the outer end is very important, for the pivot must be aligned with the blade as shown, as far ahead of the bar as the blade teeth are. If the pivot is either ahead of or behind the teeth, the blade will not return to its starting place. Make the short leg of a flat mending plate, a right-angled one, or a similar bit of metal you can bolt or rivet to the end of the strip. Carefully measure out, punch-mark, and drill the pivot hole to fit a common nail.

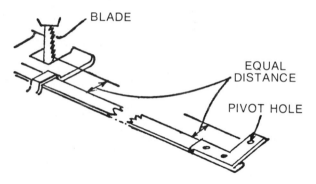

FIG. 10-36. Making a large disk with a saber saw.

CUTTING ORNAMENTAL CURVES Scallops and coves can be sawed freehand. But the circle-cutting guide makes it easy to cut out ornamental soffits, headboards, furniture and cabinet aprons, and so forth. A combination of bored holes and sawed arcs becomes interesting (and not at all difficult) scrollwork. Figure 10-37 shows such a design. Along a line parallel to the edge of a board, intervals of $6\frac{1}{4}$ inches are laid out with center marks between them. Holes 1 inch in diameter are bored at the $6\frac{1}{4}$-inch spacings. Then the circle-cutting guide is set at a 3-inch radius, and the pivot nail is driven into the center mark between two holes (the saw blade is inserted in the one at the right of the pivot). Swung around, it neatly cuts the 3-inch radius, leaving a small neck at the bottom of the 1-inch holes as part of the design. If the sawing is done from the back face, the pivot holes will not show.

The use of bored holes as a part of scrollwork is worth remembering, for the circle-cutting guide will not work at less than a $2\frac{1}{2}$-inch radius. The freehand sawing of smaller holes is not only awkward, but it rarely produces a truly round opening. Bored holes are truly circular, form

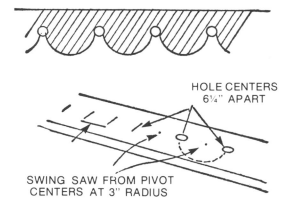

FIG. 10-37. Cutting ornamental curves with a saber saw.

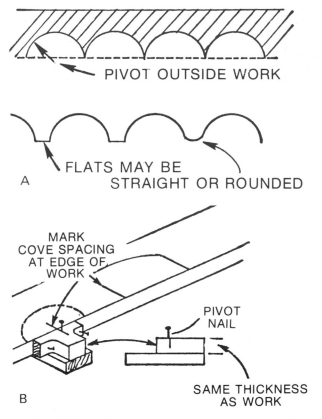

FIG. 10-38. Another method of cutting ornamental curves.

convenient starting openings for the saw blade, and are quickly made with wood bits or hole saws.

Another kind of scalloped edge with cove cuts requires pivot points outside the workpiece, as shown in Figure 10-38a. The arcs may meet to form points, or they may have short or long straight intervals between them. These intervals may also be rounded off. It is a good idea to experiment with pencil and compass on paper to decide what design and proportions best suit you. This will also show how far outside the work edge the pivot points must lie, and how far apart the radius cuts have to be made.

Mark the pivot spacing carefully on the work edge as in Figure 10-38b. Nail two pieces of scrap stock together as shown. Draw a centerline at right angles to the inner edge of the top piece, and spot the pivot center on this line as far from the inner edge as you want it from the work edge. Align the centerline with each spacing mark on the work in turn; drive the two nails into the work edge far enough to hold; and, with the circle-cutting guide set at the correct radius, swing each cut into the work from left to right. Take special care to hold up the saw near the end of each cut, for you are sawing away its support. Loosen the pivot block and tack it on at the next place. If you cut the head off the pivot nail, the saw can be lifted off and set aside while you are changing the block.

SAWING METAL With the proper blade, a saber saw can cut rods, bars, angles, and sheet stock of almost any common metal from soft aluminum to steel. The household aluminum widely sold at hardware stores is readily cut for such items as screens, railings, ornamental brackets, and house numbers. Blades for cutting metal must, in general, be finer than those used for wood; the thinner the metal to be sawed, the finer the teeth should be. A 14-tooth blade is suitable for metal $\frac{3}{32}$ inch or thicker. For thinner stock a 24- or 32-tooth metal-cutting blade should be used. Metal is cut more slowly than wood, of course. But a good saber saw with the right blade can cut 10-gauge cold-rolled steel (over $\frac{1}{8}$ inch thick) at 6 inches per minute or 22-gauge cold-rolled steel (about $\frac{1}{32}$ inch thick) at 23 inches per minute.

When sawing thick metal, lubricate the blade with a candle or with the kind of stick wax sold for easing window-sash movement. Soft metal may tend to clog the teeth; the next coarser blade may do better, but do not violate the "two-tooth rule." Stopping to brush chips out of the teeth occasionally is helpful. Start turns in metal very slowly, for the metal-cutting blade has little set and binds readily. Its harder temper also makes it more brittle and prone to break than ordinary woodcutting blades.

Thin sheet metal may bend or even tear when sawed. Use a 32-tooth blade, support the work as close to the cutting line as possible, and feed very slowly. For best results, clamp sheet-metal stock tightly between two sheets of hard composition board or thin plywood, mark the cutting line on the top sheet, and cut through all three pieces at once. Although it requires extra work, this method ensures a clean cut on the metal, with no danger of bending or tearing. It is also a good way to saw two or more thin pieces to the identical shape at once.

The fastest way to saw iron angle stock is across one leg at a time. Sawing through the flat of a leg is much slower. Another way to cut small angle stock is across the V section. Be sure to clamp the material firmly or lock it in a vise. Maintain close control of the saw at all times, as there is little support for the base when you cut such stock.

CUTTING SOFT MATERIAL Plain or corrugated cardboard, soft wallboard, acoustic tile, leather, canvas, rubber, and some kinds of floor tiles can be cut with the *knife blade* in the jigsaw. This is a toothless, keen-edged blade that cuts quickly and cleanly. (It is somewhat more dangerous than fine-toothed saw blades, and children should not be permitted to use it.) The knife blade can be resharpened and should be honed to keenness when it shows signs of dulling.

Cardboard can be cut in multiple layers if you stack it as much as an inch thick and mark the cutting lines on the sheet. It is too soft to clamp without damage, so hold it down firmly on a horizontal surface and make the cut as near the supporting edge as possible. Little pressure is needed to feed the knife.

Cloth, canvas, and soft leather must be backed by cardboard. Fabric may wrinkle under the jigsaw and, like thin sheet metal, is best cut as part of a sandwich. Tape it to a piece of cardboard, and tape or staple a second piece on top.

The knife blade makes it easy to cut vinyl or rubber floor tile to fit around pipes, wall setbacks, and built-in furniture. Asphalt-asbestos tile can be cut with a metal-cutting blade.

MAINTENANCE AND CARE OF SABER SAWS

Although any good saber/jig/bayonet saw will last for years, one preventive measure and a bit of occasional maintenance will lengthen its life. The preventive measure is easy—do not let the saw overheat. When the body gets hot, not just warm, let it run free for a few minutes. That is the quickest way of cooling it, even better than just shutting it off. Clogged vents also cause overheating. Keep them clear by frequent cleaning with a stiff-bristle brush.

Every tool needs lubrication, and the saber saw is no exception. Your instruction booklet will tell you how often it should be greased and oiled. Remove the old grease by wiping with a rag; never use solvent. Replace it with fresh lubricant of the kind recommended for your tool. The points where oil should be applied vary from one saw to another; follow the manufacturer's recommendations here also.

Motor brushes will eventually wear, causing rough or erratic operation. An occasional but regular check on the condition of the brushes will give you advance notice that they are wearing, so that you can replace them before trouble actually occurs.

Most manufacturers advise against making internal repairs and adjustments yourself. You may void your guarantee if you do.

Reciprocating Saws

Often referred to as a "plunge-cutting" or "all-purpose" saw, the reciprocating saw resembles an overgrown saber saw with the blade projecting from the front of the tool instead of from the bottom. It has a long blade that may be up to 12 inches in length. Equipped with the proper type of blade, it will cut through wood, metal, and plaster. The blade can be mounted in from four to six different positions to permit cutting in almost any direction, and it is ideally suited for plunge cutting in walls, floors, and ceilings.

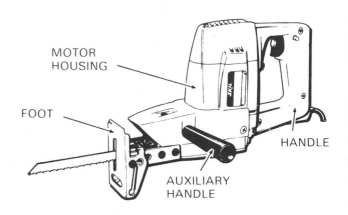

FIG. 10-39. Major parts of a typical reciprocating saw.

Although larger and heavier than a saber saw, the reciprocating saw can be used for scroll cutting as well as straight-line cutting, and most models will cut flush up against walls or other obstructions. They will slice through 2 X 4s or 4 X 4s with ease, and they are widely used by plumbers, electricians, and contractors on alteration jobs. Special blades are available for cutting through lumber in which embedded nails may be encountered, and most models can also be equipped with long, coarse blades which will cut green or gummy wood so that they can be used for pruning large shrubs and cutting off tree limbs.

When using a reciprocating saw, be sure to employ the right blade, as recommended by the manufacturer, and a sharp one. Blades for this tool, like the saber saw, are made for specific cutting purposes and should not be used for other than specified jobs. Candle wax on a saw blade will assist in cuts in heavy material. If your reciprocating saw is equipped with a variable speed control, set the control for the best cutting with the particular blade used. Follow the blade manufacturer's recommendations for the proper blade speed.

The foot of the reciprocating saw can usually be installed in several positons to suit the kind of cut being made. Note in Figure 10-39 that the typical foot supports have two tapped holes on each side. Position A shows the foot installed for flush cutting. The shoulder screw is in the top hole of the foot support. Position *B* is used for cutting bars, pipe, conduit, and sheet metal, and for scrollwork. The shoulder screw is in the bottom hole. Position *C* is used for crosscutting, rip cutting, and cutting corrugated sheet and other uneven materials. With most reciprocal saws, the shoe should never be placed at the extreme 45° position with the shoe fully extended. The blade will cut into the shoe if the saw is used with the shoe in this position.

For most wood, metal, and plastic cutting, the shoe can be left in the 90° position. The shoe should be braced firmly against the work, and the work must be braced well to avoid vibration and blade damage. Thin metal is best cut when it is clamped between two pieces of scrap plywood. Thin plywood should be C-clamped to steady the work.

To start a plunge cut with a reciprocal saw, grasp the handle with the front of the saw facing the work. Tilt the front of the saw down, place the front edge of the shoe on the work, and hold it with firm pressure. A firm stop in back of the shoe, such as a small block nailed to the work, is recommended. Turn on the power, and tilt the saw downward gradually until the blade contacts the work at the point of the cut. Continue tilting the saw downward slowly until the blade cuts through the work. *Caution*: Before making any plunge cuts in walls, check for concealed wiring, pipes, etc.

For other cutting operations, as well as safety and maintenance, the basic techniques and rules for the saber saw hold for the reciprocating saw.

Chain Saws

A few years ago, chain saws were used only by loggers and construction and nursery workers, but handymen have found that for any real quantity of pruning and tree trimming, or for felling trees and cutting firewood, the tool they want is a chain saw. Originally available only in large professional models that required a good deal of muscle to handle (some called for two operators), modern, light-duty versions that have been developed in recent years weigh as little as 7 pounds (with fuel) and are designed for the occasional user.

As its name implies, a chain-saw blade consists of an endless chain with a series of sharp cutters attached to it. The chain travels at about 1400 feet per minute around a long oval-shaped bar that projects out in front of the saw,

so that the cutters chip and slice their way through either hardwoods or softwoods when the bar is brought into contact with them. Although a few models are electrically driven, by far the most popular are the gasoline-powered saws. They eliminate the need for dragging around a lengthy extension cord, and they enable you to work anywhere that you can climb or reach. Electric saws are less expensive, but your reach is limited by the length and capacity of the extension cord. Electric chain saws do not require fuel storage and are a great deal quieter when operating. They do not have the log- or tree-cutting capacity (diameters) of gas-powered saws. If you estimate that your total cutting time will not likely exceed 5 hours annually and you can cut a lot of firewood in 5 hours, the electric chain saw is probably the one for you.

The bar and chain length and the displacement of the engine determine the price and power category of gas-fueled saws. Table 10-2 gives the basic information on chain saws.

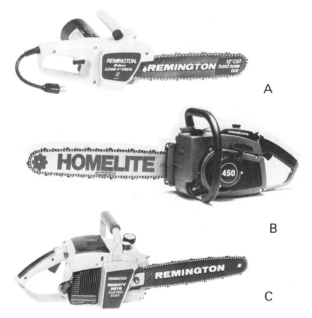

Fig. 10-40. *(a)* An electric-start chain saw; *(b)* a gasoline rope-start chain saw; *(c)* typical gasoline electric-start model.

Table 10-2 Chain-Saw Capacities

Power source	Bar and chain saw length, inches	Engine displacement) (cubic inches)	Average annual Time, hours	log or tree-cutting Capacity (diameter), inches
Electric	8 to 12		Up to 5	Limited
Gasoline	10 to 12	Up to 2.2	Up to 15	Up to 24
Gasoline	14 to 16	2 to 3.5	Up to 40	Up to 32
Gasoline	16 to 24	3 to 4	Unlimited	Up to 48

Since a chain saw can cut to the full depth of its bar, a 16-inch saw can actually cut through a 32-inch tree (or a 32-inch log) with two cuts—one from each side. The log-traction teeth at the base of the blade help considerably and should always be used on felling and top-bucking operations. Good lubrication of the chain is very important to the performance of the machine. Some machines have manual oilers, other automatic. Most have an automatic centrifugal clutch so that the chain does not move when the engine is idling; as you speed up the engine, the clutch automatically engages. Other features, which cost extra dollars but offer advantages, are chromed chains, antifriction-bearing-tipped guidebars, vibration isolation, compression releases for easy starting, and special antikickback devices. Some gasoline chain saws even feature an electric-start system rather than the conventional recoil starter.

SAFETY AND CHAIN SAWS

It is important to remember that any power cutting tool can be dangerous if it is not handled properly. Follow these precautions when using a chain saw:

1. Always hold the saw with both hands, making sure that your thumbs are hooked around the handles and that your grip is tight. This keeps the saw from jumping if the teeth should grab accidentally.
2. Be careful not to let the end of the blade hit branches, stubs, stumps, or any object other than the one you are cutting.
3. Be sure that any helpers or spectators are at a safe distance from you and the saw, and that they are not standing where they might be struck by falling branches, etc. That is, prepare the immediate cutting area by cleaning out undergrowth likely to interfere with operator and saw, and by removing dead material which could cause fire. Prepare a path of safe retreat to the rear and diagonal to the line of fall of trees or branches. Keep all bystanders from the work area.
4. Turn the saw off between cuts. Never hold it in one hand while you use the other to pick up cut pieces.

5. Do not carry the saw while the engine is running. Always turn the saw so the blade points backward when you walk with it from one cut to another.
6. Never use metal wedges or an axe to hold cuts open. Cut wooden wedges or pick up plastic wedges at your chain-saw dealer's shop.
7. Never set the saw on the ground with the engine running. There is a chance that heat from the engine might cause a fire.
8. Avoid refueling the saw in an area where spilled gasoline could soak flammable material. Never start the saw near the place where you refuel. Never refuel inside, not even in the garage. All these conditions could produce a fire hazard.
9. When you are sharpening or adjusting the blade, wear gloves or take extra precautions not to draw your finger across a saw tooth. Both the sharpness of the teeth and their shape make them inflict cuts easily.
10. Always wear short sleeves or buttoned cuffs and generally close-fitting clothes when you run your chain saw, to avoid the possibility of clothing getting caught in the saw. In other words, wear the proper apparel; safety foot-wear, snug-fitting clothes, and gloves.
11. Only make cuts within the capacity of your chain saw. Stand with your weight evenly distributed on both feet for proper balance. Do not overreach.
12. Follow the manufacturer's preparation and operating procedures, as recommended in the instruction manual, to the letter.

BASIC SAWING TECHNIQUES

Before cutting trees, practice making a few cuts on small logs. Support the log to be cut, off the ground, so the saw chain does not touch the ground as it cuts through the log. Hold the chain saw firmly with both hands.

When cutting small logs and limbs, open the throttle fully just before letting the chain touch the wood. It is safest to cut with the saw bumper up against the wood. If you cut further out along the bar, the chain will have a tendency to pull you and the saw toward the work, so you

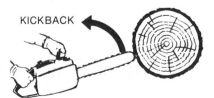

WHEN INCORRECTLY
STARTING TO BORE

WHEN NOSE STRIKES
ANY SOLID OBJECT

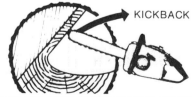

IF NOSE OF SAW HITS BOTTOM OF SAW CUT
WHEN REINSERTED INTO PREVIOUS CUT

FIG. 10-41. Situations causing the saw blade to kick back toward the operator.

must take care to brace yourself against this slight pull. (The reverse will be true if you are using the top of the bar to snip small limbs or "under-buck"). Exert light feed pressure to cut straight through the wood, but be ready to ease off on the throttle the moment the cut is completed. Try to master a steady, even cut before cutting down a tree.

LIMBING A TREE Limbing is removing the branches from a fallen tree. When limbing, leave the large lower limbs to support the tree off the ground. Remove the small limbs in one cut, as shown. Branches under tension should be cut from the bottom up to avoid pinching and binding of the chain saw.

FIG. 10-42. Antikick tip and how it helps prevent kickback.

"Kickback" is the term used for the upward motion of the chain saw which occurs when the chain contacts an object at the nose of the guidebar. To avoid kickback and maintain control of the chain saw, always hold the chain-saw handles with both hands. When the chain is moving, use a firm grip with thumbs and fingers encircling the handles. Maintain good footing and balance. Do not overreach. Some chain saws have a special safety tip that greatly reduces the chance of kickback.

CUTTING A LOG INTO LENGTHS Hold the chain saw firmly with both hands, and make sure your footing is firm and your weight is evenly distributed on both feet. The most desirable way to hold a log while cutting it into lengths is to use a sawbuck. When this is not possible, the log should be raised and supported by limbs or logs. Always stop the engine before moving from one cutting location to another.

For easier cutting, keep the following points in mind:

1. When cutting a log on a slope, always stand on firm ground and in a position away from the possible roll of the log. Release the cutting

pressure near the end of the cut to maintain complete control without relaxing your grip on the handles.
2. When the log is supported along its entire length, it should be cut from the top.
3. When the log is supported on one end, it should first be cut upward, one-third of its diameter, from the underside. Then the finish cut is made by cutting from the top to meet the first cut.
4. When the log is supported on both ends, it should first be cut downward, one-third of its diameter, from the top. Then the finish cut is made by cutting from the underside to meet the first cut.

Do not attempt to bore with the nose of the bar until you have become proficient in operating the saw and are sure of your own capabilities as well as those of the saw. Boring is something resorted to only when there is no better way to make a cut. It may be necessary to bore when some obstruction—another tree or log, a rock, or the ground—prevents you from placing the long edge of the bar against the wood. Boring is also employed to cut "blind holes" such as holes in fenceposts or cutouts for log-cabin windows. One way to minimize the danger of the saw kicking back is to begin with an angular cut, making contact with the wood as far back from the bar nose as possible; when this cut is deep enough to become a guide, exert downward pressure to bring the bar gradually into line for boring. Then bore into the wood.

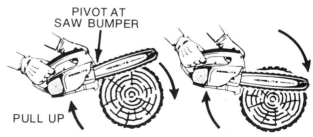

FIG. 10-43. Use the saw bumper as pivot.

TRIMMING Trimming is removing unwanted limbs from standing trees. Use a properly positioned and secured ladder to reach the higher limbs. Hoist the chain saw with a rope after you have a firm position on the ladder. Do not climb out on limbs or branches. To avoid tree damage, proceed as follows:

1. Make the first limbing cut from the underside, about $\frac{1}{2}$ foot from the trunk and one-third through the diameter.
2. Make the second limbing cut 2 to 4 inches farther out on the limb, *from above*, until the limb falls.
3. Undercut one-third the diameter of the limb

stub as close to the trunk as possible.

4. Make the final cut from above, as close to the trunk as possible to meet the undercut.

CUTTING DOWN A TREE Trees should not be cut down in a manner which would endanger any person, strike any utility line, or cause any property damage. If a tree does make contact with a utility line, the utility company should be notified immediately.

A retreat path should be planned and cleared as necessary before the felling cuts are started. The retreat path should extend back and diagonally to the rear of the expected line of fall. Before cutting a tree down, do the following:

1. Consider the natural lean of the tree, the location of the larger branches, and the wind direction to judge which way the tree will fall.
2. Clear the work area around the tree to be cut.
3. Remove all dirt and stones from the bark where the cuts will be made.
4. Make the notch cut one-third the diameter of the tree and perpendicular to the line of fall. Make the lower horizontal part of the notch cut first. This will help to avoid pinching of either the chain or the guide bar when the second notch cut is made.
5. Make the felling back cut at least 2 inches higher than, and parallel to, the horizontal notch cut. In making the felling back cut, leave enough wood to act as a hinge. The hinge wood keeps the tree from twisting and falling in the wrong direction. Do not cut through the hinge.

Guide the chain, without forcing it, through the cut. Use only enough pressure to keep the chain cutting full wood chips. As the felling cut gets close to the hinge, the tree should begin to fall. If there is any chance that the

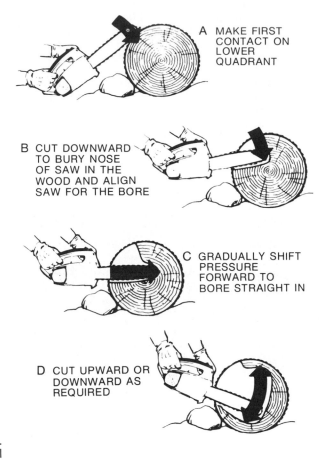

A MAKE FIRST CONTACT ON LOWER QUADRANT

B CUT DOWNWARD TO BURY NOSE OF SAW IN THE WOOD AND ALIGN SAW FOR THE BORE

C GRADUALLY SHIFT PRESSURE FORWARD TO BORE STRAIGHT IN

D CUT UPWARD OR DOWNWARD AS REQUIRED

FIG. 10-45. Steps in boring with the nose of the saw.

LIMB CUT

KEEP WORK OFF GROUND. LEAVE SUPPORT LIMBS UNTIL LOG IS CUT.

FIG. 10-44. When limbing a tree, keep the work off the ground. Leave the support limbs until the log is cut.

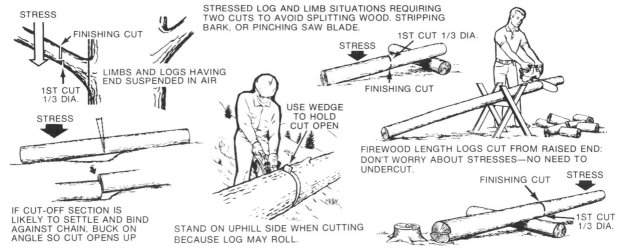

FIG. 10-46. Stressed log and limb situations sometimes require two cuts to avoid splitting the wood, stripping the bark, or pinching the saw blade.

tree might not fall in the desired direction, or may rock back and bind the saw chain, stop cutting before the felling back cut is completed. Use wedges made of wood, plastic, or aluminum to open the felling back cut to drop the tree along the desired line of fall. Never try to free a chain saw bound in a cut by starting the engine or forcing the guide bar. As the tree begins to fall:

1. *Remove* the chain saw from the cut.
2. *Stop* the engine.
3. *Move* back a safe distance on your retreat route. Watch your footing.
4. *Watch* for any flying branches.

CHAIN SAW MAINTENANCE

To keep your chain saw in top operating condition, do the following:

1. Check the chain tension frequently (with gloves on), and adjust it so it is snug on the bar but loose enough to pull around by hand. A loose chain will wear itself and the guidebar rapidly. A tight chain will rob the saw of cutting power and cause rapid wear.
2. Keep the chain cutters sharp. It is better to sharpen them too frequently than to wait until they become extremely dull.

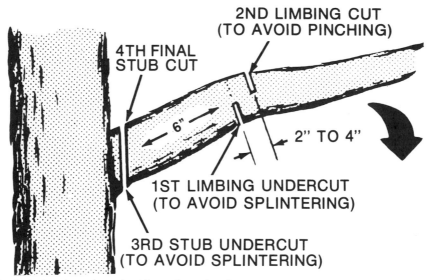

FIG. 10-47. Method of trimming a branch without damaging the tree.

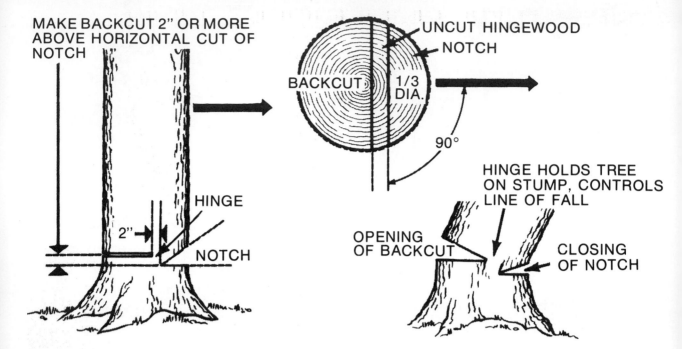

MAKE BACKCUT 2" OR MORE ABOVE HORIZONTAL CUT OF NOTCH

2"

HINGE

NOTCH

UNCUT HINGEWOOD

NOTCH

BACKCUT

1/3 DIA.

90°

HINGE HOLDS TREE ON STUMP, CONTROLS LINE OF FALL

OPENING OF BACKCUT

CLOSING OF NOTCH

FIG. 10-48. Proper method of notching and felling a tree.

3. Make sure the manual and/or automatic oilers are working. A well-lubricated chain is free and clean. A dry chain is stiff and runs hot, and resin builds up on the links and rivet heads. Always fill the oil tank when it becomes empty and each time the fuel tank is filled. Never use dirty oil or fuel.

4. Check the chain saw regularly for a frayed starter cord, loose bolts, dented guidebar groove, and general condition and appearance.

5. Check the fuel-tank vent each time you fill the tank, to be sure it is clean and operating properly. Also keep the air filter clean as per the manufacturer's directions. Never operate a saw with the filter off.

6. Clean and gap the spark plug regularly.

7. Periodically clean and check the spark arrestor and/or the muffler. Never run the engine without a spark arrestor or muffler.

8. Check to be sure that the cylinder cooling fins

1ST CUT—USE PIVOT ACTION

UNCUT HINGE WOOD

NOTCH

2ND CUT—REINSERT SAW AND DRAW IT AROUND THE BACK

NOTCH

FELLING CUT—INSERT FELLING WEDGE BEHIND BLADE. CONTINUE TO CUT FORWARD TOWARD NOTCH

NOTCH

DRIVE WEDGE INTO BACK CUT TO HELP FORCE TREE OVER. REMOVE SAW

FIG. 10-49. Normal sequence used to fell very large trees (up to twice the bar length in diameter).

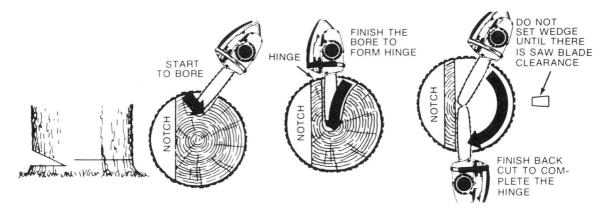

START TO BORE

HINGE

FINISH THE BORE TO FORM HINGE

NOTCH

DO NOT SET WEDGE UNTIL THERE IS SAW BLADE CLEARANCE

FINISH BACK CUT TO COMPLETE THE HINGE

FIG. 10-50. Sequence for felling very large trees close to ground level.

are clear. Use a flat stick to clean dirt, chips, and other material from between the cylinder fins.

9. Keep the guidebar oil holes free and clear of foreign material. Reverse your guidebar top for bottom each time the chain is removed from the chain saw. This will result in longer guidebar life.

10. When replacing the chain, always install a new sprocket. A chain and sprocket become a matched pair in use, owing to their common wear. A new chain on a worn sprocket or a worn chain on a new sprocket can cause early wear and possible failure of the new part. Check the sprocket and chain frequently for wear.

11. For problems or troubles beyond the normal maintenance and servicing checks, take the saw to a manufacturer's authorized service center or dealer. Always follow the manufacturer's instructions in the service manual.

12. If the chain saw is not to be used for a period of a few weeks or more or during the noncutting months, drain the fuel tank in a safe area, then run it until it stops (at idle speed) to remove most of the fuel. Remove the spark plug, and pour a teaspoon of oil into the combustion chamber. Pull the starter rope slowly several times, and replace the spark plug tightly. Clean the bar and chain thoroughly. Store the chain in a container of oil. Oil the bar thoroughly to prevent rust, and wrap it in heavy paper. Clean the outside of the saw, wrap or box it, and store everything in a dry, cool place, away from furnaces, heaters, etc.

ROUTERS

The router—more exactly, the portable electric router—is another very versatile power tool. But the router is a tool for advanced carpentry and furniture making. In its modern efficiency, it can not only make the decorative edges on tabletops, trim plastic laminates, and cut outlines for inlay jobs, but also do many ordinary and useful jobs around the house. For instance, a tool that can cut grooves and rabbets for cabinetwork, mortises for door hinges, fancy edges for bookcases and shelving, grooves for storm windows and weatherstripping, and sink openings in counter tops, can duplicate shapes of intricate design, can cut circles and ovals with perfectly smooth edges, and can round corners in all sorts of work should certainly earn its keep in anyone's shop. The router and its companions, the electric plane and the shaper table, can do all those tricks and many more.

The router is unique in that it has no hand-tool counterpart unless it be the carving chisel and mallet. Its principle of operation is quite different, however, being derived from and similar to that of the electric drill. The cutting bit is short and shaped for whatever task is desired, with three or four cutting edges of fairly small diameter. The shank of the bit is held in a small threaded chuck directly on the end of the shaft, and the cutter is driven at a very high speed. The base of the machine is arranged so that the cutter can be guided over or along the work as the particular job demands. The depth of cut can be altered by raising or lowering the motor housing in the base frame. A variety of cutting bits enables the router to do a great many jobs on wood, plastics, composition materials, and the new pressed-wood materials. Carbide-tipped cutters are available for quantity work on abrasive and tough materials such as laminated plastics.

In learning to handle many of these new materials, shop workers and carpenters have found that ordinary shop tools such as the band saw and table shaper just

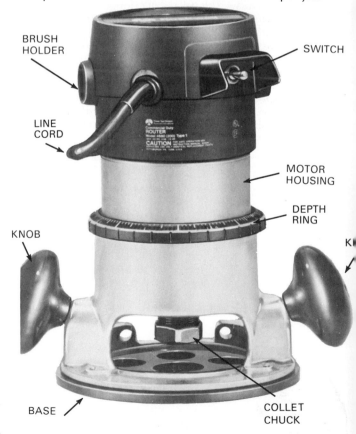

FIG. 11-1. Parts of a typical router.

could not be adjusted to cut and shape effectively. The router was found to be the answer. The small, fast cutters will cut out irregular shapes and fancy edges smoothly and quickly without chipping or splitting the material. With the planer (which also employs a variety of cutters) and the table shaper, this portable tool is just about the last word in professional shop efficiency for all woodworkers, including the home craftsman and homeowner.

ROUTER FEATURES

Routers are available in many models, but they all include three basic parts: motor, base, and bits. The motor is equipped with a chuck on one end of its shaft, and it fits upright (shaft down) in the base. Releasing a clamp screw allows the motor to rotate in the spiral-channeled base; this action raises or lowers the motor with respect to the base and therefore adjusts the depth of cut. In some models, the subbase, which provides a flat, low-friction surface for the tool to ride on, is interchangeable with other special-purpose subbases.

The motor that drives the router is usually a powerful 120-volt ac-dc universal motor which runs at a high speed of around 18,000 to 28,000 rpm. The motor case should be trim and slender and of highly polished die-cast aluminum alloy which is easy to keep clean. The switch must be a double-pole snap type, recessed into the case at the rear of the housing where it is readily accessible. As with most portable tools, the models offered by manufacturers can be considered either light or standard duty ($\frac{1}{3}$ to $\frac{1}{2}$ hp), or heavy or commercial duty ($\frac{3}{4}$ hp and up). The difference in the types is not in the scope of their applications but in the speed with which they can accomplish a job. That is, with a lighter-duty router you may have to make a cut in several slow partial-depth passes rather than one fast pass, but you can make the cut just the same. Also, some of the larger bits cannot be fully retracted in some of the smaller models.

The router rests on the work and requires little lifting. Routers vary in weight from $3\frac{1}{2}$ to 9 pounds but are, nevertheless, easy to handle.

The cutting depth is regulated by raising or lowering the motor unit in relation to the base. In some routers, the adjustment is by rack-and-pinion gearing; in others, by a spiral cam. Scale markings are usually in sixty-fourths of an inch, and you can actually control the depth that accurately. A clamping lever or locking nut holds the motor base at the desired depth. A collet chuck on the motor shaft holds the cutting tool. It is important always to use a wrench to tighten the chuck. Some models have a light which operates when the motor is on and which helps you to follow marks on the work.

ROUTER BITS AND CUTTERS

Bits and cutters come in three mounting arrangements, two materials, and an almost infinite variety of shapes and sizes. There are two basic types. The first, and by far the

A

B

C

D

FIG. 11-2. While router design varies to some extent, the following are some of the basic features: (a) The router motor (right) fits into the top of the base and has chuck at the bottom for bits with $\frac{1}{4}$-inch shafts. (b) The motor can be raised or lowered inside the base by a ring around its middle, to regulate the depth of cut. (c) The wrench which comes with the router opens and closes the collet chuck. Some models require two wrenches. (d) A chamfering or beveling bit with a $\frac{1}{4}$-inch shaft being inserted in the collet chuck of a router.

most popular, is the one-piece bit with a shank built into the cutting head. It may or may not have a pilot, or cylindrical guide tip, built into the lower cutting edge. The shank fits into the collet of the router motor. The other type has a hole threaded completely through the center of the cutting head. When this bit is used with the router, a separate shank or arbor is screwed into the top of the cutting head. Also, if a separate pilot is needed, it is screwed into the bottom of the cutting head. When the edge of a board is routed, the pilot controls the horizontal depth of the cut by riding along the edge of the work. All routers today use $\frac{1}{4}$-inch shank bits, and different manufacturers' bits are interchangeable. Arbor bits thread onto separate shanks.

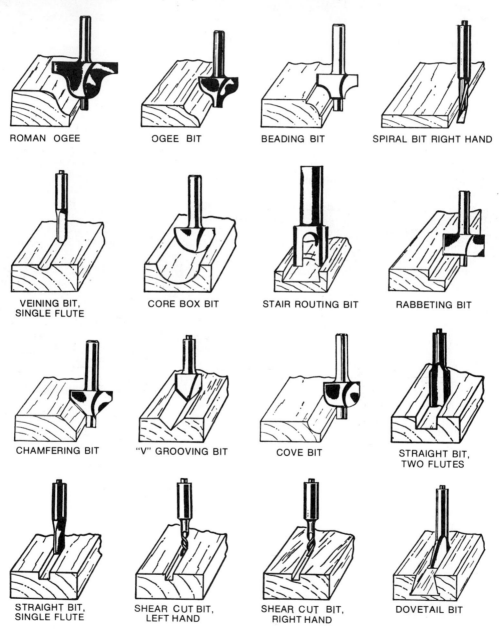

ROMAN OGEE   OGEE BIT   BEADING BIT   SPIRAL BIT RIGHT HAND

VEINING BIT, SINGLE FLUTE   CORE BOX BIT   STAIR ROUTING BIT   RABBETING BIT

CHAMFERING BIT   "V" GROOVING BIT   COVE BIT   STRAIGHT BIT, TWO FLUTES

STRAIGHT BIT, SINGLE FLUTE   SHEAR CUT BIT, LEFT HAND   SHEAR CUT BIT, RIGHT HAND   DOVETAIL BIT

FIG. 11-3. Profiles of some of the more common router bits.

Shaper cutters can also be used on some higher-power routers. The bit collet is unscrewed, and a spindle is installed in its place on the router motor shaft. A cutter with a smooth hole through its center is mounted on the spindle, along with spacing collars, and clamped tight with a nut. Sometimes, several cutters and collars are used together. Shaper cutters are particularly useful in routing the edges of boards, as the router subbase rides on the flat side of the board, rather than on the edge.

Some bits are provided with noncutting pilots that control the sidewise depth of cut; these pilots are either a solid rod or a high-speed ball bearing. Carbide bits (solid and tipped) cost two and a half to three times as much as tool-steel bits but are worth the price because they stay sharp much longer.

Figure 11-3 shows the profiles of some of the more common cutting bits; the cuts they make clearly reveal the wide variety and nature of the work the router will do. Various sizes of *straight* bits are used for routing edges, dadoes, rabbets, and grooves. *Veining* bits are used for narrow decorative grooves; their ends can be either rounded or square. Some veining bits are double ended and use a special collet.

Core-box bits scoop out a half-round groove and can be used for hollowing out trays and for making concave quarter-round edge moldings. *Cove* bits are shaped like core-box bits except that they have pilots and are used for molding edges only. *Beading* bits are used for making rounded edges that have a sharp break at each end of the round. *Rounding-over* bits (not illustrated) make a similar cut, but the molded edges are rounded over because they have pilots that are flush with the edge of the cutter. Other shapes include *V-groove* bits, *rabbeting* bits,

chamfering bits, *shear-cut* bits, *spiral* bits, *stair-cutting* bits, *ogee* bits, *Roman-ogee* bits, and *dovetail* bits.

Laminate trimmers (carbide only) are special bits for edging laminated plastic counter tops. Most are cleverly designed to combine bevel and flush cutting in a single bit.

Shaper cutters are primarily used for molding board edges or cutting tongues and grooves and other joints. They work fast, but it takes a powerful router (1 hp or better) to drive them efficiently.

Regardless of how little routing you plan to do, invest in one ½-inch carbide straight bit, and use it for everything it will handle; then buy lower-priced steel bits for your less frequent routing requirements. If your bits are not kept sharp, they will burn your work. Keep them stored in individual compartments to protect their edges. You can sharpen your bits yourself with a sharpening-kit attachment for some routers, or you can have them done by a professional sharpener.

To insert a bit into the router chuck, follow these typical steps:

1. Select the proper bit for the job. If the bit does not have a shank, add an arbor.
2. Insert the bit (with arbor) all the way into the collet, and then back it out about 1/16 inch.
3. Fasten the chuck with the wrenches furnished with the router. Some chucks must be fastened with two wrenches.
4. The depth of the cut can be set by measuring with a rule and then adjusting the depth ring.
5. Reverse this procedure when removing the bit or cutter.

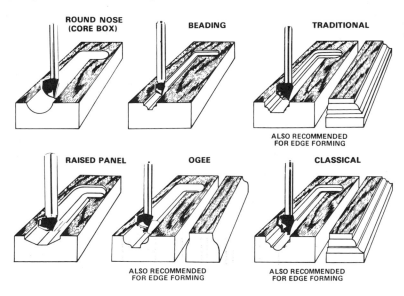

FIG. 11-4. Shapes of carbide-tipped groove-forming production router bits which are used to form decorative inlays for cabinet doors, furniture pieces, displays, etc. The traditional, ogee, and classical can also be used for edge forming.

FIG. 11-5. A special panel trim bit is used in the router to make the plywood back panel perfectly flush with the frame of the bookcase.

GUIDES AND ACCESSORIES

The router can be guided freehand to write your name in a board or to follow penciled guidelines for decorative veining. But this is only the beginning of its possibilities. There are a number of attachments, some of which you can make yourself, that enable the router to do many kinds of precision work.

STRAIGHT AND CIRCULAR GUIDE This can guide the router parallel to a straight edge or concentrically inside a round one, always keeping the bit at precisely the same distance from that edge. The guide, shown in Figure 11-6a, is a frame with two sockets for guide rods fixed on it. At one end of the rods is a flat arc-shaped bracket by which the guide is attached to the top of the router base with four screws. By loosening the thumbscrews, you can slide the head along the rods.

This accessory frequently has a vernier screw adjustment with which you can alter its setting on the rods by a hair's breadth at a time. The head also has a center slot underneath, in which a rule can be laid directly against the bit for precise settings.

To rout along straight edges, the flanged section is used as a guiding surface. When a longer or wider guiding area is needed, you can attach a wood facing, 8 to 10 inches long, with screws through two holes provided. For rabbeting an opening for storm windows and other similar frames, a triangular wood block can be attached to the straight guide, as shown in Figure 11-6b. This permits cutting around a corner without changing the position of the machine.

SLOT AND CIRCLE-CUTTING ATTACHMENT With a special bracket for mounting onto the router base, this attachment has a plate that is adjustable on two rods (Figure 11-7). On the inner edge of the plate is a pivot pin held by a screw. Set this pin into a ¼-inch hole drilled in the work, and you can swing the router to make perfectly circular slots, grooves, rosettes and the like, from 1 to 22

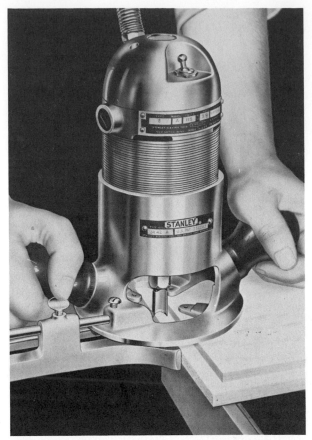

A

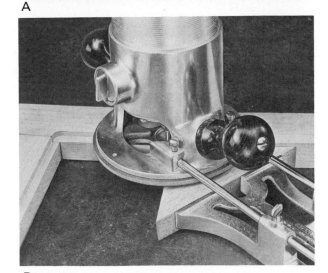

B

FIG. 11-6. (a) Straightedge guide; (b) straightedge guide with a triangular corner block.

A

B

FIG. 11-7. *(a)* By using a V-block circle-cutting attachment as an edge guide, the guided cut can be made on a radius. The rods on the edge guide slip into the sockets on the router base; the guide can then be moved in or out along the length of the rods for any cut. *(b)* By attaching a pivot pin (arrow) to the guide, many circular patterns can be cut.

inches in diameter. You can also cut out perfectly circular disks with a straight bit, lowering it a little at a time after each pass until it cuts through. With a molding cutter, you can, in one operation, cut out a disk with a shaped edge and leave a circular opening with a similar molded edge.

Remove the pivot or trammel point or pin and replace it with a straight bar, and you can rout grooves along short or long edges, or evenly spaced grooves across a surface. In Figure 11-8, for example, the first groove is made with the bar sliding along the work edge. Then it is slid inside each routed groove in turn, spacing the next one always precisely the same distance away. (With a cutter wider than the bar, you simply guide against the same side of the groove each time.)

FIG. 11-8. In making parallel cuts, the first groove can act as a channel guide. The guide is extended for each new cut, or each previous cut is used as the new guide.

TEMPLATES AND TEMPLATE GUIDES Two other devices also are used in guiding the router: templates and template guides. The guide is a thin metal sleeve through which a bit is inserted. It is used to follow the outlines of a template.

The template can be made of plywood, hardwood, or metal to form an outline of the groove to be cut. Templates for routing dovetail joints and hinge-butt mortises are two examples of manufacturers' prepared guides. They enable you to perform these operations quickly and easily and are worth the cost if you have much of this type of work to do.

You can reproduce any design by tracing it onto ¼-inch plywood or hardboard and cutting out a template. The router then follows the template and cuts the design into the wood, reproducing the design exactly.

To make a template, first draw the shape on paper; then sketch it slightly larger or smaller, depending on the kind of template, to allow for the thickness of the base ring. Draw the outline in soft pencil; then transfer the design to ¼-inch plywood by turning the paper over and rubbing it with a fingernail. Then, with the bit set at 1/16 inch below the template, move the router around the inside of the design. You can easily improvise straightedge guides for your router by clamping pieces of lumber to your work, provided they have straight, smooth edges.

SAFETY AND THE ROUTER

While the router is basically a safe power tool, the following safety precautions should be taken:

1. Be sure the motor is properly grounded.
2. Wear goggles or a face shield when using the router.
3. Mount the bit securely in the chuck, and make sure the base is tight. A slightly loose bit can "walk" partially out of the chuck, particularly when taking a heavy cut, and destroy your depth accuracy.
4. Always unplug the motor when changing bits or cutters or making adjustments.
5. Be certain the work is securely clamped so it will remain stationary during the routing operation.
6. Place the router base on the work, template, or guide, with the bit clear of the wood, before turning on the power. Hold it firmly when turning on the motor, to overcome the starting torque.
7. Make sure the bits and cutters are sharp. Know the purpose of each one before using it.
8. Always check for the correct depth adjustment before making a cut.
9. Hold the router with both hands, and feed it smoothly through the cut in the correct direction. Always maintain a well-balanced position on both feet when handling the router.
10. When the cut is complete, turn off the motor. Do not lift the machine from the work until the motor has come to a complete stop.

FIG. 11-9. Another guide attachment that converts a router into a fairly efficient edge-plane tool.

USING THE ROUTER

Besides tool sharpness, the other factor that affects the smoothness of your routing is the rate of feed, which boils down to how much material you try to remove in one pass. Clean, smooth routing can be done when the router is running close to its no-load speed. Too deep a cut or a too-fast feed will slow it down, letting the cutter take bigger bites. You have to judge this by ear. There is no set rule; the proper cut and feed depend on the size of the bit, the power of the router, and the hardness and moisture content of the wood.

The direction of feed is important. It should be from left to right along an edge, so that the cutter blades will perform a chopping action, rather than a gouging action that can cause splintering. When you start the router, hold it firmly; the initial torque will tend to twist it out of your hands. Always keep the router base flat on the work surface. Feed from left to right or, on circular work, counterclockwise. Let your sense of feel control the feed. Too slow a feed creates friction that can burn the wood; too rapid a feed wears bit edges and leaves a rough surface. The feeding speed will depend largely on the

A

B

FIG. 11-10. (a) A typical router template guide can be made from hardboard or (b) the machine used freehand.

hardness and density of the wood the bit must pass through. If the going is difficult, it is better to set the cutter to a shallower depth and make several passes to achieve the desired full depth. In fact, you should learn to "feel" a router, by practice, so that you recognize the sound and pressure of the machine. In general, the router should be moved along its work so that the speed of the motor is slowed no more than one-third. Working too fast overloads the motor; working too slowly may burn the wood or spoil the cutter. Always keep the cutting tools sharp to make the work easier for the tool. On those models with a light, the light becomes brighter as you increase the load. This can serve as a warning to reduce feed pressure.

In freehand routing, without the use of any guide, success depends upon your skill and artistry. Practice first on a piece of scrap material to get the feel of it, and to see the results of the trial-and-error process. Try writing your name in a piece of wood with a veining bit.

FIG. 11-11. Making a beaded corner molding. The noncutting pin on the bottom of the cutter governs the depth of the cut.

To prevent gouging at corners it is wise to have a close fit between the cutter and the guide opening, especially for rabbeting. Some home carpenters attach a wooden strip up to 1 inch thick to the guide when using the straight guide, allowing the cutter to make a recess as the bit is lowered. Splintering is avoided by attaching scrap wood to the edge.

FIG. 11-12. Dado and blind dado made with a router.

CUTTING A DADO OR GROOVE One of the most useful functions of the router is in making wood joints, which it does better than most other tools. (For some joints, it rates as an equal to stationary shapers.) The dado joint, for example, is much used for installing shelves in furniture, such as bookcases, cabinets, and desks. If you have a bit the same size as the thickness of the shelving, you can cut the dado to the exact size in one pass with the router. Otherwise, you can make several passes to cut it to the required width. Use the router guide to get the desired distance from the edge. Make sure that the edge from which you guide is straight and smooth. For the grooves into which drawer bottoms are to be placed, use a $\frac{1}{4}$-inch spiral bit and cut a groove about $\frac{1}{4}$ inch away from the bottom of each of the sides of the drawer. Then you can slide the drawer bottom into these grooves from the back, after the drawer is put together. The router is the only portable power tool that can cut a "blind dado," that is, a dado that does not extend to the edges of the piece and therefore does not show from either side.

FIG. 11-13. Cutting a dado with a straight bit, using a shop-made T square as an edge.

One of the simplest guides for routing dadoes is a T-square guide. This is used with the round edge of the router base guiding along the crossbar. (It does not matter if the router base turns slightly, for the cutter is centered and therefore the same distance from any part of the round edge of the base.) You can rout through dadoes that run from edge to edge (routing a like notch in the head of the T guide), or half-blind dadoes that start from one edge but stop short of the other. True blind dadoes that reach neither edge are made by lowering the router carefully into starting position, and lifting it where you want the dadoes to stop.

If you want dadoes wider than the cutter, insert a shim strip alongside the crossbar and make one pass. Then remove the strip to make a second pass directly against the crossbar. The thickness of the shim strip must be the difference between cutter diameter and the desired dado width. Thus, to make a $\frac{3}{8}$-inch dado with a $\frac{1}{4}$-inch bit, you would use a $\frac{1}{8}$-inch-thick strip. To prevent edge chipping when you make through dadoes, clamp a scrap piece against the work edge from which the router emerges.

FIG. 11-16. The back edges of a bookcase frame are recessed with a router, using a rabbeting bit, so a plywood backing can be set into the frame.

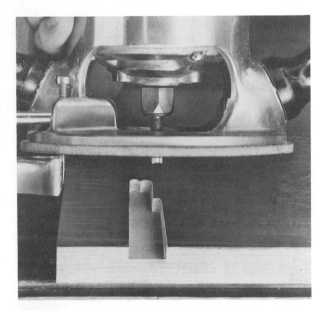

FIG. 11-14. For wider dado cuts, make repeated cuts alongside one another until the desired width is obtained.

A two-bar guide as shown in Figure 11-14 is easy to make and, when clamped to the work, it produces faultless dadoes. Figure 11-15 shows a template for making a dovetail dado, an excellent joint for fine cabinet work. The same dovetail bit is used for the dovetail dadoes and for the matching dovetails, or tongues, on the second part of the joint. The first piece of stock is held in the template. The router is guided along the jig, cutting the dovetail dadoes. The second workpiece is placed on the template, and indented one notch. Then the corresponding dovetails are cut in the same manner as the dadoes. Dadoes and dovetails can be cut wider than the bit itself by making two passes, with the router shifted the amount necessary.

FIG. 11-15. Cutting a dovetail on the end of a shelf.

FIG. 11-17. A simple jig for both spline and tongue-and groove joints.

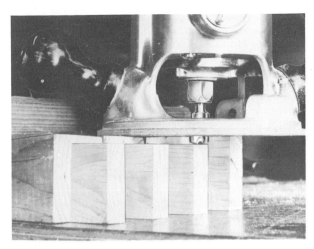

FIG. 11-18. Cutting a mortise and tenon joint with a router.

FIG. 11-19. Dovetail kit and examples of the finished work.

CUTTING A RABBET Edge and end rabbets can be made in two ways. One is with a rabbeting bit, which has a smooth shank under its blades and is both guide and cutter. The depth of the rabbet is set on the router with the knurled depth-adjustment collar; the width of the rabbet is governed by the bit itself. The smooth pilot shank is guided directly along the uncut part of the work edge under the rabbet.

With a straight bit, you would use the straight and circular guide to form rabbets. It is best if the bit is slightly larger in diameter than the desired width of the rabbet, as this makes adjustment less critical. When a rabbet is to be routed on all four sides of a piece, experts make cuts across the end grain first, and then cut with the grain, to eliminate chipping at the corners. In fact, all rabbeting should be organized so that there is minimum risk of splintering. Where an end and an edge are to be cut, cut the end first. Multiple pieces should be aligned in a continuous line when possible.

A

B

C

FIG. 11-20. Making a dovetail joint: *(a)* putting the template in place; *(b)* cutting with the router; *(c)* the results.

Inside rabbets (as at the edge of a screen door) require a guide block set at a 90° angle to the router guide. Move the router in the direction opposite the bit rotation.

To cut a stopped rabbet, start the router at the inside end; or, if the start is made at the edge, make an automatic block by attaching a properly sized piece of stock to hold the guide at the right point. A rabbet on the edge of a disk requires a shaped guide made of wood in place of the straight guide. Always be sure to use strips to protect against splintering at the edges.

CUTTING A SPLINE JOINT Another very useful joint that the router can make with ease and precision is the spline joint. This joint is strong, is used for joining two pieces of wood together, and has the advantage of holding the pieces together while the glue is setting. The spline joint consists of a groove in each piece and a spline that fits into both grooves and holds the pieces together with the aid of wood glue. The grain of the spline should run across the joint line, not with it. Plywood is a good choice for splines.

To make the grooves, mark them on one piece as for tongue-and-groove joints, and set the straight guide the same way. Rout from both faces of the workpiece to center the groove precisely. To groove across the ends of pieces such as frame members, hold them in a simple fixture such as that in Figure 11-17. The spacer must be precisely the same thickness as the stock being routed. The two side boards should be of equal thickness, great enough to give the router firm support. This same jig can be used to cut tongue-and-groove joints.

CUTTING A MORTISE-AND-TENON JOINT The mortise-and-tenon joint, laborious and difficult to cut by hand, is easy to cut with a router. The mortise is marked and cut just as the groove on an edge. Squaring the cut usually requires a chisel. The tenon is cut in the same way as a rabbet, by working from the shoulder to provide support. If a number of mortise-and-tenon joints are to be made, a jig setup is a big timesaver.

On one piece, outline the desired mortise carefully. Clamp the piece in a fixture such as that in Figure 11-18, and, with a bit smaller than the mortise width and set at zero depth, adjust the straight guide to align one side of the bit exactly on one side of the mortise outline. Then set the bit to the desired mortise depth. (In hardwood you may have to make more than one pass to bring the mortise to full depth.) Lower the revolving bit slowly into the work until the base is flat on top of the fixture. Then move it the desired length of the mortise. Next, place the straight guide against the opposite face of the fixture, and make a second pass to bring the mortise to width. This centers the mortise in the stock. It will, of course, have rounded ends which can be chiseled square if you prefer.

When a mortise is to be made to one side of center, as is often the case in furniture legs, the bit must be the full mortise width; the cut is made from one face of the fixture. Cut the tenon $\frac{1}{64}$ inch shallower than the mortise to leave space for entrapped glue. Clamp the workpiece in the fixture, and set the straight guide (by means of the vernier adjustment) to make the tenon the correct width when the router is guided along both sides of the fixture. To bring the tenon to correct length, guide the router against the closed end of the fixture. Reverse the workpiece in the fixture to cut the other end.

CUTTING A DOVETAIL JOINT The strongest, most widely used joint in professional woodworking is the dovetail. With a router and an accessory template which most manufacturers have available, it is easy to make in the following manner: Secure the template to the front of the workbench. It has two barclamps, one on the top and one in front. To cut the dovetail (when making a drawer), clamp one side piece vertically in front of the template. Then place the front piece underneath the plastic fingers on the top of the template. Make sure that (1) both pieces are butted tightly against the stops on the left side of the template; (2) the front edge of the drawer front butts against the drawer side; and (3) the top edge of the drawer side is flush with the top of the front. Secure the bar clamps. Then, screw the guide (usually a small aluminum disk) into the hole of the router subbase, and secure the dovetail bit in the chuck. Adjust the router carefully for depth of cut; it will vary, depending on the size of the bit. Begin at the left edge of the template and

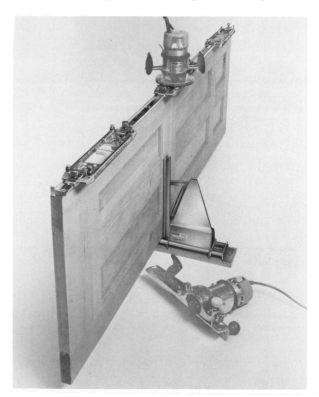

FIG. 11-21. Typical hinge-mortise template.

make a cut to the right, removing stock in front of the template fingers. This must be done before working into the finger indentations, to avoid chipping the work edge. Then, working from right to left, cut in and out, around the template fingers.

Remove the two pieces and they will fit together to make a perfect dovetail corner joint. If the fit is loose, the cut was not deep enough; if it is tight, it was too deep. Most templates will handle either flush or rabbeted dovetails on various stock thicknesses.

HINGE-MORTISE CUTTING Most manufacturers have a kit available for setting hinges in doors and shutters. The kit includes template frames that are temporarily fastened to the doors and their frames, a template guide that tracks the router in them, and a special bit and chisel for cutting the corners square. After hinge mortises have been routed in the door, the template frames are transferred to the door frame for routing perfectly aligned mortises there.

DECORATIVE MOLDINGS Molding bits with smooth pilot shanks can be guided directly against the work edge, whether it is straight, curved, or irregular, the pilot riding that part which is not cut away. Straight, convex, concave, and bead cutters can be stacked on an arbor to make moldings of your own design. You can make strip molding by shaping an edge on a board and then ripsawing it off to any desired width. Always take care to leave enough of the edge to guide against. When this is not possible, use a template or, on round work, the circular guide.

FINISHING LAMINATE EDGES You can trim Formica, Micarta, Textolite and other hard laminated-plastic counter-top materials with either a separate tool or an inexpensive kit that converts your present router to a laminate trimmer.

The laminate trimmer kit fits some but not all models of conventional routers. If you are interested in adding the laminate trimmer kit to your collection of router accessories, first check to see if it will fit your present router.

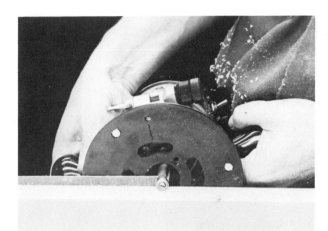

FIG. 11-23. Trimming the edge of plastic laminate with a router bit.

A feature that distinguishes the complete (separate) laminate trimmer unit from the standard router is its shape. This shape, plus a wall guide bracket, enables the laminate trimmer to be guided along an irregular wall while simultaneously scribing and trimming the back edge of a counter or other surface. The base for the kit is circular in shape, while the base for the laminate trimmer unit is square.

The laminate trimmer kit consists of a special base, a precision adjustable trim guide, and a carbide veneer-trim bit. Also available for use with the laminate trimmer are carbide bevel cutters of several different bevels, combination carbide straight- and bevel-trim bits, carbide flush-trim cutters, solid carbide trim saws, a laminate trimmer arbor for saws, and carbide slotting cutters. The special base is attached to the router by means of four screws and is easily interchangeable with the conventional router subbase. The precision adjustable trim guide has two thumbscrews, one to adjust the distance of the trim cutter from the edge of the work, and the other to lock the setting of the first thumbscrew.

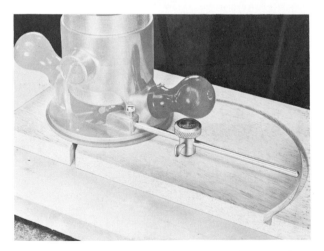

FIG. 11-22. A circle can be cut by a router with a trammel point attached to one of the guide rods. The upper knob-like portion of the trammel is held down on the work while the lower portion, which is a needle-like point, anchors into the wood and acts as a center point, similar to the action of a compass. The router is then moved in a circle around this center point, producing a perfect circle.

When constructing counter tops of decorative plastic laminates, cut the laminate material slightly oversize. When gluing this to the wood backing, be sure some of the excess overhangs each edge. Then trim this flush with your veneer trimmer.

The base of the laminate trimmer unit tilts 45° in either direction to permit bevel trimming with a straight bit. Carbide cutters cut plastics, even Formica, easily without getting dull quickly. The depth of the cut on the veneer-trimmer unit is controlled by two thumbscrews. One raises or lowers the base in parallel channels, and the other locks the adjustment of the first. This procedure can be used to position the cutting portion of the bit, cutter, or saw at the level of the surface to be trimmed. If you are using a standard router with the laminate trimmer attachment, set the depth of cut in the manner prescribed for that router.

ROUTER/BENCH SHAPER

Because it has a high-velocity motor, the router is designed by some manufacturers to be converted to a bench shaper. The advantages of using the router in this manner, rather than as a portable tool for cutting moldings and other shapes, is apparent when you consider the awkwardness of clamping small pieces of wood to a bench and attempting to move the router over them. A shaper plate, which converts the router to a bench router, is first installed in a bench. When you plan to use your router to cut moldings, unscrew the router from its base and mount the router motor on the shaper plate, underneath the bench. This permits tilting the motor 45 to 90°. The shaper cutter extends through a hole in the bench top. Work is fed into the cutter by pushing it along the shaper fence, which extends across the bench top on either side of the cutter. By using different shaper cutters and by tilting the router motor to various angles, an almost infinite variety of shapes can be produced.

Once the router-shaper table is set up, the tool can be operated in the same manner as described in Chapter 20 for the stationary type of table shaper. Of course, you should not use the router for any of the heavy-duty operations mentioned in that chapter.

The router-shaper table shown in Figure 11-25 can also be used to hold a saber saw and thus convert it to a stationary jigsaw. The table illustrated in Figure 10-35 can also be employed with a router. Of course, one of the

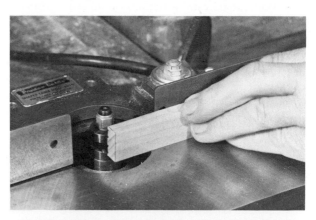

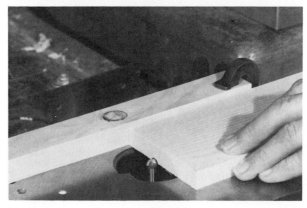

FIG. 11-24. Typical laminate trimmer. This routerlike tool operates at 28,000 rpm. Its compact and lightweight design allows one-hand operation.

FIG. 11-25. Typical router-shaper table.

most interesting of all these router conversion units is the so-called "router-crafter," which changes a router to a precision lathe for turning out wood pieces, without the bother of chisels or delicate measuring. To operate it:

1. Mount the workpiece (up to 3 inches square and 36 inches long) between the headstock and tailstock.
2. Attach the router, with a 1/4-inch-shank bit, to the sliding platform.
3. Set the depth adjustment on the router, and turn on the router.
4. Crank the handle of the tool to move the router for its lengthwise cuts.

FIG. 11-26. Typical power-plane attachment.

POWER PLANE

The power-plane attachment is another useful accessory for your basic router unit. The same motor that powers the shaper and router also powers the plane attachment. You may purchase one as part of the router kit, or later as the need arises. The power-plane attachment is a precision tool capable of exact control of the depth of cut. While its principal use is in sizing doors, screens, and the like for installation, it can be used to good advantage anywhere a hand plane can be used. Unlike some other tools that are sometimes used to trim doors, the power plane leaves smooth, clean, even edges.

Full details on the operation of a power plane can be found in Chapter 13.

CARE AND MAINTENANCE OF ROUTERS

Since the one motor drives all these tools, care and maintenance problems are minimal. Keep the motor clean of dust by blowing out the air passages frequently. Do not allow dust to collect inside the motor housing. Be sure that the current is 120 volts, and that the extension or lead wire is No. 14 or larger. Make sure that the ground wire is connected to a positive ground. The other parts of the combination kit require the same common-sense care and attention that all good tools require. Keep the parts clean and the adjustments working properly. It seems almost unnecessary to mention the need for selecting the proper collets or adapters to fit the various bits. Be sure the one selected is the right size and that the cutting bit is securely tightened before you start the motor. Again, keep it sharp.

Lubrication is usually not necessary on these tools. The precision ball bearings in the motor are greased and sealed for the life of the bearings.

As has already been stated, bits and cutters must be razor sharp for free cutting and smooth surfaces. An ingenious accessory which is available with many models makes it easy to sharpen them on the router itself. The router is inverted, and a small cup-shaped grinding wheel is mounted in it. The bit is locked in the sharpener, which is adjusted to bring the bit against the edge of the wheel. The fixture is then moved about on the inverted router base to grind the edge.

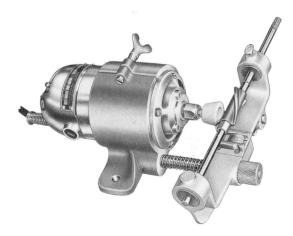

FIG. 11-27. Available sharpening kits include a universal grinding-jig attachment and stones.

PORTABLE POWER SANDERS

The portable power sander is much more than a simple smoothing tool. It also serves as a shaper if a piece of wood is held against it. Although some other power tools, especially the power drill, can be used as sanders, the electric sander is designed to do its specific job more effectively than any other tool.

There are three types of power sanders (Figure 12-1).

PAD OR FINISHING SANDERS This type of sander comes with either of three different actions: orbital, straight line, and combination orbital and straight line. The orbital pad sander has a rotary motor geared to move the abrasive platen in a tiny circular orbit (usually $3/16$ inch in diameter). Thus it cuts across the grain at one time, with it at another, and at all angles in between. But because the orbit is tiny, cross-grain scratches are microscopic, and the finish can be brought to satin smoothness. As the action is circular, it does not matter how you hold or move the sander; and because the abrasive movement is partially cross-grain,

orbital sanders work more rapidly than the straight-line type. This orbital action also tends to level the surfaces even though grain lines are of different density than the wood between them.

Straight-line pad sanders move the abrasive shoe back and forth only. Therefore they should always be held and moved so that this action is parallel to the grain. If the pad cuts across the grain or at an angle to it, the surface will show scratches. (However, some users feel it is permissible—and quicker—to sand cross-grain in the early sanding stages. Finishing strokes must always be with the grain.) Some straight-line sanders are driven by vibratory or magnetic motors. These have a short stroke and generally less power than rotary motors. Straight-line sanders can produce a fine, mirrorlike finish if grosser surface scratches are first carefully worked down.

Combination sanders theoretically give the best of both worlds, but many of them do not deliver two truly

FIG. 12-1. Three types of portable sanders (left to right): pad; disk; belt.

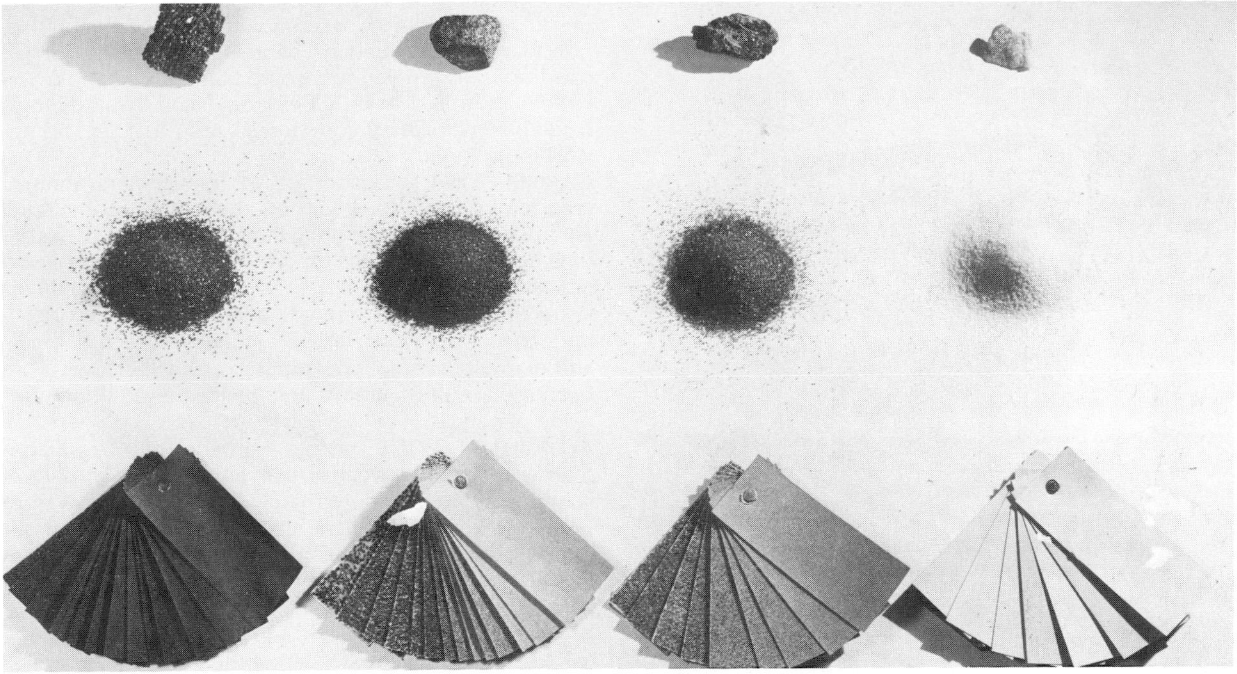

FIG. 12-2. Abrasive papers for wood finishing. They are made from silicon carbide, aluminum oxide, garnet, and flint.

different strokes. The orbital motion may have a dash of straight line in it, and vice versa. Thus, if you should decide on a dual-action pad sander, check it out most carefully.

DISK SANDERS The disk sander spins on a shank like a phonograph record. All disk sanders have a circular rubber pad mounted at right angles to the drive spindle of the motor. The abrasive disks are attached by a flange and screw that thread into the spindle. Disks are easy to change and, in the 5- and 6-inch diameter sizes, the choice of grits (degree of roughness) is great. They usually have a speed of from 3500 to 4500 rpm. (Some heavy-duty industrial models with 7- to 9-inch disks range from 5000 to 8000 rpm. The higher-speed machines are used for fast sanding.) Their main function (by design) is to remove stock rapidly and roughly. If you have a lot of paint to remove or a good amount of wood to sand off, a disk sander will do it best. They are not designed for, and hence not recommended for, finish work.

BELT SANDERS The belt sander has an abrasive belt traveling over two drums, one of them driven by the motor. The belt has far more sanding area than even a big orbital sander, and a high surface speed that can cut a wide swath through the work surface. The belt sander works so rapidly with a coarse abrasive that it can remove old paint, reduce stock thickness, or work like a plane to fit doors, screens, or storm windows to their frames. It can round off a square table edge or counter top without recourse to cutting tools; with a proper sequence of coarse to fine belts, it can surface rough wood to a smoothness fit for finishing.

Although belt sanders can do an excellent finishing job, if two sanders are available, the belt sander or disk sander is used for rough sanding, and the pad sander for finishing.

Abrasive Papers

As has been stated several times in this book, any job is easier and less time-consuming if you first familiarize yourself with the tools and materials you are working with; this is particularly true of most sanding chores. Regardless of the electric sander you are using, a knowledge of sandpaper grades and types will enable you to pick the abrasive that will work fastest and give you the smoothest finish. Thus, before discussing the operation of power sanders in detail, let us look at the various abrasives available.

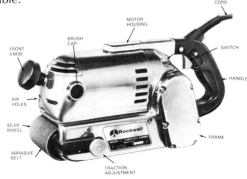

FIG. 12-3. Major parts of a typical belt sander.

A

B

C

FIG. 12-4. Steps in changing typical belts: *(a)* The lever adjustment on this belt sander relieves or restores the drum tension, permitting quick belt changes. *(b)* Tension is relieved on another belt model by simply pushing against the drum until it locks back as shown. *(c)* New abrasive belts are easily slipped onto the drums; with the tension restored, pressure holds the belt securely.

ABRASIVE MATERIALS USED

Although they are frequently called "sandpaper," sand is not used in the manufacturing of *abrasive papers*. The least expensive kind, and the one that most people think of when they mention the word sandpaper, is flint paper. Its sandy color and texture are undoubtedly the reason it was first called sandpaper, but it is actually made of white quartz, a natural mineral that is one of the oldest and cheapest of abrasives, but one that dulls and wears rapidly. Flint paper for power sanding is limited to removing old paint. In fact, most abrasive-paper manufacturers no longer make it for power use.

Another abrasive paper that is seldom used for power applications is emery—a mixture of iron oxide and corundum. It was, at one time, widely used for finishing

metal. However, it is a comparatively weak abrasive, nowadays (as described in Chapter 8) chiefly used only for hand-polishing metal. It is comparatively dull and wears rapidly and it is currently being replaced by aluminum-oxide papers for most commercial, industrial, and home-workshop applications.

GARNET PAPER This paper uses a natural mineral abrasive (a form of red quartz or garnet), the hardest of all natural abrasives. Much sharper than flint paper, garnet paper has long been popular with commercial finishers for use with power tools, as well as for hand sanding, because it cuts faster and lasts much longer than flint paper—although it does cost more. However, garnet tends to fracture easily, and many local stores no longer carry it because it has been replaced to a great extent by the newer aluminum-oxide papers.

ALUMINUM OXIDE This is a synthetic abrasive which is sharper and longer-wearing than either flint or garnet, yet it costs only slightly more than garnet (which is why most stores no longer carry both). It is actually the best all-around abrasive paper for shop use because it wears from 5 to 10 times longer than flint paper, stands up better than garnet paper, and cuts faster than both. It can be used for hand or power sanding with every type of machine, and it will work on metal, plastics, and other materials, as well as on wood.

SILICON CARBIDE This is another synthetic mineral which is actually the hardest abrasive of all, but its drawback is that it is very brittle and tends to fracture rather easily. It is widely used on abrasive papers that have a waterproof backing (wet-or-dry sandpapers), especially in the finer grades that are used for rubbing down varnish, lacquer, or enamel finishes on automobiles and furniture. Silicon carbide is also used on heavy-duty floor papers that are designed for drum and disk type floor sanders.

GRADING OF ABRASIVE PAPERS

Almost all the major manufacturers of abrasive papers now grade them according to grain size, by using numbers that indicate the size of mesh through which the grains will fall. Thus, a No. 100 paper has grains that will pass through a screen with 100 openings per square inch;

FIG. 12-5. A belt sander with a bag such as is shown here provides "dustless" sanding.

FIG. 12-6. To edge sand with a belt machine, clamp several pieces of stock together to provide a broad support.

FIG. 12-8. (Left) Major parts of a typical pad sander. (Right) The block sander operates in the same manner, except that is has a one-hand palm grip to get closer to inside corners.

FIG. 12-7. (Left) Mounted upside down in a vise, a portable belt sander becomes an excellent bench-type finisher for small work. (Right) fitted with this metal-cutting abrasive belt, a sander does a first-class job of sharpening and honing hand tools.

a No. 220 paper has finer grains that will pass through a mesh with 220 openings to the inch. In other words, the larger the number, the finer the grit. This method of grading is fairly standard now and has almost completely replaced the old-fashioned system which uses the designations $\frac{1}{0}$, $\frac{2}{0}$, etc.

In an effort to make things still simpler for the occasional purchaser, most manufacturers also mark the back of their papers with descriptive grades or names which vary from "very fine" to "very coarse," as indicated in Table 12-1. However, remember that these terms are not yet standardized among all manufacturers. "Fine," for example, may vary from No. 180 to No. 120, and other descriptive grades can vary by the same amount. For

casual sanding this will probably make little or no difference, but for the careful worker who insists on consistent results, purchases should be made on the basis of grade or grit numbers, not on descriptive names.

While many abrasive papers are made in both "closed-coat" and "open-coat" form, chances are that you will not have much choice at your local store, since it will probably stock only the most popular grades. As a rule, open-coat aluminum-oxide papers are more popular and more useful, because the grains are more widely separated and thus the paper has less tendency to clog. Closed-coat papers will cut a little faster, but they also clog more rapidly since sanding dust can accumulate in the very small spaces between the grains.

Most abrasive-paper manufacturers also make a variety of backings, but here again you will find that you have to take what is available locally. However, this should pose no problem since manufacturers usually match the backing to the grit number, so that the finer grades will have a thinner and more flexible backing, while the coarser grades will be stiffer and heavier. The very fine grades of silicon-carbide paper that you will want for the polishing and smoothing of final finishes have a waterproof backing so that you can use them wet for finest results.

To clear up any confusion in the classification of abrasives for power sanders, Table 12-1 gives equivalent numbers and grit sizes, abrasive classifications, and the abrasives recommended for various materials.

SAFETY AND SANDERS

Sanders are safe tools to use, but the following safety tips should be kept in mind:

1. Check to see that the electrical connection is grounded, unless it is of the shockproof and double-insulated type. Sanders that are not double-insulated have three-prong plugs, while the shockproof machines have two-prong plugs.
2. Arrange the electric cord so that it cannot be caught by the abrasive belt. A good arrangement for safety is to hang the cord over your

shoulder. Keep the cord free, and prevent it from being drawn between the abrasive belt and the housing.
3. Keep both hands on the tool, where they belong for good control. Remember that the moving abrasive paper can abrade fingernails to the quick.
4. Always wear goggles if work is being sanded at eye level or overhead.
5. Hold onto the handle of the sander when you plug it into the electric outlet. This prevents possible damage to the machine. Someone might have turned the switch on without your knowledge. The machine could jerk off the bench.
6. Never lay the tool on its side with the motor running; remember that the switch lock will keep it on until you squeeze the switch trigger.
7. Disconnect the plug from the power outlet when changing abrasive belts or sheets.

Belt Sanders

Belt sanders are the fastest and most powerful of all portable sanding tools. In these power sanders, a continuous belt of abrasive runs over a cylinder at each end of the tool. The belt runs across a flat shoe on the bottom of the machine. The abrasive action of the belt sander is all in one direction, from the front to the back of

Table 12-1 Abrasive Papers

Material	Abrasive to use	Grit for finish desired		
		Rough	Medium	Fine
Hardwood	Aluminum oxide	2½–1½	½–1/0	2/0–3/0
Aluminum	Aluminum oxide	40	60–80	100
Copper	Aluminum oxide	40–50	80–100	100–200
Steel	Aluminum oxide	24–30	60–80	100
Plastic	Aluminum oxide	50–80	120–180	240
Hardwood	Garnet	2½–1½	½–1/0	2/0–3/0
Softwood	Garnet	1½–1	1/0	2/0
Composition board	Garnet	1½–1	½	1/0
Plastic	Garnet	50–80	120–180	240
Glass	Silicon carbide	50–60	100–120	120–320
Cast iron	Silicon carbide	24–30	60–80	100
Painted surfaces	Flint	3–1½	½–1/0	

Abrasive	Grit numbers and abrasive grades and types				
	Very fine	Fine	Medium	Coarse	Very coarse
Flint	4/0	2/0–3/0	1/0–½	1–2	2½–3½
Garnet	6/0–10/0	3/0–5/0	1/0–2/0	½–1½	2–3
Silicon carbide, aluminum oxide	220–360	120–180	80–100	40–60	24–36

GRIT EQUIVALENTS

8/0 = 280	6/0 = 220	4/0 = 150	2/0 = 100	½ = 60	1½ = 40	2½ = 30
7/0 = 240	5/0 = 180	3/0 = 120	0 = 80	1 = 50	2 = 36	3 = 24

the machine. This gives much more satisfactory action on grained materials and allows a smoother and more accurate method of working than does the rotary disk. It is most useful on flat surfaces, although, by u. 3 a soft pad on the shoe, curved and irregular surfaces can be sanded. Belt sanders all use the same basic operating principle, but general features vary a great deal on the different sizes. As with saws, the dimensions of the cutting element determine the size of the tool. The width of the belt, from 2 to 4 inches, is the determining factor. In fact, the sizes of belt sanders are listed as the widths and circumferences of the abrasive belts that fit them. Common belt sizes are 2 X 15, 2 X 18, 3 X 18, 3 X 21, 3 X 24, 4 X 21, 4 X 24, and 4 X 27 inches. Generally, the larger the sander, the greater its work capacity.

The speeds of the belts on different models, given in surface feet per minute (sfm), range from 750 to 1600. The greater the speed, the greater the work capacity of the tool for its size, and the faster it removes material from the surface being sanded. The weights of sanders range from 5 to 25 pounds. Heavier sanders usually have greater work capacity, but they m y also be beyond your strength to control or to hold vertically against walls and doors.

With most belt sanders, the housing covers the motor, the upper surface of the abrasive belt, and one side of the sander. The other side is mostly open to make belt changing easier. Check to see if the housing allows you to sand close to a wall. Areas the belt cannot reach must be sanded by other means.

All belt sanders have two handles. The rear handles on most models are a contoured D shape for good grip. A few have pistol grips. An additional knob or bar handle in front is helpful for guiding the sander or applying even sanding pressure.

The belt sander, as stated previously, has two rollers, one idle and one powered. On some models the rear roller, powered by the motor, has a soft outer layer that grips the abrasive belt and helps prevent slippage. Other models provide a soft lining belt over which the abrasive belt is placed for good traction. In any case, the sander is powered by a universal motor which operates on ac or dc. The on-off switch is in the handle as a trigger or a slide switch. Most trigger-switch models have a button which locks the switch on for prolonged sanding. The loc! releases the instant the trigger switch is squeezed. A few models that offer two speeds have separate slide or toggle speed-selector switches.

To change a belt, you first retract the front, free-turning roller of the belt sander. Then, after the new belt is on and the front roller returned to operating position, you must align the belt so it will not run off to one side during sanding. Most belt sanders have a built-in tracking adjustment so that you can keep the belt centered between the two pulleys. If you find it moving to one side or the other, make the necessary adjustments promptly; otherwise you will wind up with either a belt flying off and ripping itself to pieces on one side or creeping over and cutting into the housing on the other side. It is a good idea to consult the owner's manual about belt changing for the model you are considering for purchase. It should be simple to understand and easy to do. Incidentally, when installing an abrasive belt, point the arrow on its back in the direction the belt will turn.

A belt sander produces large quantities of waste, or dust, that is removed from the work surface. Any one of three systems of dust collection is recommended: a built-in dust bag; a bag bought separately that can be attached as required; an accessory flexible hose that connects to a vacuum cleaner. In the first two systems, dust collection is powered by a motor in the sander. In the third, the vacuum-cleaner motor sucks dust away from the sander.

OPERATING A BELT SANDER

Because the bottom of the belt always moves in the same direction, the tool tends to roll over the work. The user must counteract this with a firm grip on the handle and knob. Always start and stop the sander off the work, and apply it to the material only after the belt is running at top speed. Some people prefer to lower the rear of the belt against the work surface first, and then tilt it down flat; others simply drop the full length of the belt onto the surface. The important thing is to start moving at once. Never leave the belt in one place for long; it will dig itself in and spoil the surface.

The sanding stroke is a simple straight, short, back-and-forth motion, with each stroke overlapping the one before. After the first stroke, the motions come naturally. It is important to work systematically to avoid resanding the same area. Remember just to guide the tool over the work without using any additional pressure. The weight of the machine will do the job. In fact, additional pressure will just slow the motor and the cutting speed. Again, always keep the sander in motion; allowing it to rest in one place will make gouges.

Where both face and end grain are exposed, start by sanding the end grain. For heavy sanding, where much material must be removed, start by sanding across the grain. Gradually angle the belt back parallel to the grain, and keep it so for medium and fine sanding. Rapid sanding can also be done with the belt sander held at an angle to the grain but moved straight along it. Cupped boards can be sanded flat on the concave side (at the cost of making them thinner at the edges) by holding the sander at such an angle that it rides both high edges.

Be cautious about tilting the sander along an edge; it works so rapidly that the edge may be chamfered or rounded more than you intend. Sand veneered work with caution, using only fine abrasive belts. A coarse belt on a powerful machine can dig right through the surface veneer and ruin the work.

By mounting the belt sander upside down in a ready-made or home-made stand, you can use it as a bench sander for shaping and smoothing small work. With

FIG. 12-9. With most dual sanders, a switch shifts the tool's action from straight-line to orbital sanding. On a few models, the shift is made with a wrench.

suitable belts, it can be used for sharpening tools, shaping plastic, and smoothing metal.

Pad Sanders

Pad or finishing sanders are probably the most practical and most popular of all portable sanding machines, since they are the ones that are most useful. They take flat sheets of sandpaper which are clamped to a pad on the bottom of the machine. This pad usually has either a felt or a rubber facing to provide a cushioned backing for the sandpaper; the machine is designed so that the pad is driven with either a straight-line (back and forth) or orbital (oval) action. Straight-line action with the grain gives the smoothest final finish but it is generally slower working. Orbital action cuts faster, but since the oval motion means that some part of the stroke is crossing the grain, the finish is not quite as smooth—although on most machines the short stroke gives a fine enough finish to satisfy all but the most finicky.

Nowadays there are comparatively few machines that provide only a straight-line action; most are orbital. However, a number of the newer models also give a choice of both actions in the same machine—you can change from straight-line to orbital motion by simply flicking a lever or turning a key. These enable you to start out with an orbital action for fast preliminary sanding and smoothing, and then switch to straight-line action for the final sanding.

Most finishing sanders are motor driven, but there are a number of smaller, less expensive units that are driven by a magnetic vibrator mechanism, rather than by a motor. That is, brush type, or universal motors, are used in almost all sanders designed for home-shop use. Lightweight, inexpensive sanders may have vibration, electromagnetic, or magnetic-impulse drive. They are not powerful, but they do not have to be.

The power of a motor is often indicated by its ampere rating. A 3.5-ampere motor is generally more powerful than a 1.8-ampere motor. But the kind of bearings a sander has, their number, and the overall tool design may be equally significant. It is not very scientific, but you can make a quick test of a sander's power by turning it on and holding it with increasing pressure against a surface. Press down hard with both hands. Can you make the motor stall? Chances are that most will seem to have about equal power, even though they may carry different ampere ratings. You may try a half dozen models before you find one that will stand out from all the rest, and it will not necessarily have the highest ampere rating. Most likely, however, it will be more costly.

Although vibrator-type pad sanders cost less, they have much shorter strokes and are obviously slower working. Nevertheless, the better-quality vibrator units are handy for small smoothing and finishing jobs. But do not count on them to remove paint or do rough work.

The work capacity of a finishing sander depends on the size of its sanding pad and the speed and length of the sanding strokes. The pad sizes of most models for home use range from $3\frac{1}{2}$ X 7 to $4\frac{1}{2}$ X 9 inches. Many catalogs and brochures list only the size of the abrasive sheet. To determine the pad size, subtract 2 inches from the sheet length and about $\frac{1}{8}$ inch from the width. Generally, a bigger pad means greater work capacity. But in tight situations and on irregular surfaces, a small pad is best. On broad, flat surfaces, the big pad is by far the best. So an in-between size is a compromise that satisfies most people most of the time. But it may not satisfy you, and you are the one who is going to be using it.

FIG. 12-10. The pad sander at the left is being used to edge sand, while the one at the right is rounding an edge.

The pad on which the paper goes may be either felt or neoprene (synthetic rubber) sponge. The felt may have a little more firmness and bite, which is especially good for flat surfaces. The neoprene may adapt to uneven contours slightly better, and can be used for either wet or dry sanding. For some sanders, you can get either kind of pad, or both kinds and use them interchangeably. Some pads extend beyond the sander sides; it is claimed that this makes them better for handling corners. The way the paper attaches to the pad may be of some significance to you, too. They all add up to the same thing, but some slight differences may appeal to different people.

FIG. 12-11. A lamb's-wool pad converts a sander to a pad polisher.

The speeds and lengths of sanding strokes are coordinated in three different ways in pad sanders. On some models the speed is between 3000 and 4500 orbits per minute (OPM); on others the speed is doubled to around 10,000 OPM but the stroke length is halved. The sanding capacities of the two arrangements are similar, but shorter strokes give a glossier surface. Reciprocal sanders with vibratory motors have a speed of 7200 strokes per minute (SPM), the equivalent of 7200 OPM, and a short stroke. They can produce a fine surface, but smooth more slowly than orbital models. If the housing extends beyond the edges of the sanding pad, hand sanding will be necessary close to perpendicular surfaces and in corners.

Most models have separate handles, but some simply have a housing palm grip. Try such a tool under power to find if it becomes uncomfortably hot to hold during extended use. Heavier units may have auxiliary handles, such as a front knob, to provide better control and more uniform pressure with two-handed use. The off-on control on a finishing sander is either a slide or a trigger switch. A trigger switch usually has a locking button nearby. A slide switch locks on automatically.

Some pad sanders feel twice as heavy as others, either because of a difference in balance or because of an actual difference in weight. Weight is important. Pressure should not be applied on a sander. This will slow its speed and cause its paper to clog. The weight of the sander alone, plus the natural weight of your hand, is all the pressure required in normal operation. A heavier sander usually has a more powerful motor and is more of a workhorse. But a lighter tool has an advantage on vertical surfaces and overhead. On such surfaces, you have to supply your own pressure, and you become aware of the weight of the tool. A lightweight sander will be less tiring. So compromise between the two, or select on the basis of the kind of work you do most.

To take a worn abrasive sheet off the pad of a finishing sander and replace it with a fresh one, you must operate a special mechanism. On some models a lever opens and closes clamps at the front and back of the sanding pad. On others you use a special key or a screwdriver to loosen and tighten pad clamps. Still others have spring-loaded clamps that must be held open while an abrasive sheet is inserted. Before you purchase a model, test the ease with which the abrasive is changed.

Finishing or pad sanders produce less waste than belt models, but you may still want a dust-collection system to keep your work and work area clean. You can buy either a model with a built-in dust bag or one that will accept a kit. A kit contains a plastic skirt to fit over the sanding pad, a flexible hose, and an adapter to connect the hose to your vacuum cleaner. Some manufacturers make dust-collection kits to fit all their models; others make kits only for some styles.

OPERATING A PAD SANDER

Familiarize yourself with the switch action for quick and easy control. For most sanding, you will want to lock an instant-release switch in the on position. To turn the locked switch off, simply squeeze and release the trigger.

Turn on the motor while you hold the sander off the work surface. Then simply lower it and start sanding. As already mentioned, it is rarely necessary to put any extra pressure on the tool; its own weight is usually enough. You can sand in any direction. Where end grain is exposed, you will find it takes longer to smooth than neighboring face grain. Remember to start with the coarsest abrasive that will not roughen the existing surface, but do not forget to switch to finer paper as the coarser scratches disappear. There is a point at which a coarse paper does no more to improve the surface. That is, begin with a grit coarse enough to accomplish the dirty work, then move on to a finer grit and a still finer grit until you are satisfied with the smoothness of the results. For a fine finish with a minimum amount of sanding, start with the finest grit that will remove the surface defects. On many projects you may want to round corners and edges slightly. They will look better, wear better, and hold the finish better.

When proceeding from coarse to fine paper, do not skip more than two grits at a time. Better, skip no more than one grit. A good and perfectly legitimate progression might be from No. 60 to 80 to 120. For between-coat sanding of enamel and varnish, you would not want anything coarser than No. 220.

Keep the sander moving. If you stop in one place for long, you will make a rut. With a straight-line sander, if you go across the grain you will tear the wood fibers. With an orbital sander, grain direction is not quite so critical.

With coarse paper especially, beware of oversanding edges and veneered stock. Clean edges can be blunted and gouged by careless sanding. (Sharp edges are vulnerable even after finish is applied; they will stand up better if rounded ever so slightly by judicious use of the sander with fine abrasive in it.) Veneer is only $\frac{1}{28}$-inch deep and can be damaged by careless sanding.

An old and favored trick for producing a super-smooth surface is to "raise the grain." Wet the already sanded surface with a damp cloth or sponge, and let it dry thoroughly. The water will swell some wood fibers more than others, so that the surface looks rougher than before. But when you finish-sand with fine paper, working down the raised particles, the result is a beautifully smooth surface. Do not, however, use this method on veneered surfaces; the moisture may loosen the veneer.

Disk Sanders

Disk sanders are for rough work only and can be used for such jobs as removing paint around the outside of the house, trimming down rough edges, and cleaning off rusted metal. They should never be used on interior paneling, furniture, or cabinets since they tend to leave swirl marks and scratches and, unless carefully handled, can gouge the surface severely. However, when used for jobs such as removing blistered or cracked paint, they work fast and are easy to handle. In addition, equipped with a lamb's-wool bonnet instead of a sanding disk, they do a fast job of polishing and waxing.

In its most common form, the disk sander consists of an arbor that is chucked into an electric drill with a semiflexible hard-rubber disk mounted at the end. Sanding disks are secured to the face side by a recessed nut and washer in the center. The only trouble with this setup is that many small $\frac{1}{4}$-inch drills are really not

FIG. 12-12. Parts of a typical disk sander.

FIG. 12-13. Typical disk grinder.

powerful enough and rugged enough for this kind of work, and many are not designed to take the sideways thrust in the bearings. However, there are some multipurpose portable tools which are specifically designed to take this kind of abuse. These consist of a basic heavy-duty drill with bearings which are designed to take sidewise pressure; the disk is usually attached by removing the chuck and threading the disk directly onto the spindle, rather than by inserting an arbor into the chuck.

If you have much use for a disk sander, your best bet is to buy one of these heavy-duty models, or a machine that is especially designed for the purpose—similar to the commercial sander-polishers used in auto-body repair shops. These often have a choice of speeds and are easier to handle because the disk is mounted at right angles to the motor body, with a second handle near the working end. For best results, always hold the tool so that the disk contacts the surface at a slight angle, with the outer half of the abrasive sheet doing most of the work. Keep the disk moving continuously, as long as the motor is on, by sweeping it back and forth with a gliding motion. Exert only a moderate amount of pressure so that the edge of the disk does not gouge the surface.

A disk grinder (Figure 12-13) looks a great deal like a disk sander, but it has a much more powerful motor. The average 7-inch grinder can handle a 7-inch-diameter disk grinding wheel, a 5-inch-diameter grinding cup, and a 5-inch-diameter wire cup brush. The 9-inch grinder handles larger units. These tools operate at from 5000 to 6000 rpm. A few models can even be used with an appropriately sized sanding disk.

Floor Sanders

Floor sanders cannot be considered standard shop equipment, except for floor layers and finishers and major builders. However, homeowners and small contractors frequently rent them when a floor must be finished or refinished. As shown in Figure 12-15, there are two basic types of floor sanders: the drum floor sander and the disk edge sander. Each is usually equipped with a vacuum-cleaner arrangement that removes the dust produced by

FIG. 12-14. Right and wrong ways to use a disk sander.

the sanding operation.

When floor sanders are used, three sanding cuts, or "traverses," are recommended for the average floor, although acceptable results sometimes are achieved with only two. The first cut may be made crosswise to the grain or at a 45° angle. Succeeding cuts should be in the direction of the grain. It generally is best to use No. 2 or 3 sandpaper for the first traverse, No. 1 or 0 for the second, and No. 00 or 000 for the third. It is impossible to sand parquet floors with the grain of the wood; hence, in this case a finer grit must be used and special care must be taken.

Start sanding by moving the drum sander slowly forward and gently lowering the sanding drum into contact with the floor. Keep the machine moving by walking slowly forward. Take short steps, and keep your feet close to the machine. At the end of the forward cut, the sanding drum must be raised clear of the floor before the machine comes to a standstill. When the backward cut is started, the machine must again be in motion as the drum is lowered to contact the floor. Sanding must be done with the grain, and enough taken off to get down to the clear wood.

After each of the three sandings with the drum floor sander, the disk edge sander is used along baseboards, stair treads, etc. (change the sandpaper each time to correspond with what was used in the drum sander). To remove the old finish or smooth the surface in corners, behind radiator pipes, or in other areas inaccessible to the disk edge sander, use a hand scraper and sandpaper.

CARE OF SANDERS

The life of the motor in your sander, as in all your power tools, depends in part on proper ventilation. Check the ventilating holes in the motor housing occasionally to be sure that they are not clogged with sawdust. It is also a good idea to follow the other maintenance procedures recommended by the manufacturer. Cleaning and lubricating your sander according to instructions supplied with it will permit many years of trouble-free operation.

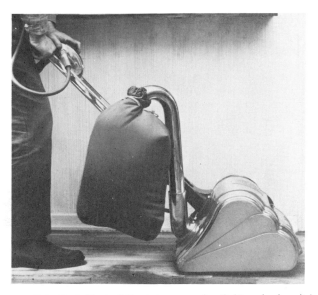

FIG. 12-15. Typical floor drum sander (left) and edge disk sander (right).

MISCELLANEOUS PORTABLE POWER TOOLS

The "miscellaneous" portable power tools discussed in this chapter include planes, polishers, impact wrenches, screwdrivers, hammer-drills, hand grinders, engravers, flex shafts, glue guns, soldering irons and guns, and paint sprayers. In addition, we include the versatile propane torch and small welding and brazing units. Some power tools such as electric staplers, powered drain cleaners, and cartridge-fired stud drivers have already been mentioned in previous chapters in Section 1.

Electric Planes

Professional carpenters have been using these for a number of years to speed the work of trimming and hanging doors or installing cabinets, but it is only in the past 5 or 10 years that home-size models have been introduced by four or five prominent manufacturers.

The cutting action of the electric plane is derived from a high-speed rotating cutter head similar to that on a stationary jointer-planer or wood shaper. Usually equipped with two blades, the cutter head is mounted in the middle of a sole plate or base so that the cutting edges project slightly below the surface. Although they are relatively compact and light in weight, electric planers must have powerful motors, since a very high speed is essential for a smooth and rapid cut. As with shapers, routers, and other tools which cut with rotating knives, higher speeds give a smoother cut.

The principal manufacturers of electric hand planes currently produce them in three basic types (Figure 13-1). The most popular—especially with professionals—is actually a planing attachment which uses a router motor as the source of power. (This attachment is fully described in Chapter 11.) The second, more standard type is a plane about 16 inches long, with its own motor. Motor sizes range from $\frac{1}{2}$ hp (light duty) to over 1 hp (professional duty), and cutter speeds vary from 15,000 to 22,000 rpm. They usually can plane boards from $2\frac{1}{16}$ to 3 inches wide, and their depth of cut is adjustable to a maximum of $\frac{3}{32}$ to $\frac{3}{16}$ inch in one pass, depending on the duty rating.

The third type of electric plane is a block plane. The width of cut of the power block plane is between $1\frac{3}{4}$ and 2 inches, but its maximum depth of cut is only from $\frac{1}{32}$ to $\frac{3}{32}$ inch in one pass, depending on the duty rating. However, because it is much smaller and lighter and is designed to be operated with only one hand, most home shop workers find it easier and more convenient to use for many jobs, including trimming doors, fitting storm sash, and shaving off end grain on lumber. Its high speed (about 22,000 rpm) gives an extremely smooth cut, even on end grain and plastics, and it is designed so that the cutter fits flush on one side to permit cutting into corners. You can use this handy little electric tool for cutting rabbets and tenons, as well as for planing flat surfaces and edges.

Made of high-speed steel, the power-plane cutter requires occasional sharpening. Also available, but more expensive, are carbide-tipped cutters, which require sharpening very infrequently. Whichever type of cutter you choose, be sure it is sharp at all times, as a dull cutter overloads the motor, causing overheating and producing work of low quality. The straight-flute plane cutter can be sharpened by hand on an oilstone, but the spiral-flute plane cutter requires a special attachment for sharpening. The spiral-flute cutter is placed in a movable holder on the grinding attachment, and a cup grinding wheel is placed in the chuck of the router motor unit, also mounted on the attachment. Moving the cutter slowly back and forth a few times against the grinding wheel sharpens it. Straight-flute cutters can also be sharpened on the plane-cutter grinding attachment.

Operating the power plane is simply a matter of setting the depth of cut and passing the plane over the work. The door, screen, or piece of wood being planed should be held in a vise, clamped to the edge of a bench, or otherwise firmly held. As previously mentioned, the depth of cut that can be made in one pass is about 3/32 inch on some models, and up to 3/16 inch on the larger models. First, make careful measurements of the piece, where it is to fit, and determine how much material has to be removed. Check the smoothness and straightness of all the edges. If a smoothing cut is desired, make that first;

then check the dimensions again. Make as many passes as necessary with the plane to reach the desired dimension, checking frequently so as not to remove too much material. The greater the depth of the cut, the slower you must feed the tool into the work. The feed pressure should be enough to keep the tool cutting but not so much as to slow it down excessively. Keep chips off the work, since they can mar the surface as the tool passes over them.

The L-shaped fence or edge guide of most planes mounts on either side of the plane and can be adjusted from 0 to 90°. For straight cuts, the edge guide should be pressed snugly against the work during planing, to ensure that the edge will be cut square. For bevel cuts, loosen the setscrew on the base, set the base at the desired bevel, and tighten the setscrew.

Except for the fact that electric power does the work, the actual wood-planing technique is the same as for the hand-powered planes described in Chapter 2.

Electric Polishers

While polishing and buffing can be accomplished with an elecric drill and a polisher attachment, or with a disk sander and a lamb's-wool bonnet, single-duty polishers are available. Most of these are of the commercial-duty variety and are used for professional work.

The speed of the average polisher ranges from a no-load rating of 1200 rpm to 2500 rpm, and the size of the motor from 3/4 to 1 3/4 hp. Most have two polishing speeds. Polishing is done by a lamb's-wool bonnet over a rubber backing pad. When installing the bonnet, be sure to pull the drawstrings tight, tie them together, and push the loose ends under the bonnet edges so that they will not fly around.

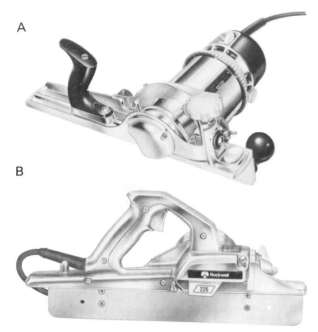

A

B

C

FIG. 13-1. There are three basic styles of electric hand planes: (a) planing attachment for the router; (b) standard plane; (c) block plane.

FIG. 13-2. (Left) Typical electric polisher at work; (right) scrubber-sander-polisher.

Cleanliness is vital to successful polishing. Grease left on the surface will prevent wax from adhering; grit will scratch the finish. Both will also contaminate the bonnet or pad, so take the trouble to clean the work well before waxing or polishing.

Tilt the polisher to make the bonnet work on less than half its area, as described for sanding. With the proper materials (rouge, buffing compound, lacquer rubbing compound, and others) you can polish brass and chrome, or rub paint and varnish to a lovely luster. To rub down lacquer and remove a faulty "orange-peel" surface, use a pile fabric pad, mounted on the rubber backing pad in the same way as a sanding disk. In all cases, hold the polisher firmly but operate it with a free, easy motion. Never force the tool by applying unnecessary pressure. As a rule, on a flat surface, the weight of the polisher alone exerts sufficient pressure for a good polishing job. Also be sure to keep the polisher moving. Employ long, sweeping motions in a back-and-forth action that advances along the surface being polished. Do not work in a spiral or circular pattern, because this will only create swirls in the finish.

Make certain to read carefully the directions that appear on the container of polish or wax that you purchase. Some materials must be buffed while dry; others must be worked when damp. Use only polishes or compounds that are designed for electric polishers. Some that are intended for hand application will mat a powered polishing pad and can smear or burn the finish.

Another interesting tool that looks very much like a polisher is a so-called "scrubber/sander/polisher." Thanks to a unique oscillating action, this tool can be used to scrub, sand, or polish just by changing the disc pad. That is, pads are available for sanding, polishing, and scrubbing. The scrubber–wax-remover head is made of ethafoam, a sturdy yet flexible woven porous material.

Power Screwdrivers

You can make short work of driving screws, as mentioned in Chapter 9, by using a screwdriver bit in your electric drill. The best drill for the purpose is a $\frac{3}{8}$-inch variable-speed job. The $\frac{3}{8}$-inch drill has double-reduction gears which give you the torque or turning power needed for driving screws. The variable-speed feature gives you the slow speed necessary for this kind of work.

There are several types of power screwdrivers or fastener drivers on the market (both cord and cordless) that drive screws quickly. Further, there are both light-duty and industrial-duty models. (Figure 13-3.) Operating at 150 to 350 rpm, light-duty screwdrivers will drive screws into any type of wood. Many have a special finder sleeve. This is usually a metal spring-loaded sleeve that helps you find the slot as you press the drill down on the screwhead. Its greatest value is in helping to keep the screw bit in the slot (for Phillips screws as well as bits up to point size 3). Magnetic bit holders for hex nuts are also available. Electric screwdrivers, as a rule, either turn on immediately or have bits that idle until forward pressure on the tool engages the screw or nut and drives it home.

The cord-type light-duty power screwdriver can drive screws up to No. 14 and set hex nuts up to $\frac{9}{16}$ inch. The motor, which uses about 0.25 ampere, has about a 100-to-1 gear reduction for high torque. The cordless-type light-duty screwdriver will drive screws from No. 8 to No. 14, depending on the model. Some even feature two speeds; the slower speed (usually about 150 rpm) will drive the larger screws. Both cord and cordless light-duty screwdrivers come with slotted and Phillips-head blades, plus a drill bit for making pilot holes.

Industrial-type screwdrivers or fastener drivers usually have an easy reversing action and have 0 to 1000 rpm no-load ratings. (A few fastener drivers operate at 2500 rpm, but these are used for drill-point fasteners.) They have easy-change bit holders to save time on the job, and manual or automatic torque-control clutches to assure proper seating of all types of fasteners—slotted screws, Philips screws, hex-head screws, cap screws, nuts, etc.

Electric Hammer-Drills and Rotary Hammers

The electric hammer-drill (Figure 13-6) is really a multipurpose electric drill. That is, by shifting its collar, the tool can easily be converted from a rotary drill (for drilling

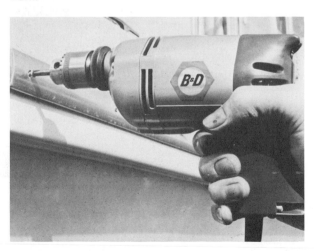
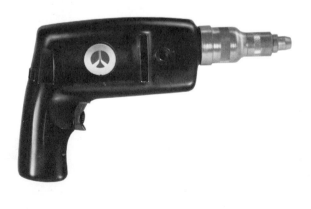

FIG. 13-3. Typical light-duty (left) and industrial-duty (right) screwdriver models.

FIG. 13-4. Fastener driver that can be converted to a $\frac{3}{8}$-inch drill with a twist of the selector collar.

A

B

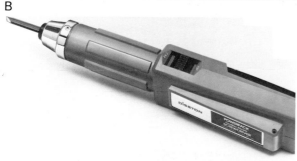

FIG. 13-5. Two cordless screwdrivers: *(a)* with a battery charger; *(b)* with a powerpack.

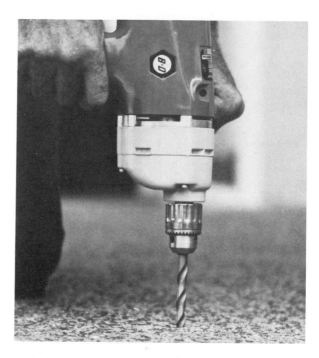

FIG. 13-6. Typical hammer drill at work.

holes in metal and wood) to a percussion drill (for making holes in concrete, brick, and tile). In the hammering mode, a typical hammer-drill can deliver about 34,000 blows per minute. With the proper attachments this tool can also drive and remove screws, nuts, and bolts, and can mortise, chisel, gouge, shape, and remove scale, rust, plaster, tile, and putty.

Most hammer-drills have $\frac{1}{3}$- to $\frac{1}{2}$-hp motors with ratings of about 3.5 amperes. Speeds may be controlled from 0 to about 850 rpm. A few hammer-drills go up to 1600 rpm. The operation of this tool is basically the same as that of the electric drill (see Chapter 9.)

Impact Wrenches

The electric impact wrench is a portable hand-type reversible wrench. The one shown in Figure 13-7 has a $\frac{1}{2}$-inch square impact driving anvil over which $\frac{1}{2}$-inch square drive sockets can be fitted. It delivers up to 280 foot pounds of torque. Wrenches also can be obtained that have impact driving anvils ranging from $\frac{3}{8}$ to 1 inch square. Driving anvils are not interchangeable, however, from one wrench to another.

The electric wrench, with its accompanying equipment, is primarily intended for applying and removing nuts, bolts, and screws. It may also be used to drill and tap metal, wood, plastics, etc., and to drive and remove socket-head, Phillips-head, or slotted-head wood, machine, or self-tapping screws.

Before you use an electric impact wrench, depress the on-off trigger switch, and allow the electric wrench to operate a few seconds, noting carefully the direction of rotation. Release the trigger switch to stop the wrench. Turn the reversing ring located at the rear of the tool; it should move easily in one direction (which is determined by the present direction of rotation). Depress the on-off trigger again to start the electric wrench. The direction of rotation should now be reversed. Continue to operate it for a few seconds in each direction, to be sure that the wrench and its reversible feature are functioning correctly. When you are sure the wrench operates properly, place the suitable equipment on the impact driving anvil and go ahead with the job at hand.

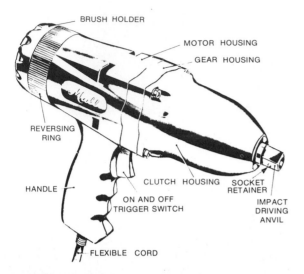

FIG. 13-7. Major parts of an electric impact wrench.

Hand Grinders, Engravers, and Flex Shafts

The hand grinder and/or the flex shaft is possibly the most versatile of all portable tools. It is literally the tool of 1001 uses. It can be used on almost any type of material—metal, wood, glass, plastic, ceramic, leather, cardboard, linoleum, and eggshell. In fact, the same saws used for slotting or cutting wood, plastics, and soft metals can be employed for the cutting and decorative fashioning of eggs.

HAND GRINDERS

The term "grinder" does not, by any means, fully describe this tool; it is really a "minishop" in its own right. The secret of the tool is its high speed. Actually, two types of motors are used with hand grinders: a rotary motor and a vibrator motor. Most of today's rotary grinders operate between 12,000 and 30,000 rpm. A few have built-in variable-speed controls that permit operation from 5000

FIG. 13-8. Two basic types of hand grinders: (left) rotary motor; (right) vibrator motor.

to 25,000 rpm. The motors in rotary grinders range from $\frac{3}{8}$ to 1 hp. The larger motors are usually found in industrial die grinders. The vibrator-type motors used in many grinders perform at from 3600 to 7200 strokes per minute.

Small grinders will take accessory tools with shanks up to $\frac{1}{8}$ inch, while the chucks or collets of the heavier-duty models will accept shanks up to $\frac{1}{4}$ inch. As for accessories, you will find high-speed steel, tungsten-carbide, and small engraving cutters; emery, silicon, and plain shaped wheel points; polishing accessories, sanding disks, wire and bristle brushes, cutting wheels, steel saws, and router bits. There is an attachment available for the grinder which permits this tool to perform many of the operations of a portable router. One manufacturer now makes over 150 different accessories for its grinders.

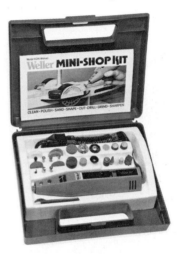

FIG. 13-9. Typical grinder kit.

While most of the grinder's operations are performed with the tool held in the hand, a variety of stands, including a drill-press type, are available to hold it stationary in the vertical, horizontal, or tipped (angled) position. There is even a stand that holds the grinder in an inverted position for use as a miniature shaper. To obtain the proper speeds for best results with rotary grinders, there are separate solid-state speed-control attachments that permit you to dial any speed from 0 to full speed with no voltage fluctuations. In fact, these speed-control units, which are usually available in 5- or 10-ampere models, can be used with any ac tool motor within that current-draw range, except capacitor-start and split-phase motors. Some solid-state speed controls are available that are foot-operated.

Most manufacturers do a fair job with the instruction manuals that come with their grinder kits. For efficient operation, it is important that accessories are balanced. To true up or balance an accessory, slightly loosen the collet or chuck, and give the accessory or collet a quarter turn. Retighten the collet and run the grinder. You should be

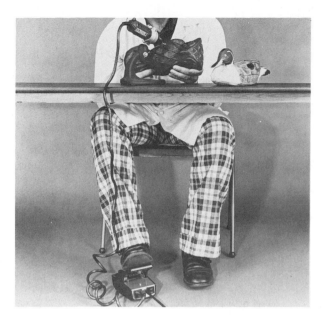

FIG. 13-10. Grinder holder and foot-pedal control in operation.

able to tell, by the sound and feel, whether the tool is running in balance. Continue adjusting in this fashion until perfect balance is achieved.

Small work should either be held in a vise or clamped to a work surface. When larger work is hand-held, grip the work in one hand and the tool in the other. It is always wise to avoid pointing the cutter toward the gripping hand. Then, if you should slip, you will not cut any more than the work.

You can engrave with a grinder as easily as writing with a pencil. For most metals, use either the carbide-tipped point or a solid carbide point. Move your hand slowly, without heavy pressure. When engraving glass, be sure to hold the point perpendicular to the surface to avoid chipping. Also be sure that the glass item is adequately cushioned, either by holding it in your hand or by resting it on a soft base. A diamond point should be used for continuous engraving and for working on very hard metals.

When cutting grooves and countersinking in soft metals such as brass and aluminum, use oil to cool and lubricate. For internal carving of plastic, a slow cutting speed is a must, to prevent the workpiece from melting. Otherwise, the gummy result can quickly clog the tool and even cause a cutter bit to be cemented in the hole you are trying to cut. The solution often lies in making only light cuts along with frequent retractions to minimize heat buildup. In general, coarser fluted cutters are used with plastic rather than with metal and wood.

Delicate wood carving and sculpture are not only possible but easy with a grinder. For instructions on this and the other many uses of the grinder, check the

instruction manual. Some manufacturers are now producing saw and chain-saw sharpening kits that make this task a great deal easier.

The disk grinder (which is really a disk sander with a grinding disk replacing the sanding disk) is frequently called a "hand grinder." The grinding disk, varying in diameter from 5 to 7 inches, is usually resinoid-toned for fast grinding of weld beads, snagging of ferrous castings, and rough finishing of heavy steel fabrications.

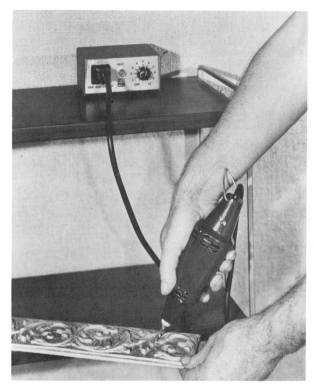

FIG. 13-11. Solid-state speed control being used in conjunction with a hand grinder.

ENGRAVERS

The electric engraver is the tool that leading law-enforcement officials recommend for guarding against burglaries. Under antiburglary programs, valuables are permanently marked with a social-security or driver's-license number so that they can be quickly traced and recovered in case they are stolen. The tough tungsten-carbide point writes on the hardest steel, glass, plastic, stone, ceramics, and wood. The high-speed reciprocating or vibrating motor delivers about 7200 strokes per minute. Incidentally, the engraver can be used to personalize jewelry, decorate glassware, engrave trophies, or decorate ceramics. The engraver, which performs only one of the grinder's many functions, is an inexpensive but valuable tool.

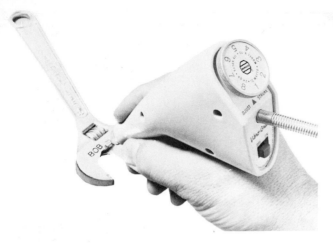

FIG. 13-12. Marking a wrench with an engraver.

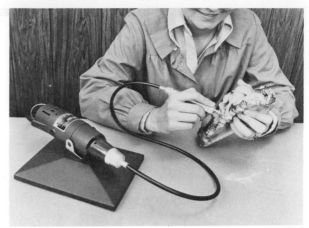

FIG. 13-13. Flexible shaft in use.

FLEXIBLE (OR FLEX) SHAFTS

The flexible or flex shaft is often called "the cutting tool with the power up front where you want it." It comes in various lengths and different diameters. You can buy flex shafts to be powered by such existing shop tools as electric drills, drill presses, and hand grinders, or to be used with special flexible-shaft tools like the one shown in Figure 13-13. This tool does most of the jobs that a hand grinder does; it grinds, polishes, slots, deburrs, sands, carves, sharpens, texturizes, routs, cuts, and engraves. Frequently, it is called a hand grinder on a long (up to 36 inches) flexible shaft. This shaft makes it easy to get into hard-to-reach spots, and the tool is excellent for delicate work. The power of a flex shaft is not, however, as great as that of a grinder. That is, the motor is smaller, about $\frac{1}{15}$ hp, and it operates at a speed of 25,000 rpm. This type of flex shaft is often operated in conjunction with a separate speed-control unit.

The flexible-shaft sizes that can be used in conjunction with shop tools are usually designated as either light duty or heavy duty. The $\frac{1}{4}$- and $\frac{5}{16}$-inch shafts are considered light-duty shafts and are suitable for such tasks as grinding, polishing, buffing, and light sanding. The $\frac{5}{16}$- to $\frac{5}{8}$-inch shafts fall into the heavy-duty category and are used for heavier sanding and grinding operations. Incidentally, all these shaft measurements include both the core, which turns, and the casing, which does not. The latter can be either a hoselike affair or a spirally wound steel tube. The core is generally made up of spirally wound, directionally alternating layers of steel wire. The "pitch" of the layers of wire indicates the direction of rotation, and this is marked on the casing or covered in the manufacturer's instructional literature. But before using any flexible shaft be sure that it can handle the horsepower of the power source. That is, a full load from a larger-capacity motor applied to a light-duty shaft, even though it fits on the motor spindle, can damage the unit.

Electric Glue Gun

The electric glue gun (Figure 13-14) can be used for such glue jobs as furniture making and repair, applying paneling and trim, installing floor and ceiling tile and carpeting, and various other tasks where a strong joint is needed. Since the strong bonding adhesive sticks to both porous and nonporous surfaces, it can be used as a waterproof caulking or sealer around tubs, tile, doors, windows, sinks, and gutters and on masonry walls. Many models of the gun are available with upwards of four interchangeable nozzles; they allow you to use the correct nozzle to apply the hot melted adhesive in different configurations to meet the needs of your specific job.

While various glue guns have different features—preset thermostat, aluminum melting chamber, self-standing design, two-cartridge storage, etc.—the following basic instructions hold for all models.

1. Insert the glue stick or sealer cartridge in the gun, in the proper chamber as detailed by the manufacturer's instructions. Some guns require the insertion of two cartridges when first used, because they feature a reserve glue compartment.
2. Plug the gun into a 120-volt electric circuit (unless it is designated as a 240-volt unit), and allow 3 minutes for warm-up. Take care not to touch the nozzle or heating chamber. The temperature in this area may reach as high as 400°F.
3. When the 3-minute warm-up period has passed, squeeze the trigger of the tool to dispense the glue or caulking sealer. From the time you start applying the adhesive to the surface to be bonded together, you have about 10 seconds of time. Work quickly. Do not try to cover a large

area. Place the two surfaces to be bonded together within 10 seconds. As with any adhesive, the two bonding surfaces must be clean.

4. After 60 seconds the adhesive will attain 90 percent of its bonding ability, which is sufficient to hold the surfaces together. It is not necessary to use clamps or other holding devices.

5. When you are finished with the glue gun, pull the line plug and rest the tool on a nonflammable material or hang it on a hook to cool. Allow the glue to remain in the tool; it can be reheated repeatedly without affecting its bonding ability. Never change the nozzle when it is hot.

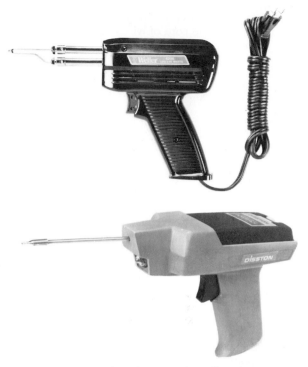

FIG. 13-15. Typical cord (top) and cordless (bottom) soldering guns.

FIG. 13-14. Typical glue gun at work.

Soldering Guns and Irons

Soldering is a metal-joining process in which a lower-melting-point metal (called solder) is heated to the point where it melts, is placed so that it wets the joint surfaces, and then is allowed to solidify in place. To enable the solder to wet the surfaces readily and be drawn into fine cracks, the surfaces and the solder must be clean and free of oxide film. When necessary, the cleaning is done with chemicals or abrasives. One cleaning substance frequently used is called "flux." Copper, tin, lead, and brass are examples of readily solderable metals. Galvanized iron, stainless steel, and aluminum are difficult to solder and require the use of special techniques which are discussed later in this section.

Soldering is a practical method of forming reliable electrical connections where bare wires are twisted together or are wound on terminals. Soldering is also used to make tight joints, such as lap seams in sheet metal, and to hold parts together physically. Soldered joints, however, do not support loads for long periods of time as well as welded joints do. Where load support is a governing factor, the usual practice calls for riveting, bolting, or some other means of fastening, followed by sealing of the joints with solder.

To solder the readily solderable metals, you need only the solder, a flux, and a heat source. The following paragraphs are primarily descriptions of the soldering equipment and procedures required for making reliable electrical connections. However, the techniques apply to most soldering work.

SOLDERS By definition, solders are joining materials or alloys that melt below 800°F. They are available in various forms: wire, bar, ingot, paste, and powder. The solders used for electrical connections are alloys of tin and lead whose melting points range between 360 and 465°F. (both extremes are approximate).

A tin-lead solder alloy is usually identified by two numbers that indicate the percentages of tin and lead in the alloy. The first number is the percentage of tin. Thus, a 60-40 alloy is made of 60 percent tin and 40 percent lead. Likewise, a 40-60 alloy is made of 40 percent tin and 60 percent lead. In general, the higher the percentage of tin in a solder alloy, the lower the melting point.

FLUXES Soldering fluxes are agents which clean solderable metals by removing the oxide film normally present on the metals and prevent further oxidation. Fluxes, classified as noncorrosive, moldly corrosive, or corrosive, range from mild substances such as rosin to chemically active salts such as zinc chloride. Rosin is an effective and nearly harmless flux used for electrical connections that must be reliable, tight, and corrosion-free. Rosin flux is available either in paste or powder form for direct application to joints before soldering, or incorporated as the core of wire solders. Unless washed off thoroughly after soldering, salt-type fluxes leave residues that tend to corrode metals. Because of their corrosive effects, so-called "acid-core" solders (which incorporate salt-type fluxes) must *not* be used in soldering electrical connections.

HEAT SOURCE The source of heat for melting solder is a soldering gun (electric) or a soldering iron (electric or nonelectric), sometimes called a "copper."

SOLDERING GUNS

The electric soldering gun uses any standard 120-volt outlet and is rated by the number of watts it consumes. The guns in general use are rated between 100 and 250 watts. All quality soldering guns operate in a temperature range of 500 to 700°F. The important difference in gun sizes is not the temperature, but the capacity of the gun to generate and maintain a satisfactory soldering temperature while giving up heat to the joint being soldered. The tip heats only when the trigger is depressed, and then very rapidly. Soldering guns afford easy access to cramped quarters, because of their small tips. Most soldering guns have a small light that is focused on the tip working area. Small cordless soldering irons are also available, as well as so-called "field" irons which can be operated from suitable batteries or low-voltage power sources supplying 12 to 14 volts.

The tip of a soldering gun should be removed occasionally to permit cleaning away the oxide scale which forms between the tip and the metal housing. Removal of this oxide increases the heating efficiency of the gun. If for any reason the tip does become damaged, replacement tips are available. Never use a soldering gun when working on solid-state equipment. Serious damage to diodes, transistors, and other solid-state components can result from the strong electromagnetic field surrounding the tip of the soldering gun.

SOLDERING IRONS

There are two general types of soldering irons in use. One is electrically heated, and the other is nonelectrically heated. The essential parts of both types are the tip and the handle. The tip is made of copper.

The nonelectric soldering iron is sized according to its weight. The commonly used sizes are the $\frac{1}{4}$-, $\frac{1}{2}$-, $\frac{3}{4}$-, 1-, $1\frac{1}{2}$-, 2-, and $2\frac{1}{2}$-pound irons. The 3-, 4-, and 5-pound sizes are not used in ordinary work. Nonelectric irons have permanent tips and must be heated over flame, or with a blowtorch or propane torch.

The electric soldering iron transmits heat to the copper tip after the heat is produced by electric current which flows through a self-contained coil of resistance wire, called the "heating element." Electric soldering irons are rated according to the number of watts (from 25 to over 400 watts) they consume when operated at the rated

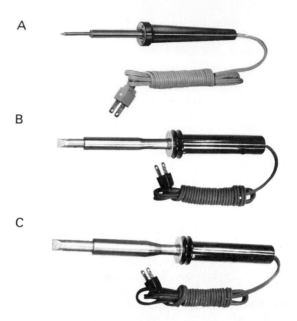

FIG. 13-16. Typical electric soldering irons: *(a)* 25 watt; *(b)* 80 watt; *(c)* 175 watt.

voltage. A 50-watt electric iron is good for most small work, while a 100-watt iron is recommended for practically all home soldering. A 200-watt electric iron is suggested for heavier soldering, and for rugged work a 350-watt electric iron should be used.

Two types of tips are used on electric irons: plug tips which slip into the heater head and which are held in place by a setscrew, and screw tips which are threaded and which screw into or on the heater head. Some tips are offset and have a 90° angle for soldering joints that are difficult to reach.

Electric-iron tips must be securely fastened in the heater unit. The tips must be clean and free of copper oxide. Sometimes the shaft oxidizes and causes the tip to stick in place. Remove the tip occasionally, and scrape off the scale. If the shaft is clean, the tip will receive more heat from the heater element, and you will be able to remove the tip easily when it must be replaced.

If a soldering tip is new or has just been forged, it will need to be tinned (coated with solder). To do so, hold it in a vise and "dress" the point with a well-chalked file. By "dressing" is meant filing to remove hammer marks resulting from the forging process and to round off the sharp corners slightly. (This is not always required when a tinned iron is to be retinned. Inspection will reveal if it is necessary.) Then heat the copper tip enough so that it will readily melt solder. Try melting solder with the copper frequently as it is being heated; as soon as it will melt the solder, it is ready for tinning. To tin the copper, first quickly dip it into rosin and then apply solder, or apply rosin-core solder, to the tip of the iron. The coating of solder should be bright and shiny and very thin. It aids in the rapid transfer of heat from the iron to the work. To retin a soldering gun, clean the tip with steel wool; then heat the tip and work in the new solder as the working temperature is attained. Wipe off any excess solder.

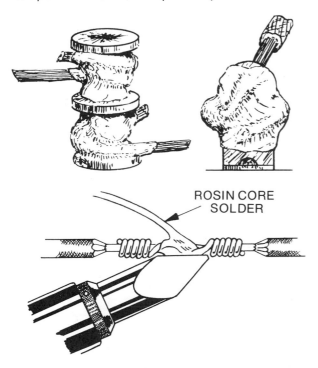

FIG. 13-17. Examples of properly made soldered joints.

ROSIN CORE SOLDER

SOLDERING PROCEDURE

The parts to be soldered must be absolutely clean (free of oxide, corrosion, and grease). During the cleaning process, and when removing insulation from wire, care must be taken not to produce cuts or nicks, which greatly reduce the mechanical strength of the wire, especially under conditions of vibration.

The joint should be prepared just prior to soldering, since the prepared surfaces will soon corrode or become dirty if they remain exposed to the air. The parts to be soldered must be securely joined mechanically before any soldering is done.

To solder electrical connections, hold the soldering iron (copper) beneath the splice being soldered, with as much mechanical contact as possible to permit maximum heat transfer. Apply rosin-core solder to the *splice*. The tinning on the soldering iron aids in the transfer of heat to the spliced wires which, when hot enough, will melt the solder. Before this temperature is reached the rosin core will have melted and run out over the wire to flux the splice. When the solder has coated the splice completely, the job is finished. No extra solder is needed.

A good, well-bonded connection is clean, shiny, smooth, and round. It also approximately outlines the wire and terminal, as shown in Figure 13-17.

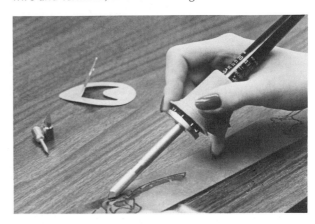

FIG. 13-18. Small-wattage soldering irons can also be used for leather tooling (above), wood burning, plastic sculpturing, and sealing.

SOLDERING PRECAUTIONS

One sizzling burn is usually enough to produce a healthy respect for hot objects. When using a soldering iron or gun, always bear in mind the following:

1. Electric soldering irons must not remain connected longer than necessary and must be kept away from flammable material.
2. To avoid burns, always assume that a soldering iron is hot.
3. Never rest a heated iron anywhere but on a metal surface or rack provided for this purpose. Faulty action on your part could result in fire, extensive equipment damage, and serious injuries.
4. Never swing an iron to remove solder because the bits of solder that come off may cause serious skin or eye burns or ignite combustible materials in the work area.
5. When cleaning an iron, use a cleaning cloth or damp sponge, but do not hold the cleaning cloth or damp sponge in your hand. Always place the cloth or damp sponge on a suitable surface, and wipe the iron across it to keep from burning your hand.
6. Hold small soldering jobs with your pliers or a suitable clamping device. Never hold the work in your hand.
7. After completing a task requiring the use of a soldering iron, disconnect the power cord from the receptacle and, when the iron has cooled off, stow it in its assigned storage area. Do not throw irons into a toolbox. When storing an iron

for a long period of time, coat the shaft and all metal parts with rust-preventive compound and store it in a dry place.

Propane or Gas Torches

Propane and Mapp-gas torches make countless household jobs, hobbies, and crafts faster, easier, and more economical. These torches operate on a very simple principle. The torch tank is filled with propane, a liquefied petroleum gas. The propane remains in a liquid state because it is under pressure. When the valve on the burner assembly is opened, propane is released through the fuel orifice. With reduced pressure, the propane converts to a gas, which burns readily when mixed with air. The tool consists of only two basic parts: the fuel tank and the burner assembly.

Some manufacturers have torches available that use Mapp gas rather than propane. A stabilized mixture of methylacetylene and propadiene, Mapp gas produces temperatures in excess of 3200°, or about 500° hotter than propane. Although slightly more expensive, it is frequently recommended for metal operations where the added heat is needed.

The fuel cylinder (tank) is constructed of heavy-gauge steel that meets rigorous safety specifications. It is engineered for adequate strength. Every tank is thoroughly tested for leaks before it leaves the factory. For easy handling, the tank is well proportioned and has a wide base that resists tipping. The gas dispensing valve at the top of the tank opens and closes automatically for convenient, economical torch assembly. When the burner assembly is screwed onto the tank, the valve releases propane if the gas dispensing knob is opened.

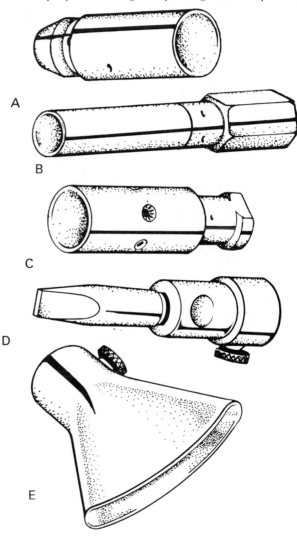

Fig. 13-20. Various types of tips: *(a)* pinpoint tip, ideal for toys, electical work, or hobbies; *(b)* standard pencil-point tip, for a general-purpose flame; *(c)* brush flame tip, recommended for soft-solder repair and maintenance; *(d)* chisel point soldering tip; *(e)* flame-spreader tip, specially designed for removing paint and ski wax, weed burning, and thawing snow and ice.

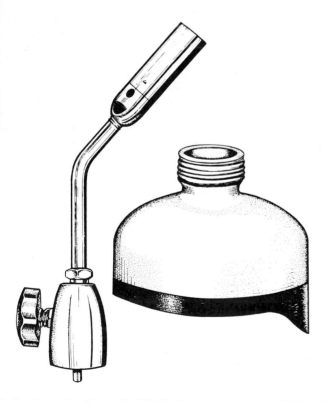

FIG. 13-19. Parts of a typical propane torch.

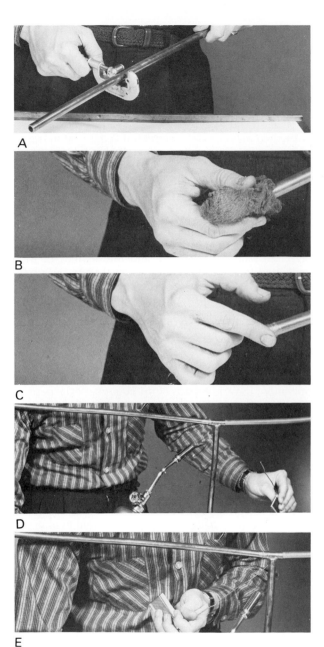

A

B

C

D

E

Fig. 13-21. Soldering copper tubing: *(a)* A tubing cutter (see Chapter 2) gives a clean, square edge when cutting copper tubing; a hacksaw may also be used. *(b)* Before joining the tubing and fitting, polish the surfaces to be joined with fine steel wool. *(c)* Apply flux to the end of the tubing, and slip the fitting over the tubing; twist slightly to spread the flux. *(d)* Apply the heat from the propane torch to the joint, playing the flame so it heats the fitting and tubing evenly. *(e)* Apply the solder to the joint; the heat in the copper melts the solder, which flows smoothly into the joint.

(*Caution*: Always inspect the inside of the cylinder outlet to make certain foreign matter has not become lodged in this area. Inspect *before* attaching the burner assembly.) When the burner head is removed from the tank, the valve closes automatically so that no propane is wasted. Every tank has an automatic pressure-release valve that eliminates the danger of the tank exploding. The valve opens automatically if the pressure in the tank is increased to a predetermined level which is above normal conditions but below unsafe conditions. Most Mapp-gas torches also have a fuel regulator. This eliminates the need for fuel adjustments since it automatically correlates fuel with flame size.

The burner-assembly unit screws onto the top of the propane or Mapp-gas tank. It can be tightened by hand; a wrench should not be used. The unit is produced under rigid quality-control standards and is thoroughly flame-tested at the factory. Caution should be exercised to prevent dropping material particles down into the center inlet valve area. Such particles could wedge the valve pin into the open position, preventing normal cylinder-valve closure upon separation of the cylinder and appliance. The burner assembly, as shown in Figure 13-19, consists of a burner head, an air-intake hole, a fuel tube, a valve assembly, and a valve control knob. A variety of burner heads or tips are available and interchangeable, to permit you to select the right type of flame for every job.

Propane and Mapp-gas torches assemble quickly and easily. First, be sure the valve on the burner assembly is completely closed by turning the on-off control knob clockwise as far as it will go. Screw the burner head onto the tank (clockwise) until it is finger tight. Avoid cross-feeding or stripping of threads. Now your torch is ready for operation. With a Mapp-gas torch, you may have to adjust the fuel regulator.

If you are using a match to light the torch, light the match and twirl or rotate it approximately 180° to create a full flame. Turn the valve control knob to the **on** position as far as it will go. Hold the match to the burner at the top of and slightly behind the tip. Never hold the match directly in front of the burner tip; the force of the escaping propane or gas will usually blow out the match. When the torch is lit, use the control knob to adjust to the desired flame.

To light the torch with a spark lighter, place the cup of the spark lighter against the end of the burner. Incline the spark lighter about 30°. Turn the valve control knob to the **on** position as far as it will go. Actuate the spark lighter. Use the control knob to adjust to the desired flame. Always allow the torch to warm up before using it in an inverted or upside-down position.

TORCH SAFETY

Like many other tools, propane and gas torches are safe when used properly. If abused, they can be dangerous. Keep the following simple precautions for safe torch storage and operation in mind:

1. Do not let unignited gas escape from the torch near any possible source of ignition.
2. Never store propane or Mapp-gas tanks in a confined, unventilated space such as a closet, or in any area where the temperature may exceed 120°F. Do not store in a room used for habitation.
3. Never use a flame to test for propane or gas leaks.
4. Never use a tank with a leaking valve or other fitting. If in doubt, test by brushing a generous amount of liquid detergent over the suspected area and looking for bubble formations.
5. Never lay a torch down unless the gas flow has been shut off. If you are maintaining a pilot flame during work pauses, use a rack or stand for the torch, and keep it away from combustible materials.
6. Do not start fires. Be very careful when working near combustible materials, and use asbestos shields when necessary.
7. Never solder a container that holds or has held flammable fluids or gases unless the container has been totally purged of these materials. If in doubt as to the previous contents of a container, thoroughly purge it. Be sure any container you work on is well vented.
8. Propane and Mapp gas consume oxygen and generate toxic fumes; therefore, use a torch only in a well-ventilated area.
9. Avoid breathing the vapors and fumes generated during torch usage. Provide ventilation that will move the vapors away from the work area.

The propane or Mapp-gas torch is a useful tool for auto-body repair, metal sculpture, burning off paint, soldering copper tubing, removing nuts, bolts, and damaged screws, repairing household and farm utensils, thawing frozen pipes, burning weeds, drying spark plugs, and annealing and case-hardening metals. Be sure to follow the manufacturer's instructions for its various uses.

BLOWTORCHES

Since the introduction of the propane torch, the gasoline blowtorch has become a thing of the past, even with old-time professionals. In fact, only a very few manufacturers still produce them, and only in limited quantities. These manufacturers supply filling and operating information with their torches. But on the whole, the successful use of the conventional gasoline blowtorch requires skill and experience. It was and still is a tool that is not recommended for amateur use. However, several manufacturers still offer small, lightweight blowtorches—some fired by alcohol—which may be used to advantage where a small soldering iron alone does not serve. That is, such torches are useful for preheating small metal surfaces which require high temperatures to be soldered. They are also useful if "hard" rather than "soft" solder is to be applied; i.e., in silver-soldering jewelry, ornaments, and the like. The manufacturer's instructions must be followed closely for best results.

Brazing and Welding Equipment

The two metal-joining methods that give the strongest joints are brazing and welding. Both require special equipment.

Brazing is done at high temperatures to join tougher metals. With such metals, ordinary soft soldering will not do, and the soldering iron or gun will not produce enough heat to melt the tougher "hard" solders. The usual equipment used industrially is an oxyacetylene hand torch. The fuel is a mixture of oxygen and acetylene. Both the flame temperature and the amount of heat generated (measured in British thermal units, or Btu) by the torch depend upon the ratio of oxygen to acetylene, or the fuel ratio. For example when a 1-to-1 oxygen-to-acetylene mixture is used, a flame temperature of about 5500°F is produced. But if we increase the oxygen to a 1.7-to-1 ratio, the flame temperature will increase to approximately 6000°F. Because the tanks containing the two gases must be kept under pressure, the oxyacetylene torch system requires numerous gauges for proper operation; in various parts of the country special permits are required by law for the storing of these fuel tanks, so they are not usually found in the average shop. The oxyacetylene system is, however, ideal for mending broken tools, gears, and auto bodies. Joints which have been brazed can stand jars and shocks which soft-soldered joints will not.

In recent years, thanks to the introduction of gas and oxygen weld-braze outfits, the home shop operator can do brazing work. In these outfits, the two necessary gases, oxygen and propane or Mapp gas, are combined in the torch and, when burned at the tip of the torch, produce a flame of intense heat. The temperature may reach as high as 5300°F, which is high enough to melt most metals, making the brazing and welding of these metals possible. In cutting, a jet of oxygen is supplied in addition to the flame. As a general rule, Mapp gas will produce a somewhat higher heat output and may allow you to complete a braze-weld or fusion-weld job quicker and with less oxygen. The choice of fuels is yours to make.

Oxygen itself does not burn but is an indispensible ingredient in the combustion process. As has already been mentioned, when a highly concentrated source of oxygen is added to the fuel, the flame temperature and rate of heat output are greatly increased. It is impossible, however, to obtain sufficient oxygen from the air to produce the temperatures needed for flame cutting or fusion welding. Therefore, as shown by the two outfits in Figure 13-22, the necessary oxygen is supplied from a "bottle" or in a solid form. That is, the oxygen necessary

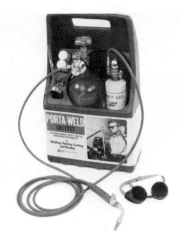
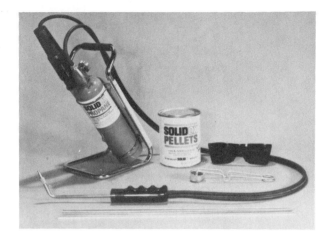

FIG. 13-22. Two portable welding-brazing outfits: one (left) uses bottled oxygen; the other (right) employs solid oxygen.

for the operation of the welder comes from small compressed-oxygen cylinders or is made in a special cylinder from pellets which are used as directed by the manufacturer.

The brazing process is almost identical to welding. The chief difference is that, in brazing, the two metal pieces are joined by another metal (the brazing rod). In welding, the two metal pieces are fused together. The brazing rod has a lower melting point than the metals to be joined; for

this reason, the brazing process is somewhat easier to complete.

When the base metal is hot all the way through the joint (not just at the surface), introduce the brazing rod into the torch flame, touching the joint at the hottest point. Rub some flux from the end of the rod onto the joint. When both joint and rod are hot enough, the rod will melt and flow easily and quickly into the joint. You can now move the torch along the joint, repeating the same sequence as required. Table 13-1 suggests the proper rods to use.

Table 13-1 The Proper Brazing Rods for Various Metals

Type rod:	Steel	Aluminum, flux-core	Bronze, flux-coated	Nickel-silver	Copper-phosphorus
Type torch to use:	Oxygen; Mapp gas	Oxygen; propane or Mapp gas	Oxygen; Mapp gas	Oxygen; Mapp gas	Oxygen; propane or Mapp gas
Apply welding, brazing, or soldering rod:	Melt rod end in molten puddle of base metal	Flux becomes a clear liquid	Rod flows freely on contact with heated metal	Flux becomes a clear liquid, and rod flows freely on contact with heated metal	Rod flows freely on contact with heated metal
Metals*					
Aluminum		X			
Chrome plate			X	X	
Nickel-base alloys			X	X	
Bronze			X	X	X
Copper			X		X
Galvanized iron or steel	X		X	X	
Silver or silver plate					
Stainless steel			X	X	
Steel	X		X	X	
Cast iron	X		X	X	

*Unlike metals can be joined using brazing rods that are suited to both metals. For example, steel and galvanized iron can be joined using steel rods, bronze flux-coated rods, nickel-silver rods, or silver solder.

In fusion welding, as in brazing, the metal pieces to be joined must be thoroughly cleaned of all dirt, paint, oil, and rust. Chemical cleaners may be used, or the metal can be sanded, filed, or cleaned with a grinding wheel. If the metal is not thoroughly cleaned before welding, the joint will be weak. The edges of the pieces to be joined should be trimmed to fit snugly together before welding. Filler or welding rods can be used to fill small gaps, but the strongest weld will be obtained if the metals match well before welding. As the metal is heated with the torch, it will expand, causing the metal to move. It is therefore important to firmly anchor the peices in position before heating. This can be accomplished with clamps, straps, or bolts. If the joint is not anchored before heating, movement could result in a misaligned repair. Here again, "practice makes perfect." Since the welding process actually requires melting the metal pieces so they will flow together, it is possible to overheat them and cause distortion near the weld. A few practice welds on scrap metal of the same thickness as the repair job will guide you to the proper application of heat.

It is best to allow the welded joint to cool slowly and naturally. This may take some time, and care should be taken not to touch the metal until you are sure it has cooled. Dipping the metal in cold water will cool the joint faster, but it may also cause distortion of the metal and weaken the joint.

ARC WELDING

Arc-welding equipment ranges from stationary types that require hundreds of amperes and 240 volts (ac, ac-dc, or dc) to small units that operate on household current. The latter, shown in Figure 13-24, are suitable for light-duty jobs: the joining of rods and plates of $\frac{1}{8}$- to $\frac{1}{2}$-inch size. Other arc-welding units are suitable for shop use, especially in the 230- to 300-ampere output range, but such welders require at least a 240-volt, 50-ampere circuit. Also, these larger medium-duty units cannot be considered portable, as are the light-duty units. Of course, dollies make their transportation a relatively easy task.

In arc welding, the power is electricity. The "torch" is actually a holder for a rod of welding metal which is fused to join the melted metal of the pieces being welded. The work is grounded through one wire; the "rod" completes the circuit; and the very hot arc caused by holding the rod near the work melts the welding rod and welded metal. The arc is so brilliant that an eye shield is required to avoid blindness and to assist the welder in seeing the work as it progresses.

Most arc welders use a carbon rod, available with the equipment or as an accessory, to braze, repair light-gauge metal, sweat copper tubing, and even construct metal sculptures. Another valuable accessory is an arc stabilizer, which converts any ac or ac-dc arc welder to a versatile tungsten inert gas (TIG) torch. Such a unit will enable you

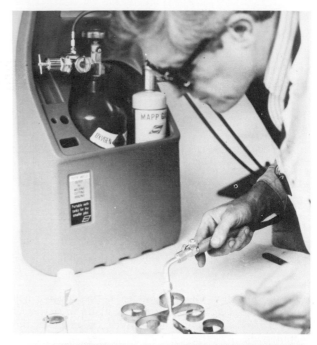

FIG. 13-23. Two styles of bottled-oxygen welding-brazing outfits at work.

to weld metals such as aluminum, bronze, nickel, and stainless steel, and metals of very light gauge up to $\frac{1}{4}$ inch thick. The arc stabilizer operates continuously to maintain a long arc. The tip need not touch the metal during welding. This process floods the molten metal with a noncombining inert gas (usually argon) to prevent oxidation and embrittlement of the weld. The TIG torch uses a tungsten electrode; it will not pass impurities on to the weld.

In joining two pieces of metal in standard arc welding, the melted rod forms a "bead" similar to the melted solder in soldering and in brazing. However, the metals

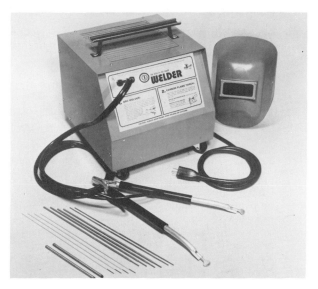

FIG. 13-24. Typical light-duty electric- or arc-welding kit.

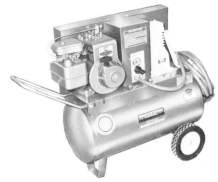

FIG. 13-25. (Top) Typical light-duty compressor sprayer-roller unit; (Bottom) typical heavy-duty paint-gun compressor.

being joined also fuse, and the rod is fused along with them. Here, too, the rod includes a flux to keep air from the joint, and to prevent corrosion and weakness. As in soldering and brazing, the right rod, suitable for the metal pieces to be welded, must be chosen. Obviously, a hard-metal rod will not melt until it attains the right temperature; if the metal pieces to be joined are softer, they will melt before the rod itself.

In comparison with the soldering technique, the welding rod must be moved slowly. If it is moved too rapidly, not enough of the rod will be melted at any one point, and the joint will be improperly filled and weak. Practice is needed, but there is little to learn so you should become skilled after a few practice sessions. Start by joining pieces of scrap in various positions; weld them together, and then try to break them apart to study your work. If you succeed in breaking them apart, your failure will be visible. If not, you have learned all you need to know with the exception of appearance. Neat welding joints, while not important from the standpoint of strength, mark your work as that of an expert.

Because of design variations in brazing and welding equipment, it is not possible to give full instructions on how to use these tools. Fortunately, the manufacturers do supply good instruction manuals which should be carefully followed.

Paint Sprayers

Paint sprayers are particularly useful for large areas and for the application of certain furniture finishes. Spraying is much faster than brushing or rolling, and, although some paint will likely be wasted through overspraying, the saving in time and effort may more than compensate for any additional paint cost. Once you have perfected your

spraying technique, you can produce a coating with excellent uniformity of thickness and appearance.

Surface areas accessible only with difficulty to the brush or roller can readily be covered by the sprayer. All coats can be applied satisfactorily by the spray technique, except for primer coats. Spraying should be done only on a clean surface, since the paint may not adhere well if a dust film is present. Preparation of the *paint* is of critical importance when a sprayer is to be used. Stir or strain the paint to remove any lumps, and thin it carefully. If the paint is lumpy or too thick, it may clog the spray valve; if it is too thin, the paint may sag or run after it is applied. Follow the manufacturer's instructions on the paint label for the type and amount of thinner to be used.

There are two basic types of paint sprayers on the market today: the airless sprayer and the compressor sprayer. The latter is the so-called conventional system and consists of a spray gun, an air compressor and motor, and an air-pressure tank and safety gauges, plus the necessary air hoses. The motor size can range from about $1/2$ hp to over 3 hp and can deliver from 3.2 standard cubic feet per minute (scfm) at 35 psi to 9.7 scfm at 40 psi. For average shop use, the smaller models are suitable. Some compressor systems can be used to apply paint by both gun and roller.

The better airless sprayers will spray at a rate up to four

times faster than conventional compressor sprayers. In fact, some professional models will deliver up to $\frac{1}{3}$ gallon of paint per minute. There is minimal overspray with airless sprayers, which means less time need be spent in masking, and less time wasted in after-painting cleanup. They also spray most latex paints unthinned. Airless sprayers run the gamut from inexpensive to very expensive. The rule here, as with all tools, is to buy the best you can afford. While the airless electric sprayers apply finishing materials faster, many old-time wood finishers still prefer the conventional compressor sprayers for fine furniture work.

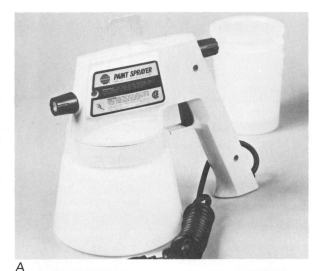

A

B

FIG. 13-26. (a) Typical light-duty airless paint sprayer; (b) typical medium-duty airless paint sprayer.

SPRAYER TECHNIQUES

Before using your sprayer, carefully read the instruction manual. Here are some additional techniques that may help you get the best possible results.

1. Adjust the width of the spray fan to the size of the surface to be coated. A narrow fan is best for spraying small or narrow surfaces; a wider fan should be used to spray tabletops or walls.
2. Before spraying any surface, test the thickness of the paint, the size of the fan, and the motion of the spray gun. Excessive thickness can cause rippling of the wet film or lead to blistering later.
3. Hold the nozzle 7 to 9 inches from the surface to be painted. Spraying from closer than 6 inches may cause the paint to pile up and run. Spraying from more than 10 inches can cause "dusting" or a sandy surface.
4. As much as possible, keep the gun level. Pointing up or down causes the paint to pile up at one edge of the spray pattern. For painting flat surfaces, such as floors and ceilings, tilt the gun no more than 45°. Better yet, order a 45° angle nozzle. Keep your wrist limber, so the gun always points "head-on" and holds the right distance throughout your stroke. Short 20-inch strokes are easiest. Angling in or out piles up paint at one end of the stroke. Arcing piles it at the middle. Piled paint may sag or run. There is an easy trick for smooth stroking: move the gun back and forth in rhythm, as if it were a baton. This is important, because slowing down or stopping produces heavy spots and possible runs.
5. Triggering, too, is a simple matter of rhythm. On a practice box, draw two vertical marks about 20 inches apart. Practice your stroke and triggering between these marks. Squeeze the trigger just before the nozzle hits the first mark; release the trigger as the nozzle passes the second mark. Start right off with a swing, stroking in both directions. Half a dozen strokes on the box, and you will get the knack of it.
6. Practice your stroking and triggering by spraying left to right, right to left, always at the same distance from the surface and with your wrist limber, never arcing or waving the stroke. To lap your strokes evenly, aim at the edge of the stroke just completed. This ensures even coverage, free of streaks and runs.
7. When spraying flat surfaces, always start at the near edge. If the spray is directed first at the far edge of the surface, your mist falls on the freshly painted surfaces as you work. This causes a sandy finish.
8. Outside corners should be sprayed with the

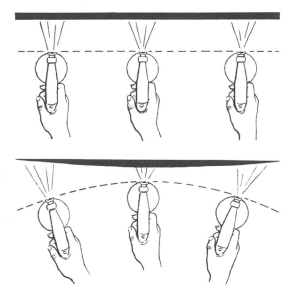

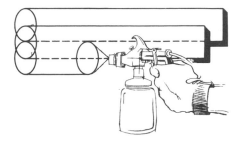

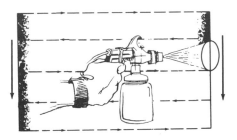

FIG. 13-27. (Top) The *right way:* move the gun parallel to the work surface, keeping the wrist flexible. Hold the gun 7 to 9 inches from the work. (Bottom) The *wrong way:* keeping the wrist too stiff causes arcing and poor distribution of the finish.

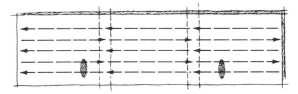

FIG. 13-28. (Top) Overlap strokes by approximately one-half; (bottom) spray bands at each end.

nozzle aimed squarely at the corner. This deposits the heaviest coat on the corner itself, where it is needed. Inside corners should be sprayed by aiming the gun at each side of the corner in turn. In this case, if the gun is aimed into the corner, paint builds up on the sides while the corner receives a thin coat only. Try it and see for yourself.

9. When spraying vertical surfaces, always start at the top and work downward with horizontal strokes. Lap evenly by aiming the nozzle at the edge of the previous stroke. Reduce overspray by painting one stroke down each vertical edge before starting the horizontal strokes.

10. Cutting down the size and volume of the spray pattern automatically reduces overspray. Practice finding the happy meeting place between good coverage and minimum overspray for each material. You will find that in most situations a 24 X 18 inch cardboard shield, handled with the free hand, eliminates any overspray problem. Newspapers overlapped and fastened with a few pieces of tape form an adequate drop cloth.

11. Cover everything close to the work area with drop cloths, tarps, or newspapers. The "bounce-back" from a sprayer may extend several feet from the work surface. Pliable masking tape is used mainly in intricate corners and to fasten

down sheets of newspapers extending over wider areas. Often only one edge of a sheet of overlapped newspaper needs to be fastened. Do not tape newly painted surfaces or leave tape on any painted surface more than a few hours.

12. Use a respirator of some type to avoid inhaling paint vapors.

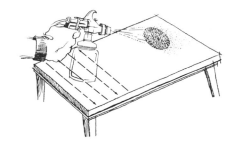

FIG. 13-29. On level surfaces, start at the near edge to avoid overspraying on coated work. Any overspraying then falls on uncoated work.

FIG. 13-30. Light-duty compressors can be used to spray paints, inflate bicycle tires and other objects (left), spray insecticides and cleaners, and apply caulking compound (right).

PAINT-SPRAYER CARE

Clean the sprayer promptly, before the paint dries. After using oil-base or alkyd paints, clean the sprayer with the same solvent used to thin the paint. After using latex paint, clean the sprayer with detergent and water. Fill the sprayer tank with the cleaning liquid, and spray it clean. If the fluid tip becomes clogged, it can be cleaned with a broom straw. Never use wire or a nail to clear clogged air holes in the sprayer tip.

Portable Compressors, Power Plants, and Heaters

The portable compressor has many uses around the home, in the shop, or on the farm other than for paint spraying. For constant pressure, a pressure regulator must be included in the rig. The compressor motor can be either electric or gasoline operated and can range from $\frac{1}{2}$ to 5 hp. (A few heavy-duty motors or engines are rated over 5 hp.) The 4-scfm at 100 psi compressor will operate most air (pneumatic) tools as well as caulking guns, inflators, sprayers for paint, fertilizer, insecticides, and herbicides, and sandblasters. (The sandblaster accessory for the compressor provides a method of removing paint, dirt, rust, and scale from castings, stone, brick, ceramic, concrete, metal, plastic, and wood. In addition to heavy-duty cleaning, it can be used to etch plastic, glass, metal, or stone—all with ordinary sand.) A single-stage compressor is powerful enough for use in the home and a small shop, while two-stage pumps are employed for heavy-duty use. A tank of at least 20 gallons capacity that meets the American Society of Mechanical Engineers (ASME) code is best. Small compressors such as the one shown in Figure 13-30 can do limited work around a home.

Portable heaters (electric or kerosene) are needed tools for many work areas such as garages and unheated shops. The kerosene type shown in Figure 13-31 is very popular. Ranging in capacity from 30,000 to over 225,000 Btu, these units require no installation and no special power source or fuel hookup. Most run on standard 120-volt, 60-hertz power with a three-prong plug. The heater uses kerosene

FIG. 13-31. Two types of portable heaters that will heat unheated work areas.

FIG. 13-32. An electric power plant.

or No. 1 fuel oil and many have optional thermostatic control. Your local dealer will help you to select the proper size for any given project.

Two other portable tools are electric pumps and electric power plants (generators). While portable water pumps are primarily used by builders and contractors to supply water to sites where there is no available water supply, electric power plants serve the same purpose for electricity, but they also take the worry and inconvenience out of power failures and brownouts. These portable gasoline-driven power plants, furnishing either 120 or 240 volts or both, are generally available with capacities of between 2000 and 7500 watts.

Table 13-2 gives the power requirements of average motors. An electric motor requires more power during starting than running. Motors of the split-phase type require more power during starting than capacitor-start motors and repulsion-induction motors. For difficult starting conditions, such as in running compressors, air conditioners, and deep-well pumps, allow about 25 percent more power for starting. To choose a generator of adequate size, add up all the watts which may be used at one time, including the *starting* loads of all automatic equipment such as furnaces, refrigerators, and freezers. The *running* watts of motors for water pumps and air conditioners may be used, assuming they will be started manually, one at a time, during an emergency. However, the generator must be of sufficient capacity to handle the individual starting load of any motor it is to power.

Table 13-2 Running and Starting Loads of Electric Motors by Horsepower

Hp	Running watts	Split-phase	Capacitor-start	Repulsion-induction
1/6	275	2050	850	600
1/4	400	2400	1050	850
1/3	450	2700	1350	975
1/2	600	3600	1800	1300
3/4	850		2600	1900
1	1100		3300	2500
1 1/2	1650		5000	3500
2	2200		6600	4600

When selecting cables to run from a portable power plant, follow the recommendations in Table 13-3.

Table 13-3 Maximum Cable Lengths for Various Electrical Loadings

Current, amperes	Load, watts		Maximum allowable cable length, feet			
	At 120 volts	At 240 volts	No. 10 wire	No. 12 wire	No. 14 wire	No. 16 wire
2.5	300	600	1000	600	375	250
5	575	1150	500	300	200	125
7.5	860	1725	350	200	125	100
10	1150	2300	250	150	100	
15	1725	3450	150	100	65	
20	2300	4600	125	75	50	

Shop Vacuum Cleaners

While industrial shops have various systems for cleaning up the dust and dirt that are bound to result from almost any tool operation, the best method for the average shop is to use a shop vacuum cleaner. The typical unit (Figure 13-33) ranges from 5 to 15 gallons in capacity and is operated by a motor that develops about 1hp. Most are complete with easy-rolling tires, hose, and wands. Other cleaning accessories usually come as extras.

FIG. 13-33. Typical shop vacuum cleaner.

STATIONARY POWER TOOLS

MULTIPURPOSE SINGLE-UNIT POWER TOOLS

There are several different types in this category, but they have certain basic characteristics. All have individual motors, and all occupy a limited amount of floor area. One well-known unit, for example, combines a circular saw, jointer, sander, and drill press in a single machine. Another unit is a radial-arm machine (see Chapter 15) to which various attachments can be connected to convert it from a saw to a lathe, drill press, sander, shaper, router, grinder, saber saw, polisher, jointer, or buffer.

While these complete and compact power plants fit into a small space and perform the work of many individual machines, there is always a time loss while you convert the machine from one purpose to another. This is not a major obstacle for the average homeowner, but for the "production worker" who needs to save time between operations, this tool is not too adequate.

SINGLE-PURPOSE POWER TOOLS

For heavy production, there is no substitute for the single-purpose power tool. The traditional idea of adding self-contained single-purpose tools to the average workshop—as you need them and can afford them—continues to be the practice of many homeowners. This is fine if you want all your power tools ready for instant action. It is also possible to save time by organizing your working procedures more efficiently. However, this is undoubtedly the most expensive way of going about building a power-tool workshop.

SINGLE-PURPOSE POWER TOOLS WITH REMOVABLE MOTOR

A power-tool workshop in which one motor serves several single-purpose tools may be erected if the floor area permits. In an arrangement of this sort, special mounting brackets on the motor facilitate shifting it from one tool to another, but this obviously prevents the use of more than one tool at a time. Although this method results in a considerable saving in motor cost, the apparent saving must be balanced against the time wasted in refitting the motor when it is moved from one tool to another.

To sum up, the important factors to be considered when planning a workshop and purchasing stationary power tools are:

1. The amount of space available
2. The type and quantity of work you plan to do
3. The amount of money you want to spend to acquire the tools you need

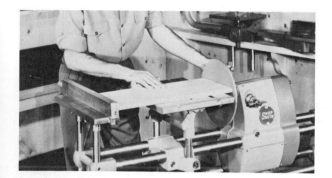
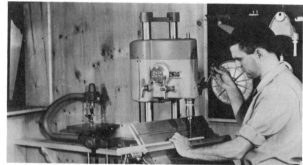
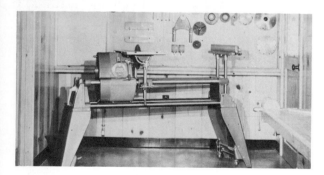

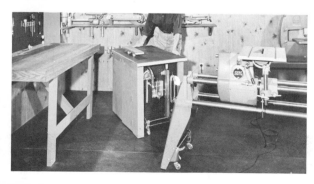

FIG. III-1. Multi-purpose tools do the combined operations of many different single-purpose stationary tools.

Although the various classes of stationary power tools may differ considerably depending upon the particular manufacturer, all standard tools are now so well constructed and designed that it would be almost impossible to make a mistake in selecting stationary power tools. However, the selection and use of the stationary power tools that best fit your needs are covered in detail in this section. This information is necessary if your shop is to fit your particular requirements.

As stated in the introduction to this book, stationary power tools are mounted on benches or stands which rest firmly on the floor. Work is brought to the tool. The proper selection of stationary power tools for the average workshop is not a very difficult problem because of the great abundance of power tools now available. Depending on the available space, floor area, individual requirements, and cost involved, selection can be made from the following three classes:

1. Multipurpose single-unit power tools which may be installed advantageously in the small workshop where space is at a premium
2. Single-purpose power tools with individual motors, ideal for quick access to every operation
3. Single-purpose tools with only one "quick-change" motor, which give you the advantage of individual units and, at the same time, eliminate the cost of buying a separate motor for each tool

NOTE: In the stationary tool chapters, blade guards and other safety devices have been removed in order to clearly illustrate the procedure described. For safe operation of any power tools, guards and other safety devices *must* always be utilized.

TABLE SAWS

The table saw (also called the bench, variety, or stationary circular saw) is one of the oldest known stationary power tools used in woodworking. Performing the fundamental operations of straight-line sawing, the circular saw is the basic machine in any woodworking shop. It is not a difficult machine to run; plain ripping and crosscutting come naturally to most operators, and other jobs requiring more "know-how" are easily learned. Popular sizes for shopwork are 9 to 12 inches, where the figures represent the diameter of the saw blade. Circular saws for industrial use range up to 24 inches in diameter, but the 14- and 16-inch sizes are most commonly employed.

Homeshop table saws, today, are of the tilting-arbor design. It features a fixed table, while the arbor and motor are made to raise and tilt. Because of the intricate mechanics involved in building a good tilting arbor, these saws are necessarily more expensive than the tilting-table type formerly made but are well worth the additional cost since they make all sawing operations easier, safer, and more convenient.

As to the controls of a tilting arbor saw, there is a handle to tilt the saw blade, a handle to lock the blade at any degree of tilt, and a scale setting to show the degree of tilt.

The ripping fence is guided by means of bars fastened to each end of the table, with the front bar calibrated to show the distance the fence is set from the saw blade. If the saw table is large, the fence must be locked to both front and rear guide bars to be rigid; also, the lock for the rear fence should be at the front of the table for convenience. The fence on a small saw is often clamped at the front end only, since with the short span it is held sufficiently rigid by one clamp. Most fences on quality saws have a microset adjustment to permit fine setting by means of a rack-and-gear movement.

FIG. 14-1. Typical 12-inch tilting-arbor saw.

FIG. 14-2. Typical 9-inch tilting-arbor bench saw.

A 9-inch table saw requires a $\frac{1}{2}$-hp motor for average work, although $\frac{1}{3}$ hp will suffice if only thin stock is to be cut. A saw of this size is made to operate at a speed of about 3400 rpm, giving a cutting speed of 7100 surface feet per minute (sfm). A 10-inch saw requires $\frac{3}{4}$ or 1 hp if the full $3\frac{1}{4}$-inch capacity of the saw is to be used. This saw runs at about 3200 to 3400 rpm, which gives a cutting speed of 8100 sfm. The 12-inch saw requires a 2-hp or larger motor and has a cutting speed of 10,000 sfm. Its full cut is about $4\frac{1}{4}$ inches. It is a mistake to run any saw faster or slower than the manufacturer recommends; this feature has been worked out carefully to allow maximum cutting capacity with minimal blade wear and moderate power consumption.

Usually, the motor is constructed so that it can be moved a little if the belt gets too loose. The metal stand bought from the manufacturer of the machine has provision for fastening the motor in the correct position. If a bench saw must be driven by a jackshaft or a slow-speed motor, it is necessary to figure out the size of pulley that will drive it at the correct speed. Never run a saw or other machine at a higher or lower speed than the manufacturer recommends.

To figure the diameter of a pulley or the speed of a shaft, use this formula:

Speed of drive shaft $\times$ diameter of driver pulley = speed of driven shaft $\times$ diameter of driven pulley

For example, suppose a motor shaft makes 1200 revolutions per minute (rpm). What diameter pulley is necessary to drive the saw arbor, which has a 3-inch pulley, at 3600 rpm?

Solution: $1200 \times P = 3600 \times 3$

$$P = \frac{3600 \times 3}{1200} = 9$$

Pulleys are fastened to shafts with keys or setscrews or both. When a key is used, both the shaft and the pulley are slotted for it so that the pulley cannot turn relative to the shaft.

The table-saw guard is a metal or plastic cover that is arranged to fall over the blade. A splitter or spreader is a metal plate mounted directly behind the saw blade; its purpose is to hold the saw cut or kerf open so that the wood will not rub against the saw to cause burning and binding. The splitter is commonly fitted with antikickback fingers or pawls which effectively grip the work and prevent it from being thrown back at the operator. Most illustrations in this chapter have the saw guard, splitter and antikickback parts removed for clarity. When operating a saw, be sure these essential parts are attached.

The saw itself can be mounted on a bench or on a suitable steel or wood stand. The saw is sometimes mounted on the same stand as the jointer, since

FIG. 14-3. Angle sawing on the tilting-arbor saw is much easier and less awkward than on the tilting-table saw. For this reason, few tilting-table circular saws are produced.

smoothing with the jointer often follows cutting with the saw. The saw table should be slightly below waist height; 34 inches from the floor is a good standard. A central location in the floor plan is almost a must, because the saw needs plenty of room in all directions. A bag or box fitted to or behind the sawdust chute will catch most of the dust. Saws of the tilting-arbor type are commonly mounted on a cabinet base which provides a self-contained sawdust box fitted with a cleanout door.

SAW BLADES AND CUTTERS

The average workshop owner is concerned with two kinds of saw blades: (1) the combination blade and (2) the hollow-ground planer blade. Both blades rip, crosscut, and miter equally well; hence their adaptability to home shop needs. Where production work is being done, two other common saw blades—the crosscut saw and the ripsaw—are useful, but each can be used only for the one operation for which it is intended. In addition to these four common blades, there are hundreds of specialized saw styles, each designed to work best under certain conditions.

CROSSCUT BLADE The crosscut or cutoff saw blade is intended for cutting across the grain and is useless for ripping. A typical tooth pattern is shown in Figure 14-4a. This drawing also gives the names of the different parts of the sawtooth (the names apply equally well to all saw blades). The gullets of the crosscut saw are quite sharp, yet they should have a slight round in order to prevent cracking. The front or face of the tooth is on a line with the center of the saw and is filed to a 15° bevel. Where fine, smooth work is to be done, the face bevel can be increased to 20 to 25°. The back of the tooth is filed on a 10° bevel (15° for fine cutting). This saw is usually spring set. Setting consists of bending successive teeth in opposite directions to secure clearance as the saw cuts through wood. Setting is done after filing, using a setting stake or suitable hand set. The set is alternately right and left on successive teeth. Only the tips of the teeth are set. The set should not exceed $\frac{1}{64}$ inch.

A fine-tooth crosscut saw is a set blade that will smoothly cut plywoods, fiberboards, and veneers with minimum splintering, as well as crosscutting wood.

PLANER BLADE The planer saw is a hollow-ground blade whose cutting edge is shaped as shown in Figure 14-4b. This same tooth pattern is also used for flat-ground saws. In this case, the teeth are set to give the necessary clearance. The hollow-ground blade does not require setting since it is tapered from the edge to the center for clearance. The planer saw has two kinds of teeth—cutting teeth and raker teeth. The cutting teeth sever the wood fibers on either side of the cut, while the raker teeth clean out the wood fibers. Raker teeth should be $\frac{1}{32}$ to $\frac{1}{64}$ inch shorter than cutting teeth. The cutting teeth are beveled alternately right and left, as shown. The raker teeth are filed square across, front and back. Sometimes called a "miter blade," it is generally used by cabinetmakers when cutting stock to finish dimensions because it cuts very smoothly, both with and across the grain, and reduces the amount of sanding required.

RIPSAW BLADE Ripsaw teeth (Figure 14-4c) are filed to many different patterns. The face of the tooth is on a line tangent to a circle one-third to one-fourth the diameter of the saw. The point of the tooth must be strong in view of the rough work for which this saw is intended. The teeth are filed square across to give a true chisel point. The blade tends to tear wood on crosscuts but cuts fast and clean when ripping. Since ripping usually puts a heavy load on the motor, this blade is recommended for general ripping jobs.

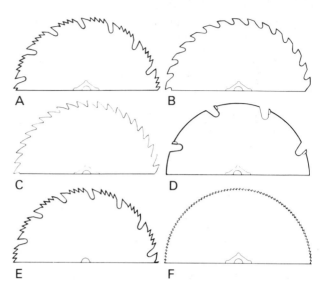

FIG. 14-5. Typical tooth patterns for (a) standard combination blade; (b) chisel-tooth flat-ground combination blade; (c) hard-tip combination blade; (d) carbide-tipped combination blade; (e) cabinet combination blade; (f) plywood blade.

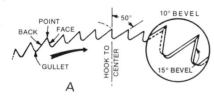

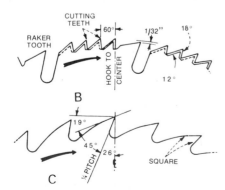

FIG. 14-4. Typical tooth patterns for crosscut, planer, and rip blades.

FIG. 14-6. Metal-slitting blade (top) and cutoff wheel (bottom) in use.

COMBINATION SAW BLADE Your table saw usually comes equipped with a combination blade which will make all cuts equally well. This blade is adaptable to most workshop needs for general-purpose work. The combination blade is divided into segments and has crosscut teeth and one raker tooth in each segment, with a deep gullet between. This arrangement permits the blade to cut freely and smoothly both with and across the grain.

PLYWOOD BLADE This fine-tooth cutting blade, with its thin-rim taper, does an excellent job on plywood and gummy, resinous woods. It makes cuts with smooth finishes, ideal for glue joints. Plywood blades are also available in the thin-kerf-line type, for use on both plywoods and veneers.

NONFERROUS-METAL BLADE This blade is taper-ground for smooth, free sawing of all metals except iron and steel. Because sparks are produced, your eyes must be protected. For best results with the blade, lubricate the teeth with tallow (candle wax) and feed the work slowly. The metal slitting blade is useful for neat and accurate cutting of light sheet metal, but cannot be used on other materials.

ABRASIVE OR CUTOFF WHEELS Abrasive wheels for use on the circular-saw arbor can be obtained in a number of different grades, thicknesses, and diameters. For average home shop use, 8-inch-diameter, $\frac{3}{32}$-inch-thick resinous-bonded wheels are the most satisfactory. Almost any material can be cut with abrasive wheels. Aluminum-oxide wheels are used for cutting steel and nonferrous metals, while silicon-carbide wheels work best for glass, porcelain, plastics, hard rubber, and similar materials. Cutting operations are performed dry and at the regular saw speed of about 6500 surface feet per minute. For production work, the speed can be increased to 10,000 sfm, but this has no particular advantages beyond prolonging the life of the wheel. Wheels are mounted on the circular-saw arbor as is any saw blade, with the addition of heavy paper washers on either side.

Masonry cutting wheels are about the only answer if you need to cut brick, cement block, or tile. These wheels are fitted on the saw arbor, just as a regular blade, but require some special care when being used. Safety glasses are a must; a filter mask will add much to your comfort when you use the masonry cutoff wheel, since it has a tendency to fill the air with fine abrasive dust. When cutting masonry, protect your saw table by placing a scrap piece of wood between the work and the table.

DADO HEADS While there are several dado heads on the market, the two most popular are still the conventional dado set and the adjustable wobble blade. The conventional or standard dado set (Figure 14-8, top) consists of two outside saws, each about $\frac{1}{8}$ inch thick, whose teeth are not given any set, and inside saws, or "chippers" as they are called: one $\frac{1}{4}$ inch thick, two $\frac{1}{8}$ inch (some heads include two additional $\frac{1}{8}$-inch chippers instead of the $\frac{1}{4}$-inch one), and one $\frac{1}{16}$ inch thick (thickness at the hub). The cutting portions of the inside

FIG. 14-7. (Top) To install the blade on the arbor, first crank the arbor up to maximum elevation. Slip the blade onto the arbor, making sure that the teeth are pointing in the right direction. Place the washer on the arbor, and run the nut up tight against it. Now fit your wrench over the nut so that the wrench handle is resting against the front edge of the well. Grab the top edge of the blade, and pull it firmly toward you, securely seating the retaining nut. (Bottom) To remove a blade, reverse the procedure, wedging the front teeth of the blade with a wood block and pulling the wrench handle toward you.

cutters or chippers are widened to overlap the adjacent cutter or saw. When assembling a cutter head, arrange the two outside cutters so that the larger raker teeth on one are opposite the small cutting teeth on the other. This produces a smoother-cutting and easier-running head. Be sure also that the swaged teeth of the inside cutters are placed in the gullets of the outside cutters, not against the teeth, so that the head cuts clean and the chips have exit clearance. And stagger the inside cutters so that their teeth do not come together. For example, if three cutters are used, they should be set 120° apart. The design of the cutting teeth of the dado-head set permits cutting with the grain, across the grain, or at an angle.

The second type is a single blade with self-contained adjustable wobbler units (Figure 14-8, bottom) that can be set to cause the blade rim to wobble from side to side a predetermined amount as the blade revolves. These blades cut kerfs from $\frac{3}{16}$ inch (or $\frac{1}{4}$ inch) minimum up to $\frac{13}{16}$ inch and are adjusted by rotation of a dial. Although the dial is calibrated in $\frac{1}{16}$-inch increments, the adjustment is continuous (not stepped), so that variations of less than $\frac{1}{16}$ inch are possible. Tightening of the arbor nut locks the adjustment while securing the blade on the arbor.

FIG. 14-8. The conventional dado set consists of two outside blades and several chippers. The number of chippers between the blades adjusts the dado width.

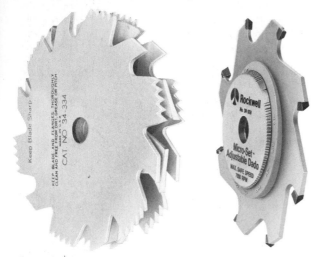

FIG. 14-9. Types of quick-setting dado heads. Both are adjustable for any cut from ¼ to ¹³⁄₁₆ inch without removing the saw arbor. The one on the right has carbide-tipped teeth for long life.

FIG. 14-10. The molding cutter is available with a variety of blades for making trim. The cutter head replaces the regular blade.

MOLDING HEAD The molding head consists of a cutter head in which can be mounted various shapes of steel knives, as shown. A special fence is required; it is cut out at the center to give clearance to the cutter head when the knives are at their highest cutting point. Alternatively, a cut-out wood facing can be clamped or screwed to a standard fence. Each of the three knives in a set is fitted into a groove in the cutter head and securely clamped with a screw. The knife grooves should be kept free of sawdust which would prevent the cutter from seating properly.

Molding-head knives are made of high-speed steel and will cut many thousands of feet of molding before becoming dull. They are ground in such a manner that sharpening is accomplished by simply whetting the flat side of the knife, and then removing the burr thus formed from the beveled edge. Extremely dull knives can also be ground on the bevel, but this is seldom worthwhile in view of the low cost of new knives. Grinding is often useful, however, in reshaping a straight knife to some particular pattern which may be needed. Grinding should be done dry, with the knife cooled frequently in water to prevent burning.

JIGS

Numerous jigs are used in table work. A few of these are so universal in application as to be considered an essential part of the saw; typical of these is the tenoning jig. Other gadgets, while less extensive in scope, are often extremely handy for some particular job, and most can easily be made right in the shop. Several of these are described in this chapter. Four of the most useful manufactured table-saw accessories and work helpers are:

1. *Hold-down clamp for miter gauge.* Attached to your miter gauge, this clamp holds a workpiece securely to the miter-gauge bar, squarely up against the miter-gauge head. It will prevent the workpiece from creeping or shifting out of squareness with the gauge, and it is of help in feeding a small workpiece for crosscutting with one hand (on the gauge handle). A firm palm push sets and locks the hold-down clamp shown in Figure 14-11*a*; it releases at a touch.
2. *Miter-gauge stop rods.* Fitted to the miter gauge, this attachment holds short workpieces to prevent creeping, and positions them for cutting off to a predetermined length. In Figure 14-11*b*, the stop rod is set in the miter gauge on the side away from the saw blade.
3. *Universal jig.* This jig slides in the miter-gauge groove at an adjustable distance from the saw blade, and holds wood up to 2 inches thick for on-edge or one-end feeding to the blade. It is especially useful for holding long, narrow stock on end, and very small work. It is also good as a tenoning jig (Figure 14-11*c*) and for other precision joints. A clamp holds the workpiece firmly and in the correct position.
4. *Hold-down attachment.* Attached to the fence

B

C

D

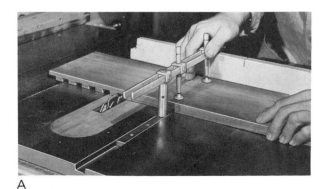

A

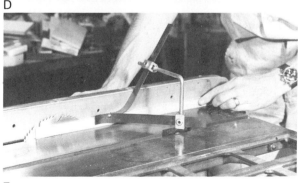

E

FIG. 14-11. Five most helpful manufactured jigs: (*a*) hold-down clamp for miter gauge; (*b*) miter-gauge stop rod; (*c*) universal jig; (*d*) tenoning jig which is used in the same manner as the universal jig; (*e*) hold-down attachment.

A

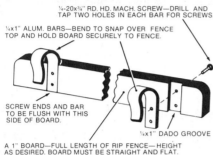

¼-20x¾" RD. HD. MACH. SCREW—DRILL AND
TAP TWO HOLES IN EACH BAR FOR SCREWS.

¼x1" ALUM. BARS—BEND TO SNAP OVER FENCE
TOP AND HOLD BOARD SECURELY TO FENCE.

SCREW ENDS AND BAR
TO BE FLUSH WITH THIS
SIDE OF BOARD.

¼x1" DADO GROOVE

B A 1" BOARD—FULL LENGTH OF RIP FENCE—HEIGHT
AS DESIRED. BOARD MUST BE STRAIGHT AND FLAT.

FIG. 14-12. (a) Miter-gauge auxiliary fence which is attached to the miter gauge with a screw-bolt arrangement. The electric tape on the facing helps to provide added friction. (b) Simple clip-on fence that can be quickly installed on the rip fence.

or locked in the miter slot (Figure 14-11d) or both, the spring leaf of this hold-down is ideal for ripping narrow pieces, since it holds the work tight against both the fence and the table.

There are also several auxiliary fences. For example, certain ripping operations can be better and more safely accomplished with the aid of a home-made additional fence such as that shown in Figure 14-12a. Be sure to attach the 1 X 4 to the miter gauge so that it cannot come loose or wobble. If a kerf is required, it can be cut during use.

Frequently, there are operations that require an auxiliary wood fence attached to the rip fence. One method is to bolt a suitable board to your fence. This necessitates the use of flathead machine screws (with nuts) which must be countersunk in the board and inserted through holes in the fence (which may have to be drilled), a time-consuming setup procedure. A clip-on fence (illustrated in Figure 14-12b) can be more quickly installed.

SAFETY AND THE TABLE SAW

The table saw can be used quite safely if reasonable care is taken and certain fundamental rules are followed. For the guidance of the beginner, the following rules are given:

1. Keep the machine lubricated and in first-class condition at all times.
2. Never use a dull saw or one that does not have sufficient set. It may cause a kickback.
3. Tighten all screws and levers before starting the machine, and make no adjustments while the saw is running.
4. Leave no tools or pieces of wood on the saw table, and keep the floor around the machine clean and in good condition.
5. Use all guards and safety devices whenever possible.
6. Stock to be ripped must lie flat on the table and have a straight, true edge to be guided along the ripping fence. Never saw "freehand."
7. The saw blade should not project more than $\frac{1}{8}$ inch above the stock being sawed.
8. Never reach over the saw to pick up stock that has been sawed.
9. Stand slightly to one side of the saw, never in line with it.
10. Always use a clearance block or push stick when cutting to length against the ripping fence.
11. Do not wear gloves and loose-fitting or ragged clothing. Always tuck your necktie inside your shirt.
12. Do not take your eyes off the work you are doing, and do not talk to anyone while using the saw.

A kickback means that stock being sawed is thrown back toward the operator with great force and speed. This is one of the greatest hazards in running a bench saw and must at all costs be avoided. A kickback may be caused by:

1. Using a dull saw or a saw with insufficient set
2. Cutting "freehand" or ripping badly warped wood
3. Failure to use the splitter guard
4. Crosscutting against the ripping fence without using a clearance block
5. Pieces of wood dropped on an unguarded saw

BLADE-TABLE ALIGNMENT AND OTHER ADJUSTMENTS

Since the rip fence and miter gauge both rely on the table for their alignment, it is of critical importance that the table itself be correctly squared with the saw blade. To check the blade-table alignment, crank the blade up to maximum elevation, and mark one of the teeth with a crayon. Turn the blade until the marked tooth is even with the surface of the table, and carefully measure the distance, at a right angle to the blade, from the marked tooth to the edge of the table. Then rotate the blade until the marked tooth is even with the surface of the table at the other end of the blade slot, and measure again. The two measurements should be identical; otherwise the blade is out of alignment and will have to be adjusted. Another way to check this alignment is to set the miter gauge at exactly 90°, using a combination square. Place the miter gauge in its slot and, again with the combination square, make sure that the face of the gauge is at 90° to the blade. (Hold the square against the flat of the blade, and not against a raked-out tooth.) If you find that the blade is out of alignment, the necessary adjustment can easily be made by loosening the bolts that hold the arbor assembly to the table.

To check the vertical blade alignment, crank the tilt control as far as it will go with the blade in the straight-up position; then check with the combination square to see if the blade is at an exact 90° vertical position relative to the table surface. If not, sawdust in the tilt-mechanism track may be preventing the tilt from riding all the way against the stop; or you may have to correct the stop itself, which is usually an easily adjusted bolt. When this has been done and the blade is positioned at 90°, check the tilt indicator. This should read exactly 0° when the blade is in the vertical position. To adjust the pointer, simply loosen the screw that holds it to the arbor and set it correctly.

The miter gauge should glide smoothly and easily in its slot. If it does not, sprinkle a bit of automotive valve-grinding compound in the slot, and slide the gauge back and forth until it moves freely; then clean and wax both the slide bar and the slot. Set the miter gauge at 90° with your combination square, and check the indicator for accuracy; if it does not read 90°, loosen the retaining screw and adjust the pointer accordingly.

With the square, check the rip fence to see that its side surfaces are vertical to the surface of the table. If they are not, turn the fence upside down and adjust the alignment bar. This is the part of the fence that rides against the table, usually the front edge, and maintains the fence's lateral alignment with the table. In each end of this bar you will find an adjusting screw or pad that can be raised or lowered, thus correcting any error in vertical alignment.

Finally, check the lateral alignments of the fence by cutting two small wood blocks to fit snugly into the ends of the miter-gauge slot, and locking the fence up against these blocks. If there is a gap between the fence and either block, there are two screws in the guide bar (where you made the vertical-alignment adjustment) that can be loosened to allow the guide bar to be shifted to the correct lateral alignment.

Check all nuts, bolts, and screws for tightness. Check the arbor bearings by cranking the blade all the way up, and then trying to wiggle it; if you can feel play, replace the arbor bearings. Check the elevation and tilt gears and tracks to make certain these are functioning properly.

No alignment procedures or adjustments should be made while the saw is operating.

LUBRICATION Most of the newer saws and motors are built with either sealed or oilless bearings, but if yours has lubrication fittings on the motor or arbor assemblies then give each a modest squirt of light machine oil every 6 months. Do not oil anything that does not have an oil fitting, but apply graphite-dust lubricant liberally on the other working parts of the saw. Oil on any exposed part will only collect sawdust and eventually clog up the works.

PLAIN SAWING

Probably 90 percent of all operations on the table or bench saw are ripping and crosscutting. It should be noted again that a table saw should not be used without the saw guard in place. In the majority of photographs shown in this chapter, the guard has been removed for the sake of clarity. While there are a few special operations which require the removal of the guard, they are exceptions to the rule and will be mentioned when those operations are described. Remember, the rule is: Use all guards and safety devices whenever possible.

RIPPING Ripping is the operation of making a lengthwise cut through a board. One edge of the work rides against the guide fence while the flat side of the board rests on the table. These contact surfaces of the work must be reasonably straight and true. If the work has a crooked edge, it will be impossible to guide it in a straight line to the saw. Then, when the work departs from a straight and true feed, the saw will become jammed in the saw cut, leading to bucking of the work and, if the piece is light, an actual kicking back of the work toward the operator. The danger in the kickback is that if your hands are near the saw blade at the time, one or both hands may be jerked loose and thrown into the blade. The approved sawing method is therefore aimed at preventing kickbacks; then, as an extra precaution, the hands are kept in the clear, "just in case."

The start of a ripping cut on a long board demands no particular method; stand where you like behind the saw, hold the work with both hands, and push it along the fence and into the saw blade. At the stage shown in Figure 14-18, the left hand is removed from the work, and the feed is continued with the right hand only. If the cut is 3 inches or wider, the right hand can safely feed the work right past the blade. After the work is beyond the saw, the feed hand is removed from the work. When this is done, the workpiece will either (1) stay on the table; (2) tilt up slightly and be caught by the splitter; or (3) if no splitter is used and if the work is long, tilt up and slide off the table to the floor. Alternatively, the feed can continue to the end of the table, after which the work is lifted and brought back along the outside edge of the fence. The waste stock remains on the saw table and is not touched with the hands until the saw is stopped, unless it is a large piece allowing safe removal. If the ripped work is less than 3 inches wide, a push stick should be used to complete the feed; the stick is brought into use at the stage shown in Figure 14-19.

When making a push stick such as the one shown in Figure 14-20, make sure that the stick is thinner than the

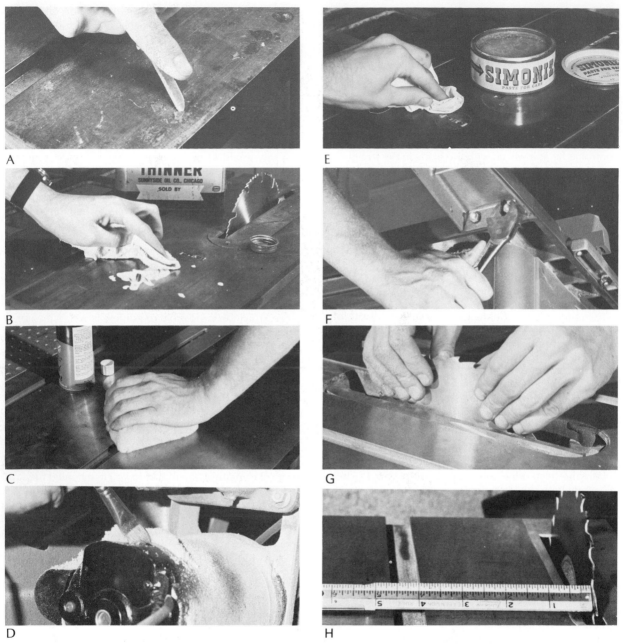

FIG. 14-13. Saw care and adjustments: (*a*) A sharp knife chips off glue spatters. (*b*) Lacquer thinner will remove paint spots. (*c*) Rub with metal polish to remove rust. (*d*) Brush sawdust from inside the machine. (*e*) Give the frame, motor, blade, table, and accessories an occasional coating of paste wax. (*f*) Tighten all nuts and bolts, both inside and outside. (*g*) To check the arbor bearing, wiggle the blade to test for play. (*h*) Measure from the blade to the table edge at both ends of the slot to check blade-table alignment. (*i*) Check the miter gauge with a combination square. (*j*) Use a combination square to check that the blade is at a right angle to the face of the miter gauge. (*k*) Check the vertical blade alignment. (*l*) Make sure that sawdust in the tilt-mechanism track is not interfering with the saw's alignment. (*m*) Apply grinding compound to the gauge slot so the gauge slides freely. (*n*) Set the miter-gauge pointer to give an accurate reading. (*o*) See that the rip fence is vertical to the table. (*p*) Adjust the alignment bar on the rip fence. (*q*) Check clamping by pushing firmly on the front of rip fence before locking in position. (*r*) To check the ripping accuracy, lock the fence against the blocks in the gauge slot.

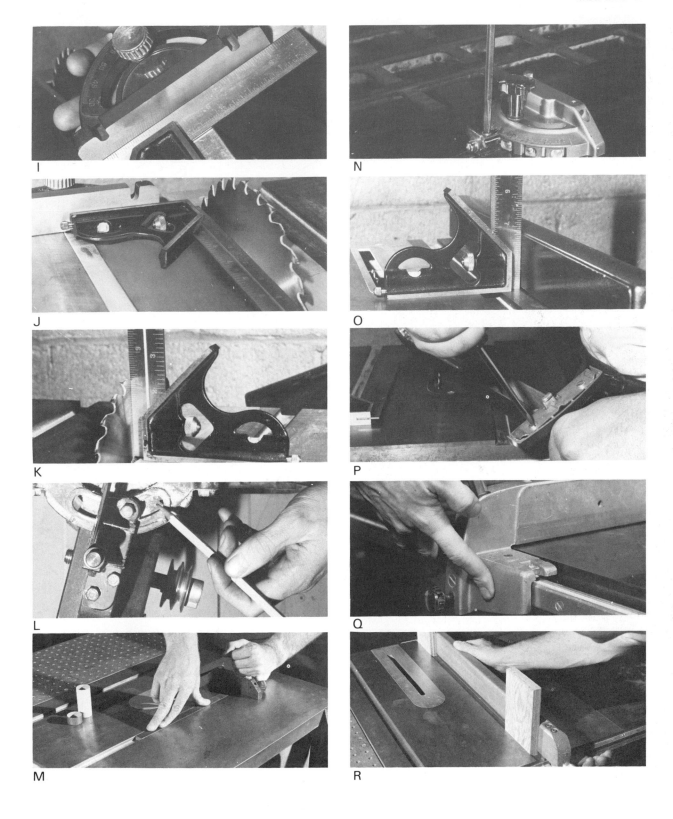

I

N

J

K

O

P

L

Q

M

R

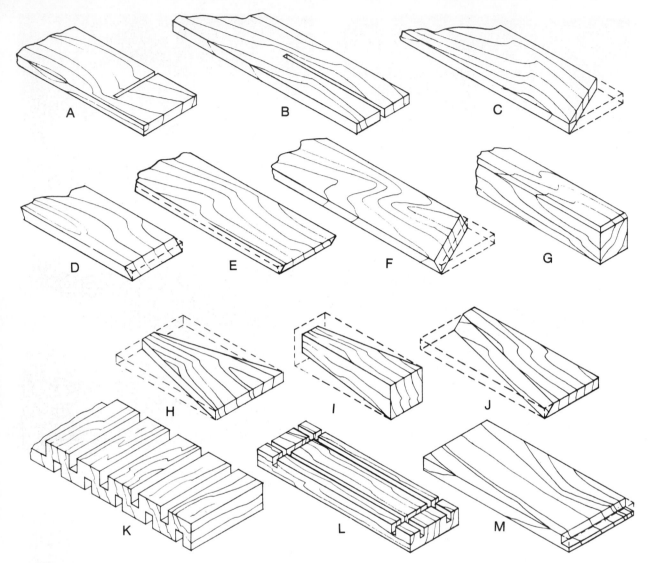

FIG. 14-14. Typical cuts that can be made on a table saw: (a) crosscut; (b) rip; (c) miter; (d) cross bevel; (e) rip bevel; (f) compound miter; (g) chamfer; (h) two-side taper; (i) four-side taper; (j) compound rip bevel; (k) kerfing; (l) kerfing; (m) rabbet (two pass).

FIG. 14-15. The safest blade cutting position is ¼ inch above the top of the workpiece.

width of the stock to be cut. If the push stick is too wide, it will not clear between the guard and the fence. Even more dangerous, if the saw cuts into the end of the stick, it may flip out of your hand, causing your hand to drop into the saw or making the stock kick back.

Any board that could sag down behind the saw before the completion of the cut must be supported in such a manner that the end you are holding cannot be whipped up off the table. Any saw-table-height support will do, but a home-made roller support (Figure 14-21) is recommended. Hold your end of the board up level while feeding, and use the appropriate feeding method.

FIG. 14-18. Hook the last three fingers over the fence, and push the work with the thumb.

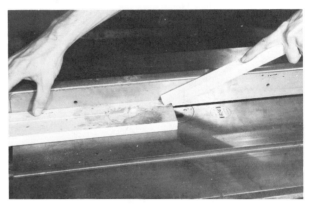

FIG. 14-19. For narrow rips, use a push stick and hold the workpiece with the other hand.

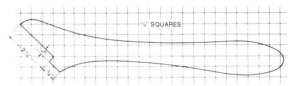

FIG. 14-20. Simple push stick.

FIG. 14-16. The table-saw teeth rotate in the direction of the operator, and enter the top surface first. Therefore, place the wood with the finished side upward (top). This applies to plain plywood, veneers, and any form of plywood with laminates attached. Where both sides of the wood are finished, use a fine-tooth blade without any set at all, or use a cabinetmaker's hollow-ground saw blade with the teeth widely spaced and without set (bottom). The saw blade can then enter from either side.

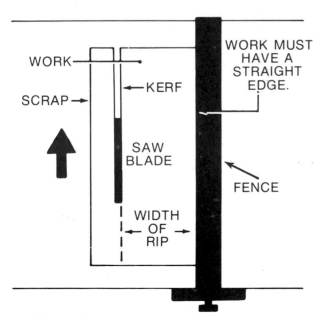

FIG. 14-17. Ripping is sawing through a workpiece while using the fence as a guide.

RESAWING Resawing is the operation of ripping a thick board to make a thin board. If the work does not exceed the capacity of the saw, the cut can be treated as a regular ripping operation. But, before attempting this operation, it is necessary to make a jig called a "fingerboard" or "featherboard." A featherboard is a board cut off at an angle of 60°. At that cut end, a series of parallel cuts is made partway through the board, as sketched in Figure 14-22a.

The featherboard is clamped to the saw table in such a way that it bears against the workpiece to be resawed and has its long edge opposite the front of the saw. It holds the

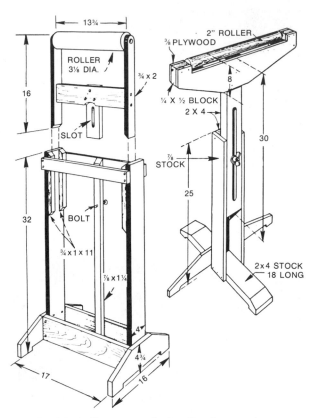

FIG. 14-21. Roller supports for handling long work on a table or jointer.

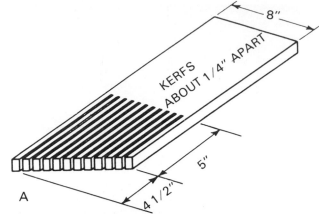

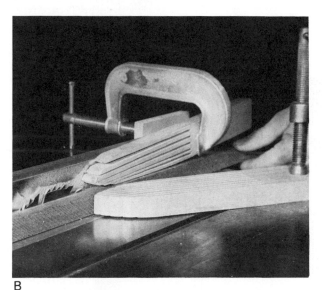

FIG. 14-22. (a) One style of fingerboard or featherboard; (b) another design of featherboard in use.

stock firmly against the ripping fence, and its "fingers" prevent it from being thrown back. If it were clamped farther forward, it would bear against the saw cut and pinch the saw.

If the board thickness is within the maximum capacity of the blade, it can be resawed in one pass; if it is thicker, but not more than twice as thick, it can be resawed in two passes (one with each edge down; see Figure 14-23a); if it is over twice as thick, two passes may come close enough to severing it (Figure 14-23b) so that the job can be finished by handsawing or on a band saw. That is, the cuts made on the circular saw help in either case to make the rest of the cut straight and to reduce the labor. It is not easy to resaw a thick plank entirely on a band saw, because the blade has a tendency to weave in and out. The cuts made on the table saw help it to keep a straight line.

When two passes are required, it is necessary to remove the saw-blade guard; hence extra care must be taken to keep your hands away from the blade. Set the blade height so that the first cut will be no deeper than halfway through the workpiece. Then (unless the blade is already at maximum height) raise the blade so that the second cut will overlap the first by $\frac{1}{8}$ to $\frac{1}{4}$ inch. To feed the

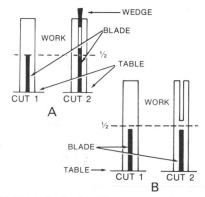

FIG. 14-23. Methods of making two cuts when resawing.

workpiece, hold it at the top and sides—never hold it at the end to push. When you make the second cut, if there is any tendency for the first-cut kerf to squeeze closed, use wedges to hold it open.

BEVEL RIPPING AND CHAMFERING In beveling, the saw blade is tilted. If the blade tilts to the right, the ripping fence remains on the right side of the saw; if it tilts to the left, the ripping fence must be moved to the left side of the saw blade. The reason for this is that the board on which the bevel or chamfer is to be cut must rest against

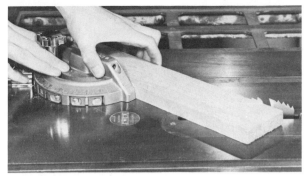

FIG. 14-26. Making a miter crosscut.

FIG. 14-24. Cutting a bevel on an edge.

FIG. 14-27. An auxiliary fence extends the miter gauge for larger crosscut work.

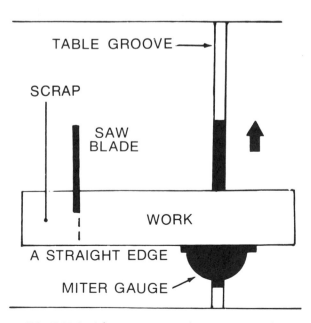

TABLE GROOVE

SCRAP

SAW
BLADE

WORK

A STRAIGHT EDGE

MITER GAUGE

FIG. 14-25. Straight crosscutting with a miter gauge. The miter gauge can be used at the right or left side.

FIG. 14-28. Attach an auxiliary fence or support to the rip fence when edge cutting a large board.

the ripping fence. Otherwise, it would be difficult to hold the board against the fence, and a kickback might result. A bevel is cut right across the edge of a board; it is therefore not square to the surface. A chamfer is cut only partway, that is, only the sharp corner between face and edge is flattened.

CROSSCUTTING Crosscutting is sawing through a workpiece while using the miter gauge to guide it. All rectangular workpieces that are to be sawed from one long edge to the other must be crosscut. It follows that when a natural-wood board is crosscut it is sawed across the grain. If the cut is at 90° to the board edge against the miter-gauge face, it is a straight crosscut. A miter crosscut is a cut for which this angle is other than 90°.

Because it slides (in its table groove) on a line parallel with the saw blade, the miter gauge will guide a workpiece held firmly against it for a true, straight-line cut. However, the work must be firmly held. Use two hands—one on the miter-gauge handle, and the other holding the workpiece in place against the miter-gauge face. To prevent a long board from wobbling use a miter-gauge auxiliary facing to provide a longer "face" against which to hold the work. To help prevent creeping, glue sandpaper to the miter-gauge (or auxiliary) face. An additional safeguard against both wobbling and creeping is the miter-gauge hold-down clamp.

The miter gauge may be used in either table groove. If you are using the left-hand groove, hold the miter-gauge handle with your right hand, and use your left hand to hold the workpiece. Reverse these hand positions if the miter gauge is in the right-hand groove. Always keep both hands at the same side of the saw blade; never place them at opposite sides (doing so could bind the blade and cause a kickback).

When making a straight crosscut, set and lock the miter gauge at 0°. Draw a line on the workpiece at the cut-off point; make the line long enough to use for sighting. Position the work against the miter-gauge face; then shift it sideways as necessary to align your cut-off line with the saw blade. If the scrap piece is at the left, the cut-off line should be aligned with the right side of the blade (so that the kerf will be in the scrap) and vice versa. Either firmly hold or clamp the work in this position; then start the motor and make the crosscut. Wait for the blade to stop before picking up the pieces or returning the miter gauge to the starting position.

In making a miter crosscut, there are two methods of setting up:

1. Set and lock the miter gauge at the desired angle. Mark the start of the cut (where the blade will enter) on your workpiece; then position the work as explained for a straight crosscut.
2. Draw the cut-off line (long enough for sighting) on your workpiece; then position the work against the miter-gauge face. Simultaneously shift the work and alter the miter-gauge angle until this cut-off line is aligned with the saw blade. Then lock the miter gauge and hold (or clamp) the workpiece in place.

In either case, the cut is made in the same way as a straight crosscut. However, there will be considerably more tendency for the workpiece to creep, and extra precautions should be taken.

CROSSCUTTING STOCK TO LENGTH If a number of short pieces are to be cut to the same length, the best method is to use the ripping fence with a clearance block clamped to it as a stop. Hold the stock against the miter gauge while cutting, but be sure to use a clearance block; otherwise a kickback is certain to result. Also use the guard over the saw and the splitter guard so that the pieces cut off will not be picked up by the back teeth and thrown forward.

To cut longer pieces to length, use the stop rod in the miter gauge, and move the ripping fence out of the way. Measure the distance from the stop block to one sawtooth set to the left. Square one end first on all the pieces, hold the squared end against the stop block, and make the cut (Figure 14-30).

If the workpieces are longer than the stop rod will reach, an auxiliary fence will have to be made and screwed to the miter gauge. Remove the ripping fence from the machine, and be sure to make the auxiliary fence long enough on both sides so that it will not tip the miter gauge. Nail, screw, or clamp a stop to the auxiliary fence at the correct length.

BEVEL CROSSCUTTING Set the blade at the desired angle, and cut in the normal crosscut manner. When setting the blade at the bevel, use the miter gauge in the right-hand table groove (so that the blade is tilted away from the gauge).

FIG. 14-29. To end cut a small board, clamp it to a larger piece of wood.

FIG. 14-30. A stop block clamped to the rip fence facilitates duplicate cutting.

FIG. 14-31. To make a compound cut, adjust both the blade and the miter gauge.

FIG. 14-32. Making a dado crosscut.

DADO OPERATIONS

The regular table insert must be replaced with a dado insert (refer to your owner's manual for the correct one) which has a slot wide enough to accommodate a full-width dado head. For dado-head mounting and width-spacing (or adjustable-dado setting) instructions, refer to the owner's manual supplied with your accessory. A dado head can be used with the saw arbor tilted (for a bevel cut), but not in all positions. Too great an angle, depending upon the width of cut of the dado, will cause the dado head to strike and destroy the table insert. Never tilt the arbor while the saw is running. Disconnect your tool, elevate and/or tilt the dado as desired, and test it by rotating it with a piece of wood to be sure it clears the insert, before turning the power on.

A dado head must never be used for through sawing—only for cutting partway through (or into) a workpiece. Therefore, the saw guard cannot be used. Remove the

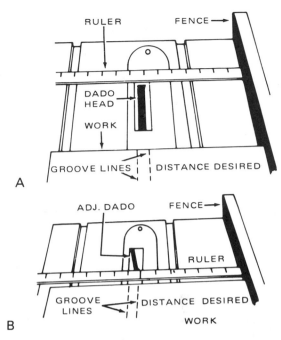

FIG. 14-33. Measuring for (a) a conventional dado head and (b) an adjustable dado head.

saw guard for dado operations, but be sure to reinstall it as soon as these operations are completed.

Dadoing operations, both ripping and crosscutting, must be done in the manner described above for these operations. Although the dado blade does not project above the workpiece top, do not forget that it will be exposed at the end of the cut; *keep your hands out of the line of the cut.* Because dadoing is done "blind" (on the underside of the work), and because of the varying widths of dado cuts, the workpiece is aligned with a dado differently than with a saw blade.

To position the head for dado ripping, the "distance desired" can be established with a ruler. When measuring to a dado head, measure to a tooth set toward the fence; when measuring to an adjustable dado, rotate the blade (by hand) to establish the nearest approach of blade teeth to the fence (they wobble nearer and further), and then measure accordingly. Instead of a ruler you can use "groove lines" (as shown in Figure 14-33a and b) marked on the workpiece top, and sight along these lines to the extreme tooth sides of the dado head (or adjustable dado). In any case, for utmost accuracy it is best to test your setting on a piece of scrap.

In positioning the head for dado crosscutting, the quickest way to locate the work in the miter gauge is to draw groove lines on the workpiece top and leading edge, and then do the aligning by eye. A more accurate method is illustrated in Figure 14-34. Mark an X on the workpiece at a measured distance from the desired

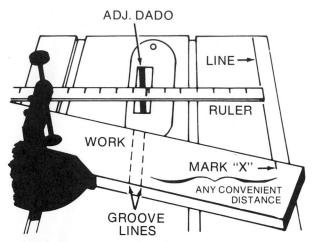

FIG. 14-34. Positioning for dado crosscutting.

groove. Measure this same distance from the dado, and mark the table with a line parallel to the dado. The X can now be aligned with this line.

To save setup time for both ripping and crosscutting operations, you can mark your dado insert as illustrated in Figure 14-35 . For each much-used dado width ($\frac{1}{8}$ inch, $\frac{1}{4}$ inch, $\frac{3}{8}$ inch, etc.), set up your dado and elevate it as high as possible. Lay a steel rule along the right side of the dado (just touching the tooth set, or wobbled to the right), and use a scratch awl to mark both ends of the insert. Code your marks. These can now be used for aligning the right sides of correspondingly wide grooves drawn on workpieces. While you are at it, also scribe "C/L" on your insert, directly over the centerline of the saw arbor. This is useful for setting the dado elevation.

When elevating a dado for the depth of a groove, keep in mind the fact that the maximum depth is produced by the tooth tips as they pass the vertical centerline of the blade. If you have marked the position of this centerline on your dado insert, setting an accurate elevation is not difficult. You can either use a ruler as shown in Figure 14-36, or make a depth-of-cut mark on the workpiece edge (or end) and use it instead. In either case, revolve the dado by hand to position a tooth tip on the centerline, and measure to this tip. If a ruler is used, measure at the left side of the blade where the dado insert is narrowest and least likely to spring down to spoil the measurement. In fact, it is best to use a wide ruler turned crosswise to the dado so it will rest partly on the solid table.

If a groove wider than the dado is needed, it must be made in two or more passes, all at the same elevation setting. It is preferable to make the two outside cuts first, aligning each carefully with its respective side of the dado. The center cuts can then be made without particular attention to alignment; simply have each cut overlap the adjacent one(s) by at least $\frac{1}{16}$ inch.

As previously mentioned, making a wide, deep dado

groove can slow down the motor. In addition to overheating the motor, this can result in a cut with ragged edges. The depth of cut should be restricted as noted in Table 14-1.

Table 14-1 Maximum Depths of Cut for Dadoes

In softwood, inches		In hardwood, inches	
Wide	Deep	Wide	Deep
$\frac{1}{4}$	1	$\frac{1}{4}$	$\frac{1}{2}$
$\frac{3}{8}$	$\frac{7}{8}$	$\frac{3}{8}$	$\frac{7}{16}$
$\frac{1}{2}$	$\frac{3}{4}$	$\frac{1}{2}$	$\frac{3}{8}$
$\frac{5}{8}$	$\frac{5}{8}$	$\frac{5}{8}$	$\frac{5}{16}$
$\frac{3}{4}$	$\frac{1}{2}$	$\frac{3}{4}$	$\frac{1}{4}$
$\frac{7}{8}$	$\frac{3}{8}$	$\frac{7}{8}$	$\frac{3}{16}$
1	$\frac{1}{4}$	1	$\frac{1}{8}$

Make each pass without altering the workpiece setup, continuing to increase the dado elevation, as indicated in the table, until the desired depth is reached.

EDGE GROOVING The long edge of a workpiece is grooved with exactly the setup used for resawing. First elevate the dado to the required depth of cut; then position the regular fence to align the dado with the groove marks on your workpiece. Position the auxiliary fence to serve its purpose, and make the cut.

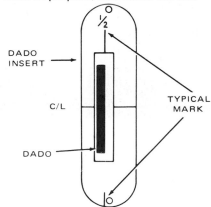

FIG. 14-35. How to mark a dado insert plate.

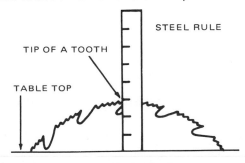

FIG. 14-36. Elevating a dado for depth of groove.

END GROOVING Because it is very difficult to feed a long board (12 inches or more) on end, the only recommended method of performing this operation is with the universal jig. Position the work on the jig so the bottom end just slides free^{ly} along the table; then adjust the dado elevation as requ ▷'. Adjust the jig to align the cut, and lock it. Handle the jig in the same way as the miter gauge for feeding the workpiece to the dado.

BEVEL GROOVING Grooves that are to be made with the dado tilted to a desired bevel angle are cut by using the ripping or crosscutting procedures previously described. Alignment is, however, more difficult; the only practical method is to draw the desired groove on the leading workpiece end (or edge) and sight from the rear of the table along the dado to set the dado elevation and workpiece position for the cut. In addition, the angled dado will produce a strong creeping tendency. When ripping, it is best to locate the fence at the right side of the dado; when crosscutting, use the miter-gauge hold-down clamp. In any case, hold the workpiece securely.

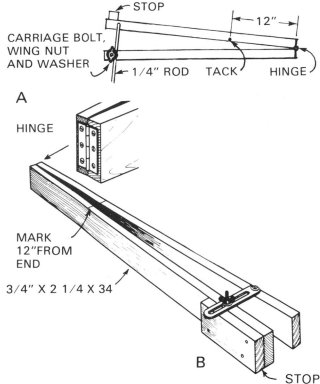

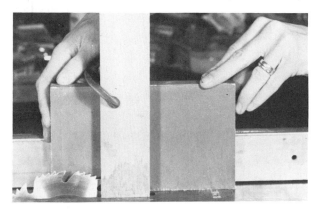

FIG. 14-37. End grooving with a universal jig.

SPECIAL SAW AND DADO OPERATIONS

Special operations performed on the circular saw include taper ripping, rabbeting, pattern sawing, cove cutting, and the sawing of compound angles. These operations are easy and safe to do, and, while the nature of the work is different, the actual handling of the saw does not vary greatly from the plain ripping and crosscutting described earlier in this chapter.

TAPER RIPPING Tapering is cutting one end of a board or table leg narrower or smaller than the other. A jig for tapering boards is shown in Figure 14-38. It consists of two narrow boards hinged together at one end and connected at the other by a slotted strip of metal which permits the jig to be locked in any position. The taper per foot is equal to the distance between the boards 12 inches from the hinged end. This jig will conveniently handle work up to 24 inches length; workpieces up to 36 inches long can be tapered if you use an auxiliary fence to extend the regular fence about 18 inches over the front edge of

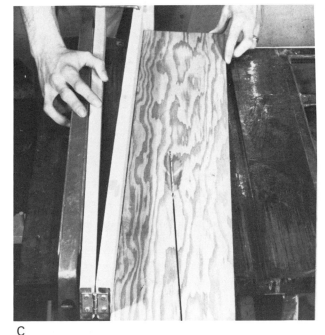

FIG. 14-38. (a) Typical taper jig; (b) how it is set; (c) how it is used.

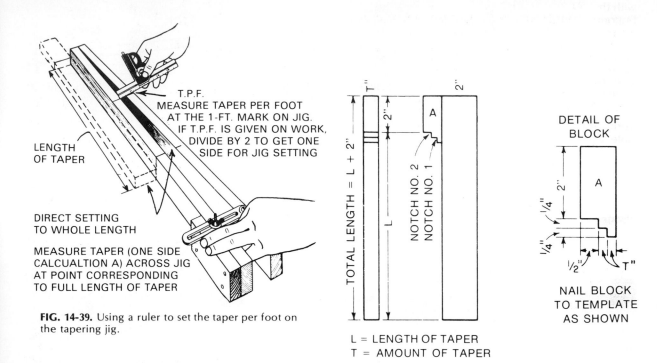

T.P.F.
MEASURE TAPER PER FOOT
AT THE 1-FT. MARK ON JIG.
IF T.P.F. IS GIVEN ON WORK,
DIVIDE BY 2 TO GET ONE
SIDE FOR JIG SETTING

LENGTH
OF TAPER

DIRECT SETTING
TO WHOLE LENGTH

MEASURE TAPER (ONE SIDE
CALCUALTION A) ACROSS JIG
AT POINT CORRESPONDING
TO FULL LENGTH OF TAPER

FIG. 14-39. Using a ruler to set the taper per foot on the tapering jig.

TOTAL LENGTH = L + 2"

NOTCH NO. 2
NOTCH NO. 1

L = LENGTH OF TAPER
T = AMOUNT OF TAPER

DETAIL OF
BLOCK

NAIL BLOCK
TO TEMPLATE
AS SHOWN

B

DETERMINING TAPER

A OVERALL TAPER

TAPER
EACH SIDE = $\dfrac{W-W_1}{2}$

EXAMPLE:

$TAPER = \dfrac{1.50 - .75}{2} = \dfrac{.75}{2} = .375 = 3/8"$

B TAPER PER FOOT EACH SIDE

$TAPER = \dfrac{W-W_1}{L} \times 6$

SAME EXAMPLE AS ABOVE:

$TAPER = \dfrac{1.50 - .75}{18} \times \dfrac{6}{1}$

$TAPER = \dfrac{.75}{\underset{3}{\cancel{18}}} \times \dfrac{\cancel{6}}{1} = \dfrac{.75}{3} = .25 = 1/4"$

C TAPER PER FOOT (ONE SIDE ONLY)

SAME FORMULA AS B BUT
MULTIPLY BY 12 INSTEAD OF 6

$TAPER = \dfrac{1.50 - .75}{18} \times \dfrac{12}{1}$

$TAPER = \dfrac{.75}{\underset{3}{\cancel{18}}} \times \dfrac{\overset{2}{\cancel{12}}}{1} = \dfrac{1.5}{3} = .5 = 1/2"$

A

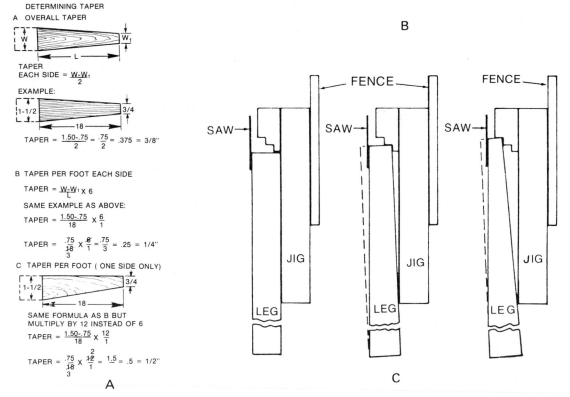

FENCE   FENCE

SAW   SAW   SAW

JIG   JIG   JIG

LEG   LEG   LEG

C

FIG. 14-40. (a) How a symmetrical taper is calculated; (b) Details of a typical tapering guide; (c) How it should be used.

the table. If the tapered cut-off line is drawn on the workpiece, the jig can be set by eye to align the cut-off line with the blade; or, you can use a ruler to equalize measurements A and B in Figure 14-39.

When only one side of a workpiece is to be tapered, you can use the following formulas to lay out your work for marking and setting up.

$$T \text{ (taper)} = 12\frac{W - X}{L}$$

$$X \text{ (small end)} = W - \frac{L \times T}{12}$$

$$W \text{ (big end)} = X + \frac{L \times T}{12}$$

$$L \text{ (length)} = 12\frac{W - X}{T}$$

To taper two opposite sides symmetrically, a 6 is substituted for the 12 in each of the formulas. For instance, the amount of taper is calculated as shown in Figure 14-40a.

When you set the jig for the first of two opposite symmetrical tapers, set it for the calculated taper per side (in the formula); however, when setting it to cut the second (opposite) side, double the jig opening. If you are symmetrically tapering all four sides of a square workpiece (like a table leg), set up for the first taper and do two adjacent sides; then set up for the second (doubled) taper and do the two remaining sides.

Another jig for cutting tapers on table legs is shown in Figure 14-40b. With the work dressed to net size and perfectly square, the saw fence is set to equal the combined width of work and guide board, as shown in Figure 14-40c. The leg is then placed in the first notch of the jig, and the combined jig and work are pushed into

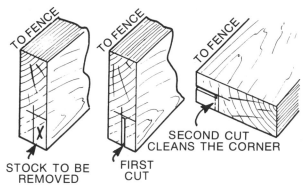

FIG. 14-42. Steps in cutting a rabbet with a standard blade.

the saw. An adjacent side of the work is cut in the same manner, while the two remaining sides are cut with the work in the second notch. No change is made in the fence setting.

Both jigs can be employed to taper-rip with the radial-arm saw and band saw.

CUTTING A RABBET A rabbet is a groove cut in an adjoining edge and side of a board; it is used in picture, mirror, and window frames. The groove is cut out by making one saw cut from the side of the board and another from the edge. Lay out the rabbet on the end of the board, and first make the shallow cut: Raise the saw blade to the depth of the rabbet, measure the width of the groove to a sawtooth pointing away from the fence, and make the cut, placing the board flat on the table. For the next cut, measure the depth of the rabbet from the fence to a sawtooth pointing away from the fence, raise the saw up enough to meet the first saw cut, place the board on edge with the rabbet against the fence, and make the second saw cut. This will cut loose a strip of wood, which will probably fly backward like an arrow. The saw guard

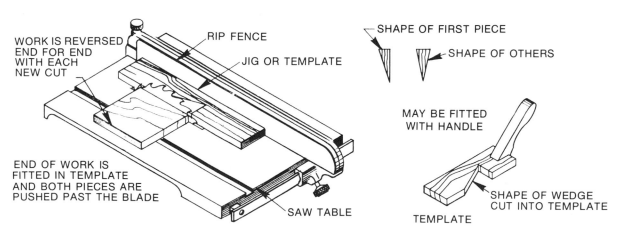

FIG. 14-41. Using a template to cut small wedges or tapers.

FIG. 14-43. Cutting a rabbet with a dado head.

cannot be used for cutting rabbets.

Sometimes a shallow rabbet is cut on the face and edge of a tabletop which later is to be rounded with a block plane. However, a shaper can be used to perform these two operations at one time. If the top is round, the rabbet can also be cut on the bench saw, provided a cradle of the same curvature as the top is made and clamped to the table with a couple of hand screws. The saw is kept below the table while the ripping fence is adjusted and the cradle is clamped to the top. The saw is then started and brought up through the cradle until it is high enough to cut a rabbet of the required depth.

RAISED PANELS The basic raised panel in Figure 14-44 is obtained by saw-blade rabbeting all four sides of a prepared square or rectangular workpiece, using a bevel angle for the cuts. If exactly the same setups are used for the four rabbets, the panel will be centered, and the face slopes and side heights will all be equal. After making a setup, cut all four sides before proceeding to the next setup. Panels B and C are like A, except that an extra setup (cut 3) is required. Panel D is produced by using only bevel-ripping and/or crosscutting procedures; for cuts 3 and 4, elevate the blade to reach only halfway into the kerfs of cuts 1 and 2.

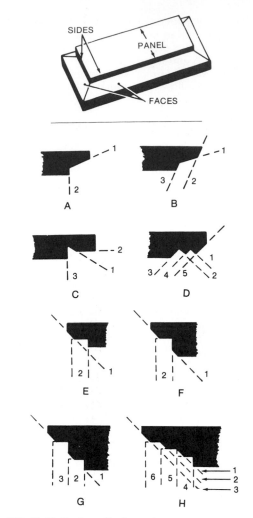

FIG. 14-44. Cutting raised panels.

Table 14-2 Table of Compound Angles

Tilt of work	Equivalent taper per inch	Four-sided butt		Four-sided miter		Six-sided miter		Eight-sided miter	
		Bevel	Miter	Bevel	Miter	Bevel	Miter	Bevel	Miter
5°	0.087	$\frac{1}{2}$	85	$44\frac{3}{4}$	85	$29\frac{3}{4}$	$87\frac{1}{2}$	$22\frac{1}{4}$	88
10°	0.176	$1\frac{1}{2}$	$80\frac{1}{4}$	$44\frac{1}{4}$	$80\frac{1}{4}$	$29\frac{1}{2}$	$84\frac{1}{2}$	22	86
15°	0.268	$3\frac{3}{4}$	$75\frac{1}{2}$	$43\frac{1}{4}$	$75\frac{1}{2}$	29	$81\frac{3}{4}$	$21\frac{1}{2}$	84
20°	0.364	$6\frac{1}{4}$	$71\frac{1}{4}$	$41\frac{3}{4}$	$71\frac{1}{4}$	$28\frac{1}{4}$	79	21	82
25°	0.466	10	67	40	67	$27\frac{1}{4}$	$76\frac{1}{2}$	$20\frac{1}{4}$	80
30°	0.577	$14\frac{1}{2}$	$63\frac{1}{2}$	$37\frac{3}{4}$	$63\frac{1}{2}$	26	74	$19\frac{1}{2}$	$78\frac{1}{4}$
35°	0.700	$19\frac{1}{2}$	$60\frac{1}{4}$	$35\frac{1}{4}$	$60\frac{1}{4}$	$24\frac{1}{2}$	$70\frac{3}{4}$	$18\frac{1}{4}$	$76\frac{3}{4}$
40°	0.839	$24\frac{1}{2}$	$57\frac{1}{4}$	$32\frac{1}{2}$	$57\frac{1}{4}$	$22\frac{3}{4}$	$69\frac{3}{4}$	17	75
45°	1.000	30	$54\frac{3}{4}$	30	$54\frac{3}{4}$	21	$67\frac{3}{4}$	$15\frac{3}{4}$	$73\frac{3}{4}$
50°	1.19	36	$52\frac{1}{2}$	27	$52\frac{1}{2}$	19	$66\frac{1}{4}$	$14\frac{1}{4}$	$72\frac{1}{2}$
55°	1.43	42	$50\frac{3}{4}$	24	$50\frac{3}{4}$	$16\frac{3}{4}$	$64\frac{3}{4}$	$12\frac{1}{2}$	$71\frac{1}{4}$
60°	1.73	48	49	21	49	$14\frac{1}{2}$	$63\frac{1}{2}$	11	$70\frac{1}{4}$

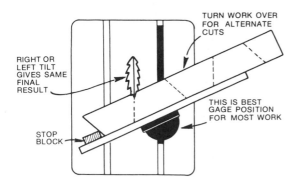

FIG. 14-45. Continuous cutting of compound angles.

As indicated by the illustrations, there are a variety of ways to decorate a raised panel. Four additional suggestions (E through H) are shown in Figure 14-44. These can be done entirely with a saw blade, but the use of a dado (as indicated) reduces the number of setups. Use a standard dado head or an adjustable dado set for maximum width of cut. These will provide surfaces that are straight enough to be sanded smooth. If desired, all cuts (even those indicated as saw-blade cuts) can be made with the dado. In any case, all the cuts can be made with the workpiece flat on the table.

COMPOUND-ANGLE SAWING A compound angle made on the circular saw requires both a tilt of the blade (or table) and a swing of the miter gauge. In other words, a miter and a bevel are cut in one pass. Cuts of this kind are required for making boxes with tilted sides, sawhorses, pedestal stands, and similar work. Compound cuts are also required in making tables with splayed legs if the outward tilt is over 10°. The basic figure is a box, which can have four, six, or eight sides, all equally tilted. Table 14-2 gives the saw settings at 5° intervals, so the work should be planned to match. Joints for a four-sided figure can be either butted or mitered. Six- and eight-sided figures are always mitered because on such work a butt joint would be poor construction.

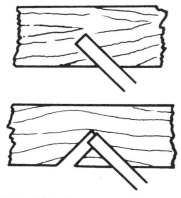

FIG. 14-46. Saw-blade V groove at 45°.

The actual sawing is as simple as a common miter. All you do is refer to the table and set the miter gauge and blade (or table) tilt to the figures given for the type of box and amount of slope required. Large work can be cut from individual boards, but, if the job allows, it is better to cut all parts from one board, as shown in Figure 14-45, turning the work over for alternate cuts. If the edges of the board are square, any miter-gauge position can be used. For general work of this kind, the closed position shown in Figure 14-45 is best.

V-GROOVE CUTTING Clean-cut (45° bevel-angle) V grooves of any depth up to the maximum blade elevation are most easily made with a saw blade in two cuts, as shown in Figure 14-46. The second cut requires rotating the workpiece 180°; the blade elevation should be reduced so the cut enters only halfway into the first-cut kerf.

V grooves also can be made with a standard dado head or adjustable dado set at the maximum width of cut. Any multiple-cut variations, such as the stepped and truncated grooves illustrated in Figure 14-47, require very precise setting up. All cuts are made by using the appropriate ripping or crosscut procedure.

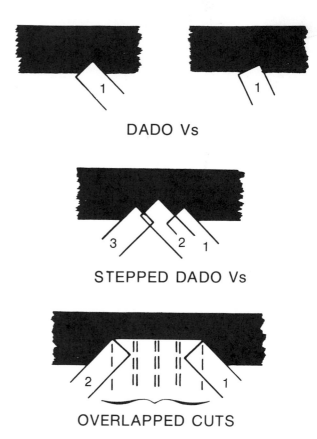

FIG. 14-47. Truncated dado V groove.

SAW-CUT MOLDINGS Several attractive moldings can be made with saw cuts only. The zigzag shape shown at the top of Figure 14-48 is commonly called a "dentil molding," although this term has broad application and can include many different shapes. The setup is made by fastening a wood facing to the miter gauge. A nail is driven into the wood facing to act as a guide pin, as can be seen in Figure 14-49; the distance from nail to blade determines the spacing of the saw cuts.

To complete the molding, the saw is set at a suitable projection, and repeat cuts are made by ripping narrow strips from the work. But ripping work as narrow and delicate as this demands a special setup, both for clean work and for safety. The best method is to fit the saw table with an auxiliary wood table (Figure 14-50) to give the work full support; otherwise the narrow work might be pulled down through the opening in the table insert. Thus, to rip the molding to a desired thickness (actually *thinness*), proceed as follows:

1. Cut the auxiliary table to size to fit the saw table.
2. Lower the blade beneath the table.
3. Set the rip fence a distance, from the blade, equal to the thickness of the strips desired.
4. Clamp the auxiliary table to the saw table.
5. Raise the blade so that it cuts its own slot in the wood.
6. Clamp the auxiliary fence to the rip fence.
7. Be sure to use a push stick when cutting the work.

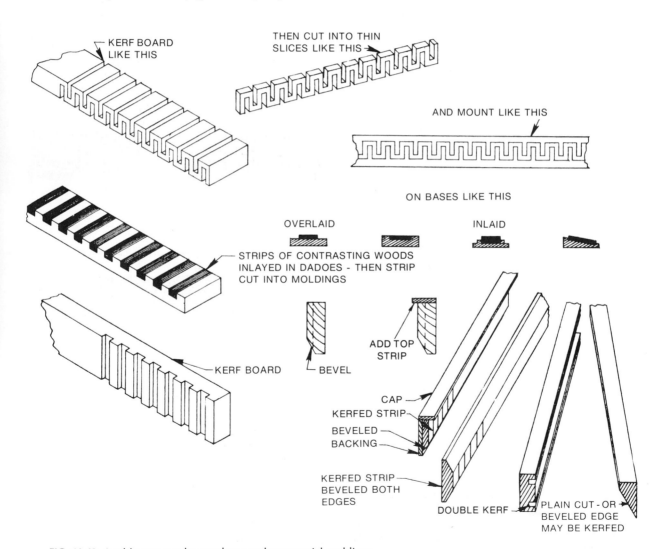

FIG. 14-48. A table saw can be used to cut these special moldings.

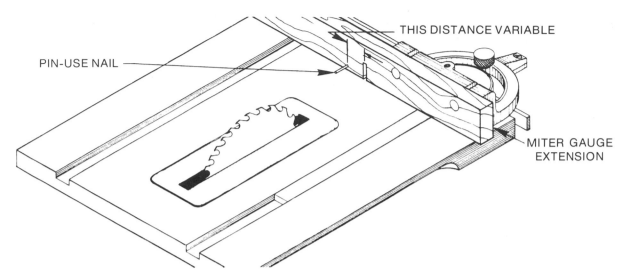

PIN-USE NAIL

THIS DISTANCE VARIABLE

MITER GAUGE
EXTENSION

FIG. 14-49. Setup for controlling the spacing of the kerfs.

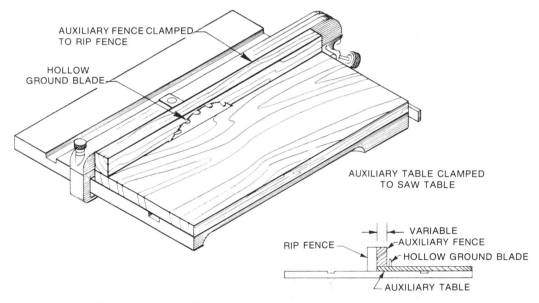

AUXILIARY FENCE CLAMPED
TO RIP FENCE

HOLLOW
GROUND BLADE

AUXILIARY TABLE CLAMPED
TO SAW TABLE

VARIABLE
AUXILIARY FENCE
RIP FENCE
HOLLOW GROUND BLADE
AUXILIARY TABLE

FIG. 14-50. Auxiliary table for cutting extra-thin strips.

Once the setup is made, the same auxiliary table may be used with different thicknesses of auxiliary fences. These should be cut to exact thicknesses. Incidentally, when this ripping method is used with a hollow-ground blade, it is possible to cut strips as fine as $1/64$ inch thick.

As shown in Figure 14-48, simple yet attractive moldings can be made with spaced saw cuts on the face of the work. The setup is the same as for dentil molding, with a spacer pin to set the various cuts. The work is then ripped in two and sliced into molding strips of suitable size.

MOLDING OPERATIONS

Once the molding head has been assembled, install it in place of the regular saw blade, with its cutting edges facing the saw. As the regular saw insert plate cannot be used in the table, it will be necessary to use a molding-cutter insert plate. Then turn the head manually to determine if (1) the head is running true and (2) all head parts clear all saw parts.

Molding operations require a specially prepared auxiliary fence. It is easy to adapt your rip fence to a

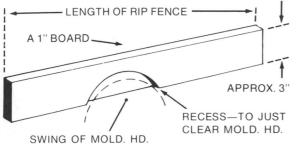

FIG. 14-51. (Top) The shaper blade is installed on the cutter head and is used to embellish straight edges as well as to form joints and rabbets. (Bottom) An auxiliary fence for molding cutting.

FIG. 14-52. Care must be taken to feed the workpiece slowly and steadily into the shaper blade, while holding it tightly against the table and rip fence.

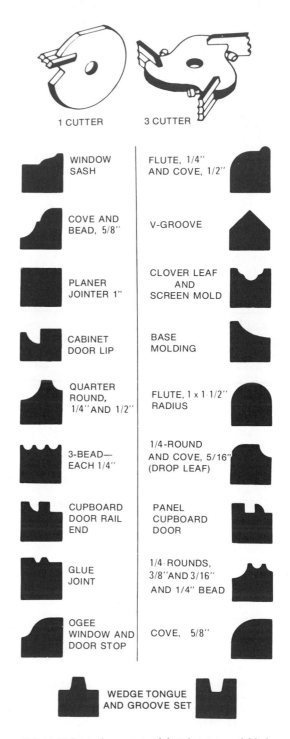

FIG. 14-53. Typical cutters (and their knives) available for table-saw molding cutting. More information on these cutters can be found in Chapter 20.

molding-cutter fence as follows:

1. Make two ¾-inch-thick auxiliary fence boards the exact height and length of the rip fence.
2. From a ¾-inch-thick piece of scrap lumber, make a shim board the exact height and length of the rip fence.
3. Place the rip fence in operating position on the saw table.
4. Place the shim board against the rip fence, and one auxiliary board against the shim board, so they will match the height and length of the rip fence.
5. All three parts should be securely clamped together, and the rip fence clamped into position, so the auxiliary board will be over the cutter head.
6. Use a set of planer and jointer cutter blades in the head to cut a semicircular notch in the bottom edge of the auxiliary board for cutter clearance.
7. The cutter blades should be below the top of the table when the work is placed in position.
8. Start the saw, and gradually raise the height of the molding head, taking as many shallow cuts as necessary to cut the notch 1 inch deep. Feed the work slowly.
9. Prepare the other auxiliary fence board in like manner, and mount the two boards on opposite sides of the rip fence with countersunk bolts and nuts.

With a molding head and an assortment of cutters, you can do both edge (or end) molding and surface decoration (like grooving with a dado). Because the workpiece can be fed flat (a ripping or a crosscut-type operation) or on edge (or end), because you can use mitering or taper-ripping techniques, and because the molding head can be tilted, you can produce an almost endless variety of patterns with the cutters shown in Figure 14-53. In short, a molding head can be used in all the ways previously described for dadoing. It must never, however, be used for "sawing through."

By combining the cuts made by two or more cutters, any number of different useful and/or decorative shapes can be molded. Cuts can be planned to just meet, to overlap, to be spaced, or to be at angles to each other. To help in the planning, it is advisable to make a file record of each cutter shape. For this purpose make ink outlines of your cutters on 4-inch squares of vellum or tracing paper. Two or more of these squares can then be stacked together and moved about to create the desired design, after which you can trace the result onto another paper on which you can also note the cutters, angles, etc., to be used for the cutting operation. Some standard-type molded patterns are shown in Figure 14-53.

Like a dado, the molding head takes a wide cut. If the cut is also a deep one, the tool must remove a considerable amount of stock. Such a cut would necessarily slow the motor, which, in turn would produce a rough cut with possible splintering. Worse, the danger of kickback would be greatly increased. For these reasons it is essential that cuts be limited in depth to no more than $\frac{1}{4}$ inch in softwood and $\frac{1}{8}$ inch in hardwood. If deeper cuts are needed, make as many passes—each so limited in depth—as necessary. To obtain the smoothest possible finish, plan to increase the depth for the final pass by no more than $\frac{1}{16}$ inch insofar as you can, and plan workpieces so that molding can be done with the grain. When cross-grain molding is also required, try to provide waste at the cut ends that can be trimmed off afterward. Never attempt to mold without a guide (fence, miter gauge, or the equivalent). As with dadoing, the saw guard must be removed, but always reinstall the guard immediately after finishing.

RADIAL-ARM SAWS

The radial saw was developed from the older swing saw, on which the blade swung back and forth above the work table. The modern radial saw is a precision machine that is capable of doing an amazing variety of woodworking operations. It is so named because the arm can be rotated 360° left or right. Because of its versatility, the radial-arm saw has become the number one multipurpose tool in the shop.

This machine, with proper adjustment and the many available attachments, can be used to crosscut, rip, miter, bevel, and compound-bevel. It can rip tapers, plow, cut dadoes, rabbets, grooves, and tongues, and make tenons. It can also be used for molding and router shaping. It also drills, sands, and polishes.

Although radial-arm saws come in various sizes and there are slight differences in design, all have the same basic parts: (1) the base, table, and fence; (2) the column and arm; and (3) the blade, motor, and carriage. The function of the steel base is obvious; it supports the table and the radial arm. The wood table supports the work, and the fence aligns it and provides the backing for crosscutting, ripping, and many other operations. In many models, this wooden fence guide is removable and can be positioned between any two of the table's movable boards, for different widths of material to be cut.

The upright column is the steel cylinder which provides the support for the overarm at the rear. It holds the radial-arm mechanism above the table and base. The column can be moved up or down, to raise or lower the saw, by means of the elevating crank. The arm provides the track in which the saw rides. It can be rotated 360° by releasing a clamp lock. Another clamp provides positive stops that position the arm at exactly 45 or 90° to the fence. Other angles may be determined with the scale and pointer at the top of the column.

The saw blade is mounted directly on the motor shaft, and the motor hangs in a yoke. By releasing a clamp lock on the yoke and releasing a stop or latch pin, the motor can be tilted to any position through a full 90° arc. The stop or latch pin allows positive positioning of the blade at 45 and 90°, and parallel to the surface of the table.

The top of the yoke usually has ball-bearing rollers that ride in grooves inside the arm. By releasing a lock clamp on the yoke and releasing a stop, the motor, blade, and lower half of the yoke can be rotated 360°. The stop pin positions the blade either at a right angle or parallel to the fence.

Radial-saw sizes are given in terms of the blade diameter and vary from 8 to 20 inches. The 10- to 12-inch saws are best for the average shop. The larger sizes are more suitable for industrial production. The types of saw blades used on the radial saw are the same as those used on the circular saw (see Chapter 14).

The motor speed on most models is between 3425 and 3450 rpm. The surface speed in surface feet per minute varies with the diameter of the blade. This speed can be easily computed: Multiply the motor speed by the blade circumference in inches, and divide by 12. The motors used with 10- to 12-inch radial saws usually develop $1\frac{1}{2}$ to $3\frac{1}{2}$ hp.

Most saws have at least four built-in safety devices:

1. A key switch which requires insertion of a key before the motor will respond to the START button. Keep the key where children cannot find it.
2. A saw guard that covers the saw blade.
3. Antikickback pawls that hang down behind the saw guard and prevent the blade from throwing a piece of lumber at you.

4. A blade brake. Shutting off the current does not stop the blade; it keeps coasting on momentum unless it has a built-in brake. If your saw has a manual brake, do not fail to use it.

Most manufacturers supply good instructions on how to assemble their saws. Usually all you have to do is bolt the table into place, attach the post and arm, and push the motor carriage onto its tracks under the arm. Once your saw is assembled, read and reread the operating instructions. The safety precautions are particularly important; while the radial-arm type is considered the safest of power saws, any saw can be dangerous. For this reason, the following general rules should be carefully read and remembered—for both your safety and that of your radial-arm saw.

1. When mounting the saw blade, use two wrenches to tighten the arbor nut.
2. Always use the safety guard with the proper adjustment when operating the saw.
3. Be sure all clamps and locking handles are tight before operating the saw.
4. The saw and motor should always be returned to the rear of the table against the column after a cut is completed.
5. The equipment should be shut off when any adjustment is made.
6. The saw blade or tool should be completely stopped before you leave the machine.
7. Material that is being cut should always lie flat on the table and be held firmly back against the guide fence.
8. Stock should not be removed from the table until the saw has been returned to the rear of the table.
9. Always use a stick to remove small pieces of scrap from the worktable. Never get your hands in the path of the saw's travel.
10. The worktable should always be kept clean; no loose material should be left on it.
11. For ripping, the direction of rotation of the saw blade is upward toward the operator. Always feed the material past the safety guard from the side opposite the antikickback fingers. (Observe the caution tag on the safety guard.) Never stand in back of, or in a direct line with, the saw when ripping.
12. When making any kind of cut, maintain a balanced position. If you are crosscutting material from the left, put your left foot forward and place your left hand approximately 12 inches to the left of the line of saw-blade travel. Pull the yoke handle with your right hand. In cutting from the right side, put your right foot forward, and hold the material with your right hand; then pull the yoke handle with your left hand.

13. Always use the antikickback assembly when ripping or plowing.
14. It is a good practice always to remove the key from the switch on the arm when changing tools or making adjustments.
15. Never use cracked or improper types of saw blades.
16. Never wear gloves or loose clothing which could come in contact with the saw. Remove your necktie.
17. Keep the saw blade sharp and properly filed.
18. Make sure the available electric current agrees with the current characteristics specified on the motor nameplate. Consult the power company if necessary.
19. The voltage should be within 5 percent (plus or minus) of the motor nameplate value; otherwise the motor will run hot, and the stator winding will be damaged.
20. If, while cutting, the motor speed decreases, it indicates that the motor is being overloaded. This may be due to low voltage, improperly filed saw blades, or material being fed into the saw too fast.
21. Do not force material into the saw or stall the motor. A stalled motor will heat up the start winding and eventually burn it out.
22. About once a month, lubricate moving parts to minimize normal wear due to friction. Apply a good grade of machine oil to the elevating screw, miter latch, swivel latch, and bevel latch. The ball bearings in the motor are grease-packed and sealed for life. No other lubrication is necessary.
23. Wipe the tracks inside the arm clean before starting the machine. Occasionally clean these tracks with lacquer thinner or a similar solvent to remove grease and dirt. It is not necessary to oil or grease these tracks.
24. The machine should always be kept in good alignment and adjustment to prevent excessive vibration, which will cause inaccurate cutting and cause the saw to grab or creep.

A tool such as a radial-arm saw, which can be turned in so many ways, naturally has more things on it that can go out of alignment than a simpler machine. The misalignments are usually minor, but they do prevent perfect accuracy and smooth operation. Such lack of alignment may be the result of misuse, vibration, or wear. This does not mean that radial saws are always out of alignment. Some misalignments almost never occur, some are occasional, and some are more frequent, depending on how the saw is used.

Here are some typical misalignments: The saw blade may not be square to the table and will therefore cut at a slant instead of at 90°; the blade may "heel," which means that the rear teeth do not follow the same path as the front teeth, with the result that one side of a cut is rough and scored while the other is scorched and polished; the arm may not be square to the guide fence, so that crosscuts are slightly slanted instead of straight; the table may be slightly lower on one end than on the other end, causing an uneven depth of cut. It is very easy to align most radial saws properly. Instructions on how to do this will be found in the operator's manual which comes with the machine.

FIG. 15-1. Two designs of radial-arm machines.

BASIC SAW CUTS

The radial-arm saw is a pull-through, cut-off type of saw that cuts in a straight line or at any angle. In crosscutting, the saw is moved in the same direction as its rotation (Figure 15-3a). Ripping must never be done in the same direction as the saw rotation (Figure 15-3b). For accurate and smooth cutting, a sharp blade must be used.

CROSSCUTTING For straight crosscutting, the radial arm must be at a right angle to the guide fence; this is indicated as 0° on the miter scale. Now the saw blade should follow the saw kerf in the tabletop. Use the elevating handle to drop the saw blade until the teeth are approximately $\frac{1}{16}$ inch below the top surface of the table in the saw kerf. This clearance is needed to cut through the board. Then return the saw all the way back against the column. Place the material on the worktable, against the guide fence. Adjust the guard parallel to the bottom of the motor, and adjust the kickback fingers down to $\frac{1}{8}$ inch above the material you will cut off. Turn on the power, and give the motor sufficient time to attain top speed. Then pull the saw blade from behind the guide fence in one steady motion, completely through the cut

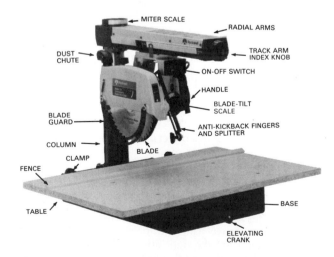

Fig. 15-2. Major parts of a typical radial saw. While designs vary, the parts are basically the same.

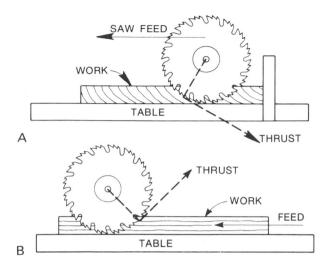

FIG. 15-3. Blade action in crosscutting (a) and ripping (b).

(Figure 15-4). Never allow it to "walk" too rapidly through the work. Return the saw to the rear of the guide fence before removing the material from the table. Practice to get the "feel" of the cutting action; let the saw blade cut— do not force it.

A big advantage of a radial saw is its ability to crosscut any length board you have the space to handle. However, if the board end overhangs the table enough to sag or to drop down as the cut is made, then the end must be supported to prevent board movement and binding of the blade. Any support of exactly the table height will do.

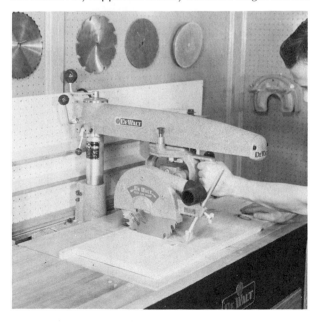

FIG. 15-4. Making a crosscut with a radial-arm machine.

To cut a board thicker than the capacity of the machine, set the blade for a cut just a little over half the thickness of the material. Pull the blade through in the same manner as for straight crosscutting; then turn the board over and complete the cut on the other side. When turning the material over, align its kerf with that on the tabletop, or use a stop block as shown in Figure 15-5a. Actually, the latter method is preferred since it is easier and more accurate. That is, after aligning the workpiece for the first cut, clamp a stop block (to the fence or table) at the work side you will hold. Alignment for the second cut can now be made by again butting the workpiece against the stop block. When the thickness of the material is greater than the capacity of the saw, cut to the limit on both sides first, and then cut the remaining stock with a hand crosscut saw.

If the length of the cut line on the work exceeds the maximum crosscut capacity of your tool but is less than twice this maximum, you can straight-crosscut a perfectly squared board in two passes (Figure 15-5b). For a straight crosscut, make the first pass as long as possible; then flop the board over (other side up) so that the opposite edge is against the fence, for the second pass.

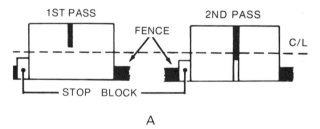

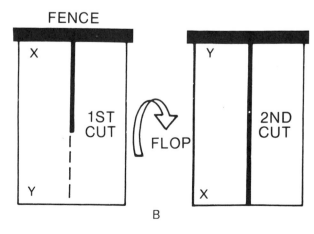

FIG. 15-5. Crosscutting (a) a thick board and (b) a wide board.

When crosscutting a bowed board, always place the concave side down. Hold one edge firmly down on the table. If the board cannot be held firmly down in place, do not attempt the cut.

If there is not a long enough straight workpiece edge to rest firmly against the fence, and the workpiece is large enough, C-clamp it to the table at one side or the front, to keep it from moving while you are sawing. Never try to hold a small or irregular piece by hand. If necessary, nail the piece to a scrap board large enough to be held against the fence. Or, you can use the home-made jig shown in Figure 15-6. Position the jig so it will hold the workpiece very firmly until the blade has been returned to behind the fence.

A number of pieces can be crosscut in one operation if all of them, together, can be held firmly down and against the fence. However, if there are four or more pieces, some may slide during the cut, thus binding the blade and spoiling the work. When all cutoffs are to be the same length, you can guard against this by using a scrap board clamped to the table as shown in Figure 15-7a.

Exact duplicate cutoff pieces, up to the maximum lengths permitted by the table size, can be made with the setup shown in Figure 15-7b. By clamping the stop a measured distance from the previously made fence groove, you can also exactly establish the cutoff length.

HORIZONTAL CROSSCUTTING This crosscut operation (Figure 15-8) is used for cutting across the end of any size of stock. To make the cut, use an auxiliary table such as the one shown in Figure 15-9, mounted on the tool table at the right side of the saw blade, with the fence of the auxiliary table mounted at the normal fence position. Place a wood block in the fence slot at the left end, so the table clamps can be securely tightened to hold the auxiliary table. Before starting, make certain that the auxiliary table is firmly clamped in place to rest squarely on the tool table, and that the saw-blade guard is in place.

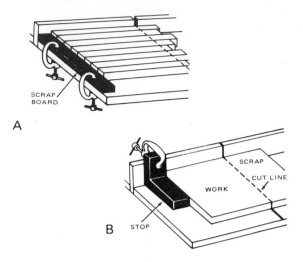

FIG. 15-7. Two jigs for gang or duplicate crosscutting.

FIG. 15-8. Making a horizontal crosscut.

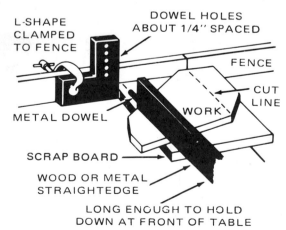

FIG. 15-6. Jig for crosscutting small pieces.

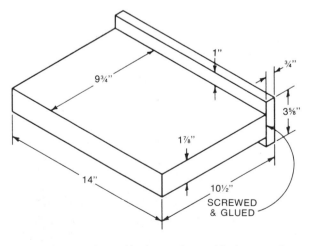

FIG. 15-9. Auxiliary table that can be used for horizontal crosscutting.

To position the blade horizontally, lock the tool arm and yoke each at 0°; lock the power unit at 90°. When installing the auxiliary table, position it so that the saw-blade teeth will just touch (without cutting) the left end of its fence when the carriage is moved along the arm. Place the board on the auxiliary table against the fence, with the depth-of-cut mark exactly aligned with the left end of the fence. Securely clamp and/or block the work so that it cannot move away from the fence. Adjust the saw-blade elevation to align it (by eye) with the height of your desired groove.

To make the cut, pull the carriage out with your left hand while holding the workpiece firmly down on the table with your right hand. Pull the carriage out just far enough to complete the cut; then return it to the rear, turn the saw off, and wait for the blade to stop before moving the workpiece.

One of the most interesting of all horizontal crosscutting operations is the making of the lock or finger joint. To make this joint, it is necessary to find the exact thickness of the saw blade. To do this, place a piece of scrap wood on the auxiliary table illustrated in Figure 15-10, and make a cut flush with the bottom edge. Now elevate the machine one turn ($\frac{1}{8}$ inch) and make a second cut. Elevate again and make a third cut. You have now made three cuts, with two tongues or fingers left standing. Break off the bottom tongue, and fit it into the top saw cut. If it fits too loosely, elevate the machine slightly more than one turn before each cut. (This is a trial-and-error situation.) Once you have found the correct elevation for spacing, you can complete the joint fairly quickly on good lumber. It is best to use a planer or plywood blade for this joint.

MITER-ANGLE CROSSCUT With the model used to illustrate Figure 15-11, this cut requires the yoke and power unit to be locked at 0°, the arm to be locked at the desired right or left miter angle, the blade to be lowered to cut about $\frac{1}{16}$ inch into the tabletop, and the fence as preceding cuts. Scribe the cut line on the workpiece top and front edge. Proceed as for a straight crosscut.

It may be difficult to align the cut line with the blade by eye, and making the cut will groove the table anyway. Therefore, it is best to set up and pregroove the table; then place the work on the table and align it with the groove. Also remember that the work may tend to creep unless it is firmly held or clamped to the table.

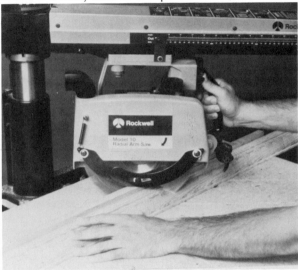

FIG. 15-11. Making a miter-angle crosscut.

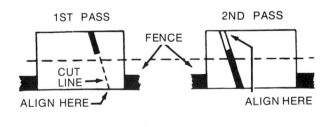

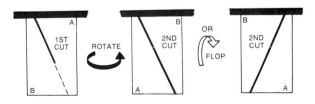

FIG. 15-12. Method of making a miter-angle crosscut in a thick board (top) and a wide board (bottom).

FIG. 15-10. Making a lock or finger joint.

BEVEL CROSSCUTTING With the model illustrated in Figure 15-13, this requires the arm and yoke to be locked at 0°, the power unit to be locked at the desired bevel angle, the blade to be lowered to cut about $\frac{1}{16}$ inch into the tabletop and the fence. If necessary, pregroove the table for the cut. Scribe the cut line on the front edge and top of the workpiece. Position the work squarely against the fence with the cut line aligned with the correct table groove (alignment with the blade is very difficult). Clamp or hold the workpiece very firmly to the table to prevent it from sliding horizontally on the table. Proceed as for a miter-angle crosscut.

Bevel-angle crosscuts are made exactly as explained for horizontal crosscutting except that the power unit is locked at some desired bevel angle between 0 and 90°. The workpiece illustrated in Figure 15-14a has a 45° beveled end that has been grooved at a 45° angle. To make a 90° splined joint, two workpieces are prepared in this manner. When setting up each piece for the groove, draw the groove and mark the depth of cut on the edge against the fence; then align this mark with the fence end as noted above.

A

B

FIG. 15-13. Making a bevel crosscut (A). Bevel cross-cutting can also be used to make a spline joint (B).

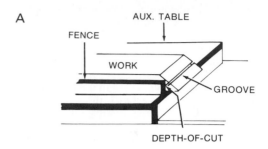

A

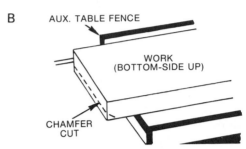

B

FIG. 15-14. (a) As viewed from behind the fence, the auxiliary table detailed in Figure 15-9 is used for a bevel-angle end cut. (b) One method of cutting an end chamfer.

To chamfer a workpiece end (Figure 15-14b), use the same procedure as above with these exceptions:

1. Position the work bottom side up.
2. Position the auxiliary table and the work (on the table) so the saw blade will cut off the end as desired without cutting into the auxiliary table.

RIPPING Straight ripping is done by having the saw blade parallel with the guide fence and feeding the material into the saw blade. You can rip from either the left or right side of the machine. How the workpiece is fed into the saw depends on the rotation of the saw blade. For ripping from the right side of the table (in-rip), the motor and saw must be swiveled to the left 90° from the crosscut position. For ripping from the left side of the machine (out-rip), swivel the motor and saw to the right 90° from the crosscut position. Generally, the in-rip is best because the motor is then on the outer side, leaving a clearer space between the blade and fence through which to feed the work.

If they are kept in proper adjustment, you can generally rely upon your tool's in- and out-rip scales to measure the cutting widths. Just remember that each scale measures from the fence to the fence side of the blade, if:

1. The fence is at normal position (or at rearmost, if there is such a scale).
2. The scale pointer was adjusted for the blade's thickness.

Changing the fence position will (and changing the blade may) alter the accuracy of the scales. With most machines, however, the readjustment of the scales is a simple task. Of course, for extreme precision, measure with a ruler.

For safety and convenience, do the following after completing other control setups:

1. Adjust the rear of the guard to just clear the workpiece to prevent kickup of the work and to collect maximum sawdust.
2. Adjust the antikickback and spreader assembly so the spreader will enter the saw kerf and the pawls will drag on the work surface to prevent kickback.
3. Adjust the sawdust chute to blow the sawdust down and away from you as much as possible.

With the saw set to the in-rip position, you must feed the work into the saw from the right side of the machine. With your left hand approximately 6 inches back of the safety guard, hold the workpiece down and back against the guide strip. Now, with your right hand, move the material into the saw by standing on the right front side of the machine and letting the work slide through your left hand. When your right hand meets your left hand, continue the balance of the rip by using a pusher board, approximately 18 inches long. Hold the pusher board back against the guide fence and against the end of the board you are ripping, and continue on through until the stock you are ripping clears the saw blade on the opposite side by 2 inches. Now pull the pusher board straight back.

When ripping wide material such as panel boards, you should swivel the saw 90° counterclockwise from the crosscut position to the out-rip position. With the saw set to the out-rip position, follow the lower edge of the rip rule on the radial arm. This rule can be used to a capacity of at least 17½ inches (depending on the model of saw) with the guide fence in its standard position. For ripping wider material, it is necessary to move the guide fence to the rear of the table boards. Make the safety guard and antikickback adjustments as previously described for in-ripping. When the saw is set for out-ripping, the workpiece must be fed into the saw from the left side of the machine.

A long board must not be allowed to sag over the table edge(s) or to spring up and down while being sawed. You can hold it up level, and steady the end you are pushing; but a support, level with the tabletop, is needed at the other end. An adjustable-height roller support is illustrated in Chapter 14, but any suitable support will do. When the cut end of the board is about 3 feet past the table edge, stop the motor, walk around, and position the support under the board. Also, if your saw does not have a spreader, put a wedge in the kerf to prevent binding of the blade. Walk back, start the motor, and finish.

If the work does not have a suitable straight edge for the purpose, never attempt to guide it along the fence or to guide it freehand. If the saw blade and table front edge are parallel (check to be sure), you can use a suitable straightedge clamped to the workpiece (at both ends) to guide it as shown in Figure 15-16. This method is also useful when the cut line does not parallel either board edge. Clamp the straightedge to the workpiece parallel to the cut line. When the straightedge is held against the table front edge, the cut line will be parallel to the blade and fence.

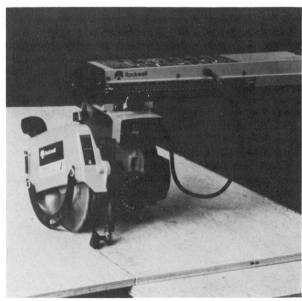

FIG. 15-15. Ripping a board in the bevel in-rip (left) and straight out-rip positions.

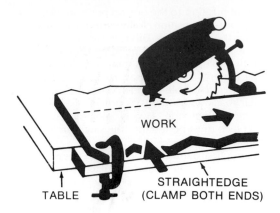
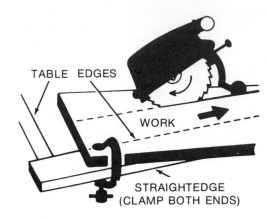

FIG. 15-16. Ripping an odd-shaped board or at an angle to the edges.

A uniformly bowed board can be ripped along the fence, but place the concave side down and be certain that the guard, spreader, and antikickback pawls are properly adjusted. A twisted board cannot be safely held against the fence by hand while feeding. One possible solution is to use a straightedge guide to slide along the table front edge, as in the preceding paragraph. For both bowed and twisted lumber, the resulting cut will necessarily be somewhat bevel-angled to the edges.

ANGLED EDGE CUTS Ordinary (0 to 90°) bevel-angle cuts can be made as detailed above, if desired. These will slant down (from the workpiece edge toward the bottom). If your auxiliary table is high enough, you can also tilt the blade upward (at an angle greater than 90°) for chamfering.

RESAWING As with crosscutting, a depth greater than your saw's maximum depth of cut (but less than twice this maximum) can be sawed straight by making two opposite meeting cuts. Ripping to accomplish this, as mentioned in Chapter 14, is called resawing. Always place a wedge in each end of the first cut (to hold it open) when making the second cut. Always use a fence at least three-fourths as high as the workpiece, and never attempt to resaw a board less than 1 inch thick. Use a push stick, at least 18 inches long, to shove the work past the blade without allowing your hand to approach closer than 8 inches to the blade.

Use either a vertical in-rip or out-rip position. Adjust the guard, spreader, and antikickback pawls in the same way as for a through ripping operation. To make the first cut, lower the blade to cut a little more than halfway through. To make the second cut, flip the board end to end to keep the same side against the fence, and do not alter the tool setup. (When resawing, never reverse the board side for side.) Be sure to follow all the safety rules for straight ripping when resawing.

HORIZONTAL RIPPING This operation is similar to horizontal crosscutting, except that the cut is made on the side of the stock rather than on the end. To place the saw

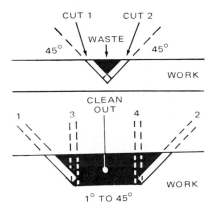

FIG. 15-17. V-grooves and notches can be made with the radial saw in the bevel rip position.

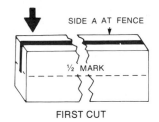

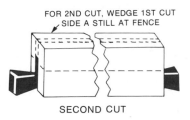

FIG. 15-18. Steps in resawing.

blade in the horizontal rip position, first set the saw in the in-rip location and then turn it to 90° as indicated on the bevel scale described in the section on horizontal crosscutting.

SPECIAL CUTTING OPERATIONS

By combining the basic cuts just discussed, you can perform such special operations as tapering, chamfering, kerfing, cove-cutting, and making saw-cut moldings. While this work may seem more complicated, it is easy and safe to do on a radial-arm saw.

KERFING It is often necessary to bend wood. When the problem of curved surfaces arises, you have a choice of three methods: (1) bend the wood by steaming it (this calls for special equipment); (2) build the curve up by sawing thick segments of the circle on a saber saw (which means that a great deal of expensive wood is wasted); or (3) cut a series of saw kerfs to within 1/8 inch of the outside surface to make the material more flexible for bending. The latter is the most practical method.

The distance between the saw kerfs determines the flexibility of the stock and the radius to which it can be bent. In order to form a more rigid curve, the saw kerfs should be as close together as possible. In determining the proper spacing, the first step is to decide on the radius of the curve or circle to be formed. After the radius has been determined, measure this same distance (the radius) from the end of the stock as shown in Figure 15-19, and make a saw kerf at this point. The kerf can be made in the crosscut position, with the blade lowered to 1/8 inch from the bottom of the stock. Now clamp the stock to the tabletop with a C clamp. Raise the end of the stock until the saw kerf is closed. The distance the stock is raised to close the kerf determines the distance needed between saw kerfs in order to form the curve. Since most bending operations require many saw kerfs, mark this distance on the guide fence with a pencil. This is a great timesaver. The first kerf is made in the standard crosscut position, with the end of the work butted against the mark. The remaining cuts are located by placing each new kerf over the guide-fence mark and making the new cut.

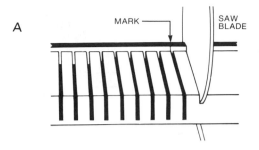

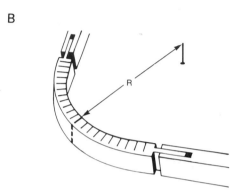

FIG. 15-20. *(a)* Crosscut sawing is used to obtain evenly spaced kerfs; *(b)* the kerfs are finished by gluing to the desired radius *R*.

When the kerfing is complete, the stock is slowly bent until it forms the required curve. Wetting the wood with warm water will help in the bending process, while a tie strip tacked in place will hold the shape until the part is attached to the assembly. Even compound curves may be formed in this manner, by kerfing both sides of the work. When kerfing is exposed, veneers may be glued in place to hide the cuts.

In bending wood for exterior use, the kerfs should be coated with glue before the bend is made. After the bend is made, plastic wood and putty may be used to fill the crevices. When the piece is finished properly, only a close examination will show the method used to make the bend.

SAUCER CUTTING This cut makes intricate decorative patterns easily. Place the stock flush with the edge of the table front, and clamp it to the tabletop. Locate the saw arm so that the lowest portion of the blade is on the centerline of the stock, and tighten the rip clamp. Lower the blade until it touches the workpiece, swing the motor to the 90° bevel position, and then lower the motor by turning the elevating handle one full turn. With your left hand on the antikickback rod, pull out the bevel latch with your right hand. Then swing the motor in an arc past the stock. Lower the saw blade one full turn of the elevating handle, and continue the cutting process until the desired depth is reached (Figure 15-21).

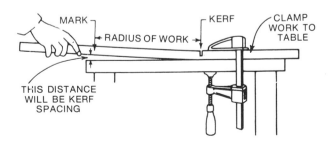

FIG. 15-19. Planning a kerf cut.

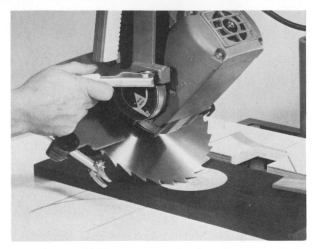

FIG. 15-21. Making a saucer or bowl cut.

COMPOUND-ANGLE CUTTING Compound-angle cutting on the radial-arm saw is a fairly simple operation. Actually, a compound angle is a combination of a miter and a bevel cut. Any frame or open structure with sloping sides requires a compound-angle cut. A peaked figure (with any number of sides) such as a doll- or bird-house roof or a fence-post top, and such house-construction jobs as cutting jack rafters and hip rafters also require compound-angle cuts.

To join two pieces of wood to form a 90° miter corner, you would set the radial arm at a 45° miter position. Strange as it may seem, when a compound-angle or shadow-box joint is made, the bevel that forms the miter must be cut at some angle, but it is never 45°. If, for example, a shadow box is to be made having the sides slanting at 25° as shown in Figure 15-22, the angle at which the miter must be cut is 40° and not 45°, although, when the pieces are assembled, the two 40° angles form a corner of 90°. The reason for this can be found in the fact that, when the pieces are assembled, they are revolved to a plane different from the plane at which they were cut. These are facts that are difficult to understand unless you are thoroughly familiar with advanced geometry.

You need not know any geometry to make a cut for a shadow-box joint on the radial-arm saw, if the chart shown in Figure 15-22 is used. The only thing you have to know is the slant at which you want to make the sides and whether you are making a box with four, six, or eight sides.

The use of the chart is quite simple and can best be explained by an example. If a four-sided shadow-box frame such as is shown in Figure 15-22 is to be made, with the sides slanting at an angle of 25°, the information is applied to the chart in the following manner. Since the frame has four sides, the quadrant on the chart marked "square box" is used. The angle of the stand, which is 25°, is located on this quadrant. The vertical line that intersects or crosses the quadrant at the 25° mark is followed to the bottom of the chart. The vertical line is marked 39¾ at the lower end. This 39¾ means that the motor must be set at the 39¾° bevel position.

In order to cut the second angle at the same time, the motor must be set in a bevel position at the angle shown at the left of the chart. To determine this angle, the original 25° is followed across the chart, either right or left, to the vertical degree markings. This vertical line shows the angle of the arm miter setting to be 23¼°. After the motor is set at the 39¾° bevel position, and the arm is swung to the 23¼° miter position, place the stock against the guide fence and pull the saw through it. Duplicate this cut (both right and left miter) for each end, positioning the stock as needed.

If a six-sided frame is to be made, the quadrant on the chart marked "six-sided box" should be used to determine the angles at which the arm and motor should be set. In the case of the 25° side slant, the motor would be set in the 27° bevel position, and the arm would be swung to the 13½° miter setting. In the case of an "eight-sided box," the motor should be beveled at the 20° bevel position, and the arm swung to a 9¾° miter position.

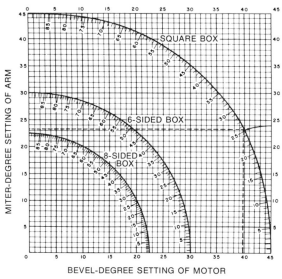

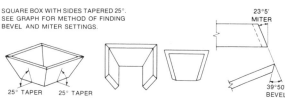

FIG. 15-22. Guide for making compound-angle cuts.

Chair and table legs are sometimes splayed outward, and this construction calls for a compound cut at the top and bottom. Work of this type is usually done at less than a 10° tilt, and for those small angles direct setting to the work tilt gives a satisfactory joint. For a 10° tilt, the saw is set at the 10° bevel position, and the arm is swung to the 10° miter position; for a 5° tilt as seen from the front and a 10° tilt as seen from the end, the bevel is tilted for one of the angles and the radial arm is swung for the other.

Diamond shapes involve another form of compound-angle cutting. After bevel ripping the stock into V strips, set the motor at the 45° right-hand miter position and the 45° bevel position (Figure 15-23). Such cuttings make beautiful decorative patterns.

FIG. 15-23. Cutting diamond or star shapes.

CIRCLE CUTTING The 360° swing of the motor housing or the turret arm makes it possible to cut circles and arcs on the radial saw without the use of a pivoting jig. As shown in Figures 15-24 and 15-25, both small and large circle cuts can be made. The material should be securely fastened to the saw, since the cutting action changes with the rotation of the motor or arm. To cut very large circles and arcs, the machine is set up for ripping, and a pivoting jig should be used to ensure accuracy (Figure 15-25).

TAPER RIPPING For taper ripping, one of the jigs illustrated and described in Chapter 14 may be used with the radial saw in the same manner as with the circular saw. But a radial-arm machine can taper without the use of a specialized jig. (This also includes taper ripping long stock which cannot be handled in the jig.) When a piece of narrow stock is clamped to the lower edge of the material to be ripped, the front edge of the tabletop becomes a second "guide fence" for this operation. You can taper rip at any predetermined angle with this method. Just decide on the degree of taper desired; then clamp on the lower guide board accordingly. The saw is placed in the out-rip position (that is, swiveled to the right rather than the left) for this taper-rip operation. This allows the blade to be positioned directly above the front edge of the worktable. Thus, the completed rip cut corresponds exactly to the angle at which the guide board is clamped to the stock.

CHAMFER CUTTING This operation is simply making bevel cuts along the top edges of stock. Set the saw in the rip-bevel position at an angle of 20 to 45°. Position the blade so that it overhangs the stock by the desired width of the cut, and lock it in place with the rip clamp. Push the workpiece along the guide fence and through the blade path. Then reverse the work and cut along the other top edge in the same manner.

Cross-chamfers are achieved by placing the blade in the crosscut-bevel position at the desired angle. Position the blade so that it overhangs the stock by the desired width (as for a rip chamfer). Then pull the motor and saw through in the prescribed crosscut method.

The octagon shape required for spindle lathe work can be cut in the manner described for chamfer cutting.

FIG. 15-24. Making a small circle with a radial-arm machine.

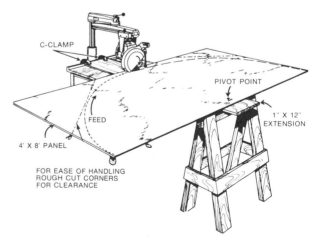

FIG. 15-25. Making a large circle with a radial-arm machine.

RAISED-PANEL CUTTING This operation can add immeasurably to the beauty of a finished door project. Actually, raised-panel cutting is simply rip-bevel sawing. For this operation, an 8-inch-diameter saw should be used in place of the standard 9-inch blade, since the latter may strike the column base and ruin it. Place the saw in the in-rip position, and turn it to the 90° bevel position. Then raise it 5 to 10° (indicated as 85 to 90° on the bevel scale). Position the blade so that it overhangs the guide fence (either on the stationary or auxiliary table, depending on the thickness of the material) by the desired width of the cut. To do this, move the saw the desired amount from the column, and lock it in position with the rip clamp. When starting the motor, make sure that the saw blade moves freely. Then push the stock along the guide fence and through the blade path. The resulting smooth finish is comparable to the most expensive millwork. A piece of hardboard under the work makes it slide easily.

It is possible to do such operations as rabbeting, grooving, dado cutting, lap-joint cutting, and tenon and mortise cutting with the blade of a radial-arm machine. But these cuts are made much more quickly, neatly, and accurately with a dado head.

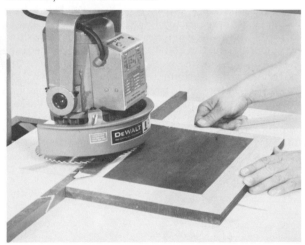

FIG. 15-26. Making a raised-panel cut.

DADO-HEAD OPERATIONS

The types of dado heads described in Chapter 14 all can be used with a radial-arm machine. But, when using a dado head, remember that it is operated in the same manner as the radial-saw blade. The settings for the various cuts are the same. The safety precautions are also the same.

PLAIN DADO A plain or cross dado is a groove cut across the grain. It can be cut in the manner described for crosscutting. With the motor in the crosscut position, elevate or lower the radial arm until the proper depth of groove is obtained. Then pull the motor past the stock, which has been placed tight against the guide fence.

FIG. 15-27. Cutting a plain or cross dado.

To locate the dado, mark a line across the workpiece to indicate one side of it. Hold the second member over it, and mark the width of the dado. Draw a line across either edge and mark the depth of the dado, usually half the thickness of the stock. You can predetermine the depth of the cut by lowering the dado to the top of the stock, barely touching it, and then lowering the arm by means of the elevating handle, recalling that one full turn equals $\frac{1}{8}$ inch.

ANGLE DADO This cut has many uses in cabinetmaking, construction work, and general woodworking. Among other applications, the angle-dado cut is used to recess treads in stepladders, in joining the sill to the upright members of a window frame, and to recess the narrow strips in shutters, louvers, etc. This cut is made in the same manner as the cross dado, except that the radial arm is moved to the right or left to the desired angle as indicated on the miter scale. Raise or lower the arm to the desired depth of the cut by means of the elevating handle.

PARALLEL DADOES These are a series of dado cuts exactly parallel to one another. With the radial-arm machine, these cuts are easy to make because the workpiece remains stationary, the cutting head doing all the moving.

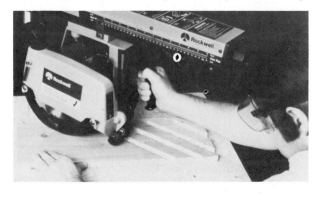

FIG. 15-28. Parallel dado cuts at a miter.

As a result, any two cuts made with the radial arm in the same position (whether crosscut or any degree of miter) are always exactly parallel to one another. Mark your guide fence, and make successive cuts the exact distance apart.

Parallel dado cuts at right and left miter can be made. Cut the right-hand angle dadoes first, and then swivel the motor 180°. Swing the arm left to the same angle as the right-hand cut. If you mark the guide fence properly, you can be assured that successive cuts will be the same exact distance apart.

BLIND DADO A blind dado or gain is cut only partly across the board. With the stock against the guide fence, mark off where you wish the dado to stop. Then place a stop clamp on the machine. With the dado head in the crosscut position and the arm set at the proper height, pull the yoke forward until it hits the stop, and then back off the motor. If a square cut is desired at the blind end of the dado, it can be made with a wood chisel.

FIG. 15-29. By using parallel dado cuts, a lattice cut can be accomplished. The depth is set at half the thickness of the wood, and diagonal dado cuts are made on each side of the work.

CORNER DADO To make a corner-dado cut, place the stock at 45° in a V block, and clamp the block against the guide fence. Raise or lower the arm until the proper depth is obtained. Pull the motor through the stock in the standard crosscut procedure. The stock can project beyond the block, or the block may be partially cut away to permit the passage of the dado head.

PLOWING The plowing or trenching operation with a dado head corresponds to the rip cut with a saw blade and is done in the same way. Set the radial arm at 0° (crosscut position); swivel the yoke 90° from the crosscut position; move the carriage out on the arm to the desired width, and lock it; raise or lower the column to the desired depth for the groove. Adjust the safety guard so that the infeed part clears the stock; lock the wing nut; then lower the antikickback fingers $\frac{1}{8}$ inch below the surface of the board. Push the work against the guide fence, past the blade from right to left, in the same manner as when ripping.

FIG. 15-30. Plowing or trenching with a dado blade.

Center or blind plowing is done by raising the column until the stock to be cut will slide beneath the dado head. Then lower the moving head into the lumber to the desired depth. Push the stock, as when ripping or plowing, until the groove is as long as you want it. Then raise the arm until the dado head is clear and the lumber can be pulled from beneath the cutting member.

BEVEL PLOWING This operation leaves a smooth, accurate V groove in the stock. The cut has many applications, both functional and decorative, in cabinetmaking and general woodworking. It also can be used to make V-block jigs. Bevel plowing is done with the radial arm and yoke positioned as for straight plowing. In this operation, however, the motor is tilted to a 45° position. To tilt the motor, release the bevel clamp and the bevel latch, drop the motor, and then reset these controls. The bevel latch on most machines locates the 45° angle automatically. (Other angles can be used and are located on the scale and locked with the bevel clamp.) With the workpiece against the fence, move the motor out on the

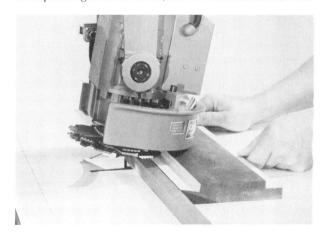

FIG. 15-31. Cutting a bevel and regular rabbet.

arm to the desired width, and lock the rip clamp. Then raise or lower the arm to the desired depth for the V, and push the stock past the dado head in the usual rip method.

RABBETING Grooving a notch from the side and top of the lumber is simple and effective with the radial-arm machine. Elevate the arm until you have sufficient space beneath the motor to allow the cutting member to swing to a vertical setting. Then release the bevel clamp and the bevel latch to put the dado head in the vertical position (horizontal sawing position.) To set the width of the rabbet, use the rip scale located on the radial arm. Then lower the arm to the desired depth for the groove, and push the work past the cutter from the right side of the table. If thin stock is to be rabbeted, use the auxiliary table.

If the cutter "burns" the stock, it indicates a minor misalignment. Simply release the arm, and swing it approximately 5° to the right-hand interposition. This will relieve the drag and result in a clean cut.

To lay out a rabbet joint, hold one edge of the second member over the end or side of the first, and mark the width of the rabbet. Then draw a line down the sides or end and measure one-half to two-thirds the thickness of the first member as the depth of the rabbet.

The bevel rabbet is made in a manner similar to the straight rabbet except that the motor is placed at some angle smaller than 90° (the vertical position), depending upon the degree of bevel desired. This cut is widely used in construction, cabinetmaking, and general millwork operations.

GROOVING Although the term "groove" is used to denote many types of dado cuts, it is properly applied to the dado operation made on the side, as opposed to the top or end surface of the stock. The operation is exactly the same as for rabbeting except that the arm is lowered so that the cutting head is below the top surface of the lumber. Thus, the finished cut is bounded on two sides by remaining stock, instead of on only one side as in the rabbet cut. Using the dado head gives you an extra-wide groove cut, eliminating several of the passes that are necessary in grooving with a saw blade.

Blind mortising or blind grooving is similar to grooving except that the cut is not carried completely through the ends of the stock. In many cases, where the ends of the lumber will be exposed, it is desirable not to show the side groove. In such cases, the stock is "heeled" or pivoted into the cutting head some inches back from the end.

MORTISING AND TENONING For both operations, the motor is placed in the vertical position (as for horizontal crosscutting). A spacing collar is inserted into the dado head at the proper place so that the stock forming the tenon is left standing. On the auxiliary table, place the workpiece against the fence, and mark the stock for the tongue or groove depth desired. The dado head should be located at the proper height, and the motor can be brought forward to the tenon.

FIG. 15-32. Making a box-joint cut with a dado head.

Mortising is actually the reverse of the cut used for tenons. Making the mortise consists simply in cutting a groove to the same width as a previously made single tenon. Be sure the lengths of the tenon and mortise are the same.

CUTTING LAP JOINTS The lap joint is found in simple furniture legs, tables, frames, and chairs, as well as in many other pieces. The basic joint is the cross-lap or middle-half-lap joint. Adaptations of this are the edge-lap, middle-lap or tee-lap, end-lap, and half-lap joints. The cross-lap joint is one in which two pieces cross, with the surfaces flush. They may cross at 90° or any other necessary angle. On modern furniture legs, for example, they frequently cross at 45°.

To lay out a cross-lap joint, mark a line across one surface of one member to indicate one side of the dado. Place the second member over it, and mark its width. Invert the pieces, and mark the width on the second member. Draw lines down the edges of both pieces, and mark the depth of the dado, which should be one-half the thickness of the piece.

The edge-lap joint is identical to the cross lap, except that the members cross on edge. The middle-lap or tee-lap joint is made with one member cut exactly as for a cross-lap joint and the second member cut as for a rabbet. The end-lap joint, which is used in frame construction, is made by laying out and cutting both pieces as rabbets. The half-lap joint is cut in the same way, except that the pieces are joined to end.

The end-lap and half-lap joints are actually two tenons with the stock removed from only one side. With the motor in the vertical position, lay the stock, side by side, against the guide fence on the auxiliary table. Raise or lower the radial arm until the lower blade is in the middle of the stock, and then pull the cutter through as in the ordinary crosscutting procedure.

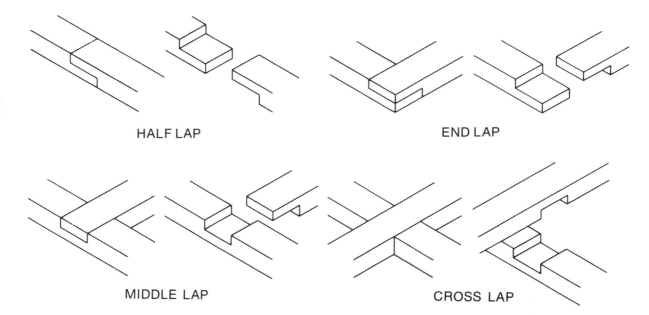

HALF LAP   END LAP

MIDDLE LAP   CROSS LAP

FIG. 15-33. Various lap joints.

Cross-lap and edge-lap joints are cut similarly to a cross dado, except that the lap joints are usually wider. Make the layout and cut in the manner described for cross dadoes.

In the middle-lap joint, one member is cut like a tenon, and the second like a dado. Follow the instructions for making each of these two kinds of cuts.

RADIUS CUTTING This is a dado operation used to produce a concave cut along the face of a piece of lumber. It is accomplished by elevating the column (the radial arm and yoke remain in the normal crosscut position) and dropping the motor to the 45° bevel position. The motor is moved in or out on the radial arm to the correct position in relation to the stock to be cut and is locked in place. The workpiece is then pushed under the cutting head as when ripping or plowing. The first cut should be about $\frac{1}{8}$ inch, and the dado head should be lowered one full turn at a time until the desired concavity is obtained. This operation is similar to contour cutting with a saw blade.

SCALLOPING For window valances, scallop cutting is ideal. Place the dado head in the horizontal ripping position. Locate the motor on the radial arm so that the dado head overhangs the guide fence as shown in Figure 15-34, and lock it in place after determining the width of cut desired. Then lower the column to position the blade to the desired depth of cut. Start the machine, and feed the stock into the dado by heeling or pivoting it on the right side of the guide fence as shown. The design may be varied by changing the position of the overhang of the dado head.

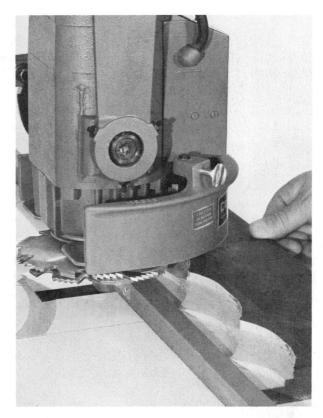

FIG. 15-34. Accomplishing a scallop cut with a dado head.

TONGUE AND GROOVE By cutting tongues and grooves, you can make your own flooring, wood panels, etc. The tongue-and-groove cut is really a combination of tenoning and grooving, previously described. With the saw in the horizontal rip position, cut the tongue by using the dado inserts with collars set to the exact dimension needed. Push the stock past the blade to complete the tongue. Cut all the tongues first; then turn the stock over and cut the grooves. The grooves must match the tongues for a good fit.

Tongue-and-groove cuts can also be made with a molding head on the shaper (see Chapter 20).

PANEL SINKING This decorative door pattern is cut by a combination of cross dadoing and plowing. Mark the layout of the design, and locate the motor above the beginning of the first cross-dado cut. Turn the machine on, and lower the blade until it is $\frac{1}{8}$ inch below the surface of the panel. Then pull the yoke to the end of the marked design, and elevate the motor. Repeat the cut at the other end.

Now swing the motor to the in-rip position, and lower the arm into the beginning of the cross-dado cut. Elevate the motor, and cut the other side of the design in the same manner. Use a wood chisel to square the corners.

CUTTING AND DADOING It is possible, by combining a saw blade and the dado head, to do both a cutoff and a dadoing operation at the same time. Install the saw blade on the arbor first, followed by the dado head. Then, with the saw in the crosscut position, pull the yoke through the workpiece. The result is a cutoff and a dado in the same operation. Use a 9-inch saw blade and an 8-inch-diameter dado head, as a rule, for deep cuts.

It is also possible to rip and plow at the same time. Mount the saw blade and dado head on the arbor, and put the motor in the rip position. Lower the column to the desired depth, and push the stock past the blade and dado head. Again the result is two cuts in a single operation.

OTHER RADIAL-SAW OPERATIONS

Many valuable and versatile accessories are available for use with the radial-arm saw. They include saber saws, shapers, routers, sanders, power drills, and jointers. Figure 15-35 shows some of the more popular other radial-saw operations.

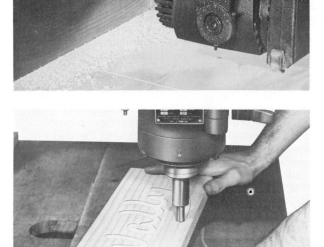

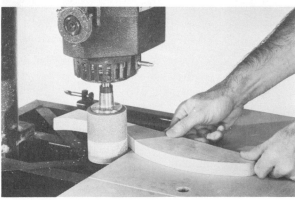

FIG. 15-35. Various other radial-saw operations.

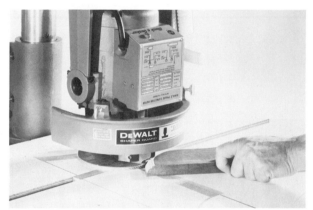

OTHER TYPES OF STATIONARY SAWS

While the table saw and radial-arm saw are the premier saws in any shop, other stationary saws are most useful. The three most popular are the band saw, the jigsaw, and the powered miter box. The first two perform many sawing operations, but the latter does only limited types of work.

Band Saws

Band saws are of various kinds: The band mill, which is the largest one, is used for sawing logs into boards; the band resaw, also a large saw, is used for sawing planks into boards; and the band scroll saw, the one most often found in the average shop, is used for general woodcutting operations. Besides these band saws, which are for sawing wood only, there are also band saws for sawing metal and band saws for sawing meat and bones. Some manufacturers now make a variable-speed band saw which cuts both wood and metal. In all cases, however, the saw itself is a flexible, continuous band of steel with teeth cut on one edge; the sawing action is also continuous.

The band saw to be discussed in this chapter is the band scroll type, which is generally made in sizes from 9½ to 42 inches. The size of a band saw is the distance from the frame to the blade (the depth of throat), which is equal to the diameter of the wheels around which the band runs. Thus, a 12-inch band saw could cut through the center of a 24-inch board. Machines with wheels of less than 14-inch diameter (14-inch band saws) are suitable for home workshops but are not practical for school or industry. Smaller wheels tend to crystallize the blades in a relatively short time. They break more easily. The cutting speed varies from 3000 to approximately 6000 feet per minute (fpm), depending upon the size of the saw.

Large band saws are fastened to the floor; smaller ones,

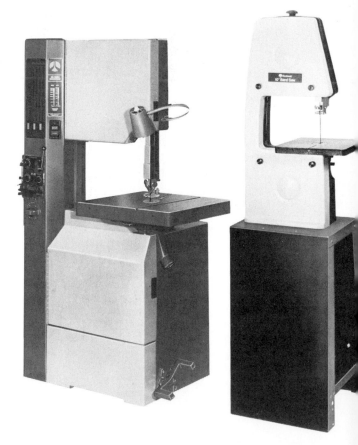

FIG. 16-1. Floor-model (left) and table-model (right) band saws.

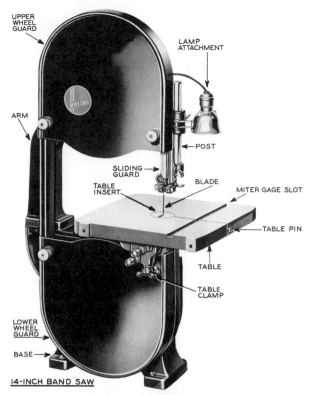

UPPER
WHEEL
GUARD

LAMP
ATTACHMENT

ARM

POST

SLIDING
GUARD

TABLE
INSERT

BLADE

MITER GAGE SLOT

TABLE PIN

TABLE

TABLE
CLAMP

LOWER
WHEEL
GUARD

BASE

14-INCH BAND SAW

FIG. 16-2. Major parts of a band saw.

to a bench or a metal stand. The height of the table above the floor should be from 42 to 44 inches.

A band saw consists of the following main parts: the wheels, the table, the guides, and the guards (Figure 16-2). Ordinarily, a band saw has two wheels which are of the same size. They are mounted on the frame so that one is directly above the other. The upper wheel is supported on an arm curving over the table, called a "gooseneck." The wheels are usually cast, and they have rubber tires on their rims on which the band-saw blade runs. The rubber tires serve to protect the teeth, act as a cushion for the saw blade, and prevent it from slipping.

When a blade breaks, the two ends can be filed to form a tapered or scarfed joint and soldered with silver solder. This, of course, makes the blade shorter. To accommodate the short blade, the upper wheel can be lowered by means of a screw. The wheel also needs to be lowered and raised again when a new blade is put on the machine. Some band saws have a tension mechanism that automatically gives the blade the correct tension. On others the tension must be judged by pressing lightly on the side of the saw with the fingers.

The saw table or tables are bolted to trunnions directly above the lower wheel. Larger machines always have two tables. The table to the left is smaller and is immovable. The one to the right is larger and can be tilted 45° to the

right and about 10° to the left. The blade runs through a slot in the larger table, the entrance to which is cut from the front of the table. It has a steel pin at the entrance. Some of the smaller bench machines have only one table, but they often have a slot milled in it for a miter gauge. Moreover, the saw blade on the smaller machine often enters in a slot cut from the side. All saws usually have an aluminum throat plate so that the saw blade will not be damaged if it breaks.

The guides serve to keep the saw blade in a straight line and prevent it from being pushed off the wheels when stock is being sawed. Two guides are used, one above the table and one below. The guide below the table is fastened to the frame with bolts, but the one above the table is fastened to the guidepost, which is a piece of steel that is moved up or down to accommodate work of different thickness. A saw guide consists of two steel jaws or guide pins between which the blade slides. Behind the side guides, a small circular wheel spins around when the saw is running, and the rear edge of the blade is pushed against it. These small wheels prevent the saw from being pushed off the wheels.

The guards on a band saw are usually two metal doors or panels for the upper and lower wheels and two channel irons for the blades on the right and left sides. The guard on the right side is fastened to the guidepost and moves up or down with it. The guard on the left side covers the saw between the wheels and is fastened to the frame. Therefore, as a rule, only the part of the saw blade between the table and the upper saw guide, where the cutting is done, is unguarded.

Band saws are driven by direct motor drive, by belt, and by chain. All such drives are well guarded on modern band saws.

BLADES There is a wide choice of blades for various operations; there is no general-purpose blade suitable for all operations. Blades differ in type and size of teeth and in width. To do a variety of work, you need a selection of blades.

The thicknesses of band-saw blades average 0.001 inch for each inch of diameter of the wheels on which they run. For example, a 12-inch band saw would use blades about 0.012 inch thick. This is a general rule for blade thickness; however, both thicker and thinner blades are frequently used. The teeth themselves are arranged just like those on the handsaw; there is always one more point than the number of teeth per inch. (Thus, a blade with five teeth per inch will have six points.) To prevent binding, the teeth are set on band-saw blades so that the saw kerf is wider than the blade.

Blades vary in width from $\frac{1}{8}$ to $\frac{3}{4}$ inch. (Blades up to $1\frac{1}{4}$ inch are available for large commercial-type band saws.) Actually, smaller-width blades will cut to a tighter radius than larger-width blades (Figure 16-4); and standard finer-tooth blades will make smoother (but generally slower) cuts than those with larger teeth. On the whole, very hard and dry (gum-free) woods and plywoods are best cut with

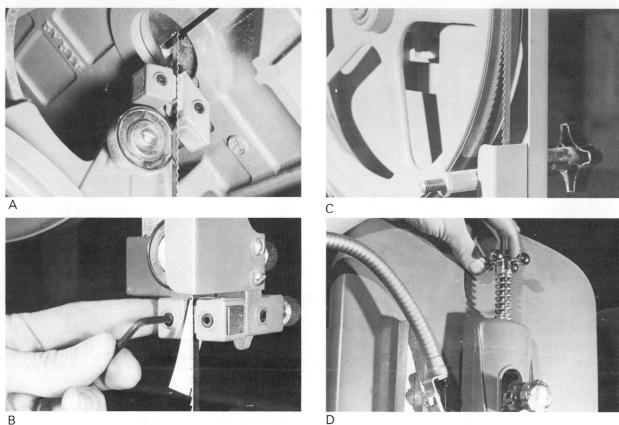

FIG. 16-3. Important band-saw adjustments: *(a)* View of the second back roller, under the table. The back edge of the blade should barely clear all back rollers, and should bear against them only when cutting. *(b)* To adjust the side guides properly, set the blade clearance equal to the thickness of a piece of paper. The blade will always twist to the side when cutting stock if the guides are too loose. *(c)* The blade should track in the center of the wheel's rubber facing. Adjust by tilting the idler wheel with the double knobs shown (right). The second knob is a lock nut. *(d)* A hand is shown setting the blade tension; prior to this, be sure the upper blade guide is set at its highest position. If light finger pressure deflects the blade 1/8 inch, the tension is set.

a fine-tooth blade, especially if little finish sanding is planned; soft and/or resinous woods (and all fast, rough work) are best cut with a coarse-tooth blade. For extremely fast and rough cutting, use a skip-tooth or buttress blade, which has widely spaced teeth that are larger than those of the standard blade (Figure 16-5). Incidentally, most plastics and other (nonmetallic) materials can be sawed with one or another of the woodcutting blades. Thermosetting plastics and light materials (like asbestos board) require a medium- to coarse-tooth blade; catalyst-setting plastics and dense materials (like wallboard) require a fine-tooth blade.

When a variable-speed band saw is used for metal work, the woodcutting blade must be replaced with a metal-cutting blade. Blades for sawing nonferrous and ferrous metals have medium-sized teeth and are generally classified by tooth design, as illustrated in Figure 16-6. Actually, three different types of tooth form and two types of set are commonly employed in metal-cutting

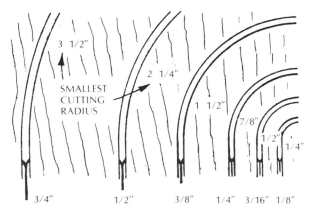

FIG. 16-4. This chart shows how to select the correct width of blade for cutting. For example, a 3/4-inch blade cannot cut a circle smaller than 3½ inches in diameter.

band-saw blades. They are:

1. *Regular tooth.* This tooth is recommended for use on all ferrous materials and for general-purpose cutting. It is usually available in widths of $\frac{1}{4}$ to $1\frac{1}{4}$ inches and a coarseness range of about 8 to 24 teeth per inch.

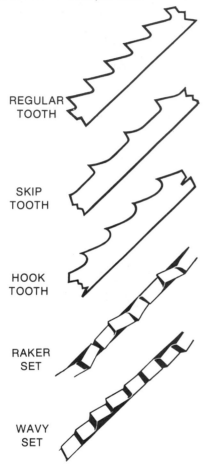

REGULAR TOOTH

SKIP TOOTH

HOOK TOOTH

RAKER SET

WAVY SET

FIG. 16-5. Tooth form for woodworking blades.

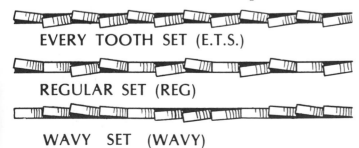

EVERY TOOTH SET (E.T.S.)

REGULAR SET (REG)

WAVY SET (WAVY)

FIG. 16-6. Tooth form and set for metal-cutting blades.

2. *Hook tooth.* The positive hook design of this tooth permits clean chip removal without increasing friction heat. The specially hardened teeth and smooth blending of radii in the gullet mean faster cutting (more bite under light feed pressures) and longer-lasting sharpness. It is recommended for use on wood, plastics, paper, and nonferrous metals. It is also effective on ferrous castings and mild steels having thick cross sections. Blade widths range from approximately $1\frac{1}{4}$ to $4\frac{1}{4}$ inches, with coarsenesses of 2, 3, 4, and 6 teeth per inch.

3. *Skip tooth.* Here is another tooth characterized by wide spacing for effective chip clearance and high-speed cutting of nonferrous metals, plastics, wood, hard rubber, etc. It holds its sharpness well for long all-around use. Blade widths are generally $\frac{3}{16}$ to $1\frac{1}{4}$ inches with coarsenesses of 2, 3, 4, and 6 teeth per inch.

4. *Raker set.* This general-purpose set is especially preferred for cutting larger solids or thick plate. It ensures a fast cutoff rate and retains a uniform saw kerf. It is also excellent for cutting contours, dies, and intricate shapes to layout lines within close tolerances. Blades are generally available in twelve widths, from $\frac{1}{16}$ inch (very narrow and fine-toothed) to $1\frac{1}{4}$ inches, covering a total of about seven coarsenesses of from 6 to 24 teeth per inch.

5. *Wavy set.* This set reduces stripping for cutting thin sections—structural shapes, tubing, pipes, sheet stock, etc. Blade widths usually run from the "threadlike" $\frac{1}{16}$ inch to 1 inch. Their coarseness range is from 8 to 32 teeth per inch.

When not installed on the tool, blades should be carefully stored. Clean them, if necessary, with a stiff-bristle or wire brush, and wipe with an oily rag. Store blades so the teeth cannot be damaged, either on wall pegs or in a cabinet tray such as is illustrated in Figure 16-7.

Band-saw blades can be easily folded for storage as follows: Hold the blade, with the back toward you, in both hands, the right hand with the thumb down and the left hand with the thumb up. Simultaneously rotate the right hand to turn the thumb up and the left hand to turn

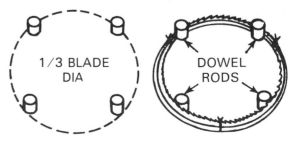

1/3 BLADE DIA

DOWEL RODS

FIG. 16-7. Good blade-storage arrangement.

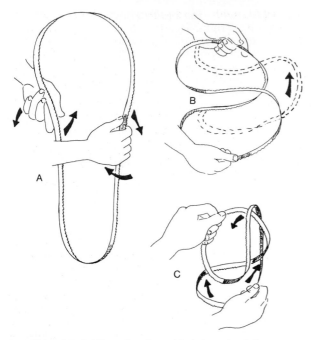

FIG. 16-8. Folding a band-saw blade into thirds for easy storage.

the thumb down, while allowing the hands to come together as they are pulled by the blade. The blade will coil into a tight triple loop (Figure 16-8) which can be stored on pegs. To unfold a blade, carefully untwist it; then check the teeth. (It is possible for the blade to untwist so that, when installed, the teeth will point up instead of down. In that case, the blade must be turned inside out.) Never use a bent, kinked, or cracked blade.

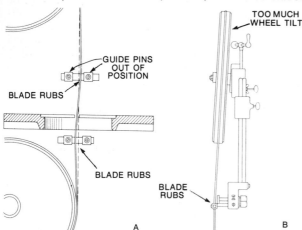

FIG. 16-9. If the guide pins are out of alignment (a), this will soon result in a broken blade. Too much wheel tilt (b) will also cause problems, making the blade ride too hard against the support wheel.

SAFETY PRECAUTIONS

Although the band saw is considered one of the safest machines in the shop, it is well to observe a few simple safety rules:

1. Take a firm, balanced stance slightly to the *left* of the front of the band-saw table. Be sure never to stand or allow anyone else to stand at the right side of either the table or the machine. If the blade breaks, it will fly out in that direction.
2. If the band-saw blade should break while the machine is in operation, turn off the power and move away until the tool has stopped.
3. Examine the blade frequently to make sure it is in good condition. There should be no breaks in it. If there are, this indicates crystallizing (brittleness). A rhythmic click indicates that the blade is cracked.
4. It is important that you use a sharp blade on the band saw at all times. Always be sure the teeth are pointing down.
5. Check the tension of the blade, following the manufacturer's specifications. Also make any other necessary adjustments before turning on the power.
6. Do not cut until the saw is moving at full speed. Feed with the right hand, using the left hand to help guide the work, but keep both hands well away from the saw blade.
7. Be sure to cut through the waste stock when possible, rather than backing your piece away from the blade. Backing out of the work could conceivably cause the blade to pull off the wheels.
8. When it is necessary to back the work out of a long cut, turn off the tool and allow the blade to come to a complete stop. Then remove the work.

OPERATING A BAND SAW

Freehand sawing on the band saw should be attempted only when the work to be sawed is resting flat on the table. That is, unless you are using a miter gauge or jig to hold the workpiece, it must be flat on the table throughout the operation, to prevent binding of the blade. Never shove a workpiece at the blade; feed with a steady, gentle pressure just sufficient to keep the blade cutting. If the blade noticeably slows or binds, stop feeding, back off about $\frac{1}{8}$ inch, and wait for the blade to regain full speed before continuing the feed. If the blade squeals or shrieks, you are either pushing it back too forcefully against the thrust bearings or twisting it against the blade guides; ease up on your feed and/or correct your line of feed to prevent the workpiece from slipping sideways. On the other hand, if your feed is too slow the blade may burn the sides of the cut and, in some cases (very soft, fast-cutting woods), can weave just enough to widen and spoil the cut. Never turn the stock (to try to cut a curve too tight for the blade) so as to twist the blade. If the blade is twisted, the blade sides and/or the guides will be rapidly worn, and the blade can crack or break. Always adjust the upper blade guide to clear the workpiece top by ¼ inch; this provides the back support necessary to prevent blade bending.

When the feed is straight, the blade should always cut straight. Occasionally, the blade may develop a tendency to veer right or left, a condition called "lead." This may be the result of unusual wood grain (corrected by temporarily increasing the blade tension) or worn and twisted blade guides. But it is most often the result of an imbalanced set to the teeth (more bite on one side of the blade). New blades of cheaper quality may have "lead." However, the condition may also result from normal wear or cutting through a nail, which would dull one side of the blade. "Leads" can be corrected by lightly touching the sides of the blade with a fine oilstone while the machine is in operation (Figure 16-10). Overuse of this remedy can dull the blade. But never continue to use a blade that leads. If you have to feed work at an angle to try to follow a line, not only will it be impossible to make a clean, true cut, but the guides and blade will be worn and the blade may crack or break.

STRAIGHT RIPPING OR CROSSCUTTING A straight line, satisfactory for some purposes, can be sawed if (1) you first draw a straight guideline on the workpiece to follow, and (2) you place both hands so as to hold and carefully guide the workpiece straight to the blade. Care must be taken not to twist the workpiece or to let it slip sideways. The thicker the workpiece and the slower the cutting action, the more difficult this is to do.

A much truer straight line (especially if the workpiece is thick) can be cut using the fence. With the workpiece on the table, adjust and lock the fence so the blade will start on the marked cut line; then simply hold the workpiece against the fence while feeding it. To crosscut a board whose end is too narrow to hold steady against the fence,

FIG. 16-11. Method of using a backing block when crosscutting.

use a backing block as shown in Figure 16-11, pressing the workpiece against this block while feeding to keep it from rocking. By the way, a straight-edged board can be clamped to the table to serve as a fence.

A true, straight cutoff or crosscut at any desired miter angle also can be obtained by using the miter gauge, with a hold-down clamp to firmly hold the workpiece for feeding to the blade. Position the stock and miter-gauge head to feed the workpiece along the desired cut line; tighten the miter gauge and hold-down clamp; and then slide the miter gauge in the table groove to feed the workpiece to the blade. If the workpiece is short, use the right hand (only) on the gauge; if the workpiece is long, use the left hand on the gauge (for feeding), and use the right hand to hold the outer end of the stock to prevent its twisting in the gauge. If the work is so wide that you cannot start the miter gauge in the table groove, plan to begin with the gauge backward and to finish (after turning the workpiece around in the gauge) with the gauge in the normal position.

Round or elliptical workpieces can be crosscut in any of the ways described above. However, if you are doing the job freehand or against the fence, instead of cutting straight through, roll the stock so as to cut a kerf all around on the cutoff line; then finish the cut. This will prevent splintering at the end of the cut.

To split a round (or rounded-bottom) piece, some type of holding device must be used to prevent the workpiece from rocking. One method is to C-clamp wood blocks (which will lie flat on the table) to the workpiece, as shown in Figure 16-12. However, since the table is small, the blocks and clamp may have to be relocated one or more times (and the operation stopped each time) if the workpiece is long. Another method is to use two blocks with brad points which can be squeezed against the workpiece sides and used both to feed the stock forward and to prevent it from rocking. Again, if the workpiece is long, you may have to stop to relocate the blocks one or more times.

The band-saw rip fence is used like the rip fence on the

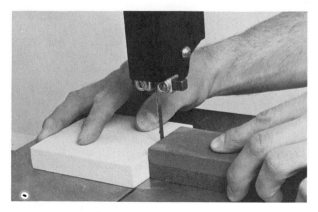

FIG. 16-10. Adjusting a blade's lead.

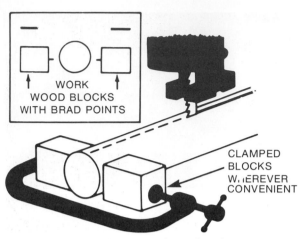

FIG. 16-12. Straight cutting of round stock.

FIG. 16-14. The band saw demonstrating its great depth-of-cut capacity on 6 X 6 inch stock.

table saw. It is positioned to maintain the width of cut as the work is moved forward against the blade. Work may be fed with both hands while you stand slightly to the left of the blade (if the fence is used on the left side), or one hand may be extended over the fence to hold the work while the other feeds it forward.

When ripping a board that is too narrow to hold against the fence (or to feed freehand) with your right hand without getting your hand too close to the blade, use a home-made hold-in or fingerboard (see Chapter 14) clamped to the table as shown in Figure 16-13. Also, to keep your left hand away from the blade, use a push stick.

The band saw does an excellent job of cutting through extra-heavy stock. One instance of its particular ability in this type of work is shown in Figure 16-14. Here, a 6 X 6 inch beam has been cut to length and is being cut to round shape for a lathe-turning job. Since a large section of the blade is actually in the stock, it is unwise to force this work beyond the cutting capacity of the blade. Feed such work slowly, and let the blade do the cutting without being forced.

When the fence is used in beveling operations, it should be positioned on the outside of the table so that both fence and work are below the blade (Figure 16-15). This makes it unnecessary to do the double job of keeping the work against the fence and feeding it forward to make the cut. With the fence below the blade, the work can rest on it, and the operator just feeds it forward. With the table tilted 45°, as it is here, diagonal cuts can be made on the ends of turning squares for lathe mounting.

The band saw does a good job of thinning out sections of stock for facings on round corners. The section to be thinned is marked out on one edge of the stock. The cut should be about 1 inch longer than the corner to be turned. Two end cuts are made first. Then, starting from somewhere in between the two end cuts, an approach is made, slanted into the straight line, and carried forward until it meets the end cut. Then the work is turned end for end, which situates it on the opposite side of the blade, and the cut is completed.

One big advantage of a band saw is its ability to resaw

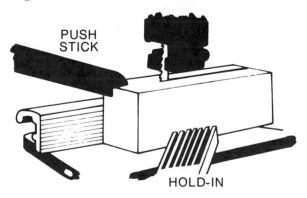

FIG. 16-13. Ripping a narrow board.

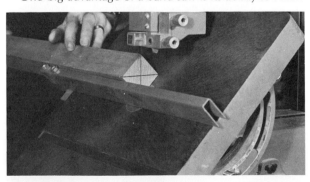

FIG. 16-15. To make a center-find end crosscut for lathe turning (see Chapter 18), tilt the table 45° and set the fence to just clear the blade. Make the cuts about 1/8 inch deep.

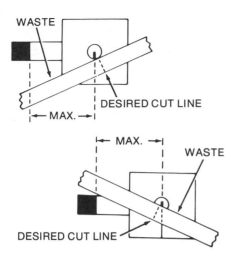

FIG. 16-16. Crosscutting when the "left end" is too long.

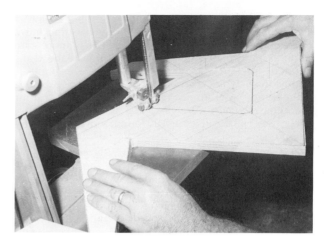

FIG. 16-17. Difficult cuts such as this one can be easy if you plan each step.

(cut into thinner pieces) boards of considerable width. Resawing is a ripcutting operation which, for a true, straight cut, should be done against a fence. If you do not have the fence accessory, use a home-made fence clamped to the table in the proper position. It is always best to use the widest blade available, although a good job can be accomplished with a 1/4-inch blade. Fingerboards may be clamped to the table to hold the work against the fence.

In ripping a long board, the stock must be flat on the table. A very long workpiece will tend to seesaw (and spoil the cut) if not properly supported. Since you must hold the infeed end of a board (and thus can hold it up), this end presents no problem; but the outfeed end (where the cut has been completed) will sag down if you rely on your hands to hold it. Use a table-height support behind the table to hold this workpiece end up level. Any support will do, but the roller support shown in Chapter 14 is exceptionally useful.

A wide piece of stock (such as a sheet of plywood) can present two problems: (1) The maximum cut-line distance from the left edge of the workpiece is limited by the tool's size. If the line is further than the depth of throat from both edges (so that the stock cannot be fed with either edge at the left), the cut must be made with some other tool. (2) If the cut line is within the maximum distance from one (left) edge but the opposite edge is far enough out to allow the stock to sag down over the table at the right, something must be done to hold it up, or the blade will bind and spoil the cut. Either provide a support, such as a roller support, at the right of the table to hold the workpiece up, or, if possible, use a fence and stand at the right side of the workpiece so you can simultaneously hold it up and walk it through the cut while holding it against the fence. Remember that the use of a fence (which must be secured to the table) reduces the effective depth of throat by approximately one-half.

If the position of the cut line presents the problem described above but the workpiece is not too wide, a cutoff can be accomplished in two cuts, in one of the two ways illustrated in Figure 16-16. The first cut can be straight or curved, and the second cut is along the "desired cut line," as shown.

To bevel-crosscut a workpiece that is not too wide, use the miter gauge with hold-down. To bevel-ripcut a narrower board, C-clamp a straightedge to the table at the right side. But if the stock is too large for either of these methods, your only remaining (and less satisfactory) choice is to use the fence (or a straightedge clamped to the table) at the left (uphill) side. In this case the workpiece must simultaneously be held down (flat on the table) and up (from the outer edge) against the fence, throughout the operation.

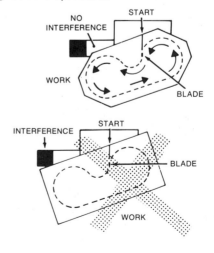

FIG. 16-18. The correct (top) and wrong (bottom) ways to plan your work.

SAWING CURVES It is best, whenever possible, to finish a cut in one continuous operation, without backtracking or sawing off waste, in order not to make two or more starts at different locations. Quite often, if you plan ahead and properly presize your stock (refer to the example in Figure 16-18), you can avoid the "interference" problem. Even when interference cannot be avoided, careful planning of where to make starts and how to remove sections of waste can reduce the number of separate starts required.

If your work generally calls for a fairly wide blade but includes some convex curves that are too tight for this blade, there are two methods of avoiding having to change to a blade narrow enough for the curves. The best method is to make preliminary radial cuts, as shown in Figure 16-19. Make the small ends of the wedges, where these touch the curve, narrower than your blade width. Then, when you saw around the curve, these wedges will drop off to leave room in which to swing the blade on around the curve.

An alternative method is to make a series of tangent cuts (which can be straight or curved) that will reduce the stock on the outside of the curve to a minimum. This excess stock can then be scraped away in one continuous operation by sawing on the desired (curved) cut line. The tangent cuts and, especially, the final sawing of the curve must be very carefully done, however, or the resulting edge will be rough. Of course, when the curve is concave, neither method will work; you must change to a narrow blade. Or, you can saw as close to the curve as possible, and then whittle, file, or sand down to the required contour.

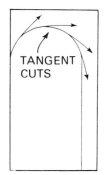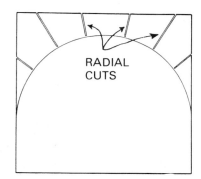

FIG. 16-19. Typical tangent and radial cuts.

Angles located on the exterior of a workpiece are easily sawed, simply by making separate cuts along the two sides that form each angle. However, when an angle occurs on an interior contour of a workpiece, a number of cuts may be needed. For instance, the best method for removing stock to leave a wide rectangular opening is illustrated in Figure 16-21. Four cuts can accomplish the job if there is space in which to swing cut 3 to saw straight along line X. Care must be exercised, when starting cut 4, to hold the

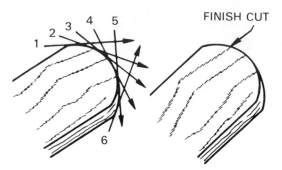

FIG. 16-20. Radial relief cuts help ease the technique of turning.

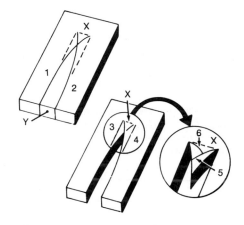

FIG. 16-21. Sawing a narrow slot.

blade to line X. If the opening is a slot too narrow to allow you to turn the blade to cut straight along line X, begin with two cuts that will remove a wedge (Y) and also will touch the ends of line X. Next make cuts 3 and 4 to straighten both sides up to line X. Finally, make as many cuts (5, 6, etc.) as you can to reduce the amount of stock in front of line X, and use a file or sandpaper for the final straightening of this line.

Another method of turning internal angles (Figure 16-22) is to drill large enough holes (preferably with a mortising chisel, if the corner is square) to swing the blade in. Be careful to keep each hole entirely in the waste. If necessary, the side of a hole can be straightened, after all other waste is removed, by straight-line cuts into the angle.

Form the habit of visualizing the cut before you begin your work. Planning the cuts will not only save work, but will produce a smoother, more professional result than can be obtained with a number of unnecessary cuts. Actually, every design presents a challenge. Typical is the valance illustrated in Figure 16-23. By first making cut 1, you can, with two more cuts (like cut 2), remove the bulk of the waste and form the sharp center angle. Afterward, one continuous straight-line cut (cut 3) will ensure both

FIG. 16-22. Use of corner cuts and turning holes.

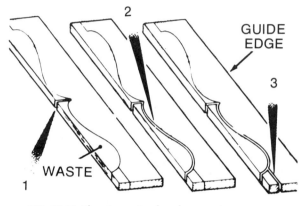

GUIDE EDGE

WASTE

FIG. 16-23. Planning a simple valance cut.

straightness and alignment of the two ends. Remember that when backtracking is necessary, it is more easily accomplished on short cuts. For this reason, when it is impossible to make a cut in one continuous pass, make the short cuts first (Figure 16-24). The jobs shown here are typical band-saw operations requiring backtracking one or more times. Follow the numbers, which indicate the order of the cuts.

Here is another point to keep in mind, especially when considerable turning of the workpiece, which might impair your accuracy, will be required to saw a design in one operation: Even though your blade will make all the turns, it is preferable to saw only the general outline in the first operation, cutting through waste to avoid details. The details can be sawed afterward, one at a time. Whenever there will be multiple outline cuts and you have the choice, make the shorter cuts first. Quite often this will allow the following longer cuts to free sections of waste, thus avoiding the necessity of backtracking through a long kerf.

When one edge of a workpiece has been cut to a curve, an identical curve can be cut along the opposite edge with the help of a guide arm. The guide arm is a wood strip with a small rounded end. Clamp it to the table, as shown

in Figure 16-25, with its center directly aligned with the blade teeth and at the desired distance from the blade. Guide the workpiece by pressing the finished edge against the guide arm, turning as needed to keep the edge at a right angle to the arm.

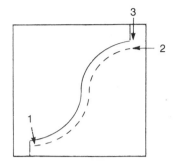

WHEN BACKTRACKING IS NECESSARY MAKE THE SHORTEST CUTS FIRST

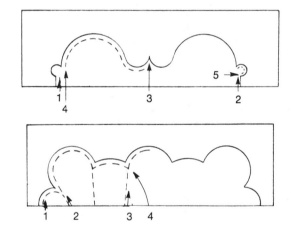

FIG. 16-24. How to "backtrack."

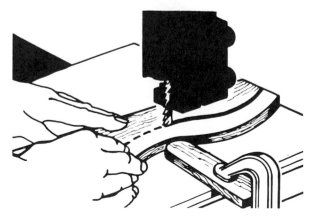

FIG. 16-25. Using a guide arm for sawing curves.

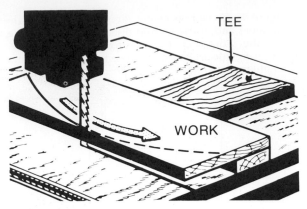

FIG. 16-26. Sawing perfect arcs.

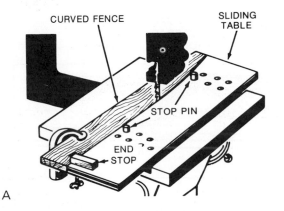

A

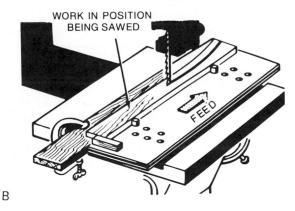

B

FIG. 16-27. Duplicating long, regular curves.

To saw perfect areas, the simple setup shown in Figure 16-26 is ideal. It consists of an auxiliary table on which a T-shaped arm is pivoted. The pivot point of the T must be exactly in line with the cutting edge of the saw blade. The work is cut by securing the stock to the T, to feed it to the blade.

Chair rockers and similar pieces usually require parallel arcs. First, saw the convex (outer) curve freehand. To saw the concave curve, use the fence (or a clamped-on straightedge). Position the fence against the blade, and mark it where the blade teeth touch it; then reset the fence (from the blade) to the distance between the two curves. Now, when you saw the second curve, keep the edge of the first curve constantly in contact with the mark on the fence.

A number of duplicate pieces having long regular (arc-shaped) curves can be sawed quickly with the setup shown in Figure 16-27a. Use a long scrap board 6 inches wide or wider, and ripcut it to the desired curve. Clamp one cut piece to the table, touching the left side of the blade, to serve as a fence. Prepare the other piece to use as a sliding table by attaching an end stop and, if desired, providing stop pins and holes, as shown in Figure 16-27b. For sawing, the workpiece is butted against the end stop so it can be fed to the blade; it is also located against the stop pins to establish the cutoff line. Workpieces of any width can be cut if the stop-pin holes are located so that advancing the pins toward the blade for each successive cut will result in making cutoffs of identical width. For example, if the finished strips are to be 2 inches wide, the holes for each pin must be spaced at 2-inch intervals.

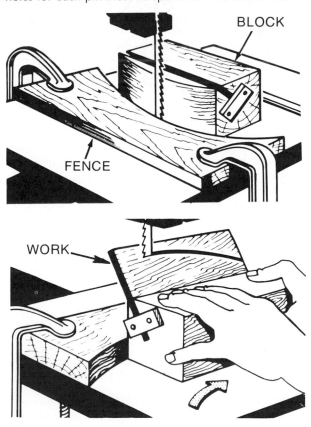

FIG. 16-28. Sawing bevel-edged curves.

FIG. 16-29. By tilting the table to any desired angle, a round can be cut with a beveled edge, eliminating most of the roughing work usually required on a lathe-shaping project.

Bevel-edged arcs can be uniformly sawed with the setup illustrated in Figure 16-28. This consists of a curved fence and a sliding block to be held against the fence edge; the block face must have the desired workpiece curvature, and the block slot must be cut to hold the workpiece at the desired bevel angle. Of course, bevel-edged curves of any type can be cut freehand, with the table tilted to the desired bevel angle (Figure 16-29). Considerable care is, however, required to prevent the workpiece from sliding down, away from the desired cut line.

SAWING CIRCLES With a steady hand you can saw freehand around a circle drawn on a workpiece. A more certain way is to use a jig.

For small circles, the two jigs illustrated in Figure 16-30 can be employed. The first has a single pivot point; the entire jig must be moved for circles with different diameters. The second provides a slide with pivot points that can be located nearer to or further from the blade for circles with different diameters For positioning, the single-pivot-point jig must have guide rails to fit snugly against the front and back table edges, and it must be clamped to the table. Wood strips screwed to the underside and arranged to fit snugly against all four table edges hold the second jig in position; however, the slide must be clamped to be held stationary after it is positioned. But with either jig the pivot point must be exactly aligned, on a straight line to the right of the tips of the blade teeth.

To use the jig, first saw one tangent to the desired circle outline, to provide a flat spot on the outline for starting the blade. Set up the jig and workpiece with the blade against the outline at this flat spot. Then start the motor, and slowly rotate the workpiece into the blade until the cut is finished.

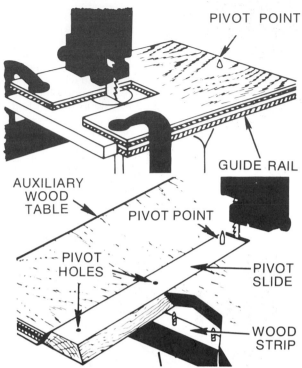

FIG. 16-30. Two small circle jigs.

The slide jig shown in Figure 16-31 can be built to fit on top of a bench or stand which can be positioned to the right of the blade the necessary distance to accommodate a large circular (or, as shown, a semicircular) workpiece. The distance from the blade to the pivot point is governed solely by the bench position; alignment of the pivot point with the tips of the blade teeth is accomplished by positioning the slide. The top of the jig must, of course, be level with the tool tabletop.

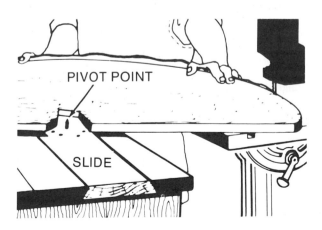

FIG. 16-31. Large circle jig.

Duplicates of any shape with straight and/or broadly curved sides, as well as circles, can be cut with a guide and pattern such as is shown in Figure 16-32. The guide is clamped at the left side of the blade. It is made so that the blade is recessed flush with the end, which is shaped to allow smooth contact with the pattern and which is also undercut to allow clearance for the waste portion of the workpiece. The pattern, shaped exactly to the finished workpiece contour, is placed on top of the workpiece for the operation. Rubber cement or prick points in the pattern are used to prevent the workpiece from slipping. To start the cut, saw into the stock until the blade is broadside to the pattern edge and the pattern is up against the guide. Then feed the workpiece into the blade while keeping the pattern against the guide, with its edge at the point of contact at 90° to the guide end. Radial lines drawn on the pattern top at 90° to its edge will help you to guide it properly.

FIG. 16-33. Multiple or "pad" sawing permits the operator to make duplicate pieces in one operation; the stacked stock is nailed together in scrap areas.

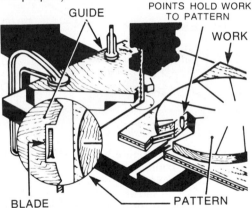

FIG. 16-32. Pattern sawing.

MAKING UNIFORM CUTOFFS To cut off the same amount from a number of identical pieces, you can use the miter gauge with stop-rod attachment if the workpieces are not too long. If the cut-off portions are not too long, a better method is to use a wood block clamped to the table, as illustrated in Figure 16-34; this does not require that the original pieces be of the same length. If neither method is practical, clamp a straightedge across the table in front of the blade so you can use it (like a ruler) to position the left (or right) end of each workpiece at the start of the cut; then feed the work freehand. Or, you can use a step gauge and duplicate cutoffs of two or more different lengths.

COMPOUND SAWING Compound sawing is often used in making chair and table legs, posts, curved railings, and other similar objects. Actually, it is the sawing of profiles on any two adjacent faces of square or rectangular stock. Two, three, or all four faces may be sawed to profile. The problem is this: In order that the profiles be accurate—especially if they are to be identical—each profile must be drawn on a flat surface. Yet, after the first profile is cut, the

FIG. 16-34. Setup for producing identical-length crosscuts when a stop rod is not available. Clamp a block of scrap stock to the saw table as shown, and use it as a measuring stop. Set the stop back from the blade so that the workpiece will not bind.

adjacent face, on which the cut has been made, is no longer flat. Its curved surface would distort the pattern if the profile were drawn on it, and any endeavor to compensate for this would be difficult.

The problem is solved by planning the layout so there will be enough waste—at each side of each profile—to be removed all in one piece. This waste is then temporarily nailed back in place (with the nails in the waste portion of the main workpiece) so that a profile drawn on its flat surface can be used to guide the next cuts. If preferred, instead of nailing you can leave the waste attached by not quite completing the first cut.

SAWING PLASTICS Most plastics tend to chip easily, and some can be cracked or shattered (like glass) if the cutting action is too coarse and rough. On the other hand, some plastics tend to soften and gum up while being sawed so that the sawteeth, if they are too fine, will become clogged and cease to cut. It follows that the only general rule for plastics is to select the finest-toothed, narrowest blade that can be used without clogging. And the amount of clogging depends somewhat on the speed of cutting as well as on the type of plastic.

Block and sheet plastics are handled like similar wood shapes; they are sawed freehand or with the aid of a miter gauge, fence, or other guide. Tubular and extruded shapes generally require some type of holding device (such as a V block, or universal jig). Always feed large sections of plastic to the blade as fast as the blade can do the cutting, to avoid possible overheating of the plastic and clogging of the blade. Thin sections (sheets) must be fed more slowly, to avoid chipping.

FIG. 16-35. (Top) To make a compound cut, tack the scrap from the first cut back in place; this affords a flat surface for making the second cut at right angles. (Bottom) At times, it is not practical or possible to replace the scrap from compound cuts for the purpose of temporarily restoring the straight-line guides. An alternative technique makes use of nail supports driven into the workpiece at an angle and depth which produces the same effect. The nail holes can be filled with putty after the second cut.

SAWING HARD METALS Most aluminum, etc., requires metal-cutting blades of the correct tooth pattern for the job, and a much slower operating speed than is used for woodcutting (from one-fourth to one-tenth the wood-cutting speed). As mentioned earlier, some band saws are designed for operation at woodcutting or metal-cutting speeds. Also, with some saws it is possible to cut metals by using a jack shaft with pulleys of the correct sizes, with a means of shifting the belt to convert to the slower speeds required. Never attempt to saw hard metal at woodcutting speed; you will burn up your blade. If you do have the required setup, metal sawing is much the same as wood sawing—except that the feed speed must necessarily be reduced so that the work is fed only as fast as the blade can cut. In other words, the feeding pressure should vary according to the size of the work (length and depth of cut) and the machinability of the material. Combined with the proper speed, a steady, moderate feed pressure is essential to good cutting and long blade life. Excessive pressure often dulls the teeth; too light a feed will cause the blade to slide over the work and result in premature blade wear. Use a light feed on thin cross sections, and a heavier feed on hard materials. Use a light feed for blades $\frac{1}{4}$ inch wide and under, as well as for radius cutting.

Because metal has no "give" like wood, workpieces must be very firmly held to prevent twisting or misalignment while feeding. That is, support the work firmly. Chattering or vibration of the workpiece is not only destructive to the blade, but often results in inaccurate or excessively wide cuts.

Table 16-1 gives suggested blades and blade speeds for various metals. Keep in mind the general admonition that with raker and wavy set blades two teeth at least should be in contact with the cross section of the work to prevent their shelling, stripping or premature dulling, and to

FIG. 16-36. Cutting metal on a band saw.

Table 16-1 Blades and Blade Speeds for Cutting Metals

Material	Hook and skip teeth, number per inch	Blade speed, feet per minute	Raker and wavy set teeth, number per inch	Blade speed, feet per minute
Aluminum	3–4	500–3500	6–10	500–3000
Brass				
Soft	3–4	1000–1500	8–12	500–1000
Hard	3–4	500–750	8–12	250–500
Bronze	3–6	100–300	8–12	75–250
Copper	3–4	1000–1500	6–10	250–500
Iron, cast	3–4	75–175	6–10	75–150
Lead	3–4	2500–3500	6–10	1500–3000
Steel				
Over 6 inches thick	3–4	50–150	6–14	50–125
Under 6 inches thick	3–4	75–125	10–14	100–150

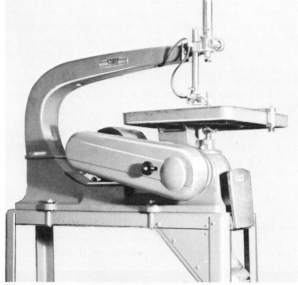

A

B

FIG. 16-37. Two types of power-driven jigsaws: (a) reciprocating-plunger; (b) magnetic motor driven.

assure long-lived, efficient performance and fast production. Broadly speaking, use the finer-tooth blades for thin cross sections, such as sheet metal and light tubing, and for extra-hard materials generaly; coarser-tooth blades for thick cross sections, soft and stringy materials or on thin stock at extremely high speeds.

Jigsaws

While it is not intended to do the work of a circular saw or a band saw, the jigsaw, also called the "scroll saw," can substitute for either in many operations. But the major feature of this power tool is its ability to cut fine decorative curves, especially "inside" curves, which are started by drilling a hole in the stock, inserting the removable blade, and then cutting in the usual manner. Metal, plastics, fiber, etc., can be also cut with special blades. In addition, files and sanding sticks can be quickly chucked to convert your jigsaw into a filing machine or fine sander.

There are two main groups of power-driven jigsaws: the reciprocating-plunger type and the magnetic motor-driven type. Most machines of the first type can be used for saber-blade work and filing; this is the most popular and most used type.

The capacity of a jigsaw is limited by the up-and-down travel of the blade and the depth of the throat. The throat is the distance from the blade to the forward edge of the post that carries the upper arm. Jigsaws operated by a magnetic-type motor (having a vibrating armature similar to that in an electric bell) are limited as to the up-and-down travel of the jigsaw blade and are intended for cutting relatively thin stock. On the types that are driven by a fractional-horsepower rotary motor ($\frac{1}{3}$ to $\frac{1}{2}$ hp), the blade may travel as much as $1\frac{1}{8}$ inches. A jigsaw with so large a blade movement can cut stock up to $2\frac{1}{4}$ inches in thickness without having sawdust clog the gullets of the blade.

The width and length of the stock that can be cut on any type of jigsaw depends on the depth of the throat. Some jigsaws are constructed to permit the teeth of the blade to face either the front of the machine, as in Figure 16-38a, or the side of the machine, as in Figure 16-38b. Called "indexing," this versatility can be appreciated in cutting large pieces of stock. On machines that do not permit the changing of blade direction, the depth of the throat limits the maximum length of a cut. If the throat dimension is 12 inches, the longest cut that can be made is 24 inches, and the cut can only be made by working from each end of the stock in turn. If the machine permits indexing, as in Figure 16-38b, a 12-inch throat will allow cuts of 24 inches or more in length without the need to reverse the stock.

Except for the magnetic motor-driven jigsaw, these machines are operated by fractional-horsepower rotary motors. Any split-phase or induction motor having a speed of either 1750 or 3450 rpm and a horsepower rating of from $\frac{1}{3}$ to $\frac{1}{2}$ hp will be found satisfactory. For heavy-duty or continuous operation, a $\frac{1}{2}$-hp motor is best. To obtain speed flexibility, the motor shaft and the shaft driving the mechanism that actuates the saw blade are frequently equipped with four-step cone pulleys. These pulleys should be matched so that changing the belt from one groove to the next will not necessitate moving the motor to take up slack in the belt. All manufacturers of jigsaws who provide their machines with cone pulleys either supply the motor pulley with the machine or specify a particular pulley in their instructions for setting up the machine. With the use of cone pulleys it is possible to obtain speeds of approximately 650, 1000, 1300, and 1750 rpm. The lower speeds are used when cutting metals and plastics and for saber-blade work or filing, whereas the higher speeds are used when cutting wood.

The various parts and controls of a jigsaw are illustrated in Figure 16-39. The correct jigsaw blade is selected for the type of work and inserted vertically in the flat jaws of the lower chuck. The squared end of a scrap of wood will be of aid in setting the blade at right angles to the table. The plunger is then raised to its highest point (by turning the pulley by hand), and the free end of the blade is clamped in the jaws of the upper chuck. The tension is usually adjusted by pulling up on the spring housing and securing it with the knurled knob at the right side of the overarm.

The purpose of the hold-down is to prevent the work from being raised from the table during the upward stroke of the saw blade. Blade guides and a blower (to clear sawdust away from the line of cut) are carried on the upper shaft. The roller guide should be adjusted to bear lightly against the back of the blade, and the slotted guide should be taken up to prevent side twist. Both guides must be adjusted so the slot does not project beyond the gullets of the saw teeth, as this would quickly ruin the blade.

Saber blades are mounted somewhat differently, being held only in the lower chuck. This saves considerable time in making inside cuts, as it is unnecessary to release the blade from the upper chuck to insert the stock.

Files and small sanding drums having $\frac{1}{4}$-inch shanks can be held in the V jaws of the lower chuck, to convert the jigsaw into an efficient tool for finishing the edges of wood or metal after they have been sawed roughly to shape.

BLADES Three types of blades are used with the jigsaw: (1) the standard or fret blade, (2) the jewelers or piercing blade, and (3) the saber blade. The first two blade types are fastened in both chucks.

In general, the kind of blade as well as the thickness, width, and number of teeth per inch are determined by the kind of material to be cut and the desired accuracy and smoothness of the cut surface. Select extremely fine-tooth piercing blades for delicate scroll and jewelry work. Thin, fine-tooth blades should be used for sawing thin woods, veneer, plastic, metal, and similar materials. Choose medium-tooth blades for sawing wood and metal of medium thickness. Coarse heavier blades are employed for sawing thick materials. Stiff saber blades are used for the ripping and heavy sawing of large inside curves. The blade selected should have at least three teeth in contact with the stock at all times. Table 16-2 will help you in choosing the correct blades for your jigsaw.

SAFETY AND THE JIGSAW

The jigsaw is basically a very safe tool, but the following precautions must be kept in mind:

1. Check all adjustments to see that they are correctly set, as directed in the manufacturer's manual. The power should be off.
2. Use the proper size of blade for the work that is to be done. Make certain that the blade is correctly fastened in the chuck or chucks and that the teeth of the jigsaw or saber blade are pointing down. If the upper chuck is fastened to the blade, be certain the tension sleeve has been adjusted properly.
3. Handle the material firmly with both hands

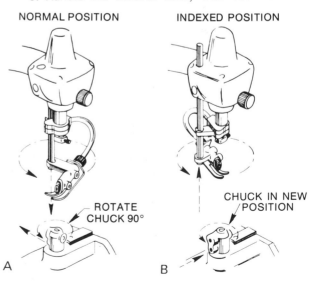

FIG. 16-38. How the indexing feature works.

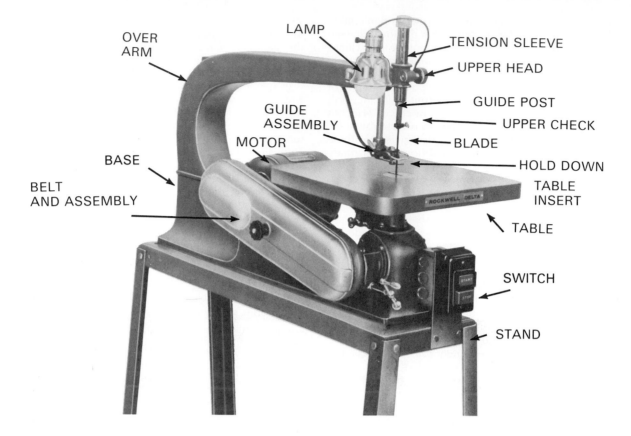

OVER ARM

LAMP

TENSION SLEEVE

UPPER HEAD

GUIDE POST

GUIDE ASSEMBLY

UPPER CHECK

MOTOR

BLADE

BASE

HOLD DOWN

BELT AND ASSEMBLY

TABLE INSERT

TABLE

SWITCH

STAND

FIG. 16-39. Major parts and controls of a jigsaw.

while sawing. Keep your fingers away from the blade.

4. When making curved cuts, do not push the stock into the blade. Turn it on the table until the curve has been cut.
5. Turn off the switch before backing the blade out of the work.

JIGSAW OPERATING TECHNIQUE

When cutting wood on a jigsaw, stand facing the teeth of the jigsaw blade. Before the saw can be used, it is necessary to adjust the hold-down for the thickness of the material that is to be cut. The function of the hold-down is to hold the material against the table while the saw is in operation. Never adjust the hold-down while the machine is running. To do so is likely to result in a broken saw blade. To adjust the hold-down, raise it far enough above the table so that the material to be cut can be placed under it; then lower the hold-down so that it is resting on the upper surface of the stock. Lock the hold-down in this position by whatever means is provided. Before turning on the power, turn the machine over by

hand to make certain that the position of the hold-down and blade guide is not interfering with the free movement of the blade. If the hold-down is too high, the upper chuck is likely to strike it, and something is likely to break if the power is turned on. When it has been ascertained that the hold-down has been set correctly, the power can be turned on and cutting started.

To keep blade breakage at a minimum and to produce perfectly cut work, several things must be kept in mind. The first is not to crowd the blade, that is, not to apply too much pressure on the wood as it is fed into the blade (in an effort to speed up the cutting). A steady, even feed pressure should be maintained. When you use the lighter blades, such as those used for cutting veneers or metal, the feed must be relatively slow.

The second point to keep in mind deals with the cutting of curves. Very sharp curves can be cut only with narrow blades. As a curve is being cut, it is necessary to swing the stock so that the blade is at a tangent to the curve at all times. Side pressure need never be applied to material being cut in order to keep the saw blade cutting on the line or parallel to it.

If the blade develops signs of pulling away from the line

Table 16-2 Requirements for Choosing Jigsaw Blades

Material to be cut	Blade thickness, inches	Blade width, inches	Teeth per inch
Hardwood and softwood	0.020	0.110	10
	0.028	0.187	10
	0.028	0.250	7
Wood panels and veneers	0.010	0.048	18
Wood veneer, laminated plastics, hard rubber, ivory, and plastics, extremely thin materials	0.008	0.035	20
Wallboard, pressed wood, wood, lead, bone, felt, paper, copper, ivory, aluminum, celluloid	0.020	0.110	15
Plastics, hard rubber, ivory, wood, celluloid	0.019	0.050	15
	0.019	0.055	12
	0.020	0.070	7
	0.020	0.110	7
Plastics, celluloid, hard rubber, ivory, wood, laminated plastics	0.010	0.070	14
	0.010	0.055	16
	0.010	0.045	18
Pearl, pewter, mica, pressed wood, seashells, jewelry, metals, hard leather	0.016	0.054	30
	0.016	0.054	20
	0.020	0.070	15
	0.020	0.085	12
Asbestos, brake lining, mica, steel, iron, lead, copper, brass, aluminum, pewter	0.028	0.250	20
Steel, iron, lead, copper, brass, aluminum, pewter, asbestos, wood	0.020	0.070	15
	0.020	0.085	15
	0.020	0.110	20
Steel, iron, lead, copper, pewter, aluminum, asbestos, felt, paper	0.020	0.070	32
	0.020	0.070	20

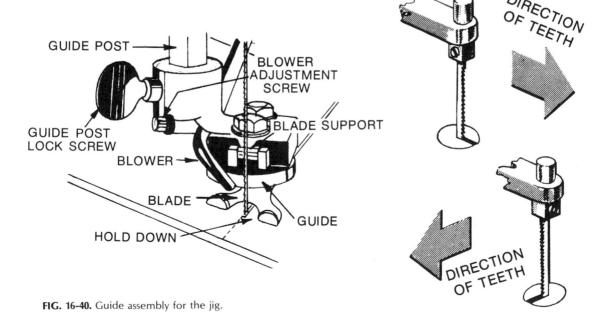

FIG. 16-40. Guide assembly for the jig.

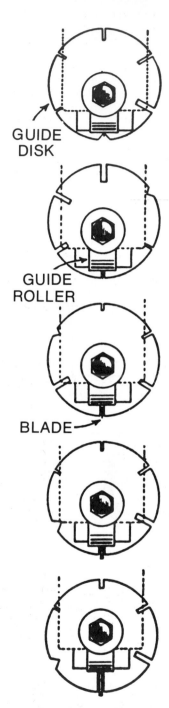

FIG. 16-41. Different settings of the universal guide can be used to fit different blades. The guide disk can be rotated, and the guide roller moved back and forth. The forward edge of the guide disk should be just behind the bottom of the blade teeth.

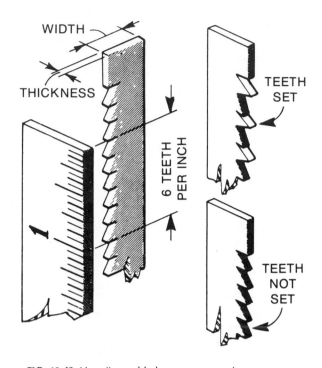

FIG. 16-42. How jigsaw blades are measured.

as it cuts, the stock is not being fed into the saw at the proper angle. An example of this is shown in Figure 16-43. If the work is revolved too far to the left, as in this sketch, the blade will cut over the line. To correct this, the work is drawn back a little until the blade is in proper relation to the line; then the stock is swung or revolved a little to the right. Cutting is then continued. If the blade shows signs of pulling away from the line in a direction opposite to that shown in Figure 16-43, the work should be swung to the left. This holds true whether a curve or a straight line is being cut on the jigsaw.

Frequently, if a thin blade or a heavy blade that is dull is used to cut thick hardwood, the blade will have a tendency to follow the grain and pull away from the line, no matter how the stock is fed. The remedy is to use the proper blade for the material being cut or to replace the blade with one that is sharp. Insufficient blade tension or the wrong blade guide may also be responsible for a blade twisting as the wood is fed into it.

CUTTING CORNERS Cutting sharp corners is the next point to be considered. Although a corner may have to be sharp, the material being cut should never be suddenly swung through a large arc; this practice will result in blade breakage. As shown in Figure 16-44a, a sharp outside corner can be produced by cutting into the waste wood. When cutting a sharp inside corner, as shown in Figure 16-44b, make the cut to point A, which is the corner; then draw the stock back until the blade is at point B. With the blade at point B, the cut that moves up to point C is started. A curve is cut into the waste wood to bring the saw blade into position so that the inside corner at A may be completed.

With the heavier jigsaw blades, the cutting of sharp corners can be accomplished only by cutting into the waste portion of the material to change the direction of the cut, as shown in Figure 16-44. This cannot be done when jigsaw puzzles and inlays are cut, as in these instances there is no waste wood to permit the cutting of loops to change the direction of the saw kerf. The blades designed for cutting jigsaw puzzles and inlays are extremely thin and narrow. When such blades are used, it is possible to cut a relatively sharp corner or double back on a cut without the need for cutting loops or backtracking.

PIERCING Piercing requires the boring of a small hole within the area of the stock that is to be removed, as shown in Figure 16-45, so that the jigsaw blade can be passed through the stock. To set up the jigsaw for piercing, remove the blade from the chucks and raise the hold-down. Place the stock on the saw table so that the small hole is directly over the slot in the table. Pass the saw blade through the hole in the stock and the table slot; then set and secure it in the lower chuck. Attach the upper end of the blade to the upper chuck, and lower the hold-down before centering. As shown in Figure 16-45, the cut is made from the hole through which the blade was passed to point 1 of the design. The blade is backed in the saw kerf to point 2; then the stock is swung to cut a curve that will bring the blade to the line at the opposite side. Cutting is done along this line to point 3, from which the blade is backed again in the kerf to point 4. A second curve is cut to bring the blade back to the line on which the cut was started. Then the cutting is continued along this line to the starting point. The machine is stopped while the freed center section is removed. The piercing is completed by cutting from point 5 to 1, and from point 6 to 3.

SABER BLADES The use of a saber blade in the jigsaw, in place of the regular blade, has some advantages and some disadvantages. Because these blades are heavy in cross

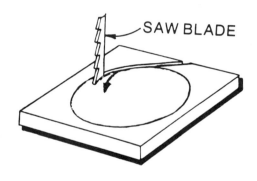

FIG. 16-43. Checking the pull of a saw blade.

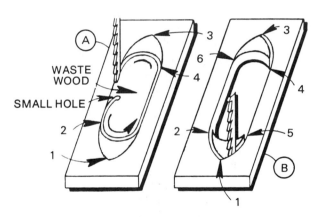

FIG. 16-45. Method of making a piercing cut.

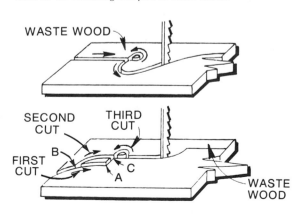

FIG. 16-44. Method of cutting sharp corners.

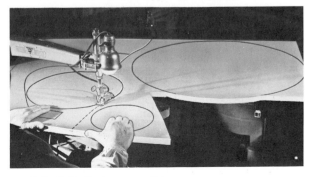

FIG. 16-46. Cutting out a disk.

section and have large teeth, they are capable of cutting much more rapidly than a blade having finer teeth. Because of its larger teeth, a saber blade that is used to cut wood will leave the sawed surface relatively rough. A certain amount of filing or sanding of the edges and underface of the stock is required to obtain a smooth finish.

The greatest advantage of the saber blade over the jigsaw blade is in piercing heavier stock. Because the blade can be held in the lower chuck only, with the upper end open, the work can be passed from one section to the next without removing the blade to pass it through holes in the pierced sections.

RIPPING While the saber blade is designed to be held only in the lower chuck, with the upper end free, the blade may be placed in both upper and lower chucks to be used as a regular jigsaw blade for fast ripping or crosscutting of relatively thick stock. If a finer jigsaw blade is used for ripping or crosscutting, there is a tendency for the blade to drift or twist. With the heavier saber blade, drifting is eliminated or reduced to a minimum. A ripping fence can be provided by clamping a piece of stock to the table. The fence must be parallel to the side of the blade if drifting is to be avoided.

CUTTING ARCS AND CIRCLES The cutting of arcs and circles, which should not be confused with the cutting of curves, can be done on the jigsaw with the aid of a device similar to the one shown earlier in the chapter. Since an arc or circle revolves around one point, this accessory is designed to hold the center point in one place as the stock is fed into the saw blade. To prepare the device, an auxiliary table made of plywood is placed on the saw table. A saw kerf is cut from one end to the center to allow passage of the blade. A line is drawn across the auxiliary table at a right angle to the cutting edge of the blade. It is on this line that the center point of the arc or circle is pivoted by means of a small brad.

PATTERNS With the exception of arcs, circles, and straight lines, most designs that are cut on the jigsaw require the use of patterns. Patterns are usually laid out on paper; then the designs are transferred to the stock. If the paper pattern is to be used only once, it can be glued or cemented directly to the stock. Rubber cement, household glue, or shellac is used to attach the pattern.

If rubber cement is used, both the back of the pattern and the face of the stock to which the pattern is to be attached should be given a thin coat. The cement should be allowed a minute or two to dry before the pattern is applied to the stock. When applying a pattern coated with rubber cement, start by placing one edge of the paper on the stock; then, as the pattern is laid down gently, brush it out with your hand. Do not try to drop the entire pattern on the stock in one movement.

If household glue is used, spread the liquid on the wood only. Apply one coat, allow a short time for it to dry, and then apply a second coat before placing the pattern on the stock. Place the pattern on the stock as described above.

If shellac is used, the stock only should be given a coat. When the shellac has dried sufficiently to become tacky, which takes no more than a minute, the pattern is rolled onto the stock in the manner described above for rubber cement.

When a paper pattern is to be used several times, the outline can be transferred to the stock with the aid of carbon paper. A sheet of carbon paper is placed on the stock with the prepared side down, and the pattern is placed over the carbon paper. The pattern should be held in position with several thumbtacks to prevent shifting. The tacks should be placed outside the areas that are to be used. A pencil or stylus is used to go over the pattern outline with sufficient pressure to transfer the design through the carbon paper onto the stock. In the absence of carbon paper, the same result can be obtained by coating the back of the pattern with graphite from a soft pencil, and then proceeding as outlined above.

If the design is to be used a number of times, or if you intend to keep the design for future use, it is advisable to prepare a wooden pattern such as that shown in Figure 16-47. Such a pattern is prepared by gluing the paper pattern to a piece of $\frac{1}{8}$- or $\frac{1}{4}$-inch plywood and then cutting the outline on the jigsaw. The edges should be finished smooth. A pattern of this type becomes a permanent piece of shop equipment and can be used indefinitely.

INLAYS OR MARQUETRY One of the most fascinating things that can be done on the jigsaw is to make pictures using woods of different colors. It is done by making a pad or pile of various veneers, each of which is $\frac{1}{28}$ inch thick,

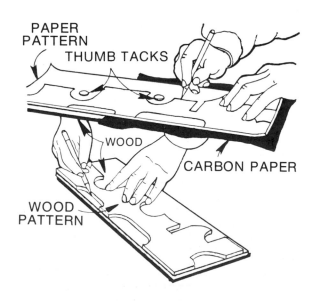

FIG. 16-47. Making a pattern.

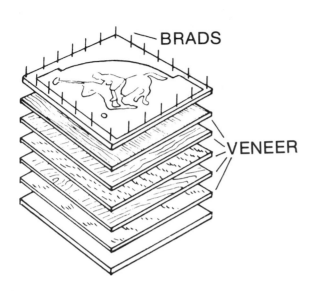

FIG. 16-48. Setting up a pad of veneers.

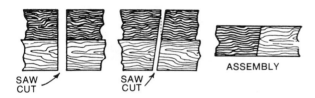

FIG. 16-49. When angle sawing, note that the pieces fit together with no visible saw kerf.

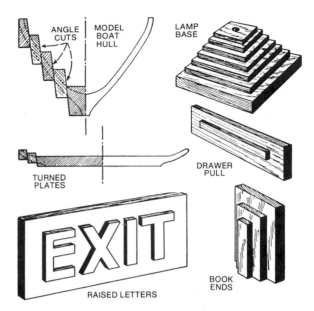

FIG. 16-50. Several items that can be made by angle sawing.

and then placing a piece of ⅛-inch plywood on the top and bottom of the pile, as shown in Figure 16-48. After the pile has been prepared, it is held together by driving brads through to the bottom.

A fine blade, with teeth that have not been set, is used to cut the pile on the jigsaw. Where piercing is required, a hole only large enough to pass the saw blade should be bored, as in work of this type there is no waste wood within the design area. The pieces that result from the cutting are put together in the same manner as a jigsaw puzzle, and then glued to a backing.

BEVEL CUTTING AND ANGLE SAWING The table can be tilted to cut stock on a bevel, that is, at an angle other than 90°. In Figure 16-49, note that, when cut at an angle, the pieces fit together with no visible saw kerf. However, for cutting on an angle or bevel, the work must always remain on the same side of the blade. The lamp base, drawer pull, and books shown in Figure 16-50 were cut from a piece of

¾-inch stock by tilting the saw table a few degrees off square. Concentric cutting of the same piece of stock at a slight angle permits the telescoping of the pieces so that when each is allowed to drop inside the outer one, depth is obtained. By applying glue to the butting edges, a permanently expanded piece is obtained.

In work of this nature, the thickness of the saw blade and the angle at which the table is tilted are vital factors. If the table angle is many degrees off square, the expansion of the sections will be limited. On the other hand, if the angle is only a few degrees off square, the pieces can be expanded to their maximum. If a thick blade is used when the table is set at only a slight angle, the saw kerf will be too wide for the angle; then, instead of the pieces holding together when expanded, they will fall through one another.

MULTIPLE CUTTING Several pieces of stock with the same outline can be cut on the jigsaw at the same time. The only limitation is the total thickness of the pieces when they are piled one on the other. All jigsaws have a limited thickness-of-cut capacity. The number of pieces that can be cut at one time will depend on this capacity.

The work is begun by arranging the pieces in a pile and applying the pattern to the face of the top piece. The various pieces should be held together with several brads or nails driven through the pile. The brads should be placed outside the areas that are to be used, in the waste wood. Then the nails or brads will not leave holes in the finished piece when they are removed. The same technique can be employed on the band saw.

CUTTING THIN STOCK Difficulties are often encountered in cutting very thin stock, either wood, metal, or plastic, on the jigsaw. Even though a fine blade is used, the material often breaks or is turned down by the action of the blade. There are several ways in which this can be overcome. In some cases only one of the methods described here need be used; in other cases it may take a combination of these to obtain the desired results.

If the saw table is provided with a center insert, this should be removed and a new one made of wood or metal should be provided. Instead of a slot being cut in the new insert to take the blade, a small hole, only slightly larger than is necessary for the blade to pass through, should be drilled in the center. Such an insert will prevent thin wood from breaking or metal from being turned down as the blade cuts. The use of an individual upper blade guide which can be lowered to come in contact with the material will eliminate the breaking of wood or the upward bending of metal on the upstroke of the saw blade. The guide should be close to the work.

You can also sandwich thin metal or wood between two pieces of $\frac{1}{8}$-inch stock so that the pad can be fastened together with brads. This will also eliminate the breaking or bending of the material that is being cut.

SANDING AND FILING A jigsaw provided with a universal lower jaw can be used for machine filing and sanding. Files designed for use on a jigsaw are factory cut to work on the down stroke, which means that the teeth of the file point toward the tang of the file. (Hand files are cut with their teeth pointing toward the toe of the file, which is opposite the tang.) The table insert must be removed to perform any filing operations.

Sanding can be done on the jigsaw with a sanding drum made and installed as shown in Figure 16-51. The table insert must be removed, and the sanding drum set in the lower chuck in the same manner as a file. For sanding or filing on the jigsaw, the speed should be low. High speeds will result in the file or sander simply scraping the wood without cutting.

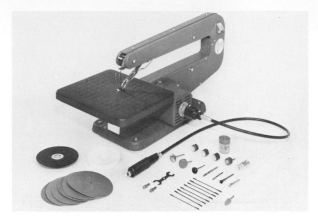

FIG. 16-52. Small jigsaw with a flex shaft that operates as a rotary grinder and disk sander.

FIG. 16-53. Typical motorized miter box.

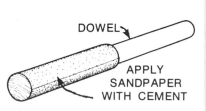

DOWEL

APPLY
SANDPAPER
WITH CEMENT

FIG. 16-51. How to make and insert a sanding drum.

Power Miter Box

The power miter box will rapidly and accurately miter, bevel, and cut compound angles in most workpieces used in carpentry work and picture framing, and in similar pieces used in cabinetmaking. The unit is usually powered by a ½-hp gear-driven motor.

Whether mounted permanently on a workbench or used as a portable tool, your miter box must be set up level, in such a way that it cannot shift position or rock while in use. A good overhead light source is also required for safe, accurate work. Also be sure each workpiece is firmly supported. Do not try to balance a workpiece on edge by hand, or to hand-hold a piece of stock too small to be firmly grasped while the fingers are kept at least 3 inches from the path of the blade. When necessary, use some type of mechanical holding device or a home-made support.

OPERATION OF THE POWER MITER BOX

Baseboard and similar molding, and even 2 X 4s, can easily be miter-angle cut by positioning the board flat on the tool worktable, against the fence. The tool can be set for any angle from 45 to 90°, right or left. To cut a bevel angle (this range is also 45 to 90°), the workpiece must be positioned on edge, against the fence.

To cut a compound angle at the end of a board, the board must be slanted at an angle to the tool worktable. Prepare a filler block to fit on the table against the fence, to support the board, as shown in Figure 16-54. The angle at the bottom of the filler block will determine the bevel angle of the cut; the tool control setting will determine the miter angle.

To miter crown moldings and similar shapes, it is necessary to hold the molding on the table and against the fence, in the position in which it will fit against the ceiling and wall. This requires the use of a filler block

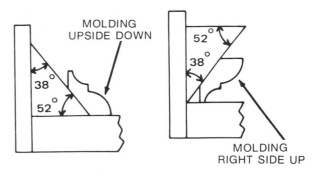

FIG. 16-55. Mitering crown molding.

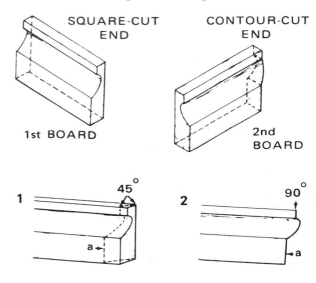

FIG. 16-56. Cutting a coped joint.

fastened to the fence, as above. Most crown moldings have the angles indicated in the illustration, but other angles (as measured) are needed for some. The filler block and molding can be positioned in either of the two ways shown in Figure 16-55.

To cope-join two moldings, cut off the first board square. Cut off the end of the second at a 45° angle. Then use a band or coping saw to cut off the end at 90° to the board face along the line established by the bevel cut on this board face. The result will be a contour-cut end (Figure 16-56) that will butt against the face of the first board at a right angle.

PICTURE FRAMING Most picture-frame moldings have a flat back. Position such a piece face up on the worktable, and miter cut the right and left ends. If the pieces are to be used on edge (to provide a shadow-box effect), bevel cut them instead, as described above. Any piece that cannot be accurately held flat on the table or against the fence with the face up must be supported from beneath or behind by a suitable scrap block.

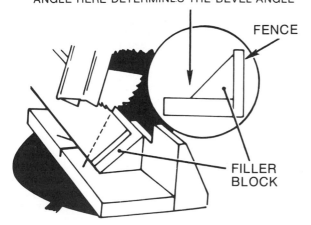

ANGLE HERE DETERMINES THE BEVEL ANGLE

FENCE

FILLER BLOCK

FIG. 16-54. Cutting a compound angle.

To exactly fit a glass or backing, first cut off one end; then measure on the back side, in the glass recess, and mark point A of Figure 16-57. Use a 45° angle on the back to mark the miter at the edges. When placing pieces on the worktable face up, use these marks to align with the 45° groove in the worktable.

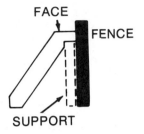

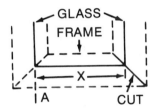

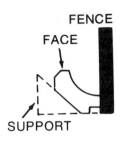

FIG. 16-57. Picture-frame making with a motorized miter box.

Horizontal Band Saws

Horizontal band saws (Figure 16-58) were designed primarily for ferrous and nonferrous metal cutting. They operate only in a horizontal position and generally feed themselves automatically, using gravity. The horizontal band saw is basically an industrial tool and is seldom found in a home workshop. On the other hand, the portable horizontal band saw is fast becoming popular with those who work with metal in the home workshop.

Although the home shop horizontal band saw can be used as a portable tool (Figure 16-59), it performs best when mounted in its own stand. This stand may be mounted on pipe legs (Figure 16-60) or on a workbench or metal stand. The height of the base above the floor will depend upon the operator's preference. The average, however, is about 42 inches. The stand turns the portable band saw into a stationary tool.

Once the portable horizontal band saw is in its stand, you are ready to cut. Clamp the material securely in the chain vise as shown in Figure 16-61. Set the speed knob

FIG. 16-58. A stationary horizontal band saw.

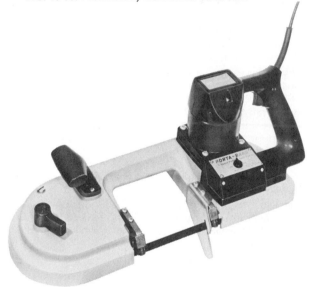

FIG. 16-59. A typical two-speed, portable band saw.

at the desired position. Incidentally, the speed of most machines with either a two-speed or variable speed arrangement, can be changed while the machine is running. Be sure that the work-stop of the saw is contacting the workpiece and the blade teeth clear the work. While keeping the saw above the work, turn the saw "ON" and lower it carefully onto the work (Figure 16-62). Allow the weight of the saw to control the cutting pressure. Additional feed pressure will slow down the speed of the blade and reduce cutting efficiency. Keep the saw cutting until the cut is completed; then raise it away from the work. Stay clear of the end pieces that might fall after being cut off.

Power Hacksaws

Power hacksawing is simply an adaptation of the hand hacksawing principle—with machine power replacing human effort. The difference is the difference between mechanically regulated operating factors and the less definite control actions of the hand and mind. In hand operations, we can deal with special situations as they arise; machine operations are intended to handle work of a more uniform character and in a more general manner. Consequently, for mass production and for reasonably unvarying types and thicknesses of stock, power hacksawing is inestimably faster, more precise, and more economical. The metal-cutting saw shown in Figure 16-63a is suitable for small machine-shop work, while the one in Figure 16-63b is a light-duty machine that can be used in an average shop operation. Since the power hacksaw is not a so-called "standard" homeshop tool, no explanation of its operation is given in this book.

FIG. 16-62. Making the cut.

FIG. 16-60. A portable horizontal band saw mounted on a pipe stand.

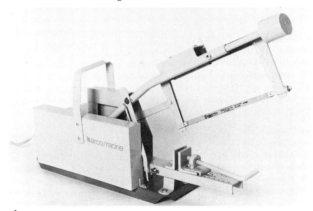

A

FIG. 16-61. Clamping the workpiece in the chain vise.

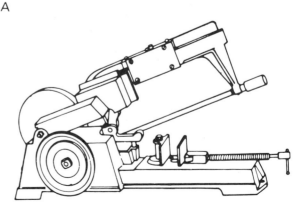

B

FIG. 16-63. Two designs of power hacksaws.

DRILL PRESSES

The drill press was originally designed for the metal-working trades, but with modern techniques of woodworking and the multitude of cutting instruments, fixtures, and attachments available, the drill press has become a basic shop tool. It not only drills in metal but also bores in wood and performs other woodworking operations such as mortising, routing, planing, sanding, and shaping. To make all this possible, it has been necessary to increase its speed range to between 600 and 6000 rpm. Drill presses made exclusively for the machine shop have a speed range of from 400 to 2200 rpm.

The drill press consists of the following main parts: a hollow steel column fastened to a cast-iron base, a table, and a head which contains all the mechanism. The cast-iron table is clamped to the column and can be moved to any point between the head and the base. The table has two or more slots milled in it to aid in clamping the work. It usually also has a central hole drilled through it. The table can be tilted to any angle, and on some models has fixed positions at 30, 45, and 90°. An auxiliary table made of plywood, which can readily be fastened to the regular drill-press table, is available on some models. The cast-iron base also has two slots for clamping work to it, and usually three drilled holes for fastening the machine to the floor or a stand.

The column is machined to a smooth finish and polished.

Floor machines range in height from 66 to 72 inches; bench machines, from 36 to 44 inches.

The head is fastened to the upper end of the column. It has a central shaft, or spindle, which rotates in a sleeve called the "quill." The quill, together with the spindle, is moved up or down by one or more bars, with a ball on the end of each. The quill has a stroke or travel of from 3 to 4 inches. It is automatically returned to its normal position

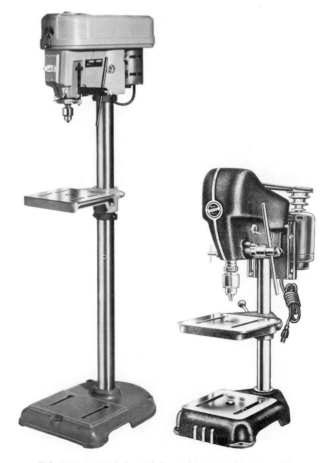

FIG. 17-1. Typical floor (left) and bench (right) models.

by a spring. Machines for production work are equipped with a power or treadle feed arrangement.

Different manufacturers have provided various means of increasing the versatility of the drill press. One type of drill press can be provided with different spindles, each with a different purpose. One is designed to take a Jacobs chuck, another to take a drill with a No. 1 Morse taper, a third to take router and mortising bits, a fourth to take shaper cutters having a $\frac{5}{16}$-inch hole, and a fifth for cup grinding wheels. Other manufacturers use the one spindle and provide adapter chucks for converting the drill press into a shaper, grinder, router, or hollow mortiser. For router, carving, and dovetail cutters, a collet chuck that takes a $\frac{5}{16}$-inch shank can be obtained. The collet chuck replaces the Jacobs chuck and is locked on the spindle by means of a threaded sleeve. Shaping with cutters having a $\frac{5}{16}$-inch hole requires the use of an adapter. This adapter is held in the $\frac{5}{16}$-inch collet chuck. Large molding cutters having a $\frac{1}{4}$-inch hole require the use of the adapter. This adapter is placed on the spindle and locked in position.

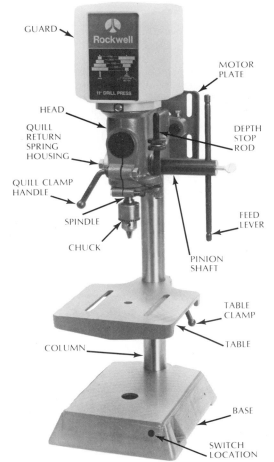

GUARD
MOTOR PLATE
HEAD
QUILL RETURN SPRING HOUSING
DEPTH STOP ROD
QUILL CLAMP HANDLE
SPINDLE
FEED LEVER
CHUCK
PINION SHAFT
TABLE CLAMP
TABLE
COLUMN
BASE
SWITCH LOCATION

FIG. 17-2. Parts of a typical drill press.

The spindle is driven by a four-step cone pulley connected by a V belt to a similar pulley on a motor, which is usually bolted to a plate on the head casting in the rear of the column. Motor sizes vary between $\frac{1}{3}$ and $1\frac{1}{2}$ hp.

The size of the press is usually expressed in terms of the chuck capacity (the maximum-diameter tool shank it will hold) or the distance between the spindle center and the column. A press with a 12-inch capacity can be used to drill the center of a 24-inch board or circle. The most practical sizes for the average shop range between 11 and 16 inches.

The radial or universal type drill press (Figure 17-3) has a tilting head that allows drilling at any angle. The head is mounted on a horizontal arm that swivels on the supporting column to position the drill bit instead of the work.

DRILLS AND BITS To be technically correct, you "bore" a hole in wood (even though twist drills are used) and "drill" a hole in metal. Today, however, this terminology is not slavishly followed, and usually the two terms—bore and drill—are used interchangeably in discussions of power drills. However, different bits are used to cut in wood and in metals.

Several types of wood bits are used for wood boring with a drill press. Most popular for clean, sharp-sided holes in softwoods, hardwoods, and plywoods are the power wood bits. These are available in the one-piece type, where each bit bores one size of hole from $\frac{3}{8}$ to $1\frac{1}{4}$ inches or larger and has a $\frac{1}{4}$-inch shank, or in the interchangeable-size type, where one common $\frac{1}{4}$-inch shank can be fitted with a number of detachable cutters ranging from $\frac{1}{4}$ to $1\frac{1}{2}$ inches or larger. Both types are very fast and accurate in operation, and easy to resharpen.

For small holes (from $\frac{1}{16}$ to $\frac{1}{2}$ inch) you can use wood drills (carbon steel, for wood only) which have $\frac{1}{4}$-inch shanks, or you can use metal-cutting twist drills available in all fractional, numbered, and lettered sizes, with shank sizes based on the drill sizes (see Chapter 9). Though similar to twist drills, the wood drills have longer lips which are better adapted to fast, clean drilling in all kinds of wood.

Very deep holes (approximately 4 to 18 inches deep) require electrician's drills, commonly available in $\frac{1}{4}$-, $\frac{1}{2}$-, and $\frac{3}{4}$-inch sizes. Holes larger than $1\frac{1}{4}$ or $1\frac{1}{2}$ inches in diameter are drilled with an expansive bit or a hole saw. The expansive bit (usually $1\frac{1}{4}$ to 3 inches in diameter capacity) is good for deep through or blind holes (up to about 6 inches deep), but the screw point must be filed to remove the threads, so that the bit will not feed itself into the work. Hole saws come in various sizes (1 to 3 inches or more). The circle cutter also can be used for removing large-diameter plugs or making circular cuts that do not go through the workpiece. (Note: A "plug" is a through cut. If it is not cut all the way through, a plug must be removed with a chisel.)

Holes for wood screws are most quickly bored with a

FIG. 17-3. Two types of radial-type drill presses. The one on the right has a so-called "solid-state" speed-control circuit, which eliminates the need for belts.

wood-screw pilot bit of a size designated for the screw to be used. This bit simultaneously (when sunk to the proper depth) drills the correct size of screw hole, counterbores for the screw shank, and countersinks for the screw head. Or, you can do the countersinking with either of the countersinks illustrated in Figure 17-4.

Twist drills up to ½ inch in diameter, together with the other typical metal-drilling accessories shown, can be used to drill iron, steel, and nonferrous metals. It is preferable to use only high-speed drills on ferrous metals; carbon-steel drills are satisfactory only for nonferrous metals, unless a slower than normal spindle speed is used.

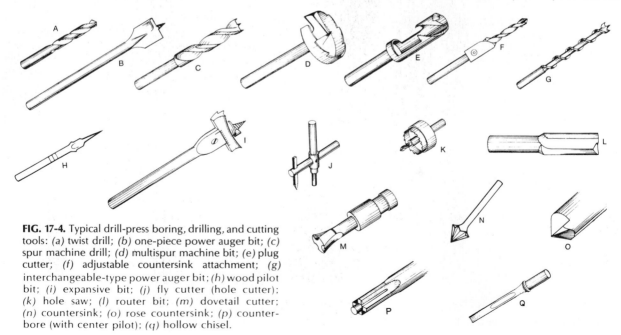

FIG. 17-4. Typical drill-press boring, drilling, and cutting tools: *(a)* twist drill; *(b)* one-piece power auger bit; *(c)* spur machine drill; *(d)* multispur machine bit; *(e)* plug cutter; *(f)* adjustable countersink attachment; *(g)* interchangeable-type power auger bit; *(h)* wood pilot bit; *(i)* expansive bit; *(j)* fly cutter (hole cutter); *(k)* hole saw; *(l)* router bit; *(m)* dovetail cutter; *(n)* countersink; *(o)* rose countersink; *(p)* counterbore (with center pilot); *(q)* hollow chisel.

More information on the drills and bits that can be used to drill and bore with a drill press is given in Chapter 9. Use only drills, bits, and cutters designed for machine or power use. Never attempt to use a *hand* auger bit unless the lead screw has been cut smooth, and the square tang cut off. The square tang of a bit cannot be centered in a drill chuck. A lead screw is undesirable for use in a drill press because it cuts too fast.

HOLD-DOWNS AND VISES To drill a small piece with a drill press, either hold the work in a drill-press vise of some type or clamp the work securely to the table. C clamps (Figure 17-5a) are excellent for holding small, flat workpieces and, in many cases, for securing a long, unwieldy piece to the table to assist the left hand in holding it.

There are also several special clamps on the market, such as the one shown in Figure 17-5b. This universal hold-down clamp is excellent for light-duty holding. The hold-down fence illustrated in Figure 17-5c has the added feature of an adjustable "shoe-shaped" hold-down clamp that rides lightly on the top surface of the workpiece and prevents it from lifting off the work table when the drill is withdrawn. The fence is useful both for guiding a workpiece (as when routing) and positioning it. The hold-down clamps the work in the exact desired position; it is adjustable on the post to accommodate various thicknesses of work.

The three work-holding vises shown in Figure 17-5d to f bolt or clamp to the drill-press table to securely hold small (especially metal) workpieces. The rotary indexing table is the best of the three. This precision machinist's tool is designed for layout, indexing, and holding for drilling, milling, etc. The large table rotates 360°; the dial is calibrated in 0.001-inch increments.

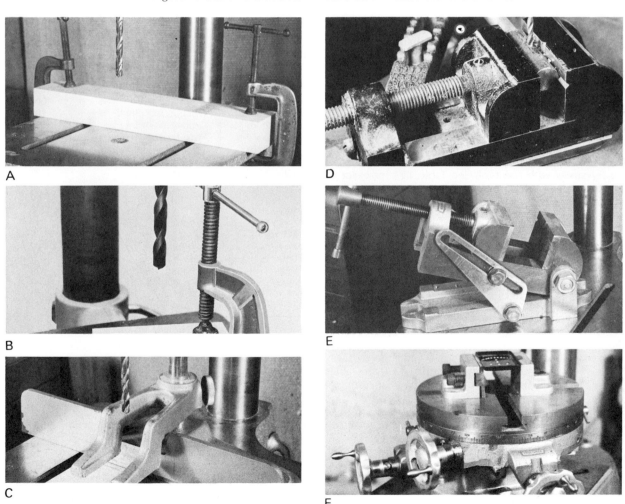

FIG. 17-5. Popular types of hold-downs and vises: (a) C clamps; (b) universal hold-down clamp; (c) hold-down fence; (d) general-purpose vise; (e) angle vise; (f) rotary indexing table.

SAFETY WITH THE DRILL PRESS

Only a few safety precautions must be remembered during drill-press operation. They are:

1. Use goggles or a face shield, especially when operating the drill press at high speed.
2. Make sure small pieces are clamped properly before drilling or boring.
3. Hold the work firmly so that it will not fly or spin off the table. It is often best to fasten the piece securely with clamps.
4. Keep the guard on the pulleys and the bell to prevent your hair and clothing from getting caught.
5. Always position the hole in the center of the table beneath the drill, and place a piece of wood beneath the work to keep from drilling holes in the table.
6. Use the recommended spindle or chuck. Most operations can be done successfully with the 0 to $1/2$-inch-capacity drill chuck.
7. When you use mortising, routing, and shaping attachments on the drill press, make certain that they have been properly fastened and adjusted.
8. Check and adjust the pulley and belt combination to ensure that the correct speed is set up. You will usually find a chart giving the various speed ratios available with your particular drill press somewhere in the instruction booklet that comes with the tool. See Table 17-1 for exact recommended speeds. Remember that each cutting tool operates best at a particular speed that also depends on the material being worked. On most drill presses, it is impossible to get the exact speed, but you can come close by adjusting the drive belt on the step-cone pulleys.

The drill press should be leveled and, depending on whether it is a bench or floor model, bolted securely to a sturdy bench or stand or screwed to the floor with lag or expansion screws. This will reduce vibration and increase accuracy.

A coat of paste wax or a rubdown with a piece of wax paper will protect the polished surface of the table; wiping with a slightly oiled cloth will discourage rusting of the column and quill. Presses not fitted with sealed spindle bearings will need a drop of oil now and then, in the lubrication holes in the quill. The rest of the press should be kept clean by dusting with a clean rag or brush.

Be careful to keep the drive belt free of oil and grease. The belt tension is adjusted by manipulating two locking bolts and a movable motor mount. Keep the belt just tight enough so the pulleys will not slip when pulled by hand; excess tension will only cause undue wear on the motor and spindle bearings. Most drill presses have a quill return spring that raises the spindle automatically when the feed

lever is released and holds the quill in the raised position. The return-spring tension may be adjusted to suit individual requirements by gripping the spring housing with a pair of pliers (to prevent the spring from unwinding when it is released), loosening the locknut or screw, and rotating the housing until the desired tension is achieved. Turning the housing clockwise reduces the tension; turning counterclockwise increases it.

Table 17-1 Recommended Speeds for Drill-Press Operations

Material	Operation	Speed*, rpm
Wood	Drilling, up to $1/4$ inch	3800
Wood	Drilling, $1/4$ to $1/2$ inch	3100
Wood	Drilling, $1/2$ to $3/4$ inch	2300
Wood	Drilling, $3/4$ to 1 inch	2000
Wood	Drilling, over 1 inch	600
Wood	Using expansion bit	600
Wood	Routing	5000–6000
Wood	Cutting plugs	3000
Wood	Carving	5000–6000
Wood	Using fly cutter	600
Wood	Using dowel cutter	1800
Hardwood	Mortising	1500
Softwood	Mortising	2200
Metal, hard†	Drilling, up to $1/4$ inch	1000
Metal, hard	Drilling, to $3/8$ inch	700
Metal, hard	Drilling, to $1/2$ inch	600
Metal, hard	Wire brushing, fine	3300
Metal, hard	Wire brushing, coarse	1200
Metal, hard	Using fly cutter	600
Metal, hard	Buffing	4700
Metal, hard	Grinding	3000
Metal, soft‡	Drilling, up to $1/4$ inch	2200
Metal, soft	Drilling, to $3/8$ inch	1300
Metal, soft	Drilling, to $1/2$ inch	800
Metal, soft	Using fly cutter	600
Metal, soft	Buffing	3800
Plastic	Drilling, up to $1/4$ inch	2200§
Plastic	Drilling, to $1/2$ inch	800
Plastic	Using fly cutter	600
Plastic	Buffing	2300
Glass	Drilling with tube	600

*When in doubt, set the speed on the "under" side.
†Mild steel and cast iron.
‡Aluminum, brass, and copper.
§Certain plastics may melt at the listed speeds; if so, reduce the speed accordingly.

WOOD BORING

Drilling in metal or boring in wood is probably the first thought that comes to mind when one considers the operations that can be performed on a drill press. Boring is usually very simple, as most holes are bored at right angles to the surface. It is therefore necessary only to clamp the work to the table, select the correct bit, and set it to depth.

In boring, the feed pressure must be determined by feel. Never force a bit; use just enough force to keep the bit cutting. If the wood is very hard, be careful not to let the bit overheat; back the bit out of the hole frequently during the operation, to let it cool. If the wood is green and chips tend to gum up and clog the bit, back the bit out and stop it to clean the chips from it, if necessary.

When you bore through a piece of stock, the center hole in the table must be centered under the bit. If the bit is too large to enter this hole (as is a hole saw), place a scrap block (preferably, ½ inch or thicker) under the workpiece. In fact, it is a good idea to use a scrap block in any case; this will prevent splintering at the underside of the work. The alternative is to bore a hole almost—but not entirely—through, and then turn the work over to finish the hole from the opposite side.

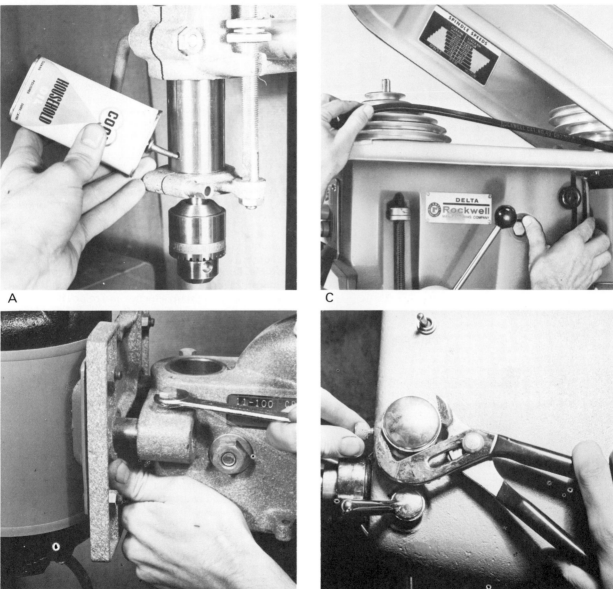

FIG. 17-6. Care and maintenance are very important. (a) Check the instruction manual for lubrication points, and oil at regular intervals. (b) The movable motor mount adjusts the belt tension; it is held in position by two locking bolts. (c) Adjust the drive belt on the step-cone pulleys for the proper speed, according to the tool used and the material worked. (d) The quill return-spring tension is adjusted by loosening the lock and rotating the spring housing.

FIG. 17-7. Some drill presses have a socket for the chuck key; otherwise, attach a spring clip or chain to hold the key.

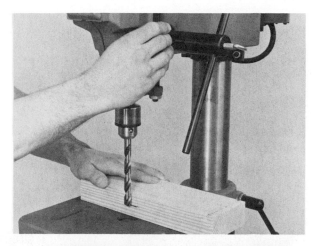

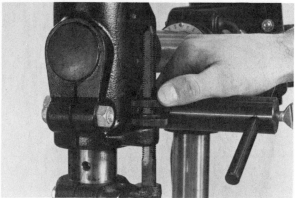

Fig. 17-8. When drilling a predetermined depth, mark the depth on the side of the stock, and run the bit down even with the mark (top); then set the depth-gauge rod (bottom).

To bore to a specific depth, mark the desired depth on the side of the workpiece, lower the bit end to the mark, and adjust the feed stop (Figure 17-8). If, instead, you wish to bore to a certain (but unmarked) depth (for instance, 2 inches), lower the bit until the point just touches the workpiece top; then set the feed stop to the desired depth. In either case, start the motor to finish the operation after completing the setup.

Holes up to at least 4 inches deep can usually be drilled on most drill presses with one feeding (movement of the chuck from top to bottom), if the table is positioned so that the bit tip just touches the workpiece top with the chuck fully raised. Of course, through holes up to 8 inches deep can be drilled in from opposite sides, if the holes are carefully set up to meet at the center. This requires perfect plotting of hole locations on both the top and the bottom of the work. However, an easier method is illustrated in Figure 17-9. Clamp a $\frac{3}{4}$-inch or thicker scrap board to the table, and drill it to a $\frac{1}{2}$-inch depth. Relocate the table to bore a 4-inch-deep hole in the workpiece, leaving the scrap piece clamped to the table. After this, fit a dowel of the proper size in the hole in the scrap piece, and place the workpiece over the dowel to locate it for boring in from the opposite side.

Deeper holes, using an electrician's bit or a similar extra-length bit, require two or more successive operations. It is best to clamp the workpiece to the table, if possible. Bore to a 4-inch depth, as detailed above. Stop the motor; raise the chuck to the top and lock the quill; raise the table straight up 4 inches and relock it; and then continue the boring operation. Repeat until the desired depth is reached. After completing the hole, raise the chuck, lock the quill, and lower the table to free the bit. Remember that any hole deeper than 1 inch may require frequent backing up of the bit to clear chips. Do this with the motor running by simply reversing the feed to raise the bit an inch or more before resuming the feeding operation. When raising the table, use extreme care not to shift the hole out of alignment with the bit; any shifting may bend the bit. The bit must be perfectly aligned in the hole before you restart the motor.

To bore a hole in a miter, tilt the table to the angle that makes the miter cut horizontal. It is necessary to devise several stop blocks if similar holes are to be bored in a number of pieces without measurement.

Holes over about $1\frac{1}{2}$ inches in diameter generally are bored with:

1. An expansive bit (with the screw threads removed from the point) if the hole is to be blind or the depth exceeds the capacity of the next two bit sizes
2. A hole saw or fly cutter, which will remove a plug having a $\frac{1}{4}$-inch hole in the center but cannot bore a blind hole
3. A circle cutter, which bores like a hole saw, but greater diameters

A

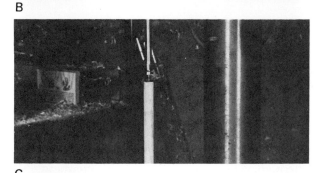

B

C

D

FIG. 17-9. When drilling a hole that is deeper than the length of your drill bit, clamp a flat scrap of wood to the table, and bore a hole through it *(a)*. Then drill as deep as your bit permits in the work *(b)*. Remove the workpiece, and use a straight length of dowel to align the hole in the scrap with the bit *(c)*. Replace this dowel with a short dowel, and fit the workpiece over it *(d)*. Drill the rest of the way through.

If the circle cutter is used, the cutter end should be ground to an 80° angle to prevent tearing of the wood. To use any of these three bit types, securely clamp or vise-mount the workpiece on the table. Use low drilling speeds as specified in the chart for your drill press; when using the circle cutter (regardless of the size hole for which it is set), use only the lowest speed.

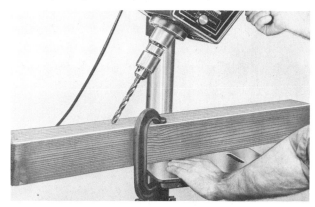

FIG. 17-10. With the radial or universal drill, the drill head can be moved and tilted to do many operations. It eliminates the necessity of holding the work at difficult angles. The work can be clamped to the table in a flat position.

If holes are to be bored in the edges of boards that are to be glued together, an auxiliary fence (Figure 17-11) should be made and clamped to the back of the table. Using a pin in previously bored spacing holes, will ensure correct spacing of the holes.

FIG. 17-11. Stop block, spacer blocks, and a fence are used to drill a series of holes.

To bore a series of evenly spaced holes in the face of a board, clamp an auxiliary fence to the table, hold the board against it, and bore the first hole in the board. Make a stop block, hold it against the auxiliary fence, and bore a hole through it of the same diameter as the holes to be bored in the board. Put a dowel or nail through the stop block, and insert it in the first hole. Place the board so that the second hole is directly below the bit, clamp the block to the auxiliary fence, and bore the second hole. Insert the dowel in the second hole, bore the third one, and so on (Figure 17-12).

FIG. 17-12. The mechanical method of locating dowel holes permits faster work on duplicate pieces.

To bore holes in round stock, support it in a home-made V block as illustrated in Figure 17-13. The block must be clamped to the table with the bit exactly centered in the bottom of the V. Any round now placed firmly down in the V will be drilled through a diameter. Rounds, as well as small odd-shaped pieces, can also be held in a vise clamped to the table. Prepare the workpiece by drawing the centerline of the hole on one end. When securing the workpiece in the vise, position it so that this centerline is exactly aligned (vertically) with the centerline of the bit to be used. Reposition the vise, with the work in it, under the bit to bore the hole.

FIG. 17-13. Round work can be held easily with either a commercial or a home-made V block.

When boring a long piece of stock, never attempt to balance it on end to drill it. Use a home-made jig such as that shown in Figure 17-14. This is simply two substantial scrap boards with a center block (to butt against the tool column) nailed between them. Position the workpiece on the table (or tool base) ready for boring; then clamp the jig to it near the top. If necessary, use a second jig near the bottom. While boring, hold the workpiece and jig squarely against the tool column.

FIG. 17-14. End drilling a long piece. Make the center block the required width to hold the side rails parallel.

When two pieces of work are to be assembled with a screw, you can either use a screw pilot bit or bore two holes. One hole is drilled through the upper piece and is large enough to pass the shank of the screw. The lower piece (into which the screw will be threaded) is bored with a core hole smaller than the first. It is preferable to assemble the two pieces, either with a clamp or by gluing. If the correct size of pilot bit is now used, it will bore both pieces and countersink for the screwhead, all at once. Otherwise, the larger shank hole is drilled first, and the smaller core hole is then drilled down beyond it. Afterward, you can countersink for the screwhead.

COUNTERBORING AND COUNTERSINKING Counterboring is enlarging the outer end of a bored hole, usually for the purpose of accommodating the head of a bolt or screw which must be sunk below the surface. In woodworking, the enlarged portion of the hole is bored first, since wood bits do not track well in previously bored smaller holes. The smaller bit can be centered accurately at the bottom of the larger hole.

Countersinking is similar to counterboring, except that the countersink accommodates the head of a flathead screw, permitting the screw head to be sunk flush with the work surface. For countersinking a series of holes with a drill press, it is good practice to set the feed stop for uniform depth of cut. Center each hole by lowering the countersink into it before starting the motor.

POCKET HOLES The pocket hole provides a good method of attaching legs to shelves, and rails to tops (Figure 17-16). Use a guide board that is beveled to about 15°, and bore with a machine spur bit. This is actually a counterboring operation, since a larger hole is needed for the head of the screw, and a smaller one for its body. Always bore the larger hole first. The same setup can be employed for a corner pocket hole, except that the work must be supported on the edge at the corner.

Fig. 17-15. Profile bits (top) are specially designed to drill the proper size holes for wood screws. Lacking a profile bit, use a countersink cutter (bottom) for flush sealing of flathead screws.

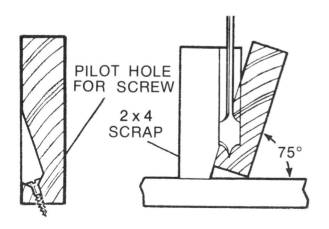

FIG. 17-16. Making a pocket hole.

PILOT HOLE FOR SCREW

2 x 4 SCRAP

75°

FIG. 17-17. A plug cutter produces perfectly fitting plugs for screw holes, or it can make small dowels.

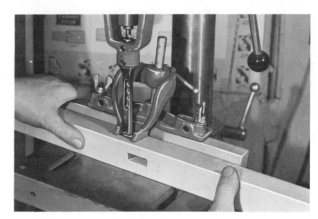

FIG. 17-18. A mortiser at work.

CUTTING DOWELS AND CIRCULAR PLUGS The plug cutter (Figure 17-19) makes it easy to cut dowel pins. The full length of the cutter makes dowels up to about 2 inches long. In addition, crossgrain plugs can be made with this cutter. Crossgrain plugs are especially useful for plugging holes in the surfaces and edges of boards. The design of these plugs makes it possible for the grain of the plug to be lined up with the grain of the board. Crossgrain plugs are also used where the heads of screws and bolts are recessed below the surface.

OTHER WOODWORKING OPERATIONS

Many other woodcutting operations can be done on a drill press, including mortising, dovetailing, routing, carving, shaping, planing, and sanding. These operations, of course, require special attachments. Also for routing, carving, shaping and planing a drill must be able to provide higher speeds—a speed multiplier arrangement, for example—or otherwise the operation will not provide satisfactory results.

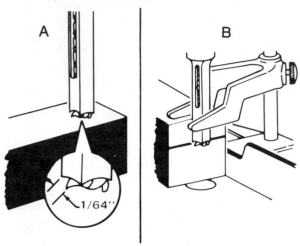

FIG. 17-19. (a) How a bit fits inside a chisel. (b) Preset the feed stop before drilling.

MORTISING Mortising differs from boring in that square or rectangular holes are made instead of round ones. A special casting is furnished to hold the hollow chisel. The casting is secured on the lower end of the quill, and the hollow, square chisel is fastened to the casting. The bit, which revolves inside the hollow chisel, is held in a special spindle or collet chuck of the required size. A special fence is clamped to the slots in the table. This fence is also provided with a "hold-down," which holds the work firmly on the table while the chisel returns to its normal position. Two bent bars keep the work against the fence.

To attach the casting to the quill, it is necessary to remove the clamp piece to which the depth gauge is attached. In most instances, the Jacobs chuck has to be removed before the clamp can be freed. If the drill press is designed to take a special spindle for the mortise bit, the regular spindle should be removed and the special spindle set in place. If the drill press is of the type to which a collet chuck can be attached to take the bit, the chuck is placed on the tapered spindle and locked in place with the threaded sleeve provided for this purpose. The chisel adapter replaces the clamp; then the depth-gauge rod is secured in the hole provided for it in the adapter. The chisel is placed in the adapter with the shoulder of the chisel tight against the bottom of the adapter, and it is secured by means of the setscrew. (When placing the chisel in the adapter, be sure to keep it square to the fence. If the chisel should be turned slightly, so that the sides are not parallel to the fence, the ends of the mortise will not be square to the stock.) The bit is passed up through the bottom of the chisel, and its shank is secured in the chuck. Hollow mortise bits have considerably wider

nibs and lips than spiral or twist bits. When securing these bits in the chuck, be certain that there is clearance between the flared end of the bit and the inside of the chisel. In order that this clearance may be obtained, the bit should project slightly beyond the end of the chisel, as shown in Figure 17-19.

The depth gauge is used to control the depth of the mortise. To set the depth gauge, the work to be mortised is set on the drill-press table, the fence is adjusted to bring the mortise in line with the mortising chisel, and the quill is racked down until the mortise bit touches the stock. The stop on the depth-gauge rod is now set for the required depth of the mortise.

Mortises longer and/or wider than the chisel width require two or more cuts. Make the first cut at one end or corner of the mortise outline—to the full depth required. Plan succeeding cuts to overlap about one-third of the chisel width; make each cut to the full depth. The work must be repositioned carefully for each new cut.

It is of the utmost importance, in mortising with a hollow mortise chisel, that both the chisel and bit be kept sharp. The feed should be slow, and never forced. If chips of wood lodge inside the chisel, the machine should be stopped and the chips removed. Failure to keep these points in mind could result in your ruining both chisel and bit. The nibs and lips of the bit are sharpened in the same manner as any auger bit. Sharpening the chisel requires the use of a cone-shaped grinding wheel.

ROUTING Shallow mortises are often cut with a router bit. A router bit is grooved throughout its length and is used for such jobs as veining, inlaying, grooving, rabbeting, and dadoing. The router bit is fastened in the same type of spindle or collet chuck as the mortising bit. The wood is pushed against the side of the bit.

All straight-line grooving and routing requires a guide. The simple auxiliary table shown in Figure 17-20 is a good one. When cutting the slot, be sure that it is not any wider than is required to contain the bit.

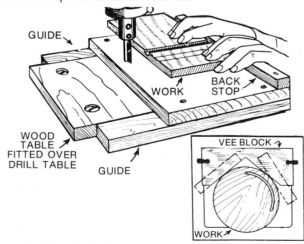

FIG. 17-20. Simple auxiliary table for routing.

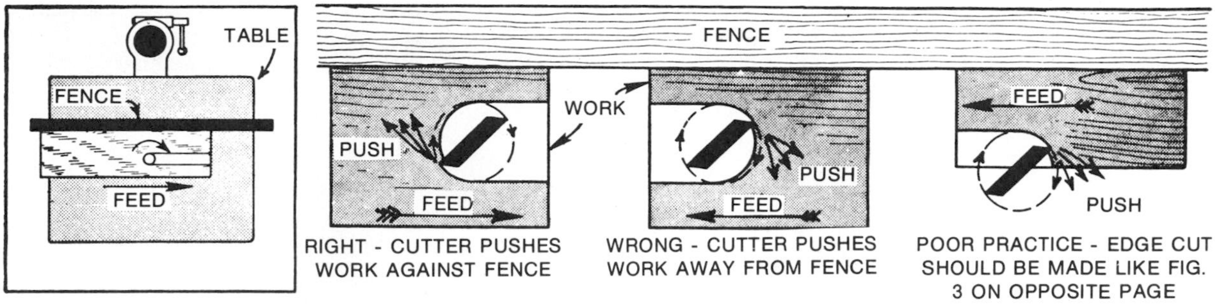

FENCE · TABLE · FENCE · FEED

FENCE

PUSH · WORK · FEED

RIGHT - CUTTER PUSHES
WORK AGAINST FENCE

PUSH · FEED

WRONG - CUTTER PUSHES
WORK AWAY FROM FENCE

FEED · PUSH

POOR PRACTICE - EDGE CUT
SHOULD BE MADE LIKE FIG.
3 ON OPPOSITE PAGE

FIG. 17-21. Why the feed must be from left to right.

Whenever possible, mark the desired depth of cut on the workpiece end (or edge), position the bit at this mark, and adjust the tool-depth setting accordingly. Otherwise, start with the bit tip resting on the workpiece top, and then adjust the depth setting by a measured distance (on the scale). Use the highest drill-press speed. If the cut will start from the outside of the workpiece, lock the quill before beginning; if it will start inside the workpiece, use the bit to bore down to the set depth, and then lock the quill before doing the routing. The bit revolves clockwise (looking down at the table), as shown in Figure 17-21. When using a bit over $\frac{1}{4}$ inch in diameter keep this in mind so you can hold the workpiece against the thrust of the bit. Also, in edge cutting, feed in the direction opposite the travel of the side of the bit that is doing the cutting (i.e., against bit rotation). Never attempt too deep a cut; it is better to make several passes at increasing depths. A cut is too deep if the workpiece is at all difficult to feed to the bit; feeding should require only very light pressure. As a rule, any cut over $\frac{1}{4}$ inch may be too deep.

For straight-line grooving and edging, as previously mentioned, a fence of some kind must be used (Figure 17-22). If the cut is along a board edge, arrange the work so

that this edge is not against the fence; otherwise, the fence must have a cutout into which the bit can be recessed as required. In making a crossgrain groove or edge trim that will extend to the workpiece edge, use a scrap block as shown in Figure 17-23, to prevent splintering. If you are edging four sides, do the crossgrain work (ends) first; then work with the grain (edges).

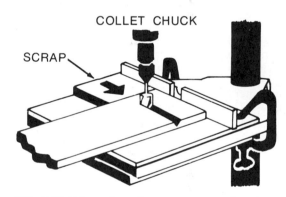

COLLET CHUCK

SCRAP

FIG. 17-23. Using a piece of scrap to prevent splintering.

As shown in Figure 17-24, some of the new radial drill presses can easily be converted into a router by turning the power head 180°. With such a unit it is not necessary to change the chuck when routing. There are, of course, other stationary routers on the market. For example, the so-called "production routers" are large units that can be raised or lowered by means of a hand screw. The router arm extends to the center of the table. In most machines the revolving part is connected to the driving mechanism by a belt (a few are now manufactured with solid-state speed controls), which gives the router speeds from 10,000 to 22,000 rpm. The table can also be raised or lowered with a treadle, and the length of the stroke can be set beforehand. Some production routers also have a chuck for holding a shaper spindle. In this case, the router cuts are necessarily made from the top, whereas a standard shaper cutter projects through the table and cuts from below. Production routers are primarily used in large woodworking shops and furniture shops.

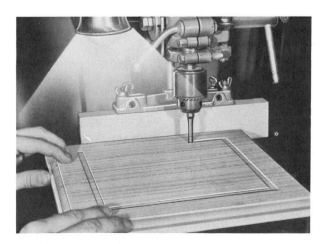

FIG. 17-22. Use a fence when straight-line routing.

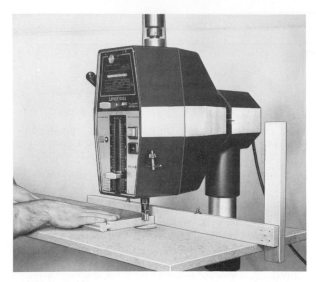

FIG. 17-24. Some drill presses have a separate router. The one shown is converted from a drill press to a router by turning the power head 180°.

CARVING Small-diameter router bits and high-speed cutters of the type sold for use with a rotary grinder (see Chapter 13) can be used to carve designs in the workpiece surfaces. Do not, however, use any bit larger than $\frac{1}{4}$ inch in diameter, and never attempt to cut deeper than $\frac{1}{8}$ inch per pass. The best practice is to cut a design outline first, down to the required depth at the outline, guiding the workpiece on the table with a firm, two-handed grip at the corners furthest from the bit. Afterward, adjust the quill for the shallowest internal cutting needed, do all of this before progressing to a deeper setting, and so on, until the design is finished. The quill must be locked at each new depth setting.

SHAPING Standard shaper cutters, of the type sold for wood shapers (see Chapter 20), can be used on the drill press if the chuck is replaced with a special adapter to hold the cutters. You must also use either a shaper fence or a collar mounted on the adapter with the cutter, to serve the same purpose as a router-bit pilot. A collar (or several, to build up to the proper diameter for the desired cut) is needed for all except straight-edge shaping; the fence is required for straight-edge work. Typical shaper cutters are illustrated in Chapter 20. Additional shapes can be achieved by combining the cuts of two or more cutters.

When the drill press is used as a shaper, the fence should be permanently mounted on a substantial ($\frac{3}{4}$-inch) plywood table cover that can be clamped to the table and that provides ample surface for holding workpieces. The cover should have an open portion in the fence, for recessing a cutter. The adapter must be securely mounted on the spindle, and the cutter must also be secure.

FIG. 17-25. Typical shaper fence in place.

When mounting a cutter, keep the direction of spindle rotation in mind; the cutter edge bevels must trail the cutting edges when the cutter is rotating. This means that some cutters having a greater diameter at one end must be mounted with this greater diameter at the bottom; others must be mounted with the greater diameter at the top. Check carefully. The collar or collars, when used, can be mounted above or below the cutter, depending upon where the uncut workpiece edge will be. Use the highest spindle speed for all operations, and always feed against the cutter rotation. Preshape the workpiece prior to shaping so the cutter will remove as little material as possible. Never cut deeper in one pass than the maximum depth shown in Figure 17-26.

LOOKING DOWN

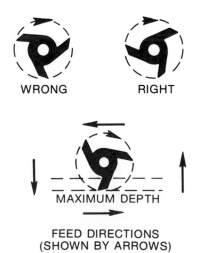

WRONG   RIGHT

MAXIMUM DEPTH

**FEED DIRECTIONS
(SHOWN BY ARROWS)**

FIG. 17-26. Rotation of shaper knives.

To accomplish straight-edge shaping, use the following procedure: Start with both fence faces adjusted for the desired depth of cut. The fence faces should also be as close to the cutter as possible, and the quill must be locked after the desired vertical position of the cutter is set. Adjust the fence spring arms to hold the workpiece firmly down and against the fence. Back the workpiece away to clear the cutter before starting the motor. If only part of the edge is being removed (leaving a part above or below the cutter untouched), finish the operation without readjusting the fence. However, if all of an edge is being cut away, stop the motor when about 1 inch of the leading workpiece edge is opposite the outfeed fence face. Adjust this outfeed face so it just makes contact with the workpiece, slide the workpiece to the left enough to clear the cutter before restarting the motor, and then finish the operation. When necessary, reset the fence faces and/or the cutter height and repeat all these steps to make a second pass. You can mount two or more cutters—up to the maximum that the adapter can securely hold—if such a combination will produce the desired shape.

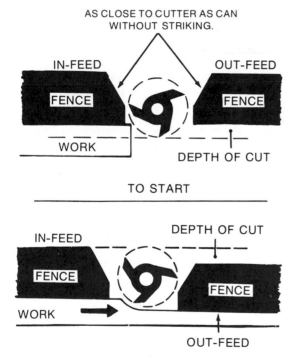

FIG. 17-27. Setup for straight edge shaping.

PLANING Planing may be done on the drill press with a rotary planing attachment such as that shown in Figure 17-28. This planing device consists of a disk about 3⅛ inches in diameter, through the base of which three cutting knives are inserted. A special collet chuck or spindle, designed to take a ½-inch shank, must be used to adapt the attachment to the drill-press spindle. The planing device is quite safe because the cutters are well inside the rim. The stock is moved in any direction while the disk is revolving.

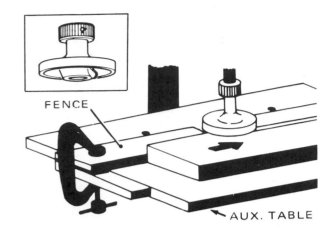

FIG. 17-28. Planer attachment in use.

To use a rotary planer, you must provide an auxiliary table constructed of flat lumber, as illustrated in Figure 17-29. This table must be bolted to the drill-press table with four bolts, washers, and wing nuts. Position the auxiliary table against the drill-press column, squared up with the drill-press table, to mark (and then bore) the four bolt holes so the bolts will engage in the drill-press-table slots. The fence is free to slide on the auxiliary table and must be secured to it with a C clamp at each end, after the fence is positioned for a cut.

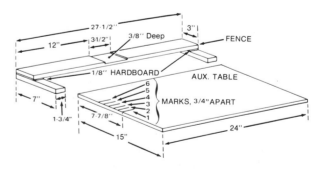

FIG. 17-29. Auxiliary table for planing. Use ¾-inch plywood for all pieces.

When using the planer attachment, never adjust the quill for more than a ¹⁄₃₂-inch-deep cut. Adjust the fence so the width of the cut will not exceed ¾ inch (even though a planer will cut a 2¾-inch-diameter circle). The quill must be locked. The drill-press table must be about 36 inches above the floor, and the head approximately 8 inches above the table. When planing a board, begin at one edge. Clamp the fence at the No. 1 mark on the table (thus providing a ¾-inch-wide edge cut). After adjusting the quill, feed the workpiece very slowly from left to right, while holding the workpiece firmly down on the table. Rotate the workpiece 180° to plane the opposite edge similarly. Afterward, (with the drill press turned off), reset the fence to the second mark to make two more cuts; and so on. If additional depth is needed, start again at the beginning, with the quill readjusted for another $\frac{1}{32}$-inch cut. (*Caution:* Keep your hands well away from the planer at all times; if necessary, use a push stick to feed the workpiece. Do not plane a warped or twisted board; the board must be flat for good, trouble-free work. Never attempt to plane freehand—the fence must be used to guide the workpiece.)

SANDING AND POLISHING Sanding and polishing require accessories such as sanding disks, sanding drums, and polishing bonnets. Sanding drums are generally available in two sizes, large and small; the larger drum usually requires a special work arbor, whereas the smaller drum and sanding disks can be mounted in a standard chuck. Use a spindle speed of from 1300 to 2300 rpm. Replaceable sleeves (for the drums) and disks (for the plate) are available in standard sandpaper grits (see Chapter 8). The polishing bonnet fits over the sanding-disk plate (which is sold with bonnet and disks as a kit for electric hand drills).

Disk sanding requires the use of a table-cover guide with fence (Figure 17-30); if you should try to feed the work without a fence, it would be very difficult to hold. Lower and lock the quill in position for the sandpaper disk to take a light bite; then feed left to right along the fence. For additional passes, reposition the table cover as necessary to reach the entire workpiece surface, without altering the depth-of-cut setting.

FIG. 17-30. Disk sander in action.

Drum sanding can be done freehand (the work is held with two hands and guided to the drum) or, better, with the use of an auxiliary table clamped to the drill-press table as shown in Figure 17-31. In either case, the quill must be locked, and the workpiece must be guided with both hands. A drum sander should not be operated at a spindle speed greater than 800 rpm.

FIG. 17-31. Drum sander in action.

To sand to depth, use a pattern and a guide. The guide is a wooden disk of the same diameter as the sanding drum, fastened to the auxiliary table and centered under the drum so that the pattern edge will contact it during operation. The workpiece must be secured to the pattern (with rubber cement or brad points) so that the desired finish contour will be achieved when the pattern is in firm contact with the guide. More data on both disk and drum sanding, adaptable to drill-press sanding, can be found in Chapter 21.

For polishing, the polishing bonnet is installed on the sanding plate, the quill is locked at a convenient chuck height, and the work is fed to the bottom side of the bonnet (never the edge). The workpiece surface should be coated with wax, oil, or polish. Use a light feed pressure.

METAL DRILLING

Drilling in metal is much the same as boring in wood, with certain differences. Since the material is much tougher and harder, speeds and feeds are more critical to the quality of the work and the life of the cutting tool. In drilling metal, there is also a greater tendency for the work to twist, particularly when the point of the drill breaks through. For this reason, care must be taken to see that the work is held securely to the table. The drill vise is best for small or round work, while large flat work can be secured with clamps. Holes can be drilled in large pieces by holding the work with a step block and clamps (Figure

17-32a). (A piece of metal of suitable size, with a hole drilled near one end, makes a suitable substitute for a clamp.) When holding work with step blocks and clamps, you may use a gooseneck clamp as shown in Figure 17-32b. Notice that the body of the clamp is approximately parallel to the surface of the drill-press table and that the bolt is held close to the work rather than close to the step block. This setup provides the most favorable mechanical advantage. Usually, two or more clamps are used on each setup.

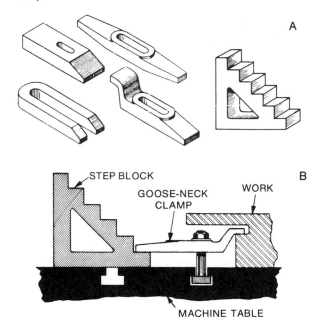

FIG. 17-32. (a) Step block and clamp; (b) how they hold work for drilling.

Every hole drilled in metal must be started with a suitable center-punch mark; if the bit tip is too large to seat in this mark, a smaller drill must be used to start a hole that the bit tip can seat in. If this is not done, the bit can wander, spoil the hole, and possibly be broken. If the bit wanders at the start, either the starting hole was not properly made, the workpiece is not being held with its surface at 90° to the bit (the surface is slanted down), or the bit has been improperly sharpened (tip off center, one tip too long, etc.). Stop, check for the cause, and correct the problem. Then (as described in Chapter 1), use a cape chisel to cut away some metal on the side toward which the drill should return. Cut out enough to drift the bit back to the center when the operation is resumed.

Always apply pressure along a line straight through the axis of the drill. (Side pressure will enlarge the hole and can break the drill.) Keep the drill steady, and apply enough pressure to keep it cutting. Too much pressure will overload the motor; too little pressure will cause the drill to "polish" instead of cut. This will quickly dull the cutting edges of the drill. You will know the pressure is correct when the drill bites continuously without overloading the drill motor. Drill large holes in stages. A pilot hole is a good idea, since it serves as a guide for the larger drill and helps to increase accuracy.

Most metals can be drilled without lubrication, but ferrous metals (especially the harder steels) and the dense aluminums should be lubricated to prevent overheating of the bit point. For aluminum, use kerosene; for ferrous metals, use a light oil. (See Chapters 3 and 9 for more details on the lubricants to use when drilling.) Place a drop on the "spot" before starting; then add lubricant as you see it is needed. Chip clearing is also important, particularly in drilling deep holes, so raise the drill often, and do not let the flutes clog with chips.

Table 17-2 lists some of the common problems that are sometimes encountered in drilling metal and their possible solutions.

Table 17-2 Metal-Drilling Problems and Solutions

Drilling problem	Cause	What to do
Drill overheats and turns blue at the corners	Cutting speed too high	Reduce spindle speed
Drill breaks or chips at cutting edges	Excessive clearance	Regrind drill; use less clearance
Drill slits up the web	Feed rate too high; insufficient clearance	Reduce feed rate; regrind drill; use more clearance
Hole drilled oversize (it should be understood that a drill normally cuts slightly oversize)	Unequal lip lengths; tool misaligned in drill holder	Regrind drill; use a drill-point gauge to check for correct angle and lip length; realign tool or change drill holder
Hole drilled undersize (common with abrasive materials such as phenolic resins, hard rubber, aluminum castings, and cast-iron scale)	Margin has been worn down	Replace drill
Bell-mouth hole	Drill not held properly in machine; work not held securely	Check and adjust drill clamping; reclamp work securely

Bits will last longer if you use the recommended spindle speeds. Also watch the rate of feed. Except when cast iron is drilled, chips should emerge as long ribbons. If the feed pressure is too light, the chips will be too thin to make ribbons; if too heavy, the chips will grow too fast and clog the bit. Hold the feed pressure steady until the bit is about to break through; then ease the pressure for the breakthrough.

COUNTERSINKING AND COUNTERBORING An 82°-angle high-speed countersink bit is used to enlarge the top of a drilled hole for countersinking a flathead machine screw or simply to remove the sharp edge from the hole prior to reaming or tapping. Choose a bit whose diameter is at least as large as the diameter of the top of the screwhead. Use the spindle speed for that diameter of bit. To sink the screwhead exactly flush, preset the feed stop so the bit will enter the workpiece up to the point at which its diameter is exactly that of the screwhead top. (If the workpiece has a flat, smooth top, hold the screw upside down on the top near an edge, so you can lower the bit alongside it to sight the matching of diameters.)

Counterboring in metal is the enlargement of the top of a hole to recess a bolt head. It usually is done in a workshop with a bit of the required diameter (larger than the hole), in which case the recess shoulders are slanted down toward the center instead of being flat. To recess the bolt head fully, a feed stop must be set so that the outer ends of the bit lips will penetrate to a depth equal to bolt-head height. *Note:* Bits designed for counterboring flat-shouldered recesses are available at machine-tool supply houses. These also are used for spot facing, the leveling of a rough (casting) surface around a hole to provide a flat seat for a bolt head.

Spot facing is similar to counterboring. It is done to produce a flat surface in a local area or a spot on which to seat a washer or bolt head.

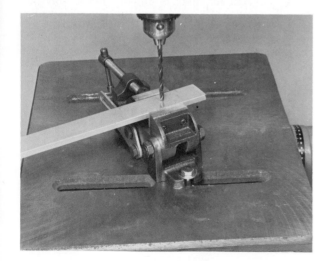

FIG. 17-33. Holding thin-gauge metal for drilling.

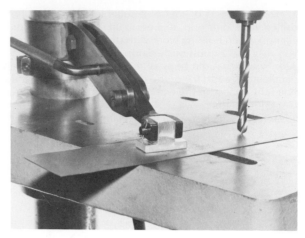

FIG. 17-34. A magnetic clamp such as the one shown holds thin-gauge metal for drilling.

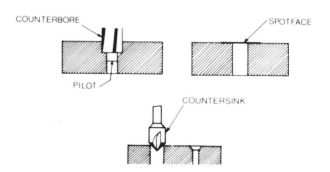

FIG. 17-35. Counterboring and countersinking a hole.

PLASTIC DRILLING

Although plastics can be drilled with ordinary metal twist drills, better operations (less "hogging" by the bit) are achieved if the bit points are reground to the lip angle illustrated in Figure 17-36a. Use the spindle speeds recommended on the drill-press chart. Lift the bit out of the hole frequently to clear the chips and prevent softening of the plastic, especially when drilling a thermosetting plastic. If the holes are for metal (nails, screws, etc.) and the material will be subject to temperature changes, it is best to drill them $1/64$ to $1/32$ inch oversize to allow for expansion and contraction. Do not turn the screwheads down very tight.

DRILLING GLASS

The most accurate and successful glass drilling is done either with a diamond-pointed bit or a specially designed tungsten-carbide-pointed bit (available at jeweler's supply houses and some specialty and hobby shops). See Figure 17-36b. The workpiece must be on a flat, clean, absolutely level wood surface (the slightest bump—even a grain of sand—under the pressure point can start a crack). The bit must be kept well lubricated; turpentine or kerosene is best, though water will do. Use the spindle speeds recommended for stainless steel. Heavy, very steady feed pressure is required to keep the bit grinding (there are no visible chips), but the pressure must be eased off considerably just after the bit point breaks through. In fact, if practical, it is best to turn the workpiece over and finish from the other side at this point.

Glass can also be drilled by using a piece of brass tubing with an outside diameter equal to the size of the hole to be drilled. The tubing should be slotted with one cut, using a very narrow saw. The cut need not extend more than about 1/4 inch from the end of the tube. Similar results

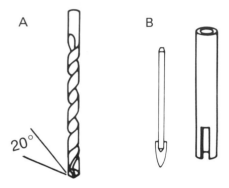

FIG. 17-36. Special drills: *(a)* plastic drill; *(b)* glass drills.

are effected by notching the end of the tube in two or three places. The tube is not sharpened in any way; it is simply cut square on the end and then slotted or notched as noted. The glass should be supported on a perfectly flat piece of wood or, better, on a piece of felt or rubber. A dam of putty is built around the place where the hole is to be drilled (Figure 17-37a), or a felt ring can be used for the same purpose. The well is fed with a liquidy mixture of 80-grit silicon-carbide abrasive grains combined with machine oil or turpentine. Use enough feed pressure to keep the bit grinding, but no more (Figure 17-37b). Do not attempt to drill through; about halfway through, restart the hole from the other side.

Very hard glazed ceramic tiles and clay pottery should be drilled in the same way as glass.

A

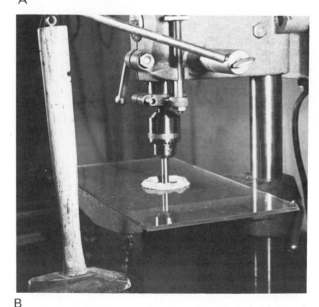

B

FIG. 17-37. A home-made brass or steel rod can be used for drilling glass. Make a putty dam, and fill it with silicon carbide and turpentine. A weight on the feed lever will maintain the required pressure .

LATHES

The lathe was probably the first powered woodworking machine. In its early form, it consisted of two holding centers with the suspended stock being rotated by an endless rope belt. To operate it, one person pulled on the rope hand over hand, while the cutting was done by a second person holding crude hand lathe tools on an improvised beam rest.

The wood turning performed on modern lathes is still done almost exclusively with woodturner's hand tools. In fact, the lathe, more than any other woodworking tool in the shop, is in itself a complete unit capable of producing finished work. The machine is not difficult to operate; indeed, any beginner can make a creditable turning on the very first try by using scraping methods. True wood turning, however, is a cutting operation, and the acquisition of the skill necessary to fashion turnings quickly and well in this manner demands some knowledge of the methods and considerable practice in their application.

In recent years, the lathe has declined a little in popularity as a shop tool. But with the increased interest in early American colonial and contemporary furniture, as well as the various provincial lines, the lathe may well make a comeback. In any case, wood turning is a fascinating art. Under the chisel, the whirling wood is molded like clay on the potter's wheel, and only imagination limits the forms than can be evolved. Table legs, lamp bases, bowls, gunstocks, pepper mills, lazy Susans, and candlesticks shaped into countless designs are but a few of the items to be made with a lathe.

WOOD LATHES AND LATHE EQUIPMENT

The terms "wood lathe" and "speed lathe" are generally used to describe wood-turning lathes to avoid confusion with machine or metal-turning lathes. Wood lathes are designated according to the maximum diameter of work which can be swung over the bed; a lathe capable of swinging an 11-inch-diameter disk of wood is called an 11-inch lathe. (Remember that the maximum swing of a lathe is twice the distance from the centerline of the headstock spindle to the bed.) The gap-bed lathe shown in Figure 18-1 has a swing of 11 inches over the bed, and a swing over the gap of 13½ inches with 4-inch-thick stock. This gap feature makes it possible to do larger face-plate turning on the inside of the lathe.

The standard wood lathe shown in Figure 18-2 has a maximum swing of 12 inches and a working-center capacity of 37 inches. (The latter is the maximum distance between the headstock and tailstock centers.) The miniature lathe illustrated in Figure 18-3 has a maximum swing of 4 inches and center capacity of 10 inches.

A lathe may have a direct-drive motor, it may be belt driven (employing step pulleys), or it may have a variable-speed pulley. The speed range of a lathe depends, of course, on the drive arrangement used. For instance, the

FIG. 18-1. Typical gap-bed bench wood-turning lathe.

gap-bed lathe shown in Figure 18-4 has a variable-speed control drive which permits it to turn at any speed from 240 to 3600 rpm. A lathe equipped with a standard four-step pulley may have speeds of 960, 1575, 2100, and 3150 rpm. On some wood lathes, speeds up over 4000 rpm are obtainable.

The principal parts of any wood lathe (Figure 18-5) are the headstock, tailstock, tool rest, and bed. The headstock is mounted on the left end of the lathe bed, and all power for the lathe is transmitted through the headstock. There are two general types of headstocks, depending on whether the spindle is hollow or solid. Most standard

FIG. 18-3. Miniature woodworking lathe in use.

FIG. 18-2. Standard wood-turning lathe with its own bench.

FIG. 18-4. Heavy-duty gap-bed lathe.

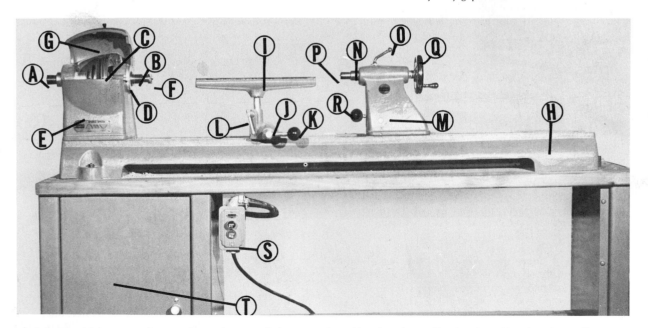

FIG. 18-5. Major parts of a typical wood-turning lathe: (a) outboard headstock spindle; (b) inboard headstock spindle; (c) spindle pulley (note the cone-pulley arrangement for adjusting the belt for various speeds); (d) indexing stop pin (used for face-plate work and for spacing cuts in fluting); (e) headstock; (f) live (spur) center; (g) pulley cover; (h) lathe bed; (i) tool T rest; (j) tool-rest base; (k) tool-rest base clamp; (l) tool-rest clamp; (m) tailstock; (n) tailstock quill; (o) quill clamp; (p) dead (cup) center; (q) quill wheel crank; (r) tailstock clamp; (s) on-off switch; (t) stand and motor housing.

lathes employ a hollow spindle, internally tapered at both ends to take No. 2 Morse shanks. Smaller lathes have either a hollow spindle with a No. 1 Morse taper, or a solid spindle. The spindle of the tailstock is usually made to match the headstock spindle so that various attachments can be used in either position. The two main attachments are the spur center, which fits the headstock spindle and is consequently known as the "live" center, and the cup center, which fits the tailstock spindle and is known as the "dead" center. In operation, the work is mounted between these two centers for turning, the spurs of the live center serving as the driving member.

The tailstock of the lathe usually has three adjustments. First, it can be moved bodily along the lathe bed and can be clamped at any position by means of a wrench which fits over the tailstock clamp screw. Second, it can be moved within slight limits across the bed of the lathe by means of the set-over screws. Third, the spindle can be projected or retracted inside the body of the tailstock by manipulating the feed handle. Any desired position can be fixed by clamping the spindle with the tailstock spindle clamp.

The tool rest consists of two main parts, the base and the rest or support itself. Different types of rests are interchangeable in the same base. The turning tool is worked back and forth along the horizontal guide of the tool rest during the wood-turning operation.

The lathe bed is the supporting body of the lathe. It holds the headstock and tailstock assemblies, as well as the tool rest and its support. The lathe bed should be

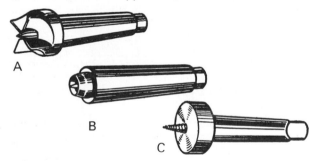

FIG. 18-6. Three types of centers: *(a)* spur or drive center; *(b)* cup center; *(c)* screw or dead center. The latter furnishes a quick and satisfactory method of mounting small face-plate turnings.

constructed of heavy steel. Those constructed of either rods or sections of pipe set up vibrations which make accurate wood turning an impossibility.

The lathe can be mounted on any workbench or on a special frame with metal legs, as shown in Figure 18-2. The lathe-spindle centerline should be 40 to 44 inches above the floor—in other words, at waist level. If the lathe is not self-contained, the motor can be mounted below or to the rear of the lathe, depending on the method of installation. The motor should be at least a $\frac{1}{4}$-hp, 1750-

rpm capacitor or repulsion-induction motor for average wood turning. A switch rod or electric off-on switch should be installed to bring the power control within convenient reach.

TURNING TOOLS The wood lathe is different from any other woodworking machine because hand tools are used in conjunction with the power-driven machine. The hand tools used are a series of chisels. But these steel chisels are longer and heavier than similar chisels used in ordinary woodworking (see Chapter 2). The handles are also proportionally longer and heavier. Since turning chisels are never driven into the wood, they have no shoulder. The common wood-turning tools are shown in Figure 18-8.

Gouge This tool is used in spindle turning (turning between centers) for reducing stock to a cylinder and for making rough and concave cuts—for example, cones and circular grooves. In face-plate turning, gouges are used for these same purposes, and sometimes for turning beads. In use, the tip of the handle ordinarily is held several inches below the top of the rest, and the gouge is rolled over on its side in the direction of the cut. That is, the round side of the gouge should rest on the tool-rest and should be turned or rolled a little to the right, with the wooden handle always held down. This produces a *shearing* cut.

Gouges are made in sizes varying from $\frac{1}{8}$ to 2 inches or more. The most commonly used sizes are $\frac{1}{4}$, $\frac{1}{2}$, $\frac{3}{4}$, and 1 inch.

Skew The cutting edge of this tool is ground at an angle

FIG. 18-7. The tool rest can be placed in any position. This "phantom" photograph shows many of the positions which tool rests may take to handle work.

of about 70° with the narrow side of the chisel. It is called a skew chisel because the cutting edge is skewed or angled to the side. Skew chisels are used in such a manner as to produce a shearing cut. They are employed for making smoothing cuts after the stock has been reduced to approximately the desired size, for making V cuts and convex cuts (turning beads), and for trimming shoulders and ends. Skew chisels are made in sizes varying from $\frac{1}{8}$ to $1\frac{1}{2}$ inches or more.

The right and left skew chisels are like ordinary skew

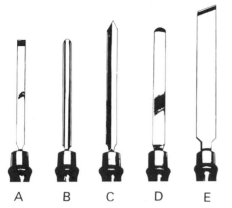

FIG. 18-8. Basic chisels: *(a)* squarenose; *(b)* gouge; *(c)* parting tool; *(d)* roundnose; *(e)* skew.

chisels, except that they are ground with only one face bevel. Such chisels are used to finish-turn recesses where it would be inconvenient or impossible to use a square-nosed tool.

Parting Tool This tool is used for cutting narrow grooves, for cutting recesses with straight sides and a flat or square bottom, or to serve as a depth guide to facilitate the turning of a true cylinder. The parting tool should be held with the narrow edge on the tool rest and the point of the tool in the same plane as the centerline of the work, or slightly above. Held thusly, the tool makes a scraping cut. Parting tools range in size from $\frac{1}{8}$ to $\frac{3}{4}$ inch.

Roundnose This scraping tool is used principally for rough turning, forming concave recesses, coves, and circular grooves, chiefly in face-plate turning. The roundnose is placed flat on the tool rest, with the bevel side of the chisel down. Roundnose tools are made in a number of sizes; the most commonly used are $\frac{1}{8}$, $\frac{1}{4}$, and $\frac{1}{2}$ inch.

Squarenose This tool resembles an ordinary flat chisel, except that the bevel is ground at an angle of 45°. It is a scraping tool and is used principally for smoothing convex or flat surfaces, chiefly in face-plate turning. In spindle turning, it is frequently used to smooth off the cylinder and make it perfectly straight just before the sanding operation. The squarenose chisel is usually held with the beveled side down. The tool is available in various sizes, the most common being $\frac{1}{2}$ and $\frac{3}{4}$ inch.

Spearpoint This tool—frequently called a "diamond point"—is used for smoothing the insides of recesses or

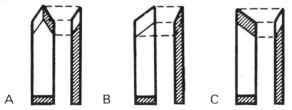

FIG. 18-9. Other chisels: *(a)* spearpoint; *(b)* right skew; *(c)* left skew.

square corners and for convex or bead cutting where it is necessary to round off corners. Frequently the spearpoint serves the same purpose as the left or right skew chisel. To avoid catching when the tool is used to smooth a square corner, the cutting edges should be ground on each side at an angle of from 30 to 35°. As a rule, the spearpoint chisel is placed flat on the tool rest, with the point of the tool above the centerline.

A spearpoint tool can be made by grinding a skew chisel of suitable size to the shape desired, or it can be purchased in various sizes. The sharpening of wood-turning tools is discussed in Chapter 22.

Tungsten-carbide-tipped wood-turning chisels are available in all shapes and in most common sizes. Such tools hold their sharpness much longer than steel but are more expensive to purchase. However, in addition to being used on wood, the carbide-tipped tools can be employed in freehand turning on plastics and metals at woodworking speeds.

When working with carbide-tipped chisels on hard materials, it is usually best to employ slow speeds. The angle at which the tool is held can help you do a better job with carbide-tipped tools. As a *general* rule, for wood and plastics, the chisel handle should be slightly below the tool rest. For steel, keep it about level; for nonferrous metals, raise it. Also remember that carbide edges are quite brittle. Therefore, make certain that the cutting edges are protected; avoid banging them against hard surfaces.

MEASURING TOOLS Most lathe work requires certain measuring tools, namely, a 1- or 2-foot rule, inside and outside calipers for checking the diameter of the work, and dividers for laying out circles, especially on face-plate work. Spring-type calipers are best, since they are often applied directly to the revolving stock and must be depended on to hold a set dimension when in this position. Full details on the use of these measuring tools can be found in Chapter 7.

LATHE ACCESSORIES Figure 18-10 illustrates various accessories which are frequently used in wood turning. The *24-inch tool support,* for example, is invaluable for doing turnings which cannot be covered from end to end with the shorter tool rest. The *right-angle support* is used for face-plate work; it permits operations on both the rim and face of the turning. The *face plate* is used for face-plate turning; the 6- and 3-inch-diameter sizes are usually needed. The *screw-on arbor* is valuable as a means of mounting a grinding wheel, wire brush, or buffing wheel; this is available with both right- and left-hand threads to fit either end of the spindle. Sanding accessories are worthwhile aids, the two most common types being the *sanding drum* and the *sanding disk.* The *steady rest* is used as a support for long, slender turnings, or as an end support for shorter work. Accessories for any specific lathe model may vary slightly in construction to suit the mechanics of the lathe.

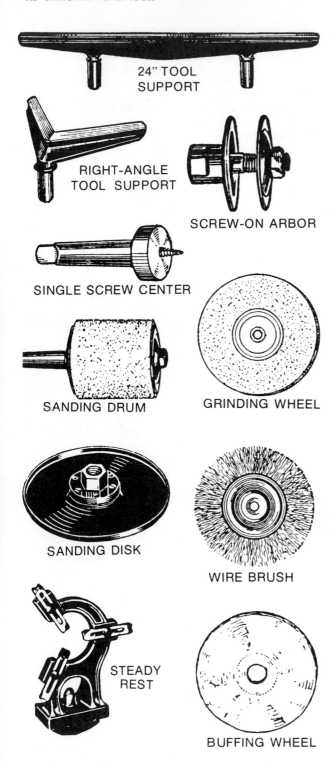

FIG. 18-10. Various lathe accessories.

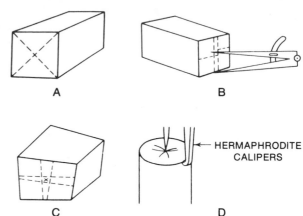

FIG. 18-11. Methods of determining the exact center.

LATHE SAFETY

While the lathe is one of the safest tools in the shop, accidents can and do happen. Before attempting to do any work on a lathe, it is advisable to become familiar with certain precautions for your own safety.

1. Make sure that the wood you are going to turn is free of knots, checks, and other defects. Do not turn stock that is badly cracked. It might come apart when run at high speed. If you are turning glued stock between centers, it is advisable to cut it a little longer than needed, insert a screw between the centers or to the face plates, and tighten the two clamps on the tailstock and tool post, because work thrown from the lathe strikes with tremendous force.
3. After tightening all the clamps, revolve the stock by hand to make sure that it clears at all points.
4. Remember to put soap or oil on the end running on the dead center, because the friction at this spot will usually burn the wood, and its exact center may be lost. It may also become loose and possibly fly out of the lathe.
5. Place the tool rest as close to the work as possible; do not change its position while the lathe is running, because you might injure your hand. Always stop the lathe before making any adjustments.
6. Never allow any other person to stand near the lathe when it is in operation.
7. Hold all tools firmly, and use only sharp tools. Dull tools are always very dangerous to use.
8. Do not turn stock that is too far out of center, as it causes excessive vibration and may be thrown from the lathe.
9. Plane off the sharp edges of large-diameter stock; this will allow it to run smoother and prevent large splinters from flying off the stock.

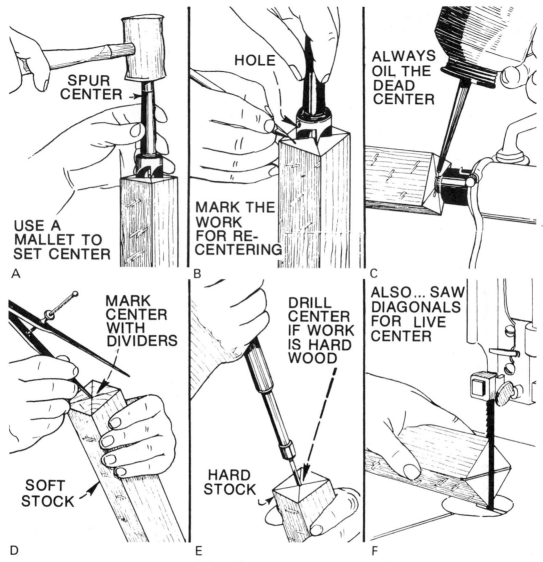

FIG. 18-12. Various operations in centering lathe work.

10. Do not screw a face plate partway onto the live spindle and then turn on the power, since this will generally cause the face plate to jam very hard against the live spindle, and it will be difficult to remove.

11. Do not run the lathe at a high speed, especially not until the stock has been rounded off. Keep in mind that slower operating speeds are by far the safest to use. For stock over 6 inches in diameter, maintain a slow speed; from 3 to 6 inches, medium speed; under 3 inches, a faster speed.

12. Remove the tool rest when sanding or polishing.

If you do not, there is always the possibility of getting a finger caught between the stock and the tool rest.

13. Always wear goggles or a face shield when working on a lathe.

14. It is especially important that your sleeves be tight and your necktie off, and that you wear no loose clothing when working at the lathe.

Woodworking lathes, like all other pieces of machinery, will not stand overloading or indefinite overworking. A person about to operate a machine should first become acquainted with its capacity, and

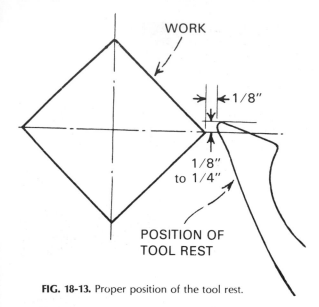

FIG. 18-13. Proper position of the tool rest.

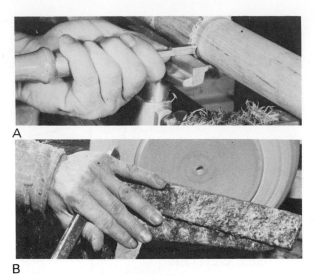

FIG. 18-14. Two methods of holding a chisel.

then, when operating it, do so safely within its capacity. Ordinarily, a woodworking lathe will need only nominal care to keep it in good working order. If cap screws, setscrews, and nuts are kept properly tightened, and revolving parts properly lubricated, little difficulty will be experienced in keeping the machine in good working order. Lack of lubrication is the most frequent cause of wear and vibration in a woodworking lathe.

Spindle Turning on the Lathe

Spindle turning, or turning between centers, means the turning of work held between the live and dead centers. This is the principal type of wood turning, as typified by the making of table and chair legs, lamp stems, etc. Spindle turning can be done with either a scraping or a cutting technique.

The scraping method is the simplest and easiest for the beginner to learn. All the tools are used as scraping tools, and the wood is removed by wearing away the fibers. It does not produce as smooth a surface, but with sanding it is very satisfactory. For the operator who makes only an occasional piece on the wood lathe, this method can be recommended. All face-plate work is done by the scraping method.

With the cutting or paring method, the wood fibers are sheared off. This requires considerably more practice. If you plan to do a good deal of wood turning, it will pay to learn this method.

CENTERING AND MOUNTING WORK

If the true center points on the ends of the stock are not properly located, a considerable amount of vibration will result, and it will be impossible to make an accurate turning. The common methods of determining the exact center are shown in Figure 18-11.

On approximately square stock, one method (a) consists of drawing diagonal lines from corner to corner, the intersection marking the center of the work. In another square-stock method (b), a distance a little more or a little less than one-half the width of the stock is set off from each of the four sides. The small square thus set off in the center can then be used in marking the true center. If the stock is lopsided, the true center can be found by laying it on a bench and scribing the ends with a pair of dividers as shown in c. On round material, determine the center point quickly with a pair of hermaphrodite calipers or dividers (d).

FIG. 18-15. The first rough cuts can also be made with a parting tool.

To make mounting easier, make two diagonal saw cuts across the end that is to be at the headstock of the lathe (Figure 18-12a). If the wood is extremely hard, saw a kerf about $\frac{1}{8}$ inch deep across each corner and drill a small center hole, $\frac{1}{16}$ inch in diameter and $\frac{1}{8}$ inch deep, in either end for insertion of the centers (Figure 18-12b). In softwoods, mark the center with a prick punch or scratch awl (Figure 18-12c).

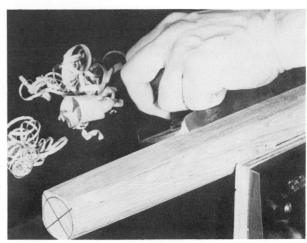

FIG. 18-16. Sometimes it is easier to do rough work with a chisel or plane before mounting the work in the lathe.

Remove the spur center from the headstock spindle. This is usually accomplished by loosening the hex-head screws. With a soft-face mallet drive the spur of the headstock into the saw cut at the center point, about $\frac{1}{8}$ inch deep (Figure 18-12d). Never drive the piece of wood against the headstock of the lathe by hammering on the far end. This will damage the bearing on the lathe and in time will knock the headstock out of alignment. Replace the spur center on the headstock spindle, and lock it in place (usually by tightening setscrews). If the work is to be removed from the lathe before completion, an index mark should be made as a guide for recentering (Figure 18-12e). A permanent indexer can be made by grinding off one corner of one of the spurs.

Move the tailstock of the lathe so that its point of dead center is approximately $\frac{1}{2}$ inch from the end of the stock. Secure the tailstock in place by tightening the adjusting wrench. Then, continue by turning the hand wheel of the tailstock so that when the dead center enters the stock it will be set in so firmly that the work cannot be turned by hand. Turn the handwheel in the opposite direction to loosen it just enough so that the work can now be turned by hand. Tighten the dead-center clamp at the top of the tailstock to hold the stock firmly in position.

Lubricate the dead center of the tailstock with oil, or, if the stain will be objectionable, fill the cup with soap, paraffin, or some other solid lubricant so that the stock will not be burned by friction on the dead center (Figure 18-12f).

ADJUSTING THE TOOL REST Proper location of the tool rest is the last preliminary operation before starting the actual turning. The tool rest should be adjusted so that its top is $\frac{1}{8}$ to $\frac{1}{4}$ inch above the center. The top of the tool rest should be parallel to the stock and about $\frac{1}{8}$ inch away from the furthest-projecting edge of the material being turned (Figure 18-13). Turn the stock by hand to be sure that it has the proper amount of clearance. Check that all clamps and adjusting wrenches are tight, and all necessary adjustments made, before turning on the motor switch on the radial arm.

LATHE SPEEDS Generally speaking, the larger the work, the slower the speed should be. Turning large work at excessive speed is very dangerous and should never be attempted. Suitable speeds for various sizes of turnings (with regard to both safety and procedure) have been established, and these should be followed. The four-step pulleys provided with many standard wood lathes give adequate speed adjustment for most wood-turning operations. Table 18-1 gives the basic speeds for most woodturning.

Table 18-1 Wood-Lathe Cutting Speeds

Diameter of stock, inches	Cutting speeds, rpm		
	Roughing to size	General cutting	Finishing
Under 2	900–1300	2400–2800	3000–4000
2–4	600–1000	1800–2400	2400–3000
4–6	600– 800	1200–1800	1800–2400
6–8	400– 600	800–1200	1200–1800
8–10	300– 400	600– 800	900–1200
Over 10	200– 300	300– 600	600– 900

SHAPING SQUARE STOCK TO A CYLINDER

The first step in the process of shaping a rectangular piece of stock into cylindrical form on the lathe is called "roughing." This process consists of cutting off the square edges of the material until the piece is approximately cylindrical.

Take a position in front of the lathe, with your left side turned a little nearer to the lathe than the right. Take an easy position that permits you to sway from side to side. Start the lathe, but not at its highest speed, and proceed to round off the piece with a 1-inch gouge. If you are right-handed, hold the gouge in your left hand, using whichever of the following methods is most suited to you.

1. Grasp the gouge about an inch from the cutting end, with the thumb on the inside and the other fingers around the outside or convex side. The index finger will then act as a stop against the tool rest (Figure 18-14a).
2. Place your hand over the concave side of the gouge, with the thumb underneath. The wrist must be bent to act as a stop against the tool rest (Figure 18-14b).

Hold the handle of the turning tool firmly in the right hand. Place the convex side of the gouge against the tool rest, about 2 inches from the dead center. (Never start a cut at the end of the stock; the cutting tool is apt to catch and be forcibly thrown from your hand.) Your index finger or wrist should be held firmly against the rest, and the cutting tool against the top. Twist the turning tool slightly to the right and force it into the revolving stock until cutting begins. The beveled edge should be tangent to the cylinder. Then push the tool slowly toward the tailstock. Start the second cut several inches to the left of the first, and continue in the direction of the first cut until both meet. When rounding off the material, do not take long cuts; large chips or slivers of wood are apt to fly off and cause injury to you and to the material.

After each cut, move the tool several inches more toward the headstock and repeat. When the cylinder is formed to within 2 inches of the headstock, twist the tool to the left, pushing it toward the headstock. At first the cutting will be done only on the edges, then gradually on the whole cylinder. It is easy to tell if the stock is round by laying a tool lightly against the revolving surface.

When making a roughing cut, do not attempt to shape the material to a perfect cylindrical form of the required dimension. When roughing, occasionally check the dimensions of the cylinder with calipers. Continue to move the gouge back and forth from right to left on the tool rest until the entire piece of stock is cylindrical in form and approximately $\frac{1}{8}$ inch larger than the largest diameter of the finished turning. Then turn off the motor.

The next series of cuts, called "sizing" cuts, are made with a parting tool. Set the lathe at the proper speed, readjust the position of the tool rest to $\frac{1}{8}$ inch from the cylinder, and tighten it in place. Adjust the caliper to a diameter $\frac{1}{16}$ inch greater than that required for the finished work. This is the allowance for the finishing cuts and final sanding.

With the caliper held in the left hand and the parting chisel in the right (Figure 18-17), start the lathe. Using the parting tool, cut a narrow groove in the stock several inches from dead center. Take light, thin shavings, and do not exert too great a pressure on the chisel. As the work progresses, check the depth of the cut with the caliper. Stop cutting when the legs of the caliper pass over the cut without any pressure. Repeat the operation at intervals of approximately 1 inch over the entire length of the work. These grooves are sizing or parting cuts.

Smoothing and cutting the cylinder to the required dimension is the final operation. This is called the "finishing" cut. When making this cut on the lathe by the scraping method, use a large skew or a squarenose chisel (Figure 18-18). Use the recommended speed for this job.

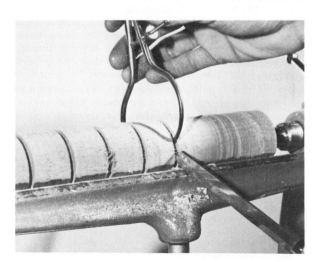

FIG. 18-17. Use calipers and the parting tool to make guide cuts every few inches along the work.

FIG. 18-18. Use a large skew or squarenose chisel to turn the work to size.

Hold the cutting edge parallel to the cylinder, and force it into the stock until the scraping begins. Then move it from one side to the other. Always start the scraping some distance in from the ends to prevent the tool from catching and splitting the wood. Check occasionally with an outside caliper until the finished size is obtained.

For the cutting or paring method, use a large-size skew. Place the skew on its side with the cutting edge slightly above and beyond the cylinder. Start at a point 2 to 3 inches in from the end. Hold the side of the tool firmly against the tool rest. Slowly draw the skew back until the cutting edge is over the cylinder at a point about halfway between the heel and toe (Figure 18-19). Keep the edge at an angle of about 40 to 60° with the axis of the work. Be careful not to catch the toe of the tool in the revolving cylinder. Tip the skew slightly until the cutting edge can be forced into the wood. Then push the skew along toward the tailstock, taking a shearing cut. Reverse the direction and cut toward the headstock.

The operation of squaring an end can be done with a parting tool or spearpoint chisel (Figure 18-20). However, both tools are rough cutters, so that ultimately the skew must be used in cleaning the cut. The whole operation can be done with the skew, and this technique is illustrated in Figure 18-21. The first movement is a nicking cut with the toe of the skew. This cut cannot be made very deep without danger of burning the chisel, so a clearance cut is made by inclining the skew away from the first cut and again pushing the tool into the work. This procedure, side cut and clearance cut, is repeated as often as needed. The important point to note is that while the skew can be pushed into the wood in any direction, the cutting edge itself must be inclined a little away from this work plane. In Figure 18-19, note that if the full cutting edge of the skew bears against the cut surface, the tool will have a tendency to run. Now observe the proper way to make the cut, as shown at the left end of Figure 18-19. The chisel is pushed straight into the work, but the cutting edge is inclined away from the cut surface; only the extreme toe end cuts. This is the most important principle in skew handling, and you will run into it repeatedly in making shoulders, beads, and vee cuts.

The beginner's major difficulty is in holding the tool at too great an angle to the work, thus making the tool dig in, or in holding it in one position too long, which results in too small a diameter.

CUTTING A SHOULDER

When the stock has been turned to a perfect cylindrical form of the required dimension, it is ready for turning or forming to the shape or combination of shapes that constitute the finished turning.

Make a full-size dimensional drawing of the desired turning. Then determine the points where shoulder or sizing cuts are to be made, and mark them on the drawing. With a pair of dividers, transfer these points from the drawing and locate them on the cylinder. Place the point of a pencil on each of the marks made by the dividers, and revolve the cylinder by hand to mark the entire circumference. Adjust the caliper for a diameter $\frac{1}{16}$ inch larger than required by the drawing or pattern at the point where the first shoulder or sizing cut is to be made.

Place the narrow edge of a parting tool or spearpoint chisel on the tool rest, with the point above the line of the centers. Locate the point on one of the pencil marks on the turning, start the lathe, raise the handle of the parting chisel, and push the point into the stock. Check the accuracy of the sizing or shoulder cut by holding the previously adjusted caliper in the groove that has been cut. Continue cutting until the caliper slips easily over the stock. Adjust the caliper for each of the subsequent shoulder cuts, and proceed in the same way.

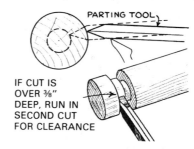

FIG. 18-20. Making a parting cut.

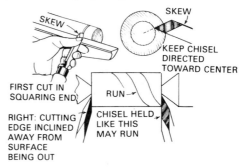

FIG. 18-21. Squaring an end with a skew. Note the clearance angle, which is essential in skew manipulation.

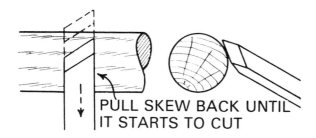

FIG. 18-19. Smoothing a cylinder with a skew.

FIG. 18-22. An effective and easy way to turn down a straight section is with a wood plane. Set the blade for a very fine cut, hold plane at an angle to work, and move it from end to end.

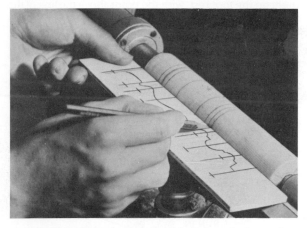

FIG. 18-23. Trace the pattern of half the cylinder, and mark it on the work with colors: red for deep spots, green for high, etc.

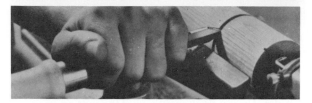

FIG. 18-24. As work is turned (top), use a caliper to check the depth of cuts, and check these cuts against the pattern at frequent intervals. Continue cutting (bottom) and checking until the piece is complete. Then cut out the pattern and rest it against the finished work to check the overall dimensions.

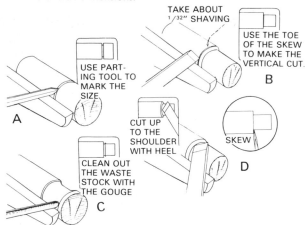

FIG. 18-25. Successive operations in roughing out and finishing a shoulder.

In cutting a shoulder, the parting tool is first used to reduce the wood to within 1/16 inch of the required shoulder diameter, as shown in Figure 18-25a and b. The waste stock is then cleaned out with the gouge (Figure 18-25c). The actual cutting of the shoulder is done with the skew, as shown in Figure 18-25d, and is the same as squaring an end. The horizontal cut is also made with the skew, but in a little different manner from that used in doing plain cylinder work. If the shoulder is long, the ordinary skew position can be used for the outer portion of the cut; but, at the angle between the horizontal and vertical cuts, the heel of the chisel moves into a tangent position between the skew and the cylinder, as shown in Figure 18-26. In this position, the handle of the chisel is raised slightly to allow it to cut as the tool moves along the rest. A very light cut should be taken, to produce smooth work. The heel of

the skew can be used to make the entire cut if desired, but the cut, whether in this position or any other position, should not be started at the very end of the stock. It is quite evident that any horizontal cut started directly at the end of the work will have a tendency to bite into the wood, often ruining the entire piece. Always run *off* the end, and not *into* it. Where a very short shoulder makes this impossible, it is best to use the skew flat in a scraping position. If the cutting technique is used, engage only the heel of skew in a very light cut.

CUTTING A LONG TAPER

The gouge or roundnose chisel is used to make taper cuts in the scraping method. Cut from the larger to the smaller end of the taper. With the tool, cut the taper down to within about 1/8 inch of the entire depth of the shoulder cuts (previously made with the parting or sizing chisel), using the procedure described above for forming the stock to cylindrical form. Finish with a skew or squarenose chisel. As the cutting progresses, check the work with the caliper set from the full-size drawing.

The skew chisel is used to make taper cuts in the cutting method. Place this chisel on the tool rest at an angle of approximately 60° to the surface of the stock and slightly above it. After starting the lathe, draw the chisel back just a little, until the heel starts the cut; then draw it slightly further down and back to the original position. Repeat this procedure until the actual cutting is being done by the heel of the chisel, but the direction of cutting is always downhill. The entire taper cut can be made with the heel.

CUTTING LARGE RECTANGULAR RECESSES

First turn the cylinder to the largest diameter, as previously discussed. Then hold a rule on the tool rest and mark the locations of the recesses. With a parting tool cut a groove at the end of each recess, to the desired diameter and about $\frac{1}{32}$ to $\frac{1}{16}$ inch inside the layout line. Scrape the recess to size using a gouge, and trim the shoulders of the recesses with the toe of a skew. Finish the recesses with a skew chisel.

CUTTING A LINE

The simplest ornament in spindle turning is an incised line. After the cylinder has been cut, set the tool rest about level with the lathe center, and touch a lead pencil against the revolving work. Rest the skew on its edge with the toe down and the handle lowered. Lift the handle until the point digs in, and you have an incised line. A shallow line can be made by scraping the cylinder with a diamond-point chisel laid flat on the tool rest.

Enlarged, the line becomes a V groove. Simply hold the diamond-point tool flat and force it into the wood until the desired width of the V is obtained (Figure 18-28). As the V angle on this tool is rather blunt, you may want to grind a sharper angle—possibly 90 or 80°—which will also enable you to work in close quarters when scraping the ends of spindles or shoulders. Of course, a scraped V

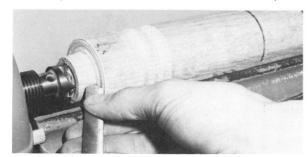

FIG. 18-26. To true up the ends of a spindle, use a spearpoint chisel and a scraping cut. The pencil marks at the right were made on the stock to indicate the locations of further cuts.

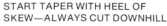

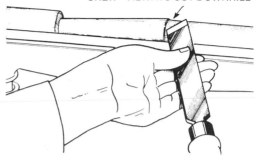
START TAPER WITH HEEL OF SKEW—ALWAYS CUT DOWNHILL

FIG. 18-27. Method of making a long taper.

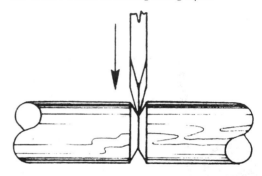

FIG. 18-28. Cutting a shallow or narrow V with a diamond point chisel.

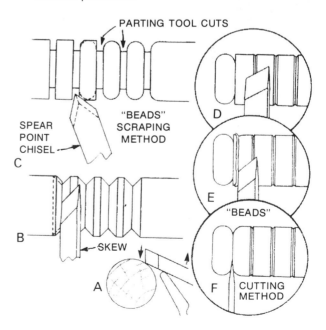

FIG. 18-29. Cutting of V's and beads.

groove can be blunted by swinging the handle from right to left, with care being taken to prevent scoring opposite sides with the point.

The V groove can also be cut with a skew (Figure 18-29a) which is held hinged position straight into the workpiece without rotation. Only half the V is made at a time, and one, two, or more cuts may be needed on each side to obtain the desired shape. As in all cutting with the skew, the bevel next to the cut must be used as a fulcrum (Figure 18-29b) without at the same time allowing the full edge of the chisel to catch and cause a run. V grooves can also be made with the toe of the skew, in the manner already described for squaring an end.

Beads can be scraped or cut. The easy method of scraping makes use of the spearpoint chisel and works to best advantage on beads separated by parting-tool cuts, as shown in Figure 18-29c. Scraping is slower and less productive of clean work than cutting, but it has the advantage of perfect safety: you will not spoil the work with long gash runs.

Cutting beads quickly and accurately with the small skew is one of the most difficult lathe operations. Various working methods can be used, the usual system being as shown in Figure 18-29d to f. The first cut is a vertical incision at the point where the two curved surfaces will eventually come together. This cut can be made with either the heel or toe of the skew. Now place the skew at right angles to the work and well up on the cylinder, as shown in Figure 18-29d. The chisel is flat on its side at the start, and is evenly rotated through the successive stages of the cut, as shown in Figure 18-29d, e, and f. At the same time, the chisel is pulled slightly backward to maintain the same cutting point. The entire cut is made with the heel of the chisel. The opposite side of the bead is cut in the same manner, one cut serving to produce the full shape in each instance. Beads cut in this manner are beautifully smooth and polished, and the technique is well worth mastering.

CUTTING COVES

Second to forming a perfect bead, the cove or concave cut is the most difficult to master. This cut is made with the gouge, the size of the tool depending upon the size of the cut.

The size of the intended cove is first laid out, and the gouge is pushed directly into the work to remove the surplus stock, as pictured in Figure 18-30a. The cove cut can now be made. The gouge is placed on edge on the tool rest in such a position that the grind of the chisel forms an approximate right angle with the work, as shown in Figure 18-30b and c. The chisel contacts the work at the center of the cutting edge, the tool being held so that the centerline of the gouge is pointing directly toward the center of the revolving stock, as shown in Figure 18-30d. This starting position is important; otherwise the gouge will have a tendency to run along the surface of the work.

From the starting position, the gouge is pushed into the revolving stock, and the tool is rolled on the rest. A triple

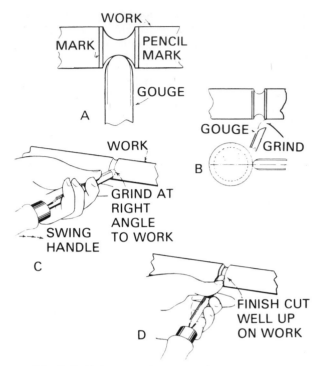

FIG. 18-30. Various steps in cove cutting.

action takes place here: First, the chisel is rolled to follow the shape of the cut; second, the handle is dropped slightly so that the portion already cut will force the lip of the chisel sideways; third, the chisel is pushed forward so that at the end of the cut (Figure 18-30d) it will be well up on the work and tangent to the cut surface. Only one half of the cut is made at one time; then the chisel is reversed to cut the other half. The occasional turner is advised to make cove cuts with a scraping technique, using either the small gouge or roundnose chisel.

CUTTING REVERSE CURVES

Reverse curves can be treated as combinations of beads and coves. The skew chisel, in turning the convex parts, is rolled on its edge and then rolled back to the flat position as the curve flows into the cove. Use the heel of the skew to clean the angles against isolated beads and shoulders, and use the point in narrow places. A parting tool is useful for dressing narrow fillets and small coves.

SQUARE SECTIONS

When the turning has a square section, the stock should be jointed before turning. Good centering is essential, since any error will show at the shoulder where the round meets the square. The turning of the shoulder from square to round can be done in various ways, one method being illustrated in Figure 18-32a to d. If the parting tool is sharp, the nicking cut with the skew (Figure

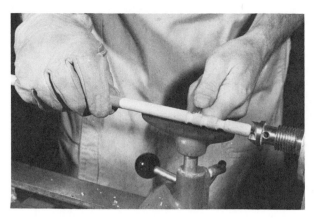

FIG. 18-31. To eliminate chatter and whip when turning fine work between centers, support the work with your free hand. A leather glove protects the hand from heat and splinters.

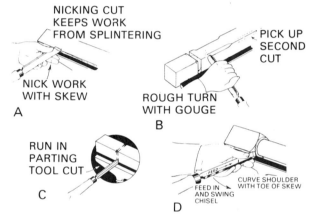

NICKING CUT KEEPS WORK FROM SPLINTERING

NICK WORK WITH SKEW

A

PICK UP SECOND CUT

ROUGH TURN WITH GOUGE

B

RUN IN PARTING TOOL CUT

C

CURVE SHOULDER WITH TOE OF SKEW

FEED IN AND SWING CHISEL

D

FIG. 18-32. Steps in making a shoulder cut from the round to the square.

FIG. 18-33. Cutting work to shape on a band saw.

18-32a) can be omitted. The final trimming operation (Figure 18-32d) can be done with either the skew or spearpoint chisel. This is a scraping operation. While the shoulder can be cut with the same technique used for cutting a bead, the simpler scraping method pictured does clean work and is easier.

CUTTING STOCK TO LENGTH

After the cylinder is worked to the correct diameter, mark the length with a pencil. In the scraping method, force a parting tool into the stock exactly at the layout line at the tailstock, and cut to a ⅛-inch diameter. Repeat at the headstock end. If you wish to cut the end off completely at the headstock, hold the parting tool in your right hand and place your left hand loosely around the revolving stock. Continue to force the parting tool into the wood until the cylinder drops off. Remember to allow enough wood at the headstock end to keep from hitting the spur center. (This cutting can also be done with a small skew held on its side.) Never cut the stock off at the tailstock end, as the work might be thrown.

In the cutting method, hold a small skew on edge with the heel up and the toe down. Then turn it at an angle so that one bevel is parallel to the cut to be made. Force the skew in slowly; then back it out and cut a half V in the waste stock. It is of the utmost importance to keep one cutting edge of the skew parallel to the wood, since it is easy for the tool to "hog in" and damage the stock. Make this same cut at both ends.

In either method, trim off the waste stock on the ends with a saw, and sand smooth.

You can remove a live center by driving a dowel or a soft metal rod through the spur center. The dead center is removed simply by backing off the tailstock wheel until the center is loosened and can be taken out of the cup center of the tailstock.

Face-Plate Turning

When the work to be turned cannot be held between the live and the dead centers, a face plate is used. All cutting in face-plate work is done by scraping; any attempt to use a cutting technique on the edge grain of large work will result in a hogging, gouging cut which may tear the chisel out of your hands. The work is held to the face plate by means of screws.

MOUNTING THE WORK

Before attaching the face plate, remove all surplus wood from the material by drawing a circle on it slightly larger in diameter than is desired for the finished piece. Cut this circle out with a saber saw or band saw (Figure 18-33). Make sure that there are no checks or defects in the wood which might crack or split during the turning. Center the work accurately when screwing it to the face plate. If the material is hardwood, drill small holes in it to start the screws. Use short, heavy flathead screws that will enter the work no more than ⅜ to ½ inch. Make sure that the work is securely fastened to the face plate and that the ends of the screws will not come in contact with the cutting chisel.

When the shape of the finished piece is such that contact with the screws cannot be avoided, the work must be backed up with a disk of the same size. Bore and countersink the holes for the screws at points where they will not come in contact with the chisel. Screw this extra disk or backing plate onto the work and attach it to the face plate (Figure 18-34).

Place the face plate on the headstock spindle, and tighten the setscrew. Move the tool rest so that its top edge is about $\frac{1}{8}$ inch above the center of the revolving cylinder; then lock it with the adjusting wrench.

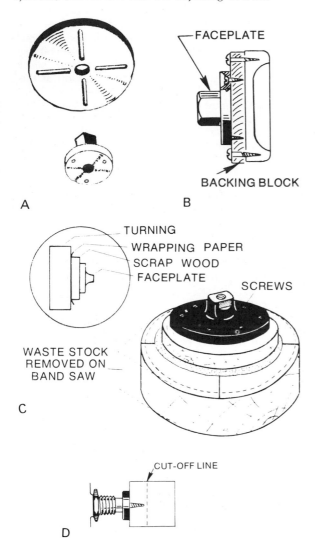

FIG. 18-34. Various methods of applying work onto the face plate.

SIMPLE TURNING

With the lathe rotating at a slow speed, use a squarenose chisel, skew, or gouge to true the face. Hold it on its side with the cutting edge parallel to the front of the cylinder. Start at the center, and take a scraping cut toward the outside nearest yourself. Take several cuts until the stock is the correct thickness (Figure 18-35). Hold a rule or square against the face to make sure it is true.

Locate the center of the stock. Adjust the dividers to half the largest diameter that must be turned, and mark a circle around the face of the work. Readjust the tool rest until it is parallel to the edge of the stock. Use the same tool to turn the edge until it is the correct diameter.

With the dividers, mark the location of the recess or bead on the face of the cylinder. Readjust the tool rest across the face and turn to shape, using the proper tools. For a simple recess, a roundnose tool is usually preferred. For cutting a bead, choose a squarenose or skew. Sometimes the tool rest must be readjusted at an angle to the work for certain kinds of turning. A spearpoint chisel is often used to cut a sharp shoulder on the face of the work.

FIG. 18-35. On inboard face-plate work, use the gouge and scraping cut for all roughing. Keep the tool rest as close to the work as possible, and make cuts from the center toward the outside edge.

DEEP BORING

The deep boring required for bowls, boxes, and similar face-plate work is not difficult, but it is slow. To speed up this operation, rough out the recess by drilling a series of holes to the required depth with a drill. If this is not done, at least drill a center starting hole. The cutting tools used for deep boring are the skew, roundnose, and spearpoint chisel. The skew is used for sliding down the edge of the hole; it can also be used, with a series of jab contacts, to rough the wood at the bottom of the recess. For the bottom cuts use a roundnose chisel, starting at the center, with overlapping short strokes directed toward the

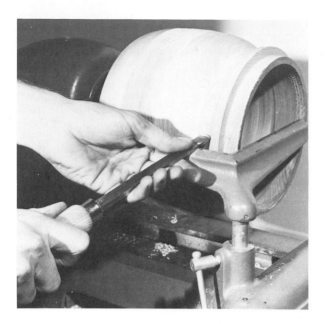

FIG. 18-36. An object that is going to require deep boring.

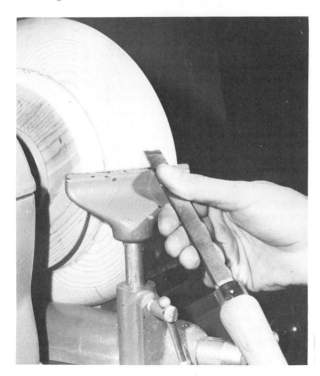

FIG. 18-37. Turning the back of an inboard face-plate project is easier if you use a short T rest that can be moved in closer to the workpiece. The bowl is being finished at high speed with a skew.

center. The tool rest should be positioned at an angle into the hole to provide maximum support to the chisel. The accuracy of the boring can be checked with a combination square held against a parallel edge spanning the work opening. The final finish cuts down the side should be made with a skew. Shoulders on the deep boring can be made with the spearpoint chisel.

TURNING BOTH SIDES OF THE STOCK

Many face-plate jobs require that both sides of an object be turned; an example is a simple bowl. For work of this type, it is generally objectionable to have the screw hole in the stock. Therefore, cut a piece of stock slightly larger that the finished bowl is to be. Cut a piece of *scrap* stock thick enough to fasten screws into. Glue these two pieces together, with a piece of paper between them for easy separation. Next fasten the stock to the face plate, installing the screws in the scrap piece. Then place the face plate on the headstock spindle, and tighten the setscrew. Turn the front or top and the edge of the bowl. When this is completed, separate the scrap stock from the finished piece by driving a sharp chisel between them.

To hold the bowl on the face side, make a simple wood chuck. Cut a piece of scrap stock slightly larger than the diameter of the bowl. Fasten this to the face plate. Turn it to a cylinder, and cut a recess in this scrap stock that the bowl will just fit, with a tight press fit.

Press the stock into the home-made chuck, and turn to the back side of bowl. The bottom side should be finished in the same manner as the top side. The work can usually be removed by pulling it out. If necessary, the recessed edge of the chuck can be cut away to release the bowl.

FIG. 18-38. Large turnings are mounted on a 6-inch face plate or handwheel and are worked on the outboard end of the spindle. A floor stand is needed to hold the tool rest.

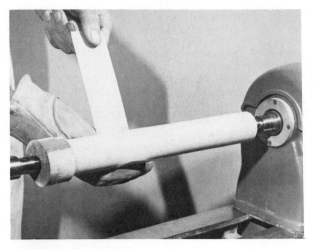

FIG. 18-39. Sand a finished spindle with sandpaper cut in strips. The position shown allows pressure to be applied without tearing the paper. A glove protects the hand from friction.

FIG. 18-40. Water stain being applied with a cloth while the bowl is turning on the lathe. Use a slow speed.

FIG. 18-41. Typical metal-turning lathe.

Finishing Lathe Work

There are several methods of finishing turned parts. Often the parts are removed from the lathe, assembled, and the finish is applied to the completed project.

SANDING TURNINGS Medium, fine, extra fine, and very fine sandpapers are usually used to sand turnings on the lathe. Cut strips of sandpaper about 1 inch wide. These must be held in both hands, with the right hand above and the left below the turning. To avoid cutting grooves, keep the sandpaper in motion while the work is turning in the lathe. Fold the sandpaper, and use the edge of the fold to get into the bottoms of V-shaped cuts. Always remove the tool rest, and adjust the lathe to a high spindle speed. Never wrap the paper around the work. To sand the inside of a bowl, hold a pad of paper over your fingers and follow the contour of the bowl.

FRICTIONAL POLISH A handful of fine shavings taken from the work is cupped in the hand and pressed against the revolving spindle. This causes the work to shine somewhat, but it is usually done only as an initial step before some other form of finishing.

OIL FINISH This entails the use of hot boiled linseed oil as the only polishing medium. The oil is brushed on, and the surface is thoroughly rubbed with a soft cloth as the lathe revolves. Considerable rubbing is necessary to dry the oiled surface entirely.

For small bowls and accessories used for food, mineral oil should be substituted for the linseed oil.

FRENCH POLISHING Mix equal quantities of 4-pound commercial shellac and wood alcohol. Make a pad of cheesecloth about 2 inches square. Dip this into the diluted shellac, and then put several drops of a good grade of machine oil on the pad. Hold the pad lightly on the revolving turning, keeping it in contact with all parts of the work and in motion all the time. The heat generated by friction will harden and glaze the shellac so that it becomes necessary from time to time to redip the pad. Each time the pad is dipped into the shellac, additional oil must also be dropped on the pad. Continue in this way until the desired finish is obtained.

WAX FINISH Apply paste wax to the work with your fingers or a cloth. Allow about 10 minutes for the wax to flat out. To polish, run the lathe at low speed and hold a piece of soft cloth against the revolving spindle. A second coat can be applied 1 hour after the first. Harder waxes can also be used—beeswax, paraffin wax, or carnauba wax. These are in lump form; apply them by pressing the lump against the revolving spindle so that the wax will become soft and adhere to the turning. After the piece is evenly coated, rub with a soft cloth. If a higher polish is desired, repeat the entire operation.

Completed turnings of all types can, of course, be finished with commercial wood finishes, varnishes, or paints. When using any of these materials, follow the manufacturer's application instructions to the letter.

Metal-Working Lathes

Metal lathes are generally found only in machine shops. For this reason, no operating and detailed explanation of the tool is given. One of the major differences between wood and metal lathes is the range of speeds. A typical metal lathe ranges from about 160 to 2100 rpm in direct drive, and 25 to 350 rpm in back-gear drive. The average metal-working lathe will turn most metals, plastics, and even wood. It will cut screw threads, repair machine parts, or fabricate new ones. With the average metal lathe and the proper attachments, it is possible to perform a whole range of operations including milling, tapering, grinding, boring, spinning, knurling, and more.

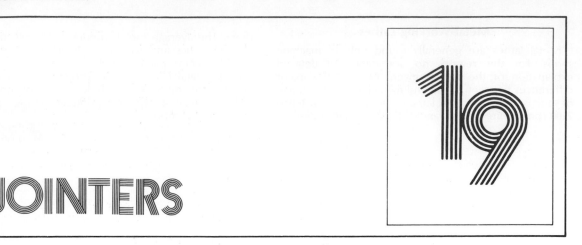

JOINTERS

The jointer is a planing machine, used primarily to finish edges and surfaces of boards cut on a power saw. It can also be employed to cut or plane tapers, bevels, chamfers, stop chamfers, rabbets, octagons, and other shapes.

The principal parts of a typical jointer, except the cutter head, are shown in Figure 19-1. The size of a jointer is based on the length of the knives carried in the cutter head, or, in other words, the maximum width of board which the machine can surface. Sizes range from 4 inches (most popular in home workshops) to 36 inches (used in furniture-making plants).

TYPES OF JOINTERS

The jointer and the other planing machines described in this chapter cut with two or more thin knives fastened in a steel cylinder. The first cutter heads were square, with square-head screws holding the knives. This, of course, was very dangerous, as half the hand might easily slip in between the tables and cutter head. Modern machines all use the round cutter head (Figure 19-2), which fits closely in the opening between the tables and therefore is very much safer.

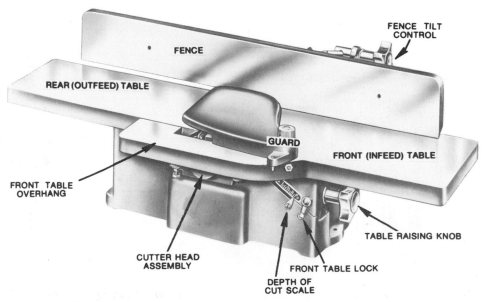

FENCE TILT CONTROL

FENCE

REAR (OUTFEED) TABLE

GUARD

FRONT (INFEED) TABLE

FRONT TABLE OVERHANG

TABLE RAISING KNOB

CUTTER HEAD ASSEMBLY

FRONT TABLE LOCK

DEPTH OF CUT SCALE

FIG. 19-1. Principal parts of a jointer.

The cutter head revolves in two bearings fastened to the main casting. On large machines, this casting stands directly on the floor; on smaller machines it is bolted to a floor stand or a wooden bench. Most modern jointers have ball bearings and run at a speed of from 3500 to 4500 rpm.

Every jointer has two tables, the front or "infeed" table and the rear or "outfeed" table. The work to be planed is first placed on the front table. It is then run across the revolving cutter head and onto the rear table, from which it is then removed. All jointers have a guide or fence, which is fastened to either the front or rear table. The fence can be moved across the tables and fastened at any point. On some jointers the most-used angles are quickly located with an automatic plunger. The fence can also be tilted to any angle from 90 to 45°.

A guard covers the cutter head. There are two basic types in general use. One type swings on a pivot, is pushed aside as the work approaches the cutting head, and then automatically closes when the work has passed. The second type raises and permits the work to slide

under it. The advantage of the latter type is that it covers the revolving head at all times, while the swinging type allows a portion of the knives to be exposed from the time the rear of the work clears the head until it passes the guard. The type that permits the work to pass under it provides greater protection, but many craftsmen prefer the other because they can maintain a firmer grip on the work while it is passing over the knives. A few jointers are equipped with a back guard which adjusts behind the fence. This is especially useful when the fence is adjusted to cut rabbets, because it covers the cutter head behind the fence.

The jointer may be driven either by belts or by a motor head drive in which one end of the cutter head forms the rotor of the motor. The former is the most popular today.

ADJUSTING THE TABLES

For satisfactory work, the rear table must be exactly level with the knives in the cutter head, as shown in Figure 19-4. To make this adjustment on most modern jointers, release the locking device at the back of the jointer and

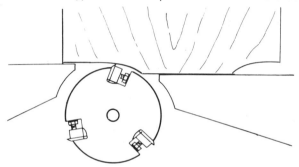

FIG. 19-2. Typical jointer cutter head.

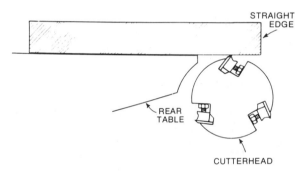

FIG. 19-4. Correct adjustment of the rear table of the jointer with the cutting edge of the knives.

FIG. 19-3. Frequently, the jointer and table saw are located on the same worktable.

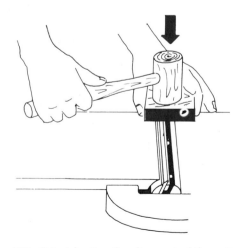

FIG. 19-5. Adjusting the alignment of the cutter knife with the rear table.

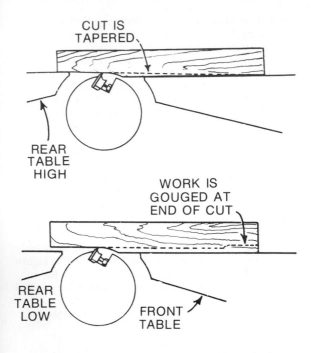

FIG. 19-6. Effects of a high and low rear table on the jointer cuts.

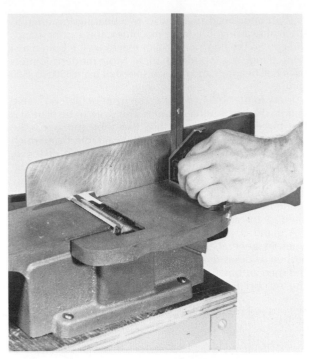

FIG. 19-7. Check the fence with a square edge before use, since an incorrect fence angle will distort a joint.

then turn the adjusting handwheel to raise or lower the rear table until it is level with the knives. An accurate straightedge at least 10 inches long should be used, as in Figure 19-4. The initial check is made on any one knife, which should be in such a position that its cutting edge is at the highest point of the cutting circle. A similar check should be made on all knives, to check the projection of each. The adjustment should be checked at both ends and at the center of each knife, to determine if any knife is improperly mounted in the cutter head. If a knife is out of alignment, the screws which hold it in place should be loosened slightly so that the knife may be tapped down or pried up to the proper position, as shown in Figure 19-5. Once the rear table has been adjusted perfectly level with the knives, it is locked in place by means of the locking wheel and is not touched again until further adjustment is required (after sharpening the knives or after the rear table has been lowered for some special operation, such as chamfering). The effect of an improperly adjusted rear table is shown in Figure 19-6. If the rear table is higher than the knives, the work will be cut on a taper; if the rear table is lower than the knives, the work will be gouged at the end of the cut. After the rear table is set with a straightedge, a secondary check can be made by setting the machine in motion and running a piece of wood slowly over the knives for a distance of a few inches. It should slide onto the rear table perfectly, neither bumping the table nor being above it by as much as a hair.

On a few jointers, the rear table is fixed (stationary) and cannot be moved. In such machines, the adjusting handwheel controls the movement of the front table and thus regulates the depth of the cut. On still other jointers both tables are adjustable, but the front table is usually moved to regulate the depth of cut. Adjustment of the rear table on such machines is only for the purpose of bringing it into alignment with the knives, or for lowering it to cut a recess parallel to the edge of the board at some intermediate point, for example, a stop chamfer or a straight recess. Each table, of course, has its own adjusting handwheel.

OTHER ADJUSTMENTS The depth-of-cut indicator or gauge must be set so that it will show the correct cut on the scale. To adjust this, make a test cut of exactly $\frac{1}{8}$ inch, and then set the pointer to this mark on the scale in the manner described in the manufacturer's literature. All other markings will then be correct. The depth-of-cut indicator will generally require slight adjustment each time the cutter-head knives are sharpened.

Before doing any work on the jointer, check the fence to make certain it is at a right angle (90°) to the tables. Do this with a try square (Figure 19-7). There is a tilt scale for checking this on most jointer fences.

RATE OF FEEDING SPEED Stock is fed against the cutter or knives by hand. The rate at which stock is fed is determined by the following factors:

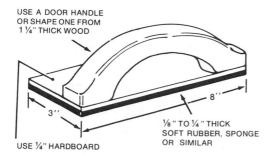

USE A DOOR HANDLE
OR SHAPE ONE FROM
1 ¼" THICK WOOD

8"

3"

⅛" TO ¼" THICK
SOFT RUBBER, SPONGE
OR SIMILAR

USE ¼" HARDBOARD

FIG. 19-8. Simple hold-down/push block that you can make.

1. *Quality of work desired.* Where a very smooth surface is required, the work is fed slowly.
2. *Depth of cut.* When a very heavy cut is taken, the work must be fed slowly. Rapid feeding tends to choke and slow down the machine and greatly increases vibration.
3. *Kind of material.* For the same depth of cut, harder materials (oak, maple) should be fed more slowly than softer materials (pine), to avoid choking.
4. *Width of the material.* For the same depth of cut, a wider board should be fed more slowly than a narrower board, to avoid choking the machine.
5. *Condition or sharpness of the knives.* A dull knife will not cut as rapidly or as easily as a sharp one. Using the machine when the knives are dull greatly increases the risk of accident, owing to the fact that the speed of the machine is decreased by the increased friction between the knives and the stock. As a result, the knives, instead of striking the work a series of sharp, quick blows, strike a series of slow, heavy ones. This is very likely to result in the work being kicked from under the operator's hands, thus allowing them to come in contact with the knives.

JOINTER SAFETY

The following safety suggestions pertaining to the use of the jointer should be followed:

1. Never run a piece of stock shorter than 10 inches across the jointer. Use hand tools to plane such small parts, or surface the stock before cutting it to length. The latter is good practice even at the expense of wasting moderate amounts of material, since it eliminates the hazard of jointing short pieces.
2. Use a push block (Figure 19-8) when surfacing stock thinner than ¾ inch. In fact, it is not wise to attempt to surface any boards less than ⅜ inch thick, since they may split and shatter.

3. Always keep your hands on top of the work. Do not hold them too near the end of the stock, because they might easily be jarred loose and come in contact with the cutter-head knives. In addition, make certain the work is kept firmly on the table or against the fence.
4. Do not operate the jointer when the knives are dull or chipped. Dull knives will cause kickbacks, especially when edging short stock or angle-cut stock.
5. Use the safety guard whenever possible. On some jointers the guard cannot be employed for rabbeting or stop chamfering. The spring tension should be checked regularly to ensure satisfactory operation of the guard.
6. Before using a jointer, check to be certain that all parts of the machine are locked securely; this is especially important for the cutter-head knives. Never adjust the fence while the machine is in motion.
7. Avoid taking too deep a cut. The maximum cut is determined by the type of stock being run, but overcutting is a frequent cause of kickbacks. One-sixteenth inch is a good average cut. The only exception is when cutting a rabbet.
8. Never attempt to run a piece across the jointer until the machine is running at full speed.
9. Always try to plane in the direction of the grain. Never plane the end grain of narrow stock (less than 8 inches). It is best to surface the concave (hollow) side of a warped board first.
10. Make it a practice to stand at the left of the jointer. Never stand at the end of the front table, because a board may accidentally kick back. Keep the floor around the machine clean and in good condition. This will reduce the possibility of your feet slipping.
11. The use of jigs is strongly recommended because they permit jointing without the necessity of your hands ever being close to the cutting head.

JOINTING AN EDGE

Jointing an edge is the simplest and most common jointer operation. Set the guide or fence square with the table, and to the desired width. Then fasten it securely. Stand at the edge of the infeed table, with the feet well apart and the left foot forward. Set the jointer to the desired depth, and hold the best face of the work against the guide with both hands. Figure 19-9 shows the cut as the work is pushed over the revolving cutter head. The hand over the rear table presses the work down so that the newly formed surface will make perfect contact with the table. The hand over the front table (usually the right hand) exerts no downward pressure, but simply advances the work to the knives. Both hands exert side pressure to keep the work in contact with the guide fence.

FIG. 19-9. In pushing material over the cutters, all parts of the hands and fingers should be above the table.

The position of the hands is important. The fingers or thumb must not be allowed to pass dangerously close to the revolving knives, and the work must be kept in solid contact with the tables if a straight, true cut is to be made. Some operators never pass either hand directly over the knives; they make the cut as follows: Both hands are over the front table at the start of the cut. As soon as the stock is resting solidly on the rear table, the left hand is lifted and placed on this portion of the stock. As the right hand approaches the cutter head, the work is held down tightly with the left hand, while the right hand is lifted and placed on the stock over the rear table. Both hands are now over the rear table, and the balance of the cut is completed in this position.

In the more usual method of feeding the stock, both hands are over the front table at the start of the cut, and both hands pass over the cutter head as the cut is made. While there may be some reluctance to advance the hands over the cutter head, actually there is no danger involved, providing the feed is made carefully. It is faster and easier to feed in this manner. The right hand, always in position at the end of the work, affords positive protection against the most common and most dangerous jointer hazard, the kickback. The first method is safer for surfacing, especially when the stock is less than 1 inch thick.

If a board has one concave and one convex side, it is usually easier to plane the concave side by first taking a few cuts off the edge at both ends, and then finally planing the whole edge. If the board has to be the same width throughout, it should be cut to width on a saw after one side is planed. Then the other side is run over the jointer.

Edges on thin stock like veneer may be planed smooth on the jointer if they are clamped between two boards. In some cases the boards may be held together with nails.

Side pressure is always required to keep the work in contact with the guide fence, and is very important when jointing wide stock. Where a considerable amount of wide work is to be handled, it is advisable to fasten an auxiliary high fence to the standard fence, as shown in Figure 19-10, for a more positive means of support.

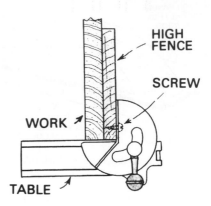

FIG. 19-10. How to install an auxiliary fence.

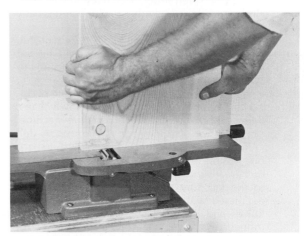

FIG. 19-11. One method of jointing an end.

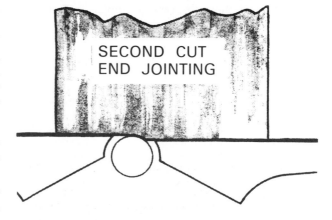

SECOND CUT
END JOINTING

FIG. 19-12. Another method of jointing an end.

JOINTING AN END

An end can be jointed in the same manner as jointing with the grain. The one big difference is that the surface should be formed with light cuts. A single heavy cut will invariably tear the grain at the end of the cut unless the knives are very sharp. In a second method of working, a short cut is made at one end, as shown in Figure 19-11. The work is then reversed and fed from the opposite side, to blend with the first cut at A, as shown in Figure 19-12. This method has the disadvantage of a possible poor blend of the two cuts unless the rear table and guide fence are set to hairline perfection. Where the work is to be jointed all around, the final cuts with the grain (Figure 19-13) will remove any splintered edges formed by the initial cutting across the ends. Stock less than 8 inches wide should not be end jointed unless some form of guide jig is used.

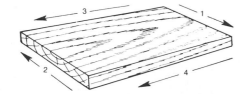

FIG. 19-13. Steps in squaring the edges of a board on the jointer.

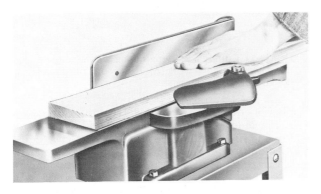

FIG. 19-14. Correct positioning of the hands, guard, and fence in the surface planing of boards.

SURFACING

The face of a board is one of its wide surfaces. This should always be planed with the grain. The direction of the grain can be found by noticing the grain on the edges. Remember that opposite faces or edges are always planed in opposite directions. As the face is usually wider than the edge, a lighter cut should be taken. In planing shorter boards, it is generally best to use the pusher, holding it in the right hand. A pusher is indispensable for planing thin stock, if the jointer is not equipped with a dual-purpose guard.

Warped boards are hollow on one side and round on

the other. It is better to plane the hollow side first and then finish the round side on a surface planer. Boards "in wind" are more difficult to plane, because only two corners will touch a flat surface at a time. Hold the board so that two corners are touching the table, take a light cut, and plane it off until flat. Make sure that the first corner does not butt against the lip of the outfeed table. If a thickness planer is not available, saw the other side of the board on a circular saw and then smooth it on the jointer.

Thin boards such as T-square blades or the slats used in venetian blinds may be planed safely if a slot is cut for them in heavier wood (Figure 19-16). T-square blades may also be cut from a solid block several inches thick, which has been planed on all four sides and which has the traditional hole bored right through it. The other side may be finished with a cabinet scraper and a piece of sandpaper.

FIG. 19-15. For wider boards, remove the fence and guard, and pass the outer edges, then the center, over the cutters.

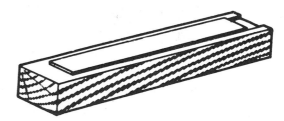

FIG. 19-16. Typical recessed block for planing thin stock.

SQUARING STOCK TO DIMENSIONS

If a board must be squared on all six surfaces, the first step is to surface one face just enough to clean it up. Next, hold that face against the fence, and joint the end grain. Cut the board to length (plus $\frac{1}{16}$ inch). Reverse the stock, and joint the second end. Then hold the surfaced face against the fence, and joint the first edge. Next cut to width plus $\frac{1}{16}$ inch, and joint the second edge. Now, from the working face, mark the thickness along the edges and ends. If the piece is not uniform in thickness, it will be necessary to take several lighter cuts on the thicker portion before making the final cut (Figure 19-17).

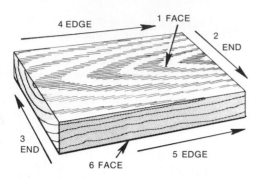

FIG. 19-17. Steps in squaring up the six sides of a piece of stock.

TAPER JOINTING

Taper jointing is one of the most useful jointer operations, and it can be used to good advantage on a wide variety of work. The simplest kind of tapering involves stock which is shorter in length than the length of the front table. On the 6-inch jointer, this includes stock up to about 14½ inches long. In making the cut, the front table is lowered to the necessary depth of cut. The stock is then placed against the fence. The far end of the board is in such a position that it will land on the rear table at the start of the cut. From this position, the board is moved forward to cut the taper. Work longer than the front table can be handled similarly with a home-made front-table extension, as shown in Figure 19-18.

Where long tapers are to be cut without the use of an extension, a slightly different procedure must be followed. The basic rule is that the stock must be divided into a number of equal divisions, each division being slightly shorter than the front table. For example, a 28-inch board would be divided into two divisions. The depth of the cut must be divided into a corresponding

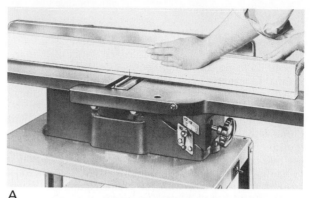

A

B

FIG. 19-19. Cutting a full-length long taper. Note the halfway mark on the work (A). The second portion of the cut (B) is also shown.

number of equal parts, which, in this case, would be two. Thus, if a 28-inch board was to be tapered ⅜ inch from end to end, the board would be divided into two equal parts, and the front table would be set to a depth of ³⁄₁₆ inch. Two cuts are necessary, the first cut being started by dropping the cut mark over the knives. Figure 19-19 shows the completion of this first cut. The second cut is started at the far end of the board and proceeds the full length of the board to complete the ⅜-inch taper. Any length of board can be handled in this manner. A 36-inch long board, for example, would be divided into three divisions of 12 inches each. If the required taper is ¾ inch, the front table is set to one-third of this, or ¼ inch.

Short tapers are planed as follows: Mark the taper on the wood with a pencil. Set the infeed table to the depth of the taper, and put the mark indicating the beginning of the taper over the lip of the outfeed table. Stand behind the outfeed table, slide a block of wood under the piece to be tapered, and nail it to the piece with fine brads. Clamp a stop block to the infeed table, start the machine, and pull the stock over the cutter head. This is the safest way to plane short tapers.

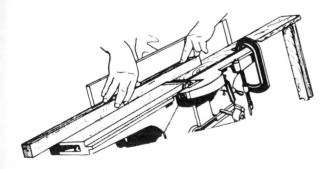

FIG. 19-18. Tapering with an extension table.

RABBETING

Figure 19-21 shows the cutting of a rabbet. The rabbet may be made as wide as the knives are long. On some jointers the edge of the outfeed table is rabbeted, and a rabbet can therefore be planed to that depth. The stock to be rabbeted is supported on this recess as well as on a rabbeting arm screwed to the infeed table. When you are ready to plane, the width of the rabbet should be measured in two places from the rabbet in the outfeed table to the fence, and the infeed table should be lowered to the depth of the rabbet in the outfeed table.

On some other machines, there is no rabbet in the outfeed table. Instead, these have a larger rabbeting arm on which to support the stock. The depth of the rabbet that can be planed on these machines depends upon the height of the cutter-head bearing over which the stock must pass.

BEVELING AND CHAMFERING

A bevel is an edge at an angle other than 90° to the face. A chamfer is a bevel which does not extend all the way across the edge. It is usually cut at 45°. A stopped chamfer is a chamfer which does not extend from end to end. It may be stopped at one or both ends of a board (Figure 19-23).

A bevel or chamfer is cut by tilting the fence (in or out) to the desired angle. (Generally, it is safer to do the cutting with the fence tilted in.) If this angle is not shown on a scale attached to the fence, it can be set with a sliding T bevel held between the table and the fence. Hold the face of the stock against the fence, and plane it in the usual way. Several passes may be necessary to achieve the desired bevel or chamfer.

FIG. 19-21. In cutting the rabbet, the cut-out section is on the underside and the fence side of the piece being cut.

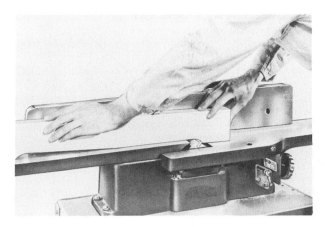

FIG. 19-22. More intricate work on tapering can also be handled; here a cutout is made as a taper.

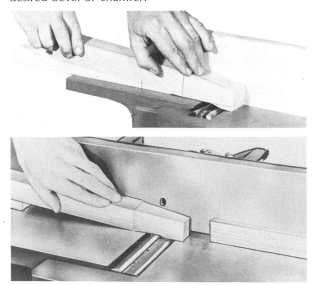

FIG. 19-20. Eventually, you can manage without the stop block, but it is still good for cutting multiple pieces.

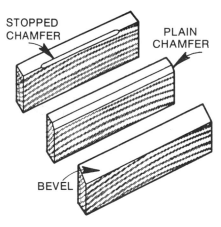

STOPPED CHAMFER

PLAIN CHAMFER

BEVEL

FIG. 19-23. Various chamfers and bevels.

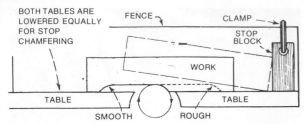

FIG. 19-24. Typical stop-chamfer setup; both tables are lowered.

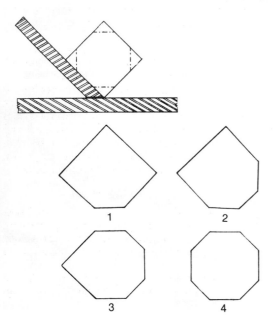

FIG. 19-25. Forming an octagonal shape.

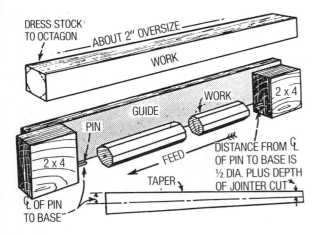

FIG. 19-26. Jig necessary for tapering in the round.

Stop chamfering requires that both the front and rear tables be lowered an equal amount or that the cutter head be raised. Stop blocks are clamped on each side of the cutter head so the chamfer will be cut to the desired length. Tilt the fence to the desired angle or width. Since the guard cannot be used, it is advisable to move it as far as possible toward the front edge. Start the machine, hold the stock against the stop block, and carefully let it down onto the revolving knives. Push it ahead until it reaches the stop block on the outfeed table, and then pick it up with both hands.

CUTTING AN OCTAGON

To cut octagonal shapes, set the fence at a 45° angle and make the necessary passes (Figure 19-25) so that the corners of the square are removed to form four new faces. The same number of passes is made on each surface.

TAPERING IN THE ROUND Tapering in the round requires a setup such as that illustrated in Figure 19-26. The stock is first dressed to an octagonal shape, not tapered, and is then mounted between the two end blocks. The pin in the block which is to rest on the rear table is located at a distance of one-half the diameter of the large end of the required taper, measured from the base of the 2 X 4 inch block. The distance of the other pin from the base of the block is one-half the diameter of the small end of the taper, plus the depth of the cut (which is quite deep, usually ½ inch). One screw through each end of the guide board holds the two end blocks snugly in place. In operation, the two end blocks are considered as opposite ends of a long board, the cut being made in the same manner as for ordinary tapering. Successive cuts, with the work turned about 15° for each new cut, result in a taper which can readily be sanded to a perfect finish.

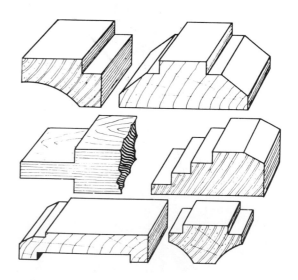

FIG. 19-27. Molding cut on a jointer (no scale).

MAKING MOLDINGS

A jointer can make only moldings with a combination of flat and beveled surfaces. The various cuts and surfaces can be placed at different depths and at varying angles. Attractive moldings can be made by combining cuts (Figure 19-27). The procedure is exactly the same as for conventional cuts.

SHARPENING JOINTER KNIVES

The two most important factors in the care and maintenance of a jointer are proper lubrication of all moving parts and proper sharpening and adjustment of the knives or cutters. Dull knives and cutters deteriorate the machinery by causing it to "labor" and to "chatter" or vibrate. Besides, a dull knife or cutter on a power shaving machine is very dangerous. A dull knife or cutter tends to "catch" in the wood, and since the machine is cutting toward the operator, the result of a catch is a violent throwback of the stock toward the operator. The piece may strike the operator; but more serious than this is the fact that the operator's hands, when the piece is torn out of them, may be driven against the knives or the cutters. Full details on sharpening jointer knives are given in Chapter 22.

HONING KNIVES Grinding is not always necessary for sharpening the jointer knives, since careful honing at regular intervals will keep a head sharp for some time. To hone the knives, partly cover a fine carborundum stone with paper so it will not mark the table, and place it on the front table as shown in Figure 19-28. Turn the cutter head until the stone rests flat on the bevel, and fix the head in this position by clamping the belt to the stand. Whet each knife by stroking the stone lengthwise with the blade; treat each knife with the same number of strokes.

JOINTING THE KNIVES Knives can be sharpened and brought to a true cutting circle by jointing their edges while the head is revolving. In this operation, the stone is placed on the rear table as shown in Figure 19-29, and the table is lowered until the stone barely touches the knives.

SETTING JOINTER KNIVES Place the knife in the slot in the cutter head, and set it a little above the correct height, tightening the setscrews only slightly. Set a level or straightedge on the outfeed table, letting it project over the knife. If the knife lifts the level when the cutter head is revolved by hand, it is too high and must be set further down in the slot. This is best done by tapping it lightly with a mallet. Remember that the knife must be at the same height all along its length. When the knife is set correctly, tighten the setscrews, little by little. It is not a good plan to tighten each setscrew all at once; rather, begin at one end and give each a little twist. Repeat until all are tightened. Replace the other knives in the same manner.

Another method of setting knives in the cutter head is with a magnet, as shown in Figure 19-30. An index mark should be scribed on the magnet, and a stop block should be clamped to the front table at such a position as to bring the index mark in line with the cutting edge of the knife when it is at its highest point. The knife is placed in its slot and is pulled up to the required level by the magnet.

Planers or Surfacers

The planer, also called a "surfacer" or "thickness planer," is a single-purpose woodworking machine employed for making a smooth planed surface on a piece of stock. In other words, it planes or surfaces the stock to a uniform thickness.

While the thickness planer is basically an industrial woodworking machine, a small one adds greatly to the

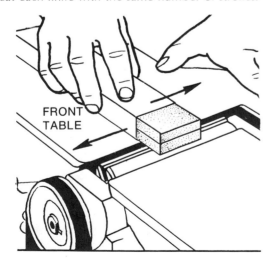

FIG. 19-28. Honing the cutter heads with the cutter locked in place. Use a fine abrasive stone with heavy kraft paper tapered around.

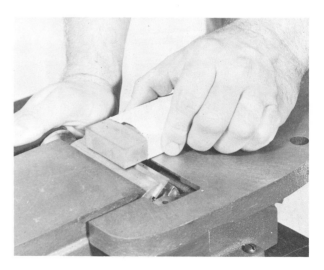

FIG. 19-29. Simple method of jointing the knives.

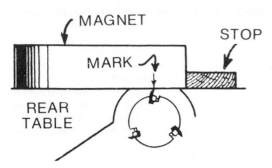

FIG. 19-30. Simple method of setting the jointer knives.

home craftsman's independence. As any home craftsman knows, it is difficult to obtain stock dressed to a specified thickness. A great deal of fine furniture making and cabinetmaking is done with hardwoods, and the home craftsman usually has to order material by mail because lumberyards in most localities do not stock hardwood. Those local lumberyards that do stock this type of lumber have it either in the rough or dressed only in the heavier sizes. When various thicknesses are required for a particular project, the craftsman is therefore forced to order the stock specially dressed to specifications. This, of course, increases the cost of the material.

In a shop equipped with a surface or thickness planer, this problem is eliminated. Material can be ordered in the

A

B

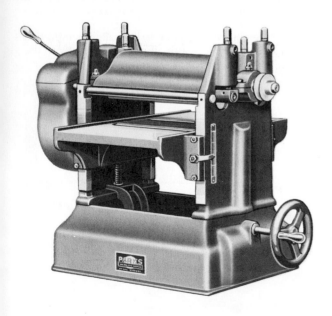

FIG. 19-31. Typical 12 x 4 inch planer. This is the size generally found in the average woodworking shop.

FIG. 19-32. A molder-planer such as the one shown can be used to make moldings (A) or plane lumber (B).

rough and in standard sizes (at a much lower cost), and the planer used to reduce it to the desired thicknesses. For example, the craftsman could lay in a stock of 1-inch mahogany. If a project required material dressed to $\frac{7}{8}$ inch, it could be passed through the surfacer, and the stock would come out dressed to the desired size. If a project called for $\frac{1}{4}$-inch mahogany stock, the 1-inch rough stock could be resawed, and each board passed through the planer; the craftsman would end up with two pieces of material where originally there was only one.

Another use to which the planer can be put is that of reclaiming stock that has been painted or marred. Passing it through the planer will remove the imperfections or the painted surface. A board that has developed a cup warp can be made true again in short order with a planer. Odd thicknesses, too, can be quickly reduced to a uniform size.

The size of a planer indicates the maximum width and thickness of stock it will handle. A planer whose size is 12 X 4 inches will dress a piece of wood up to 12 inches wide and 4 inches thick. While planers range in size up to 42 X 8 inches, the 12 X 4 inch size (Figure 19-31) is the most used for small shop work. But because these tools are not commonly found in the home shop no operation instruction is given in this book.

SHAPERS

Woodworking shapers are used principally for edging curved stock and for cutting ornamental edges, such as on moldings; they can also be used for rabbeting, grooving, fluting, and beading. The shaper is simple to operate, and it produces superior work quickly and accurately. However, the versatility of the shaper depends on the types of cutters available.

While shapers are made in many designs and sizes, the basic machine has a flat, horizontal table through which one or two vertical spindles project. The two-spindle shaper is a production machine, and will not be discussed in this book. The average machine has only one spindle, which revolves at a speed of from 7000 to 18,000 rpm. Some shapers are equipped with a reversing switch so that the cut can always be made with the grain, but this is hardly necessary with high-speed shapers, as they cut smoothly even against the grain. Incidentally, in normal use the spindle moves counterclockwise, with the work moving from right to left.

On account of the high speed, the spindle is usually driven by a belt from a motor bolted to the frame of the machine. The spindle is mounted in two ball bearings, which in some bench machines are lubricated for life and in others are lubricated with oil under pressure. The spindles on some machines can be moved up and down; on others the spindle remains stationary and the table is moved up and down. The hole in the table through which the spindle projects is fitted with rings, some with raised edges, which act as a guide for stock being shaped (Figure 20-2).

Most light-duty production floor models and all bench shapers are equipped with an adjustable metal or wood fence resembling the ripping fence of a circular table saw. It is employed primarily for grooving or shaping straight edges. (On larger machines the fence usually consists of a board straightedge, clamped to the table with a hand-screw arrangement.) For shaping end grain, most bench shapers have another fence that slides in a groove in the table, similar to the cutoff gauge on a table saw. Some machines also have clamping devices or spring hold-downs in which the work can be fastened to shape end grain, or to hold the work firmly against the fence or table.

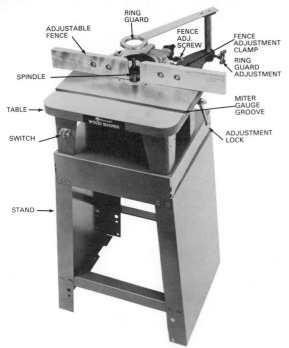

FIG. 20-1. Major parts of a typical woodworking shaper.

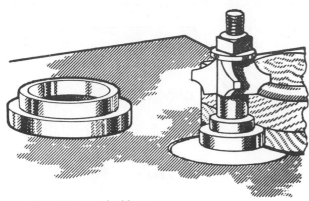

FIG. 20-2. Typical table rings.

Another convenient accessory is a sliding shaper jig which can be used in many horizontal shaping operations such as cutting grooves and tenons. A few machines are even designed so that a portion of the table can be tilted.

For shaping curved or irregular edges, there are usually a couple of holes in the table, one on either side of the spindle, in which vertical starter pins can be inserted. When a curved edge is being shaped, the piece is guided by and steadied against the starter pin and the collar on the spindle. The part of the edge that is to remain uncut runs against the so-called "rub" or "depth" collar on the spindle and starter pin. On some machines a cutter or ring guard is supplied and should be used to protect you from injury when making cuts without a fence.

The spindle has a top which is a round steel bar that screws into it. Spindle tops are of different lengths and diameters, according to the size of the machine. Actually, the size of a shaper is measured by the diameter of the spindle and the size of the table. Most bench machines and light-duty floor-type shapers are equipped with $5/16$- to $3/4$-inch spindles. The spindles are usually interchangeable. That is, they permit the use of a rather complete range of cutters. Included, usually, are the $5/16$-inch spindle for small cutters, with $5/16$-inch holes; the $1/2$- and $3/4$-inch spindles for regular cutters, with $1/2$- and $3/4$-inch holes; and the $1/2$-inch stub spindle for cope cutters, which usually fasten on the top of the spindle. While a $1/2$-inch spindle can be driven by a $1/2$-hp motor, it is best to use a $3/4$- or 1-hp unit for any shaper with a $3/4$-inch spindle.

Shaper knives are either single, flat knives or solid three-lip or wing cutters. The latter have a central hole so that they can be slipped over the spindle. These knives are the safest to use because they cannot get loose. They are made of special alloy tool steel or are carbide tipped, and they come in a wide variety of shapes which offer almost unlimited possibilities in woodcutting.

The flat or open-face knife cutters are the oldest and are used on all production machines, but they are not recommended for general use. The flat knives are held between two slotted collars. The knives have beveled or angled edges fitting the slot in the collars. Two flat knives

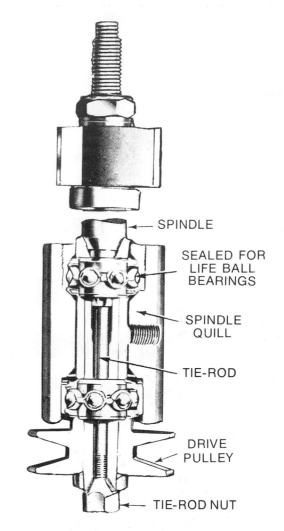

FIG. 20-3. Typical shaper spindle assembly.

SPINDLE

SEALED FOR LIFE BALL BEARINGS

SPINDLE QUILL

TIE-ROD

DRIVE PULLEY

TIE-ROD NUT

are always used, and they must be exactly the same width, so that they can be held securely between the collars, as shown in Figure 20-5. If the knives are not held tightly in place, they may fly out of the machine while it is running at high speed. In fact, it is best not to use this clamp-type cutter head unless you are experienced with it. Flat-knife cutters are made in a wide variety of shapes to do many kinds of cutting; in addition, blank flat knives are available which may be ground to any desired cutting-edge shape.

Most modern shapers with either $1/2$- or $3/4$-inch spindles can use the two-knife flat cutter head. A wide variety of interchangeable two-knife sets can be used with this cutter head (Figure 20-5). The knives can be installed and removed with a special tool. Since a special unit keeps these flat knives in place in the cutter head, they cannot fly off when properly installed.

FLAT KNIFE

GROOVED SHAPER COLLAR

ASSEMBLED
KNIFE SHAPER
HEAD

FIG. 20-5. These flat or open-face knives with collars may be purchased blank or already ground.

FIG. 20-4. Profiles of standard shaper cutters.

FIG. 20-6. Typical three-knife cutter head. The head is made of alloy steel and fits either ½- or ¾-inch spindles.

All shaper knives or cutter heads are held on the spindle with collars, which are highly polished circular disks of different diameters. They are slipped over the spindle and tightened with a nut on its end. As a rule, the remainder of the spindle, either above or below the cutter, is filled in with spare collars before the nut is fastened to the top. Collars should be of smaller diameter than the cutting edges of the cutter if a fence is to be employed. But, if you are using one of the collars as a rub or depth collar when working on curved or irregular edges, place it either directly below or directly above the cutter, depending on where it is to make contact with the wood edge. The diameter should be large enough to serve as a fence. To prevent burning the work, frictionless or ball-bearing collars are available for use as guides on irregular work, where the fence is not used.

SHAPER SAFETY

The shaper can be considered a relatively dangerous machine because it must operate at a high speed and its cutters are difficult to guard completely. For this reason it would be a good idea for beginners to memorize the few safety rules that follow.

1. Dress properly. Avoid wearing loose clothing, sleeves, or neckties which might accidentally be caught in the knife. Always wear safety goggles or a field shield when operating the shaper.
2. Whenever possible, install the cutter head on the spindle so that the bottom of the stock is shaped. In this way the stock will cover most of the cutter and will act as a guard.
3. Make certain that the cutters are sharp. Also check that the cutter or the cutter knives are fastened securely to the spindle. Rotate the spindle by hand to make sure it clears all guards, jigs, and fences before turning on the power.
4. Keep the work table clean. Remove all tools and materials from the shaper before starting it. Also keep the floor around your machine neat and uncluttered. Some machines have an exhaust or shaving chute that can be connected to a dust-collection system to clear away chips as the shaping is done.
5. Use a fence, cutter guard, jig, or clamping

devices when possible. When shaping irregular work, make sure that the starting pin is securely in place on the table.

6. Inspect the stock very closely before cutting, to make certain that it is free of defects such as loose knots, cracks, and splits.

7. Feed the work *against* the rotation of the knives. Never "back up" any work, because it may be thrown out of your hands. Start all over again if necessary. Some shapers, as mentioned earlier, have a reversing switch so that the spindle can be rotated either clockwise or counterclockwise.

8. Boards less than 10 inches wide should not be shaped on the ends unless the shaper has a sliding jig to clamp on the stock and hold it in place. Also use a push block for close work.

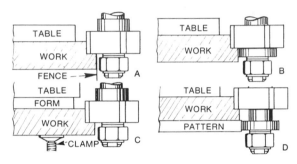

FIG. 20-7. Four major shaping operations: *(a)* shaping with a fence; *(b)* shaping against a collar or ring; *(c)* shaping with a pattern or template; *(d)* shaping with a form or jig.

All moving parts of the shaper should be kept well lubricated. Fortunately, most modern machines have spindle and motor bearings that are sealed and never require lubrication. To keep the table surface free of rust, apply a thin coat of paste wax to it. This will also provide a clean, smooth working surface.

The knives of your machine are very important to the quality of your work. Dull knives will burn and tear. The knives should be honed occasionally on the flat side adjacent to the cutting edge, with a flat 60- to 80-grit stone. Be careful to remove the same amount from all three faces. Keep the knives and collars free of pitch by cleaning them with kerosene. Leave a light film of kerosene or oil on the knives when they are not in use, to prevent rusting.

Shaper Operations

Shaper operations may be divided into four main groups, according to the methods used in guiding or holding the stock against the cutters. These are:

1. Holding the stock against wooden or metal

fences. This method is used for cutting stock with straight edges or faces.

2. Holding and guiding the stock against shaper rings or collars. This method is used principally for cutting stock with curved edges or faces.

3. Cutting stock according to patterns and templates. This is used in production work, when many pieces of the same shape have to be made.

4. Holding the stock on special forms or jigs. This is used mainly for stock that cannot readily be held except on the special forms.

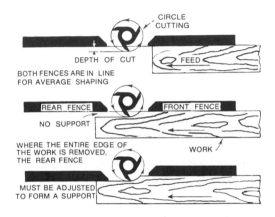

FIG. 20-8. How the shaper fence must be adjusted for various cuts.

SHAPING STRAIGHT EDGES

Straight shaping is the process of cutting a profile or contour on the straight edges of tabletops or bench tops, or cutting moldings on straight lumber. Select the desired cutter, cutter head, or knife assembly. Fasten it securely on the spindle. Remember that the cutter must be put on the spindle so the cutting edge faces in the direction of rotation, which is normally counterclockwise when viewed from the spindle end. Place enough shaper collars below and above the cutter, and tighten the nut on top. See that the collars are small enough to permit the cutter to project sufficiently. Then pull out the pin so that the spindle can revolve. Place the stock in position, and raise or lower the table or spindle until the cutter is at the correct height for the desired cut.

To adjust the cutter to depth, screw the fence to the table and adjust the left part (or front fence) so that it is in line with the right part (or rear fence). Hold the stock against the front fence, and move the whole fence back until the cutter projects the correct amount. Finally, set and adjust the guard. Large stock can usually be held quite safely in the hands only. Metal springs can be obtained to hold smaller stock down on the table and press it against the fence. To ensure accurate work, make a trial cut on a piece of waste wood.

For cutting a molding on a straight edge, two or even three wing cutters may sometimes be used simultaneously on the same spindle. When this is not possible, a compound molding must be cut with one cutter at a time (Figure 20-9). If the whole edge is to be shaped, make the cut so that the stock is well past the spindle, and then stop the motor. The front fence will then have to be moved back until the shaped end touches the rear fence and is supported by it. It is always a good idea to make a trial cut first, on scrap material.

FIG. 20-9. Making a compound molding with one cutter.

A rule joint is used on tables with folding leaves. It is rather hard to make by hand, but on a shaper it is made easily and quickly (Figure 20-10). A table usually has two leaves which are hinged to the central part that is fastened to the rails of the table. When laying out a rule joint, first set a marking gauge to half the thickness of the knuckle of the hinge, and gauge the ends of the boards as shown in Figure 20-11. The centers of both the concave and convex cuts lie in the gauge lines. The radius is the distance from the gauge lines to the upper surface, less $\frac{3}{16}$ inch for the square edge. Select a cutter that will fit the convex curve, and cut both edges of the central part of the tabletop. The cutter for the concave cuts in the leaves should be the reverse of the first cutter, but with a radius $\frac{1}{32}$ inch larger, so that there will be clearance for the two moving leaves. Turn the top and leaves upside down, and place them flat on a bench. The kind of hinges used are called "backflaps" and have one leaf longer than the other. As screw holes are countersunk on the reverse side of the hinge, the knuckles must be set into the wood as shown in Figure 20-11. If it is difficult to obtain the right kind of hinges, ordinary hinge hasps may be used.

When end grain is to be shaped, a miter gauge can be employed to help support the work. The stock can also be clamped to the sliding shaper jig before cutting to keep it from being whipped from your hands.

As mentioned earlier, the work is fed into the cutter head from right to left. Occasionally the shaper cuts may

be such that the motor should be reversed through the switch, the cutter head inverted (turned upside down), and the piece fed from left to right. Figure 20-12 illustrates the difference between making cuts from right to left and from left to right. It also shows the direction of the cutter blade.

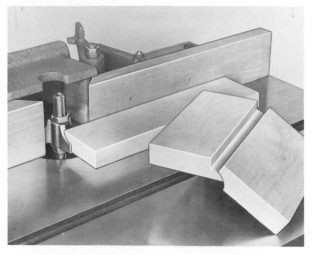

FIG. 20-10. Shaping a rule joint.

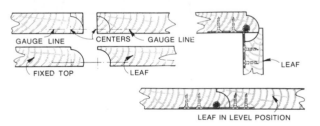

FIG. 20-11. Laying out a rule joint.

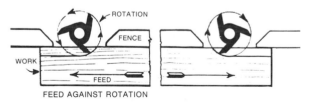

FIG. 20-12. Feed against the rotation.

For shaping all four straight edges on a piece of stock, either of two methods may be employed. One is to start on one edge and progress completely around in one continuous cut. Rub or depth collars are used in this method. The second way—often called "start-and-stop" cutting—is accomplished by following the sequence of cuts shown in Figure 20-13.

Shaping the edge of a wood face is very similar to shaping a straight edge. Figure 20-14 illustrates the similarity. It is simply a matter of how the board is placed against the fence and table. Sometimes, for face-shaping long or wide stock, it is a good idea to use a high wooden fence (Figure 20-15) to support the work. To hold the fence in place, clamp it to the shaper table with C clamps.

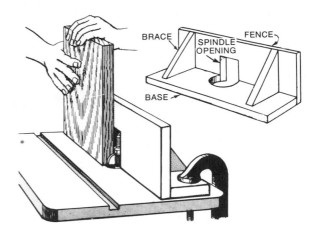

FIG. 20-15. High auxiliary fence.

SHAPING IRREGULAR AND CIRCULAR EDGES

Irregular shaping is the process of shaping the irregular edges of oval-shaped tables, curved legs, table stretchers, and decorative moldings on all types of curved, irregular stock. For this type of shaping, the edge of the stock must be smooth and without any irregularities. The stock should, of course, be cut to the exact shape of the finished piece.

For irregular shaping, you must remove the fence assembly. Insert the starting pin into the threaded hole in the table in front of and to the right of the spindle. Select the knife you plan to use and mount it on the spindle, along with a depth or rub collar of the correct diameter. On heavy cuts in hardwood, you might want to use a large-diameter depth collar first, and then a smaller one, to remove the stock in two passes. Always use a ring for the depth guard when shaping curved work directly against collars. Besides offering protection, the guard provides a hold-down by pressing the work down on the table surface.

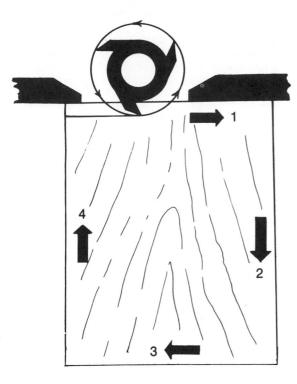

FIG. 20-13. Steps in shaping all four straight edges of a board.

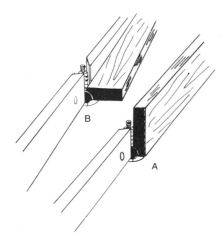

FIG. 20-14. The similarity between face and straight-edge shaping: (a) the face of the board; (b) the edge.

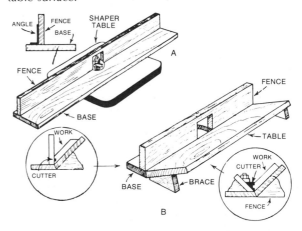

FIG. 20-16. Construction of (a) long and (b) miter fences.

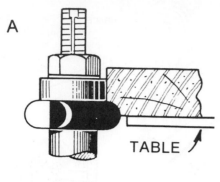

A

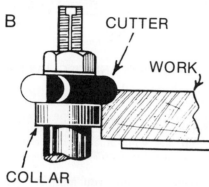

B

CUTTER

WORK

COLLAR

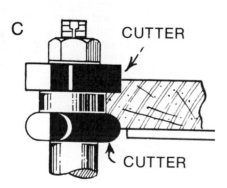

C

CUTTER

CUTTER

FIG. 20-17. Positioning of the rub collar *(a)* above the cutter shapes the lower side of the edge; *(b)* below the cutter shapes the top side of the edge; *(c)* between the two cutters shapes both the top and bottom sides with one pass.

After selecting the proper knife and collar, place your workpiece flat on the table, and use the starting pin furnished with your machine as a fulcrum. Begin feeding from right to left into the cutter. Through experience you will soon determine the correct feed rate for the smoothest cut. Keep a firm grip on the stock. The starting pin will prevent the knives from hogging in. As soon as the cutter has cut into the workpiece to where the collar is

bearing against the uncut portion, you may move the workpiece away from the starting pin and feed it along the rest of the edge, simply using the depth collar as a guide.

When shaping the entire edge of an irregular piece, start the cut as illustrated in Figure 20-18. Continue to cut carefully and accurately until the shaping has been completed.

The collar rubbing against the workpiece will sometimes burn the wood. This is caused by feeding the work too slowly. It can be removed by light sanding. However, to eliminate the possibility of burning, use a ball-bearing depth or rub collar. Or, a pattern can be made, to attach to the workpiece in such a way that only the pattern will rub on the collar.

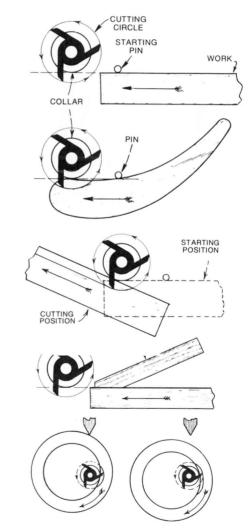

FIG. 20-18. Details of a piece being moved (worked) in position and away from the starting pin.

SHAPING WITH PATTERNS

Patterns are also used as guides when a great many pieces of the same shape have to be made, or when the whole edge of a tabletop has to be shaped or rounded. The pattern must be of the exact shape of the article wanted. It is generally made of some close-grained hardwood such as maple or birch, or of plywood. Patterns are generally best made of material from $\frac{1}{2}$ to $\frac{3}{4}$ inch thick.

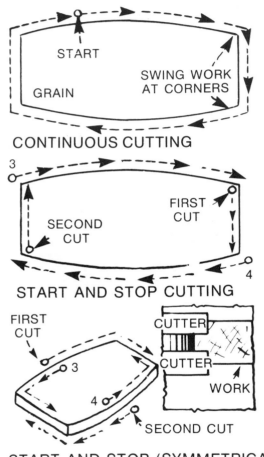

FIG. 20-19. Details of continuous shaping around an irregular edge.

The pattern is guided against the collar, and the work may be placed either on top of the pattern or on its underside (Figure 20-20). The cut is started as for irregular shaping. It is very important to cut the pattern accurately and to make certain that the edges are smooth. When only a portion of the edge is to be shaped, the workpiece should be exactly the size of the pattern. If the entire edge of the stock is to be shaped, it should be roughly sawed

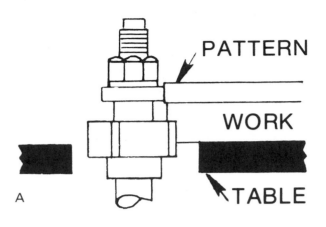

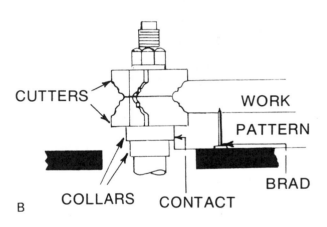

FIG. 20-20. Details showing a pattern fastened (a) to the top of the work and (b) underneath the work. In the latter, note the brad anchor points.

about $\frac{1}{16}$ to $\frac{1}{8}$ inch oversize. Then, anchor pins (sharp-pointed nails or screws) must be installed to hold the work on the pattern (Figure 20-21a). Sometimes two patterns, *exactly* alike, may be used for the same article, one on top and one below (Figure 20-21b). This is done so that the work can be turned over so it is always shaped with the grain. In this case the patterns must be not only of the same shape, but also of the same thickness. A register block is also necessary (Figure 20-21c) for lining up the stock and patterns. When a high-speed shaper is used, however, it makes little difference whether the cut is made with or against the grain. In furniture factories many patterns and templates are used for shaper work.

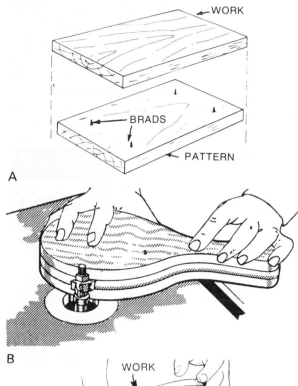

A

B

C

FIG. 20-21. Shaping with a pattern: *(a)* relationship of the pattern to the piece being shaped; *(b)* using a double pattern for shaping an edge; *(c)* a typical register block.

SHAPING ON SPECIAL FORMS OR JIGS

Many special cuts and grooves can be successfully made on the shaper with the use of jigs and special types of forms. Some of these can be custom made for the particular job; others are standard accessories which are available from shaper manufacturers. For instance, the sliding jig is an excellent accessory with which to hold narrow stock while it is being shaped on the end. Another manufactured jig which can be used to good advantage for many shaper operations is the sliding tenoning jig.

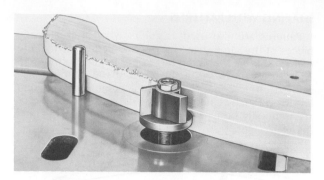

FIG. 20-22. Shaping an edge with a pattern. Note that the entire thickness of the edge is being cut.

Reeding or fluting a round table leg, on the other hand, requires a specially built jig, which is a board having an iron dividing head, a live center, and a dead center. Figure 20-23 shows a detail of the fluting process.

Possibly one of the most valuable of jigs is the guide shown in Figure 20-24, which can be used for shaping a wide variety of circle sizes. It is a flat piece of wood which is as thick as, or thicker than, the piece being shaped. It

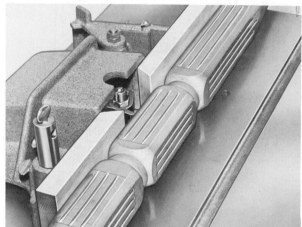

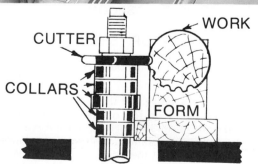

FIG. 20-23. Shaping operation and details of the fluting process.

has a 90° V opening cut in the center. The size of the opening should conform generally to the size of the circular piece. This wooden jig can be set for use with pieces of many different diameters. It must, however, provide two contact points for the circular work.

The variety of cuts and grooves that can be made with jigs is dependent entirely upon the ingenuity of the operator, the cutters available, and the shape of the specially built forms. Shaping, as mentioned in earlier chapters, can also be done (with special attachments) on the radial-arm saw, the drill press, and the router.

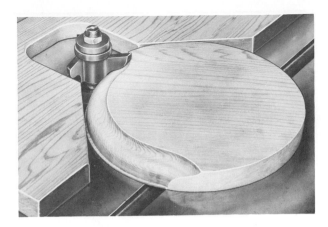

FIG. 20-24. V-block jig at work.

STATIONARY COMBINATION SANDERS

Portable power sanders, described in Chapter 12, take a great deal of the work out of sanding. For the more-than-casual woodworker, however, the stationary type of sander permits a more professional looking finish on any piece of work.

The three most commonly used stationary types are the spindle (drum) sander, which is designed primarily for finishing concave curves; the disk sander, which is used to finish convex curves and small flat surfaces; and the belt sander, which is used for large flat surfaces. While they can be employed for fine finishing such as is found on high-grade cabinet work, these sanders were designed basically for fast cutting operations. Most craftsmen use portable pad sanders (see Chapter 12) for finishing work.

While all three sanders are available as separate units, disk and belt sanders are usually sold as a combination unit (Figure 21-1). To get the most out of it, the combination sander should be properly mounted. The best arrangement is to bolt it to an individual stand about 30 inches high, with the motor on a shelf or bracket below. If desired, the stand can be on casters for portability. These sanders, however, are built so the motor can also be placed to one side; thus the complete outfit may be set up on a workbench, as shown in the photos. The important thing is to have plenty of space all around the tool and to have it accessible from both sides. There will be many times when you will want to work on the belt from the far side; so do not mount it on a bench or table against the wall. The motor used to drive the belt-disk combination sander is usually a ½- or ¾-hp, 1725-rpm motor.

Spindle or drum sanders are seldom found in the average shop as individual tools. They are generally set up as attachments to a drill press, a radial-arm saw, or some other multi-purpose stationary tool.

ABRASIVES

There are five things to consider in choosing the proper abrasive for a stationary sander: type of abrasive material, grit size, backing, type of coating, and form. The information given in Chapters 8 and 12 holds for the abrasives used with stationary spindle, disk, and belt sanders. As to form, all abrasive-coated materials can be obtained in sheets, rolls, disks, drums, and belts. Of course, the most common sheet form measures 9 by 11 inches and is generally used for hand sanding. It can also be cut into disk form for use on power-driven sanding disks. Abrasives are also obtainable in rolls of various widths, but these are seldom used by the home craftsman, except for cutting disks.

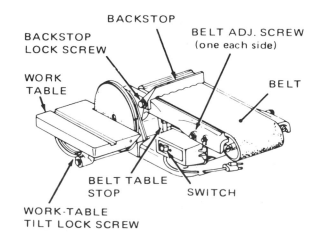

FIG. 21-1. Typical disk-belt combination sander.

For power-driven sanders, most abrasive manufacturers supply precut disks in diameters from 1 inch upward. These can be obtained with paper or cloth backing, coated with aluminum oxide, garnet, or silicon carbide. Flint-coated abrasive can be obtained in paper-backed disks only.

Abrasives in belt form for the belt sander are available with paper or cloth backing, coated with garnet, aluminum oxide, or silicon carbide. Because of the constant flexing of belts as they travel over the drums, a cloth backing will stand up much better than paper.

Spindle or drum sanding machines require a sleeve of a diameter equal to that of the spindle over which it is slipped. Sleeves are available with the same abrasives and backings as belts.

BASIC RULES FOR STATIONARY POWER SANDING

The following basic rules should be kept in mind when power sanding with stationary sanders:

1. Always select the grade of abrasive carefully for the job you are doing. See the abrasive chart in Chapter 8.
2. Wear a face shield or goggles. Sanding dust can be blown into your eyes, harming them.
3. Check the installation of an abrasive belt after it has been put on. Make certain it tracks (runs evenly on the pulleys) and that the sanding belt is neither too loose nor too tight.
4. Make sure that an abrasive disk is fastened firmly to the metal plate.
5. Always sand with the grain of the wood. Note the direction in which the belt, disk, or drum turns. This helps you to decide how to hold the piece being sanded or how to hold the pressure of the belt on the project.
6. Do all the cutting operations before sanding. Except for special jobs, the sander is designed to finish the surface of the work, not to shape it.
7. Apply enough pressure to complete the work. The tendency of the beginner is to press too hard and attempt too big a pass, thus cutting scratches in the surface.
8. At frequent intervals clean off the abrasive paper or cloth with a brush.
9. Always sand surfaces square. The tendency in sanding is to round all edges and surfaces. Do not spoil the accuracy of your work by careless sanding.
10. "Break" all edges slightly to prevent splintering. The corners should be rounded to about the diameter of the lead in a pencil.
11. Move the work about, to avoid heating and burning a portion of the abrasive disk, belt, or wood.
12. Do not sand small pieces unless you have devised a jig to hold them securely, or use a push stick.

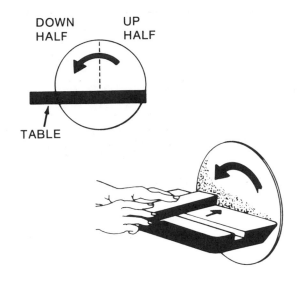

FIG. 21-2. How to use a disk sander.

Disk Sanders

The disk plate of a disk sander is usually 9 to 12 inches in diameter. (Larger ones are available for production work.) The 12-inch disk is usually operated at 1725 rpm. This produces a surface speed at the outer edge of the disk of about 5500 feet per minute. The smaller the disk, the higher can be the speed at which it operates, provided the machine is heavy enough to withstand the speed. The speed at the exact center of a sanding disk is zero.

Resinous materials or materials likely to clog the abrasive when heated should be worked closer to the center of the disk, where the speed is not so great. While a sanding disk has a large surface, only that portion, from the center to the outside edge, that is traveling *downward* can be used safely. The section that is traveling upward is likely to throw the stock being sanded. Thus, sanding should be done on the "down" side of the disk. Although it is permissible to sand small pieces on the "up" side, and while it is necessary to use both sides of the disk when sanding end grain on wide work, the surface produced will not be quite so smooth as that sanded only on the side of the disk moving down. But with a versatile tilting-arbor disk sander, it is possible to sand large areas with only the downward-moving portion of the disk.

The abrasive used on the disk sander will depend upon the work. Garnet can be used for all types of woods (both soft and hard), while aluminum oxide is recommended for hardwoods and metals (see Chapter 11). Since the disk sander is commonly employed for edge work, the abrasive can be somewhat coarser than that used for surfacing. A $\frac{1}{2}$ or $\frac{1}{0}$ disk cuts rapidly to a fairly smooth surface. Fine woodworking, however, requires final sanding with a $\frac{2}{0}$ or $\frac{3}{0}$ disk so that abrasive scratches will not show.

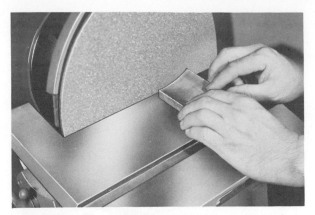

FIG. 21-3. The bench-type disk sander is available with an adjustable tilt table for angled and beveled sanding.

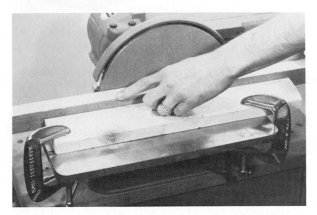

FIG. 21-4. Two clamps and a scrap board serve as a fence for edge sanding long strips to exact dimensions.

The abrasive disk must be cemented or glued to the plate as directed in any owner's manual.

When working small wooden or plastic parts requiring two grades of abrasive for finishing, good use can be made of a double sanding disk. This is made by cutting out the center of the coarser disk, and cementing a smaller disk of fine abrasive in the opening thus provided. The work is first sanded on the outer portion of the disk and then, without stopping the machine, is finished by means of the finer abrasive.

OPERATING THE DISK SANDER

Sanding on the disk sander is usually done freehand, the work being held flat on the table and pushed into the sanding disk. A smooth, light feed should be practiced. Avoid heavy pressure. Best results on curved work can be obtained by going over the work two or three times with light cuts. Remember, sanding is done on the "down" side of the disk; working on the opposite side would, of course, push the work away from the sanding table.

Sanding can be done on the right or left side of the disk, depending on the rotation of the motor. The feed should never be forced (the paper will clog and burn), so gently engage the moving disk, applying only enough pressure to keep the abrasive cutting.

When you are sanding edges longer than the diameter of the disk, take particular care to prevent the disk edge from digging into the work. The best approach is to start the end of the workpiece at the down side of the disk and, with gentle pressure, feed the full length across the face. Keep the work moving at all times when it is in contact with the abrasive.

While the disk sander is not particularly suited for sanding long straight edges, good work can be done using the setup shown in Figure 21-5. A wood fence to which is fastened a hold-down block is clamped to the sander table at the required distance from the sanding disk. The wood fence should be mounted at a slight angle to make sure that the work, which is fed from the "up" side of the disk, will not come in contact with the sanding surface until it reaches the "down" side. The angle should be very slight; it is purposely exaggerated in the illustrations to show the method. A smooth feed is essential. Any length of work can be handled in this manner; or, short pieces can be run through one after another.

Where the work being sanded is so large that it cannot be easily held on the sander table, an auxiliary wood table of suitable size should be made and clamped or otherwise fastened to the standard sanding table.

Workpieces that are too small to be held in the hand can be held with a suitable tool. Do not use ordinary pliers; the jaws close at an angle to each other and cannot securely grip a workpiece against side thrusts. You can use locking pliers, a hand vise, a glue clamp, or any holding device having parallel jaws that will securely grip the workpiece to prevent movement in any direction. Secure the workpiece in the holding device; then rest the holding device on the worktable at the downward moving half of the disk to accomplish the sanding.

A miter gauge—one from a table saw will do—can be used to advantage in sanding square or mitered ends.

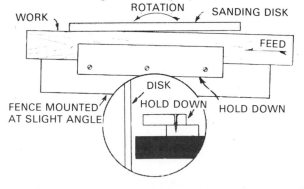

FIG. 21-5. Another method used in sanding long, straight edges.

Where miters are being sanded, the preferred position is as shown in Figure 21-6a; it permits better handling than the reverse position shown in Figure 21-6b. Square ends are sanded by moving the work along the miter gauge until it contacts the disk. Sanding to exact length can be done by presetting the stop rod at the required distance. The rod is free to slide in the hole in the end of the gauge, as shown in Figure 21-6c; the exact length is set when the rod comes to a stop at the bottom of the hole. Square posts are easily beveled by using the miter gauge with a stop rod in this manner.

Circular work should always be sanded with the use of a pivot jig. Top and bottom views of a simple jig are shown in Figure 21-7. Cleats on the underside provide a positive stop against the front and side of the standard table. The sliding strip can be set at any position; it is locked in place by pushing down on the locking lever, the end of which works like a cam. In use, the work is first band sawed to shape, after which it is mounted on the pivot point. The sliding strip is locked at the required distance from the sanding disk. Pushing the table into the disk sets the cut, and rotation finishes the entire edge to a perfectly circular shape. The jig can be clamped to the sander table or simply held with one hand while the other hand rotates the work.

Any other style of pivot jig will work equally well. The simplest setup is a brad driven into a board which is clamped to the sander table at the required distance from the sanding disk.

The sanding of corners is allied to circular work in that the edge being worked is part of a true circle. Most work of this nature can be done freehand, by sweeping the corner of the work across the face of the sanding disk two or three times until the desired round is obtained. More accurate results are possible if the pivot jig is used in the manner shown in Figure 21-7. The sliding strip is first locked in place at the required distance from the face of the sanding disk. A pencil mark is then drawn on the table of the jig; this mark is the same distance from the pivot point as the pivot point is from the sanding disk, as shown in Figure 21-7a. The work is placed against a guide fastened to the rear edge of the jig as shown in Figure 21-7b, and it is brought down on the pivot point in alignment with the pencil mark. Rotating the work rounds the corner (see Figure 21-7c). Figure 21-7d shows how the jig table can be marked with pencil lines as a guide in placing work of any radius.

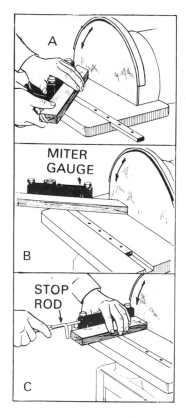

FIG. 21-6. How to use a miter gauge.

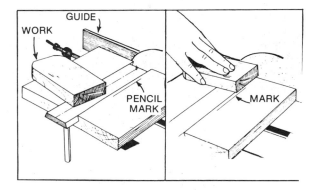

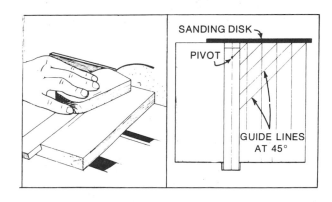

FIG. 21-7. Method of rounding corners.

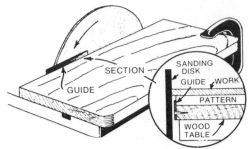

FIG. 21-8. Clean, accurate work in production runs can be done by sanding with a pattern.

In production work, a pattern can be used to ensure perfect sanding. A thin but rigid strip of metal is screwfastened to one side of a wooden table. The table is clamped in place over the regular sanding table, as shown in Figure 21-8. The guiding edge of the metal strip should be about $\frac{1}{8}$ inch from the surface of the sanding disk, and the pattern should be made $\frac{1}{8}$ inch undersize to correspond. Anchor points permit fastening the pattern to the work, after which the work is band sawed about $\frac{3}{16}$ inch outside the edge of the pattern. The work is then sanded smooth, the pattern being held in contact with the metal guide as the work is moved into the sanding disk.

Metals and plastics are finished on the disk sander in practically the same way as wood, except that an aluminum-oxide abrasive disk must be used.

Belt Sanders

The belt sander is probably the one type of stationary sanding machine most used both for production and in the home crafts shop. Sanders of this type should be operated at about 3000 feet per minute. All manufacturers of belt sanders recommend a definite size of pulley as well as the motor speed to be used for the operation of their machines. If these recommendations are followed, there is no need to figure out the pulley size or motor speed necessary to operate the sander at the required speed.

The belt sander can be used to do almost any operation that can be accomplished on the disk sander, besides sanding large surfaces. Abrasive belts are less likely to become impregnated with resin and dust because of the lower operating speed and the flexing of the belt over the drums—which has a tendency to throw out dust embedded between the grains of abrasive.

All belt sanders are provided with two drums over which the abrasive belt travels. The powered drum, the one on which the power pulley is placed, is covered with a rubber sleeve to give traction to the belt. The other drum, which is the idler, is provided with an adjusting device that produces the belt tension and keeps the belt tracking. This device consists of two handwheels or knobs, one at each end of the idler-drum shaft. A lock nut on each adjuster is provided, to lock in the adjustment after it has been made.

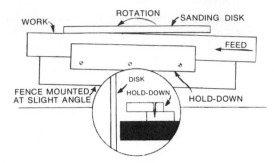

FIG. 21-9. A fully adjustable accessory guide fence allows accurate positioning for beveling long edges.

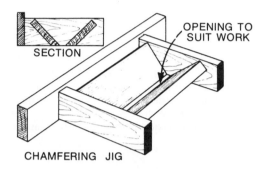

FIG. 21-10. Simple beveling or chamfering jig.

When placing a belt on the sander, release the tension by unscrewing the adjusters; then slip the belt over the pulleys. (Be sure the arrow on the inside of the belt points toward the guide fence.) Tighten both adjustments back to their original positions so that there will be sufficient tension for the belt to move when the power pulley is turned over by hand.

Turn the power pulley over several times to determine if the belt is tracking properly. If the belt shifts to the right when you do this, slightly loosen the right outside nut and tighten the right inside nut; this throws the belt to the left. If this does not solve the problem, slightly loosen the left-side inside nut and tighten the left outside nut; this will help to throw the belt to the left. Alternate the adjustments until the belt tracks properly. But remember to loosen lightly and not radically, as the adjustments are sensitive.

If the belt is tracking to the left, reverse the procedure described in the previous paragraph. Do not start the machine until you are certain that the belt is tracking on the center of the pulleys.

When the machine is started, it may be necessary to adjust the tension on the belt. To increase the tension, loosen the outside knurled nuts about a quarter turn, and tighten the inside nuts until the assembly is forced against the outside nuts. Sometimes it may be necessary to adjust the tension on one side or the other to prevent the belt from shifting to the right or left.

To decrease the tension, reverse the procedure described in the preceding paragraph. Too much tension will act as a resistance to your motor and will shorten the life of the abrasive belt.

OPERATING THE BELT SANDER

Work on a belt sander is generally done freehand; that is, the material to be surfaced is simply placed on the table. Use a light but firm pressure to keep the piece in the proper position. Avoid excessive pressure, since it will scratch the surface being sanded. If the work is longer than the table, it is started at one end and gradually advanced in much the same manner as surfacing on the jointer. Where long work is to be surfaced, it is advisable to use the sanding fence as a guide, especially if the board is close to 6 inches wide.

Most belt sanders used by craftsmen are provided with a fence which extends across the face of the belt. This fence may be set at any angle from 90°, or square to the belt, to 45°. This permits the sanding of long edges or ends at any angle. The work is pushed down along the fence until it contacts the surface. Figure 21-9 shows how beveling is done on the edge of the stock. Chamfering can be done in the same manner. For all operations in which the fence is used, feed the wood against the direction in which the belt is traveling; otherwise the stock will be pulled from your hands.

The cleanest and most accurate chamfering or beveling (especially on short pieces and end grain) is done with the use of a simple V-shaped jig. Figure 21-10 shows the general construction. The two pieces forming the V groove are fitted together at right angles and are separated at the bottom by a suitable distance to make the required cut. The work is simply placed in the V groove and held there until the sanding belt ceases to cut. If the jig is mounted close to the belt, the bevel will be wider than when the jig is mounted higher. The wear on the sanding belt is kept even by moving the fence. Overcutting is impossible, and, provided the jig is parallel to the sanding-belt surface, the bevel will be perfectly uniform and straight from one end of the work to the other.

Straight pieces shorter than the belt table can be sanded on the sides by holding the workpiece lightly against the belt and moving it back and forth across the belt. Use the stop fence to keep the piece from slipping off the table. Pieces longer than the belt-sander table should be sanded by starting the work at one end and gradually pushing it to the other end; feed slowly across the width at the same time. Ends can be sanded square by locating the work against the miter and feeding back and forth across the disk from the center to the left outside edge. Some belt sanders are equipped with a fence which extends parallel to the abrasive belt. On such sanders, long edges can easily be sanded at any angle.

The use of a diagonal feed, as shown in Figure 21-11, permits the surfacing of work considerably wider than the

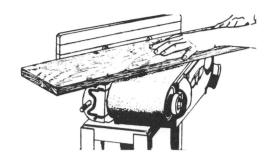

FIG. 21-11. Use of diagonal feed.

belt. The angle at which the work is fed across the belt should be kept as small as possible so as to hold to a minimum the scratches that may appear on the surface because of the diagonal sanding. A belt with a fine abrasive will also help to reduce scratches.

Small, flat stock can best be sanded with the fence set across the belt. When the table is in this position, it acts as a stop for the material being sanded.

Inside contours larger than about $1\frac{3}{4}$ inch in radius can be sanded on the drums at either end of the machine. Hold the work firmly, press the start of the contour lightly against the drum on one side, and move the work slowly across the drum while moving up the contour against the drum. (See Figure 21-13.) Outside curves can be sanded on the belt table. Hold the work firmly, begin the curve lightly against one side at the end of the belt table, and feed across the belt and toward the opposite end of the belt while moving up the contour of the workpiece.

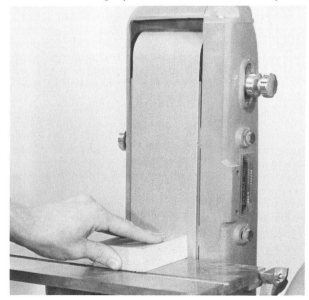

FIG. 21-12. With the belt in a true vertical position and the table horizontal, you are set up for end work.

FIG. 21-13. When positioned as shown, with the guard removed, the end drum can sand an inside curve.

Outside curves on the end grain can also be sanded against the disk on the tilting table. Feed the work lightly against the disk, and move it back and forth from the center of the disk to the left outside edge while moving along the contour of the workpiece. Note that, if the curve runs with the grain of the workpiece, a better finish would result from sanding with the grain on the sanding table.

In production work, sanding can often be done more quickly with forms. These are made from wood cut to the proper curvature; the form is screw-fastened to the standard sanding table. It is necessary, in most cases, to make a sanding belt to fit, although a very shallow form can be used with the standard sanding belt. A common shape is the circular form (see Figure 21-14a). This form is a portion of a true circle; hence, the work can be pushed along it because the curve is the same at all points. A suitable fence is made and clamped to the standard fence, thus providing a side support for the work and ensuring square edges. The irregular form (Figure 21-14b) is not a part of a circle; work sanded over this type of form must be set down in a certain position, with the placement controlled by means of a stop block. Hollow forms (Figure 21-14c) have curves which do not conform to the belt shape. In this case the belt is run rather loose so that it will take the same shape as the form when the work presses against it.

Forms can be built up, with the work surface being covered with plywood, as shown in Figure 21-15; or the shape may be cut from a solid piece of wood. Cloth-backed abrasive belts are preferred for use with forms. A heavyweight backing can be used for most work, the exception being very abrupt curves where a light backing gives better results. Forms of that type require a light, flexible belt that will conform to their shape.

The manner in which these forms work can be seen in Figure 21-16. The fence is aligned with the shaped portion of the form so that the work will be in the proper position when it is pressed against the fence and moved into the belt. Under pressure, the belt takes on the same shape as the form and sands the work to the desired shape. A knowledge of just when to lift the work from the belt must be acquired by practice. With a lightweight backing

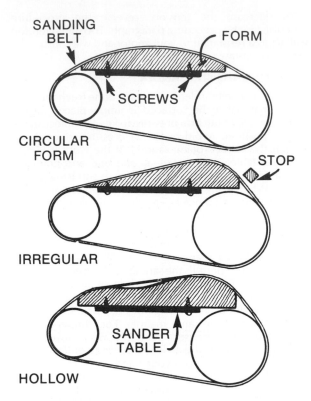

FIG. 21-14. Various sanding forms.

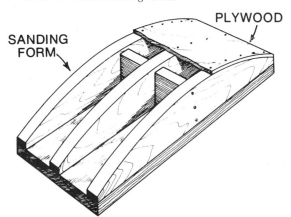

FIG. 21-15. How a sanding form is constructed.

surfaced with a fine-grit abrasive, sanding of practically any molded shape is possible. Where the shape of the form is composed of very abrupt curves, slashed belts should be used. This type of belt, as the name implies, is not a solid surface but is slashed into strips about $\frac{1}{8}$ inch wide. Short sections of the belt are left uncut, and these uncut portions serve to hold the numerous narrow belts together.

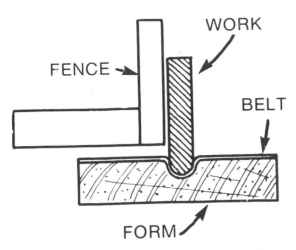

FIG. 21-16. How a sanding form is located on a belt sander.

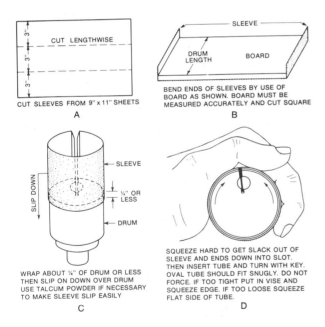

CUT SLEEVES FROM 9" x 11" SHEETS

A

BEND ENDS OF SLEEVES BY USE OF BOARD AS SHOWN. BOARD MUST BE MEASURED ACCURATELY AND CUT SQUARE

B

WRAP ABOUT ¼" OF DRUM OR LESS THEN SLIP ON DOWN OVER DRUM USE TALCUM POWDER IF NECESSARY TO MAKE SLEEVE SLIP EASILY

C

SQUEEZE HARD TO GET SLACK OUT OF SLEEVE AND ENDS DOWN INTO SLOT. THEN INSERT TUBE AND TURN WITH KEY. OVAL TUBE SHOULD FIT SNUGLY. DO NOT FORCE. IF TOO TIGHT PUT IN VISE AND SQUEEZE EDGE. IF TOO LOOSE SQUEEZE FLAT SIDE OF TUBE.

D

FIG. 21-17. Replacing the abrasive paper on a drum sander.

Slashed belts are ideal for sanding odd-shaped edges. This type of work is done without a backing plate; hence either the sander table must be removed or the work must be done on the back side. The latter is preferable for occasional work, since it is much easier to remove the back plate than the table. In use, the belt is run rather slack so that the work, when moved into it, will cause the belt to assume the proper shape. Edges finished in this

manner will show a very slight curvature, but for all practical purposes the effect is a right-angle cut. Production runs are best done with the sander table, since this provides a rest for the work while ensuring proper contact with the belt. It is necessary, of course, to remove the main sander table before the tilt table can be used.

Spindle or Drum Sanders

As was stated earlier, some self-contained spindle or drum sanders are available, but in the average crafts shop, the drum sander is an attachment that is used in conjunction with the drill press, the scroll saw, the shaper, the radial-arm saw, or some multipurpose tool. The sanding drums used with these tools range in size from 1 to 3½ inches in diameter. The most popular is the 2½-inch size. Both the drums and abrasive sleeves are inexpensive and very efficient for edge sanding curved work.

Directions for replacing sleeves are shown in Figure 21-17. Cut a 9 X 11 inch sheet of abrasive paper with the proper grit into three 3 X 11 inch strips by tearing it against a metal straightedge or a hacksaw blade. (Never cut the abrasive paper with scissors or a knife, as this will damage the cutting edge of the tool.) Bend the ends of the sleeves by using a board as shown. The board must be measured accurately and cut square. Then wrap the sleeve around the drum, approximately ¼ inch below the top, and slip the ends in the slot. Now slip the sleeve on over the drum. A little talcum powder on the soft-rubber drum will make the sleeve slip on more easily. Squeeze hard to get the slack out of the sleeve, and push the ends down into the slot. Then insert the tube that comes with the drum, and turn it with a key. The oval tube should fit snugly; do not force it. If it is too tight, put it in a vise and squeeze the edge; if it is too loose, squeeze the flat side of the tube.

OPERATING THE SPINDLE SANDER

Sanding drums of various sizes are used extensively for edge work; they can be satisfactorily worked on a drill press, lathe, or flexible shaft, or direct-coupled to a motor shaft. The size most commonly used measures between 2½ and 3 inches in diameter and should be run at a speed of about 1800 rpm. Drums of smaller diameter may be operated at a slightly higher speed. In fact, within reasonable limits, the higher the drum speed, the smoother the finish. However, excessive speed causes overheating, and, where wood is being finished, the heat extracts a gummy pitch from the work which quickly clogs the abrasive sleeve.

Standard sanding drums usually measure 3 inches long and have a projecting nut on the free end. Narrow-face drums are 1 inch wide and are flush on the bottom, with the tightening nut on the shank end. All standard operations can be performed with these drums; the face width of 1 inch is sufficient to handle average ¾-inch-thick work. The flush bottom also permits the finishing of inside corners, as shown in Figure 21-18. When doing this kind of work, it is advisable to mount the sleeve so that it projects about $\frac{1}{32}$ inch beyond the bottom of the drum, in order to prevent the drum bottom from burning the work. Narrow-face drums are fitted with a special "trishape" shank which permits mounting in either $\frac{5}{16}$-inch collets or three-jaw chucks.

The drums used on lathes are fitted with taper shanks or screw-on fittings to permit fastening to the lathe headstock. Sanding can be done freehand, but where edge work is being done a vertical support greatly

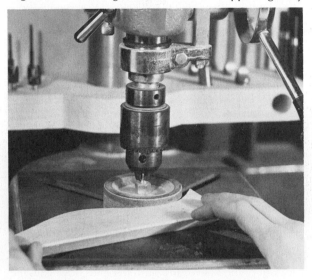

FIG. 21-18. Spindle-type narrow-face drum-sander accessory in action. This type of sander does not usually require an auxiliary table.

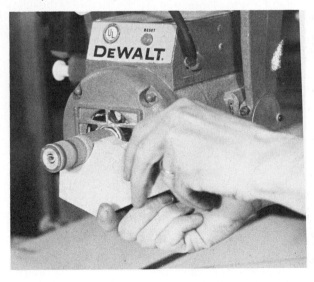

FIG. 21-19. With the power drive and drum positioned vertically, the radial-arm machine helps in sanding the edges of long work.

simplifies the work. Drums with taper shanks can be safeguarded from coming loose by supporting the end with the tailstock, using a 60° plain center.

The drums used on drill presses run in a vertical position most useful for average work. But when a standard drum or spindle sander is used, some surface against which the material being sanded can be supported is an absolute necessity if the angle of the finished surface is to be maintained. When the drill press is used as a spindle sander, an auxiliary table made of wood must be provided so that the drum or spindle can be let into it. The lower edge of the drum must be a little below the surface of the auxiliary table, in order that the entire edge of the stock being finished will come in contact with the abrasive. The common arrangement for a radial-arm saw is illustrated in Figure 21-19.

In conjunction with the radial-arm machine (and some other multipurpose tools), it is possible to use the drum sander in a horizontal position. As shown in Figure 21-20, it can be used to sand intricate curves freehand. It will also do an effective job of surfacing narrow work. For this operation, use either the auxiliary or stationary table. With the motor raised to its full extent, set the motor shaft in a horizontal position. Place the material tight against the fence, and lower the radial arm until the abrasive hits the start of the stock. Withdraw the stock, turn on the motor, and feed the work against the rotation of the drum. If more smoothness is desired, keep lowering the arm, a quarter turn at a time. Wider boards may be handled in the same manner, except that several passes will have to be taken with the sander at the same height. Remember, in any surface-sanding operation, not to attempt too deep a bite in one pass; two or more passes will result in a better job.

Another accessory is the shaping sanding drum, for working in and around irregular shapes and bends. It is a small drum with a series of stiff-bristle brushes around its surface. Abrasive cloth is attached to the front of each brush; as the unit rotates, the bristles force the cloth into and against small corners, turns, and crevices.

CARE AND MAINTENANCE OF STATIONARY SANDING TOOLS

Keep the stationary sander clean. When necessary, take it apart and remove all sawdust from operating parts. Make sure the air vents are not plugged. Keep the tool well lubricated. On the stationary abrasive belt sander, lubricate the idler drum bearing, belt-tension knob screws, and tracking-handle screws. On the stationary disk sander, lubricate the spindle bearing when needed. Use SAE 20 or 30 machine oil for lubricating.

Check the belt, disk, or drum sleeve frequently to make sure the abrasive cloth or paper is not worn. Replace it as necessary. Also make sure the paper or cloth is attached properly. Remember, on belt sanders, that the arrow on the belt indicates the direction of rotation. Always be sure to maintain the proper motor-belt tension.

FIG. 21-20. Long, thin drum sander, good for small, intricate curves.

SANDER/GRINDER

The sander/grinder shown in Fig. 21-21 is basically a belt sander which can be employed for both external and internal wood-surface sanding. As described in Chapter 22, it can also be used for some grinding, sharpening, and polishing operations. While the sander/grinder is especially useful for small workpieces, it can be used on large ones, too. (Fig. 21-21b).

FIG. 21-21. A sander/grinder at work.

GRINDERS AND KEEPING YOUR TOOLS SHARP

A great many of the tools mentioned in this book require sharpening if they are to work properly. When an edge starts to become dull, more pressure is needed to keep it cutting. More pressure means more wear, more nicks, and other damage. If it is not badly nicked, worn out of shape (bevels destroyed), or otherwise damaged, a dulled edge can be restored simply by sharpening. If it has, however, been badly damaged, an edge must be reshaped before it is sharpened. Some tools are "case hardened" so that the hard metal capable of holding an edge is only skin deep. Other tools have specially hardened, not-too-deep edge material set into softer metal bodies. Either of these types is limited as to the amount of reshaping that can be done; when a tool is reshaped enough to remove the hard skin (or inset edge), it becomes useless.

Most tools can be sharpened with a proper hone or, at worst, a fine file lightly used prior to honing. Reshaping requires filing or grinding. Remember that grinding with a dry stone creates heat. A large tool can absorb much heat without damage, but a small tool (such as a knife blade) cannot. If too much heat is absorbed, the edge will lose its temper (hardness) so that it will afterward be dulled very easily. Therefore, when dry grinding, never let metal become any warmer than is comfortable to your touch; air-cool or (quicker) water-cool the metal as frequently as necessary. Also, when sharpening, always restore the tool's original bevel angles and edge shape insofar as is possible. Altering the bevel and edge shape alters a tool's usefulness.

Grinding Equipment

As mentioned previously, grinding wheels can be used in conjunction with the radial-arm machine, drill press, and portable electric drill. As mentioned in Chapter 13, hand electric grinders can be used to sharpen tools. However, most grinding operations are performed on motorized grinders.

MOTORIZED GRINDERS

The electric grinder is available in either the bench type (which is fastened to the top of the workbench) or the pedestal model (which has its own stand that is fastened to the floor). The latter is usually a heavy-duty type; the bench type is more popular for the average shop.

While some bench grinders are belt driven (a pulley mounted on the shaft drives the grinding wheels), most today come with integral motors, as in Figure 22-1. All such tools are equipped with two grinding wheels (usually with two different grits), adjustable tool rests, guards,

FIG. 22-1. Typical motorized grinder.

safety eye shields and an on-off switch. Models differ principally in the grinding-wheel size (diameter), rated motor horsepower, and such features as type of bearings, type and convenience of switch, and type of tool light (if any).

Grinders are classified according to the diameter of the grinding wheel. For instance, a "6-inch grinder" is designed to operate with a 6-inch grinding wheel. For average shop use, the most practical grinders are those in the 5- to 7-inch category, and they should have motors ranging from $\frac{1}{4}$ to $\frac{1}{2}$ hp. If you plan to do any heavy-duty grinding, then an 8-inch grinder powered by a $\frac{3}{4}$-hp or stronger motor might be a better selection.

GRINDING WHEELS A grinding wheel is composed of two basic elements: the abrasive grains, and the bonding agent. The abrasive grains may be thought of as many single-point tools embedded in a tool holder of bonding agent. Each of these grains extracts a very small chip from the material as it makes contact on each revolution of the grinding wheel.

An ideal cutting tool is one that will sharpen itself when it becomes dull. This, in effect, is what happens to the abrasive grains. As the individual grains become dull, the pressure that is generated on them causes them to fracture and present new sharp cutting edges to the work. When the grains can fracture no more, the pressure becomes too great and they are released from the bond, allowing new sharp grains to be presented to the work.

Grinding wheels come in various sizes and shapes. The size of a grinding wheel is given in terms of its diameter in inches, the diameter of the spindle hole, and the width of the face of the wheel. Grinding wheels come in too many shapes to list in this book, but Figure 22-2 shows most of the more frequently used wheel shapes. The type numbers are standard and are used by all manufacturers. The shapes are shown in cross-sectional views. The specific job will dictate the shape of wheel to be used.

Grinding-wheel markings are comprised of six parts or sections. They are shown in Figure 22-3 and are:

1. Kind of Abrasive There are, as mentioned in Chapter 8, two types of abrasives: natural and manufactured. Natural abrasives, such as emery, corundum, and diamond, are used only in honing stones and in special types of grinding wheels. The common manufactured abrasives are aluminum oxide and silicon carbide. They have superior qualities and are more economical than natural abrasives. Aluminum oxide (designated by the letter A) is used for grinding steel and steel alloys, and for heavy-duty work such as cleaning up steel castings. Silicon carbide (designated by the letter C), which is harder but not as tough as aluminum oxide, is used mostly for grinding nonferrous metals and carbide tools. The abrasive in a grinding wheel comprises about 40 percent of the wheel.

2. Grain Size Grain sizes range from 10 to 600. The size is determined by the size of the mesh of a sieve through which the grains can pass. Generally speaking, they are rated as follows:

> Coarse: 10, 12, 14, 16, 20, 24
> Medium: 30, 36, 46, 54, 60
> Fine: 70, 80, 90, 100, 120, 150, 180
> Very fine: 220, 240, 280, 320, 400, 500, 600

Grain sizes finer than 240 are generally considered "flour." Generally speaking, fine-grain wheels are preferred for grinding hard materials, as they have more cutting edges and will cut faster than coarse-grain wheels. Coarse-grain wheels are generally preferred for rapid metal removal on softer materials.

3. Grade (Hardness) The grade is designated by a letter of the alphabet; grades run from A to Z, or soft to hard. The grade of a grinding wheel is a measurement of the ability of the bond to retain the abrasive grains in the wheel. Grinding wheels are said to be of soft to hard grades. This does not mean that the bond or the abrasive is soft or hard; it means that the wheel has a large amount of bond (hard grade) or a small amount of bond (soft grade). Figure 22-4 illustrates magnified portions of a soft-grade and a hard-grade wheel. You can see that a part of the bond surrounds the abrasive grains and the remainder of the bond forms into posts that both hold the grains to the wheel and hold them apart from each other. The wheel having the larger amount of bonding material has thick bond posts and will offer great resistance to

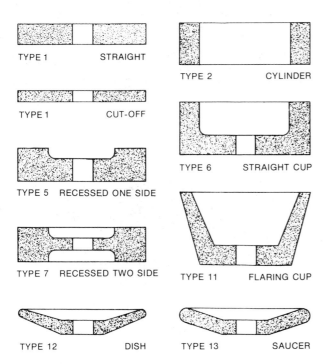

TYPE 1   STRAIGHT

TYPE 1   CUT-OFF

TYPE 5   RECESSED ONE SIDE

TYPE 7   RECESSED TWO SIDE

TYPE 12   DISH

TYPE 2   CYLINDER

TYPE 6   STRAIGHT CUP

TYPE 11   FLARING CUP

TYPE 13   SAUCER

FIG. 22-2. Grinding-wheel shapes.

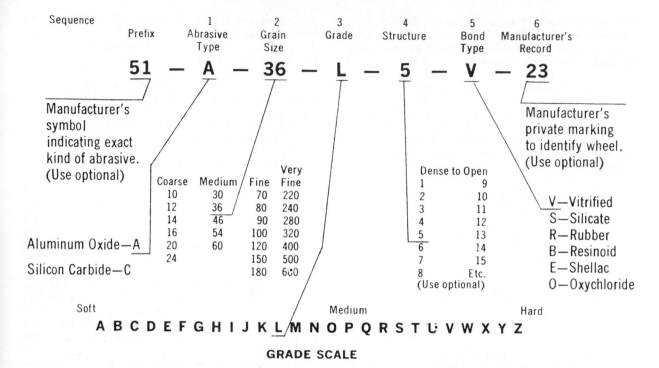

FIG. 22-3. Standard system of marking grinding wheels, adopted by the American Standards Association. Although the standard greatly facilitates ordering from the standpoint of uniform marking of wheels, there is no assurance that competitors' wheels that are marked alike will cut in the same way. Each manufacturer may describe the wheel further in the first and last symbols of the identification mark.

pressures generated in grinding. The wheel having the least amount of bonding material will offer less resistance to grinding pressures. In other words, the wheel with a large amount of bond is said to be a hard grade, and the wheel with a small amount of bond is said to be a soft grade.

4. Structure The structure of a grinding wheel is designated by a number from 1 to 15. The structure refers to the open space between the grains, as shown in Figure 22-4. Grains that are very closely spaced are said to be dense; when grains are wider apart, they are said to be open. Generally speaking, more metal is removed by open-grain wheels than by close-grain wheels. Also, dense or close-grain wheels will normally produce a finer finish. The structure of a grinding wheel comprises about 20 percent of the grinding wheel.

5. Bond Type The bond comprises the remaining 40 percent of the grinding wheel and is one of the most important parts of the wheel. The bond determines the strength of the wheel. There are six basic types of bonds in general use, as follows:

Vitrified bond, designated by the letter V, is not affected by oil, acid, or water. Vitrified-bonded wheels are strong and porous, and rapid temperature changes have little or no effect on them. Vitrified wheels should

not be run in excess of 6500 surface feet per minute.

Silicate-bonded wheels are designated by the letter S. Silicate-bonded wheels are used mainly for large, slow-speed machines where a cooler cutting action is desired. Silicate-bonded wheels are said to be softer than vitrified wheels, as they release the grains more readily than vitrified-bonded wheels. This wheel, like the vitrified-bonded wheel, should not be run in excess of 6500 surface feet per minute.

Rubber-bonded wheels, designated by the letter R, are strong and elastic. They are used for the manufacture of thin cutoff wheels and are used extensively for regulating wheels on centerless grinders. Rubber-bonded wheels produce a high finish and can be run at speeds up to 16,000 surface feet per minute.

Resinoid-bonded wheels are designated by the letter B and are shock resistant and strong. They are used for rough grinding and cutoff wheels. Resinoid wheels also can be run at speeds up to 16,000 surface feet per minute.

Shellac-bonded wheels, designated by the letter E, give a high finish and have a cool cutting action when used as cutoff wheels. Shellac-bonded wheels can be run up to 12,500 surface feet per minute.

Oxychloride bonded wheels are designated by the letter O. They are not to be run at speeds greater than

6500 surface feet per minute.

6. Manufacturer's Record. This may be a letter or number, or both. It is used by the manufacturer to designate bond modifications or wheel characteristics.

SELECTION OF GRINDING WHEELS The selection of grinding wheels for precision grinding can be discussed generally in terms of such factors as the physical properties of the material to be ground, the amount of stock to be removed (depth of cut), the wheel speed and work speed, and the finish required. A grinding wheel having the proper abrasive, grain, grade, and bond is selected by considering one or more of these factors.

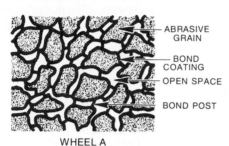

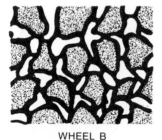

FIG. 22-4. How the bond affects the grade of the wheel. Wheel A is softer; wheel B, harder.

An aluminum-oxide abrasive is most suitable for grinding carbon and alloy steel, high-speed steel, cast alloys, and malleable iron. A silicon-carbide abrasive is most suitable for grinding nonferrous metals, nonmetallic materials, and cemented carbides.

Generally, the softer and more ductile the material being ground, the coarser the grain should be. Also, if a large amount of material is to be removed, a coarse-grain wheel is recommended (except on very hard materials). If a good finish is required, a fine-grain wheel should be used.

For soft materials, small depth of cut, or high work speed, use a soft-grade wheel. If the machine you are using is worn, a harder grade may be necessary to help offset the effects of wear of the machine. Using a coolant also permits the use of a harder grade of wheel. Table 22-1 lists *generally* recommended grinding wheels for various motorized grinder operations.

GRINDING SAFETY

The grinding wheel is a fragile cutting tool which operates at high speeds. For this reason, the following guidelines for safe grinding must be practiced:

1. The wheel must be properly installed according to the tool manufacturer's instructions. Before a wheel is installed, however, it should be inspected for visible defects and "sounded" by tapping lightly with a piece of hardwood to determine whether it has invisible cracks. A good wheel gives out a clear, ringing sound when tapped, but if the wheel is cracked a dull thud is heard.
2. Secure all loose clothing, and remove rings or other jewelry.
3. Inspect the grinding wheel, wheel guards, tool rest, and other safety devices to ensure they are

Table 22-1 Recommendations for Selecting Grinding Wheels

Operation	Wheel designation					Material
	Abrasive	Grain size	Grade	Structure	Bond	
Cylindrical grinding	A	60	K	8	V	High-speed steel
	A	60	L	5	V	Hardened steel
	A	54	M	5	V	Soft steel
	C	36	K	5	V	Cast iron, brass, aluminum
	A	54	1	5	V	General purpose
Surface grinding	A	46	H	8	V	High-speed steel
	A	60	F	12	V	Hardened steel
	A	46	J	5	V	Soft steel
	C	36	J	8	V	Cast iron and bronze
	A	24	H	8	V	General purpose
Tool and cutter grinding	A	46	K	8	V	High-speed steel or cast alloy milling cutter
	A	54	L	5	V	Reamers
	A	60	K	8	V	Taps

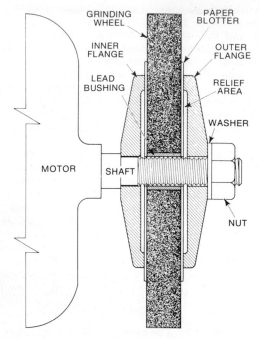

FIG. 22-5. Typical method of mounting a grinding wheel.

in good condition and positioned properly. Set the tool rest so that it is within $\frac{1}{8}$ inch of the wheel face and level with the center of the wheel.

4. Transparent shields, if installed, should be clean and properly adjusted. Transparent shields do not preclude the use of goggles, as the dust and grit may get around a shield. Goggles, however, provide full eye protection.

5. Stand aside when starting the grinder motor, until the operating speed is reached. This prevents injury if the wheel explodes from a defect that has not been noticed.

6. Use light pressure when starting the grinding; too much pressure on a cold wheel may cause failure.

7. Grind only on the face or outer circumference of a grinding wheel unless the wheel is specifically designed for side grinding.

8. The grinding temperature must be kept low. Use a coolant to prevent overheating the work.

9. The wheel direction should always be away from the cutting edge toward the body of the tool. This positioning of the tool directs heat travel away from the cutting edge.

10. Wear goggles and respiratory filters to protect your eyes and lungs from injury by grit and dust generated by grinding operations. Also, wear ear plugs or muffs during extended periods of operation.

GRINDING METAL STOCK

Besides sharpening tools, there are an almost endless number of odd jobs that can be done on the grinding wheel. Smoothing a welded joint is typical of this class of work. Cutting thin metal that has been folded, by grinding through the fold, is another example. But a major use is to grind metal stock to shape. For instance, to grind a straight edge on metal stock (Figure 22-6a), adjust the tool rest so that it just clears the wheel and is approximately at the centerline of the wheel. Then, keeping the edge of the stock parallel with the centerline of the grinder shaft, pass the stock across the face of the wheel. Grind across the entire width of the workpiece, using that pressure which will keep the wheel cutting but will not appreciably decrease its speed. By grinding across the entire width of the piece and the wheel, you wear the wheel evenly and help prevent overheating.

To grind a bevel on an edge (Figure 22-6b), hold the stock as shown so that it is resting both on the wheel and on the edge of the tool rest. The edge being ground is away from the tool rest and therefore is not liable to get caught between the tool rest and the wheel. Pass the stock across the face of the wheel, just as you do when grinding a square edge.

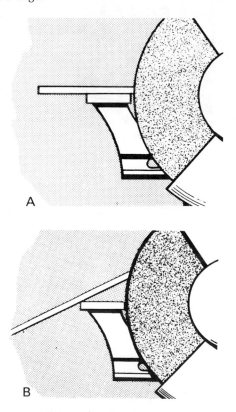

FIG. 22-6. (a) Grinding a straight edge on metal stock; (b) grinding a bevel on metal stock.

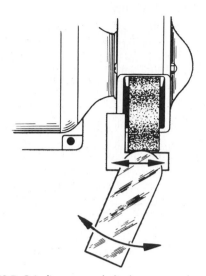

FIG. 22-7. Grinding a rounded edge on metal stock.

To grind a rounded edge, set the tool rest at the centerline of the wheel. With one hand, hold the end of the stock being ground so that you can move it from left to right, across the face of the wheel, as shown by the small double-headed arrow in Figure 22-7; also hold it down firmly on the tool rest. With the other hand, swing the arc shown by the longer curved double-headed arrow at the opposite end of the stock. The motion indicated by the curved arrow will produce the rounded edge on the stock. The travel indicated by the short straight double-headed arrow will prevent the wearing of a groove in the wheel (which would then have to be removed by dressing).

SPARK TESTING Spark testing provides a rapid, economical method of separating and classifying types of irons and steels and some nonferrous metals. Iron and oxygen are regarded as necessary elements for brilliant grinding sparks from common metals. The oxygen may be mixed with other gases as in air. Carbon is a necessary element for spurts or bursts. Some nonferrous metals, such as copper and aluminum, yield no true grinding sparks in air.

Table 22-2 and the sketches in Figure 22-8 point out important differences among the sparks from a wide variety of metals. The terms are relative rather than absolute. The length of the spark stream depends, for one thing, upon the pressure between the grinding wheel and the work. The apparent color depends upon the light in which the inspection is made. The order of colors is: red (darkest), orange, light orange, straw, white (brightest). A "forked" spurt is simple in form, with all branches emanating from a single source. Machine steel affords a striking example of forked spurts. A "fine, repeating" spurt is one whose branches "repeat" or explode again, sometimes several times. A striking example is provided by plain high-carbon steel. Some steels produce both types of spurts in the same stream. For simplicity, the bursts from each sample are specified as "forked" or "fine, repeating" according to which predominates.

TRUING AND DRESSING THE GRINDING WHEEL Grinding wheels, like other cutting tools, require frequent reconditioning of the cutting surfaces to perform efficiently. "Dressing" is the term used to describe the process of cleaning the periphery of a grinding wheel. This cleaning breaks away dull abrasive grains and smooths the surface so that there are no grooves. Truing is the term used to describe the removal of material from the cutting face of the wheel so that the resultant surface runs absolutely true to some other

Table 22-2 Metal Sparks Resulting from Grinding

Metal	Volume of stream	Color of stream close to wheel	Color of streaks near end of stream	Quantity of spurts	Nature of spurts
Wrought iron	Large	Straw	White	Very few	Forked
Machine steel	Large	White	White	Few	Forked
Carbon tool steel	Moderately large	White	White	Very many	Fine, repeating
Gray cast iron	Small	Red	Straw	Many	Fine, repeating
White cast iron	Very small	Red	Straw	Few	Fine, repeating
Annealed malleable iron	Moderate	Red	Straw	Many	Fine, repeating
High-speed steel	Small	Red	Straw	Extremely few	Forked
Manganese steel	Moderately large	White	White	Many	Fine, repeating
Stainless steel	Moderate	Straw	White	Moderate	Forked
Tungsten-chromium die steel	Small	Red	Straw	Many	Fine, repeating
Nitrided nitralloy	Large (curved)	White	White	Moderate	Forked
Stellite	Very small	Orange	Orange	None	
Cemented tungsten carbide	Extremely small	Light orange	Light orange	None	
Nickel	Very small	Orange	Orange	None	
Copper, brass, aluminum	None			None	

surface, such as the grinding-wheel shaft.

The diamond-pointed wheel dresser shown in Figure 22-9 is used for dressing grinding wheels on bench and pedestal grinders. To dress a wheel with this tool, start the grinder and let it come up to speed. Set the wheel dresser on the rest as shown, and bring it into firm contact with the wheel. Move the wheel dresser back and forth across the face of the wheel until the surface is clean and approximately square with the sides of the wheel.

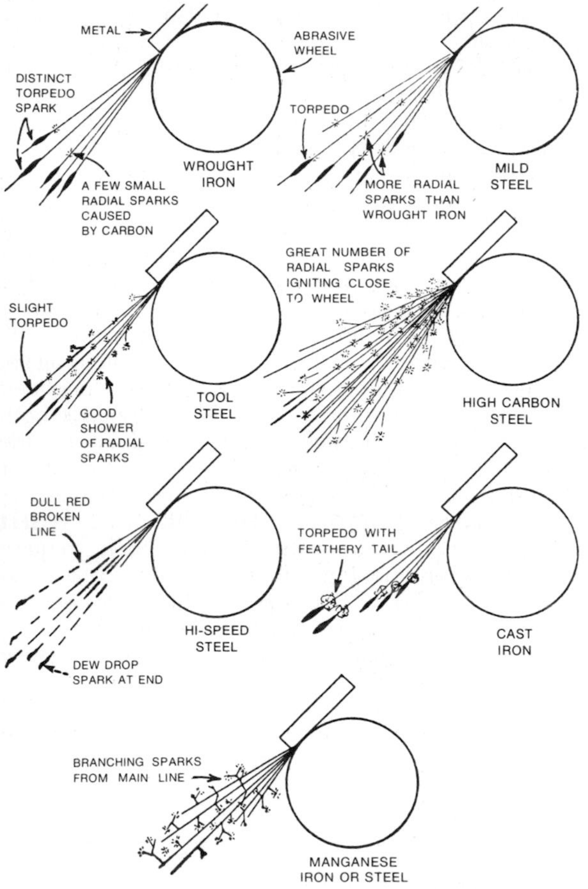

If a grinding wheel gets off balance because of out-of-roundness, dressing the wheel will usually remedy the condition. A grinding wheel can get out of balance if it is left with part of the wheel immersed in the coolant; if this happens, the wheel should be removed and dried out by baking. If the wheel gets out of balance axially, the efficiency of the wheel will probably not be affected. This unbalance may be remedied simply by removing the wheel and cleaning the shaft spindle and spindle hole in the wheel and the flanges.

Each time a wheel is dressed, it is necessary that you check the clearance between the tool rest and the wheel. Reestablish the clearance at $\frac{1}{16}$ inch as required. Adjustments must be made with the machine secured, to preclude possible injury to the operator.

In addition to grinding and sharpening, any motor-driven grinder can also be used, with the typical accessories, for buffing, polishing, and wire brushing (removing burrs, rust, etc.). Wire wheels for grinders generally come in three sizes: 3, 4, and 6 inches. There are fine and coarse grades in each size; in addition, the 6-inch size includes a medium grade and a two-section (or double-thick) coarse grade. Wire cup brushes come in three sizes and two grades: $1\frac{1}{2}$-inch fine and coarse, $2\frac{1}{2}$-inch fine and coarse; and 3-inch coarse. Cotton buffs come in three sizes: 3, 4, and 6 inches. All are $\frac{1}{2}$ inch thick. They have no grades. Polishing bonnets come in two sizes (5 and 7 inches) and, like the buffs, have no grades. Incidentally, most of these grinding-wheel attachments can be used with electric portable drills and drill presses (Chapters 9 and 17).

FIG. 22-8. Characteristics of sparks generated by the grinding of some of the more common metals.

FIG. 22-9. Using a grinding-wheel dresser.

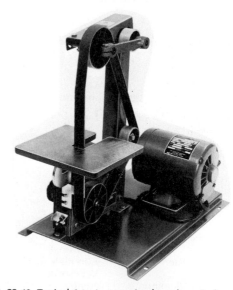

FIG. 22-10. Typical 1-inch motorized sander-grinder.

OTHER TYPES OF GRINDERS

The following types of equipment also may be purchased for grinding and/or sharpening.

MOTORIZED SANDER-GRINDER This tool (Figure 22-10) usually provides a 1- or 2-inch wide aluminum-oxide sanding belt together with a plate arrangement for holding a sandpaper disk. Both the belt and the sandpaper disk can be obtained in various grits suitable for light grinding and sharpening operations on knife blades, chisels, and similar tools. The sander-grinder generally has a 1/3- or 1/2-hp built-in motor.

To grind metal, feed the work to the belt lightly so that the abrasive (not your force) does the work. If a sharp edge is to be broken or rounded, do not push it straight in; round it from each side to avoid tearing the belt. If the workpiece becomes too hot to hold, you can cool it in water, but never apply a coolant to the belt or to the work while grinding. If the workpiece contact edge is smaller than the belt width, you can hold the work steady; otherwise, move the workpiece constantly.

Bevel-edged tools can be sharpened with the work platform tilted to the proper angle, as shown in Figure 22-11. Clamp a scrap block to the table, notched as indicated to fit close to the belt, to provide a bearing surface on which you can hold the tool flat to be sharpened. Press the bevel edge lightly against the belt, and cool it frequently during the operation (with air or water) to prevent overheating. Keep the edge in constant motion to equalize stock removal.

FIG. 22-11. A tilted work platform for sharpening bevel-edged tools.

Metal that is pitted or rusted can be restored by using this tool with a slack belt. To slacken the belt, you must remove the platen (refer to the owner's manual as to how this is done) and adjust the upper idler pulley. Feed the work gently to the belt, holding it as necessary to make the contact required, but take care not to force the belt from its pulleys. Cool the workpiece in water as necessary.

One of the main purposes of this tool is, of course, sanding. Wood or plastic ends, edges, and small surfaces are sanded quickly with this machine. Keep the feed pressure light and the work moving uniformly from side to side so that the belt edge cannot dig in to leave a mark. Beveling is done by tilting the worktable.

HAND-DRIVEN GRINDERS These are small grindstones for hand operation, generally driven (by handle rotation) through gears which impart a desirable wheel speed without excessive effort. They may be designed for clamping or bolting to a bench. A tool rest is usually provided (Figure 22-12).

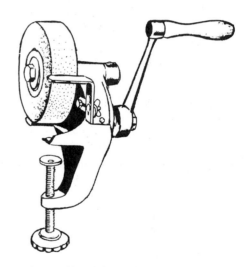

FIG. 22-12. Typical hand-driven dry grinder.

OTHER TOOL-SHARPENING TOOLS

There are other tool-sharpening implements available: files and sharpening or honing stones. These tools have been fully described in Chapters 3 and 8, respectively. Here is a summary of their uses in sharpening tools.

FILES AND FILING TECHNIQUES Many tools cannot be ground, but must be filed to reshape their edges. Files also are used for the preliminary sharpening (to remove slight nicks) of edges to be finished by honing. The shape, type, and tooth grade of a file determine its use. Select a shape (round, flat, etc.) suited to the contour of the edge to be filed. Choose a type and tooth grade according to the amount of material to be removed. Double-cut files work faster and rougher than single-cut files; use double-cut files for shaping, and single-cut files for sharpening operations. In either case, select a tooth grade (fine, medium fine, medium, medium coarse, or coarse) suited to the operation. Just remember: larger, coarser teeth leave deeper, rougher scratches.

SHARPENING OR HONING STONES For honing you can choose from a variety of types and shapes of both natural and artificial stones (see Chapter 8), or, for knives, use a sharpening steel. Artificial (aluminum-oxide or silicon-carbide) stones of the vitrified types are the most durable. Fine-, medium-, and coarse-grit stones of this type are available. A popular general-use rectangular "oilstone" is offered with two grits (usually medium and fine) on opposite sides. However you begin, final razorlike edging generally requires a fine-grit stone.

All hones work best when wet with light oil, water, or petroleum jelly, according to choice. Honing, whether you hold the hone or the tool, is done by alternately stroking the opposite edge bevels, at the correct angle, with progressively lighter pressure, until the desired edge is obtained. If a razor-type edge is desired, stroke as if the edge were slicing into the stone. For a wire edge, stroke so that the hone travels toward the edge; however, stop before too much stroking breaks the wire edge off (to leave a microscopically ragged razor edge). Exactly the correct bevel angle, and equalized pressure and stroke duration at the two sides, must be maintained throughout the operation (otherwise, the edge will be lopsided).

A stone must be clean and smooth. Remove dried oil and glaze with gasoline. Light dressing can be done with emery cloth; to remove large irregularities, hold the stone against the flat side of a revolving grinding wheel.

Sharpening Wood-Slicing and Scraping Tools

This group of tools includes wood hand chisels, plane irons, wood-turning chisels, cabinet scrapers, drawknives, spokeshaves, and jointer knives. All except the parting tool and straight-edged cabinet scraper have edges that are beveled on one side only. All can be ground on a power grinder. If a dry stone is used, frequent air or water cooling is absolutely necessary.

Tools may need rough grinding, on a medium- or even coarse-grit stone, to remove bad nicks or reshape the edges and bevels. However, such grinding should be avoided unless it is really necessary. If your tools are kept in good condition, light grinding on a fine-grit stone (or honing, as explained later) will do until repeated sharpenings finally make reshaping necessary.

WOOD CHISELS

Woodcutting chisels should be hollow-ground. Move the chisel straight into the wheel to remove nicks, as shown in Figure 22-13a; then adjust the tool rest or the chisel-grinding attachment to the required position to grind the bevel (Figure 22-13b), working the chisel squarely across the face of the wheel (Figure 22-14). Worked on the face of the wheel, the bevel will have a slight hollow, making it easy to hone to a perfect edge several times before regrinding again becomes necessary.

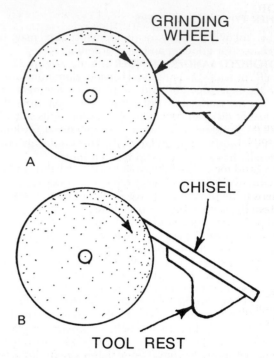

FIG. 22-13. (a) Remove nicks by pushing the chisel straight into the wheel. (b) Tilt the tool rest to grind a bevel to the required angle.

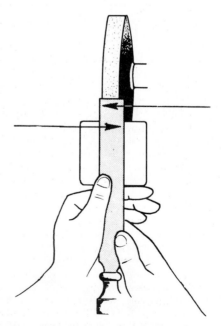

FIG. 22-14. To sharpen, move the chisel evenly across the face of the wheel.

(Remember that while a slightly concave—never convex—bevel is preferable, a straight bevel can be used.) The bevel should be about 30°; it is obtained by making the bevel twice the thickness of the chisel, as shown in Figure 22-15. A 20° bevel can be used for softwood, but this thin wedge will crumble on hardwood, as illustrated in Figure 22-16.

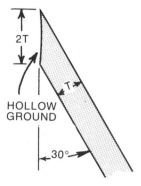

FIG. 22-15. A 30° bevel is obtained by making a bevel twice the thickness of the chisel.

FIG. 22-16. A short bevel is best for hardwoods, and a long bevel for softwoods.

A file can be used to sharpen wood chisels, too. But if you use files, support the tool in a vise so that the bevel face is horizontal, with the edge away from you, and file toward the edge while holding the file level.

HONING Whether you are sharpening on a grinder or with a file, the next step is honing the edge. Either an aluminum-oxide or a silicon-carbide oilstone will give good results in honing or whetting the chisel edge. In most cases, begin with a medium-grit stone; finish with a fine-grit stone. (Most common oilstones used for this sharpening operation have a coarse to medium grit on one side, and fine grit on the other.) Make sure the stone is firmly held so that it cannot move. Cover the stone with light machine oil so that the fine particles of steel ground off will float and thus prevent the stone from clogging.

Hold the chisel in one hand with the bevel flat against the coarser side of the stone. Use the fingers of your other hand to steady the chisel and hold it down against the stone. Using smooth even strokes, rub the chisel back and forth, parallel to the surface of the stone (Figure 22-17). The entire surface of the stone should be used, to avoid wearing a hollow in the center of the stone. Do not rock

the blade. The angle between the blade and the stone must remain constant during the whetting process. After a few strokes, a burr, wire edge, or feather edge is produced. To remove the burr, first take a few strokes with the flat side of the chisel held flat on the fine-grit side of the stone. Be careful not to raise the chisel even slightly; avoid putting the slightest bevel on the flat side, for then the chisel must be ground until the bevel is removed.

After whetting the flat side on the fine-grit side of the stone, turn the chisel over. Place the bevel side down, and hold it at the same angle you used to whet it on the coarse side of the stone. Take two or three light strokes to remove the burr. To test the sharpness of the cutting edge, hold the chisel where a good light will shine on the cutting edge. A keen edge does not reflect light in any position. If there are no shiny or white spots, it is a good edge.

High-carbon-steel wood chisels should be sharpened in the same manner as the wood-turning type.

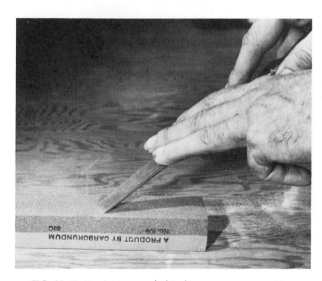

FIG. 22-17. Honing a wood chisel.

PLANE IRONS

Plane irons are sharpened in the same way as wood chisels. A bevel of 30° and a honing angle of 35° are satisfactory in most cases. Bevels can be checked by using a combination rule or protractor. Use an accurate square to check the squareness of the plane-iron edge. The cutting edges of plane irons are shaped as shown in Figure 22-18. The corners of the plane iron should be slightly rounded—just enough to prevent them from grooving the work surface. By the way, when forming a rounded jack-plane edge, be careful not to start the curves exactly at the center, and not to leave a break where each curve starts. A very slight curve is desirable.

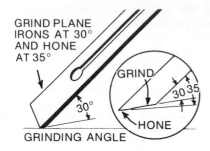

GRIND PLANE
IRONS AT 30°
AND HONE
AT 35°

GRIND

30 35

30°

HONE

GRINDING ANGLE

FIG. 22-18. Plane-iron shapes and proper grinding and honing angles. It is a good idea to grind plane irons at 30°, and hone at 35°.

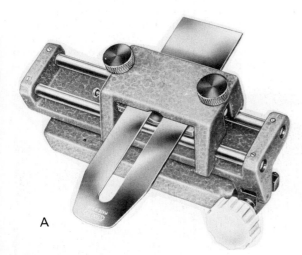

A

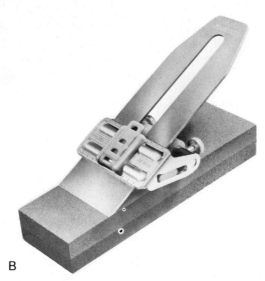

B

FIG. 22-19. (a) Plane-blade grinding attachment; (b) typical honing fixture.

Mechanical devices that hold the plane iron or chisel at the proper angle for grinding are advantageous. Figure 22-19a pictures a plane-blade grinding attachment. A carriage table is clamped to the adjustable arm on the grinder. The table tilts so that any desired angle may be obtained. The adjustable quadrant is located on the left side, which permits accurate grinding of angle knives as well as an accurate right-angle position for straight knives. The attachment has a knurled adjusting nut which allows you to control the amount of "cut" when grinding. It will take knives up to 3 9/16 inches wide. A diamond-pointed wheel dresser may also be clamped in the holder for wheel dressing. Figure 22-19b shows a honing fixture that holds the plane blade steady and at the proper angle during honing or stropping. Use stropping or buffing to obtain a super edge. To buff, hold the tool so that the buffing-wheel edge moves outward, toward—not into—the sharp edge; give each side a very short, light buffing with a small amount of red- or white-rouge compound. To strop, use a piece of leather, as from a belt glued hair side up to a wood block. Stroke only toward you, as in Figure 22-20, a few times on each side of the blade. Press lightly.

FIG. 22-20. When stropping, stroke only toward yourself.

SPOKESHAVE

The small blade of this tool is much like a plane iron and is sharpened in the same way. The bevels range from 25 to 30° and may be slightly concave.

DRAWKNIFE

The blade cutting area has a single, preferably flat or slightly concave, bevel at approximately a 30° angle to the sides. The cutting area must be straight, from end to end. Grind it on the wheel face in the same manner as a plane iron (the blade tangs would interfere with the use of the wheel's side). Check with a straightedge such as a small steel rule, to maintain the blade straightness. Finish by honing and buffing or stropping. To hone, use either a handled knife-sharpening oilstone or a combination oilstone held similarly in your hand. Be careful to hold the stone at the correct bevel angle and to move it uniformly back and forth so as to maintain edge straightness. If you turn over a slight wire edge, remove it by honing lightly on the flat side of the blade with the stone flat against the blade.

WOOD-TURNING CHISELS

Wood-turning chisels usually are made of select, very hard tool steel. If a dry wheel is used, cool the tool frequently in water. All bevels should be flat except those on the parting tool, which can be slightly concave. Therefore, final grinding should be done on the side of the wheel, even though the wheel face may have been used at first for removing nicks, etc. After grinding, the edges should be honed on appropriately shaped oilstones. For cutting tools (gouges, parting tools, and skews), hone both sides to completely remove any wire edge; but for scraping tools (spearpoint, flatnose, and roundnose), hone only the bevel side to turn the wire edge over toward the unbeveled side. The bevels and angles are as illustrated in Figure 22-21.

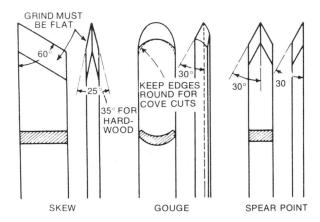

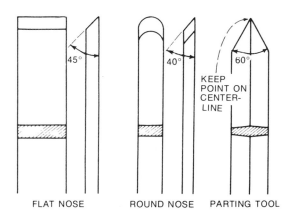

FIG. 22-21. Grinding angles for wood-turning tools.

PARTING TOOL This tool can be ground against the wheel face. Mark the center, where the point is to be, and grind just up to the center from each side.

GOUGE AND ROUNDNOSE CHISEL Each of these tools has a round edge whose curvature must be regular and symmetric. If much metal is to be removed, start on the face of the wheel. Adjust the tool rest so that the tool will lie flat on it while making the proper bevel angle with the wheel face. Hold your left thumb as shown in Figure 22-22a, and use it as a fulcrum for swinging the tool edge against the wheel. Since the gouge is round (instead of flat like the roundnose), when grinding the gouge you must roll the tool while swinging it. Finish grinding on the side of the wheel, providing a similar setup, and continue the swinging or the swinging-and-rolling motion.

To hone the curved inside (unground) edge of the gouge, use a curved abrasive surface. One method is to use a tapered grinding point, which can be chucked in a lathe headstock (Figure 22-22b). Another method is to use a round slipstone as shown in Figure 22-22c. To hone the ground edge of either the gouge or the roundnose, use a flat oilstone, and use the motion described for grinding.

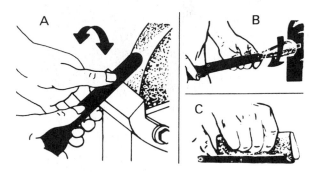

FIG. 22-22. Grinding a gouge and roundnose chisel.

SKEW, SPEARPOINT, AND FLATNOSE CHISELS If much metal needs to be removed, start on the face of the wheel, using the tool rest. Otherwise, it is best to use a lathe tool rest (or a similar rest) bolted to a wood block, or to make a guide block such as is shown in Figure 22-23, and to do all the grinding against the side of the wheel. Advance the edge, held at the proper bevel angle, straight into the wheel side. Do the final honing on a flat oilstone, holding the tool carefully at the bevel angle already established by grinding.

STRAIGHT-EDGE WOOD OR CABINET SCRAPER

This has a straight, unbeveled edge which is, however, slightly turned to one side for good scraping action. Generally made of low-carbon steel, scrapers may be ground or filed for sharpening.

To remove nicks in the blade, preferably grind it on the side of the wheel, where it is easiest to maintain the long, straight edge simply by holding blade at exactly 90° to the wheel surface in both directions. If the wheel face is used, employ the technique used for grinding plane irons. If filing is preferred, place the blade low down in a vise, and hold the file exactly horizontal but with the handle end swung 45° to the right. Start at the right end of the edge, and move the file to the left end while simultaneously pushing it across the edge to cut. Return to the starting position for the next stroke. In all cases, check as necessary with a square to keep the edge at 90° to the sides and ends.

Whether you grind or file to remove nicks, finish the edge either by drawfiling (the easiest way) or by honing (for the smoothest edge). Do the drawfiling exactly as described above, but use a fine mill file, and continue until fine wire edges are formed along the two sharp edges. To hone, use a medium to fine oilstone supported squarely in a vise. Hold the blade exactly perpendicular, and move the edge as if along a track, back and forth, until wire edges appear. In both cases, remove the wire edges by carefully honing the flat sides on a fine oilstone.

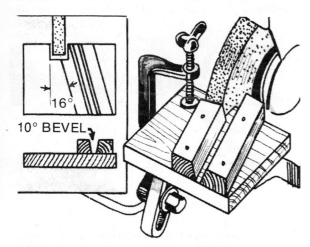

FIG. 22-23. Wood-turning chisel guide block.

TURNING THE EDGE The edge should be turned at an angle of approximately 15° toward one side. Preferably use a burnisher (a ribbed steel rod), though a screwdriver blade or similar round rod will do. Place the scraper in the vise, and put oil along its edge. Hold the burnisher straight across the edge, with the handle end tipped down at an angle of 10° to the scraper side. Bear down on the burnisher, and pull it along the full length of the edge. If properly done, this one stroke should turn the edge 10°. Make a second stroke with the burnisher tipped down at a 15° angle to finish turning the edge to this angle.

After turning the edge, run the tip of the burnisher once along the full length of the underside of the edge, bearing upward with a very light force. This will turn the underside of the edge slightly outward to improve its

scraping action. Re-turning the edge will often suffice to recondition a scraper, without sharpening.

BEVEL-EDGE WOOD OR CABINET SCRAPERS

These are sharpened like the straight-edge type, except that their edges are beveled on one side at approximately 30°. The edge is turned at approximately 15° toward the side having the sharp edge. When drawfiling or honing, create a wire edge along the sharp side of the bevel; then hone the one flat side only to remove this wire edge.

POCKETKNIFE

Pocketknives may be sharpened on a medium- or fine-grade sharpening stone, with a few drops of oil spread on the surface. Hold the handle of the knife in one hand, and place the blade across the stone. Press down with the fingers of the other hand, and stroke the blade, following a circular motion as shown in Figure 22-24. After several strokes, reverse the blade, and stroke the opposite side, following the same type of motion. Use a light, even pressure. A thin blade overheats quickly and can lose its temper. The wire edge or burr that may be left on a knife blade after whetting may be removed by stropping both sides on a soft wood block, or on canvas or leather.

FIG. 22-24. Sharpening a pocketknife.

JOINTER KNIVES

For the smoothest possible, best controlled (no digging in) planing operations, the jointer knives must have identical straight edges with single (no secondary) bevels and must be set squarely in the jointer head at identical heights (so as to contact the workpiece uniformly). The bevel angle is usually 36°, and a slight concavity (as produced by the face of a 6-inch-diameter or larger grinding wheel) is permissible. A secondary bevel of up to $\frac{1}{64}$ inch in height (as illustrated in Figure 22-25) can be tolerated but, since even the smallest secondary bevel will tend to produce chattering (and less than perfectly smooth results), it is better to sharpen carefully and avoid secondary bevels. For this reason (and because it can be hazardous) we do not recommend jointing or honing operations performed by operating the jointer to grind or hone the knives while they are installed in the head, unless you are experienced in this technique. Such operations frequently produce undesirable secondary bevels.

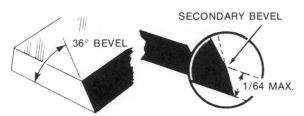

FIG. 22-25. Bevels of a jointer knife.

If your knives need sharpening, remove them for grinding and/or honing; then reinstall them very carefully, according to the instructions contained in the owner's manual.

GRINDING If the knives are ground on a dry grinding wheel, they must be air-cooled frequently. Grind only when necessary, to remove nicks or straighten the edges, and remove as little metal as possible. It is not necessary to grind all the knives the same amount; if one has deeper

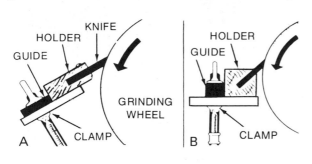

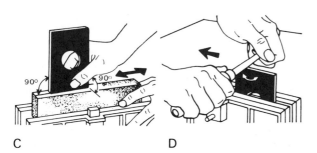

FIG. 22-26. Sharpening a jointer knife.

nicks, it can be ground deeper. Grind on the face of the wheel. Do not attempt to hold and guide a knife by hand; it would be impossible to hold a true bevel or produce a true, straight edge. Clamp a straightedge guide to your tool rest (as illustrated in Figure 22-26a); then adjust the tool rest so that the knife (held in a home-made wooden holder, as shown in Figure 22-26b) will slide straight across the wheel face and just make contact with it at the proper bevel angle (either 36° or the original angle, if it is not 36°).

To begin grinding, place a thin shim between the guide and holder to advance the knife edge toward the wheel (a strip of thin sheet metal or such will do). Add shims as needed for additional metal removal. This use of shims will help you determine the total amount of metal removed, which will make reinstallation of the knives easier. While grinding, keep the knife holder firmly back against the shim(s) and guide, and move it from side to side uniformly so as to grind a true, straight edge on the knife.

HONING If the grinding is done on a fine-grit wheel, very little honing is required. Use a fine-grit oilstone of sufficient size to more than cover the length of your knife edge. With the knife still in its holder, place it bevel edge up on a flat surface, and stroke the bevel edge lightly with the oilstone. The stone must be held flat against the bevel throughout and must be moved back and forth in a straight line while in constant contact with the full bevel edge. Four to six strokes should suffice. Afterward, turn the knife over and stroke the back side (two to four strokes) to remove the wire edge. Hold the stone absolutely flat against the knife back while stroking.

SHAPER CUTTERS

The single-cutter types are easy to sharpen, but the multiple-blade types require the use of a home-made jig (Figure 22-27) to ensure that all the blades in a set are identical in shape and length. Moreover, if a cutter is to be resharpened to the exact original contour, a good template of the original is needed. However, cutters can be reshaped as desired. Many craftsmen use straight (planer) cutters or blanks, and shape these for special cuts.

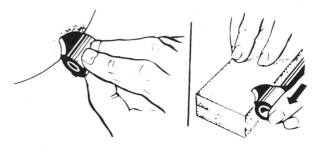

FIG. 22-27. Single-cutter types can be hand held.

Therefore, we shall cover here all the steps in creating and sharpening cutters. Use only those steps which you require.

All cutters are beveled on the top (cutting) edge, on one side only. The bevel is generally 30° and is uniform from one side to the other, regardless of edge contour. Each step of the jig must be exactly as wide as the cutter is thick. For a 30° bevel, the rise from one step to the next must be two-thirds of the cutter thickness. (For a 25° bevel, this fraction would be approximately nine-sixteenths; for a 20° bevel, approximately seven-sixteenths; for a 15° bevel, one-third.) Mount all the cutters in the jig, on their respective steps, with the bevel slopes paralleling the step descents and clamp them securely in place. The basic steps in making a shaper knife pattern from a blank are shown in detail in Figure 22-28.

GRINDING Use a dry medium-grit or fine-grit power

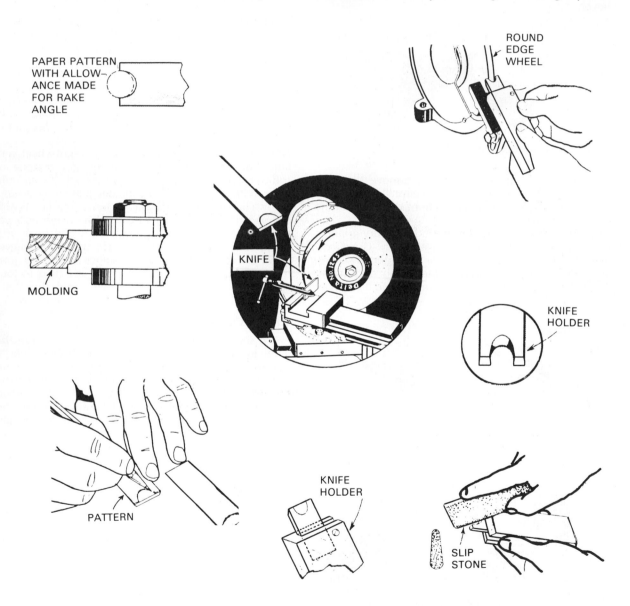

Fig. 22-28. Steps in shaper knife making.

wheel, stopping often to air-cool the cutters. That is, take care not to overheat the cutters. Grind them to shape, insofar as is possible. Always hold jig so that the wheel revolves into the bevels, and maintain the bevel angle for which you have designed the jig. If the contour is such that it can be completed on the grindstone, do as much of the final edging as you can on the wheel side, so there will be no more concavity in the bevels than necessary.

The best method of grinding a single cutter is to hold it against the side of the grinding wheel. Remove as little metal as possible to eliminate the nicks that necessitate this type of grinding.

HONING Honing is accomplished on single cutters by whetting the flat side of each cutter on an oilstone. Always stroke a cutter as if peeling a small slice from the stone. Never work on the bevel edge, as this will destroy the contour of the cutter. Remove burrs formed on the bevel edge during sharpening by taking very light file strokes along each edge. Honing is seldom attempted on multiple-cutter knives. The filing step follows grinding.

FILING This is the only step needed for slightly dulled cutters, and the final step for ground ones. With all the blades in the jig, clamp the jig in a vise at exactly the bevel angle for which the jig was designed. It is best to use a protractor to measure the angle. File the edges, on the push strokes only, holding the file horizontal. Check all cutters carefully to make certain that they are uniform in length. If more shaping is required, use fine files. File until the contours are exact and the cutting edges are true and sharp.

MORTISING CHISELS

The internal surface of the hollow mortising chisel should be ground to an included angle of 78°. The simplest method of working is to use a small electric hand grinder (see Chapter 13), dressing the wheel to the required angle. After the inside corners are sharpened on the wheel, use a triangle to remove any burrs. Finally, slide each of the four sides flat against a fine oilstone, just enough to remove the wire edge, if there is one.

A conical-shaped grinding point can also be dressed to a desired angle in a drill-press chuck. A drill vise can be employed to hold the mortising chisel while the grinding stone is fed down into it; or, the chisel can be fed upward by hand. All that is necessary is to grind the bit to the desired pattern, and to do this without burning the bit. When grinding special tools for special work, simply keep in mind the shapes and angles for the standard tool bit and the shape wanted; apply the same principles to obtain front, side, and back clearance in the special tools being ground.

There is no point in honing the edge of a tool bit that is to be used for heavy roughing cuts in steel. When turning steel, a fine edge lasts for only a few feet of cutting; then the edge rounds off to a more solid edge and remains in approximately this same condition until the bit breaks down. For fine finishing cuts, however, the bit should be honed with a reasonably fine stone. You can either fasten the bit in the lathe tool holder and work an oilstone against the cutting edge, or hold the bit in one hand and work it back and forth over the stone. When honing, sharpen against the cutting edge. In most fine-finishing operations the excellence of the work depends directly upon the keenness of the edge of the tool. Tools for soft metals should be carefully honed to as fine an edge as possible.

Sharpening Saws

All saw blades, except those of a chain saw, should be sharpened by professional blade sharpeners. The cost of sharpening a saw blade is very inexpensive.

When sharpening a chain-saw blade, although a superior filing job can be done with the chain locked in a chain filing vise, you can do a satisfactory job "on the bar" if you tighten up the chain tension enough so that the chain does not wobble. Do all the filing at the midpoint of the bar. Most saw manufacturers sell a sharpening kit which contains the proper file and a file guide. The proper filing angle is easily maintained by lining up the visual control lines inscribed on the guide. The file guide also controls the filing to the proper depth.

When filing the cutters, wear gloves for protection. Be sure to file all cutters to the same length, because if some are longer than the others, only the "longs" will get a chance to cut. If you replace damaged cutters, you must file the new cutters back to the same length as the other cutters. That is, all cutters must be filed back to equal lengths to give them equal "bite," or the chain will not cut well.

Other points to keep in mind when filing cutters are:

1. The filing stroke is made in one direction only, toward the front corner of the tooth.
2. Hold the file against the cutter face at an angle of 30° to the line of chain travel.
3. Hold the file level (90° to the cutter side plate).
4. Stroke each tooth firmly but lightly. Lift the file away from the tooth on the return stroke. Press mostly toward the back of the tooth. Avoid heavy downward pressure. Try to keep one-tenth of the file diameter above the top plate of the tooth.
5. Do not let the file dip or rock or sway off angle. Holding the angles accurately and using correct pressure as described above will result in the proper cutter contour (30° top plate angle and 85° side plate angle) and a hollow-ground under edge of 60°.
6. Put a few firm strokes on every tooth, filing all the cutters on one side of the chain, then all the cutters on the other.
7. As mentioned previously, a sharp edge will not reflect light. Examine the edge to see if the dulled area has been removed. Refile if necessary.

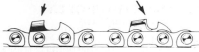

IF SOME CUTTERS ARE LONGER THAN THE OTHERS, FILE THEM BACK TO THE LENGTH OF THE SHORT CUTTERS

Fig. 22-29. General method of filing cutters to correct faults.

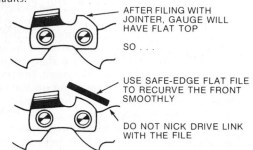

AFTER FILING WITH JOINTER, GAUGE WILL HAVE FLAT TOP

SO . . .

USE SAFE-EDGE FLAT FILE TO RECURVE THE FRONT SMOOTHLY

DO NOT NICK DRIVE LINK WITH THE FILE

FIG. 22-30. How and when to set depth-gauge clearance.

Other Tools

As has been emphasized in previous chapters, many other tools must be sharp if they are to work properly. These include the following.

AXES, ADZES, AND HATCHETS

There are many specialized types of axes, adzes, and hatchets. In general, those used for splitting wood have a short bevel, and the axe blade is thick just back of the cutting edge; those used for cutting, hewing, peeling, etc., have long bevels and thin, tapered blades. Most hatchets and many axes have straight edges with square corners, but many axes and most adzes have rounded edges of varying contours. As the entire head of a good-quality tool has been designed for a specific job, it is best not to alter the original bevel.

GRINDING Grind the tool slowly on a wheel that is kept very wet; or, grind dry but cool the tool often in water. Do not use a high-speed dry grinding wheel. Careless grinding will ruin any axe, either by destroying the temper with the heat caused by friction or by making the edge too thin. If a file is used for sharpening, be sure that all scratches are removed with a whetstone or hone. When regrinding, start 2 or 3 inches back from the cutting edge, and grind to about $\frac{1}{2}$ inch from the edge. Sharpen the remaining $\frac{1}{2}$ inch with a hone or whetstone. Work for a fan shape, leaving reinforcement at the corners for

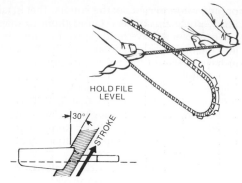

HOLD FILE LEVEL

30°

STROKE

strength. See the cross section (Figure 22-31) for the right way to shape the edge in grinding axes. Other illustrations show wrong ways to grind axes.

HONING To finish, or maintain, a truly sharp edge, use a flat oilstone as illustrated in Figure 22-32. Start on the coarser side, but finish on the finer side of the stone. Hold the stone steady to maintain the bevel angle right at the edge, and stroke back and forth a few times on one side, then on the other side. Continue until the edge is as sharp as desired.

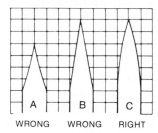

A WRONG   B WRONG   C RIGHT

FIG. 22-31. Wrong and right ways to shape an axe.

FIG. 22-32. Honing an axe blade.

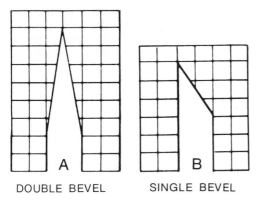

DOUBLE BEVEL   SINGLE BEVEL

FIG. 22-33. Shapes of hatchets.

AUGER BITS

If the screw point is in good shape, a bit will feed itself without the need for driving pressure; otherwise, it is not worth resharpening. A rough or out-of-round hole means that the spurs are dull or damaged; chips of uneven size mean that the cutters are dull. Bent spurs can be straightened; dull spurs or cutters can be sharpened.
STRAIGHTENING AND SHARPENING SPURS To straighten a spur, use a metal block drilled to receive the screw point, as illustrated in Figure 22-34a. Tap the spur top lightly with a hammer, over the edge of the block. After straightening, file or hone the spur to restore the outer contour, which must conform to the circumference of the bit (Figure 22-34b); however, never remove metal inside the required circumference. This is easiest to do if you can spin the bit on its center (as in a drill press) while touching the file or oilstone to the outer sides of the spurs. The spur can also be honed by hand, on a flat oilstone (Figure 22-34c).

To sharpen a spur, use a special auger-bit file (fine cut, thin, and flat, with one edge smooth). Place the smooth (noncutting) edge down against the cutter, and file the inner side of the spur at approximately a 60° angle, until the outer edge is sharp and true. Then hone the outer side, just enough to remove any wire edge.

SHARPENING CUTTERS Use the same auger-bit file, with the smooth edge inside, and file the shaft side of each cutter, filing from the edge toward the back through the flute below. Hold the file carefully to maintain the bevel angle as it was. File until the edge is sharp and straight, but file both cutters identically. Afterward, remove any wire edges formed by filing straight across the flat screw-point' sides of the cutters, but do not alter the cutter shape.

WOOD-BORING AND SCREW-PILOT BITS

Use a medium-fine mill file with one edge ground smooth so that the adjacent edge will not be filed when you file the point or the cutter. Maintain the bevel angles shown in Figure 22-35. Do not file the screw-pilot bit shank (which must not be reduced in size); when filing the screw-pilot cutters, maintain the 30° slope. The two halves of each bit must be kept identical. Remove as little metal as possible; then hone the flat sides on a fine oilstone to remove wire edges.

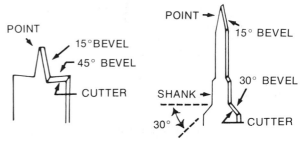

FIG. 22-35. How to sharpen wood-boring and screw-pilot bits.

ROUTER BITS

If the bits are of low-carbon steel, they can be sharpened with a file; high-speed steel bits must be touched up with an aluminum-oxide abrasive stick. Since metal removed from the outside of a bit changes its size, avoid sharpening on the outer surface more than absolutely necessary. Sharpen on the top, maintaining the bevels illustrated in Figure 22-36. Touch the edges around the outer surfaces lightly to remove burrs. On bits such as the dovetail cutter, which must be sharpened on the outer surface, remove as little metal as possible.

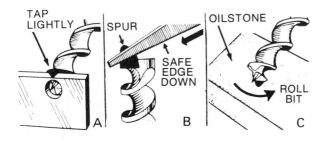

FIG. 22-34. How to straighten and sharpen spurs.

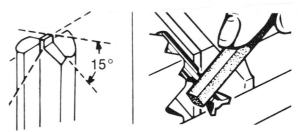

FIG. 22-36. How to sharpen router bits.

There are special router-bit attachments (see Chapter 11) that can sharpen bits easily on the router.

TWIST DRILLS

The importance of properly sharpening a metal twist drill cannot be overemphasized, since a drill which is incorrectly ground will break, burn, or drill off center or oversize. Experienced mechanics can resharpen a drill accurately by eye; the average craftsman will save money by purchasing a drill-guiding attachment.

HAND SHARPENING The following requirements are of greatest importance in twist-drill grinding: (1) equal and correctly sized drill-point angles, (2) equal-length cutting lips, (3) correct clearance behind the cutting lips, and (4) correct chisel-edge angle. All four are equally important in grinding either a regular point (Figure 22-37) used for general purposes, or a flat point (Figure 22-38) used for drilling hard and tough materials. Figure 22-39 shows the results of correct lip grinding and how equal drill-point angles and two cutting lips of equal length help achieve correct drilling results. Figure 22-40 shows a drill being checked during grinding. The drill-point gauge is being held against the body of the drill and has been brought down to where the graduated edge of the gauge is in contact with one cutting edge. In this way, both the drill-point angle and the length of the cutting edge (or lip) are checked at the same time. The process is repeated for the other side of the drill.

The lip clearance behind the cutting lip, at the margin, is determined by inspection. This means that you look at the drill point and approximate the lip clearance angle (Figures 22-37b and 22-38b), or compare it with an angle that has been set up on a protractor. The lip clearance angle need not be exact, but it must be within certain limits. Notice that in Figure 22-37b this angle ranges from 8 to 12°, and that the range given in Figure 22-38b is 6 to 9°. Whatever angle in the range is used, however, the lip clearance should be the same for both cutting lips of the drill. There must be lip clearance behind the entire length of the cutting lip, which extends from the margin of the drill to the chisel edge. This means that there must be "relief" behind the cutting lip along its entire length.

When lip clearance is being "ground into" a drill, the lip clearance angle and the chisel edge angle (Figures 22-37c and 22-38c) will be your guide to the amount of clearance you have ground into the drill behind the cutting lip along its entire length. The greater these angles are, the more clearance there will be behind their respective ends of the cutting lip. Too much lip clearance, which occurs when both the lip clearance angle and the chisel edge angle exceed their top limits, weakens the cutting edge or rip by removing too much metal directly behind it. Too little or no lip clearance prevents the cutting edge from producing a chip, or cutting, and the drill will not drill a hole.

To sharpen twist drills, first get the grinder ready. If necessary, dress the face of the wheel so that it is clean, a

true circle, and square with the sides. Before starting the grinder, readjust the tool rest to $\frac{1}{16}$ inch or less from the face of the wheel. This is an important safety measure which will help keep the work from wedging between the tool rest and the face of the wheel.

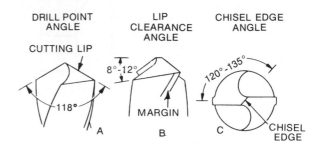

FIG. 22-37. Specifications for grinding a regular-point twist drill.

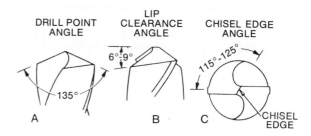

FIG. 22-38. Specifications for grinding a flat-point twist drill.

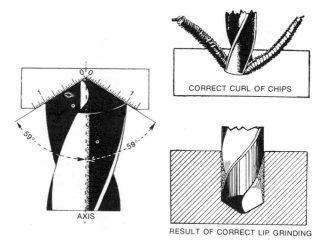

FIG. 22-39. Grinding drill lips correctly.

After starting the grinder and letting it come up to speed, you can begin grinding the drill point. Hold the twist drill as shown in Figure 22-41a, which is a top view of the first step in grinding a drill. The axis of the drill, in the first step, should make an angle of about 59° (half the drill-point angle) with the face of the wheel. The cutting lip should be horizontal. All motions, taking place at the same time, combine to produce a point satisfying the four requirements mentioned above: (1) equal and correctly sized drill-point angles, (2) equal-length cutting lips, (3) correct clearance behind the cutting lips, and (4) correct chisel-edge angle. A check with a drill-point gauge (Figure 22-40) and inspection will show when these four requirements have been met.

SHARPENING A TWIST DRILL FOR DRILLING BRASS To grind a drill for drilling brass, hold the cutting lip against the right side of the wheel as shown in Figure 22-42. Grinding the flute slightly flat, in line with the axis of the drill, greatly reduces the included angle of the cutting lip. This will give the drill a scraping action, necessary for brass, rather than the cutting action used for steel. This scraping action will prevent the tendency of drills not ground for brass to stick in the hole being drilled. This sticking is troublesome, especially in drilling through a pilot hole.

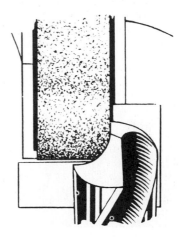

FIG. 22-42. Grinding a twist drill for brass.

THINNING THE WEB OF A TWIST DRILL Repeated sharpening, which shortens the drill, or resharpening the remainder of a broken drill, results in an increase in the web thickness at the point. This may require web thinning. Correct web thinning, when it becomes necessary, is important for satisfactory drilling.

To thin the web of a drill, hold the drill lightly to the face of a round-faced wheel, as shown in Figure 22-43a, and thin the web for a short distance behind the cutting lip and into the flutes. This is shown in Figure 22-43b. Notice that the cutting lip is actually (but only slightly) ground back, reducing its included angle only a very little, not enough to affect the operation of the drill.

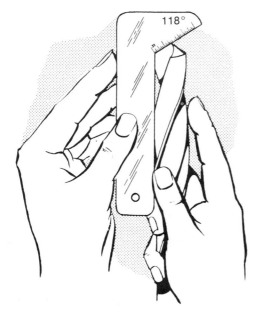

FIG. 22-40. Checking the drill-point angle and cutting edge.

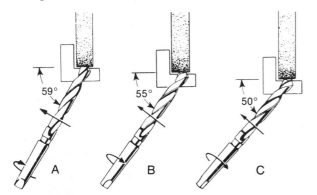

FIG. 22-41. Three steps in grinding a twist drill with a grinder.

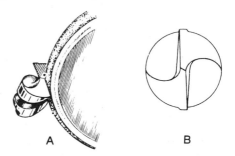

FIG. 22-43. Thinning the web of a twist drill.

SHARPENING A TWIST DRILL BY MACHINE Sharpening a twist drill by hand is a skill that is mastered only after much practice and careful attention to details. Therefore, whenever possible, use a tool grinder in which the drills can be properly positioned, clamped in place, and set with precision for the various angles. This machine grinding (Figure 22-44) will enable you to sharpen drills accurately. As a result, they will last longer and will produce more accurate holes.

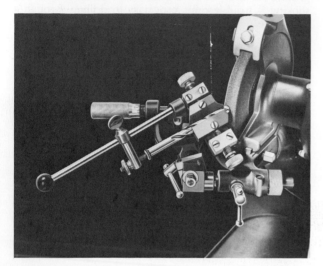

FIG. 22-44. Sharpening a twist drill with a tool grinder.

Whether you are sharpening a drill by hand or by machine, it is very necessary that the temperature at the point be kept down. As the point gets hot, it approaches the temperature at which the temper of the steel will be drawn. Keep the point cool enough to be held in your bare hand. Do this by making only a few light passes over the grinding wheel before letting the point cool for a few seconds. Then repeat this alternate grinding and cooling. Once you notice the appearance of a blue temper color at the point, it is too late. You have drawn the temper, and the steel is now too soft to hold a cutting edge. Then the only thing you can do is continue the sharpening process, first one lip and then the other, until you have finally ground away the soft tip of the drill. The blue color indicates softness throughout the entire point of the drill, and not only on the blue surface. This means that you must grind away all of that portion of the tip which is blue. This operation must be done very slowly and carefully, with the point kept cool to prevent continual bluing of the metal.

SPECIAL DRILL POINTS Ordinary twist drills are manufactured for use in hard metals, and each cutting edge is formed along the line of intersection between the lip (at the end of the drill) and the face of the twist on which the lip is situated. Because the face of each twist spirals upward and approaches the lip at an angle, the cutting edge, in effect, is somewhat like a chisel edge. The slight backward sweep under the cutting edge is called its "rake."

When an ordinary drill is used in soft metals or plastics, this rake gives the drill a tendency to hog into the material and take excessive bites. For drilling in such materials, it is advisable to reduce the rake of the cutting edges by grinding a slight flat into the face of each flute where it meets the lip. This flat need not be more than $\frac{1}{32}$ inch in width, as measured at the outside of the drill. The lip angle can also be reduced, as shown in Figure 22-45.

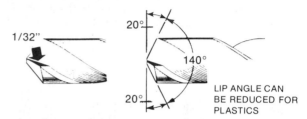

FIG. 22-45. Special drill point.

A countersink which is worn or nicked is restored to service by honing the face of the cutting edges with a triangular-shaped stone; the harder the stone, the finer the edge will be.

Tungsten-carbide masonry drills are ground very slowly on an ordinary grinding wheel. Hold them at about a 30 to 40° angle, but do not rotate or swing the drill to increase the cutting angle. Take care not to let a sharp corner dig into the softer wheel, as it may embed itself with such force as to tear the bit out of your fingers.

DRILL-BIT SHARPENER A drill sharpener (Figure 22-46) makes it easy to sharpen twist drills to their proper shape

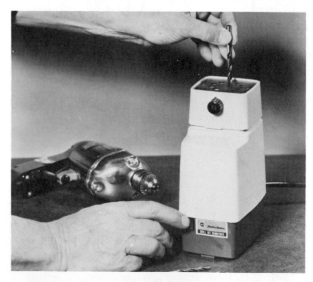

FIG. 22-46. Typical twist-drill sharpener.

and angle. Just insert the drill in the proper-size hole, run the tool 1 to 4 seconds, depending on the size of drill, and then remove it from the tool. Thanks to the properly angled grinding wheel in the tool, the drill should be correctly sharpened.

SCREWDRIVERS

Figure 22-47a and c show front views of a properly dressed screwdriver; Figure 22-47b and d show side views. To dress a common screwdriver, dress the sides so that the blade is symmetrical in shape. Then square off the end. Check the squareness of the end by resting the tip on the handle of a try square and moving the shank of the screwdriver close to the blade of the square. If the blade and the shank appear to be parallel, the tip is square (Figure 22-48).

On the common screwdriver, grind the faces of the blade so that they are parallel or nearly parallel at the tip, as shown in parts b and d of Figure 22-47. The thickness of the blade at the tip should be such that the tip will just enter the slot of the screws you intend to turn. With such a tip thickness, and the sides parallel or nearly so, the screwdriver will have the least tendency to climb out of the screw slot when the screw is being turned.

The screwdriver shown in Figure 22-47d has been ground by resting it flat against the grinding wheel. A 6-inch wheel produces about the right grind on a screwdriver used for small screws. Hold the blade high on the circumference of the wheel, and rest the shank on the tool rest (Figure 22-49).

When grinding a screwdriver, do not let the tip get too hot, or the temper will be drawn. You can file the edge of the screwdriver with a medium-fine mill file, if preferred.

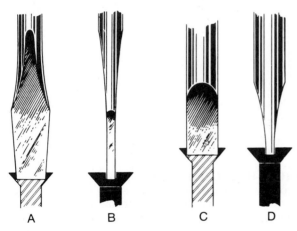

FIG. 22-47. Shapes of screwdrivers when properly dressed.

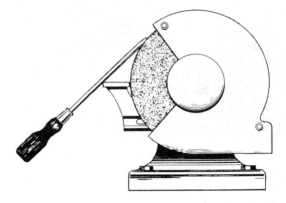

FIG. 22-49. Grinding a screwdriver tip with a bench grinder.

METAL-CUTTING CHISELS

Metal-cutting chisels are sharpened by grinding. These chisels are designed to cut cold metal, so the general term "cold chisel" is often used. The angle of 60° shown in Figure 22-50 is for a general-use cold chisel. Increase this angle somewhat for cutting harder metals, and decrease it for those that are softer. Grinding should be done on an aluminum-oxide wheel.

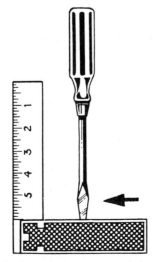

FIG. 22-48. Checking the squareness of the end of a screwdriver.

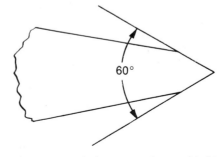

FIG. 22-50. Proper angle for a general-use cold chisel.

To sharpen a metal-cutting chisel, hold the chisel to the wheel, resting it on the tool rest (Figure 22-51a). Notice that the index finger, curved beneath the chisel, rides against the front edge of the tool rest. This affords good control of the chisel and will help you grind a single, equal bevel on each side.

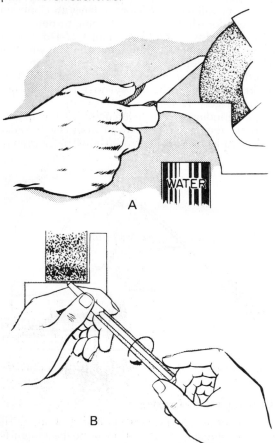

FIG. 22-51. (a) Sharpening a chisel with a grinder; (b) dressing a center punch with a bench grinder.

Let the chisel rest only lightly against the wheel when grinding. Less heat will be developed and, because the speed of the wheel is reduced only slightly, the air currents created by the wheel will have the maximum cooling effect. If the temperature of the cutting edge rises to the point where the metal begins to turn blue in color, the temper has been drawn, the cutting edge has been softened, and the edge will not stand up in use. The cutting edge will have to be resharpened, drawn to the proper temper (hardness), and the sharpening continued. As long as you can touch the cutting edge you are grinding with your bare hand and keep it there, you are in no danger of drawing the temper. Notice that it is the temperature of the cutting edge that is important. This

means the very tip of the chisel, where the bevel is being ground. The chisel may be cool an inch or less from the cutting edge while the cutting edge itself turns blue from overheating. Check this carefully while grinding.

Figure 22-52a shows a cold chisel ground with a slight curvature, and Figure 22-52b shows a straight cutting edge. Both types of edges are used. The curved cutting edge is ground by swinging either end of the chisel slightly from left to right as the two faces of the cutting edge are being ground.

For shearing metal in a vise, the chisel with the straight edge may be better. The chisel with the curvature will probably work better when you are cutting metal on a flat plate.

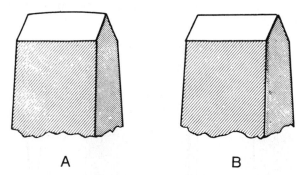

FIG. 22-52. Two cutting-edge shapes for cold chisels.

CHISEL-HEAD GRINDING In Figure 22-53a you will see a properly ground chisel head. Keep it that way through frequent grinding, before it begins to mushroom as shown in Figure 22-53b. Never use a chisel whose head has been allowed to mushroom. You, or others, can be injured by chips or metal flying off the head when it is hammered.

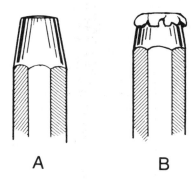

FIG. 22-53. Good and bad chisel-head shapes.

Remove the ragged edges of such a head by grinding them off. One way to do this is to hold the head against the wheel as shown in Figure 22-54. Turn the chisel with one hand as you apply pressure with the other. Grind across the entire face of the wheel to keep it flat.

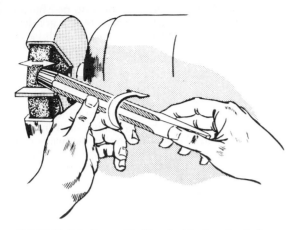

FIG. 22-54. Grinding a chisel head with a bench grinder.

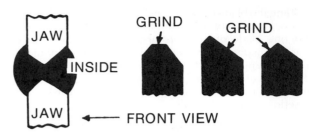

FIG. 22-55. How to sharpen carpenter's nippers.

PUNCHES

The various punches described in Chapters 1 and 3 require slightly different grinding techniques. For example, the starting and pin-punch heads are ground flat. Use the side of the stone, moving the tool constantly to prevent stone grooving. After grinding, the long, straight neck of a pin punch should be polished with fine emery cloth, preferably on a lathe.

Center-punch heads are beveled from 15° for steel to 60° for very soft metals and wood. Use the face or side of the stone. Hold the tool in one hand at the bevel angle; use the other hand to roll the tool constantly to center the point exactly. The cup of a nail set can be reformed by drilling, preferably on a lathe. Always finish the grinding on a fine-grit stone and buff afterward to make the tapers smooth.

CARPENTER'S NIPPERS

The grinding is done on an aluminum-oxide wheel, and the work is cooled with water frequently. The correct bevel angles for nipper jaws are shown in Figure 22-55. To obtain these angles, three successive grinds are required. The first grind is intended to remove nicks, and it should go deep enough to obliterate any inequalities along the edges. This grind is obtained by holding the face of a jaw against the side of the grinding wheel. After removing the nicks, make the second and third grinds by holding the jaw against the side of the wheel at the proper angle for the grind.

WIRE-CUTTING PLIERS

Pliers which are not too highly tempered can be sharpened with a small file. Those which are highly tempered must be sharpened with a thin abrasive stone. Sharpen to the original bevel by stroking lightly; then remove any wire edge produced by honing from the opposite side.

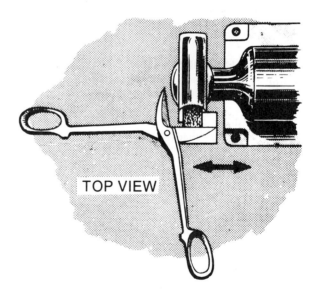

FIG. 22-56. Sharpening snips on a grinder.

TIN SNIPS

To sharpen the snips on a grinder, open the snips as shown in Figure 22-56, resting the blade on the tool rest. Hold the handle of the blade being ground so it is level, and rotate the other blade to whatever angle is necessary to grind the cutting edge to an included angle of 80 to 85°.

Holding the blade lightly against the rotating wheel, move it from left to right across the face of the wheel. Sharpen first one blade of the snips and then the other. While sharpening one blade, be careful to keep the other blade from coming into contact with the side of the wheel. Sharpening tin snips requires close and careful attention; improper techniques may wreck the snips or even result in serious personal injury.

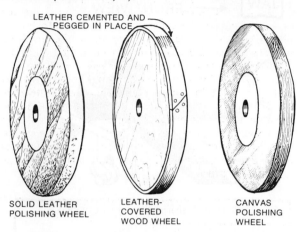

LEATHER CEMENTED AND PEGGED IN PLACE

SOLID LEATHER POLISHING WHEEL   LEATHER-COVERED WOOD WHEEL   CANVAS POLISHING WHEEL

FIG. 22-57. Metals, plastics, and lacquer-coated surfaces can be brought to a smooth and flawless finish by the application of suitably graded abrasive grains carried on a polishing wheel.

REDRESSING HAMMER HEADS

When the head of any hammer becomes chipped, spalled or mushroomed, it should be discarded. If these faults are only minor the head may be redressed.

The basic procedure of redressing hammer heads is the same as chisel-head grinding. When grinding be sure to keep the head's basic pattern intact. Always finish grinding on a fine-grit stone; preferably by buffing afterwards to make the contour smooth.

Buffing and Buffers

Buffing and polishing are the general terms applied to the complete process of removing tool marks, scratches, etc., from metals and other substances to produce a high-luster finish. The process is divided into three distinct parts. The first of these is "roughing." Roughing is done dry with abrasives in grit numbers from 40 to 80. "Dry fining" or "fine wheeling," as the second operation is called, can also be done dry, but is often done on a greased wheel. The grits used are from No. 120 to 180. "Finishing," also called "oiling" and "buffing," is the final operation. It is done with fine-grain abrasives combined with lard oil, tallow, beeswax, water, etc. The exact size of grain used in any of the operations will depend upon the original finish on the work and the desired finish on the completed product. Buffing and polishing, as mentioned

earlier in the chapter, may be done with polishing and buffing wheels in conjunction with a power grinder, or they may be accomplished on a special tool, called a buffer, which is very much like a grinder except that it does not have guards. Buffing and polishing may also be done with the power attachments on table saws, radial-arm machines, drill presses, lathes, and portable electric drills.

The first operation, roughing, can be done on a solid grinding wheel. However, because this is hard and has no flexibility, polishing is usually done on leather or canvas wheels made especially for this purpose. If the work is a flat surface, a solid leather or leather-covered wood wheel can be used; if the work is curved, it demands a cemented canvas wheel or some other type that has the required flexibility.

To set up the polishing wheel, the old abrasive is first cleaned off by applying an abrasive stick about three numbers coarser than the abrasive on the wheel. The wheel is then coated with glue, after which the abrasive grains are rolled and pounded in. (Ordinarily, one coat of abrasive is enough, but two or more coats can be applied to roughing wheels to lengthen their period of service; each coat should be completely dry before the next is applied.) After the wheel is dry, it should be balanced. If any heavy spots are found, they should be corrected by nailing small pieces of lead to the wheel or by any other method which gives the desired result.

Animal-hide ground glue is commonly used for applying abrasives to polishing wheels. The glue should be soaked in cold water from 2 to 4 hours, and then brought to a heat of 140°F in a suitable gluepot. Use the proper proportions of water and glue. Equal parts, by weight, is the right consistency for abrasive grains from No. 20 to 50. Finer grains demand a thinner glue: 60 to 70 grit takes a 40-60 mix (glue-water); 80 to 120 grit takes a 33-

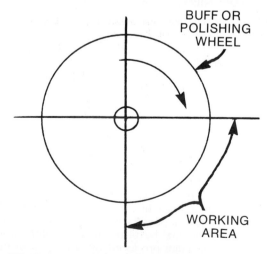

BUFF OR POLISHING WHEEL

WORKING AREA

FIG. 22-58. How work is fed to a polishing wheel.

67 mix; and very fine abrasives from 150 to 220 grit require 20 percent glue to 80 percent water. Wheels should set at least 48 hours before they are used. Instead of using glue, many workers prefer special polishing cements made for this purpose. These have the advantage of being already mixed, and they require a shorter drying time.

The work is presented freehand to the wheel on the lower quarter of the area of the wheel surface, as shown in Figure 22-58. Avoid using too much pressure, as this tears out the abrasive grains and shortens the life of the wheel. Apply grease or other lubricant if required. An occasional application of lump pumice will clean the wheel if it becomes clogged. Work systematically over the area to be polished, inspecting the work frequently for defects which must be worked out.

Fine wheeling is done in the same manner as roughing, except that finer abrasive grains are used. Also, at this stage there is a greater use of the softer polishing wheels, and frequent use of grease or other lubricant to prevent the wheel from clogging.

Buffs are disks of muslin, felt, flannel, leather, etc., sewn in a wide variety of patterns as shown in Figure 22-59, to produce hard or soft wheels. The loose buff (stitched once around the hole) is a popular style. The ripple buff can be made to run with either a hard or soft edge by reversing it on the spindle. As in polishing, the work must be done on the lower side of the wheel. Work presented as shown by the dotted lines in Figure 22-60 will be torn from the hands with considerable force. The edges of the buff should be kept clean and round. Frayed edges can be dressed down with a buffing-wheel rake while the buff is running. Any rough edge, such as a household food grater, can be used to dress buffs.

Buffing compounds are various natural abrasives, such as emery, tripoli, pumice, crocus, lime, and rouge, which are combined with a suitable wax or grease to form a mixture which can readily be applied to the revolving buff. The compound should be applied to the buff lightly and frequently as the work progresses.

You can make your own buffing compounds by melting beeswax in a double boiler, and then adding the abrasive until a thick paste is formed. Then pour the molten mass into cardboard tubes or make it into cakes; when cold, it is ready for use. Very fine abrasives can be bonded with oil or water. The most common types of readily available commercial compounds are red rouge, pumice, and tripoli.

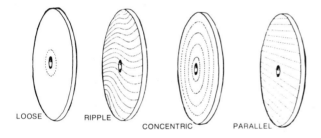

FIG. 22-59. Buffing is the final polishing and is done with soft cloth or leather wheels.

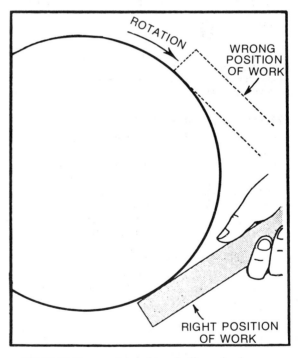

FIG. 22-60. How work is fed to a buffing wheel.

Index

DATE			